SCHOLARS' GUIDE
TO WASHINGTON, D.C.
FOR
SOUTH ASIAN STUDIES

সলার্স গাইড
টু ওয়াশিংটন,ডি.সি
ফর সাউথ এশিয়ান স্টাডিজ

SCHOLARS' GUIDE
TO WASHINGTON, D.C.
FOR

SOUTH ASIAN STUDIES

AFGHANISTAN, BANGLADESH, BHUTAN, INDIA, MALDIVES,
NEPAL, PAKISTAN, SRI LANKA

ENAYETUR RAHIM

Consultants
PURNIMA M. BHATT
LOUIS A. JACOB

Series Editor
ZDENĚK V. DAVID

WOODROW WILSON INTERNATIONAL CENTER FOR SCHOLARS

SMITHSONIAN INSTITUTION PRESS
WASHINGTON, D.C.
1981

This work was developed under a grant from the U.S. Department of Education. However, the content does not necessarily reflect the position or policy of that agency, and no official endorsement of these materials should be inferred.

Library of Congress Cataloging in Publication Data

Rahim, Enayetur.
  Scholars' guide to Washington, D.C., for South Asian studies.

  (Scholars' guide to Washington, D.C.; no. 8)
  Bibliography: p.
  Includes indexes.
  1. South Asia—Library resources—Washington, D.C.
  2. South Asia—Archival resources—Washington,D.C.
  3. South Asia—Societies, etc.—Directories.
  I. Title. II. Series.
  Z3185.R34   [DS335]   016.954'0720753   81-607847
  ISBN 0-87474-778-3   AACR2
  ISBN 0-87474-777-5 (pbk.)

Designed by Elizabeth Dixon.

CONTENTS

FOREWORD

This *Guide* is sponsored by the Woodrow Wilson International Center for Scholars, the nation's "living memorial" to its twenty-eighth president. It is the eighth in a series of reference works describing the scholarly resources of the Washington, D.C., area. These *Guides* arose from the accumulated lore about scholarly materials that was developing among fellows in the Wilson Center.

South Asia represents an ancient crossroad of civilizations, at which Buddhism, Hinduism, and Islam have encountered and affected one another. In more recent times, South Asia has become the seat of the world's second most populous country which is also its largest parliamentary democracy. The area has served as an important battleground for influence among competing great powers, particularly China and the Soviet Union. American interest in South Asia has increased because of the region's proximity to the major world reserves of oil and, most recently, because of Soviet presence in Afghanistan. While the Wilson Center has no program specifically designed to cover South Asia, the Center has supported research on South Asian topics in its existing programs and divisions.

Taken as a whole, the series of *Guides* exemplifies the Wilson Center's "switchboard function" of facilitating connections between the vast resources of the nation's capital and those with scholarly or practical needs—or simple curiosity. These *Guides*—like the Center's annual fellowship program—are designed to serve the national and international scholarly communities. At least 20,000 visiting scholars come each year to Washington with serious proposals from elsewhere in America and abroad. The *Guides* are designed to inform scholars, many of them outside the major university research centers in the United States, about possibilities for engaging in research on particular topics in Washington. The *Guides* cover the metropolitan area of Washington, but they are not thereby merely of local importance. In the city's libraries, archives, and data banks; its universities and research centers; and especially in the federal agencies and international organizations concentrated here, Washington holds resources that are of national—and even worldwide—significance.

The series of *Guides* is under the general editorship of Zdeněk V. David, the Wilson Center Librarian, who has devised the basic format. Elizabeth Dixon is largely responsible for the design and publication arrangements. Louis A. Jacob, Head of the Southern Asian Section in the Library of Congress, and Purnima M. Bhatt, Assistant Professor of Anthropology and Interdisciplinary Studies at Hood College, Frederick, Maryland, served as consultants in the preparation of this particular

Guide. Wilson Center staff members providing advice and assistance were Prosser Gifford and George Liston Seay. The author of this volume, Enayetur Rahim, has taught history at Georgetown University, Edgecliff College in Cincinnati, Ohio, and Rajshahi University in Rajshahi, Bangladesh. A special feature of this *Guide* is the independent prefatory essay by a former Wilson Center Fellow (1978–1979), Manakkal S. Venkataramani, now Professor at the School of International Studies, Jawaharlal Nehru University, New Delhi, India.

The Center thanks the United States Department of Education for its indispensable financial support of the *Guide's* preparation (under the authority of Title VI, Section 602, NDEA), as well as the Morris and Gwendolyn Cafritz Foundation of Washington, D.C., for additional support.

The Center has now prepared *Guides* for scholars in the fields of Russian/Soviet (1977), Latin American and Caribbean (1979), East Asian (1979), African (1980), Central and East European (1980), and Middle Eastern (1981) studies, as well as a *Guide* covering film and video collections (1980). All were published by the Smithsonian Institution Press (P.O. Box 1579, Washington, D.C. 20013). Forthcoming volumes will survey resources in the Washington area for scholars interested in Southeast Asia and Northwest Europe.

James H. Billington, *Director*
Woodrow Wilson International Center for Scholars

PREFACE

Long years ago Horace Greeley preached to restless Americans the *mantra*: "Go West, young man, go West." Today's researcher on South Asian affairs should draw inspiration not from Greeley but from the Bonus Army and A. Philip Randolph and set about organizing his own "March on Washington." If the reader will kindly bear with me for a while, I shall demonstrate to the satisfaction of all reasonable souls that the Washington metropolitan area does, indeed, possess the richest variety of facilities available anywhere for research on contemporary South Asian affairs.

It has not always been that way. How then did Washington attain the position of distinction that I ascribe to it? Having posed that question to myself, I am impelled to present to you my version of the history of that exciting development before I offer tantalizing glimpses of the array of facilities that await our researcher once he makes the sensible decision: On to Washington! If you find my narrative rather involved, do not despair or give up. Remind yourself that you are a dauntless researcher on the peoples and problems of South Asia and that even this rambling tale may offer you some insights concerning the South Asian psyche.

It is but fair to let you know that the present narrator is a Wily Oriental Gentleman, a scion of the ancient race of Tamils, a Hindu in religion, a Brahmin by caste, and an alumnus of the Madras Christian College, who traces his origin to a charming village located on the delta of the sacred Kaveri River in peninsular India's "deep South." Do I have any credentials, ask ye? All I can say is that I have documents in my possession that will conclusively establish that I was a Fellow at the Woodrow Wilson International Center for Scholars from 23 April 1978 to 22 June 1979. I shall say no more about the matter at this point because, located as I am in distant Delhi, nostalgia wells up in my mind over my happy days with colleagues at the Center— and with the vast research facilities of Washington that had been available to me just a short walk or bus ride away. But enough of sentimentalism! Let me get on with my story.

A Founding Father's Order of Priorities

In 1784 a brilliant American with a broad range of intellectual interests and boundless curiosity left for France on a diplomatic assignment. He informed an old friend of his in Paris that one of the reasons that had induced him to accept the assignment was to see countries "whose improvements in science, in arts, and in civilization" had long excited his interest and admiration. When he returned to the United States five years later, he brought with him from the Old World fifteen packing cases filled with books. A man of meticulous habits, he had listed the titles of the books in a notebook under such categories as history, law, natural philosophy, religion and ethics, politics, mathematics, geography, and fine arts, among others.

The arrival of the packing cases on American shores deserves to be depicted as a landmark in the intellectual history of the United States—indeed of mankind. For on the foundation that the contents of those fifteen packing cases represented has grown, in the capital city of Washington, a great storehouse of the world of intellect— the Library of Congress. Around it, in the District of Columbia, have risen other depositories with a wealth of materials chronicling and depicting the multifarious activities of man in America as well as in every other part of the globe. These resources, a standing testimony to the American spirit, constitute a common treasure for all mankind.

The man who brought the packing cases full of books from Europe was, of course, Thomas Jefferson. "I cannot live without books," he once wrote to John Adams. To him, reading books was the "greatest of all amusements." The quest for knowledge was his lifelong passion. "An honest heart being the first blessing, a knowing head is the second," he once wrote to a fifteen-year-old nephew of his. While he modestly described himself as only an "amateur," he was probably as well read a man as could be found in the Western world of his time.

"In modern history," Jefferson wrote to a correspondent in October 1825, "there are but two nations with whose course it is interesting for us to be intimately ac- quainted, to wit: France and England." He believed that the acquisition of some broad knowledge concerning the history of the rest of the European continent could suffice for the time being. "For modern continental history," he wrote, "a very general idea may first be aimed at, leaving for future and occasional reading the particular histories of such countries as may excite curiosity at the time."[1]

The cultures and civilizations of Asia figured hardly at all in the thinking of even such a one as Jefferson. This is rather intriguing in view of his enormous interest, if not in distant and exotic cultures, at least in plant and animal life on earth. If the fragrance of the famed spices of the "Indies" and the delicacy of the muslin and calico from the East could not arouse his curiosity, what about the teeming fauna of those distant parts? As a student at Williamsburg, Jefferson had recorded the amount that he paid to see a tiger. Despite the hectic pace of his life in the year of the Declaration of Independence, 1776, Jefferson found time to go out and take a look at a monkey. His later investigations relating to prehistoric animals, the "me- galonyx" and the mammoth, led him to argue strenuously that those huge beasts of the past were different from elephants. Tigers, monkeys, and elephants! The con- templation of even these fascinating animals could not arouse in Jefferson some slight interest concerning one of their principal habitats—the distant subcontinent of India.

Could it be that Jefferson did not regard a study of the history, culture, civilization, and institutions of the peoples of the distant subcontinent and areas adjacent to it as worth the effort required? By nature and training, he tended to apply the yardstick of utility to any expenditure of time and effort to a task. "I revolt against metaphysical reading . . .," he wrote in 1825, near the very close of his illustrious life. He pro- claimed that "the business of life is with matter that gives us tangible results." Earlier, in writing about the university that he desired to found in Virginia, he envisaged it as a place where "every branch of science, deemed useful at this day, should be taught in its highest degree." It was this yardstick that probably led him to believe that the university need not devote attention to "Oriental learning" and such other fields as had no practical relevance or usefulness "at this day."

Determine what is useful "at this day." Examine whether a venture that is at- tempted will lead to some "tangible results." If so, embark on the enterprise, developing your skills "in the highest degree." Those were watchwords that guided Jefferson's life—watchwords that are distinctively American. They provide, indeed, the clue to the way in which facilities for research in various branches of knowledge, including South Asian studies, have been developed in the United States in general and the Washington area in particular.

Sailors, Missionaries, and Transcendentalists

If Jefferson and other southern planters had hardly any dealings with the Indian subcontinent, it was a different story in New England. The shrewd Yankee horse-traders were, in the early days of the Republic, actually making money out of business dealings with that region! Writes Samuel Eliot Morison:

> An "East-India merchant," in ante-bellum Boston possessed social *kudos* to which no cotton millionaire could pretend. . . . To have an office on India Wharf, or to live in the India Row that comprised the fine old square-built houses of many a seaport town, conferred distinction. Among sailors, the man who had made an East-India voyage took no back-wind from anyone; and on Cape Cod it used to be said of a pretty, well-bred girl, "She's good enough to marry an East-India Cap'n."[2]

The merchants prospered, the sailors were admired, and the "Cap'ns" undoubtedly found charming brides and lived happily thereafter. But those felicitous developments were not accompanied by any noticeable interest, even among the New England intelligentsia, concerning "East-India" itself.

The earliest Americans, even in New England, to concern themselves with the peoples of South Asia, their religion, customs, manners, and mores were missionaries. Church circles in the young Republic were fired by a desire to emulate the work of British missionaries in preaching the Gospel to the unsaved millions of South Asia. In June 1810, the American Board of Commissioners for Foreign Missions came into existence, and its avowed aim was "to devise, adopt, and prosecute ways and means for propagating the gospel among those who are destitute of any knowledge of Christianity." Less than two years later, five American missionaries sailed for the shores of India. They were followed in time by others, as different church groups began sending out missionaries to propagate their own particular brands of Christianity.

Letters and articles from the missionaries—published in church journals—and, in time, books written by them, constituted the first American sources of information concerning the peoples of South Asia. By and large, the writings of the missionaries tended to leave a negative image of the people and culture of India among their American readers; but translations, by British Indologists, of Indian religious and literary classics—beginning to come to the attention of the New England intellectuals—produced a very different impact on at least some individuals. Ralph Waldo Emerson and Henry David Thoreau were the outstanding American products of an environment that emerged in New England as a result, partly, of the combination of these circumstances. In some of Emerson's works, as in Thoreau's *Walden*, many references to Hindu philosophical concepts and to Indian literary classics are to be found. Perhaps never before, and never afterwards to this day, had there been a time when American luminaries—of the caliber of Emerson, Thoreau, and their associates of the Transcendentalist school—had spoken in such admiring terms of the cultural and literary heritage of India.

Emerson's work had little effect in stimulating popular interest in South Asia. He was a maverick and a target of abuse to "Cambridge theologians." John Quincy Adams regarded him as an atheist, while Edward Everett scoffed at his "conceited, laborious nonsense. . . ." Pundits and panjandrums as well as "plain folk" could believe and respond to heart-rending missionary sermons on the superstitions and depravities of the unsaved heathens of Hindustan, while Emerson's *Brahma* sounded to them nonsensical, if not downright pagan. The Transcendentalists themselves had little interest in the contemporary state of affairs in Asia, even as they discoursed on the sublime thoughts of its seers and poets of antiquity. However, their work, coupled with reports of the progress of Indology in Britain and Germany, prepared the ground for a new development of some significance.

Leaving It to John Bull

In 1841 a young man of twenty-seven named Elbrige Salisbury was appointed by Yale University as Professor of Sanskrit and Arabic. Few Americans of today can probably identify Salisbury or his successors, William D. Whitney and Edward W. Hopkins, or Charles R. Lanman of Harvard, Maurice Bloomfield of Johns Hopkins, or A. V. William Jackson of Columbia. These men were pioneering students of Sanskrit, whose lonely and dedicated labors hardly find any mention in general works on American intellectual history. A mere handful of individuals devoted themselves to "Indic Studies" until that watershed episode of the twentieth century, the First World War. Important as was their role as pioneers, their work was not concerned with contemporary affairs of the subcontinent. In Washington itself, Indic studies of even the traditional kind found no home because of the absence of well-developed and well-endowed universities.

"Before the First World War," wrote Dr. Norman Brown of the University of Pennsylvania, "there was in the United States no body of social science knowledge concerning India—the term then applied to the whole cultural area that we now call South Asia—and hardly an American economist, anthropologist, sociologist, geographer, political scientist, or recent historian who was competent in respect to India. None of the social sciences was represented in any American university by a chair designated for India."[3]

Such a state of affairs was due to the very low level of interest in India on the part of intellectual Americans. In turn, it was a reflection of the meager economic, political, and cultural interaction between the United States and South Asia. In the swirling melting pot of America, that distant region was virtually unrepresented. Few from the region had ventured to seek their fortunes in the United States even during the decades before the Oriental Exclusion Act (1924) slammed the door against the feared flood of nonwhites. When Americans spoke of "Orientals" they usually had in mind the Chinese and the Japanese, not South Asians. They had views on the so-called yellow peril and, on occasion, they could get worked up over "Chinks" and "Japs." They had little contact with, and thus little interest in, the "brown" men of South Asia.

The political status of South Asia, as a part of the British Empire, meant that even such consular, commercial, and missionary contacts that the United States had with the region were what London was willing to countenance. It is worth remembering in this connection that official U.S. representation in India had been initiated by the very first president of the United States, George Washington. In 1792 he nominated Benjamin Joy of Massachusetts to serve as consul general in Calcutta. President Martin Van Buren named Philemon S. Parker of New York as the first U.S. consul in Bombay in 1838. A U.S. consular agency was established in Madras in 1867 during the administration of President Andrew Johnson. To the State Department, until virtually the outbreak of the Second World War, these posts were of minor importance since U.S. security concerns and investments in the region were small, and missionary and educational activities were on a modest scale. The representatives of the Raj treated the U.S. consular establishment with a lofty disdain that they did not even try to conceal. The missions themselves functioned in a manner that made them well-nigh invisible to the people of South Asia.

The American "Establishment" was quite content to accept South Asia as a British preserve. God in his heaven, the monarch in Windsor, and the Anglo-Saxon race in South Asia nobly discharging the task of civilizing the teeming millions of the region! President Theodore Roosevelt summed it up neatly when he told a group of Methodist missionaries in Washington that the work of the British in India "is the greatest feat of the kind that has been performed since the break up of the Roman Empire." He proclaimed that "the successful administration of the Indian Empire by the English has been one of the most notable and most admirable achievements of the white race during the past centuries."[4]

To the American literati, with its sizable component of persons with strong Anglophile proclivities, whatever was to be known about exotic India was best learned from British scholars and officials. A title before a British name usually evoked deferential attention from American audiences whether the person was Lord Pooh-Bah or Lord Halifax. It was a perfectly satisfactory situation from the point of view of London's Whitehall.

The very low level of general American interest in South Asia meant that even the one great repository of books and documents that was steadily growing in Washington, the Library of Congress, had only relatively modest holdings of materials on South Asia. Unlike South Asia, zealously controlled by the British, China and Japan were "open" and thus came to attract far greater American interest. While South Asia figured hardly at all in the pronouncements of American presidents and members of Congress, such was not the case in regard to China and Japan. A Chinese collection was begun in 1869 by the Library of Congress, and in time Chinese and Japanese materials became the most important segments of the Orientalia Division of the Library.

In contrast, the Library's holdings on South Asia at the turn of the century consisted of little more than forty volumes in Bengali that had been received as a gift. In 1904 the Library purchased the collection of the noted Indologist, Albrecht Weber, which consisted of 3,018 volumes and 1,002 pamphlets. For over three decades thereafter, nothing of much significance was attempted. It was only in 1938, thanks to the efforts of the small group of Indologists organized in a Committee on Indic and Iranian Studies, and a grant from the Carnegie Corporation, that the Library of Congress undertook the setting up of an Indic section to acquire a broad range of materials for "the study of India in all its phases and periods." To the position of Director of Project F, "Development of Indic Studies," The Librarian named Dr. Horace I. Poleman. A most happy choice, indeed.

In the initiatives that it took at this time, the Library of Congress showed—and not for the last time—greater perceptiveness of what was going on in the world arena than did the gentlemen in pin-striped suits in the State Department. Indeed, the Library, in launching its efforts, had apparently not visualized the active cooperation of the top officials of the State Department and of U.S. consular representatives in South Asia. Had the Library of Congress sought such cooperation, it might probably have encountered surprise and amusement. As late as 1937, we find the U.S. consul general in Calcutta, J. C. White, writing to the State Department:

It does not seem to me that India offers much of political interest to Americans. As long as our missionaries are able to continue their work of teaching, curing and enlightenment and no one seems to desire to stop them—and as long as we can sell goods, the political events of India seem to me of very secondary importance from our point of view.[5]

Neither Secretary of State Cordell Hull nor President Franklin D. Roosevelt would have disagreed seriously with the consul general's appraisal. They too had little interest in the problems of the South Asian peoples, while their reverence for the British Empire was almost as passionate as that of Teddy Roosevelt. Hull stated on February 18, 1937, that "the British Empire was the greatest stabilizer of human affairs in the world today" and that "it meant everything to the future progress and civilization for the British Empire to continue to function for the human race, as well as itself." He asserted that "neither I nor my country would in any circumstances see anything said or done which would weaken a single link in the British Empire. . . ."[6]

While such sentiments were also widely held among the intelligentsia, there was greater awareness among some of them that all was not altogether well with the efforts of the British to play the role of "the greatest stabilizer of human affairs" in South Asia. The nationalist movement was growing in that region, and Gandhi was on the march. The slumbering giant, South Asia, representing about a sixth of the human race, was beginning to stir, even as mighty forces were propelling the world toward the cataclysm of war. It was at such a time that the American Council of Learned Societies sponsored the first survey ever made of "Facilities for Indic Studies in America." Published in May 1939, the survey revealed that there were but eight libraries in the United States that held more than 3,500 volumes on South Asia. In six libraries, the bulk of the holdings related to ancient philosophical and literary works and philology. The only two libraries having collections that covered a broader range were the Library of Congress and the New York Public Library. The latter's holdings were more comprehensive than those of the Library of Congress. Both were, however, puny compared to the massive collection on South Asia held by the British Museum and the India Office Library located in London. No American university could match the holdings of Oxford and Cambridge. A sensible scholar from Europe or elsewhere at that time would scarcely have thought of Washington as a place to visit in connection with any sort of research project on South Asian affairs.

"We've Got To Hold India and Ceylon"

Adolf Hitler and Hideki Tojo changed it all! The military disasters that followed in the wake of the Japanese attack on Pearl Harbor brought South Asia for the first time squarely to the attention of the American government, Congress, and the public as a region of significant importance for the U.S. war effort. Rommel's German panzers were on the rampage in North Africa, while Singapore surrendered to the Japanese on February 15, 1942. In Washington, an Army officer named Dwight David Eisenhower, assistant chief of the War Plans Division, wrote in a frantic memorandum on February 19, "We've got to hold India and Ceylon." The division's study, submitted to chief of staff, General George C. Marshall, listed the maintenance of the Allied position in the "India-Middle East" area as one of the three most vital objectives of the war. The Board of Economic Warfare, headed by Vice President Henry A. Wallace, discussed ways and means by which an American technical mission could stimulate Indian war production. The Council on Foreign Relations proffered a report—on which, men like Allen Dulles, Hanson Baldwin, and George Fielding Eliot had labored—asserting that since a great deal of manpower for military campaigns in the Far East would have to come from India, an American military mission should be dispatched forthwith to New Delhi.

On February 23, General Marshall approved Operation AQILLA—a project for the stationing of U.S. Army Air Force units in India. The decision marked the beginning of the end of the British Raj in India—and the start of an American military presence in South Asia. On February 25, members of the Foreign Relations Committee of the Senate, for the first time in the history of the U.S. Congress, discoursed on American security concerns in South Asia and harangued a hapless assistant secretary of state on Britain's errors of omission and commission in that area. On March 6, 1942, the State Department announced the decision of the United States Government to send a technical mission to India to examine and report on the possibilities of American assistance in developing the industrial resources of the country. Shortly thereafter, Roosevelt designated former assistant secretary of war, Colonel Louis Johnson, as the personal representative of the president in India.

Never previously had the Library of Congress's modest holdings on South Asia been so intensively mined by various agencies of the U.S. government as at this time. The most avid users were undoubtedly the eager-beavers of William "Wild Bill" Donovan's Office of Strategic Services. On May 27, 1942, the makeshift "area specialists" of the Research and Analysis Branch of OSS were able to turn out quite a respectable mimeographed report entitled "Survey of India." Such were the beginnings of Washington as a location for research on South Asian affairs. Those were the days when a young political scientist from Georgia who had joined the Army was posted to Washington on G-2 duties and assigned to familiarize himself with Indian affairs. He had come to the right spot, for soon he was ready to move to New Delhi's Imperial Hotel to serve on the staff of the commanding general, China-Burma-India Theatre, "Vinegar" Joe Stilwell. This particular "India-hand" was to be named by President John F. Kennedy in 1961 as secretary of state—Dean Rusk.

I may mention at this point that the account I have presented in this section is based largely on materials that I gathered in Washington in my own research on the evolution of U.S. security concerns in the South Asian region.

How To Turn Wheat into Books

If the Second World War gave the first significant boost to the acquisition of research materials on South Asia, the withdrawal of British rule and the emergence of independent nations in the area provided the next stimulus. The Carnegie Corporation of New York and the Rockefeller Foundation made grants to some universities for the promotion of South Asian Studies. The attention of the United States government and of Congress came to be directed towards the area by successive developments in the Cold War—the explosion of a nuclear device by the Soviet Union, the victory of Mao Tse-tung and the communists in the Chinese civil war, mounting hostilities between the French and the Viet Minh in Indo-China, and the outbreak of war in Korea.

Reflecting the growing national security concerns, the Joint Committee on Southern Asia of the American Council of Learned Societies and the Social Science Research Council, in its 1951 report, stated somberly that in the entire United States there were no more than 160 persons with "special competence" on South and Southeast Asia. The report offered eight recommendations aimed at remedying the state of affairs. On one issue, however, the report had nothing concrete to suggest: who would pick up the tab?

Enter the American farmer. The wheat that the sturdy yeomen of Kansas, Nebraska, North Dakota, and other states had raised, and were to raise in the years ahead, was to be the crucial factor in developments that led to the rapid growth of research materials on South Asia in Washington and certain other locations in the United States. My own India had a role in starting it all by managing to develop a serious food shortage in 1950 and seeking to purchase two million tons of wheat from the United States.

Public Law 48, enacted by Congress in connection with the "Wheat Loan" to India, provided, *inter alia*, that, from the interest paid by the government of India, a certain percentage could be utilized for the purchase and dispatch to the United States of documents that might be useful for higher education in the U.S. It was an impressively far-sighted move, but some years were to elapse before action was initiated to take advantage of this provision of the law. While scholars and librarians grew increasingly impatient, the government and Congress were preoccupied with what they regarded as the far more urgent task of countering "Communist expansionism." When officials and members of Congress were worrying over Dienbienphu and the Geneva Conference, SEATO and the Baghdad Pact, Quemoy, and Matsu, they could not pay much attention to the pleadings of scholars concerning the importance of acquiring research materials in some obscure South Asian languages with unpronounceable names.

The American farmer was doing his part. India and, subsequently, Pakistan had done what they could by developing food shortages and seeking American grain. A law was on the statute books. But still the operation would not get started, much to the anguish of South Asian researchers. Perhaps many of them turned their eyes upward in prayer. The answer to their prayers was, indeed, to emerge out there in the blue skies in the form of Sputnik, launched by the Soviet Union on October 4, 1957. A month later, a second Soviet satellite was aloft bearing an animal held in as great reverence in the U.S. as the cow supposedly is in India—a dog. The soft "beep-beep" of the Soviet satellites as they traversed the skies over the United States had a profound impact on the American people, spurring them to call for urgent action to promote scientific and technological research and to tone up the educational system itself.

The Library of Congress Takes the Lead

The time was opportune, and the Library of Congress was quick to move. In November 1957, a conference, on the need to expand American library resources of South Asian materials, was held at the Library of Congress. Andrew D. Osborn of Harvard University Library explained the need in language most likely to be comprehended by government officials and members of Congress:

> This century is increasingly being called by historians "the age of color" and the peoples of Southern Asia are among the most important of the underdeveloped countries for the United States to study and understand. Accordingly, it is of strategic importance that our resources for Southern Asia be built up retroactively and currently. . . .[7]

One Congressman whose support was enlisted for the cause was John Dingell of Michigan. He successfully piloted, to Public Law 480, an amendment, which provided that part of the local currencies generated by U.S. shipments of foodgrain under P.L. 480 could be used for the acquisition of books, periodicals, documents, and other materials of cultural or educational importance. The Dingell Amendment was viewed by scholars and librarians as a dream fulfilled. The earlier P.L. 480 had only provided for the purchase of Indian central and state government documents. Such a restriction no longer applied. Unfortunately, however, owing to foot-dragging in Congress and the Executive Branch, it was only in 1961, after John F. Kennedy had become president, that funds were appropriated for the enlarged program. They were far smaller than what the advocates of the program had fondly hoped for. It was nonetheless the beginning of a massive venture.

What was of significance for the future was that the operation of the program was to be centralized under the leadership of the Library of Congress. The vigorous manner in which the task was tackled by the Library of Congress was in no small measure due to the dedicated and imaginative labors of its specialists like Dr. Horace I. Poleman of the Orientalia (now Asian) Division. By March 1962, the first consignment of materials acquired by the Library's field offices in India and Pakistan reached Washington. While keeping a full set of materials for itself, the Library of Congress distributed other sets to selected institutions that had been invited to participate in the program.

The magnitude of the task undertaken by the Library of Congress can be gauged by this: by the end of fiscal year 1980, the total number of "pieces" acquired under the program was over seventeen million. The following table, based on information obtained from the Library of Congress in January 1981, shows the countries of origin and the number of pieces acquired from each:

Country	Number of Pieces
India (including Bhutan)	13,436,585
Nepal	422,203
Pakistan	3,187,089
Sri Lanka	173,908
Bangladesh	130,737

The range of materials being acquired can be seen from the breakdown for fiscal year 1980:

Country	Newspapers	Serials	Monographs	Other	Total
India (including Bhutan)	82,865	307,363	121,580	1,154	512,962
Nepal	6,166	10,078	2,810	5	19,059
Pakistan	38,855	41,877	18,604	34	99,370
Sri Lanka	10,081	10,687	2,223	15	23,006
Bangladesh	9,056	6,941	3,958	—	19,955

The figures show what was acquired by the Library of Congress for itself as well as for the small number of other institutions that had been invited to participate in the program. Field offices of the Library of Congress function in New Delhi and Karachi. The New Delhi Field Office, with which I am acquainted, is a very impressive operation. Its energetic director and a staff of over a hundred (including a small complement of U.S. specialists) make the place a veritable beehive of activity. The New Delhi office is in charge of acquisition of materials from India, Bangladesh, Sri Lanka, Nepal, Bhutan, and the Maldives, while the Karachi office takes care of Pakistani materials. Apart from the acquisition and selection of materials in numerous languages, the field offices prepare accession lists that serve as a valuable tool for libraries and scholars. The field offices also microfilm newspapers and official gazettes and microfiche old books that cannot otherwise be preserved. Users of the Library of Congress's extensive holdings on South Asia owe a deep debt of gratitude to the unseen but dedicated labors of the men and women in the field offices of New Delhi and Karachi.

A Plenitude of Riches

In 1951, shortly after I arrived in the United States on my first visit, I traveled to Washington. I wandered into the Library of Congress of which I had heard a great deal even while I was a college student in distant Madras. The ease of access to the vast collections for a user and the total absence of bureaucratic fuss made a deep impression on me. The present Librarian of Congress, Dr. Daniel Boorstin, whom I have the privilege of knowing, stressed this important point in an interview a couple of years ago, saying, "The Library of Congress is the library of the citizens who elect that Congress, and they should have free access to this great national intellectual repository—no matter how unfashionable their political beliefs or how esoteric their scholarly interests." What is remarkable is that the repository is available to non-citizens, too, on exactly the same basis. As Dr. Boorstin pointed out, unlike other national libraries, the Library of Congress does not require any admission cards or letters of recommendation. Its riches are open for use to "anyone who behaves himself!"

Contrary to the impression that may be entertained in certain quarters I must be a well-behaved person indeed, because I have worked in the Library in the course of several visits to the United States, especially during three periods of stay in the Washington area covering four years. On each visit I have seen, as in so many facets of American life, the changes and improvements in the services available to users.

In 1976 I made a brief visit to the United States to observe the presidential campaign and participate in an international conference in observance of the Bi-centennial. At that time, during a visit to the Librarian's office, Dr. Boorstin told me of his gifted, versatile, and tireless helper, SCORPIO (Subject-Oriented Retriever for Processing Information On-Line), the computer system with terminals silently waiting and ever ready to respond to the researcher's commands if they are couched with logical accuracy in the language in which SCORPIO has been raised. I was fascinated on my first encounter with SCORPIO and, two years later, having returned to Washington as a Fellow at the Wilson Center, I found that SCORPIO's usefulness had significantly increased.

I heard, with some dismay, that the old familiar catalogue cards were to be "frozen" before too long, and that the computer would handle all cataloging. Some old-timers mourned the imminent demise of the catalogue cards as the abandonment of "five hundred years of the cultivation of printing, of the sedulous search for clarity and beauty in type faces. . . ." What would be the impact on the sensitive scholar of "mechanical devices,. . . the shimmering green cathode-ray tube, the domino squares of microfiche, or the palely loitering sheets of machine-readable printouts. . . ."?[28] My guess is that the sensitive scholar will survive—and learn to love the cathode-ray tube that can ease his labors. Civilization marches on and nothing can stand still—certainly not the dear, old Library of Congress.

The amiable Library of Congress employee that you run into may well be a "Senior Information Systems Specialist," and if you are rash enough to ask what he is up to, you may get an earful of exciting abracadabra. You will hear the latest tidings on MARC (Machine-Readable Cataloguing), COMARC (Co-operative MARC), MUMS (Multiple-Use Marc System), RLIN (Research Libraries Information Network), and, of course, the forthcoming colloquium of CCLN (Computerized Library Network), where our Senior Information Systems Specialist expects to cross wands with a fellow magician from UTLAS (University of Toronto Library Automation System). Translated into man-readable language, what he is saying is that he expects to provide us with even faster and more comprehensive services in the days ahead. All of which means that in the Library of Congress the researcher on South Asian affairs, too, will have at his service the best technological facility available anywhere. If he does not complete his *magnum opus,* he knows exactly with whom the fault lies, whatever ingenious explanations he may offer to his wife, his chairperson, or other insistent interrogators.

Today the Library of Congress describes as "comprehensive" its holdings of materials on South Asia in the following languages: Arabic, Assamese, Bengali, English, French, Gujarati, Hindi, Kannada, Kashmiri, Konkani, Malayalam, Manipuri, Marathi, Mongolian, Nepali, Newari, Oriya, Pali, Persian, Portuguese, Prakrit, Punjabi, Sanskrit, Sindhi, Tamil, Telugu, Tibetan, Turkish, Urdu, dialects and tribal languages, and European languages (apart from English, French, and Portuguese). My own mother tongue happens to be the ancient language of Tamil. I was enormously gratified to see how comprehensive, indeed, were the Library's holdings of materials in Tamil. One who wants to work on, say, agrarian unrest, as portrayed in contemporary Tamil fiction, will find more materials available more conveniently in the Library of Congress than anywhere else in the world. To find an equivalent collection, one will have to go to the Connemara Library in Madras, capital of the state of Tamil Nadu.

Apart from studies falling within the purview of traditional disciplines, the collections available at the Library of Congress provide ample scope for topically oriented studies on such issues as population, pollution, energy, conservation, community development, urban problems, and affirmative action, among others. Those who are engaged in comparative studies of issues pertaining to selected countries in different parts of the world may find that the material on any South Asian country in the Library is adequate for their purposes.

The researcher in South Asian affairs will benefit from an opportunity to discuss his project and requirements with Mr. Louis Jacob, Head of the Southern Asia Section of the Asian Division of the Library. Working with him are two well-informed reference librarians, one on India and the other on Pakistan. It is advisable to take counsel with these gentlemen first, and as often as necessary, to get at what one wants quickly.

The South Asian collection in the Law Library deserves special mention. The Manuscripts Division contains the personal papers of many prominent Americans. The material is not, at present, a significant source for researchers on South Asian affairs. Those interested in finding out the response of some American notabilities to South Asian developments may be able, after considerable effort, to find a few items of interest. That was my own experience. The situation will undoubtedly change over the years as the papers of prominent Americans with close associations with South Asia are acquired by the Manuscripts Division. The Library of Congress also has very large collections of maps, phonographic records, photographs, and films, and the interested researcher should talk with specialists of the divisions concerned to ascertain whether items of possible use may be available in the collections.

Will the Library's acquisitions of South Asian materials continue to grow at the same pace as during the last fifteen years, or will they slacken if "local currencies" are available only in reduced volume or not at all? Scholars and librarians have been anxiously discussing the issue during the last few years. They are putting forth various arguments, including once again the tried and tested one of "national security." They point to South Asia's "strategic location," population, resources, institutions, and other factors, throwing in Islam for good measure. Will Congress listen?

I hope that there were some prominent members of Congress present among "the black-tie audience gathered in the Library's Great Hall" in May 1977, when Dr. Boorstin proclaimed that the "true commodity" at the Library of Congress was a nondepletable resource—Knowledge. A few months later, the Librarian of Congress rose to even greater heights of eloquence as he called for a national effort to make the Library "a staging ground for the Renaissance of the Book." Why the Library of Congress? "Because . . . we serve all libraries, scholars of all sorts and conditions, teachers, readers, quasi-readers, semi-readers, and even, we suspect, non-readers."

You and I certainly belong to one or another of those categories listed by Dr. Boorstin. We have thus a clear stake in praying that the Library of Congress should continue to thrive—and that its holdings on South Asia should continue to grow.

Harvest at the Archives

Washington is the home of the U.S. National Archives. When I approach the Archives, I think, strangely enough, of President Herbert Hoover, probably the first American president who, earlier in life, had some business interest in South Asia—in the Kolar Gold Fields of the present state of Karnataka. He was also the first former president to visit the subcontinent on an official mission. In 1946 he was deputed by President Harry S Truman to visit India and assess its requirements for food imports. In the course of his visit, Hoover met Mahatma Gandhi, thus becoming the highest-ranking American leader to have had a face-to-face discussion with India's Mahatma. Well, Hoover it was who, in 1932, laid the cornerstone of the National Archives Building.

The writings of American "statesmen, soldiers and all the others" who had toiled to build the structure of American national life constitute an indispensable storehouse of materials for the student of American affairs. But since those soldiers, statesmen, and others, in the course of service to their land, dealt with or worked in numerous foreign countries, the holdings of the National Archives are of considerable use to a researcher on South Asian affairs. It is true that the material one obtains will be a version of a situation presented by an American official. The local material that the American official occasionally appended to his dispatches or memoranda would be what he had chosen to select or highlight. Yet these too are often useful. Sometimes such items might not be available in the archives of the country of origin. The American version might provide information as well as leads that might set the researcher on a further search for evidence. That was my own experience when, animated by the spirit of the venturesome prospector of old, I panned the vast holdings of the Archives in the hope of finding at least a bagful of nuggets.

Perseverence pays at the National Archives, and few are the prospectors who emerge from the edifice in total disappointment. Let me illustrate from my own experience. For a study of some aspects of the Great Bengal Famine of 1943, in which three million persons perished by starvation, I found valuable materials in the National Archives. Great Britain ruled over India at that time, and war-time censorship was in force. That a tragedy of colossal dimensions might overtake the people of eastern India was predicted on the basis of a perceptive analysis in a report prepared by the Board of Economic Warfare's Technical Research Branch as early as July 1943. That document had remained undisturbed in its aging folder in one of the myriads of racks of the National Archives. But now its time had come, and it had made a half-sleepy reader from distant New Delhi sit up and take notice. More was to be found in other folders. Dispatches from the U.S. consul general in Calcutta gave a graphic account of the toll of the famine and the apathy of the British-controlled officialdom. Reports from the U.S. mission in New Delhi described the attitude of British authorities in the capital of India, while London's course was occasionally described in dispatches from the U.S. embassy. Useful information on Anglo-American discussions was found in the files of the bureau of Foreign and Domestic Commerce.

While for the pre-Independence period of the countries of South Asia the most comprehensive materials are to be found in British repositories and the respective archives of the countries concerned, the holdings of the National Archives may yield valuable supplementary information. A wide range of "Record Groups" in the

National Archives provided me with indispensable information on political, economic, and military developments in India during the crucial decade before the withdrawal of British rule and for a few years after India, Pakistan, and Sri Lanka became free. Similarly, for instance, some documents among the National Security Council material were useful in indicating U.S. security interests in, and policies towards, countries of the region.

It has ever been a tantalizing experience for me to go through the pages of the *Guide to the National Archives of the United States* (Washington, D.C.: Government Printing Office, 1974). In just a few minutes, my eyes close and I get transformed into a brown Walter Mitty, the great researcher and discoverer of profoundly significant information on international and South Asian affairs that had hitherto remained unknown to mankind. A splendid psychedelic vision, in full color, and with stereophonic sound too, may possibly occur to other fortunate individuals as the march of the Record Groups (RGs) of the Archives takes place before their closed eyes: RG 40, General Records of the Department of Commerce; RG 59, General Records of the Department of State; RG 84, Records of the Foreign Service Posts of the Department of State; RG 151, Records of the Bureau of Foreign and Domestic Commerce; RG 166, Records of the Foreign Agricultural Service; RG 266, Records of the Office of Strategic Services. . . .

The diligent researcher should have as his motto: "Seek and ye shall find." Perhaps I should modify the motto slightly: "Seek and ye may find it; Ask and ye shall find it!" The members of the professional staff of the Archives are very friendly and can be quite helpful—if only the researcher can tell them with a modicum of clarity what his research project is and for what he is looking.

For consulting certain categories of materials in the Archives for which access is restricted, the researcher is directed to a special room. I used to feel slightly claustrophobic in that room, especially since the three or four other researchers working there usually seemed to be totally lost to the world in the intensity of their concentration. In the files requested for examination, one may find large cards each indicating that an item has been removed for reasons of security classification. I learned from an American colleague, who worked in the room on a project broadly similar to mine, that, as a citizen of the United States, he was being permitted to see certain materials that were being withheld from me as a noncitizen. That was, of course, a somewhat disconcerting situation for me personally, though it did not detract from my appreciation of the general "openness" of the Archvies. I raised the issue subsequently with American colleagues at a meeting organized in Washington some years ago by, if I remember correctly, the Archives and the Society for Historians of American Foreign Relations. I received the polite response from an official of the State Department's Historical Division that the American practice in providing access to diplomatic documents to citizens and noncitizens was far more liberal than those of many other countries, including my own. Incidentally, the place to go for assistance concerning access to security-classified documents and guidance in seeking material under the Freedom of Information Act is the Records Declassification Division of the Archives.

The Archives is much more than a repository of U.S. government documents. The Audiovisual Archives Division publishes guides that could provide leads of sound recordings, still pictures, and film clips that might be of some interest to students of South Asian affairs. To those working on geographical themes, the Cartographic Division will be the area of exploration. Researchers on military history pertaining to the South Asian theater during the Second World War may launch reconnaissance operations in the Military Archives Division, which, apart from U.S. Army and Navy records, also has captured German and Japanese documents.

Specialized Libraries, Erudite Specialists

While New York, New Haven, Cambridge, Chicago, and Berkeley have magnificent libraries, they do not have the National Archives nor the array of support facilities that Washington alone provides for a researcher on South Asian affairs. The various departments and agencies of the U.S. government, Congress, and congressional committees, a host of national and professional organizations, international agencies, such as the World Bank and the International Monetary Fund, and the embassies of foreign countries have so rich an aggregation of materials and personnel to be tapped by the researcher that no other location in the United States can match them.

Specialized material may often be more quickly and conveniently available for examination in the library of the appropriate government agency or a concerned nongovernmental organization than from a huge general library. The librarian at such a place probably experiences some enhanced inner satisfaction when the exotic stranger from Allahabad, Quetta, Colombo, Kathmandu, or Dacca anxiously inquires about some document that the librarian believes may be found among the materials he has devotedly gathered for his institution over the years. I have very pleasant memories of encounters with such people.

I first found out about the potential that exists in Washington for such pleasurable and exceedingly fruitful activity when I needed to get at whatever material was available—of all things—on the state of manganese mining in India. I knew as much about manganese as I did about molybdenum—I could just barely spell the words correctly. The information that I needed was for a political-strategic study, in which Indian manganese, urgently needed by the United States at a certain time, was the central character. I wanted to know about mining operations in India, the locations and companies involved, estimates of reserves, other sources of manganese supply to the United States, locations where U.S. corporations were engaged in prospecting or mining for manganese ore, and other data.

At the Bureau of Mines of the Interior Department, I was able to obtain, in a few days, all the information on Mn that I would probably need or want in my lifetime. My vocabulary was enriched by the acquisition of words like "beneficiation." For the benefit of lay readers who do not have my amazing "expertise," may I add that "Mn" stands for manganese and "beneficiation" means the process by which low-grade ore is upgraded. Beneficiation was exactly what happened to me after my few days at the Bureau of Mines. If you do not believe me, try it out for yourself by visiting the library of a government bureau or a private organization. These organisms grow and thrive in more luxuriant profusion in Washington than in any other place.

Suppose our research scholar is working on some issue relating to economic development in South Asia. He has already taken the measure of the vast holdings of the Library of Congress. As a respite from that giddy experience, he will be well advised to wend his way to the Development Information Center of the Agency for International Development (AID) located in Arlington, Virginia. The Center contains a broad range of materials produced by AID as well as other organizations on such fields as agriculture, population, education, urban development, and rural development. If he needs additional materials on agriculture in South Asia, he knows, as a man of keen intelligence, that the place to go will be the Department of Agriculture. Of special interest to him will be the Foreign Agricultural Service as well as such units of the Economics, Statistics, and Co-operative Service as the Developing Countries Program Area, the Agricultural History Branch, and the Documentation Center of the National Economic Analysis Division. He can also schedule a visit to the Joint Library of the International Monetary Fund and the International Bank for Reconstruction and Development.

A researcher interested in energy issues can find in the Library of Congress virtually all he needs in terms of materials published in the countries of South Asia. He can check with individual embassies regarding information they may have on major recent developments, and it will be useful for him to talk to specialists at the U.S. Department of Energy, where he can find them in such units as the Office of International Programs, Bureau of International Policy Development, Bureau of Energy Research, Bureau of Energy Data, Office of Nuclear Affairs, and International Energy Analysis Division. Private research organizations, such as Resources for the Future, Overseas Development Council, and the Washington Office of the Battelle Memorial Institute may be able to offer additional leads. Persons with competence in a variety of fields can be found on the staffs of congressional committees, the Congressional Research Service, and also in the World Bank, the International Monetary Fund, the Brookings Institution, and the American Enterprise Institute. Since Washington is one of the favorite haunts of ministers, officials, and scholars from South Asian countries, the researchers may be able to run some of them down for a chat.

I found that association with the Woodrow Wilson International Center for Scholars insured prompt and courteous opening of many Washington doors to me that otherwise might have required a little pushing. The best thing that can happen to one whose research materials and sources are basically to be found in Washington is to be chosen as a Wilson Fellow. The next best thing, especially for the young researcher, will be to befriend a Wilson Fellow and get invited to the Center's programs that may be of special interest to him. All through the year, the Center organizes discussions, colloquia, and conferences featuring distinguished scholars, officials, and specialists from around the world.

The Washington area has many fine universities, but none of them has a major program of South Asian Studies comparable to those of the Universities of Pennsylvania, Chicago, Wisconsin, and California (Berkeley). Some very competent South Asian specialists serve in the capital's universities, and the researcher who is new to Washington's ways can benefit by their advice and assistance. The universities themselves have modest collections of monographs and journals of interest to the scholar. The attractiveness of the local universities lies in the fact that such materials as are available in their libraries can be conveniently consulted. Further, nothing else can reinvigorate a jaded researcher, especially an academic on his sabbatical, as the sight of lively youngsters whose demeanor, even in the libraries, seems to proclaim the profound truth that there is more to life than research.

Embassies of South Asian countries have not cared to maintain libraries worth the name. However, they can furnish the researcher with a selection of current newspapers and journals. Since the embassies get them by air freight, one can keep track of South Asian developments with a time lag of just about one week. The Indian Embassy's reading room is especially good in this respect. It is useful to become acquainted with officials of the embassy relevant to one's research. Since Washington is one of the most important capitals, officials posted to the various embassies in the city are usually those regarded as quite bright by their home offices. The official machinery of South Asian embassies tends to move at a rather leisurely pace, but a friendly soul at an embassy can be a potential source of help.

Washington has a small group of South Asian journalists representing some major newspapers. While America is their beat, they are usually well informed on the national and state politics of their respective countries. As is customary in their tribe, they can be expected to have a fund of stories that are "not fit to print." As one who had been a member of the tribe years ago, I continue to harbor the notion that the time you spend with a journalist will seldom be dull and may occasionally be even rewarding.

Concerning contemporary South Asian affairs, it is my view that there is hardly a subject that one can think of, on which one cannot locate in Washington—fairly quickly—a substantial volume of basic and secondary materials; also, competent persons with whom to talk abound. In what other location in the United States can a researcher find comparable opportunities?

The Wonderful World of Ethnicland

In and around the Washington Metropolitan area live several thousand persons of South Asian origin representing virtually every linguistic group of the region. Among them are many with advanced professional degrees who are serving in various institutions, including agencies of the federal government. In Washington, as in every other area of the South Asian "diaspora," these people have established a wide range of cultural and religious organizations. The researcher should tap this resource for whatever it is worth; the embassies of the countries concerned will provide him with a list of ethnic organizations. Given the generally extroverted attitude of the South Asian, the researcher can be reasonably certain that an indication of his interest in having a discussion or in observing a cultural or religious function will be warmly received by his prospective host. For a researcher who has had no previous experience of living in a South Asian country, contacts with the ethnic organizations in the Washington area can serve as a useful orientation.

Since South Asia itself is so diverse, a scholar who has made a few visits to the region may only be familiar with the customs of the linguistic areas in which he has lived. This is often true in the case even of natives of South Asia who, living in one part of a country, may have only hazy notions on how people in a distant part of the same country live. During my most recent stay in Washington, I came to know more about Gujarāti and Marāthi customs, mores, and festivities than I had picked up in many decades of living in Madras and New Delhi. If you are willing to take some initiative, you will meet many interesting persons and make contacts that may prove useful in the future. South Asians and Yankees have at least one thing in common: they love to talk and they relish the sound of their own voices. They can talk on any subject and at any distance from the subject. Our researcher, as a skilled interviewer, should gently lead his loquacious South Asian away from the extended digression of the moment and towards the main subject under discussion. It isn't easy, but it can be accomplished after some practice.

Ethnic newspapers are a good source of information on what is going on among various groups and on activities that are planned. There is at least one such newspaper in English published in the Washington area. On Sundays at 2 P.M. a local radio station presents a half-hour of Indian film songs interspersed with announcements of forthcoming community activities and film shows. A couple of theaters screen Indian films regularly on weekends and a Pakistani film occasionally. South Asians love music—their own kind—and you can win your way into their hearts by learning to hum one of two popular tunes. Records and cassettes are available in South Asian stores located in several places in the Metropolitan area.

Washington offers a wide choice of swamis, gurus, yogis, fakirs, mullahs, lamas, bhikkus, priests, and reverends from South Asia. They come in all sizes, shapes, and fancy costumes, and they are ready to impart to the earnest seeker their own respective recipes for inner peace, spiritual bliss, knowledge of the Ultimate, or whatever. The guru business shows no signs of slackening, and the only complaint of some South Asian holy men is that too darned many Americans are getting into the act, assuming Sanskrit names, and offering all sorts of crash programs. A sensible rule of thumb for the researcher who is not a seasoned South Asia hand will be to give a wide berth to gurus whose following is almost entirely or even largely American. For the genuine article, look for the visiting guru around whom ethnic South Asians throng. While waiting for such an encounter, one should plan visits to the Islamic Center on Massachussetts Avenue, the Gandhi Memorial Center on Western Avenue, and the Buddhist Vihara on Sixteenth Street to observe services and meet South Asian Muslims, Hindus, and Buddhists.

There are many South Asian restaurants in the Washington area where you can encounter natives of the region and also make your acquaintance with various dishes having exotic names. A South Asian who sees an American struggling with the menu in such a restaurant tends to regard the latter rather favorably on the ground that an American who has mustered the courage and sophistication to try South Asian food cannot be all bad. You have only to extend a benign smile in the direction of the South Asian and the chances are excellent that you will soon be engaged in a spirited conversation with him.

You may also collect other dividends at these South Asian restaurants. At one such establishment on New York Avenue, one block from the White House, the American working skillfully on the *Bombay thali* may be a specialist on subcontinental affairs in the National Security Council. The American standing at the head of the line at another place, serenely asking for the Tamil delicacy, *masala dosa*, may be a State Department official who had written a doctoral dissertation after extensive field research in India. At other South Asian restaurants, you may run into former Fulbright professors, AID consultants, warriors against the mosquito, Seventh Day Adventist missionaries, retired "spooks," Hare Krishna evangelists, and other assorted gentry who have "done time" in South Asia and have gotten hooked on South Asian cuisine in the bargain. As you listen to their tales, it may slowly dawn upon you that you may yourself, after a field trip or two, become an aficionado of things South Asian and an authoritative commentator on the region's affairs whenever you can collect an audience of at least two persons. Then, you will have your own tall tales to tell—including the one about the opus on South Asia that you have been working on for years and years.

Of course you will add that the triumphant completion of the opus calls for just one final spell of concentrated work in the place that has the best research collections on contemporary South Asia in the whole world—Washington, DC.

Manakkal S. Venkataramani
School of International Studies
Jawaharlal Nehru University
New Delhi, India
(*Fellow, Woodrow Wilson International Center for Scholars, 1978–1979*)

Notes

1. Saul K. Padover, comp., *A Jefferson Profile as Revealed in his Letters* (New York: John Day, 1956), pp. 338–41.

2. Samuel Eliot Morison, *The Maritime History of Massachusetts 1783–1860* (Cambridge, Mass.: Houghton Mifflin, 1961), pp. 279–85.

3. W. Norman Brown, "South Asia Studies: A History," *The Annals* of the American Academy of Political and Social Science (Philadelphia), 356 (November 1964):56.

4. Theodore Roosevelt, *Works*, vol. 14 (New York: Scribners, 1926), pp. 260–61.

5. Consul General White's dispatch addressed to Wallace Murray, Chief, Division of Near Eastern Affairs, Department of State, was provided by a State Department source.

6. *Foreign Relations of the United States 1937*, vol. 2 (Washington, D.C.: Government Printing Office, 1954), pp. 13–14.

7. Quoted by Poleman, "American Research Library Resources," in Richard D. Lambert, ed., *Resources for South Asian Area Studies in the United States* (Philadelphia: University of Pennsylvania Press, 1962), p. 194.

8. Ruth Gay, "The Machine in the Library," *The American Scholar* (Washington), 49 (Winter 1979–80):75.

INTRODUCTION

Purpose: This volume is intended to serve as a basic reference aid for scholars interested in utilizing the extraordinarily rich, varied, and often unique resources of the nation's capital for research in the field of South Asian studies. Although aimed primarily at serious researchers, this work should also prove useful and informative to many others with a more casual interest in South Asia.

It cannot be overemphasized that the wealth of resources available in the metropolitan Washington area, where history is both made and preserved, provides tremendous opportunities for scholarly research in South Asian studies as in many other fields. Washington's distinction for housing the most prolific and proliferating research resources on the area of our interest is shared by such eminent national institutions as the Library of Congress, the National Library of Medicine, the National Agricultural Library, the National Archives and Records Service, and the comprehensive museum systems and research facilities of the Smithsonian Institution, as well as by the numerous fine academic institutions, research centers, private organizations, and government departments and agencies.

In addition to the various interest groups zealously promoting their common concern and consultants vying for research and technical assistance contracts, the host of scholars, diplomats, technocrats, bureaucrats, politicians, and political activists who reside in the nation's capital contribute to the development of national perspective and decision-making processes affecting many vital areas of significance, including foreign policy. The myriad documents and records generated by these groups' divergent activities are usually deposited in the various libraries and archives described in the *Guide*.

Furthermore, the accumulated treasure of artifacts in the museums and other institutions and the presence of a large international community in the city present the scholar pursuing foreign area studies with experiential opportunities. It is with the objective of introducing, locating, and identifying the scope and extent of research potentials available in Washington in the field of South Asian studies that this volume was undertaken.

In spite of the abundance of rich materials in the area, there is a general lack of knowledge about them. The purpose of a volume such as this is to focus on the specific quantum and content of research resources in South Asian studies available in the D.C. area, thereby enabling a keener awareness of its facilities among individuals and institutions concerned with this field of study.

Scope and Content: In addition to providing a basic directory with information of names, addresses, and telephone numbers, this *Guide* is primarily designed to be a descriptive and evaluative survey of research resources in the metropolitan area. More than 500 collections, organizations, and agencies have been surveyed in the preparation of this work. While efforts have been made to make this volume comprehensive, it is by no means an exhaustive or definitive inventory of all source materials. The main body of the work is divided into two parts.

Part I examines Washington-area resource *collections*: libraries; archives, and manuscript repositories; art and artifacts; music and other sound recordings; and maps, films, and data banks. Each individual entry describes the size, content, and organizational format of a specific collection's South Asian holdings and, whenever possible, qualitatively evaluates the subject and area strengths and most outstanding aspect of the materials in those holdings.

Part II focuses on the Washington-based public and private *organizations* that are concerned with South Asia and are potential sources of information or assistance to researchers. Included in this part are: research centers; academic departments and programs in local educational institutions; United States government agencies; South Asian embassies and international organizations; academic, professional, and cultural associations; cultural-exchange and technical-assistance organizations; religious organizations; and publications and media.

Each entry in Part II describes the individual organization's South Asia-related functions, delineates its pertinent research activities, materials, and products—both published and unpublished, classified and unclassified—and notes restrictions on scholarly access to unpublished and restricted materials. Brief introductions preceding each section underscore the special features of the section and provide supplemental information.

Additional information relevant to South Asian studies is provided in a series of appendixes: South Asian press representatives in Washington; South Asian ethnic, cultural, social, and religious organizations; a listing of libraries by size of South Asian holdings; a list of area bookstores; suggestions on orienting oneself in the metropolitan area; a list of federal government holidays; and standard entry formats. A brief bibliography, and indexes (personal-papers collections, library subject-strength and evaluation table, and name and subject indexes) conclude the volume.

The *Guide's* topical coverage concentrates on the disciplines of the social sciences and the humanities, traditionally considered to fall under the rubric of area studies, although the fields of science and technology have been included where relevant. The volume's geographic scope includes Afghanistan, Bangladesh, Bhutan, India, Maldive Islands, Nepal, Pakistan, and Sri Lanka. The time frame stretches from antiquity to the present.

The problem in determining the criteria for inclusion of materials in the category of religion and philosophy was resolved somewhat arbitrarily. In addition to including all the materials on Hinduism, Jainism, Sikhism, and Zoroastrianism, all materials on Islam and Buddhism (with the exception of those dealing with a specific region or country outside of South Asia) has been counted in assessing the numerical strength of the collections. Consequently, most tabular information on religion and philosophy tends to reflect a broader than usual scope in this *Guide*.

In other categories, no materials have been taken into consideration unless they were directly relevant to South Asia. Because of the recognized link of South Asia to its peripheral geographic regions, scholars may find it useful to consult the volumes of *Scholars' Guide* for *Middle Eastern Studies* by Steven R. Dorr (1981), *East Asian Studies* by Hong N. Kim (1979), and the forthcoming *Southeast Asian Studies* by Patrick M. Mayerchak (1982). Because of the nature of the coverage, Bonnie G. Rowan's *Film and Video Collections* (1980), another Wilson Center *Guide*, may also be of assistance.

Methodology: Preparation of the volume began with the compilation of a list of all Washington-area collections and organizations considered to be potential sources of information or assistance for scholarly research on South Asia. The bibliography at the end of the volume contains some reference sources consulted in the preparation of this preliminary list. From September 1979 to November 1980, the author investigated in person or by telephone each potential collection and organization. Information was collected from on-site examination, discussion with the staff members, and relevant printed materials.

While attempts have been made to make this *Guide* as accurate and inclusive as possible, certain resources may have been overlooked, or descriptions of some collections may not be as complete as desirable. For possible future editions of this work, suggestions for additions, changes, and improvements are most welcome and may be sent to the Librarian, Woodrow Wilson International Center for Scholars, Smithsonian Institution Building, 1000 Jefferson Drive, S.W., Washington, D.C. 20560 (202/357-2567).

South Asianists will understand that much of the rich heritage of Pakistan will be recorded under "India before 1947," when the British departed and India and Pakistan became separate nations. Similarly, Bangladesh was part of India until 1947, and from 1947 to 1971 was known as East Pakistan. For this reason, the numerical assessments of Washington collections undercount the volume of materials on these two nations and their peoples.

Acknowledgments: The author wishes to thank the U.S. Department of Education for financial support (under the authority of Title VI, Section 602, NDEA), which made the preparation of this work possible. Grateful acknowledgment and appreciation are due Zdeněk V. David, editor of the Wilson Center's *Scholars' Guide* Series, and Purnima M. Bhatt and Louis A. Jacob, consultants for this volume, for the valued advice, guidance, and counsel given.

The author of this current volume, having benefited immensely from the foregoing *Guides* in the series, would like to thank the authors of those volumes whose labors made his task easier: Steven A. Grant, Michael Grow, Hong N. Kim, Purnima M. Bhatt, Bonnie G. Rowen, Kenneth J. Dillon, and Steven R. Dorr. He wishes also to have the privilege of expressing his deep appreciation to the numerous members of the staff in the institutions and organizations discussed in this *Guide* for contributing their time and knowledge to its preparation.

It is difficult to acknowledge adequately the author's indebtedness to Joyce L. Rahim for smoothing many rough edges from the original draft, for typing the manuscript, and for valuable research assistance. Thanks go also to Zaved Iqbal Apu for his contribution of the calligraphy on the title page, and Elizabeth Dixon, of the Wilson Center, for her design and production arrangements. Finally, I would like to express my gratitude to Judith F. Wilder, editor for the publisher, for copyediting the manuscript and seeing it through to the completed volume. It is needless to mention that the author alone is responsible for all commissions and omissions in this work.

HOW TO USE THIS *GUIDE*

Format: The main body of this *Guide* is divided into seven collection sections and eight organization sections. Within each section, entries are arranged alphabetically by the name of the collection or organization. In the collection sections as well as the organization sections, all entries referring to United States government agencies, have the functional descriptors preceding the generic name; i.e., *State Department* rather than *Department of State*. In the organization section containing South Asian embassies and international organizations (K), the South Asian embassies are entered under their official names as indicated in the *Diplomatic List* (August 1980), but are arranged alphabetically according to their geographic name and listed as a group before the international organizations.

Standard Entry Form: At the beginning of each section, a brief introductory paragraph is followed by a standard entry form, which indicates the category and numerical sequence of information contained within each entry. (All standard entry forms also appear together in Appendix VII.) Users of the *Guide* may find it helpful to consult the entry form before examining each section. If a particular number does not appear in an entry, that category of information was either not applicable or not available. Combining two numbers in an entry denotes overlapping of information or insufficient information to warrant separate categories. If a single institution or organization has more than one entry in the *Guide*, references to all entries are gathered under the main entry and also in the Name Index.

Names, Addresses, and Telephone Numbers: All data are subject to change, particularly for government departments, complex organizations, and associations where reorganization and personnel changes occur often. For example, while this *Guide* was being prepared, new telephone numbers were introduced for the Smithsonian Institution; the U.S. Education Department was reorganized after it was separated from the former Health, Education and Welfare Department; the Library of Congress renamed its Thomas Jefferson Building the "John Adams," and its Main Building the "Thomas Jefferson"; and the Smithsonian Institution changed its National Museum of History and Technology to the "National Museum of American History" and its National Collection of Fine Arts to the "National Museum of American Art."

All telephone numbers without an area code are within the District of Columbia (area code 202). For numbers in suburban Maryland and Virginia, area codes (301 and 703, respectively) precede the numbers. When dialing from within the Washington metropolitan area, the above mentioned area codes should be ignored since most of these would be toll free calls.

Indexes: Four indexes provide access to information in the text from several perspectives. The *Name Index* contains the names of organizations and institutions but not individuals. The *Personal-Papers Index* includes the names of individuals whose papers and manuscripts are located in libraries or other depositories in the area. The *Library Subject-Strength Index* ranks the major library collections in the area by subject and by country, based upon a scale explained in the introductory note of the libraries section. The ranking table used to evaluate the quantitative strength of the collections is also reproduced with this index. Some ratings are based on subcategories of major subject categories; for example, collections with particular strength in finance or trade are ranked within the broader category of economics. The *Subject Index* covers rather broad categories and includes geographic headings. Because of the size and relative significance of India in South Asia, most collections and organizations focus on India more than on any other country in the region. However, the *Subject Index* indicates other countries also whenever they feature in any particular collection or organization.

Transliteration: The transliteration system used in this volume is essentially that of the Library of Congress. Certain apparent inconsistencies are due to the author's attempt to facilitate retrieval by adopting names and titles as they appear in the catalogs or other bibliographic aids in the collections surveyed.

Common Acronyms:
AID—Agency for International Development
FBIS—Foreign Broadcast Information Service
FOIA—Freedom of Information Act
GPO—U.S. Government Printing Office
IBRD—International Bank for Reconstruction and Development (World Bank)
ICA—International Communication Agency
IMF—International Monetary Fund
JPRS—Joint Publications Research Service
LC—Library of Congress
NARS—National Archives and Records Service
NTIS—National Technical Information Service
UN—United Nations

COLLECTIONS

A Libraries

This *Guide* follows the evaluation methodology determined for the Wilson Center's *Scholars' Guide* series through the pioneering work of Steven A. Grant on *Russian/ Soviet Studies* (1977). South Asia-related holdings in most large general collections, and in several smaller specialized collections, are evaluated on a scale of A through D. These rankings are based on the quantity and quality of 13 major subject categories.

The Library of Congress's holdings were taken as the standard of evaluation for an A collection, which is defined here as a comprehensive collection of primary and secondary source materials.

The B collection is defined as a substantial collection (approximately one-tenth the size of the Library of Congress collection) of primary and secondary sources.

The C collection is considered to be a substantial collection (roughly one-half the size of a B collection) of secondary sources, with some primary materials, sufficient to support graduate instruction.

Finally, a D collection is defined as a collection (approximately one-half the size of a C collection) of predominately secondary sources, sufficient to support undergraduate instruction. The rating of D − (minus) indicates a collection that is not sufficient to qualify for a D rating.

In most cases, the numerical strength of various subject and geographic categories are derived from the measurement of library shelflist on the basis of a formula of 100 index cards or 85 titles per inch of shelflist catalog cards. With the exception of the category of religion and philosophy, only those call numbers, extracted from the Library of Congress classification schedule, that are devoted to South Asia or to the different subregions and countries of South Asia were taken into consideration. However, all the libraries surveyed in the area do not follow the LC classification schedule. Some follow the Dewey Decimal system, and others have devised their own systems.

Furthermore, because of the several shortcomings in the method used for shelflist measurement—including the absence of an LC classification schedule for South Asian holdings in law, the difficulty of extracting call numbers for South Asian materials in certain subject categories, the periodic modification and changes in the LC classification schedule and introduction of better numbers, and the fact that all LC classification categories are not amenable to geographic categories—the impression rendered of the relative strengths of a library collection tends to underestimate rather than overestimate. Thus the figures obtained by this measurement technique should be viewed as a rough approximation only. All figures in the tables are numbers of titles.

Numerical totals in country or geographic categories are calculated by computing the shelflist measurements of certain selected call numbers in the subject categories of history, economics, politics and government, and bibliography and reference. Important subject categories, such as religion and philosophy, and language and literature, could not be incorporated into the country figures since obviously these categories cannot be adequately separated on a geographic basis. It may also be pointed out that the Library of Congress cataloging system favors the category of history for classification of materials over politics and government, international relations, sociology, religion, geography, anthropology, and military sciences. Holdings in the category of history, therefore, in most collections, reflect the over-all numerical strength of South Asia-related holdings and may explain the relatively small number of holdings in other subject categories.

The country figures generated here are only intended to be a general indicator of the geographic strengths of the collection surveyed. It is assumed that for most average collections the cumulative totals of some highly selective but weighty call numbers in the four subject categories may provide a standard denominator in readily assessing the country or geographical strengths in the collection. All materials assigned in the LC classification schedule to the geographic category of South Asia—as opposed to the countries of that region—have been counted in the geographic category of India because they are relatively few and, in most cases, reflect India more than any other country in the region.

The Library of Congress subject categories and call numbers used in arriving at the numerical totals in the country categories are as follows:

History

DS 350–375	Afghanistan
DS 393–369.9	Bangladesh
DS 485.B503	Bhutan
DS 401–498	India (excluding call numbers for Bhutan, Nepal, Sri Lanka or Ceylon, and Maldive Islands)
DS 486.5.M3	Maldive Islands
DS 493–495.8	Nepal
DS 736–388	Pakistan
DS 488–490	Sri Lanka (Ceylon)

Politics and Government

JQ 1760–1769	Afghanistan
JQ 630–639	Bangladesh
JQ 200–620	India (excluding call numbers for Pakistan)
JQ 1825.N4	Nepal
JQ 540–559	Pakistan
JQ 650–659	Sri Lanka (Ceylon)

Economics

HC 416–420 and HA 1671–1680	Afghanistan
HC 440.8 and HA 1730.8	Bangladesh
HC 497.B	Bhutan
HC 431–440 and HA 1711–1730	India
HC 497.M27	Maldive Islands

HC 497.N5 and	
HA 1950.N5	Nepal
HC 440.5 and	
HA 1730.5	Pakistan
HC 424 and	
HA 1697	Sri Lanka (Ceylon)

Bibliography and Reference

Z 3016–3020	Afghanistan
Z 3186–3190	Bangladesh
Z 3201–3209	India
Z 3207.N	Nepal
Z 3191–3199	Pakistan
Z 3211–3215	Sri Lanka (Ceylon)

In assessing the numerical strength of a South Asia collection in the subject category of religion and philosophy, one inevitably encounters the problem of setting the criteria for selection of materials or call numbers to be included. The great religions of Buddhism, Hinduism, Jainism, and Sikhism are all of South Asian origin, and—with the exception of Buddhism, which had its greater impact beyond the South Asian frontiers, and the historic influence of Hinduism in Southeast Asia—all generally remained confined to South Asia. Another major South Asian religion, Islam, originated outside of South Asia but its impact in the region is unquestionably enormous. Similarly, the unique faith of Zoroastrianism was founded in antiquarian Iran but in the course of time found its sustenance in South Asia.

In view of these considerations, it seems appropriate that in determining the numerical strength of a collection in religion and philosophy all LC classification call numbers on Buddhism and Islam should be accounted for, excluding only those call numbers that deal specifically with a region or country outside of South Asia. For example, in the case of Buddhism, all materials on sacred literatures and commentaries are included, but Buddhism in Japan is excluded. Similarly, all call numbers concerning Islamic law (*Fiqh*), *Qur'ān* (*Koran*) and *Hadīth* (traditions of Muhammad) are included, but call numbers on Islam in Algeria or Yugoslavia are excluded. Concerning Hinduism, Jainism, and Sikhism, it seems advantageous to include all call numbers dealing with these religions since there is only an insignificant amount of material concerning them outside the confines of South Asia. For Judaism and Christianity, only those call numbers dealing directly with South Asia are included in the cumulative totals on religion and philosophy.

Aside from the above-mentioned methodological considerations, a few generalized comments may facilitate the reader in the use of this section of the *Guide* to the best advantage. The superb collection of the Library of Congress is unquestionably the most important source of printed South Asian resources in virtually every subject and category. Because of the obvious reason of very limited programs in South Asian studies in the local universities, South Asian collections in most university libraries are modest. However, the combined holdings of the local major university libraries and that of the Library of Congress could provide excellent support for any advanced research or graduate program in South Asian studies.

The excellent, selective holdings of the National Library of Medicine, National Agricultural Library, State Department Library, and the libraries of other specialized government agencies and organizations add further strength and diversity to the South Asian resources in the area. While all the major libraries are listed in this section, smaller collections or collections with significant South Asia-related materials are discussed along with the government agencies or organizations of which they are a part.

The reader's attention is called to Appendix III, Library Collections: A Listing by Size of South Asian Holdings and the Library Subject-Strength Index.

Libraries Entry Format (A)

1. General Information
    a. *address; telephone numbers*
    b. hours of service
    c. conditions of access (including availability of interlibrary loan and reproduction facilities)
    d. name/title of director and heads of relevant divisions

2. Size of Collection
    a. general
    b. South Asia

3. Description and Evaluation of Collection
    a. narrative assessment of South Asian holdings—subject and area strengths/weaknesses
    b. tabular evaluation of subject strengths:

Subject Categories	*Number of Titles (t)*	*Rating (A–D)**
Philosophy and Religion		
History and Auxiliary Sciences of History		
Geography and Anthropology		
Economics		
Sociology		
Politics and Government		
International Relations		
Law		
Education		
Art and Music		
Language and Literature		
Military Affairs		
Bibliography and Reference		

Afghanistan		
Bangladesh		
Bhutan		
India		
Maldive Islands		
Nepal		
Pakistan		
Sri Lanka (Ceylon)		

4. Special Collections
    a. periodicals
    b. newspapers
    c. government documents

d. miscellaneous vertical files
e. archives and manuscripts
f. maps
g. films
h. tapes

5. Noteworthy Holdings

6. Bibliographic Aids (catalogs, guides, etc.) Facilitating Use of Collection

---

*A—comprehensive collection of primary and secondary sources (Library of Congress collection to serve as standard of evaluation).

B—substantial collection of primary and secondary sources sufficient for some original research (holdings of roughly one-tenth those of the Library of Congress).

C—substantial collection of secondary sources with some primary materials, sufficient to support graduate instruction (holdings of roughly one-half those of the B collection).

D—collection of secondary sources, mostly in English, sufficient to support undergraduate instruction (holdings of roughly one-half those of C collection); collections rated below D are indicated by "D – ".

A1 Action Library (Peace Corps Library)

1. a. *806 Connecticut Avenue, N.W.*
    Washington, D.C. 20525
    254-3307

    b. 9:30 A.M.–4:00 P.M.   Monday–Friday

    c. The library is open to the public for on-site use only. Interlibrary loan services are available, but there is no photoduplication facility.

    d. Rita Warpeha, Chief Librarian

2. The bulk of the collection of this library consists of the holdings of the former Peace Corps Library, which was assembled to support the global program of the Peace Corps. Although currently limited to Nepal (an agreement was signed in 1979 for Peace Corps volunteers to begin projects in Bangladesh), Peace Corps operations were formerly fairly substantial in South Asia. Of the estimated 38,000 books and documents currently maintained by the library, some 1,400 titles are on South Asia. In addition, the library also holds approximately 400 periodicals of American and Western origin, of which about 15 are relevant to South Asia.

3-5. This is a small collection of mostly secondary materials in English with relative emphasis on history, government, and general cultural studies. The library's significance, however, is to be found in its collection of Peace Corps documents.

The library serves as an archive of the extensive materials generated by the Peace Corps operation since 1961 when the international volunteer program was launched. The vast array of Peace Corps program documents include regional plans and analyses, training manuals, project reports, country-program evaluations, news releases and volunteers' newsletters, correspondence, memoirs, and journals. Generally the pre-1970 program evaluations are not available for private research, but the staff will assist in obtaining those pre-1970 evaluations that already may have been cleared for release. Restricted materials may also be obtained by invoking the Freedom of Information Act.

6.   A card catalog using the LC classification schedule is available for the collection. A list of current periodical subscriptions, prepared by the library reveals its serials holdings. The library also maintains, on its vertical folders, a separate card index, which contains miscellaneous Peace Corps materials and pamphlets.

American Red Cross National Headquarters Library See entry M7

A2 American University Library

1.   a. *Massachusetts and Nebraska Avenues, N.W.*
         Washington, D.C. 20016
         686-2325

      b. Fall and spring semesters:
         8:00 A.M.–Midnight   Monday–Friday
         9:00 A.M.–6:00 P.M.   Saturday
         11:00 A.M.–Midnight   Sunday

         Summer sessions:
         9:00 A.M.–10:00 P.M.   Monday–Thursday
         9:00 A.M.–5:00 P.M.   Friday–Saturday
         For holiday hours and between-sessions, call 686-3839.

      c. The library is open to the public for reference use. Interlibrary loan and photocopying services are available.

      d. Donald D. Dennis, University Librarian

2.   American University Library's holdings are currently estimated to exceed 485,000 volumes. The library subscribes to about 3,000 journal titles and 50 newspapers. South Asian materials in the collection consist of approximately 4,600 titles, including more than 40 periodicals emanating from South Asia and 2 newspapers in microfilm: *Hindustan Times* (New Delhi) and *Pakistan Times* (Lahore).

3.   a. A comparatively better South Asian collection in the area, the library's holdings are diverse with particular strengths in history, religion, economics, language, and literature. The library has a good collection of South Asian census reports. Back files of *Asian Recorder* since 1959 are also available. Within the consortium of universities in the metropolitan Washington, D.C., area, the American University offers the most programs in South Asian studies.

b. Subject categories and evaluations:

Philosophy and Religion	703t	D –
History and Auxiliary Sciences of History	2,071t	C
Geography and Anthropology	19t	D –
Economics	618t	D
Sociology	163t	D
Politics and Government	402t	C
International Relations	16t	B
Law	15t	D –
Education	60t	D
Art and Music	27t	D –
Language and Literature	410t	D –
Military Affairs	15t	D
Bibliography and Reference	13t	D –
Afghanistan	56t	C
Bangladesh	20t	D
Bhutan	8t	B
India	2,397t	C
Maldive Islands	—	—
Nepal	15t	D
Pakistan	198t	C
Sri Lanka	69t	C

4-5. The Wesley Seminary Library (363-0922), the Washington College of Law Library (686-2625), and the Performing Arts Library (686-2165) contain a few insignificant titles on South Asia. Duplicate copies of the titles in these collections, however, are to be found in the American University Library.

6. The library follows the LC classification system. Card catalogs are divided into two parts: author/title and subject. A serials list provides holding records of all periodicals and newspapers held by the library. A printed *Library Guide* and several useful reference guides are available.

A3 Army Library (Army Department)

1. a. *The Pentagon*
    Washington, D.C. 20310
    697-4301

    b. 9:00 A.M.–4:00 P.M. Monday–Friday

    c. The Army Library serves the personnel of the Department of Defense. Persons who do not have access to the Pentagon must have a sponsor. Unclassified materials may be borrowed through interlibrary loan. Photocopying facilities are available.

    d. Mary L. Shaffer, Director

2-4. The library's collection exceeds 280,000 volumes, 1,000,000 documents, and 2,000 periodicals, covering such fields as military science, economics, geopolitics, social sciences, business administration, biography, technology, international relations, and history. Special collections include unit histories of World War II and army publications. The South Asia-related collection is very small and consists of approximately 100 volumes of English-language secondary literature on government and international relations.

5.   Finding aids include card indexes and the following printed reference works: *Periodical Holdings of the Army Library*; *Selected Current Acquisitions of the Army Library*; and *A Handbook: The Army Library Pentagon*. The library occasionally assembles selected bibliographies on important topics, such as nuclear proliferation and terrorism. Through its automated system, the library has access to the data bases of the Defense Documentation Center (see entry G6), the Educational Resources Information Center, the National Technical Information Service, and a dozen others.

Brookings Institution Library See entry H7

A4 Catholic University of America Libraries—Mullen Library

1.   a. *620 Michigan Avenue, N.E.*
         Washington, D.C. 20064
         635-5077

         b. Academic year:
         9:00 A.M.–10:00 P.M.   Monday–Thursday
         9:00 A.M.–6:00 P.M.   Friday
         9:00 A.M.–5:00 P.M.   Saturday
         1:00 P.M.–10:00 P.M.   Sunday
         Call for holiday and summer hours.

         c. The library is open to serious readers for on-site use. Visitors may inquire for temporary borrowing privileges at the office of the director (635-5055). Interlibrary loan and photocopying services are available.

         d. Fred M. Peterson, Director

2.   The total collection of the library exceeds 1,000,000 volumes including 2,000 titles on South Asia. Of the more than 6,200 newspapers and periodicals received by the library, approximately 30 are relevant to South Asia. The library, however, currently receives no newspapers from South Asia. The dominant focus of the collection is in the areas of theology, philosophy, and history. A good general collection, the library is designed to support the academic and instructional program of the university.

3.   a. Catholic University, with the exception of a limited program in Sanskrit, offers no advanced courses of study on any South Asian subject. Consequently, the library's holdings on South Asia are slim. As to be expected, there are more titles on India than any other country of the region. Also religion and philosophy, language and literature, and history claim preeminence in the South Asian holdings. Holdings on church history in South Asia include titles on Malabar Catholics of the Syrian Rite, Malabar Jacobite Church, and Syro-Malanka Rite.

b. Subject categories and evaluations:

Philosophy and Religion	800t	D –
History and Auxiliary Sciences of History	495t	D –
Geography and Anthropology	10t	D –
Economics	130t	D –
Sociology	96t	D
Politics and Government	85t	D –
International Relations	5t	D
Law	55t	D –
Education	26t	D –
Art and Music	17t	D –
Language and Literature	305t	D –
Military Affairs	3t	D –
Bibliography and Reference	9t	D –

Afghanistan	17t	D –
Bangladesh	7t	D –
Bhutan	3t	D
India	528t	D –
Maldive Islands	—	—
Nepal	4t	D –
Pakistan	81t	D
Sri Lanka	18t	D –

4-5.   Several special collections of the Mullen Library contain scattered materials on South Asia. Located on the third floor, the Clementine Collection (635-5091), the Canon Law Collection (635-5492), and the Theology-Philosophy Division (635-5088) hold an indeterminable number of titles on early European travel accounts and descriptions and a wide range of literature generated by the Catholic missionary activities on the subcontinent. For a scholar of Indic Islam, the Clementine Collection may be particularly interesting. This 10,000-volume collection is comprised of a third of the libraries of Pope Clementine XI and the Clementine family, spanning the years 1453–1850, and provides a window to European attitude and thought towards Islam. For a description of the collection, see Michael Olmert, "A Pope's Library is Brought to Light after 200 Years," *Smithsonian* (January 1978):70–77.

The Department of Archives and Manuscripts, located on the first floor (635-5065), contains many significant papers relating to the Catholic church, labor history, social welfare, immigration, and ethnicity. Several of the manuscripts on labor history include materials pertaining to international labor organizations. A preliminary inventory of these manuscripts is available in the department.

The 32,000-volume library of the Institute for Christian Oriental Research (ICOR), located on the ground floor (635-5084), is a special collection of books on the Semetic and Egyptian languages. The collection contains approximately 200 volumes on South Asian subjects, including several rare works on Sanskrit grammar and lexicon and travelogs written by European travelers and missionaries from the sixteenth through the nineteenth centuries. Examples: Theodor Benfey, *Kruze Sanskrit Grammatik* (Leipzig: F.

A. Brockhaus, 1855); A. Bergaigne and V. Henry, *Manuel Pour Étudier Le Sanscrit Védique* (Paris: Émile Bouillon, 1890); M. Garcin de Tassy, *Histoire de la Littérature Hindouie et Hindoustanie*, 2 vols. (Paris: Oriental Translation Committee of Great Britain and Ireland, 1847); *Voyages de François Bernier . . . Contenant la Description des Etats du Grand Mogol*, nouvelle edition (Amsterdam: 1724); M. Demeunier, *État Civil, Politique et Commerçant du Bengal* (Amsterdam: 1775).

The library has also retrospective runs of several learned journals including the *Journal of the Royal Asiatic Society, Journal Asiatique,* and several publications of the Hakluyt Society. The library has an author/title card catalog and a printed list of its 180 periodical holdings. Materials in this collection are not interfiled in the central card catalog of the Mullen Library. The ICOR collection is open only to serious scholars; permission to use the facility may be obtained in advance. Hours vary according to staff and reader requirements. Further information may be obtained from Aloysius Fitzgerald, Director of ICOR, and Carolyn T. Lee, Librarian.

Another distinguished collection is the Oliveira Lima Library (635-5059) housed on the ground floor of the Mullen Library. This unique collection, mostly in Portuguese, of more than 50,000 printed items and thousands of extremely rare manuscripts, photographs, and memorabilia, focuses upon the Luzo-Brazilian world: Brazil, Portugal, and their present and former territories or spheres of influence overseas. The collection is open to scholars for on-site use. However, it is advisable that researchers make advance appointments with the curator, Manoel Cardoza. Materials in the Lima collection do not circulate. Limited photoduplication facilities are available. The following hours are maintained: 1:00 P.M.–8:00 P.M., Tuesday; Noon–7:00 P.M., Wednesday–Friday; and 9:00 A.M.–5:00 P.M., Saturday.

Within the library's printed materials, there are several valuable works on India, especially Goa. One extremely rare and unusual item is the first edition (1563) of the famous work of Garcia da Orta, printed in Goa, on the drugs, spices, medicinal plants, and fruits of India. The work was rapidly known in Europe through immediate translations into Latin (1567), Italian (1582), and French (1609). A physician, Garcia went to India with an official title and practiced medicine for many years in the East, where he died.

Colóquios dos Simples e Drogas e Cousas Medicinaes da India, as Garcia's monumental work was called in Portuguese, has a real scientific value as it may be called the revelation of the botanical realm of India to Europe. It is written in a "simple unaffected charming way," comments Ruth E. V. Holmes (*Bibliographical and Historical Description of the Rarest Books in the Oliveira Lima Collection,* 1926, pp. 25–26), and "many of the fruits and plants described therein were transported and acclimatised in the New World, especially by the Jesuits. . . . Besides their documentary value as regards natural history, the *Coloquios* help to give a good insight into the social life of the Portuguese in India, immediately after the conquest, and show that there was by the side of the military adventures, some taste for intellectual research." The collection also contains several volumes, published by the Royal Academy of Sciences in Lisbon, on Portuguese conquests and activities in Malabar and other regions of India.

A shelflist and an author/title catalog provide access to the collection. There is also a 2-volume printed *Catalog of the Oliveira Lima Library* produced by G. K. Hall of Boston in 1970. Many of the books are also listed in the *National Union Catalog*. A brief printed booklet, the *Oliveira*

Lima Library, with a separate Portuguese version, may be obtained free by visitors. The items in the Lima collection are not interfiled in the central card catalog of the Mullen Library.

6. On the second floor of the Mullen Library is located the central dictionary card catalog for all recorded materials in the library system with the exception of the ICOR, Oliveira Lima, and the Law Library collections. The Mullen Library follows the LC classification schedules for its collection, except for materials on ecclesiastical literature, theology, canon law, and church history. For literatures in these subjects, *An Alternate Classification for Catholic Books* is used. For current periodicals received by the library, separate mimeographed lists on humanities, social sciences, and theology-philosophy are available in the respective divisions. A useful pamphlet, *General Library Information*, is available.

A5 Census Bureau Library (Commerce Department)

1. a. *Federal Office Building*
   Suitland, Maryland 20233
   (301) 763-5042

   b. 8:00 A.M.–5:00 P.M.   Monday–Friday

   c. Open to the public; interlibrary loan and photoduplication services are available.

   d. Betty Baxtresser, Chief of the Library Branch

2-5. The library's total holdings consist of over 375,000 volumes and approximately 3,400 current periodicals. Subjects include demography, population studies, economics, political science, education, and certain social sciences. The bulk of the collection comprises U.S. and foreign statistical materials (censuses, yearbooks, and bulletins). The library's holdings of South Asian census and other statistical materials are substantial.

6. There are 2 separate dictionary card catalogs, both of which should be consulted by the researcher: a catalog for holdings cataloged prior to 1976, and an active catalog for acquisitions since 1976. The pre-1976 materials are listed in *Catalogs of the Bureau of the Census Library*, 20 vols. (Boston: G. K. Hall and Co., 1976). A monthly list of acquisitions and current periodicals is available to researchers.

Note: Also see entry A6.

Chief of Engineers Library See entry J9

A6 Commerce Department Library

1. a. *Main Commerce Building, Room 7046*
   14th Street and Constitution Avenue, N.W.
   Washington, D.C. 20230
   377-2161

b. 8:30 A.M.–5:00 P.M.   Monday–Friday

c. Open to the public for on-site use; proper identification required. Interlibrary loan and photoduplication services are available.

d. Stanley J. Bougas, Library Director

2-3.   The library houses and services a collection of over 250,000 volumes, arranged mostly by LC classification, of current and contemporary interest to the department. Primary focus on the collection is in the areas of economic theory and history, agricultural economics, industries and commerce, technology and marketing, and political science and history. The holdings contain an extensive collection of official foreign-trade reports and official and nonofficial publications from more than 100 foreign countries, one-third of which are in foreign languages.

The small number of South Asia-related materials consist of some 500 titles. Some of the notable holdings include: the annual *Review of the Trade of India* from 1884 to 1947 with some gaps; *Annual Reports on the Post and Telegraphs of India*, 1914–29; *Statistical Statements Relating to the Co-operative Movements in India*, 1914–15; and several other retrospective and current reports of the government departments of South Asian countries. Some of the U.S. Census Bureau publications on South Asia are also available; e.g., *Afghanistan, A Demographic Uncertainty* (1978).

The library's extensive collection of some 1,350 periodicals include approximately 50 South Asian government serials and statistical abstracts.

The reference room (Room 7043) contains an extensive collection of abstracts, indexes, business services, and commercial and business directories, in addition to reference books in the fields of economics and business. Particularly useful to the South Asianist is the Hong Kong-based weekly, *Business Asia*, which provides economic and commercial data as well as sophisticated political analysis.

4-5.   The law branch of the library, located in Room 1894, consists of some 50,000 volumes of legal materials and congressional and governmental documents on microforms. The branch maintains the same hours as the main library; visitors and general public are admitted by permission.

The library's maritime collection of approximately 50,000 volumes covers a wide variety of subjects, including shipping, shipbuilding, navigation, marine engineering, nuclear propulsion, and technical periodicals.

6.   Two dictionary card catalogs provide access to the collection: entries for publications received prior to 1975 are listed in the 1914–1974 catalog; entries for publications received in 1975 and after are listed in the 1975— catalog. The library provides data-base access for computerized information retrieval through several commercial and government systems. Professional reference assistance is provided to the general public and visitors. Users may request reference staff to conduct on-line information retrieval searches from approximately 150 data bases.

The library distributes monthly *Commerce Library Bulletin,* listing new accessions, bibliographies compiled by the staff, and other research activities. A series of business-information seminars is conducted from time to time by the library on topics of current interest. A descriptive pamphlet, the *Department of Commerce Library,* is a useful guide to the library and contains a list of other commerce libraries in the metropolitan Washington area.

Note: Also see entry A5.

A7   Development Information Center (DIC) (Agency for International Development (AID))

1. a. *(Main) Development Information Center*
    Department of State Building
    320 21st Street, N.W.
    Washington, D.C. 20523
    632-9345

    Rosslyn Branch—DIC
    1601 North Kent Street, Room 105
    Arlington, Virginia 22209
    (703) 235-8936

    b. 8:45 A.M.–5:30 P.M.   Monday–Friday

    c. DIC's primary function is to serve the AID personnel, contractors, and AID grantees. However, with prior approval, DIC facilities may also be used by others for reference purposes. Interlibrary loan and photoduplication services are available.

    d. Joanne M. Paskar, Chief
    Susan Weintraub, Branch Head

2-3.   DIC's collection in both centers of cataloged reference materials, reports, and documents related to development assistance total approximately 125,000 items, roughly 3,000 of which are on South Asia. There is also a vast quantity of uncatalogued materials. Included in the collection are both classified and unclassified materials. Staff guidance is available in the filing of Freedom of Information requests. While the majority of the DIC's reports are in English, foreign-language reports are also retained.

The collection reflects AID's areas of interest and covers a broad spectrum of subject matters: agriculture and rural development, population and family planning, health and nutrition, urban development, technical-assistance methodology, development administration, and planning strategy. Although it functions mainly as the archive—or memory—for the program and project documentation and for technical information generated by AID and its predecessor agencies, the center selectively acquires appropriate technical and methodological documentation produced by other non-AID sources, including government, professional organizations, and international agencies (International Bank for Reconstruction and Development [World Bank], International Monetary Fund, Asian Development Bank, U.N. agencies).

The small Rosslyn Branch collection of monographs, periodicals, and research reports combines the materials held before by several AID technical-assistance offices. The Rosslyn Branch also holds on microform all reports contained in the 2-volume *AID Catalog of Research Literature for Development* (covering the period from 1962 through 1976) and the quarterly *A.I.D. Research and Development Abstracts.* A few examples of these reports are: M. A. Zaman, "Land Reform in Bangladesh," University of Wisconsin, 1976; M. S. Mudahar, "Dynamic Models of Agriculture Development with Demand Linkages," Cornell University, 1973; T. T. Poleman, "Food, Population and Employment; Ceylon's Crisis in Global Perspective," Cornell University, 1971.

AID's Development Information Center holds important resources for ·South Asian economic-development studies and research on U.S. development-assistance programs. Numerical evaluation of the geographical card catalog revealed the following approximate number of items: Afghanistan 300, Bhutan 2, Bangladesh 35, India 1,200, Nepal 260, Pakistan 850, and Sri Lanka 80.

4-5. The DIC provides a one-step access point to AID's program, project, and research documentation. These materials contain annual reports, project reports, project design and evaluative documents, and budget and program submissions to Congress.

Also noteworthy is the 6,000-volume cataloged Population Reference Library in the Rosslyn Branch, containing a fairly comprehensive literature on population-related studies and data.

6. Since the bulk of the complex material in the DIC continues to be uncataloged, staff assistance is essential in identifying and locating materials. Access is also available through the card catalogs in two locations arranged by author, title, subject, geographical category, and contract number, and through on-line retrieval of the AID computerized bibliographic data base, RANDD, which contains approximately 8,000 entries. The center also provides access to AID's automated, project information data bases: PAISHIST and DIS. While the PAISHIST data base generally includes all completed projects, the DIS system includes active projects.

In addition, the two centers have access to all major, special, academic and technical libraries nationwide and have on-line access to some 100 automated, specialized data bases citing development literature published worldwide.

A8 Dumbarton Oaks Research Library (Harvard University)

1. a. *1703 32nd Street, N.W.*
   Washington, D.C. 20007
   342-3240

   b. 9:00 A.M.–5:00 P.M.   Monday–Friday

   c. The collection is open to qualified researchers for reference use. Prior authorization to use the collection is recommended. Photoduplication facilities are available.

   d. Irene Vaslef, Librarian

2. This research library contains upwards of 100,000 volumes, including 800 current periodicals, and continues to grow. The principal focus of the collection is Byzantine studies, which also incorporates Islamic studies within the Byzantine frame of reference.

The South Asian portion of the collection consists of approximately 200 titles, many of which are renowned as scholarly and pioneering works. In addition to several early European works on description and travel, and historical accounts of the Macedonian invasion of the Indus Valley, there are a few authoritative studies in the collection dealing with the theme of Hellenism in Bactria and India and its magnificent cultural efflorescence, the Gandhara school of art, much of which has survived the ravages of time.

The collection also holds a few volumes edited by John Watson (1825–1913) designed to contain annotated translations of all texts in Greek and Latin literature that relate to ancient India. Among other items, an Indologist will find in the collection the following classical books on Indian archaeology; Sir John Huber Marshall, ed., *Mohenjo-daro and the Indus Civilization,* 3 vols. (London: 1931); also by Marshall, *A Guide to Sanchi* (Delhi: 1936) and *A Guide to Taxila* (Delhi: 1936); Ananda Kentish Coomaraswamy, *History of Indian and Indonesian Art* (New York: 1927); Sir Alexander Cunningham (1814–1893), *The Geography of Ancient India: Illustrating the Campaigns of Alexander and the Travels of Chinese Pilgrims* (London: 1870); Sir Mark Aurel Stein, *Archaeological Reconnaissance in North-Western India and South Eastern Iran* (London: 1937); also by Stein, *Alexander's Track to the Indus* (London: 1929).

6. Finding aids include a dictionary card catalog with its 12-volume printed version, *Dictionary Catalogue of the Byzantine Collection of the Dumbarton Oaks Research Library* (Boston: G. K. Hall, 1975) and the continuing series, *Dumbarton Oaks Bibliography.*

Energy Department Library See entry J11

Environmental Protection Agency Library See entry J12

Export-Import Bank of the United States Library See entry J13

Federal Research System's Research Library See entry J14

A9 Folger Shakespeare Library

1. a. *201 East Capital Street, S.E.*
    Washington, D.C. 20003
    544-4600

    b. 8:45 A.M.–4:30 P.M.   Monday–Saturday

    c. Designed to be an advanced-research facility, the collection is open to serious scholars for on-site use. Proper identification is required. Photoduplication and microfilming services are available, but there is no interlibrary loan.

d. O. B. Hardison, Jr., Director
Nati Krivatsy, Reference Librarian

2-3. Housed in an elegant building that is classical in approach and Tudor in interior decorative details, the carefully selected collection exceeds 200,000 volumes and 40,000 manuscripts on the theme of Elizabethan England and Renaissance Europe. Within the collection, popularly known as Shakespearana, are to be found about 300 South Asian titles on early European descriptions and travels, maps, trade, settlements, and voluminous missionary accounts, including Jesuit letters and accounts of sixteenth-century India. Also to be found in this collection are the extensive publications of the Hakluyt Society; e.g., *The Travels of Abbé Carré in India and the Near East, 1672–1674.*

6. The library follows LC classification schedules. Finding aids include: a dictionary card catalog; *Catalog of Printed Books of the Folger Shakespeare Library,* 28 vols., 1970 and a 3-volume *Supplement,* 1976; and a 3-volume *Catalog of Manuscripts of the Folger Shakespeare Library,* 1971.

Food and Agricultural Oganization Library See entry K7

A10 Foreign Service Institute Library (State Department)

1. a. *1400 Key Boulevard, Room 300*
   Arlington, Virginia 22209
   (703) 235-8717

   b. 8:45 A.M.–5:30 P.M.   Monday–Friday

   c. Although the library is designed to service the institute's language and area-studies program, its facilities are open to the public for on-site use. Interlibrary loan and photoduplication services are available.

   d. Mary Schloeder, Librarian

2. The library's collection consists of about 40,000 very select volumes, including 300 periodical titles emphasizing political science, economics, history, and social problems. Special collections have been established to support such programs as the Executive Seminar in National and International Affairs and the School of Area Studies.

3. South Asian materials in the library consist of approximately 1,000 titles including 10 periodicals from South Asia. Materials for supporting area studies in South Asia and language-training form the core of this small secondary collection.

6. A card catalog using LC classification schedules is available. There is also a separate periodical list.

A11 Freer Gallery of Art Library (Smithsonian Institution)

1. a. *12th Street and Jefferson Drive, S.W.*
   Washington, D.C. 20560
   357-2091

   b. 10:00 A.M.–4:30 P.M.   Monday–Friday

   c. Open to the public for on-site use; photocopying facilities are available. Loans from the collection, including the library, are forbidden. However, slides are lent to institutions and individuals.

   d. Priscilla P. Smith, Librarian

2-3.   The library is a reference collection supplementing the objects of art in the gallery and staff studies. Approximately half of the specialized holdings of 30,000 volumes are in the Japanese and Chinese languages. The South Asian portion of the collection consists of some 400 volumes—mostly in English—devoted to antiquities, archaeology, description and travel, and sculpture and painting.

4.   The library has a fairly comprehensive set of serial titles in fine arts. Of its some 100 current periodical subscriptions, several are related to the area of our interest.

5.   Three major gifts, informally referred to as the Islamic Archives—consisting of the Herzfeld Archive, the Islamic Archive of Myron Bement Smith, and the Raymond Arthur Hare Collection—may contain some materials of interest to South Asianists. Scholars interested in exploring the Islamic Archives may contact the librarian or Esin Atil, Curator, Near Eastern Art (357-2873).

   The library also contains 38 microfilmed items, including correspondence of Charles L. Freer. An audio collection of lectures, presented by scholars at the Freer Gallery between 1966 and 1976, is also available.

6.   A dictionary card catalog and a printed *Freer Catalogue* (Boston: G. K. Hall, 1968) facilitates researchers' access to the library's holdings. The library does not use the LC classification schedules; instead, a modified Dewey Decimal system is used.

Note: Also see entry C3.

General Accounting Office Library See entry J15

A12 Geological Survey Library (Interior Department)

1. a. *12201 Sunrise Valley Drive*
   Reston, Virginia 22092
   (703) 860-6671

   b. 7:15 A.M.–4:30 P.M.   Monday–Friday

      c. Open to the public; interlibrary loan and photoduplicating facilities are available.

      d. George H. Goodwin, Jr., Librarian

2.   The U.S. Geological Survey Library, established in 1879, is one of the largest earth-science libraries in the world. The main library in Reston, together with its branches, contain more than 1,000,000 bound and unbound monographs, serials, and government publications, 350,000 pamphlets and reprints, 350,000 maps, 12,000 field-record notebooks and manuscripts, 200,000 album prints, transparencies, lantern slides, and negatives, as well as doctoral dissertations on microfilm, and report literature on microfiche. A very extensive international and domestic exchange program formed the basis for the library's current extensive collections.

        Although the collection is devoted to all aspects of the geosciences, the major subjects of interest are geology, paleontology, petrology, mineralogy, geochemistry, geophysics, ground and surface water, cartography, and mineral resources, augmented by important holdings in physics, chemistry, and zoology. A significant number of books and periodicals reflect the Geological Survey's present interest in the environment, earth satellites and remote sensing, geothermal energy, marine geology, land use, lunar geology, and the conservation of resources. Holdings include nearly complete sets of the various national geological-survey publications and earth-science literature issued by almost every country.

3.   The geographical distribution of the South Asian holdings in the library, excluding maps, are as follows: Afghanistan 70; Bangladesh 5; Bhutan 3; India 725; Pakistan 85; Nepal 35; and Sri Lanka 40. A comprehensive numerical strength, however, cannot be ascertained since all materials are not cataloged under geographical subject headings.

4.   Currently the library maintains more than 9,500 serial and periodical titles.

5.   The library's Map Collection is described in entry E3.

6.   The library's Catalog and Classification Section maintains a card catalog file that is published periodically in book form by G. K. Hall of Boston as a supplement to its 25-volume *Catalog of the United States Geological Survey* (1964). The classification system used to organize books and other materials was especially devised to meet the particular requirements of the survey's scientific work, and it is revised when necessary to accommodate changing concepts and subject matter. A library brochure is available on request.

A13 George Washington University Library

1.   a. *2130 H Street, N.W.*
       Washington, D.C. 20052
       676-6047

      b. 8:30 A.M.–Midnight Monday–Friday
       10:00 A.M.–6:00 P.M. Saturday
       Noon–Midnight Sunday

      For hours during holidays and between sessions call 676-6845.

c. The library is open to the public for on-site use. Interlibrary loans and photoduplication facilities are available.

d. Rupert C. Woodward, University Librarian

2. The library holdings exceed 500,000 volumes. Its small South Asian collection consists of approximately 2,500 titles. Of the 4,000 periodicals and 45 newspapers received by the library, approximately 65 are from South Asia including one newspaper, *Overseas Hindustan Times.*

3. a. In the absence of any specific instructional program in South Asian studies, the South Asian holdings tend to be a secondary collection with some significant literature in history, social sciences, philosophy, and religion.

b. Subject catagories and evaluations:

Philosophy and Religion	712t	D –
History and Auxiliary		
Sciences of History	863t	D
Geography and Anthropology	16t	D –
Economics	209t	D –
Sociology	103t	D
Politics and Government	211t	D
International Relations	7t	C
Law	37t	D –
Education	20t	D –
Art and Music	33t	D –
Language and Literature	187t	D –
Military Affairs	6t	D –
Bibliography and Reference	13t	D –

Afghanistan	32t	D
Bangladesh	15t	D
Bhutan	8t	B
India	692t	D –
Maldive Islands	—	—
Nepal	13t	D –
Pakistan	118t	D
Sri Lanka	27t	D –

4-5. The Media Resources Department, located on the lower level (676-6378), maintains a sizable collection of microforms, audio-cassettes, films, video-tapes and other audiovisual equipment. Within this collection may be found a few South Asian books, documents, items of music, and interviews. The department's resources also include microfilms of several major newspapers and journals.

An important item in the collection is a 6-reel microfilm reproduction of the Office of Strategic Services/State Department Intelligence Report on India and China, 1941–1949. Another significant holding is the Vanderbilt Television News Archive, which has recordings of ABC, CBS, and NBC evening network news and news specials since 1968. These materials are available for loan on videotape. The Television News Study Service (676-7218) provides finding aids, access, information, and playback facilities for using the library's television news archive collection as well as other resources. For a scholar researching the U.S. news media's approach and reaction to contemporary South Asian issues, the collection is immensely useful.

The George Washington University Library is a depository for U.S. Census Bureau materials. It is also a depository for U.S. Geological Survey topographic maps and for international maps from the U.S. Defense Mapping Agency. Indexes and other finding aids are available at the reference desk. At least 7 maps of different divisions of South Asia are in the collection. The Institute for Sino-Soviet Studies Library, located on the seventh floor (676-7105), holds several periodicals of general interest and current affairs on Asia, including the Foreign Broadcast Information Service (FBIS) reports since 1962. The institute's library contains about 10,000 volumes and back files of 150 periodicals.

A South Asianist may also note that the Special Collections Division (676-7497) holds a few items of interest, including the manuscript of the Papers of Frederick Kuh (1924–1967)—a foreign correspondent with the *Chicago Sun Times* and the Associated Press—who was especially noted for his reporting of World War II and the postwar era. Kuh travelled to India in 1957 and returned with an award-winning series of articles on that country. His articles and loose notes appear in the subject file, *India, 1957,* while his 8 notebooks on the trip are in the separate notebook file. A finding aid for the collection is available.

6. The general card catalog is divided into three sections: author, subject, and title. All materials in the library, including periodicals and reference materials, can be located through the card catalog. The library follows the LC classification system. In addition to the card catalog, lists of periodicals currently received by the library are also available. These lists indicate the earliest issue the library has and the subject section for current issues. Several information guides to the resources and services of the library are available.

A14 Georgetown University—Fred O. Dennis Law Library (Georgetown University Law Center)

1. a. *600 New Jersey Avenue, N.W.*
      Washington, D.C. 20001
      624-8375

   b. Academic Year:
      9:00 A.M.–10:00 P.M. Monday–Friday
      9:00 A.M.–5:00 P.M. Saturday
      2:00 P.M.–10:00 P.M. Sunday

      For library hours during summer sessions, examination periods, and holidays, call 624-8260.

   c. Open to the public for use of materials within the library; interlibrary loan and photoduplication services are available.

   d. George J. Roman, Head, Foreign and International Law Section

2-3.   The library's holdings total approximately 236,000 volumes, plus almost 200,000 physical microfilm units, and the library currently subscribes to approximately 3,000 serial publications.

The library's South Asia collection contains approximately 150 titles and 4 current periodicals. The special strength of the library's rather small South Asia collection is its approximately 300 bound volumes of several *Indian High Court Law Reporters* and *Law Journals*, some dating back to 1875, but with none more recent than 1943. These increasingly scarce materials are securely located in the basement of the Law Center but are listed in the card catalog and are accessible to serious scholars. The library's excellent topical collections cover a vast array of materials, some of which are pertinent to South Asia. The library also has a good collection of bibliographic and reference literature on South Asian legal materials.

A15   Georgetown University—Joseph Mark Lauinger Memorial Library

1.   a. *37th and O Streets, N.W.*
       Washington, D.C. 20057
       625-4173

     b. Academic Year:
        8:30 A.M.–Midnight   Monday–Thursday
        8:30 A.M.–10:00 P.M.   Friday
        10:00 A.M.–10:00 P.M.   Saturday
        11:00 A.M.–Midnight   Sunday

        For information on summer hours, call 625-3300.

     c. The library and the stacks are open to scholars for on-site use. Interlibrary loan and photoduplication facilities are available.

     d. Joseph E. Jeffs, University Librarian

2.   The library collection numbers over 800,000 volumes, including South Asia-related holdings estimated at over 4,000 titles. Of the more than 5,000 serials the library currently receives, 86 are on South Asia. The library also subscribes to 39 newspapers including the *Times of India* (New Delhi).

3.   a. One of the average university collections in the Washington area, its holdings are comparatively stronger in history, religion and philosophy, language and literature, and economics.

     b. Subject categories and evaluations:

Philosophy and Religion	1,443t	D
History and Auxiliary Sciences of History	1,432t	C
Geography and Anthropology	18t	D –
Economics	205t	D –
Sociology	73t	D –
Politics and Government	170t	D
International Relations	10t	C
Law	5t	D –

Education	18t	D –
Art and Music	6t	D –
Language and Literature	600t	D –
Military Affairs	7t	D –
Bibliography and Reference	41t	D –

Afghanistan	102t	B
Bangladesh	48t	C
Bhutan	4t	B
India	1,406t	D
Maldive Islands	—	—
Nepal	30t	D
Pakistan	181t	C
Sri Lanka	52t	D

4. Since 1969 the Lauinger Library has served as a selected depository for the U.S. government documents, including congressional hearings and various State Department reports. These documents, which total over 90,000, are on microforms and are located in the Audiovisual Department (625-4213).The U.S. government depository documents are not listed in the library's card catalog. The main tool used for locating these documents is the *Monthly Catalog of U.S. Publications* and the classification system of the U.S. Superintendent of Documents.

    The Archives, Manuscripts and Rare Books Division (625-3230), located on the fifth floor, holds a number of special collections and contains a few scattered items on South Asia. The Audiovisual Department of the library maintains its international census collection, which includes approximately 150 reels of microfilms of census reports and data on Bangladesh, India, Nepal, Pakistan, and Sri Lanka, mostly since 1951. The majority of these census series is complete. The library is rapidly filling the existing gaps and expanding its census collection.

    The Audiovisual Department also holds a few 16-mm feature films on South Asia in addition to some slides, filmstrips, music, and spoken tapes. Six reels of microfilm reproduction, of the Office of Strategic Services/State Department Intelligence Reports on India and China 1941–1949, are also in the collection.

5. The library has an excellent holding on Islam and Middle Eastern Studies (13,000 volumes). Many of these materials are valuable to South Asian scholars especially interested in Islam in South Asia.

6. Except for *A Guide for Users of the Government Documents Depository,* there is no other printed catalog for the library's collection. The Lauinger Library follows the LC classification schedules and maintains subject/author/title card catalogs.

Note: Also see entries A14 and A16.

A16 Georgetown University—Woodstock Theological Center Library

1. a. *37th and O Streets, N.W.*
    Washington, D.C. 20057
    625-3120

    b. 9:00 A.M.–5:00 P.M.   Monday–Friday

    c. The library is open only to qualified researchers for on-site use. Interlibrary loan and photoduplicating facilities are available.

    d. Henry Bertels, S. J., Director

2-3.   Located in the rear lower level of the Lauinger Library, Woodstock is strictly a research library primarily for Jesuit studies. Its total collection of 156,000 volumes and 950 old and current bound periodicals is recognized as one of the best on "Jesuitica" in the United States. The library's meager holding of approximately 300 basic, historical works on South Asia may be over-looked. What may, however, prove fascinating to a South Asianist is the rich collection of Jesuit documents, records, letters, and journals. The bulk of these scattered materials, some of which date back to the sixteenth century, are in Latin, French, and German. Primarily concerned with evan-gelical and ecclesiastical matters, these materials also reflect on the con-temporary socio-cultural scene in South Asia as seen by those involved in the missions.

A17 Health and Human Services Department Library

1. a. *330 Independence Avenue, S.W.*
    Washington, D.C. 20201
    245-6791

    b. 9:00 A.M.–5:30 P.M.   Monday–Friday

    c. Open to the public for on-site use; patrons are required to register each day. Interlibrary loan and photoduplication services are available.

    d. Charles F. Gately, Director

2-3.   The department library contains approximately 818,000 items and receives approximately 9,500 current periodicals and serials. It has one of the coun-try's outstanding collections in social sciences, public welfare, and health sciences. There is a comprehensive collection of the department's publi-cations and an active vertical file of miscellaneous materials. South Asia-related materials in the collection are rather limited and consist of some 500 titles.

6.   The card catalog is the library's main resource for locating materials proc-essed since 1965 in the various collections. A printed book catalog covers

materials from 1807 through 1964. Materials are accessible by author, title, subject entry, and by serials entry. Materials in the library are classified according to the LC classification adapted in some areas to meet special needs. The library has recently added the capability to provide automated information-retrieval service in a wide variety of subject areas. About 100 data bases are available. A *DHHS Library Booklist: New Accessions* is issued monthly.

A18 House of Representatives Library

1. a. *Cannon House Office Building, Room B 18*
Washington, D.C. 20515
225-0462

   b. 9:00 A.M.–5:30 P.M.   Monday–Friday

   c. Open to the public for on-site use only; photoduplicating facilities are available but no interlibrary loan. Researchers may call before visiting the library.

   d. E. R. Lewis, Librarian

2-6.   The collection exceeds 200,000 volumes and contains complete sets of House and Senate Reports, documents, and journals, as well as the *Congressional Records, House Bills and Debates, House and Joint Committee Hearings, Supreme Court Reports*, and other materials including globes, annals, and directories.
   This collection is of immense value especially for research in U.S. relations with the South Asian countries. The library has no catalog. A brief flyer, the *House Library* is available on request.

Housing and Urban Development Department Library
See entry J17

A19 Howard University—Founders Library

1. a. *500 Howard Place, N.W.*
Washington, D.C. 20059
636-7253

   b. Academic year:
   8:00 A.M.–Midnight   Monday–Friday
   8:00 A.M.–5:00 P.M.   Saturday
   Noon–Midnight   Sunday
   Founders Library also offers limited service from Midnight to 8:00 A.M.   Sunday–Friday.

The schedule of hours for the special collections and the branch libraries is also available at the reference desk of the Founders Library.

c. Open to serious researchers for on-site use; standard interlibrary loan and photoduplication facilities are available.

d. Binford H. Conley, Director of University Libraries

2. The Founders Library, which is the general library of the university and houses the general collection, together with 13 other branch libraries and units, contains over 1,000,000 volumes, including approximately 7,000 serials. The Founders Library collection is classified partly under the LC classification schedule and partly under the older Dewey Decimal system, which renders any quantitative evaulation of its resources complicated. The South Asian holdings of the library are estimated to be about 2,500 titles, including 4 newspapers and about 35 periodicals of South Asian origin.

3. a. An average university collection, Howard University's holdings are relatively stronger in the areas of history, religion, and politics. Founders' collection of South Asian serials is also significant. Currently the university does not have any program in South Asian studies, but its resources seem to be adequate to support some programs in selected disciplines.

b. Subject categories and evaluations:

Philosophy and Religion	818t	D–
History and Auxiliary Sciences of History	858t	D
Geography and Anthropology	6t	D –
Economics	105t	D–
Sociology	97t	D
Politics and Government	142t	D
International Relations	1t	D –
Law	27t	D–
Education	25t	D–
Art and Music	22t	D –
Language and Literature	131t	D–
Military Affairs	5t	D –
Bibliography and Reference	15t	D–

Afghanistan	32t	D
Bangladesh	7t	D –
Bhutan	—	—
India	923t	D
Maldive Islands	—	—
Nepal	9t	D –
Pakistan	80t	D
Sri Lanka	19t	D –

4-5. The Serial Room of the Founders Library maintains the current files of 2 South Asian newspapers, the *Hindu* (Madras) and *Hindustan Times* (New Delhi). In addition, it receives a number of government documents and periodicals including: *Indian Quarterly, Indian Journal of Political Science,*

Indian Journal of International Law, Indian Economic Journal, Indian Journal of Public Administration, Indian Journal of Social Work, Indian Literature, Indian Law Institute Journal, Indian Mathematical Society Journal, Indian Medical Journal, Indian Journal of Pure and Applied Mathematics, Pakistan Development Review, Pakistan Review, Indian Economic and Social History Review, Indian Historian, and *Gandhi Marg.*

One of the special collections housed in the Founders Library (Room 300, 636-7261, 8:30 A.M.–5:00 P.M., Monday–Friday) is the Bernard B. Fall Collection. This noncirculating collection of books, documents, pamphlets, and maps deals with the theme of "Modern Nationalistic and Revolutionary Movement of East and Southeast Asia" and contains few volumes of interest to the South Asianist. The staff reported, however, that the collection will expand eventually to incorporate South Asia.

The Moorland-Spingarn Research Center, located in Room 109 (636-7240), is one of the finest repositories on Black history and culture. A South Asianist will find in this collection several titles of interest, especially on the Indian diaspora in Africa. The collection also contains some South Asian periodicals including *India and the World* (Calcutta, 1932–1940) and *Africa Quarterly* (New Delhi, Indian Council for African Affairs, 1961—).

Approximately 100 general titles on South Asia may be found in the Social Science Reading Room (Carnegie Building, Room 11, 636-7264). This small noncircualting collection is geared to the graduate student. Other branch libraries and units contain only a few volumes on South Asia.

6. The union (main) catalog, located in the Circulation Hall of the second floor of Founders Library, contains the record of all books and periodical titles in the university libraries system. It is divided into two parts—author/title and subject. Each unit of the library system also maintains its own separate catalog, which may be consulted on site. Reference assistance is provided throughout the entire system. The university has recently initiated a computerized, on-line, integrated, library-information network, which provides essential support for a broad range of library services including on-line catalog access. A good finding aid for locating current serials is the computer printout, *Howard University Library Subscription Holdings,* which is updated regularly. Also available is the computer-generated *Consortium Title Sequence List,* which may be consulted for determining the serials holdings of the local universities.

Indian Embassy Library See entry K3

Institute for Christian Oriental Research Library See entry A4

A20 International Communication Agency (ICA) Library

1. a. *1750 Pennsylvania Avenue, N.W., Room 1011*
   Washington, D.C. 20547
   724-9126

   b. 8:45 A.M.–5:30 P.M.   Monday–Friday

c. The USICA (formerly the United States Information Agency) Library primarily serves the reference and research needs of the agency personnel and as such its facilities are usually closed to the general public. However, permission to use the collection may be obtained upon application to the agency office of Congressional and Public Liaison (724-9103). Interlibrary loan and photoduplicating facilities are available.

d. Jeanne R. Zeydal, Librarian

2. With its primary emphasis on Americana, the library contains about 61,000 titles, 475 periodicals, and 72,750 microforms. The South Asian portion of the collection is in excess of 1,000 titles and some 15 major periodicals pertaining to South Asia.

3. Established in 1942, the library's collections are carefully selected to serve the programming and other needs of the agency, especially in the thematic areas of international security, diplomatic relations, economics, political and social processes, arts and humanities, science and technology, and communications and media. For a South Asianist, the library's main collection contains little more than basic reference materials on the area.

4-5. The Documents Branch (724-9364) manages the General Documents Collection of the library, which combines a current information file (some 770 drawers, about 4 on South Asia) of newspaper clippings or morgue from the national press, and recent documents including U.S. government documents, U.N. materials of all kinds, "think-tank" studies, and annual reports from foundations, associations, interest groups, and corporations. These materials, especially geared to agency concerns, are arranged by subject in chronological order. There is an index card file of subject headings for the documents.

A separate biographical file covers approximately 25,000 prominent persons, including a number of persons from South Asia, in the fields of government and culture. The Documents Branch also maintains the Classified Documents Collection, which contains approximately 65,000 classified reports, airgrams, telegrams, and field messages issued by USICA and other foreign-affairs agencies, arranged by areas and subjects. All agency-classified documents of historical import are listed in the computerized Documents Index system, and every year a list of all declassified documents is placed in the agency archive for reference by government and nongovernment personnel.

The Voice of America (VOA) branch library, located at 330 Independence Avenue S.W., HEW-N Building, Room 1350 (755-4649), has a small, general reference collection and serves the reference needs of the broadcasting staff.

The library's Special Collection is entrusted with the custodial responsibility of the Agency Archives that contain internal documents and public records of USICA and its predecessors, U.S. governement materials about the agency, a selection of agency publications, and other materials on the agency.

6. The USICA Library follows the LC classification system. A card catalog lists books by author, subject, and title. There is also a separate periodical

card index and a list of periodicals in the library. The library has access to the automated bibliographic data bases of the New York Times Information Bank, the Lockheed/DIALOG, Systems Development Corporation/OR-BIT, and the Library of Congress/SCORPIO. The library also announces bi-weekly acquisition lists of *New Books, New Documents,* and *Classified Documents* for agency use.

A21 International Labor Office (International Labor Organization)— Washington Branch Office Library

1. a. *1750 New York Avenue, N.W.*
   Washington, D.C. 20006
   376-2315

   b. Open to the public; photocopying facilities are available but no interlibrary loan. Publications are on sale.

   c. Patricia S. Hord, Librarian

2-5. This small collection of some 16,000 volumes is a potential source for South Asian research. In addition to a good selection of materials in the categories of labor legislation, trade unionism, social security, industrial relations, unemployment, labor statistics, labor management, manpower planning, vocational training, labor welfare, migration, cooperatives, occupational safety and health, women and children as a working force, and other related fields, the library also contains numerous ILO publications and documents since the inception of the organization.

Particularly valuable are the relevant reports and studies prepared by the World Employment Programme (WEP) and the Asian Regional Team for Employment Promotion (ARTEP). Recent WEP studies include: *Urban Development and Employment, The Prospects for Calcutta; Generating Employment for the Educated in India; Internal Migration in Developing Countries;* and *Rural and Urban Income Inequalities in Pakistan.*

Examples of ARTEP studies are: *The Challenge for Nepal, Growth with Employment; The Rural Works Program in Bangladesh; Labour Absorption in Asian Agriculture; Organization and Management of Human Resource Planning in Afghanistan;* and *Women Workers in Asian Countries.*

The library's extensive serial collection includes current and retrospective runs of the *Official Bulletin of the ILO, International Labour Review, Bulletin of Labour Statistics, Social and Labour Bulletin, Labour Education, Cooperative Information, Women at Work,* and the annual *ILO Yearbook of Labour Statistics.* The comprehensive documents collection maintained in this library include the Legislative Series of national laws and regulations on labor and social security; International Social Security Association publications; documents from the International Conference of Labor Statisticians; ILO Conference documents; minutes of the ILO Governing Body; reports, resolutions and proceedings of ILO regional conferences (including Asian Regional Conferences) and industrial conferences (e.g., mining, petroleum, steel, textiles, transportation); and numerous ILO studies and reports on international labor conditions, trade unionism, labor-management relations, social security, and occupational health and safety.

One can also find such other ILO publications as *Poverty and Landlessness in Rural Asia* (1977) and a number of reports of the ILO Technical Assistance Program (TAP) that deals with India, Pakistan, Sri Lanka, and Afghanistan. The library's collection of TAP reports includes: *Report of the ILO Mission on Social Security in Pakistan* (1952); *Report to His Majesty's Government of Nepal on the Establishment of a Manpower Assessment and Planning Program* (1968); *Report to the Government of Ceylon on Consumer Cooperative Retail Stores* (1964); and *Report to the Government of India on the Qualitative Improvement of the Vocational Guidance Program of the National Employment Service* (1973).

The library also maintains a separate country file of national laws and regulations on labor and social security drawn from the *ILO Legislative Series*. In addition, the library has a small film collection and a collection of photographs devoted primarily to the operation of the ILO. The photo collection has been drawn from the much larger photo library at the ILO headquarters in Geneva, Switzerland. A printed inventory of the Geneva collection, *ILO Photo Library: Catalogue*, is available in the Washington office. A film catalog is also available in this office.

6. There is no comprehensive card catalog for the collection. However, several useful guides to ILO publications are available: *ILO Catalog of Publications in Print* (1979); *Subject Guide to Publications of the International Labor Office* (1919–1964) (Geneva, 1967); *International Labor Documentation*, a 12-volume cumulative index to the holdings of the ILO Central Library in Geneva and an on-going monthly supplement with the same title which contains information concerning new books cataloged by the ILO library in Geneva, major new ILO publications, and labor-related abstracts from about 1,000 international journals.

Islamic Center Library See entry L43

A22 Joint Bank-Fund Library (Library of the International Bank for Reconstruction and Development and the International Monetary Fund)

1. a. *700 19th Street, N.W.*
   Washington, D.C. 20431
   477-3167

   b. 8:30 A.M.–6:00 P.M.   Monday–Friday

   c. Accessible to the public for on-site use on the basis of special permission; interlibrary loan and photocopying facilities are available.

   d. Charles D. Olsen, Librarian

2-5. The library contains over 150,000 cataloged volumes, 3,000 current periodicals, and 160 daily newspaper subscriptions. With particular emphasis on materials from the 134 member countries, the collection represents some 30 languages, although English-language materials predominate. The focus in the collection is in the areas of banking, public finance, planning, development economics, international economics, and international monetary systems. South Asia-realted holdings in the collection exceed 6,000 titles, among them: Afghanistan 150, Bangladesh 100, Bhutan 25, India 3,300, Nepal 200, and Pakistan 1,200.

6.   In addition to the dictionary card catalog—based essentially on the Dewey Decimal classification, preceded by a numerical letter designator for the country—and a geographic catalog, arranged alphabetically by country, a printed catalog published by G. K. Hall, entitled *The Developing Areas, A Classified Bibliography of the Joint Bank-Fund Library*, 3 vols. (1976), and its *First Supplement*, 4 vols. (1979), provide access to the collection. Also available is a monthly *List of Recent Periodical Articles*, a monthly *List of Recent Additions* of books and monographs, and a *Guide to the Joint Bank-Fund Library*.

Labor Department Library See entry J22

A23 Library of Congress (LC)

1.   a. *10 First Street, S.E.*
     Washington, D.C. 20540
     287-5000

     b. General Reading Rooms: Thomas Jefferson Building
        (Main), First Floor; and John Adams Building (Annex), Fifth Floor

        8:30 A.M.–9:30 P.M.   Monday–Friday
        8:30 A.M.–5:00 P.M.   Saturday
        1:00 P.M.–5:00 P.M.   Sunday

        Stack service generally ends one hour before closing. Closed on all holidays except Washington's Birthday, Columbus Day, and Veterans' Day when the hours are: 8:30 A.M.–5:00 P.M.. Hours of other divisions and services are noted below.

     c. For on-site use, LC's facilities and services are available free to all scholars. With few exceptions, its resources are available through the interlibrary loan service provided by the Loan Division. Several photoreproduction devices are located in the reading-room area for public use, and the library also extends its photoreproduction service to scholars who would like to use its variety of specialized services.

     d. Daniel J. Boorstin, The Librarian of Congress. Division chiefs and section heads are listed below.

2.   The Library of Congress is the national library of the United States. Its holdings exceed 75,000,000 items. The South Asian portion of total LC holdings is relatively small, an estimated 205,000 monographic titles; it is, nevertheless, the largest and most comprehensive collection in the country. Of the total South Asian holdings, approximately 85,000 monographic titles are in South Asian vernacular languages, the rest being in Western languages. The LC's collections contain over 250 South Asian newspapers, of which 89 are currently received. In addition, the Library of Congress re-

ceives more than 6,000 vernacular- and English-language periodicals and government publications from its field offices in South Asia. Since the 1950s the Library's South Asian collections have grown steadily. LC's Overseas Operations Division maintains 3 field offices in South Asia for direct acquisition of materials.

Because of the size and diversity of its collections, the users of the library may encounter certain problems. Holdings are so extensive and dispersed among various divisions and special collections that it is often difficult to identify and retrieve materials on a given topic. In addition, many acquisitions remain uncataloged or available only through a special custodial division.

Furthermore, there is no comprehensive catalog or finding aid incorporating all of the collections. The readers may also expect a frequent "not-on-shelf" response to a request for materials. Thus it is mandatory for a scholar, wishing to explore the rich resources of the LC, to visit the various divisions and collections described below to examine thoroughly all available catalogs and reference tools in the reading rooms and special collections, and to confer with the professional reference staff concerning the scope of the research to be pursued.

To facilitate research projects involving extensive use of its collections, the library makes available a number of private study desks, reserve-book shelves, advance book-reserve service, and limited stack passes. The Study Facilities Office (287-5211) of the General Reading Rooms Division (287-5530) receives all applications and requests. In addition, the Southern Asia Section of the Asian Division extends separate study facilities to South Asian scholars and assists in obtaining stack materials in vernacular languages. All stack services for the general collections are handled by the Collections Management Division (287-7400); difficulties in obtaining materials may be brought to the attention of this division, which has also a Special Search Section (287-7400 or 287-6568) for retrieval of mis-shelved items.

3. a. In spite of many drawbacks, LC is the premier research facility for a South Asianist in this country and contains resources for substantive research in many fields. Its wealthy resources cover all disciplines and materials, including monographs, retrospective runs of periodicals, government publications, newspapers, maps, manuscripts, prints, photographs, microfilm, music, and films. The collection is particularly strong in vernacular languages and literature, philosophy and religion, history, economics, and legal materials.

In terms of area strengths, India undoubtedly has the precedence, followed by Pakistan and Sri Lanka. Materials on the other national states of South Asia are relatively limited because there is a general shortage of published literature in those areas. Also, a bulk of the relevant materials on the newly emergent national states of South Asia continue to remain classed under their former jurisdictions. For example, much of the history and antiquity of Pakistan is to be found under India.

The following tabular evaluation of subject strengths are based on a selected shelflist measurement and do not include all cataloged materials. Inevitably, the figures under-represent actual LC holdings on South Asia and, as such, may reflect relative strengths at best rather than the actual numerical strength in each category. The readers are especially reminded of the remarks in the "How to Use the *Guide*" section concerning the significance of the numerical strength of the geographic categories. It may also be noted that atlases and maps of the Geography and Maps Division are described separately in entry E4.

b. Subject categories and evaluations:

Philosophy and Religion	39,865t	A
History and Auxiliary Sciences of History	28,029t	A
Geography and Anthropology	1,127t	A
Economics	15,678t	A
Sociology	3,576t	A
Politics and Government	5,668t	A
International Relations	126t	A
Law	14,640t	A
Education	2,105t	A
Art and Music	1,912t	A
Language and Literature	82,025t	A
Military Affairs	507t	A
Bibliography and Reference	2,747t	A

Afghanistan	908t	A
Bangladesh	534t	A
Bhutan	30t	A
India	32,311t	A
Maldive Islands	6t	A
Nepal	727t	A
Pakistan	2,676t	A
Sri Lanka	1,288t	A

Note: An examination of the LC Classification on Medicine (Class R) revealed approximately 283 titles on indigenous medicine or folk medicine in South Asia; e.g., *ayurvedic, siddha, unani, tibbi,* and Hindu *yogic* systems of therapeutic medicine. Some of these systems are still practiced in South Asia and in recent times have received academic and government patronage.

4. ASIAN DIVISION (formerly Orientalia Division)

John Adams Building First Floor, Room A 1024
287-5420
Richard Howard, Acting Chief

Southern Asia Section
John Adams Building, Room 1018
287-5600, 287-5428

Louis Jacob, Head
Samuel Iftikhar, Reference Librarian
Ranjan Borra, Reference Librarian

8:30 A.M.–5:00 P.M. Monday–Friday
8:30 A.M.–12:30 P.M. Saturday

The recently reorganized Asian Division consists of 3 sections: Chinese and Korean Section, Japanese Section, and Southern Asia Section. The Southern Asia Section is comprised of 2 wings: Southeast Asia—providing coverage of the countries of Burma, Thailand, Laos, Cambodia, Vietnam, Singapore, Malaysia, Brunei, Indonesia, and the Philippines—and South Asia—with responsibility for Pakistan, India, Nepal, Bhutan, Bangladesh, Sri Lanka, and Maldive Islands. Afghanistan, beyond the parameter of the Southern Asia Section, is a charge of the Near East Section of the African and Middle Eastern Division. To avoid possible confusion, unless otherwise indicated, all references henceforth to Southern Asian Section of the LC will be exclusive of Southeast Asia.

In spite of academic and political interest in South Asia being marginal until recently, the Library of Congress steadily built up a truly comprehensive collection on South Asia. Its South Asian holdings are undoubtedly the most outstanding in the United States and compare favorably with the other known collections on the region in the British Library, the India Office Library and Records, and the Calcutta National Library. Prior to 1947, the collection of the India Office Library had undoubtedly an edge over that of the Library of Congress, but, since then, the LC has continued to be the finest-known South Asian resource in the world.

The principal weakness in the LC's South Asian holdings is its very limited archival and manuscript resources. Also, LC's superb collection of government documents and newspapers are somewhat impaired by frequent gaps, especially before 1947. Certainly the last great war interrupted the flow of materials, but it seems that the British India Office, which generally served as the clearing house for supplying much of the materials from South Asia to the LC, did not pursue a planned acquisition scheme for its client.

The accelerated and planned acquisition of South Asian materials in the LC was initiated in 1962 with the commencement of the Public Law (PL) 480 book-acquisitions program. Within the short period of two decades of PL 480 funding, the collection grew remarkably, providing broad coverage in most fields and disciplines. The collection's particular strength, acquired in recent years, is in the areas of vernacular language and literature, modern history and politics, vernacular press and periodicals, and government publications.

For the South Asian specialist and novice alike, it is rewarding to visit the South Asia Section as the point of entry in the LC. The section has custody of all the South Asian-vernacular materials, with the exception of legal materials that are held in the Law Library. The extensive South Asian-language collection embraces all subject areas and contains monographs, periodicals, newspapers, pamphlets, tracts, and microforms. Works pertaining to South Asia in Western languages belong to the general collection managed by the Collections Management Division.

The LC's South Asia monographic collection in vernacular languages contains over 85,000 titles while Western-language monographs in the general collection total more than 115,000 titles. There are also considerable South Asian holdings in other LC-specialized collections and divisions.

Following is a tabular breakdown of selected vernacular materials in languages and literature (Class P) in order of numerical strength:

Hindi	13,430t
Bengali	11,770t

Urdu	8,670t
Tamil	6,120t
Telugu	4,675t
Marathi	4,080t
Malayalam	3,865t
Kannada	3,485t
Punjabi	3,315t
Gujarati	3,189t
Oriya	2,380t
Sinhalese	1,700t
Nepalese	1,445t
Assamese	1,065t
Sindhi	680t
Bihari	595t
Afghan Pashto	510t

The Southern Asia Section does not have any separate bibliographic control of the enormous vernacular holdings under its charge. Consequently, a scholar has to depend heavily on the published, general catalogs and the Main Reading Room Card Catalog which, unfortunately, do not reflect the entire dimension of the South Asian collections in the LC. It may be noted that the LC's computerized bibliographic data bases include South Asian vernacular materials. Section reference staff are available to provide assistance in identifying and locating materials, some of which are uncataloged or unclassified.

Reference inquiries are entertained by the staff in person, by telephone, or by correspondence. The staff, however, does not offer such services as translating, selecting research topics, or compiling ad hoc bibliographies. The general reading rooms and the Science Referral Center might be of assistance in referring specialists who would be willing to perform some of these vital services. Printed cards or magnetic tapes for the South Asian publications currently cataloged are sold by LC's Cataloging Distribution Service.

The Southern Asia Section, in conjunction with the Asian Division, contributes to the development of national library resources for research and study of South Asia, a region that nourished a high level of culture and civilization throughout history and is of considerable strategic significance in modern times. The facilities of the section benefit the individual scholar, government agencies, and academic and research institutions alike. The head of the section, Louis Jacob, serves as the Chairman of the Association of Asian Studies' Advisory Committee on the Bibliography of Asian Studies. Also, the section's staff is currently compiling separate bibliographic studies on Muhammad Iqbal and Subhas Bose, two outstanding personalities of the region.

The Southern Asia Section shares an adjoining reading room (Room 1016) with other sections of the Asian Division. Some basic reference works are available in the reading room, which is also equipped with a microfilm reader and provides short-term shelving space for materials in use by scholars. Additional reference materials are located in the section's office. An index of books charged to the South Asian reference collection is maintained in the office and is available for consultation by visitors. Books on South Asian languages cannot be obtained through the general reading rooms;

all requests for these materials are to be processed by the section. There are no photoreproduction facilities in the reading room of the section, but one may use the copying devices in the Newspaper and Current Periodical Room adjacent to the Asian Division office.

A bibliographic reference tool of somewhat limited use is the series of *Accession Lists* published in South Asia at varying frequencies. Materials in these lists represent titles purchased for the program by field staffs of the LC's Overseas Operation Division, stationed in multiple locations in southern Asia.

Currently there are 6 such South Asian *Accession Lists:* Afghanistan (Karachi), Bangladesh (New Delhi), Pakistan (Karachi), India (New Delhi), Sri Lanka (New Delhi), and Nepal (New Delhi). These lists are arranged by language of publication, with each language section separately alphabetized by author. Within each language section, commercial and government monographs are listed in a single alphabetical sequence. Serials are listed in separate alphabetical sequence, arranged by title in Romanized form, following the appropriate LC transliteration tables. In the case of India and Pakistan, separate cumulative *Accession Lists* on serials have also been prepared. It may be noted that the *Accession List* contains only certain preliminary citations, and LC call numbers are not yet assigned.

Of special interest to the South Asianist is the section's impressive collection of approximately 160 vernacular newspapers representing major South Asian national and regional languages. Most of these materials are on microfilm and are not accessible either through the Main Catalog or the card catalogs maintained by the Newspaper and Current Periodical Room. There are, however, other reference tools available for locating these materials. A "black file" folder-record of South Asian newspapers on microfilm is maintained by the section; however, the file has many gaps and does not follow a uniform format in recording information. Other sources include the following LC publications: *Newspapers in Microform: Foreign Countries, 1973–1977,* 1978; *A Checklist of Foreign Newspapers in the Library of Congress,* 1929; and *Supplement to 1929 Checklist, 1929–1961,* 1962.

Following is a tabular breakdown of the vernacular newspaper collection by languages. The figures here are not absolute since the reference sources used for the compilation of the data do not indicate the language of many newspapers. Only the major languages are considered. Many of these newspaper holdings are incomplete.

Urdu	37t
Hindi	25t
Bengali	19t
Gujarati	11t
Tamil	11t
Marathi	7t
Nepali	6t
Malayalam	6t
Oriya	5t
Kannada	4t
Assamese	4t
Punjabi	4t
Telugu	4t

Sindhi	3t
Sinhalese	3t
Pashto	1t
Manipuri	1t

A breakdown by country yields the following:

India	109t
Pakistan	20t
Bangladesh	13t
Nepal	5t
Sri Lanka	4t

The section does not receive current files of vernacular newspapers, and ordinarily there is a time lag of 6 months before microfilms are received.

In addition to the vernacular newspapers, the section also maintains files of over 975 magazines and journals in South Asian languages. The only available bibliographic control of this important collection is an awkward "visible file" located on Deck 8 of the John Adams Building, where most of the South Asian collection in vernacular languages is housed. The file is alphabetically arranged and contains certain binding records. On the same deck, there are 2 file cabinets containing vertical files of approximately 330 short-lived regional vernacular magazines and periodicals. A few of these little-noticed, uncataloged serials may prove useful for research in local history and literary trends.

Other uncataloged materials held by the section include a scattered pamphlet collection, many of which are in English. Also located on Deck 8, these materials include no fewer than 2,300 bound pamphlets, tracts, and brochures, shelved according to certain selected subject categories; 78 boxes marked with some subject labels and containing approximately 1,450 documents, records, reports, proceedings, catalogs, and posters of varying topics and authorship; and another 3,200 pieces of loose material that is shelved without any organization.

Seldom explored, the pamphlet collection is liable to yield interesting and weighty materials but only after time-consuming research efforts. For an illustration of the nature of this collection, a random selection of a few of these materials includes: *Hindu Objection Refuted*, North Indian Tract Society, Mirzapore, Orphan School Press, 1860, 2d edition; *Report of the General Secretary*, Indian National Congress, 1937–38, 1938–39; *1943 Lecture Series on the Formation of Federation*, Gokhale Institute of Politics and Economics; *Souvenir of the First All India Boy Scouts Jamboree*, 1937; and several volumes of *Foreign Trade Statistics of Pakistan*.

Under certain conditions, materials in the South Asia collection may be made available to other libraries through interlibrary loan. This service is limited to books required by scholars for use in their personal research. All requests for loans are handled by the LC's Loan Division (287-5441).

AFRICAN AND MIDDLE EAST DIVISION

Near East Section
John Adams Building, Room 1005
287-5421

George N. Atiyeh, Head
Ibrahim Pourhadi, Persian and Central Asian Area Specialist

8:30 A.M.–5:00 P.M.   Monday–Friday
8:30 A.M.–12:30 P.M.   Saturday

In the organizational structure of the Library of Congress, Afghanistan is the responsibility of the Near East Section of the African and Middle East Division. The Near East Section also enters within the scope of this *Guide* for another reason: a paramount segment of its vast collection is on Islam and the development and ramification of Islam, which are germane to several aspects of South Asian studies.

Vernacular materials on Afghanistan are primarily in Pashto and Dari (also known as Kabuli Persian or Afghan Persian), the two Afghan national, as well as official, languages. While a large quantity of the Afghan language materials are yet to be classified, it is estimated that the section's current holdings are in excess of 1,000 titles. Most of the literature in Pashto originates from Peshawar (Pakistan). The recently established Pashtū Talūnā or Pashto Academy in Kabul is also generating substantial materials in Pashto. The LC has an on-going but often interrupted exchange arrangement with the academy and other Afghan institutions for procuring their publications. An inventory of the materials thus obtained—and other publications from Afghanistan acquired by the LC in support of the National Program for Acquisition and Cataloging—is published in the form of an *Accession List: Afghanistan* (Karachi).

The Near East Section has a title/author/subject dictionary card catalog in progress on its Afghan holdings. A reference guide prepared by Ibrahim Pourhadi, *Persian and Afghan Newspapers*, Library of Congress, 1979, lists 23 Pashto and Dari newspapers in the LC collection, including *Anis, Islah, Jamhuriyat, Pamir,* and *Seramiasht.*

The section receives a handfull of journals and magazines in Afghan vernacular languages and plans to complete its series on Afghan *Government Gazettes* and other official publications. A few selected reference materials on Afghanistan are for consultation in the section's reading room (Annex 1016), which it shares with the Asian Division. Readers can request vernacular materials on Afghanistan through the reading room. Since much of the material on Afghanistan cannot be located by a routine search of the catalogs and other reference tools, a researcher will save time and effort by discussing the bibliographic problems with the area specialist of the section.

LAW LIBRARY

American-British Law Division
James Madison Memorial Building, Second Floor
287-5081

Marlene C. McGuirl, Chief
Krishan Nehra, Senior Legal Specialist
Kersi B. Shroff, Senior Legal Specialist

8:30 A.M.–9:30 P.M.   Monday-Friday
8:30 A.M.–5:00 P.M.   Saturday
1:00 P.M.–5:00 P.M.   Sunday

The Law Library's holdings of over 1,600,000 volumes constitute the world's largest and most comprehensive legal collection. Its staff claims to have competence in more than 50 languages and can provide reference and research service concerning all the world's legal systems, contemporary and historical. The initial imbalance in favor of American and common-law materials is disappearing steadily as foreign-law jurisdictions are growing rapidly.

One of the 5 divisions of the Law Library, the American-British Law Division, entrusted with the custody of legal materials of all the countries of South Asia—except Afghanistan, which is the charge of the Near Eastern and African Law Division—has a collection of approximately 15,000 titles, which undoubtedly constitutes the largest collection of its nature in the United States.

The Law Library does not circulate books out of the building to the general public. Photoduplicating equipment and microform reader-printers are located in the microtext facility adjacent to the division's reading room. A computer terminal in the division provides access to the data bases of the library. A 3-day reserve may be placed on materials to be used in the reading room or in the foreign-law rare-book reading area. A wide selection of frequently used reference books, digests, treatises, indexes, and periodicals, including the *Index to Foreign Legal Periodicals* are available in the reading room.

An LC classification schedule for law materials (Class K) on South Asia has not yet been devised; neither is there a specialized printed catalog on South Asian legal collections. However, a reliable reference tool available to the public is the division's temporary card catalog based on main division by country and class subdivisions under each country. All the materials in the collection are also to be found in the LC's Main and Official Catalogs as well as in the printed *National Union Catalog* and the LC *Subject Catalog*.

Reference assistance for using the resources in the collection is provided by the divisional legal specialists, who are also often called upon to respond to reference and research inquiries from the executive, legislative, and judicial branches of the U.S. government. These responses often generate printed analyses and are available on a selective basis for general distribution. Helpful information about the collection can be found in an LC leaflet, *A Guide to the Anglo-American Law Reading Room*, and an LC publication, *The Law Library of the Library of Congress: Its History, Collections and Services* (1978), prepared by Kimberly W. Dobbs and Kathryn A. Haun.

The division's South Asian collection is very comprehensive, especially for the post independence period. Materials in English dominate, vernacular holdings consisting of only some 450 titles. A particular strength of the collection is its many complete runs of court reports and digests. Rare books in the collection include: Sir William Jones, *Manu: Institutes of Hindu Law*, London, 1796; Nathaniel Brassey Halhed, *A Code of Gento Laws* or *Ordinances of the Pundits*, London, 1777.

Following is a tabular breakdown of its holdings:

India (central)

constitutions, session laws, annual laws	127t
compilations, revisions, collections of general law	138t
codes—civil, criminal, commercial, political	280t
editions of the laws on a special subject	709t
court reports	170t
digests, indexes, notes to court reports, court rules	295t

treatises	4,620t
miscellaneous	665t
India (states)	3,700t
Pakistan	1,608t
Nepal	22t
Bangladesh	119t
Bhutan	—
Sri Lanka	302t
Maldive Islands	1t

Near Eastern and African Law Division
Thomas Jefferson Building, Second Floor
287-5073

Zuhair E. Jwaideh, Chief

8:30 A.M.–4:15 P.M. Monday–Friday

Custodial jurisdiction of the legal materials on Afghanistan is held by the Near East and African Law Division which is one of the 5 constituent divisions of the LC's Law Library. Published legal material on Afghanistan is very limited, and this is reflected in the division's holdings, which consist of about 350 items including monographs, bound serials, and periodicals.

Any serious research in the Afghan legal system, which until recently was based on Hanafi school of Muslim law, requires a competency in Pashto and Dari (also known as Afghan Persian or Kabuli Persian), since most of the materials are in vernacular languages. However, there are some titles in Russian and English. A useful English rendering of the laws of Afghanistan, known as the *Compiled Translation of the Laws of Afghanistan,* compiled by the United Nations' Development Program (Kabul, 1975), is available in the collection.

Some other titles of interest are: *Afghan Judicial Reporters; The Civil Law of the Republic of Afghanistan;* and *Rasmi Jaridan,* or the *Official Afghan Gazette.* The division is committed to strengthen its collection of legal materials from Afghanistan and has recently taken some steps in that direction.

A visit to the Near East Law Division is indispensable to a South Asianist for another reason. The division is responsible for an outstanding collection of some 1,465 titles on Islamic law and jurisprudence. Written in Arabic, Persian, and Urdu, as well as in Western languages, these materials are essential ingredients for scholarly research into many aspects of South Asian legal systems that have organic linkages with Islamic Law.

A small reading area is available in the division office for visitors to use. An LC classification schedule for law materials (Class K) of the division has not yet been developed, nor is there a printed bibliography on the collection; however, a card catalog and a shelflist are available in the division, and a reference staff entertains requests for assistance in identifying and locating materials.

SERIAL AND GOVERNMENT PUBLICATIONS DIVISION

Newspaper and Current Periodical Room
John Adams Building, First Floor, Room 1026
287-5690

Donald F. Wisdom, Chief
Robert W. Schaaf, Senior Specialist in United Nations and International Documents

The Serial and Government Publications Division's principal public outlet for research is provided through its Newspaper and Current Periodical Room, which is primarily a reading room equipped with several microform readers. The well laid-out reading room is staffed by a score of reference librarians who are responsible for providing reader and reference service in person, by correspondence, and—on a limited basis—by telephone. Names of experienced researchers, who will do extensive research for a fee, are available at the desk. Photoduplicating facilities in the room include microfilm reader-printers. The LC's Photoduplication Service can accept orders for detailed or extensive photographic reproduction. Most newspapers on microfilm are available for interlibrary loan to other libraries for use by their readers. Bound and unbound newspapers and serials, however, do not circulate.

All loan requests are processed through the LC's Loan Division. Items requested from the collections in person are usually retrieved within 30 minutes, with the exception of bound newspaper volumes, which are housed in a storage area away from the building and, therefore, require 24- to 48-hours' notice for retrieval. All newspaper acquisitions since 1962 have been microfilmed, and the entire pre-1962 collection is scheduled to be microfilmed within the next decade.

A very frequented facility in the LC, the Newspaper and Current Periodical Room, provides access to the Serial Division's most extensive collections of periodicals, newspapers, and government documents. In addition to the indeterminate, but very large, retrospective holdings of both domestic and foreign newspapers, the library receives over 1,500 current newspapers, retaining approximately 1,200 in its permanent collection.

The serial collection includes unbound domestic and foreign periodicals and government publications. Approximately 70,000 titles of serial publications are currently received, and unbound pieces in the division's custody number close to 4,000,000. Unbound holdings, serviced through the Newspaper and Current Periodical Room, generally date within the last 2 current years. Once bound or microfilmed, serial publications are serviced along with other items from the general collections of the LC through its general reading rooms or the Microfilm Reading Room. However, law and music periodicals, bound and unbound, are serviced through the Law Library and the Music Reading Room, respectively.

Insofar as the South Asian materials are concerned, the division maintains only newspapers, periodicals, and government publications in Western languages. All newspapers and periodicals in vernacular languages are held and serviced by the Southern Asia Section of the Asian Division.

The LC currently receives 89 newspapers from South Asia. A country-based breakdown follows:

India	62t
Pakistan	10t
Sri Lanka	6t
Bangladesh	5t
Nepal	3t
Afghanistan	3t

The LC collection in Western languages of South Asian periodicals and government publications, including statistical bulletins, exceeds 4,000 titles. An estimated breakdown, by country, follows:

India	3,632t
Pakistan	300t
Bangladesh	25t
Nepal	20t
Sri Lanka	10t
Afghanistan	6t

Locating a serial is not always an easy task. The LC's computerized catalog does not provide periodical call numbers. Newspapers do not have call numbers and are not listed in the public catalogs. Microfilmed periodicals are assigned a microfilm number by which materials are retrieved. Microfilm numbers for Western-language titles are found in the Serials File in the Microfilm Reading Room.

Although not always reliable, there are several printed LC reference guides and card indexes to the collection. For an update on acquisitions, a researcher should check the latest volumes of *Newspapers Currently Received in the Library of Congress* and *Newspapers in Microform.* For the retrospective holdings, a good source is Henry A. Parson, ed., *A Check List of Foreign Newspapers in the Library of Congress,* 1929, and its loose-leaf supplementary updates through the 1960s. One should also consult the LC cumulative volumes entitled *Newspapers in Microfilm: Foreign Countries, 1948–1972,* 1973, and its 1978 quinquennial supplement for the years 1973–1977. For serials, the standard reference is the *New Serial Titles* and its compendium volume, *New Serial Titles—Classed Subject Arrangement,* published monthly with annual cumulations as well.

A dictionary card index of foreign, Western-language newspapers in microfilm—available at the reference desk of the periodical room—contains some fragmentary information on the commencement dates of the publication and the date spans in LC's holdings. Another card catalog of Western-language periodicals and government publications, arranged by country, is also maintained, for consultation by the readers in this room, which also houses a large selection of useful reference books for browsing.

A small brochure, *Newspapers and Current Periodical Room,* is issued by the Serial Division as a public service. A mimeographed pamphlet, *How to Find Newspapers and Periodicals in the Library of Congress,* 1979, prepared by the General Reading Rooms Division, has some useful advice. It may also be pointed out that the separate Periodical Card Catalog in the general reading rooms should not be overlooked; it is particularly strong on earlier publications.

In consideration of the unique significance of newspapers as primary source materials for conducting research in several disciplines, a selected list of South Asian newspapers in English, currently received by the LC, is provided below:

Afghanistan
   Kabul Times, Kabul

Bangladesh
   Bangladesh Observer, Dacca

India

Tripura Times, Agartala
Times of India, Ahmedabad
Northern India Patrika, Ahmedabad
Deccan Herald, Bangalore
Madhya Pradesh Chronicle, Bhopal
Economic Times, Bombay
Financial Express, Bombay
Times of India, Bombay
Hindustan Standard, Calcutta
Statesman, Calcutta
Tribune, Chandigarh
Eastern Times, Cuttack
Coalfield Times, Dhanbad
Assam Tribune, Gauhati
National Herald, Lucknow
Hindu, Madras
Nagpur Times, Nagpur
Hindustan Times, New Delhi
Indian Express, New Delhi
Patriot, New Delhi
Statesman, New Delhi
Times of India, New Delhi
Financial Express, New Delhi
Navhind Times, Panjim
Indian Nation, Patna

Nepal

Commoner, Kathmandu

Pakistan

Dawn, Karachi
Morning News, Karachi
Pakistan Times, Lahore
Khyber Mail, Peshawar
Baluchistan Times, Quetta
New Times, Rawalpindi

Sri Lanka

Ceylon Daily News, Colombo
Ceylon Observer, Colombo

MUSIC DIVISION

Thomas Jefferson Building. Room G-146
287-5507

Donald L. Leavitt, Chief

8:30 A.M.–5:00 P.M.   Monday–Saturday

The collections of music and music literature assembled in the LC are remarkably diverse and comprehensive. International in scope and spanning many centuries, the holdings include some 30,000 books, periodicals, and pamphlets, about 700,000 sound recordings, and over 4,000,000 pieces of music, scores, sheet music, librettos, and miscellaneous items. The over-whelming quantity of these materials, however, reflects the development of music in Western civilization.

A significant quantity of the music collection remains unindexed and uncataloged and is identifiable and retrievable only with the assistance of the reference staff of the division. Furthermore, all of the cataloged materials under the custody of the division do not appear in the Main Card Catalog. There are, however, several finding aids in the reading room of the division. One is a useful but discontinued card index to articles appearing in U.S. and foreign music periodicals (1902–1940); another card catalog of the division, based on LC classification schedules for the field of music, is available.

A comprehensive printed bibliography of the cataloged resources of the division is an LC cumulative publication, *Music, Books on Music and Sound Recordings,* and its predecessor, *Library of Congress Catalog: Music and Phonorecords; a cumulative list of works represented by Library of Congress Printed Cards.* Both of these titles are available as volumes of the *National Union Catalog.* A free leaflet prepared by the division, *The Music Division: A Guide to Its Collections and Services,* provides useful assistance to visitors. Photoduplication services and microfilm readers are available in the reading room area. With few exceptions, much of the collection circulates on interlibrary loan.

Publications on South Asian music are certainly not prolific, and this is reflected in the holdings of the division. A shelflist measurement, accompanied by other searches, revealed over 1,150 titles on various aspects of South Asian music. A dominant feature of the collection is its concentration of works on national music and on literature and history of music. For obvious reasons, the collection contains more materials on India than on any other country of the region. The collection also contains a number of titles on South Asian traditional musical instruments; e.g., shehnai, sitar, vina, vihuela, and some 50 titles on *ragas,* the traditional melody patterns with characteristic intervals, rhythms, and embellishments used by South Asian musicians as source materials for improvisation.

RARE BOOK DIVISION

Thomas Jefferson Building, Second Floor, Room 256
287-5434

William Matheson, Chief

8:30 A.M.–5:00 P.M.   Monday–Friday

This custodial division has assembled in its enormous collection over 300,000 volumes and another 200,000 broadsides, pamphlets, theater playbills, title pages, prints, manuscripts, posters, and photographs acquired with various collections. Materials in the swelling collection are selected for a variety of reasons, such as monetary value, importance in the history of printing, binding, association interest, or fragility, but the paramount reason is their long-term interest to scholars. The division's holdings of more than 5,600 incunabula consitute the largest such collection in the Western hemisphere.

The division maintains an elegant reading room that houses all of the divisional card catalogs and the reference collection. The division has its own central card catalog, containing over 650,000 cards and providing access to almost all of its collection. In addition to this predominantly author-indexed card catalog, the division has created over 100 special-aspect card files, describing individual collections or special aspects of books from many collections.

In addition, 2 printed LC leaflets facilitate access to the collections: *Some Guides to Special Collections in the Rare Books* and *Special Collections in the Library of Congress.* The former lists available printed catalogs that specifically describe individual special collections or annotate the division's holdings. Reference assistance is also offered by the professional staff. It may be noted that not all of the items in the collections appear in the general card catalog or in the LC computerized card catalog.

The division does not have facilities for photocopying. Requests for photoduplication can be accommodated through the library's Photoduplication Service, if the physical condition of the original permits. None of the division's holdings are available on interlibrary loan. The resources of the division are available to scholars following registration and presentation of identification.

There is certainly no over-abundance of materials or any special collection on South Asia in the division's holdings, but its small collection of some 300 books mostly on description, travel, evangelism, and history contain many early imprints of English, Dutch, Portuguese, Spanish, and French works.

A selected list of these materials includes: François Bernier (1620–1688), *The History . . . of the Great Mogul . . .,* Englished out of French, 2d ed., London, M. Pitt, 1671; Abū al-Faẓl ibn Mubārak (1551–1602), *Ayeen Akbery . . .,* translated from the original Persian by Francis Gladwin, Calcutta, 1783–86; Olfert Dapper (d. 1690), *Asia . . . des Grooten Mogols . . .,* Amsterdam, J. Van Meurs, 1672; William Robertson (1721–1793), *A Historical Disquisition Concerning . . . India . . .,* 1st American ed. from the 5th London ed., Philadelphia, John Bioren, 1812; Bartholomew Burges, *A Series of Indostan Letters . . .,* New York, W. Ross, 1790; John Cary (d. 1720), *A Discourse Concerning the East India Trade . . .,* London 1698 (reprint of Bristol, 1695); Charlés Vergennes (1717–1787), *Mémoire Historique et Politique . . .,* Paris, 1802; Florence Nightingale, *Observations . . .on the Sanitary State of the Army in India,* London, E. Stanford, 1863; Rudyard Kipling, *Letters of Marque,* Allahabad, A. H. Wheeler, 1891; Alexander Hamilton (d. 1732), *A New Account of the East Indies . . .,* Edinburgh, J. Mosman, 1727; Nathaniel Brassey Halhed (1751–1830), *A Grammar of the Bengali Language,* Hooghly, Bengal, 1778; John Fryer (d. 1730), *A New Account of East India . . .,* London, R. Chriswell, 1698; Ravîndranāth Thakura, *Chitra,* London, The India Society, 1913; Indian National Congress Civil Disobedience Enquiry Committee, *Report of the Civil Disobedience Enquiry Committee,* Allahabad, 1922; *Draft Constitution of India,* New Delhi, Government of India Press, 1947; India Archaeological Survey, *Archaeological Survey of Western India,* in 12 vols. (missing vol. 7), Bombay, Central Government Press, 1874–91.

Finally, the division's Lessing J. Rosenwald Collection contains an exceptionally valuable and beautiful rare Persian manuscript written in India in large nasta'líq and illustrated with 120 miniatures including portraits. Completed in 1825, this manuscript, entitled "Kitāb-i-tashrîh al-aqvām" was compiled by James Skinner (1778–1841). The manuscript is divided in two parts: the first discusses the history of the origin and distinguishing marks of the different castes of India; and the second describes the social position of Indian Muslims, including an account of the poor Muslims and their standing in Indian society. For a discussion of the manuscript, see Ibrahim Pourhadi, "The Indian Caste System in an Exquisite Persian Manuscript" in *The Quarterly Journal of the Library of Congress* (July 1977).

MICROFORM READING ROOM SECTION

Thomas Jefferson Building, First Floor, Room 140-B
287-5471

Robert V. Gross, Head
Pablo A. Calvan, Reference Librarian

8:30 A.M.–9:30 P.M.   Monday–Friday
8:30 A.M.–5:00 P.M.   Saturday
1:00 P.M.–5:00 P.M.   Sunday

The section's growing microform collections are currently estimated to exceed 1,500,000 items. The reading room is equipped with several microform readers and printers. Materials not otherwise restricted can be obtained through interlibrary loan, which is processed by the LC Loan Division (287-5441).

Generally, the materials in the collection are not included in the Main Card Catalog or the computerized catalog but are accessed primarily through specialized guides and indexes, prepared for the collections by the micropublishers, and through the assistance of the reference staff of the section. Scholars should also consult the subject/title/author card catalog located in the reading room and the mimeographed preliminary reference guide, *Selected Microform Collections in the Microform Reading Room*, 1978, a revised version of which will be published soon. This reference guide, compiled by Lois Korzendorfer and prepared by the General Reading Room Division, represents all major collections which the section has acquired. Entries have been designed to present the user with a basic idea of the scope and format of each collection. There is also another card file in the reading room for its periodical holdings in microfilm.

The section's holdings on South Asia are comprised of over 500 titles. Highlights of the collection include many valuable out-of-print census reports, government gazettes, scattered proceedings, and reports of the All India Muslim League, reports on the famines and food situation in India, and speeches and letters of Gandhi, Jinnah, Nehru, and Fazlul Huq. Also of special interest to a South Asianist are the microfilm reels of the Indian National Archives, Tagore manuscripts, and selections from the records of the Government of India (nineteenth century), and several British Command Papers dealing with the Raj.

Other items of general importance include the following: materials from the U.S. Foreign Broadcast Information Service (FBIS), U.S. Joint Publications Research Service (JPRS), Inter Documentation Company (Zug, Switzerland), Human Relations Area Files (HRAF), National Technical Information Service, Congressional Information Service (research reports), and technical translations of federal government departments and agencies; documents and official reports of the League of Nations and the United Nations; college catalogs of selected foreign universities; House of Commons (Great Britain) Sessional Papers; New York Times Information Bank;

Urban Affairs Library Newsbank; transcripts of various TV programs; selections from early British periodicals; and twentieth-century economic development plans of selected developing countries in Africa, Asia, and Latin America. All U.S. doctoral dissertations microfilmed by the University Microfilm International (Ann Arbor, Michigan) are also available in the section and are conveniently retrievable by the catalog numbers assigned by the manufacturers.

The section also maintains an undeterminable number of titles from the general book collection of the LC through its preservation program. These are retrievable by the serial or sequential numbers given to them by the section and are noted in the Main Reading Room Card Catalog entry.

SCIENCE AND TECHNOLOGY DIVISION

John Adams Building, Fifth Floor
287-5639

John Price, Acting Chief

The Science and Technology Division maintains the same service hours as the general reading rooms. This division is entrusted with the supervision of LC's holdings on science and technology and, in addition, it manages the Science Reading Room, providing a variety of bibliographic and reference services. The reading room is equipped with a computer terminal and has a reference and microfilm collection.

The division maintains no separate catalogs or indexes on the LC holdings in science and technology. A computer-generated catalog, *Science and Technology Room Collection, Books and Serials* (1979), produced by the division with the assistance of the LC Automated Systems Office, is available to the users in the reading room.

Although primarily responsible for natural sciences, the division's holdings contain materials on social sciences as well. The impressive collection of the division consists of over 3,000,000 monographs, 20,000 current periodicals and about 2,500,000 technical reports. Various directories and references prepared by the division are listed in a bibliography entitled *Publications Prepared by the Science and Technology Division, 1940–1975*.

The division issues a series of bibliographic guides on a variety of subjects under the title *LC Science Tracer Bullet*. The division is currently revising its 1973 brief guide to the division, *Mission and Services of the Science and Technology Division*. Researchers may direct inquiries by phone, mail, or in person to the several reference librarians of the division. The services of the division are usually free, but a charge for special or lengthy searches may be imposed. An immensely valuable research aid provided by the division is through its National Referral Center described below.

National Referral Center

John Adams Building, Fifth Floor
287-5670 (referral services)
287-5680 (registration of information resources)

John Feulner, Head
Monica Bowen, Referral Specialist for Humanities
John Hass, Referral Specialist for Social Sciences
8:30 A.M.–4:30 P.M. Monday–Friday

A section of the Science and Technology Division, the National Referral Center in the Library of Congress is a free referral service that directs those who have questions on any subject to organizations that can provide the answers. The referral center is not equipped to furnish answers to specific questions or to provide bibliographic assistance. Instead, its purpose is to direct those who have questions to resources that have the information and are willing to share it with others. Some of these resources exist within the LC itself.

The referral service uses a subject-indexed, computerized file of 13,000 organizations, which the center calls "Information Resources." A description of each resource includes its special fields of interest and the types of information service it is willing to provide. The National Referral Center file, which is maintained by professional analysts, is used primarily by the center's referral specialists. It is also accessible to readers at the Library of Congress through computer terminals located in various reading rooms and to many federal agencies nationwide through the RECON computer network operated by the Department of Energy.

When the center was established in 1962, it made referrals in the areas of science and technology. Today it handles referrals in virtually all subject areas, including the social sciences, the arts, and humanities. The center maintains systematic coverage for resources in the United States only, although its file also includes some international and foreign resources.

The concept of information resource is broadly defined to include any organization, institution, group, or individual with specialized information in a particular field and a willingness to share it with others. This includes not only traditional sources of information such as technical libraries, information and documentation centers, and abstracting and indexing services, but also such resources as professional societies, university research bureaus and institutions, federal and state agencies, industrial laboratories, museums, testing stations, hobby groups, and grassroots citizens' organizations. The criterion for registering an organization is not its size but its ability and willingness to provide information to others on a reasonable basis.

The center will accept requests for referral services on any topic. When a subject is not covered in the data file, the center will attempt to locate new information resources from its extensive contacts. In each case, responses to requests are individually tailored to the specific inquiry.

The center occasionally compiles directories of information resources covering a broad area. These are published by the Library of Congress under the general title, *A Directory of Information Resources in the United States* with subtitles. Some of these volumes are: *Social Sciences*, rev. ed., Washington, Government Printing Office, 1973; *Federal Government, With a Supplement of Government Sponsored Information Analysis Centers*, rev. ed., Washington, Government Printing Office, 1974.

The center also prepares a guide entitled *Directory of Federally Supported Information Analysis Centers*, which is distributed by the National Technical Information Service (see entry J6). A useful guide to the scope and services of the center is a short pamphlet distributed free by the center. A preliminary check of the center's computer by its staff revealed a multiple number of entries relevant to South Asia.

GENERAL READING ROOMS DIVISION

Thomas Jefferson Building, First Floor
287-5530

Ellen Z. Hahn, Chief

The primary responsibility of the division is to maintain the two general reading rooms: the Main Reading Room, located on the first floor of the Main Building (287-5455), and the Thomas Jefferson Reading Room, located on the fifth floor of the Annex (287-5538). Another facility of the division, the Microform Reading Room (287-5471), is described above. The division's reference librarians are on duty in both locations during the regular hours of service and will attend to reference and bibliographic questions and, when necessary, will direct inquiries to appropriate divisions or collections. A computerized printout, *Subject Specialities of Reference Librarians,* prepared by the division, notes the expertise of the reference staff for the convenience of the scholars requiring reference assistance. The division's Telephone Inquiry Section (287-5522) also provides limited reference assistance, and the Union Catalog Reference Section (287-6300), located on Deck 33 of the Main Building, can provide bibliographic reference assistance regarding the *National Union Catalog* and its other auxiliary union catalogs—both published and unpublished.

Researchers with time constraints may find it convenient to note that, if requested, the division will furnish names of stenographers, typists, translators, and free-lance researchers whose services may be hired. The division's pamphlet, *Special Facilities in the Library of Congress,* contains other useful information.

The spacious and lavishly decorated Main Reading Room houses a reference collection of some 50,000 volumes including a few periodicals, maps and atlases, government publications, statistical abstracts, indexes, and directories. An author/title dictionary catalog and a shelflist of the reference collection are available in the reading room. In addition, the division, in collaboration with the LC Automated Systems Office and the Serial Record Division, has produced a computer-generated Classed Catalog (shelflist) and a Subject Catalog of the Main Reading Room Reference Collection. Another useful reference tool generated by the division is a mimeographed printout, *How to Find Periodical Call Numbers in the Library of Congress* (1979). Other finding aids located in the reading rooms, including the Main Card Catalog, will be discussed below.

PHOTODUPLICATION SERVICE

John Adams Building, Room G-1009
287-5654

Norman J. Shaffer, Acting Chief

8:30 A.M.–4:15 P.M.   Monday–Friday

For all scholars, especially those with time constraints, the Photoduplication Service provides invaluable assistance. Individuals and institutions, for a fee, may obtain photoreproductions—in different formats—of the requested materials, excluding those restricted by copyright regulations or by other established reasons. Through one of its programs known as Document

Expediting, the service receives, duplicates, and sells materials from government agencies, including unclassified CIA reports.

The service also maintains the LC Master Negative Microfilm Collection, numbering more than 150,000 reels, which includes selections from the manuscript division, U.S. and foreign government documents, and periodicals and newspapers. Some of these items are on sale. Information about the holdings of the division may be found in *National Register of Microfilm Masters, Newspapers in Microfilm, Microfilm Clearinghouse Bulletin,* and *Guides to Microfilms in Print.* An information brochure describing the facilities provided by the Photoduplication Service, a price list, and a flyer listing the catalogs of accessible materials are available without charge.

Requests for photoduplication are entertained either in person or by mail. It should be noted that additional photoduplication facilities are available in most divisions and sections; appropriate information concerning these services are included in the descriptions of those divisions and sections.

LOAN DIVISION

Thomas Jefferson Building, Room G-155
287-5441

Jack McDonald, Chief

8:00 A.M.–5:15 P.M.   Monday–Friday

As a research library, the LC extends the use of its collections outside its facilities through an interlibrary-loan service provided by the Loan Division. The service is intended to aid scholarly research by making available unusual materials that are not readily accessible elsewhere. The service is available to most U.S. libraries and also to any major library of the world. All loan requests must originate from libraries and not from individuals. Loan requests are entertained only when such requests do not conflict with the LC's internal needs and its primary service obligation to the Congress. Certain kinds of materials, including rare books, manuscripts, newspapers, periodicals, collected sets, sheet music, librettos, motion picture films, and books that are ordinarily available do not circulate.

5.   Most of the noteworthy holdings of the Library of Congress have been described above under appropriate divisions and collections. However, it may also be appropriate to note again that LC's holdings, in all of the 21 categories evaluated, constitute one of the most outstanding collections in the world both qualitatively and quantitatively. It may be noted further that specialized publications and titles on advanced technology in agriculture, health, and medicine may abound more in the National Agricultural Library and National Library of Medicine respectively.

6.   Of the numerous bibliographic aids available for providing access to LC's collections, the one most commonly used and easily accessible is the Main Catalog. Located in the Main Reading Room, it consists of more than 20,000,000 cards interfiled alphabetically by author, subject, and title. There is no generally available card catalog in the John Adams Building; researchers there must rely on printed book catalogs or computer catalogs (described below). Separate periodical card catalogs, which duplicate cards in the Main Catalog, are in both general reading rooms.

Although the Main Catalog is the most comprehensive reference aid to LC's monographic and serial holdings, it does not reflect the bulk of the materials in the specialized collections that are managed by several divisions and sections, namely: rare book, serial, prints and photographs, music, motion pictures, broadcasting and recorded sound, manuscript, microform, science and technology, and geography and map. Thus the Main Catalog is to be used in conjunction with other specialized catalogs and finding aids. It may be repeated again that it is advisable to consult the reference librarians before concluding that needed materials are not available.

On January 2, 1981, the LC "froze" all existing card catalogs. New acquisitions will not be added; instead, they will be entered into the LC's computerized cataloging system, already in operation, and will also be added to a new back-up, second card catalog. Introduction of computer technology in LC's bibliographic control promises to revolutionize many aspects of scholarly research, but it will not render obsolete the time-honored card catalog, which will continue to be the only reference tool for those concerned with retrospective materials. It will be a long time before all the cards will be transformed into a computer data base.

The Library of Congress Computerized Catalog (LCCC) contains bibliographic information about books and certain other items cataloged since 1968. Although materials in English have been processed since 1968, materials in South Asian languages have been processed in Roman transliteration only since the summer of 1978. While for current bibliographic searches the use of LCCC can save scholars vast amounts of time and effort, only when bibliographic data for pre-1978 South Asian vernacular-language materials is converted into machine-readable form, can LCCC be of maximum use to a South Asianist. So far, more than 1,250,000 items have been processed into the LCCC, and approximately 1,000 titles are added to the system every day.

Computer terminals are located in the general reading rooms and in other public reference facilities. The Computer Catalog Center (287-6213), located in the Main Reading Room area, provides free instruction to researchers in the use of terminals. For a fee, the Cataloging Distribution Service (287-6172) will conduct bibliographic searches and produce printed outputs. A free, printed leaflet, *MARC Search Service,* outlines the details about this service. Several loose-leaf binders, users' manuals, and a printed pamphlet, *Information on the MARC System,* explain the retrieval technique and are available at the various terminal points.

A lengthy description of the LC's computer system is not within the scope of this *Guide.* For the users of the system, the most important components to be aware of are MARC (Machine-Readable Cataloging) records and the retrieval systems, MUMS (Multiple-Use MARC) and SCORPIO (Subject-Oriented Retriever for Processing Information On-Line).

Primarily a cataloger's data system, MARC also provides access to the LCCC and can be used to conduct bibliographic searches by author and title. A more generalized data retrieval system of considerably greater utility to researchers, SCORPIO can be used for general bibliographic searches based on LC subject headings, LC classification categories, or call numbers, as well as by authors and titles, or by certain characterizing indicators such as country or area.

SCORPIO is designed to respond to a group of simple, logical commands that require a minimum of training and provide a maximum amount of flexibility. Four data files can be tapped through the SCORPIO:

LCCC bibliographic data on recent monographs;

bibliocitation file, containing references to topical periodical articles—including foreign affairs—subject- and country-indexed by the LC's Congressional Research Service (CRS) from nearly 1,500 major journals, mostly American;

a subject-indexed National Referral Center Resources file containing data on some 13,000 organizations and institutions qualified and willing to provide information on a large number of topics in sciences, technologies, and social sciences; and

congressional information files containing basic data on legislative bills considered by Congress since January 19, 1976.

In addition to the published reference tools listed under appropriate divisions above, scholars may consult the publications listed below, which are more general in nature. It is best to examine a free LC brochure, *Library of Congress Publications in Print* (1979), for identifying availability, frequencies, cumulations, and other publication data of these catalogs:

The National Union Catalog, Pre-1956 Imprints, 610 vols.; *A Catalog of Books Represented by Library of Congress Printed Cards Issued* (from August 1898 through July 1942), 167 vols.; *Supplement: Cards issued August 1, 1942–December 31, 1947*, 42 vols.; *The National Union Catalog: A Cumulative Author List Representing Library of Congress Printed Cards and Titles Reported by Other American Libraries* (1953–1979), total cumulation, 558 vols.; *The Library of Congress Author Catalog, a Cumulative List of Works Represented by Library of Congress Cards, 1948–52*, 24 vols.; *Library of Congress Catalogs—Books: Subjects, a Cumulative List of Works Represented by Library of Congress Printed Cards* (1950–74), total cumulation, 209 vols., continued by *Subject Catalog* (1975–78), total cumulation, 37 vols., continues *Library of Congress Catalog—Books: Subjects; Monographic Series* (1974–78), total cumulation, 17 vols.; *The Library of Congress Classification System; Library of Congress Name Headings with References; Library of Congress Subject Headings*, supersedes *Subject Headings Used in the Dictionary Catalogs of the Library of Congress; The National Union Catalog: Reference and Related Services; Combined Indexes to the Library of Congress Classification Schedules*, 15 vols.; *Annual Report of the Librarian of Congress;* and *Quarterly Journal of the Library of Congress.*

A recently completed project provides access to the shelflist of the Library of Congress thereby adding a valuable tool to scholarly research. Microform copies of the shelflist are available for purchase in microfiche from University Microfilms International, 300 North Zeeb Road, Ann Arbor, Michigan 48106 (800/521-0600) or on film from U.S. Historical Documentation Institute, 1911 Fort Myer Drive, Arlington, Virginia 22209 (703/525-6036).

Note: Also see entries B4, B5, D3, D4, E4, F5, and F6.

A24 Martin Luther King Memorial Library (District of Columbia Public Library)

1. a. *901 G Street, N.W.*
    Washington, D.C. 20001
    727-1111

    b. 9:00 A.M.–9:00 P.M. Monday–Thursday
    9:00 A.M.–5:30 P.M. Friday–Saturday

    c. Open to the public; interlibrary loan and photoduplication facilities are available.

    d. Cathy Woods, Head Librarian

2-3. The Martin Luther King Memorial Library is the main collection in the District of Columbia public library system that supplements the system of public education in the district. The library contains nearly 2,000,000 volumes in addition to periodicals, newspapers, and other materials. South Asia-related collections in the library exceed 800 titles: India 550; Pakistan 150; Sri Lanka 85; Nepal 30; Bangladesh 8; and Bhutan 7. The collection is strong in history, description and travel, and politics and government. There are approximately 250 titles on Islam and 100 titles on Hinduism. Works on Mahatma Gandhi in the collection are significant.

4. For the films collection, see entry F8. Also see entry D5 for its music collection.

6. The library maintains a card catalog that combines title, subject, and author listings. The library uses the Dewey Decimal system of cataloging. Free brochures, describing special library programs and events, are made available to visiting patrons.

A25 Middle East Institute—George Camp Keiser Library

1. a. *1761 N Street, N.W.*
    Washington, D.C. 20036
    785-1141

    b. 10:30 A.M.–5:00 P.M. Monday–Friday
    10:00 A.M.–5:00 P.M. Saturday

    c. The library is open to the public for reference use. Interlibrary loan and photocopying services are available.

    d. Lois M. Khairallah, Librarian

2. The George Camp Keiser Library of the prestigious Middle East Institute is a small but significant collection of about 15,000 volumes devoted to Islam and the Middle East. Both the institute and the library have a special interest in South Asia, particularly Afghanistan and Pakistan, as part of the world of Islam. The South Asian portion of the collection consists of approximately 300 titles, mostly in English, dealing with travel, description,

and history. A few books in this very small South Asian holding may be worth mentioning: C. U. Aitchison, *A Collection of Treaties, Engagements and Sanads*, 24 vols., Calcutta, 1929; J. W. Kaye, *History of the War in Afghanistan*, 2 vols., London, 1851.

The library's periodical collection of some 400 titles include more than 10 from South Asia. A few titles of interest are: *Iqbal Review* (Lahore); *Islamic Culture* (Hyderabad, India); *Islamic Literature* (Lahore); *Islamic Thought* (Aligarh); and *Islam and the Modern Age* (New Delhi). A card catalog, divided into author-title and subject sections is the main reference tool for the collection. A card file for periodicals is available.

The collection contains many of the U.S. government documents on Middle East and documents generated by the governments in the Middle East. An uncataloged map collection and vertical files, by country, of miscellaneous materials are maintained. (For the film collection of the institute, see entry F9.)

National Aeronautics and Space Administration Libraries
See entry J23

A26 National Agricultural Library (Agriculture Department)

1. a. *Main Library*
       U.S. Route 1
       Beltsville, Maryland 20705
       (301) 344-3755; 344-3756

       D.C. Branch and Law Library
       U.S. Department of Agriculture
       South Building
       Independence Avenue and 14th Street, S.W.
       Washington, D.C. 20250
       447-3434; 447-7751

    b. Main Library:
       8:00 A.M.–4:30 P.M.   Monday–Friday

       D.C. Branch Library and Law Library:
       8:30 A.M.–5:00 P.M.   Monday–Friday

    c. The services of the library are available to persons with interests in the library's resources. Interlibrary loan and photocopying facilities are available.

    d. Richard A. Farley, Director
       Melba Bruno, Chief, D.C. Branch Library
       Spurgeon Terry, Law Librarian

2. The resources of the National Agricultural Library represent the most outstanding collection of published literature on agriculture and its allied subjects in the United States. Its current holdings are estimated to be in excess of 1,500,000 volumes including more than 25,000 items on South Asia. It also holds approximately 24,000 periodicals—two-thirds of which are ac-

quired through international exchange programs—and more than 130,000 microfilm items. With agriculture as the central subject, the collection includes technical agriculture, farming, veterinary science, entomology, botany, chemistry, soil science, food and nutrition, agricultural products, rural sociology, economics, statistics, and laws pertaining to agriculture.

To support the work of the Department of Agriculture, the library also collects material in physics, biology, natural history, wildlife, ecology and pollution, genetics, natural resources, energy, meteorology, and fisheries. The library collects literature related to agriculture from world-wide sources and in all major languages, including several South Asian languages.

The library also maintains a collection of historical books and manuscripts, with particular strength in various aspects of agriculture. The holdings of the D.C. Branch Library include materials on statistics, economics, and social sciences. The Law Library maintains a vast array of legal journals, law publications and legislative history.

The library's holdings pertaining to South Asia are most extensive and of particular significance to scholars investigating technical and experimental aspects of agriculture as well as the fields of rural sociology, nutrition, public health, agricultural economics, agricultural law, environment, and population control.

3. The National Agricultural Library maintains a dual system of classification. Prior to the introduction of the LC classification scheme in 1966, the library followed its own classification system. Consequently, an accurate quantitative evaluation of its South Asian resources is not possible. However, an indication of the collection's geographical strengths can be revealed through a search of the library's computerized bibliography, AGRICOLA (Agriculture On-Line Access), which contains more than 1,000,000 citations to monographs and periodical articles selected from 6,000 serial titles processed since January 1970. Following is a tabular evaluation of geographic categories based on a search of AGRICOLA's data bases:

Geographic categories	Number of entries
Afghanistan	370t
Bangladesh	377t
Bhutan	38t
India	18,056t
Maldive Islands	3t
Nepal	472t
Pakistan	1,580t
Sri Lanka (Ceylon)	770t

The computer search by language descriptions also revealed the existence of a few items in South Asian vernaculars: Bengali 6; Hindi 36; Malayalam 2; Nepalese 5; Oriyan 2; Punjabi 1; Sinhalese 5; Tamil 3; and Urdu 13. The staff indicated that a bulk of vernacular materials had not yet been processed. Also, based on an ad hoc examination of the public catalogs, the library is estimated to contain some additional 3,500 titles. Included in the collection are many standard works in history and civilization, description and travel, and politics and government. Several rare volumes of census reports from 1881 are also available.

4. Approximately 250 journals originating from South Asia are currently received by the library: Bangladesh 2; India 210; Pakistan 15; and Sri Lanka

6. Some of these journals are in vernacular languages. Besides an updated computer listing of the serial titles on-line, 2 other published serial indexes prepared by the library are available: *Serials Currently Received by the National Library of Agriculture* (1975), and *List of Journals Indexed by the National Agriculture Library* (1974–76). Publications and documents of the FAO and other international organizations related to agriculture are acquired by the library in microform; these materials are not cataloged and are retrievable by the manufacturer's catalog numbers.

Located in Room 304 of the main library, is the Food and Nutrition Information and Education Resources Center, which provides information in the areas of food and human nutrition. A computer-based information storage and retrieval system, known as the Current Research Information System, serves as the documentation and reporting system for agricultural and forestry research. The library also provides a computer-based literature searching system—Current Awareness Literature Search Service. Materials generated by the specialized services of the library are generally available to qualified researchers.

5. The extensive collection of South Asian serials, including those acquired through exchange arrangements, is undoubtedly an outstanding aspect of the holdings of the library. Some of these serials are not available in the Library of Congress.

6. Several finding aids facilitate access to the collection. An inactive dictionary catalog in the main reading room provides reference to all materials acquired from 1862 to 1965. For materials cataloged since 1966, the card catalog is divided into a convenient name catalog and a subject catalog. There is also a card file of some 22,000 foreign-language research publications translated into English during the last 3 decades. A publishing company—Rowman and Littlefield, of Totowa, New Jersey—that prepares the monthly *National Agriculture Library Catalog,* has also compiled the following catalogs on the resources of the library: *Dictionary Catalog of the National Agriculture Library, 1862–1965,* 73 vols., (1967–1970); *National Agricultural Library Catalog 1966–1970,* 12 vols. (1973) and a 1971–75 supplement, 2 vols. (1978).

In addition, the U.S. Department of Agriculture publishes a monthly bibliography with an annual cumulative index, *The Bibliography of Agriculture.* This subject/author bibliography is a comprehensive index to the vast literature of agriculture and allied sciences, and includes citation of journal articles, pamphlets, government documents, special reports, and proceedings. A convenient retrieval for materials acquired since 1970 is provided through the library's computerized bibliographic data bank, AGRICOLA, which can be searched by author, title, subject and many other categories.

Computer terminals are also available in the D.C. branch of the library. Researchers may obtain assistance from the staff in conducting on-line literature searches. The automated retrieval service of the library also provides access to the data bases of the on-line interactive systems offered by Systems Development Corporation, Lockheed Information Systems, and the Bibliographic Retrieval Service. Other available data files include: MEDLINE (the data base of the National Library of Medicine); JURIS (the retrieval and inquiry system of the U.S. Department of Justice); New York Times Information Bank; SCORPIO, produced by the Library of

Congress; and OCLC, a cooperative national cataloging data file.

Other useful information on the collection may be obtained from the following publications: *List of Available Publications of the United States Department of Agriculture* (1979); a *Guide to Services of the Library; The Card Catalogs of the National Agricultural Library: How to Use Them;* the *AGRICOLA User's Guide* (1979); and the *CAIN On-Line User's Guide* (1976)—a manual to introduce the library's cataloging and indexing system.

A27 National Geographic Society Library

1. a. *1146 16th Street, N.W.*
    Washington, D.C. 20036
    857-7787

    b. 8:30 A.M.–5:00 P.M.   Monday–Friday

    c. Open to visitors for on-site use; there are no interlibrary loan or photocopying facilities available to the public. Readers may place materials on the reserve shelf for 3 days.

    d. Virginia Carter Hills, Head Librarian

2. The collection is carefully assembled to serve primarily the reference needs of staff of the society. Its holdings exceed 69,000 volumes spanning a wide variety of subjects, including geography and allied sciences, natural history, travel, ethnography, wildlife, and the society's research and exploration materials.

3. Shelflist measurement indicated that the collection contains more than 1,000 English-language titles on South Asia, among them: Afghanistan 87; Bangladesh 12; Bhutan 8; India, including the Indian Ocean, 565; Nepal 25; Pakistan 88; Sri Lanka 90. Some of the South Asian titles are early and rare imprints from the sixteenth century on the subject of description and travel. It is of interest to a South Asianist to note that the library has a complete set of publications of the Hakluyt Society.

4-5. The periodical holdings of the library exceed 1,800 titles, of which approximately 25 are on South Asia. Periodical collections can be determined by using the card file at the circulation desk or the Periodical Indexes located in the Bibliographies Room (Room 115). A selected list of the South Asian periodicals includes: *Agricultural Geography of Afghanistan; Bio-Climate of Afghanistan; Geographical Review of Afghanistan; Pakistan Geographical Review; Geographical Review of India; Association of Indian Geographers; Bombay Geographical Magazine; Punjab Geographical Review* (India); and *Indian Geographer.*

    The library maintains a complete file of National Geographic Society's publications: *National Geographic, World,* books, maps, and news service releases.

    The society's Clipping Service (857-7053) offers a unique source of information. Contained in its 68 files and 340 drawers are newspaper clippings from 13 U.S. newspapers, foreign magazines, government publications, and over 200 unindexed periodicals, newsletters, and ephemeras on a variety of topics including cyclones, population, relief, religion, castes, antiquities, and flora and fauna. Arranged alphabetically by geographic categories and main headings, the service has a sizable total collection of approximately 4 drawers on South Asia. These vertical files are constantly weeded and updated. For staff use, the library compiles bibliographies on certain approved subjects.

The National Geographic Society's Map Library (Cartographic Division) located in the Membership Center Building, Gaithersberg, Maryland 20760 (301/857-7000, ext. 1401) maintains an extensive collection of maps and atlases (see entry E6). Its services, however, are restricted to the members of the society and authorized visitors for on-site use.

6. The principal finding aid for the collection is the card catalog in the main reading room. This aid is in dictionary form, with author, title, and subject access. The classification system used by the library follows a unique word-arrangement device. The library also maintains a very detailed separate reference card index to the articles published in the *National Geographic* since 1883. Also useful to researchers are the various cumulations of the *National Geographic Index:* 1888–1946, 1947–1976, 1977–1979. A pamphlet, *National Geographic Society Library* may be examined as a preliminary step to the collection.

Note: Also see entry E6.

A28   National Institute of Education Library (Education Department)

1.   a. *1832 M Street, N.W.*
Washington, D.C. 20208
254-5060

b. 10:00 A.M.–4:00 P.M.   Monday–Friday

c. Open to the public; interlibrary loan and photoduplication facilities are available.

d. Charles Missar, Director

2-6.   The collection exceeds 130,000 volumes and 1,200 periodicals, focusing mostly on the history of American education, U.S. legislation pertaining to education, educational psychology, and urban issues related to education. The collection also contains selected literature on comparative education and international education. However, the library's South Asia collection is insignificant; no South Asian magazines are subscribed to.

Finding aids consist of a dictionary catalog and G. K. Hall's *Subject Catalog of the Department's Library* (1965), 20 vols., with an additional supplement (1973), 4 vols. Researchers may also consult the *Periodical Holdings List: Educational Research Library* (1977).

A29   National Library of Medicine (NLM) (National Institutes of Health)

1.   a. *8600 Rockville Pike*
Bethesda, Maryland 20014
(301) 496-6095

b. Reading Room:
Regular hours (Labor Day to Memorial Day):
8:30 A.M.–9:00 P.M.   Monday–Friday
8:30 A.M.–5:00 P.M.   Saturday

Summer hours (Memorial Day to Labor Day):
8:30 A.M.–5:00 P.M.   Monday–Saturday

History of Medicine Collection:
8:30 A.M.–4:45 P.M.   Monday–Friday

c. The NLM facilities are open to serious scholars. All first-time users are required to obtain a registration number at the reader service desk. In addition, each user must sign a daily log. Interlibrary loan and coin-operated copying machines are available.

d. Martin M. Cummings, Director

2-3.   Originally established in 1836 as the Library of the Army Surgeon General's Office, the library was renamed the National Library of Medicine in 1956 by an act of Congress. The mission of the NLM is to collect, preserve, disseminate, and exchange information important to the progress of the health services.

The library is the world's largest research library in a single scientific and professional field. It collects materials exhaustively in some 40 biomedical areas and to a lesser degree in other related subjects. The holdings exceed 1,500,000 items in more than 70 languages. The library's collection is predominantly technical in nature, but a bulk of materials, especially in the History of Medicine Division, are also significant for study and research in the fields of history and social sciences.

NLM's collection on South Asia is sizable: approximately 5,000 items covering technical medical fields as well as govenrment documents and statistics; private and institutional publications, particularly concerning health, sanitation, nutrition, population control, and mortality; and literature produced by the concerned international agencies.

For medical titles, generally the NLM does not follow the LC classification system; instead it uses its own device, the *National Library of Medicine Classification: A Scheme for the Shelf Arrangement of Books in the Field of Medicine and Its Related Sciences*, 3d ed., 1964, with a 1969 supplement. Consequently, an accurate assessment of the numerical strength of the collection is not possible. A search of computer data bases of CATLINE (Catalog On-Line), which contains references to books and serials cataloged in NLM since 1965, indicated an approximate holding of about 600 titles on South Asia in Western and vernacular languages: Afghanistan 3, Bangladesh 11, India 524, Maldive Islands 2, Nepal 11, Pakistan 47, Sri Lanka 18. Similarly, a computer search of SERLINE (Serials On-Line) yielded some 760 journals and government publications from South Asia: Bangladesh 14, India 588, Pakistan 74, Sri Lanka 27. Another query to MEDLINE (Medical Literature Analysis and Retrieval System On-Line) file revealed about 1,300 current journal articles indexed in the collection: Afghanistan 22, Bangladesh 69, India 1,079, Pakistan 73, Sri Lanka 34.

The following titles are a few random examples of the quality of materials in the collection. A. P. Howell, *Note on Jails and Jail Discipline in India, 1867–68*, Calcutta, 1869; *Indian Plague Commission, 1898–9*, London, 1900–

1901; *Indian Epidemics and Mofussil Sanatory Reform*, Calcutta, 1851; P. M. Levincent, *Considérations sur le choléra épidémique, et sur celui des Indes Orientales en particulier*, Paris, 1829; *Annual Report, Family Planning Association of Pakistan;* A. R. Kahn, "Contraceptive Distribution in Bangladesh Villages: the Initial Impact," *Studies in Family Planning* (August–September 1979). In addition, NLM's manuscript depository includes the papers of Louis L. William (1917–1967) on the study and control of malaria in India.

4-5.   Housed in the library is the collection of the History of Medicine Division (496-5405), one of the four collections of the NLM (the others being General, Documents, and Reading Room). Its resources for historical scholarship in the medical and related sciences are among the richest of any institution in the world. Collected over many years, they include, in addition to rarities, exhaustive materials for the support of studies in the history of human health and diseases. To an Indologist investigating epidemics and famines, especially during the British period, this collection is of tremendous significance.

The History of Medicine Division is responsible for the custody and servicing of 500,000 pieces of printed materials, 850,000 items of manuscripts, and 70,000 items of prints, photographs, genre scenes, and graphic art. In the manuscript collection, an Indic scholar may find 11 palm-leaf manuscripts written in Sinhalese, Pali, and Sanskrit. These well-preserved original manuscripts are mostly of seventeenth-century origin and delve into such subjects as veterinary medicine, *ayurvedic* practice, herbal medicines, medical charms, astrology, human anatomy, and *jātaka* stories. For a preliminary report on these manuscripts, see Dorothy M. Schullian's *A Catalog of Incunabula and Manuscripts in the Army Medical Library* (1950).

Other printed guides of the division include: Richard J. Darling, *A Catalog of Sixteenth Century Printed Books in the National Library of Medicine* (1967), and its *Supplement* (1971), by Peter Krivatsy; John B. Blake, *A Short Title Catalog of Eighteenth Century Printed Books in the National Library of Medicine* (1979); *The National Union Catalog Pre-1956 Imprints;* and the *National Union Catalog of Manuscript Collections*. An article by Francis E. Sommer in *Journal of Oriental Studies* (April–June 1946) examines the NLM Sinhalese manuscripts. It may be of interest to note that the collection also contains 92 Arabic manuscripts, including a part of al-Razi's monumental work *Kitab al-Hawa fil al-Tibb* (1094), and 28 Persian manuscripts, some of which are of Indian origin. A computer search of the HISTLINE (History of Medicine On-Line) file revealed 376 items on India, 4 on Pakistan, and 16 on Sri Lanka.

6.   The NLM has taken several measures in disseminating information and in fostering research and training in tropical diseases in the developing countries. *The Quarterly Bibliography of Major Tropical Diseases* is a cooperative undertaking of NLM and the Special Program for Research and Training in Tropical Diseases sponsored by the United Nations Development Program, the World Bank, and the World Health Organization (WHO). This special program is a concerted effort to control 6 tropical diseases including leishmaniasis, leprosy, and malaria.

In September 1979 a Memorandum of Understanding was signed between NLM and WHO for the provision of MEDLARS (Medical Literature Analysis and Retrieval System) computer searches and interlibrary loans for the 84 developing countries. This experimental arrangement is expected to develop a mechanism to respond to the needs of the developing countries. In another extramural activity, the NLM supports the preparation and publication of biomedical studies in 7 cooperating countries, including India and Pakistan, which enables the library to draw upon foreign scientific personnel and resources in obtaining and disseminating information important to the U.S. health educators, practitioners, and researchers.

The 3 U.S. national libraries—the LC, the NLM, and the NLA (National Library of Agriculture)—have recently committed themselves to building an on-line name-authorities data base, cooperative acquisitions, and cooperative cataloging. Cooperation is also expected to extend to shared use of foreign language capacities among the 3 institutions.

As a selective depository of government documents, the library hopes to develop a comprehensive collection of legislative reference materials, relating to health sciences. Also, a collection of federal laws, congressional committee reports, hearings, and statistics relating to public health is being assembled in microfilm.

The quality of bibliographic data and the timeliness in making records and materials available to the public is a primary concern of the library. The library's computer-based MEDLARS, which became operational in 1964, provides rapid bibliographic access to NLM's vast store of biomedical information. MEDLARS bibliographic retrieval capabilities are also available thorugh a nationwide NLM network of centers at more than 1,000 universities, medical schools, hospitals, government agencies, and commercial organizations. MEDLARS contains some 4,500,000 references to journal articles and books in the health sciences published after 1965. Most of these references are published via MEDLARS in *Index Medicus* or in other printed NLM indexes and bibliographies. The NLM, through MEDLARS capabilities, periodically produces lists—termed *Recurring Bibliographies*—of citations to journal articles in specialized biomedical fields. Most of these lists are printed and distributed by nonprofit professional organizations and other government agencies with whom the library cooperates. Two examples are: *International Nursing Index* and *Population Sciences*.

One of the 18 on-line bibliographic data bases, MEDLINE (MEDLARS On-Line) contains 600,000 references to biomedical journal articles published in the current and two preceding years. An English abstract, if published with the article, is frequently included. The articles are from 3,000 journals published in the U.S. and 70 foreign countries. MEDLINE also includes a limited number of chapters and articles from selected monographs. Coverage of previous periods (back to 1966) is provided by backfiles that total some 2,500,000 references. Using the MEDLINE capabilities, the NLM assembles bibliographies from time to time on specific topics felt to be of wide interest. More than 100 of these printed *Literature Search* bibliographies are available free of charge. Examples: *Foreign Medical Graduates in the United States* (No. 79-14), *Population Control with Emphasis on Developing Countries* (No. 79-7).

Other data bases are CATLINE (Catalog On-Line) containing about 200,000 references to books and serials cataloged at NLM since 1965, and SERLINE (Serials On-Line) containing bibliographic information for about 34,000 serial titles including all journals which are on order or cataloged for the NLM collection. HISTLINE (registered acronym for History of

Medicine On-Line) contains some 40,000 references to articles, monographs, symposia, and other publications dealing with the history of medicine and related sciences. This data base is the source of NLM's annual printed bibliography of the History of Medicine. Although there are selected references back to 1964, most of the materials cited in the HISTLINE file were published after 1970. AVLINE (Audiovisuals On-Line) contains citations to some 8,000 audiovisual teaching packages used in health-sciences education.

Each of these data banks, which are described briefly in the free brochures, *MEDLARS* and *National Library of Medicine Users Guide,* can be searched geographically. Staff assistance for on-line searching is available for a fee.

Materials in the library may be located by using other finding aids. The card catalog is divided into a name catalog (authors and titles since 1946) and a subject catalog. The latter is further divided into two sections—one for items cataloged before 1960 and one for items cataloged after 1959. Many books and journals cataloged before 1946 are to be found in the author/title card file of the old public catalog. There is also a geographically arranged shelflist of U.S. and foreign documents located in the catalog room. The History of Medicine Division has its own card catalog arranged by century of publication for its pre-1801 holdings.

Several printed bibliographic tools facilitate the use of the collection: *Index-Catalogue of the Library of the Surgeon General's Office* (1800–1961, 61 vols. in 5 series); *Armed Forces Medical Library Catalog* (1950–1954, 6 vols.); *National Library of Medicine Catalog* (1955–1965, 12 vols.). These dictionary catalogs of serials and monographs again changed their publication pattern and name to become the *National Library of Medicine Current Catalog,* which has been computer produced since 1966 using CATLINE files.

The *Current Catalog* is published quarterly and cumulated annually and quinquennially. The *Bibliography of the History of Medicine* (1964—) is published annually with a five-year cumulation. It focuses on the history of medicine—including medical history of famous nonmedical persons—or with medical aspects of the work of literary figures, composers, and artists, as well as contributions from other professions related to health. In addition, the researchers may want to consult the various cumulations of the *Index Medicus* (1879—) for periodical articles and *Medical Subject Headings* for effective determination of appropriate subject headings for conducting a bibliographic search.

Printed finding tools for serials consist of the 2-volume key-word-out-of-context *Index of NLM Serial Titles* (3d ed., 1980); *List of Journals Indexed in Index Medicus;* and the 9-vol. computer printout, *Serial Titles of the NLM.* The latter provides a complete inventory of all serial holdings in the NLM and are available in microfilm also.

National Museum of American History (Smithsonian Institution)— Dibner Library See entry C9

National Museum of Natural History (Smithsonian Institution)— Anthropology Branch Library See entry C8

Natural Resources Library See entry J18

National Science Foundation Library See entry J25

Oliveira Lima Library See entry A4

Overseas Private Investment Corporation Library See entry J27

Pakistan Embassy Library See entry K5

Peace Corps Library See entry A1

Population Reference Bureau Library See entry H31

A30 School of Advanced International Studies (Johns Hopkins University)—Mason Library

1. a. *1740 Massachusetts Avenue, N.W.*
    Washington, D.C. 20036
    785-6296

    b. Academic year:
    8:30 A.M.–10:00 P.M.   Monday–Thursday
    8:30 A.M.–6:00 P.M.   Friday
    10:00 A.M.–5:00 P.M.   Saturday
    Noon–9:00 P.M.   Sunday

    When classes are not in session:
    8:30 A.M.–5:00 P.M.   Monday–Friday

    c. Open to serious researchers for reference use for a limited time; a fee is charged for borrowing material and for visiting privileges beyond a month. Interlibrary loan and photoduplicating facilities are available.

    d. Peter J. Promen, Director

2. The Mason Library's total collection is in excess of 80,000 volumes with South Asian holdings of nearly 1,900 titles. Of the approximately 900 periodicals received by the library, about 6 emanate from South Asia. The library also receives in microfilm a South Asian daily, *Hindustan Times* (New Delhi).

3. a. The collection contains largely English-language secondary literature published since the Second World War and focuses on international relations, government, foreign trade, and economics. The resources of the library are carefully developed to meet primarily the academic program of the graduate

school, which concentrates on comparative politics and modernization, international economics, international relations, and several area studies, including South Asia.

b. Subject categories and evaluations:

Philosophy and Religion	239t	D–
History and Auxiliary Sciences of History	890t	D
Geography and Anthropology	6t	D–
Economics	307t	D
Sociology	81t	D
Politics and Government	185t	D
International Relations	7t	C
Law	10t	D–
Education	9t	D–
Art and Music	—	—
Language and Literature	20t	D–
Military Affairs	6t	D–
Bibliography and Reference	19t	D–

Afghanistan	50t	C
Bangladesh	35t	C
Bhutan	4t	C
India	1,005t	D
Maldive Islands	—	—
Nepal	7t	D–
Pakistan	130t	D–
Sri Lanka	47t	D

4-5. The highly selective periodical and government-documents collection of the library contains many learned titles published in the West but relevant to South Asia. Back files of the FBIS *Daily Reports, American Universities Field Staff Reports,* and the *Asian Recorder* are available.

6. The library follows the LC classification. Principal finding aids are the card catalogs divided by author/title and subject categories. A separate periodical card catalog is available in the periodical reading room.

Secretariat for Women in Development—Documentation Center
See entry L58

A31 Senate Library

1. a. *Capitol Building, Room S-332*
   Washington, D.C. 20510
   224-7106

   b. 9:00 A.M.–5:00 P.M.   Monday–Friday
   9:00 A.M.–Noon   Saturday

c. The library is restricted to the use of the Senators and Senate establishments. Private researchers may, however, visit the library with a letter of introduction from a Senator. No interlibrary loan services are available, but the library provides photoduplication facilities.

d. Roger K. Haley, Librarian

2-6. This 300,000-volume reference collection of Senate legislative history is of potential value to the scholars dealing with U.S. relations with South Asia. Holdings include Senate and House bills, legislation, reports, records, hearings, resolutions, and other publications. The library prepares bibliographies, chronologies, digests of legislation, and the *Index of Congressional Committee Hearings*. The library has a dictionary card catalog. A descriptive brochure, *General Information and Services of the Senate Library* is available.

Smithsonian Institution Libraries See entry J30

A32 State Department Library

1. a. *Department of State Building, Room 3239*
    2201 C Street, N.W.
    Washington, D.C. 20520
    632-0535

    b. 8:45 A.M.–5:30 P.M.   Monday–Friday

    c. The collection primarily serves the staff needs for the personnel of the Department of State, the Agency for International Development, and the Arms Control and Disarmament Agency. However, others may obtain prior permission for on-site use of the library for materials not available elsewhere in the metropolitan area. Interlibrary loan and photoduplication facilities are available.

    d. Conrad Eaton, Librarian

2. The library of the Department of State, the oldest federal library, was established in 1789, along with the department itself. Currently the collection has grown in excess of 780,000 volumes, including more than 8,000 titles on South Asia. The collection is growing by 16,000 volumes per annum, of which 30–40 percent are acquired from foreign countries. The collection is particularly significant in economics, history, government, international relations, foreign law codes, and other subjects related to the work of the department; e.g., disarmament, arms control, security studies, and nuclear nonproliferation.

    As well as its collection of foreign-government documents, including official gazettes from 100 countries, the library also contains many unique items of a diplomatic nature not available elsewhere. Its inventory of the department's press releases and other publications, including foreign-service and consular lists, is the most comprehensive in the area. The library is also a depository for U.S. government documents.

3.   a. The South Asian collection in this library ranks second only to the LC. Its holdings of South Asian government documents, including the census materials, are quite exhaustive. Also, many early imprints on travel, description, and history may be found in the collection. The library's collection in the category of South Asian international relations exceeds that of the LC.

   b. Subject categories and evaluations:

Philosophy and Religion	257t	D –
History and Auxiliary Sciences of History	2,695t	B
Geography and Anthropology	12t	D –
Economics	2,575t	B
Sociology	230t	C
Politics and Government	1,145t	B
International Relations	300t	A
Law	390t	D
Education	157t	C
Art and Music	—	—
Language and Literature	110t	D –
Military Affairs	75t	B
Bibliography and Reference	145t	C

Afghanistan	115t	B
Bangladesh	75t	B
Bhutan	11t	B
India	4,185t	B
Maldive Islands	3t	B
Nepal	49t	C
Pakistan	442t	B
Sri Lanka	188t	B

4.   The library receives about 1,000 current periodicals, including some 40 from South Asia. Scholarly journals on Asia and the Third World are also subscribed to by the library. No current South Asian newspapers are received in the library.

6.   Library materials are cataloged on the basis of the LC system of classification. Basic finding tools are: an author/title/subject dictionary catalog and a geographic catalog which provides a subject approach to books and periodicals about geographical locations—countries, regions, cities, and islands. For periodical holdings, a geographically arranged index is available at the information desk. An informative brochure, the *Department of State Library* (1978) is available free.

   Using several computerized information services, including ORBIT, DIALOG, MEDLINE and RECON (developed by the Systems Development Corporation, the Lockheed Corporation, the National Library of Medicine, and the Oak Ridge National Laboratories, respectively), the library can search some 90 individual data bases by subject, organization, and geographic area. The data bases include: CRECORD (Congressional Records Abstracts), 1976 to date; CIS (Congressional Information Service), citations and abstracts from congressional publications, 1970 to date; SO-

CIAL SCISEARCH, over 500,000 citations to social science literature, 1972 to date; NTIS (National Technical Information Service), over 600,000 abstracts of government-sponsored research, 1964 to date; and the New York Times Information Bank, over 1,400,000 abstracts of news and editorial materials from newspapers and periodicals, 1969 to date.

The library publishes a monthly *Acquisitions* list of selected titles added to the collections during the month. Each month an annotated subject bibliography of current acquisitions is also included in the *Department of State Newsletter.* Also, from time to time, lists of periodical articles on topics of current interest are compiled. In addition, *Library Booklist*(s) on specific topics are prepared. Some of the topics are: "Disaster and Disaster Assistance;" "The United States and World Affairs;" "Current Publications on Foreign Affairs;" and "The Indian Subcontinent: A Selection of Recent Books." Another useful library publication is the *International Relations Dictionary* (1978), which identifies and provides information about many terms, phrases, acronyms, catchwords, and abbreviations used in the conduct of foreign relations.

Note: Also see entry A10.

Textile Museum Library See entry C11

Transportation Department Library See entry J32

A33 United Nations Information Centre

1.   a. *2101 L Street, N.W.*
Washington, D.C. 20037
296-5370

b. 9:00 A.M.–1:00 P.M.   Monday–Friday

c. Open to the public; interlibrary loan and photoduplication facilities are available.

d. Marcial Tamayo, Director
Vera P. Gathright, Reference Librarian

2-5.   The U.N. Information Centre in Washington, the first such office to be established, maintains a 15,000-volume reference library of U.N. documents, official records, and U.N. sales publications on economic, statistical, financial, international trade, legal and social questions, and human rights. However, documents generated by U.N. specialized or regional agencies are not available here. The center also maintains a small collection of U.N. photographs and films which may be borrowed by individuals and institutions without charge (see entry F15). For general reference inquiries, the center maintains a collection of pamphlets on varying subjects such as decolonization, disarmament, economic and social questions, human rights, and background materials on upcoming, major U.N. conferences. These materials are available free of charge upon request. No publications are sold at the center in Washington.

6.   For reference assistance, the library maintains a complete set of *U.N. Documents: Index* (monthly, with an annual cumulation) and a catalog of *U.N. Publications in Print* (1979–1980). Interested individuals may request that they be placed on the mailing list to receive the *Weekly News Summary, Objective: Justice*, and *U.N. Monthly Chronicle*.

A34 University of Maryland Libraries at College Park

1.   a. *McKeldin Library*
College Park, Maryland 20742
(301) 454-5704

Undergraduate Library
(301) 454-4737

Architecture Library
(301) 454-4316

East Asia Collection (McKeldin)
(301) 454-2819

Art Library
(301) 454-2065

Music Room (McKeldin)
(301) 454-3036

b. Academic year:
8:00 A.M.–11:00 P.M.   Monday–Thursday
8:00 A.M.–6:00 P.M.   Friday
10:00 A.M.–6:00 P.M.   Saturday
Noon–11:00 P.M..   Sunday

These hours are for the McKeldin Library, which is the main general library in the College Park campus. Other schedules may be obtained by calling the telephone numbers listed above.

c. The libraries are open to the public for on-site use. Interlibrary loan and photoreproduction services are available.

d. Joanne Harrar, Director of Libraries

2.   The university's libraries contain an estimated 1,300,000 items, with South Asian holdings exceeding 6,500 titles. Out of some 15,800 serials currently received, approximately 70 emanate from South Asia. The College Park libraries maintain current files of some 33 foreign newspapers, of which 2 are from South Asia.

3.   a. The South Asian resources of the College Park campus are quite diverse and constitute a potential nucleus for supporting academic programs in South Asian studies. Areas of particular strengths are history, philosophy, religion, and economics. Holdings in art and music are also noteworthy as well as those in language and literature. The South Asian collection of the University of Maryland is the strongest university collection in the area and ranks third after the LC and the Department of State Library.

b. Subject categories and evaluations:

Philosophy and Religion	1,807t	C
History and Auxiliary Sciences of History	1,928t	C
Geography and Anthropology	42t	D
Economics	925t	C
Sociology	321t	B
Politics and Government	310t	C
International Relations	13t	B
Law	50t	D−
Education	75t	D
Art and Music	315t	B
Language and Literature	379t	D−
Military Affairs	—	—
Bibliography and Reference	82t	D

Afghanistan	62t	D−
Bangladesh	30t	C
Bhutan	9t	B
India	1,860t	C
Maldive Islands	—	—
Nepal	23t	D
Pakistan	209t	B
Sri Lanka	68t	C

4.   The Periodical/Microform Room, located on the second floor of the McKeldin Library, is equipped with several microform reader-printers. A computer printout of the Serials List provides records of all serial subscriptions received by the College Park libraries. A separate checklist of foreign newspapers currently received is also available. In addition to the current files of two Indian newspapers, *Hindu* (Madras) and *Statesman* (New Delhi), the South Asian serials holdings include the following periodicals and yearbooks among others: *Pakistan Archaeology; Pakistan Development Review; Pakistan National Bibliography; Pakistan Review; Bangladesh Development Studies; Bangladesh Economic Review; Indian Press Digests; Indian Political Science Review; Journal of the Indian Philosophical Association; Indian Journal of Technology; Indian Journal of Public Administration; Indian Journal of American Studies; Indian Books in Print; Indian Council of World Affairs;* and *Indian Economic and Social History Review.*

McKeldin Library is a regional depository for United States government documents. Currently the holdings in this area exceed 500,000 items and are virtually complete since 1925, with a substantial holding of earlier series. Documents and reports of the League of Nations, United Nations, and other international organizations and agencies are also available in the library. The majority of these materials do not appear in the main card catalog, but the Government Documents/Maps Room on the third floor has some special finding aids. The U.S. government documents are classed according to the Superintendent of Documents classification system. The room also receives maps, including a few on South Asia, issued by the Defense Mapping Agency (formerly U.S. Army Map Service and U.S. Army Topographic Command) and the U.S. Geological Survey.

The East Asia Collection, located on the third floor of the McKeldin Library, contains some 50 Japanese-language titles on South Asia in the fields of religion, philosophy, history, description, and travel. These materials constitute a small fragment of the eminent Gordon W. Prange Collection, which is a vast array of published and unpublished Japanese-language materials from the Allied Occupation of Japan, 1945–52.

The Nonprint Media Services (454-4723), located on the fourth floor of the Undergraduate Library, holds several recordings of South Asian music and culture and also audio cassettes of contemporary historical documentaries. A few titles of interest to a South Asianist may also be found in the rare book collection serviced by the Special Collections Division (McKeldin, 4th floor, 454-4020). Phonographic holdings of South Asian music in the McKeldin Library are serviced through its Music Room (4th floor, 454-3036). Also, the Architecture Library and the Art Library contain some scattered materials appropriate to those collections. While most of the South Asian general materials are located in the McKeldin Library, approximately 1,000 items are housed in the Undergraduate Library.

6. The card catalogs, housed on the second floor of McKeldin, list materials in all University of Maryland (College Park) libraries. Divided into author/title and subject files, these catalogs, however, do not list all the library materials available on campus. Reference assistance is available at the information desk. At a small cost, a computer-assisted research service (454-5704) is provided. No printed bibliographic aid to the collection is available.

Woodrow Wilson International Center for Scholars Library
See entry H35

B Archives and Manuscript Repositories

The extensive archival resources on South Asia in the Washington area are highlighted by the holdings in the National Archives and Records Service. Its collection of regular dispatches and special reports (RG 59 and RG 84) from American consular and diplomatic missions located in different South Asian cities (Calcutta, Bombay, Chittagong, Colombo, Karachi, New Delhi, and Madras), which in some cases date back to the 1790s, provide not only information on commerce, trade, and manufacture, but also on social development, political conditions, and regional conflicts and diplomacy. Although most of the reports dealing with political aspects tend to reflect generally the analysis provided by the British officials in India, they nevertheless also furnish insights into American perceptions of the political processes and social changes in South Asia.

Enclosures of these dispatches include newspaper clippings, political and social pamphlets, speeches and addresses, and practically all printed matter about India generated by the British Government. Thus, for many, it may be refreshing to know that some of the rare documents, for which one would instinctively think of searching the holdings of the India Office Library in London or the archives in South Asia, are readily available in Washington. Manuscript collections and collections of private papers related to South Asia are not as rich and large as the archival materials, but in the repositories in the Library of Congress, the National Library of Medicine, and the Freer Gallery of Art, scholars may find some unexpected materials of interest.

Archives and Manuscript Repositories Entry Format (B)

1. General Information
   a. *address; telephone numbers*
   b. hours of service
   c. conditions of access
   d. reproduction services
   e. name/title of director and heads of relevant divisions

2.   Size of Holdings Pertaining to South Asia

3.   Description of Holdings Pertaining to South Asia

4.   Bibliographic Aids (inventories, calendars, etc.) Facilitating Use of Collection

---

B1 American Red Cross Archives

1.   a. *17th and D Streets, N.W.*
     Washington, D.C. 20006
     857-3712

     b. 8:30 A.M.–4:45 P.M.   Monday–Friday

     c. Open to scholars for on-site use

     d. Photoduplication facilities are available.

     e. Odette Binns, Archivist

2-3.   Materials in the archives deal with American Red Cross (ARC) activities both in the United States and abroad. Archival materials in the collection are arranged by subject within 5 chronologically determined record groups (RG). The first 3 record groups: RG 1 (1881–1916), RG 2 (1917–1934), and RG 3 (1935–1946) have been transferred to the National Archives and Records Service. A list of folder captions of these 3 record groups is available at the American Red Cross Archives. RG 4 (1947–1964) and RG 5 (1965–present) are located at the ARC archives. Included in some of these record groups are files on numerous disaster-relief operations in South Asia, especially in India, Bangladesh, and Pakistan since 1934.

4.   Unpublished indexes to all the record groups are available. Information Research Specialist, Rudolf A. Clemen, Jr. (857-3647), may assist scholars in locating South Asia-related materials.

B2 Archives of American Art (Smithsonian Institution)

1.   a. *Fine Arts and Portrait Gallery Building (library)*
     8th and F Streets, N.W.
     Washington, D.C. 20560
     357-2781

     b. 10:00 A.M.–5:00 P.M.   Monday–Friday

     c. The archives is open to researchers but access to some materials is restricted.

     d. Photoduplication services are available.

     e. Garnett McCoy, Senior Curator

2-3.   This extensive archival holding consists of manuscripts, letters, notebooks, sketchbooks, clippings, exhibit catalogs, and rare publications pertaining to United States artists, craftsmen, critics, dealers, collectors, art historians, museums, societies and institutions. Scattered among this vast collection is a very limited amount of South Asia-related material. An example is the journal of an American artist, Elliot Clark, who spent a year in India (1937). The Clark manuscript contains some contemporary wood carvings and a relief portrait of Rabindranath Tagore.

4.   Finding aids facilitating access to the collection include an alphabetical card catalog; Garnett McCoy's *Archives of American Art: Directory of Resources* (1972); and the periodically updated *Archives of American Art: A Checklist of the Collection* (1979).

Army Center of Military History See entry J9

B3 Church of Jesus Christ of the Latter Day Saints (Mormon Church)—Genealogical Libraries

1.   *Annandale Branch Genealogical Library*
      3900 Howard Street
      Annandale, Virginia 22033
      (703) 256-5518

      9:30 A.M.–10:00 P.M.   Tuesday, Wednesday, Friday
      Marge Bell, Librarian

      Oakton Branch Genealogical Library
      2719 Hunter Mill Road
      Oakton, Virginia 22124
      (703) 281-1836

      9:30 A.M.–2:00 P.M.   Monday, Wednesday, Friday
      7:00 P.M.–10:00 P.M.   Wednesday

      Mimi Stevenson, Librarian

      Silver Spring Branch Genealogical Library
      500 Randolph Road
      Silver Spring, Maryland 20904
      (301) 622-0088

      9:00 A.M.–5:00 P.M.   Monday, Wednesday
      7:00 P.M.–10:00 P.M.   Tuesday, Wednesday, Thursday
      9:00 A.M.–5:00 P.M.   1st and 3rd Saturday of each month

      Barton Howell, Librarian

      c. Open to the public; the Genealogical Society of the Church of Jesus Christ of the Latter Day Saints is headquartered at 50 East North Temple, Salt Lake City, Utah 84150 (801) 531-2323. The records collected and maintained there can be obtained on loan by researchers through any of the church's 3 genealogical libraries in the Washington, D.C., area for the price of mailing and handling. Delivery can take up to 6 weeks.

      d. Microfilm readers and reader-printers are available.

2-3. The Genealogical Society has undertaken a massive program of microfilming religious and civil records in archives throughout the world. The collection totals well over 1,000,000 rolls of film and is growing at the rate of 5,000 rolls per month. South Asian holdings include some nineteenth and early twentieth century ecclesiastical returns from India, and currently some civil registration documents that are being microfilmed in India.

4. No comprehensive index to the microfilm collection is available. A computerized catalog, however, is currently being developed.

Freer Gallery of Art—manuscript collection See entry C3

B4 Library of Congress—Manuscript Division

1. a. *James Madison Memorial Building, First Floor*
   Library of Congress
   Washington, D.C. 20540
   287-5383

   b. 8:30 A.M.–5:00 P.M.   Monday–Saturday

   c. Open to serious researchers; proper identification and registration required. Restrictions on the use of certain materials are for reasons of national security or have been imposed by donors.

   d. Subject to preservation and copyright restraints, most manuscripts may be photocopied for research use. There are coin-operated photoduplicating machines and a microreader-printer in the spacious Manuscript Reading Room. The Library's Photoduplication Service (287-5654) also provides the full range of copying facilities. Special permission is required for use of cameras in the reading room. With few exceptions, microfilm reproductions of manuscripts are available for consultation through interlibrary loan. Publication of manuscripts requires prior clearance. A leaflet concerning photocopying and publication of manuscripts is available upon request.

   e. Paul T. Heffron, Acting Chief
   David Wigdor, Specialist in 20th Century Political History

2. The holdings of the division encompass approximately 10,000 separate collections, some numbering more than 1,000,000 items. Foremost among the division's holdings are the presidential papers and papers of government officials. Certain family papers and records of a number of nongovernmental organizations are also in the custody of the division. However, materials on South Asia are both limited and scattered and, therefore, even an approximate estimate of its size cannot be provided.

3. Since there is no established geographic and subject approach to isolating South Asian materials in the collection, inevitably a South Asianist has to sift arduously through various collections of presidential papers, papers of the secretary of state, diplomats, officers of the armed forces, statesmen, scholars, journalists, missionaries, financiers, and others.
   On the basis of preliminary investigation and consultation with the staff, it seems that examination of the following collections may prove rewarding:

Joseph Alsop Papers (1910—): journalist and author; correspondence covers most major events and personalities of the late 1940s through the early 1960s.

American Council of Learned Societies Records (1919–1946): records of the council include materials relating to international intellectual cooperation.

American Peace Commission to Versailles Records: the following materials on India may be found in these records—"Memorandum on Some Aspects of Social, Religious, and Political Conditions in India, 1918;" "History of India;" "India: Agriculture and Allied Industries;" "India Economics: Famines in India;" "India Economics: Industries;" "India Economics: Irrigation;" "India Economics: Railways;" "India Economics: Mining and Mineral Resources;" "India Economics: Trade and Commerce;" "Education in British India;" "India Government: Certain Aspects of Finance;" "India Government: Political Structure and Activities;" "India Government: The Tariff in British India;" "Certain Outstanding Features of Recent Indian Reform Movement with Special Reference to Muslim Participation Therein;" and "Forest Resources in British India." (No dates are given for most of the above references.)

H. H. Arnold Papers (1886–1950): commanding general of the U.S. Army Air Forces, original member of the Joint Chiefs of Staff and World War II American-British Combined Chiefs of Staff.

William E. Borah Papers (1865–1940): senator, 1907–1940; chairman, Senate Foreign Relations Committee, 1924.

Claire Lee Chennault Papers (1890–1958): records of this army officer and aviator of the famed Flying Tigers in China (1941–1954) include operations reports from India.

Thomas T. Connally Papers (1877–1963): senator, 1929–1953; chairman, Senate Foreign Relations Committee, 1941–46, 1949–53.

Ira Clarence Eaker Papers (1896—): Air Force officer, aviator, and author.

George Foulke Papers (1856–1893): U.S. naval officer. Papers contain letters from Bombay and Colombo (1884), describing details of the social scene and religious practices in South Asia.

Huntington Gilchrist Papers (1891–1975): League of Nations and United Nations official, U.S. foreign aid program administrator, international relations expert, and business executive. Collection contains some materials on U.S. foreign aid programs to South Asia, 1950–1954, and United Nations Technical Assistance Board, Pakistan, 1955–1957.

Theodore Francis Green Papers (1867–1966): Senator, 1937–1961; chairman, Senate Committee on Foreign Relations.

Malcolm S. Hensley Papers (1913–1976): United Press correspondent during World War II. This collection contains materials on India, Pakistan, and Afghanistan.

Lewis Graham Hines Papers (1888–1960): labor leader, public official, member, International Development Advisory Board (Point Four Program).

John Haynes Holmes Papers (1879–1964): Unitarian clergyman and author. Materials include correspondence with M. K. Gandhi and Jawaharlal Nehru, and a manuscript of an unpublished book on Gandhi (1953).

Cordell Hull Papers (1871–1955): congressman, senator, and secretary of state.

Philip Jessup Papers (1897—): author, diplomat, educator, jurist, international lawyer, and statesman. Papers contain materials on his Asian lecture trip 1960–1961, and memoranda and observations on Ceylon, India, Nepal, and West Pakistan.

Nelson T. Johnson Papers (1887–1954): state department official.

Henry A. Kissinger Papers (1933—): educator, secretary of state. Collection not yet open for research at this writing.

John R. Latimer Papers (1793–1865): merchant. Papers contain letters, invoices, insurance policies, and accounts on the opium trade between India and China, 1805–1844.

Breckinridge Long Papers (1881–1958): assistant secretary of state, 1940–1944.

Moral Re-Armament Records: this collection of the ideological and religious movement of worldwide moral and spiritual reawakening contains the correspondence of many prominent national and international figures, including Rajmohan Gandhi (1956–1957) and Jawaharlal Nehru (1926). In addition the collection contains materials on the Islam and Moral Rearmament movement (1953–1958), and articles (1933–1966), clippings (1938–1960), speeches, reports, and other printed materials concerning the development of the movement in India. Subject files include Allahabad (1915–1917), Bangalore (1915–1918), India (1915–1918, 1940–1959), Calcutta (1915–1929), Lahore (1915–1918), Lucknow (1915–1918), Madras (1915–1926), Agra and Delhi (1915–1920), and Ceylon (1915–1927).

Daniel Patrick Moynihan (1927—): educator, diplomat, and senator. No register assembled as of this writing.

National Association for the Advancement of Colored People (1909–1970): materials in this large collection contain files on Indian situation 1942–1946; Indian delegation, 1942; Indian League of America 1949–1950; Famine Conditions in India, 1950; and general materials on India, 1942, 1943–1951.

Key Pittman Papers (1872–1940): senator, 1912–1940; chairman, Senate Foreign Relations Committee, 1933–1940.

Carl Andrew Spaatz Papers (1891–1974): career Army and Air Force officer.

Arthur Sweetser Papers (1888–1968): Associated Press correspondent at the State Department, member of the American Commission to Negotiate the Peace (1919), official of the League of Nations and the United Nations. Collection also deals with Allied Peace Planners of World War II, and other world organizations.

Thomas Tingey Papers (1750–1829): naval officer. Papers include journal kept on board the U.S.S. *Ganges* of a voyage from Philadelphia to Madras and Bengal and return to Philadelphia.

In addition, some of the presidential papers and papers of other American missionaries and journalists may contain materials pertaining to South Asia. It may also be reiterated here that the above list is based on preliminary investigation and is, therefore, not exhaustive. Furthermore, not all of the papers listed above may contain substantial South Asian references.

Scholars trying to locate materials in the division may note that the LC Main Card Catalog does not contain references to the holdings of the division, but advanced reference assistance on its collections is provided by the professional staff. The division maintains a collection of reference books that relate primarily to its manuscript holdings and to subjects reflected in these holdings.

In the division's reading room are located the division's catalogs, indexes, and finding aids. These include catalog cards that briefly describe the collections available for reader use, an updated, bound master record, *Collections in the Manuscript Division*, which provides current bibliographical data on all the collections, a computer printout of the Profession List—recording professional identifications of the individuals who generate the manuscripts—registers that contain information on the scope, content, and organization of most of the large groups of papers and records and other inventories. A brochure containing finding aids for the collection is available on request.

Among publications that contain descriptions of some of the holdings are: Librarian of Congress, *Annual Report*, 1897–date; Library of Congress, *Handbook of Manuscripts*, 1918, and its supplements; Curtis W. Garrison, *List of Manuscript Collections in the Library of Congress, July 1931 to July 1938*, 1939; Library of Congress, *Quarterly Journal* (until 1964 the *Quarterly Journal of Current Acquisitions*), 1943–date; Library of Congress, *National Union Catalog of Manuscript Collections*, 1959—; Philip M. Hamer, ed., *Guide to Archives and Manuscripts in the United States*, Yale University Press, New Haven, Connecticut, 1961; and Library of Congress, *Manuscripts on Microfilm: A Checklist*, 1975. A useful preliminary guide to the collection is provided in a leaflet, *The Manuscript Division of the Library of Congress*.

B5 Library of Congress—Southern Asia Section—Manuscript Collection

1. a. *John Adams Building*
    Library of Congress
    Washington, D.C. 20540
    287-5428

    b. 8:30 A.M.–5:00 P.M. Monday–Friday
    8:30 A.M.–Noon Saturday

    c. Open to scholars for on-site use

    d. Special arrangements may be made for obtaining photocopies.

    e. Louis Jacob, Head, Southern Asia Section

2-3. The Asian Division's special collection of rare books and manuscripts, securely located on Deck 8, contains several valuable South Asian manuscripts. Included in the collection are 3 Sinhalese Buddhist manuscripts on palm leaves (18th and 19th centuries); a thirteenth-century Nepalese palm-leaf manuscript of *Aṣṭasāhasrakaprajñāparamitā*; a Pali Cambodian manuscript of Buddhist text on palm leaves; 7 Sanskrit manuscripts of different segments of the *Mahabharata* completed during the late eighteenth century; 5 Sanskrit manuscripts on Hindu scriptures of uncertain dates; one scroll containing a manuscript of Indian chemistry of medicine in the Oriyan language on palm leaves of uncertain date; a family tree of the Mughal emperors; a manuscript of a letter by Mohandas K. Gandhi; a 4-volume manuscript dictionary of uncertain date and author on the customs, manufactures, production, religion, and political state of the inhabitants of India; and 54 volumes of manuscripts transliterated in Roman script of religious scriptures of Hinduism, Buddhism, and Jainism, most of which were executed by A. Weber of Berlin, Germany, during 1860–1865, and by Poona College and Deccan College.

A few of these manuscripts contain beautiful miniatures and illustrations in vivid colors. In addition, there is the Indo-Persian miniature collection of K. Minassian, which contains 13 seventeenth- and eighteenth-century original paintings of Hindu religious themes, court and royal scenes, and portraits of the Mughal nobility. The collection also contains several illuminated Persian manuscript leaves and illuminated copies of the *Qur'ān*.

4.   No inventory is maintained for this collection. Nor is a description available except for a printed index to the Weber volumes. The Southern Asia Section will assist scholars desiring to examine the collection.

Marine Corps Historical Center See entry J9

B6 National Archives and Records Service (NARS) (General Services Administration)

1.   a. *8th and Pennsylvania Avenue, N.W.*
Washington, D.C. 20408
523-3218 (Central Research)
523-3232 (Central Research Room)
523-3285 (Microfilm Research Room)

     b. Central Research Room and Microfilm Reading Room:
8:45 A.M.–10:00 P.M.   Monday–Friday
8:45 A.M.–5:00 P.M.   Saturday

     Branch Research Rooms:
Hours vary, call 523-3218

     c. Open to all serious researchers with a National Archives researcher identification card obtainable from the Central Reference Division, Room 200-B

     d. Extensive reproduction facilities are available for a fee.

     e. Robert M. Warner, Archivist of the United States

2-3.   The National Archives and Records Service, established in 1934, is the central depository for the permanently valuable records of the legislative, judicial, and executive branches of the government of the United States. The nearly 1,200,000 cubic feet of records in the National Archives, which serves as the nation's memory, span 2 centuries and total billions of pages of textual materials, 6,000,000 photographs, 5,000,000 maps and charts, 100,000 films, 80,000 sound recordings, and 350,000 rolls of microfilm.

While the bulk of the records are of the post-1940 period, a researcher may not have access to many of these materials, especially those since 1949, because the records have not as yet been declassified or because the material is incumbered by other restrictions. However, researchers may obtain authorization for use of restricted or classified materials by applying under the Freedom of Information Act or by requesting special permission from the relevant government agencies.

Generally, records in the archive are arranged not by subject matter but by "provenance;" that is, they are kept in the order in which they were arranged by the federal agency, bureau, or department that produced them. The entire accessioned collection in the National Archives is organized into some 400 Record Groups (RG). A basic unit for custodial and retrieval control of records, the Record Group is officially defined as a body of organizationally and functionally related records established with particular regard for the administrative history, complexity, and volume of the records and archives of an agency.

A typical record group consists of the records of a bureau or some other comparable unit of an executive department at the bureau level, or the records of an independent agency of somewhat comparable importance in the government's administrative hierarchy. Three practical variations of this record-control concept are:

the record groups with titles beginning "general records," which include the records of the office of the head of the department or agency and the records of other units concerned with matters that affect the department as a whole—e.g., General Records of the Department of the Navy (RG 80);

collective record groups that bring together the records of a number of relatively small and short-lived agencies that have an administrative or functional relationship, the records of each such agency constituting a separate subgroup—e.g., Records of the United States Army Overseas Operations and Commands (RG 395); and

record groups that include documents not created by a single entity or by a group of organizations, but which were collected from a variety of sources and had an arrangement scheme imposed on them—e.g., the National Archives Gift Collection (RG 200).

Unlike libraries, the National Archives does not maintain a central index of its holdings. Furthermore, even though the records of a particular federal agency are assigned specific record-group numbers, its records may be dispersed in the custody of different divisions or branches of the NARS. Also, records may be shifted from one custodial branch to another. With the exception of a brief, out-of-print, outdated, but extremely useful introductory report prepared by Purnendu Basu, *Materials in the National Archives Relating to India* (National Archive Reference Information Circular No. 38, 1949), there is no other guide or reference aid to South Asian holdings in the NARS. Some of the descriptions of South Asian materials in this entry are heavily drawn from the report prepared by Basu. It is needless to mention the pressing necessity of a South Asian volume similar to the specialized and descriptive *Guide to Materials on Latin America in the National Archives of the United States* (1974) or the *Guide to the Federal Archives Relating to Africa* (1977).

The indispensable reference aid to all scholars for orientation and overview of the vast array of materials in the archive, especially for materials accessioned since 1949, is the NARS *Guide to the National Archives of the United States* (1974) and its annual updated loose-leaf version, which contains brief descriptions of the record groups. A good many of the record groups, however, have varying kinds of indexes created by the agencies generating the records.

In addition, the NARS has assembled numerous finding aids to analyze and describe its holdings, including preliminary or provisional inventories, final inventories, reference information papers and circulars, special lists, descriptive pamphlets, and accession lists, some of which are available in manuscript form only.

Because of the sheer enormity and diversity of materials and their administrative dispersal among several custodial divisions or branches, and the absence of comprehensive finding aids, it is imperative that scholars discuss their research problems with the consultants of the Central Reference Division and with other reference staff, technicians, and archivists in the divisions.

Although the records in the archive primarily document the United States government and aspects of U.S. history and culture, they also constitute a unique source relating to different regions of the world, including the area of our interest. Materials on South Asia are both extensive and significant, covering a wide range of subjects that include economic and commercial affairs as well as political and military subjects. South Asian materials are scattered in at least 75 record groups.

Following is a brief account of some of the significant South Asian holdings within the record groups, which are listed under the operating division or branch having custody of the records. The account here is neither complete nor comprehensive, for within the vast collections of the National Archives, it is difficult to isolate thoroughly all references and materials pertaining to a particular geographic or political entity. This entry is, therefore, only an indicator of the rich and enormous South Asian resources in the National Archives.

CIVIL ARCHIVES DIVISION

Jerome Finster, Acting Director
523-3239

Diplomatic Branch
Milton Gustafson, Chief
523-3274
8:45 A.M.–5:00 P.M.   Monday–Friday

RG 11: General Records of the United States Government. The files on international treaties, executive agreements and related records, 1942–1969, contain documents related to South Asia. See Preliminary Inventory (PI) 159 for details.

RG 43: Records of International Conferences, Commissions and Expositions. Materials dealing with South Asia may be located in the records of post–World War II conferences (1945–1953), records relating to international trade matters (1934–1952), and international exposition and exhibitions (1856–1963). Most records in this group dated later than 1949 are restricted and may be used only with the permission of the Department of State. For further information on this record group see PI No. 76 (1955) and its 1965 supplement.

RG 59: General Records of the Department of State. Within this massive collection, the principal archival source for documentation of U.S. diplomatic history and foreign relations, South Asian materials abound. The bulk of documents pertaining to South Asia primarily consist of approximately 126,000 pieces of consular and diplomatic correspondence from 1794 to 1949 and their numerous enclosures. All these documents are contained in 3 main series of this record group: consular dispatches 1789–1906; numerical file 1906–1910; and decimal file 1910–1949.

The first American consulate in South Asia was established in Calcutta during 1792. Subsequently, U.S. consulates were established in Bombay, Madras, Karachi, Chittagong, and Colombo. No independent diplomatic relationship between India and the United States was established until 1941. Although initial intercourse between India and the United States was limited primarily to trade and commerce, the consular reports from India covered political and numerous other current subjects of interest.

Some of the typical subjects covered in the consular reports are: competition between American and Russian kerosene in India; tariff regulations and currency system in India; U.S. participation in exhibitions and expositions held in India, and the participation of India in those held in the United States; Indian river and harbor regulations; the production and quality of Indian cotton, wool, tobacco, rubber, jute, and wheat; detailed studies of means of communications in India and Ceylon; natural resources and their development in India and Ceylon; regulations governing residence, trade, and travel in India; mines and mining; fisheries; trade in the Persian gulf; India's trade with different countries; the use of U.S. ships to carry cargo to England; restrictions on the export of saltpeter; reports of depredations of the Confederate ship *Alabama;* and court cases pertaining to U.S. ship personnel on charges of fraud, physical mistreatment, and murder.

Besides these routine reports, which were often accompanied by statistical returns, the U.S. consuls also reported on such matters as the Second Punjab War (1848); the Burmese War (1852–1853); the possible advance of the Russian army into India (1854); the development of British political authority in India; the Imperial Assembly at Delhi on the occasion of Queen Victoria's receiving the title of Empress of India; a plan for steam navigation across the Pacific (1852); a proposal by the Parsees and Hindus of Bombay to contribute half of the cost of a hospital or orphanage for sufferers of the American Civil War (1864); Hindu missionaries in the United States; Hindu hatred of British India; the American School of Indo-Iranian Research in India; Bolshevik activities in India; political affairs of Afghanistan; and Hindu revolutionary movement in the U.S.

Other subjects to which some of the consular reports relate are labor conditions, floods, earthquakes, famines, general economic conditions, suffrage, hygiene, sanitation, police organization, municipal government, educational systems, civil service, legislation, justice, religion, ethnological specimens in India, trigonometrical survey of India (1881), meteorological studies in India, and the Standard Oil Company in Burma and India. Included among the documents is a translation of the *Mahabharata.* Also interspersed throughout the series are such documents as occasional memoranda prepared by other State Department officials, communications from British government officials in India, from Indian officials, and letters from private citizens.

In the years following World War I, separate monthly economic and political reports, which also embraced Afghanistan, were prepared by the consulates. Particularly valuable, these political reports summarized the political events of the month, recorded the conversations of consular officials with the British bureaucracy, and provided copious enclosures. The following excerpt from such a report, for the month of November 1924, submitted to Washington, D.C., by Julius G. Lay, American consul general, Calcutta, is inserted here to provide an example of the nature and quality of analysis that may be found in these reports:

"During the month of November several events occurred of political interest, some of which were commonly known to the public in general and others which have not been made public and are known only to the few.

"Among the first mentioned group are the Conference, held in Calcutta at which Mahatma Gandhi surrendered practically everything that he still had left to surrender to Mr. C. R. Das and to his fellow Swarajists, which Conference was followed by a meeting of the All India Congress Committee at Bombay which adopted by a large majority the pact signed in Calcutta by Gandhi and Das. There were also four occasions on which the Governor of Bengal, Lord Lytton, had an opportunity of making forceful addresses to the public in which he explained the necessity for having passed the Criminal Amendment Ordinance, 1924, and in which he effectively replied to the criticisms of him made by the extremists following on the arrests of numerous anarchists immediately after the publication of this Criminal Amendment.

"The events which are of a more confidential nature are those particularly connected with Mahatma Gandhi and show a phase of his character that is not suspected by many people and which, if widely known, would serve to change the high opinion of his character entertained by many of his present admirers. At the time of his recent visit to Calcutta, when he permitted himself to enjoy the hospitality of Mr. C. R. Das, he was visited by a member of the Legislative Council of Bengal and was asked whether he thought that the Criminal Amendment Ordinance was really directed against the Swaraj Party. Although his reply was in the negative, a few hours later on the same day when addressing a public meeting at the Town Hall called by Mr. C. R. Das, he came out openly and boldly with the announcement that, although he hated violent and anarchistic methods, he believed that the Ordinance was directed primarily against the Swarajist party by the bureaucratic Government. It has also come to the attention of the Consulate General that certain letters from him have been intercepted, which, if made publicly known, would compromise him in a most embarrassing manner. Even the moderate Indians when speaking of him as a politician call him an enigma and many of them openly suggest that he should keep out of politics. He may still be considered as a sincere social reformer, but he has proved conclusively that he is no politician. He himself admits that he has lost the power of commanding universal acceptance of his opinions, that he is no safe guide, and 'it was for want of ability' that he had entered into an agreement with the Swarajists."

This Record Group 59 also contains other materials valuable to South Asian studies. Very fruitful sources of information about political conditions in India may be found in the dispatches and other materials sent to the Department of State by the U.S. embassy in London. To illustrate the point, a good deal of material on the activities of the Hindustan Ghadr

Party and the British discussions with the U.S. government is to be found in the records of the U.S. embassy in London. Similarly consular reports from other countries containing significant Indian communities provide additional research materials. For example, some dispatches from South Africa review Gandhi's first experience with *satyagraha* or the passive resistance movement (1918–1919).

Other accessioned materials in this record group, containing materials on South Asia, are: Foreign Service inspection records, including inspection reports on consular posts in India and Ceylon 1896–1939; files of War History and Foreign Policy Studies Branches of the Division of Historical Policy Research 1939–1947; passport applications and other records of the Passport Office (1784–1925); records of the Visa Office including correspondence regarding immigration visas, and visa case files, 1910–1945; intelligence reports, studies, and surveys prepared or filed by the Research and Analysis Branch of the Office of Strategic Services and the Department of State, 1941–1961; records maintained by Hubert Havlik, Chief of the Division of Lend-Lease and Surplus War Property Affairs, 1944–1947; files of the Military Advisor to the Office of Near Eastern, South Asian and African Affairs; daily and weekly summaries prepared by the Executive Secretariat, 1945–1951; files of Hubert A. Fierst, special assistant to the director of the Office of United Nation's Affairs, 1946–1954; and other selected papers of State Department officials dealing with South Asian affairs.

The following finding aids and indexes are available for the materials in this record group: *Preliminary Inventory of the General Records of the Department of State* (PI 157, 1963) and *Inspection Reports on Foreign Service Posts, 1906–1939* (Special List 37, 1974). There are also card indexes and registers to the consular and miscellaneous correspondences through 1906, the Numerical and Minor Files 1906–1910, and Decimal Files, 1910–1949; also purport lists or subject indexes to the records that form the central files of the Department of State, 1910–1949. For information concerning microfilm publications of the record group, consult *National Archives Microfilm Publication*. When they are available, it is useful to consult the printed pamphlets that accompany the microfilms and summarize the records reproduced in the microfilm publications.

RG 84: Records of the Foreign Service Posts of the Department of State. Although containing somewhat similar information to that in RG 59, the records of RG 84 are distinguished from the former by the fact that the materials in this group were maintained by consular posts, as their records, and not by the Department of State, and they were transferred to the National Archives, in most cases, directly. Preserved in bound volumes and containing registers and some not-so-helpful indexes, the post records serve a useful purpose; they also may contain the enclosures sent out with instructions by the Department; and when dispatches are missing from the Department's files, copies may usually be found in post records.

Materials of interest in this very extensive record group consist of records of the consular posts in Calcutta (1885–1936), Chittagong (1866–1920), Colombo (1870–1935), Bombay (1855–1935), Karachi (1887–1935), and Madras (1867–1944). In addition to being partially duplicative in information content, the post records contain much valuable additional material on South Asian affairs, including: records of passports and visas issued; records of births, marriages and deaths of American citizens; records concerning the disposal of property; the settlement of estates and the protection of American citizens; journals, events and memoranda; notes on administrative changes; financial records and property inventories of the consulates; and various maritime documents dealing with American ships and seamen. The consular reviews of local political events, state of trade and commerce, economic outlook, and other related matters also have much research value, especially for the voluminous enclosures, which are otherwise difficult to locate.

RG 256: Records of the American Commission to Negotiate Peace. The United States began studying and preparing for the postwar settlement after its entry into the war in April 1917. Soon afterwards, at the behest of the president, a group of experts, to be known as "The Inquiry," was assembled to collect and collate data on geographical, ethnological, historical, economic, and political problems of the different regions of the world in preparation for the anticipated peace conference following the war.

The Inquiry, in fulfilling its task, gathered a number of typed reports, relating to South Asia. These are noted below with their document numbers: "History of India," 60p, Doc. 292; "India: Agriculture and Allied Industries," 71p, Doc. 294; "India Economics: Famines in India," 46p, Doc. 293; "India Economics: Industries," 106p, Doc. 295; "Empire of India— British and Native States—Area and Population Charts," 10p, Doc. 826; "Memorandum on Some Aspects of Social, Religious and Political Conditions in India," 78p, Doc. 65; "Certain Outstanding Features of Recent Indian Reform Movement with Special Reference to Extent of Moslem Participation Therein," 6p, Doc. 91; "Forest Resources of British India," 3p, Doc. 829; "Important Economic Changes in Ceylon since the Beginning of the War," 10p, Doc. 280; "India's Cotton Crops, 1913–1918," 6p, Doc. 234; "Rubber Planning Industry in South India," 2p, Doc. 307; "Further Information Regarding Shellac Market in India," 4p, Doc. 286; "Economic Conditions in Bombay District," 22p, Doc. 280; "Economic Conditions in India and Changes Resulting from the War," 38p, Doc. 280; "Supplementary Report Concerning Articles Which Would Be Required After the War," 9p, Doc. 280; and "Economic Conditions in Madras Consular District," 12p, Doc. 280. See *Inventory of Record Group 256* (1974).

Industrial and Social Branch
Jerome Finster, Chief
523-3119
8:45 A.M.–5:00 P.M.-Monday–Friday

RG14: Records of the United States Railroad Administration (1917–1945). A few documents on the history and mileage of Indian railways, complied in 1919, are located in the files of the director general.

RG 20: Records of the Office of the Special Advisor to the President on Foreign Trade. Materials relating to India for the period 1934–1936 are to be found in the records of the special representative on the Committee for Reciprocity of Information; in special studies related to foreign commercial restrictions; and in the copies of consular reports and other materials on foreign trade filed in the office.

RG 23: Records of the Coast and Geodetic Survey. Reports on earthquake and seismological registers from foreign countries (1899–1948), including some scattered materials on South Asia, are contained in this group, even though no regular survey of Indian waters was undertaken by the U.S. government.

RG 29: Records of the Bureau of Census. In its responsibility for collecting and compiling foreign trade statistics, the bureau maintains files on many foreign countries. South Asian documents in this collection are comprised of data on trade between the United States and India. In addition, the tabulations and compilations of the Division of Foreign Trade Statistics (1914–1938) provides monthly figures of imports and exports in the U.S. by ports of entry and separated by country, commodity, quantity and value. The bureau's agricultural census records are also useful for information concerning the Indian immigrants who settled in Arizona and California as farmers and agriculturists.

RG 32: Records of the United States Shipping Board. Data concerning taxes and duties on American goods imported into India and discrimination against American shipping by the Government of India (1919–1923) are among the records of the board. Also in the record of trade routes and services is provided a detailed coverage of the regular shipping services between India and the U.S. and the commercial firms participating in those services. The collection also contains some studies and consular reports on commerce and industries in India and Indian revenues from customs.

RG 81: Records of the United States Tariff Commission. Information regarding Indian tariff laws and rates are to be found in relevant parts of the consular reports for the period 1909–1944.

RG 88: Records of the Food and Drug Administration. Documents concerning South Asia in this group are to be found (with a card index) in the records relating to foreign food and drug legislation (1910–1940) and in the records of the supervising tea examiner (1912–1937), whose function was to establish standards of purity and quality for imported teas into the United States. Because large quantities of tea from South Asia were imported into the U.S., this collection contains numerous examination reports, located by ports of entry and shipment, on Ceylonese and Indian teas.

RG 90: Records of the Public Health Service. Materials of interest relating to South Asia include reports on diseases such as cholera, plague, smallpox, malaria, leprosy, and dysentery. Included in the records are also periodic mortality figures in India dating back to 1897.

RG 151: Records of the Bureau of Foreign and Domestic Commerce. A fair amount of information on India is available in the reports and other communications received from commercial attachés, foreign offices, and trade commissioners (1920–1940). Also, bureau reports on foreign trade opportunities and the records of the bureau's Office of International Trade contain information of interest. The most valuable of these records, however, are the monthly reports of the trade commissioners attached to the U.S. consulates. These reports contain data, with supporting statistics, on foreign trade of India arranged by ports; reports of the total size of foreign trade of India; summaries of annual trade and economic reviews; notes on specific items of export and import; reports on central and provincial budgets; construction activities; and weekly financial reports.

RG 178: Records of the U.S. Maritime Commission. Records of the division of operation (1917–1941) contain logs of merchant ships plying between the U.S. and India. Some of these contain references to local events at the time the vessels were in Indian ports; port regulations; weather conditions; and other related information.

RG 234: Records of the Reconstruction Finance Corporation. Included are records of U.S. businesses acquiring strategic and critical materials throughout the world during World War II.

RG 250: Records of the Office of War Mobilization and Reconversion. A general classified file on foreign operations and stockpiling (1945–1947) may contain interesting materials on India.

RG 262: Records of the Foreign Broadcast Intelligence Service. Central files contain English translations of monitored foreign radio broadcasts (1940–1946). Transcripts of several Ceylonese and Indian radio stations include the broadcasts of the Indian revolutionary movement of Azad Hind, India Freedom, and other clandestine broadcasts in Hindi from Saigon.

Judicial and Fiscal Branch
Clarence Lyons, Chief
523-3059
8:45 A.M.–5:00 P.M.   Monday–Friday

RG 36: Records of the Bureau of Customs. Records of the collector of customs (1789–1954) document the sailings of vessels from Indian ports to various ports in the United States. These records include cargo manifests, crew and passenger lists, import books, and information concerning the entrance and clearance of vessels.

RG 39: Records of the Bureau of Accounts. This record group contains some scattered materials on India during the interwar period.

RG 56: General Records of the Department of Treasury. The central files (1917–1956), on international economic, monetary, and fiscal policies, contain some materials on South Asia.

RG 60: General Records of the Department of Justice (1790–1945). Contained in this group are some interesting materials on controversies relating to Indian immigration to the U.S. during the passage of the Immigration Act of 1924; a fairly large collection of documents dealing with the activities of the Hindustan Ghadr Party and its relations with Germans during World War I; noncooperation movement in India (1920–1922); activities of Hindu missionaries or *swamis* in the California region; questions relating to the holding of land by Indians in the western states; and enemy property held in India during World War I.

RG 85: Records of the Immigration and Naturalization Service. The general immigration files (1882–1952) contain the personal records of Indians, Pakistanis, Ceylonese, and other South Asians applying for naturalization and the decisions in such cases, as well as the records of U.S.-Canada consultations on the Indian-immigration controversy in North America. In addition, the files contain the records of activities of the Indian revolutionaries of the Yugantar and Ghadr groups in the U.S. during World War I.

RG 104: Records of the Bureau of the Mint. These files contain a fair amount of material on India; namely, records about the amount of gold and silver coinage, coinage executed in India for other governments, the weight of gold and silver used in industrial arts and returned from industrial arts for monetary use, total imports into India of United States gold and silver, gold and silver production in India, laws affecting coinage, currency, banking, the import and export of gold, and the operation of mints.

RG 154: Records of the War Finance Corporation. Some materials relating to trade in South Asia are to be found in the foreign-trade information series, 1919–1939, of the corporation that was established in 1918 to give financial support to industries essential to the war effort. Subsequent to the armistice, its activities were extended to assist in the transition to peacetime.

RG 216: Records of the Office of Censorship. In its task of wartime (1939–1945) censorship of international communications, the office maintained card records of foreign-language broadcasts monitored by the broadcasting division. Additional materials on India may also be found in the British censorship materials.

RG 217: Records of the United States General Accounting Office. Accounts of living expenses of U.S. consular officials in India and Ceylon (1814–1925) may be found in the records of the fifth auditor. Records of the register also contain statistics on foreign commerce and U.S. merchant vessels.

RG 220: Records of Presidential Committees, Commissions and Boards. A good quantity of materials relating to South Asia may be found in the numerous classified documents of this record group, including: records of the president's committee on foreign aid, 1947–1948; records of the president's commission on immigration and naturalization, 1952–1953; records of the president's committee to study the U.S. military assistance program, 1958–1959; and records of the president's task force on international developments, 1969–1970.

RG 429: Records of Organization in the Executive Office of the President. Included in these materials are records of the Council on International Economic Policy (1969–1970).

Legislative and Natural Resources Branch
Harold Pinkett, Chief
523-3238
8:45 A.M.–5:00 P.M.   Monday–Friday

RG 7: Records of the Bureau of Entomology and Plant Quarantine (1863–1953). Scattered in the general files of the bureau and in the correspondence of the Federal Horticultural Board (1912–1928) is a variety of information on plants and insects in India, including documents on mosquito control and sericulture. Some of this, and other relevant information, has been generated by the foreign field staffs and inspectors of the Branch of Foreign Plant Quarantine.

RG 16: Records of the Office of the Secretary of Agriculture. South Asian agricultural resources and methods have been of interest to the United States. In the central files of the collection are correspondence and reports, relating to Indian agriculture, that were compiled by special agents of the department and were sent to the Section of Foreign Markets from 1895 onwards. These records contain information about Indian markets. Other reports made by consular officials and special agents to the various bureaus of the department contain information of specific interest to those bureaus (namely, Office of Foreign Agricultural Relations, the Bureau of Entomology and Plant Quarantine, the Bureau of Chemistry and Soils, the Bureau of Animal Industry, and the Forest Service). These reports cover the period 1889–1940.

RG 27: Records of the Weather Bureau. Some fragmentary meteorological data concerning South Asia is included in the records of surface and land observations (1819–1941) and marine observations (1842–1930).

RG 46: Records of the United States Senate. Records of the Senate Committees on Immigration, involving the passage of the Immigration Act of 1924—popularly known as the Exclusion Act—contain many petitions and memoranda concerning the issue of Indian immigration. Other materials on South Asia are also to be found in the records of the Senate Committee on Commerce and Foreign Relations and other committees, as well as in Senate journals, records, and documents.

RG 54: Records of the Bureau of Plant Industry, Soils and Agricultural Engineering (1881–1953). Materials relating to plant pathology, agricultural technology, tropical plants, crop disease, and plant nutrition may contain relevant materials.

RG 70: Records of the Bureau of Mines. Documents on petroleum and fuel (1905–1945), foreign activities (1913–1945), and reports of the Bureau of Foreign and Domestic Commerce (1920–1925) may contain some useful materials for South Asian research.

RG 83: Records of the Bureau of Agricultural Economics. Records concerning international organizations, committees, and conferences, relating to postwar foreign relief requirements (1941–1952), contain some material on South Asia.

RG 95: Records of the Forest Service. Certain materials about forestry in India, comparative studies of Indian and United States timber, and similar topics may be found in the Research Compilation File—a collection of special documents, mostly unpublished, relating to forest production, management, and utilization, 1897–1935.

RG 115: Records of the Bureau of Reclamation. Materials on foreign activities (1927–1929) in the general files of the bureau contain reports on Indian irrigation, construction of dams, reclamation of waste lands, water power, water resources, commerce, and industry.

RG 166: Records of the Foreign Agricultural Service. The records of the service contain correspondence relating to coordination of departmental activities in the area of foreign trade (1942–1949) and reports from abroad— prepared by American consuls, agricultural attachés, and special agents— that relate to such phases of foreign agriculture as production, market trends, prices, consumption statistics, imports, exports, trade regulations, and international agricultural conferences and agreements (1904–1954). Collections in this record group also contain reports, assembled by the Forest Service, 1901–1941, on all phases of forestry in foreign countries.

A fair amount of material relating to India and Ceylon will be found among these records. Of varying details and significance, these reports provide information on crop production and crop forecasts, tariffs and trade regulations, livestock and meat production, foreign trade, economic conditions, and other related subject matters. The forestry and forest-product reports contain information on planting, the commercial industry, protection legislation, silviculture, and forest products.

RG 233: Records of the United States House of Representatives. Extensive materials concerning South Asia are to be found in the bills, resolutions, and other records and documents, as well as in the proceedings and hearings of the various committees. One example of interesting material in the records of the House is a piece of legislation passed in 1918 (before direct U.S. relationship was established with India) to help Britain counteract German propaganda in India. For contemporary materials, scholars may examine public records of the House committees on Foreign Affairs; Interstate and Foreign Commerce; and the Judiciary.

RG 253: Records of the Petroleum Administration for War. This record group contains the records of the Foreign Operations Committee on production and distribution facilities abroad (1941–1946).

RG 350: Bureau of Insular Affairs. General files (1898–1945) contain correspondence between the British embassy and the State Department, regarding restrictions on the export of arms and ammunition to India and regarding the U.S.-based revolutionary Ghadr Party, formed by the immigrant Indians. During the period 1901–1910, the bureau also collected certain reports on India—the monetary system, irrigation, and administration, for example—with the expectation that the British experience in India might provide certain guidelines in formulating U.S. policy in the Philippines.

MILITARY ARCHIVES DIVISION

Meyer Fishbein, Director
523-3089

Modern Military Branch
Robert Wolfe, Chief
523-3340
8:45 A.M.–5:00 P.M.   Monday–Friday

RG 18: Records of the Army Air Forces. This record group contains World War II, security-classified "foreign files" on the India-China Theater, especially concerning air transport, supply of equipment and spare parts, lend-lease supplies, strategies, and training. An interesting item in the collection is a memorandum of understanding between the headquarters of the U.S. Air Force in India and the government of India, regarding the use of Hindustan Aircraft Ltd. of Bangalore. The records also contain several reports concerning expansion of airfields in India and Ceylon.

RG 77: Records of the Office of the Chief Engineers. Records related to army mapping activities during the World War II period contain materials of interest relating to South Asia.

RG 107: Records of the Office of the Secretary of War. This collection contains records of the War Department during World War II to 1947, including the special report of the Joint and Combined Chiefs of Staff (1940–1945) and miscellaneous speeches, statements and newspaper clippings (1940–1945).

RG 160: Records of the Headquarters Army Service Forces. Some South Asia-related documents may be located in the materials pertaining to logistic plans and projected supply operations for overseas theaters of war, 1941–1946.

RG 165: Records of the War Department General and Special Staffs. This massive collection contains vast materials on South Asia. OPD files of correspondence relating to operation and mobilization planning (1941–1946), in the Office of the Director of Plans and Operations, contain a number of interesting reports including: complaints regarding the HUMP operations in India (Oct. 25, 1945); furloughs for troops in India (Oct. 25, 1945); shipment of supplies from the China Theater to the India-Burma Theater (Nov. 24, 1945); political situation in India (Aug. 5 and 13, 1942); notes on Indian classes (Aug. 13, 1942); economic aid to India (Sept. 17,

1942); operations report from India (Sept. 27, 1942); jurisdiction over American forces in India (Oct. 8, 1942); combined U.S.-British intelligence activities in India (May 31, 1943); European population in Ceylon (Apr. 30, 1942); recommendation of the U.S. military attaché in Afghanistan that a U.S. military mission be sent to Afghanistan (June 6, 1942, and Mar. 30, 1944); transport route to China through Afghanistan (Aug. 20, 1942). The OPD files also contain several reports from India to General Eisenhower and General Stilwell.

Additional South Asia-related materials are to be found in the American-British-Canadian (ABC) organizational planning and general combat operation files (1940–1948). Some of the reports in the ABC country folders on South Asia are noted below.

Afghanistan: defense plans for the area (Mar. 10, 1942); supply of armaments under lend-lease program (July 31, 1942); memorandum to General Wedemeyer from Colonel Lindsay on Afghanistan route to the U.S.S.R. (Nov. 10, 1942); analysis of foreseeable U.S. military assistance needs during the next 3 to 5 years (Mar. 20, 1947); and a lengthy country report (July 18, 1947), analyzing the basic political-economic forces, objectives, and methods of the great powers.

Ceylon: a memo to the Chief of the French Naval mission, concerning the active cooperation of the French government against the common enemy in French Indo-China (Dec. 16, 1944); a message from the Prime Minister of Australia on strengthening the garrison at Ceylon with Australian forces (Feb. 14, 1943); and several other documents concerning strategy studies.

India: trials of Japanese war criminals in India and China by U.S. tribunals (Nov. 8, 1943); expansion of India as a base of operation (Dec. 4, 1943); appreciation of the Japanese threat to India (Mar. 10, 1942); summary of agreements between the government of India and Chiang Kai-shek (Jan. 20, 1942); and a lengthy country report on India, dealing with its economic and political problems and its prospects (Mar. 20, 1947). Other documents on India include: shipping conditions in India, oil projects in Assam, U.S. technical mission to India, lend-lease silver for India, pipeline from India to China, coordination of weather services, and a variety of other subjects.

RG 179: Records of the War Production Board. Documents in this collection, concerning coordinating control of raw materials at the international level during World War II, contain many items of an economic nature on South Asia: periodic reviews on the Indian economic situation; U.S. postwar economic policy towards India; production, export, and prices of burlap, manganese, belladonna, benzene, chromite, cotton, and carpet wool; several price-control and cost-of-living analyses of Bengal and India; reviews of food and nutrition in India; rice and rubber shortages in Ceylon; and a list of shipping priorities from accessible ports in India.

RG 218: Records of the United States Joint Chiefs of Staff. Geographic files (1942–1953) on Ceylon, Afghanistan, Nepal, Kashmir, and India contain several documents on strategic and political issues, economic conditions, industrial progress, the food situation, railways and shipping, ocean area, war supplies, technical assistance, and intelligence activities in the India-Burma Theater.

RG 226: Records of the Office of Strategic Services (OSS). The vast holdings in this record group contain numerous classified reports and analyses on South Asian political, economic, social, and military conditions during World War II and the early postwar years. To illustrate the quality and nature of the OSS reports, a few synopses follow: "Strategic Survey of Northeastern India" (175p, Jan. 19, 1943)—covers population, ethnic groups, characteristics of the people, living conditions, labor, religion, government, political parties, manufacturing, railroads, shipping, commercial aviation, commerce and communication, and maps and charts; "Pakistan, a Muslim Project for a Separate State in India" (100p, Feb. 5, 1943)— covers the background of the Pakistan movement, promotion of Pakistan, Muslim League, and M. A. Jinnah, opposition to Pakistan, Muslim world and Pakistan, and maps. Similar, lengthy essays are to be found on Germany's plan to conquer India, American troops and civil disobedience in India, industrial war efforts in India, America and India's war morale, and an economic estimate of Calcutta and environments.

Other OSS records note British hostilities to its operation in India, payoff to undercover agents in India, and the OSS India-Ceylon Project to establish an intelligence network that could function in the event that India or Ceylon or both were occupied by enemy forces. For further selections of the records, see *War Report, Office of Strategic Services* (1949), 2 vols., compiled by the History Project of the War Department.

OSS records also contain several important documents concerning the Indian revolutionary movement, the Azad Hind and its leader Subhas Chandra Bose. These materials include proclamation of the provisional government of Azad Hind, Bose's plans for administration of the area to be liberated, Bose's broadcast for revolt and Indian response, and allied counter-intelligence operations. Other OSS documents mention the Khaksar movement, M. N. Roy, the communist movement, and anti-British attitude in Bengal.

RG 263: Records of the Central Intelligence Agency. Materials include records of the Foreign Broadcast Information Branch. These consist of daily transcripts and summaries in English of monitored, foreign-radio broadcasts, 1947–1948, daily teletypes of materials selected for transmission to government agencies, and daily reports of such broadcasts, with a few miscellaneous reports and notes.

RG 319: Records of the Army Staff. This group contains military-intelligence reports, 1942–1954.

RG 330: Records of the Office of the Secretary of Defense. Important South Asian materials are scattered in this record group, especially in the general record files (1941–1955) and files relating to international security affairs (1944–1955).

RG 407: Records of the Adjutant General's Office. Military attaché reports concerning India, Ceylon, and Afghanistan provide, besides intelligence reports, a variety of information, such as battle casualties, personnel records, movement orders, facilities for military personnel, and requirements of equipment.

Note: Central Intelligence Agency (CIA) and National Security Council (NSC) documents: Modern Military Branch maintains files of recently released or declassified documents generated by both the CIA and NSC. Some of the CIA documents include: consequences of Gandhi's assassination; India-Pakistan conflict over Kashmir; the problem of Hyderabad; military budgets of India and Pakistan; and U.S. security interests in the region. Most of these CIA documents are pre-1950. NSC documents involve: periodical reviews of U.S. policy towards South Asia; military assistance to India and Pakistan; air defense for India; appraisal of the Sino-Indian situation; appraisal of U.S. national interests in South Asia; and relations between India and Pakistan. NSC documents span the period of time from 1949 to 1964. For further information see *Declassified Documents Quarterly Catalog,* published by Carrolton Press.

Navy and Old Army Branch
Robert Krauskopf, Chief
523-3229
8:45 A.M.–5:00 P.M.   Monday–Friday

RG 24: Records of the Bureau of Naval Personnel. During World War II, the activities of the Recreation Section, of the Special Services Division of the Bureau of Naval Personnel, extended to the China-Burma-India Theater, and the records of those activities contain some references to the recreational facilities available in India for soldiers and the entertainment programs for United States military personnel in that area.

RG 38: Records of the Office of Naval Operations. This collection contains files of the Naval Attaché Reports relating to the world crisis (1937–1943) and miscellaneous records of the Foreign Intelligence Branch (1936–1945). The latter was responsible for obtaining, evaluating, and disseminating information concerning foreign countries—especially that affecting naval and maritime matters. The branch, in addition, compiled "naval monographs" on all countries with sea power that supplied essential naval, political, and economic information in regard to possible enemies or allies.

South Asian materials in this collection include the following documents: Japanese commercial relations with India (1937–1939); India—political conditions (1918–1939); reports of the Indian Statutory Commission (1930); Russian relations with Afghanistan (1926); political conditions in Afghanistan (1929–1934); political conditions in Ceylon (1916–1938); and importation of arms and ammunition in Nepal (1925).

RG 45: Naval Records Collection of the Office of Naval Records Library. Some fragmentary records, concerning India, in the form of letters from officers commanding naval vessels that touched Indian waters or Indian ports are contained in this collection. For instance, among the letters of Commodore Robert W. Shufeldt of the Flagship *Ticonderoga,* during its cruise along the coasts of Africa and Asia in 1878–1880, there are sparkling accounts of British India and observations on the political, industrial, and commercial affairs of these countries.

There are also journals and logs of certain British warships among these records; for example: the log of H.M.S. *Ceres,* on a round-trip voyage from London to Canton via Madras (1797–1798), which contains a detailed description of the town and harbor of Madras, its people and their manners and customs, and drawings of Fort St. George. Such accounts are interesting and often include some references to contemporary incidents of local importance.

Another appealing item in this collection is a journal of astronomical experiments and observations made by Sir William Burrough, judge of the supreme court of Bengal, which contains his amendment of LaLande's methods of finding the longitude at sea based on observations made at Madras, Calcutta, and at sea. Additional information on India and the

Indian seas in the record group may be found in the area file on the Indian Ocean.

RG 72: Records of the Bureau of Aeronautics. The central correspondence files, 1917–1945, of the bureau contain information about activities of the Indian army paratroopers against the Hur bandits in Sind.

RG 80: General Records of the Department of the Navy. This record group contains some isolated materials pertaining to South Asia, mainly consisting of correspondences, intelligence reports, and documents concerning visits of U.S. ships to different parts of the world.

RG 165: Records of the War Department's General and Special Staffs. Among the records of the Army War College and the War College Division (1900–1945) may be found a small quantity of fragmentary materials relating to Indian army organization and military incidents of interest. Some of the subjects dealt with are: military administration in India, Indian troops in France and Mesopotamia during World War I, and the equipment, pay, and appointment of army officers.

Some examples of the other records in this collection, in the care of the Navy and Old Army Branch, are routine military attaché reports dealing with the Indian demand for home rule and a British plan for constitutional advancement in India after World War I; movements of British Indian forces in Turkistan (1918); Lenin's plans against India and Afghanistan (1920); tribal uprisings in Afghanistan (1920); and the Afghan military mission to India (1926).

Note: Certain record groups in the custody of the Military Archives Division, dealing with twentieth-century military records, are maintained jointly by both the branches in the division. Generally all pre-1940 records are in the domain of the Navy and Old Army Branch, and post-1940 records are held by the Modern Military Branch.

PRINTED DOCUMENTS DIVISION

Printed Archives Branch
Carmelita Ryan, Chief
523-3371

RG 287: Publications of the U.S. government. A complete collection of all government documents printed by the Government Printing Office, including all reports and documents related to South Asia. Documents are available through the Archives Library (523-3286).

GENERAL ARCHIVES DIVISION

Washington National Records Center
4205 Suitland Road
Suitland, Maryland
Mail: Washington, D.C. 20409
Daniel T. Goggin, Director
(301) 763-7410
8:00 A.M.–4:15 P.M.   Monday–Friday
Daily shuttle bus service available from the main Archives Building.

RG 84: Records of the Foreign Service Posts of the Department of State. Records of the Foreign Service Posts of the Department of State are generally a continuation, with some overlapping, of the series held by the Diplomatic Branch of the Civil Archives Division, located in the main NARS building. Holdings in this division cover mostly the 1935–1955 period, open through 1949.

A preliminary typed inventory, prepared by James Edward Miller and entitled "List of Foreign Service Post Records in the General Archive Division" (1976), indicates the custody of the following records of RG 84 in the Suitland facility. Diplomatic Posts: Nepal, 1946–1949, 2 cu.ft.; Afghanistan, 1936–1955, 13 cu.ft.; Ceylon, 1850–1955, 45 cu.ft.; India, 1941–1952, 64 cu.ft.; Pakistan, 1923–1955, 41 cu.ft.; Consular Posts: Bombay, 1936–1952, 79 cu.ft.; Calcutta, 1936–1952, 78 cu.ft.; Karachi, 1936–1952, 26 cu.ft.; Lahore, 1947–1952, 3 cu.ft.; and Madras, 1936–1952, 38 cu.ft. Also consult Special List No. 9, *List of Foreign Service Post Records in the National Archives* (1967).

RG 169: Records of the Foreign Economic Administration (FEA). The FEA was established in 1943 to centralize responsibilities relating to foreign economic affairs. Its records—dated between 1939 and 1947, with a few as late as 1952—are important sources of statistics and economic conditions during World War II. A *Preliminary Inventory of the Records of the Foreign Economic Administration* (PI 29, 1951) is available. Materials on South Asia include the following:

Subject File of the Area Officer, 1942–1944: correspondence, with related interoffice memoranda, exchanged between the administration's mission in India, the British Supply Mission, and private firms, regarding exports and export licensing for India. Included are a number of reports and statistical data on exports to India and Indian economic conditions. Records are arranged alphabetically by subject.

Administrative File, 1944–1947: correspondence, interoffice memoranda, organizational charts, administrative orders, copies of reports, and other papers pertaining mainly to the organization and personnel of the India Section and the India Mission, and the administration of the supply program for India.

Reports of India Lend-Lease 1941–1944: copies of reports of the India Mission, regarding war production developments, development projects, the political situation, and lend-lease requirements, arranged in part by report number and alphabetically.

Inventories of Lend-Lease Goods, 1945–1946: the inventories are under such headings as excess goods, capital goods, machine tools, complete plants, consumable stocks, capital goods, government stocks, and others.

Letters and Memoranda Sent, 1944–1946: copies of letters and memoranda sent by the administration's India Section to its personnel in the India Mission, to other government agencies, and to FEA offices.

Reading File, 1944–1947: contains letters and cables dealing with requirements, requisitions, exports, and economic programs for India. Arranged chronologically.

RG 182: Records of the War Trade Board. Materials contain some information on India's commercial economy during World War I (1917–1921). In the records of the Bureau of Research and Statistics and Bureau of Foreign Agents and Reports may be found reports and studies on the economic status of India before and during the war, industries and natural resources, and the availability of key commodities. Additional materials on trade, industry, and joint stock companies in India were covered in the studies conducted by the war-trade intelligence division. There are card indexes to the separate country studies files.

RG 208: Records of the Office of War Information (OWI). Established in 1942, OWI conducted all activities relating to U.S. propaganda abroad. Records of the Overseas Operations Branch (1941–1946) include several civil- and military-intelligence reports on India; reports on civil disobedience and anti-British attitudes in India; review of Indian press reports; reports on the war efforts in India; reports on 2 U.S. Senators' (Meade and Brewster) visit to India; and New Delhi Outpost reports. Audiovisual records include "Indian News," made in India, 1945.

RG 255: Records of the National Aeronautics and Space Administration (NASA). NASA records, which are mostly classified, may contain some scientific and technical data on Indian space programs.

RG 286: Records of the Agency for International Development (AID). This small record group contains several items on India, such as cables, correspondence, and processed materials pertaining to the background and development of the economic aid program in South Asian countries, 1950–1952; information on labor in India, 1948–1950; congressional presentation materials on India; files on Indian agricultural disease, commodities, minerals, trade, welfare, and finance; and separate files on Ceylon, Afghanistan, Pakistan, and Nepal. Most of the material in the collection is still classified.

RG 332: Records of United States Theaters of War, World War II (1939–1950). After strategic direction of the war was made a joint Army-Navy and Allied responsibility, the term "theater of operations" came to embrace a specific geographical area and all commands in it. Records of the China-Burma-India Theaters include historical files, correspondence, and messages of General Albert C. Wedemeyer, 1941–1946. See *Federal Records of World War II*, Vol. II (1951), and *United States Army in World War II, China-Burma-India Theater* (1959).

RG 338: Records of the United States Army Commands, 1942—. Records of U.S. Army overseas commands and subordinate organizations (1940–1952) include records of the China-Burma-India Theater. The records relate to maneuvers and combat operations, staff and command conferences, inspections by high-ranking officers, visits by important civilians, relationships with foreign governments, and tables of organization and equipment.

RG 354: Records of the Economic Research Service. Dated between 1934 and 1964, the records of foreign regional analysis, foreign developments and trade, and documentation relating to world-trade statistics may contain some materials of interest.

RG 407: Records of the Adjutant General's Office. World War II operations reports, 1940–1948, contain summaries of events, journals, and supportive documents, with an index.

4. In addition to the bibliographic aids mentioned above, some other published finding-aids that may be of assistance to researchers are: *Catalog of National Archives Microfilm Publications* (1974) and its supplement; *The National Archives and Foreign Relations Research* (1974), edited by Milton O. Gustafson; *Commerce Data Among State Department Records* (Reference Information Paper No. 53, 1973); *List of Record Groups of the National Archives and Records Service* (1976); *Cumulative Subject Index to the Declassified Documents Reference System* (1975), edited by Annadel Wile; and

the Department of State's on-going series, *Foreign Relations of the United States.*

Useful general information leaflets include: *A Researcher's Guide to the National Archives* (1977); *Regulations for the Public Use of Records Service* (1972); *Select List of Publications of the National Archives and Records Service* (1977); *Location of Records and Fees for Reproduction Services in the National Archives and Records Service* (1979); *General Restrictions on Access to Records in the United States* (1976); and *Suggestions for Citing Records in the National Archives of the United States* (1972).

For recent accessions in the National Archives, scholars may find it convenient to consult *Prologue: The Journal of the National Archives;* the American Historical Association's *Newsletter; The Historian,* published by Phi Alpha Theta; and the *Newsletter* of the Society for Historians of American Foreign Relations. Information on the latest archival accessions may also be obtained from the Central Reference Division, Room 200-B, or from the respective divisions.

Note: Also see entries D6, D7, E5, F12, F13, and G10

National Library of Medicine—manuscript collection
See entry A29

Naval Historical Center
See entry J9

Office of Air Force History
See entry J9

B7 Smithsonian Institution Archives (SIA)

1.   a. *900 Jefferson Drive, S.W.*
Washington, D.C. 20560
357-2240

   b. 9:00 A.M.–5:00 P.M.   Monday–Friday
Researchers wishing to use the archives before 10:00 A.M. should make special arrangements.

   c. Open to the public; researchers should make arrangements in advance to insure service from the archivist best acquainted with the records to be consulted.

   d. Photoduplication facilities and microfilm viewers are available. Permission and proper acknowledgement are required to quote from any SIA documents.

e. Richard H. Lytle, Archivist

2. This archive is the official depository for the Institution's records and some private papers that document the growth of the institution and the growth of science and art in the United States. Current holdings in the archives exceed 5,500 cubic feet. South Asia-related materials are, however, very limited. The following Record Units (RU) may contain materials pertaining to South Asia. Some of the SIA records are marked "restricted," which indicates that some staff review is necessary before the records could be made available to researchers.

3. RU 45: Office of the Secretary (Charles D. Walcott), 1907–1924. Contains records about the founding of the Freer Gallery, including Freer's gifts.

RU 91: Office of International Activities, 1964–1967. These records include correspondence, memoranda, and other information about the activities of the office, which establishes cooperative research programs with institutions of higher learning in other countries and fosters programs for the international exchange of persons in those fields of science and humanities related to Smithsonian interests.

RU 104: Assistant Secretary for History and Art, 1965–1972. Contains records related to the Freer Gallery.

RU 145: Assistant Secretary for Public Service, 1961–1974. Some records of the Office of International Activities are included in this unit.

RU 150: Assistant Secretary for Science, 1965–1971. Contains research award proposals, awards, and contracts.

RU 158: United States National Museum, 1881–1964. Curator's Annual Reports. Contains department, division, and section reports not reproduced in their entirety in the published *Annual Report* and generally contains more information than is to be found in the published version.

RU 180: Office of International Activities, Foreign Currency Program, 1965–1973. Files include grant proposals and awards, project status-reports, and correspondence related to Smithsonian excess Foreign Currency Programs (PL 480) in India, Ceylon, and Pakistan.

RU 189: Assistant Secretary in charge of the United States National Museum, 1860–1908. Incoming correspondence, mainly documents, museum accessions, Smithsonian expeditions, and field collecting trips.

RU 192: United States National Museum, 1877–1975. Permanent administrative files, some of which document museum accessions, Smithsonian expeditions, and field trips.

RU 218: Office of International and Environmental Programs, 1962–1975. Fiscal information, relating to Foreign Currency Program, and environmental information relating to marine, ecology, specific fauna, and other scientific projects, are included.

RU 223: Division of Plants, 1899–1947. Correspondence with foreign botanists and expeditions to Asia is found in this record unit.

RU 6999T: Registrar, 1834–1958 (accretions to 1976). Records include accession documents.

4. A comprehensive and detailed record of the archives is contained in the *Guide to the Smithsonian Archives* (1978) which superseded the 1971 *Preliminary Guide to the Smithsonian Archives*. Separate, unpublished finding aids for some of the record units are also available.

C Museums, Galleries, and Art Collections

A scholar in search of South Asian art and artifacts may find it fruitful to visit the Freer Gallery of Art, which houses several exquisitely beautiful South Asian miniatures and elegant sculptures. Superb specimens of a few South Asian textiles, tapestry, and shawls are to be found in the depositories of the National Gallery of Art, the National Museum of American History, and the Textile Museum. The vast numismatic and philatelic collection in the National Museum of American History contains extensive materials on South Asia. A good collection of South Asian botanical specimens and a modest collection of South Asian anthropological, archaeological, and ethnographic objects are to be found in the National Museum of Natural History.

Museums, Galleries, and Art Collections Entry Format (C)

1. General Information
    a. *address; telephone numbers*
    b. hours of service
    c. conditions of access
    d. reproduction services
    e. name/title of director and heads of relevant divisions

2. Size of Holdings Pertaining to South Asia

3. Description of Holdings Pertaining to South Asia

4. Bibliographic Aids (inventories, calendars, etc.) Facilitating Use of Collection

C1 Division of Performing Arts (Smithsonian Institution)

1. a. *2100 L'Enfant Plaza, S.W.*
    Washington, D.C. 20560
    287-3420

b. 8:45 A.M.–5:15 P.M.   Monday–Friday

c. Open to the public

d. Reproduction services are available.

e. James R. Morris, Jr., Director

2-4.   The division organizes public concerts, releases records, and explores the history of the American musical theater. The division's World Explorer series periodically sponsors performances by artists from abroad. In 1979 the historic Yakshagana troupe from India gave a performance at the Smithsonian Institution. Another performance by an Indian group was scheduled for 1981. For further information, contact Shirley E. Cherkasky (287-3420). The division's bimonthly publication, *Notes on the Arts*, available for purchase, has an international dimension.

C2 Folklife Program (Smithsonian Institution)

1.   a. *2600 L'Enfant Plaza, S.W.*
Washington, D.C. 20560
287-3424

b. 9:00 A.M.–5:00 P.M.   Monday–Friday

c. Open to the public

d. Reproduction services are available.

e. Ralph Rinzler, Director

2-4.   Research, presentation, and preservation of American cultural diversity is the goal of the Folklife Program. The annual Festival of American Folklife, sponsored by the Folklife Program, receives participants from foreign countries. In the 1976 festival, 38 Indians and 25 Pakistanis participated. In 1978–1979, the Folklife Program supervised three research trips funded by the Smithsonian Foreign Currency Program. Noted scholars were sent to India and Pakistan to locate the oldest surviving forms of traditional puppetry, with a view to bringing groups of folk puppeteers to the Smithsonian as part of the World Puppetry Festival held in June 1980. Two groups of puppeteers and one group of opera singers from India participated in that festival. Various reports regarding these festivals are available to researchers.

C3 Freer Gallery of Art (Smithsonian Institution)

1.   a. *12th Street and Jefferson Drive, S.W.*
Washington, D.C. 20560
357-2104

b. 10:00 A.M.–5:30 P.M.   daily except Christmas.

c. Open to the public; scholars wishing to view objects not on display should make special arrangements in advance. No objects from the museum's permanent collection are for loan.

d. Prints and slides of major objects in the collection are available for purchase. Objects on exhibition may be photographed; however, special permission must be obtained to use tripods.

e. Thomas Lawton, Director
Esin Atil, Curator, Near Eastern Art

2. The Freer Gallery of Art houses one of the world's most renowned collections of oriental art. Over 12,000 objects in the oriental section, which represent the arts of the Far East, the Near East, Indochina, and South Asia, include paintings, manuscripts, scrolls, screens, pottery, metalwork, glass, jade, lacquer, and sculpture. The international reputation of the Freer Gallery rests in part on the significant contributions to oriental studies made by its staff in the areas of research in art history, conservation, and education. Members of the curatorial staff spend considerable time studying objects in or related to the collection and publish results in scholarly journals and books. Furthermore, they regularly serve as advisors to students, scholars, and the general public on matters pertaining to their areas of expertise. The gallery also presents 6 or 7 free public lectures each year by distinguished scholars in oriental art. Programs in recent years have included such subjects as Islamic architecture and Nepalese crafts.

An extensive library is open to the public during gallery office hours (see entry A11). The gallery also possesses a conservation laboratory and an oriental picture-mounting studio.

A proposed new Asian Art Gallery, an adjunct to the Freer, will provide room for expansion and will enable the Freer to increase its programs for exhibitions, research, and public service.

3. The Freer collection contains approximately 350 South Asian objects, including metalwork, painting, sculpture, and manuscripts. Following is a list of significant South Asian manuscripts preserved at the Freer:

Shāhnāmah (Part IV): late seventeenth century, Mughal, tooled-leather binding, Persian text in Indian nasta'līq script, illuminated 'unwān and chapter headings, 14 miniatures. There are at least 2 other illustrated manuscripts of *Shāhnāmah* at the Freer, executed in India during the Mughal period.

Kalpa Sūtra and *Kalakācāryakathā:* fifteenth century, 123 leaves on colophon, Gujarati Rajput, Jaina (Svetāmbara), fifty miniatures in color and gold, Prakrit script.

'Ajā'ibu-l-Makhlūkāt (Marvels of Creation) by al-Ḳazwīnī: late eighteenth century, 525 paper leaves, Mughal, Persian translation from original Arabic written in Indian nasta'līq, 272 illustrations in color and gold.

Gulistān of Sa'dī: late eighteenth century, 111 leaves, Mughal, Persian Text in Indian nasta'līq script. One 'unwān and 12 miniatures in color and slight gold.

Mahābhārata (selections): eighteenth through nineteenth century, 258 paper leaves, northern Hindu style, Sanskrit text in black, red, and occasional gold, 29 illuminated pages, 22 miniature paintings, bound in watered blue muslin.

Rāmāyana of Vālmīkī: late sixteenth century, 346 leaves plus 5 end leaves, Mughal (School of Akbar) style, Persian translation in small Indian nasta'līq script, 130 miniatures in opaque colors and gold.

Ḥamlah-i-Ḥaidarī (combats of the lion) by Bazil: late eighteenth century, 312 leaves, Mughal style, a metrical history of the life of Muhammad and the first Khalifs, Persian text in Indian nasta'līq script, red leather binding, gold tooled, one 'unwān, 44 miniatures in color and gold.

Prajñāpāramita: early twelfth century, 69 palm leaves containing 81,000 *slokas* (aṣṭasahasraka), Buddhist (Bengal), text in black *ranjā* script, 2 pages adorned with miniatures.

Vasanta Vilāsa (a poem on spring): fifteenth century, illuminated scroll, Gujarati, text in red, black, blue, and yellow script, 79 miniatures.

In addition, there is a fragmentary Jaina (Svetāmbara) manuscript in Gujarati (or Rajput) style with Prakrit text from the fifteenth century; and a sixteenth- through seventeenth-century Mughal album containing paintings and calligraphies. There is also a seventeenth-century copy of the *Qur'ān* in Indian-Arabic style in minute *naskhi* script, tooled with gold.

The Freer's collection of South Asian metalwork includes a fifteenth-century Nepalese saṁvara and ṣakti male figure with 4 heads and 12 arms, embracing his escort; a knife made for emperor Jahangir, partially of meteoric iron, decorated by cut design and gold inlay; and a few other daggers, silver jars, and necklaces with inscriptions in relief.

The Freer's limited but rich collection of South Asian sculpture includes: an early second-century-B.C. Sūṅ ga high relief of the Great Miracle of Srāvastī from Bharhut; a late first-century-A.D. Kushana Nāgarāja (serpent king) image in red sandstone from Mathura; a fifth-century-A.D. Gupta-period torso of a standing Buddha in Mathura style; an Andhara-period (A.D. 100–200) head of a lion from Amarāvati region; a second-century-A.D. Kushana frieze showing 4 scenes from the life of Buddha; and an eleventh-century-A.D. image of Visnu from Trivikrama.

South Asian paintings in the gallery are organized under the following groups of styles: Agra-Bengal, Deccani, Gujarati, Hindu, Jaipur, Lucknow, Mewar, Mughal (Akbar, Jahangir, Shahjahan), Mughal Rajput, Nepal, Rajput, and Sultanate. Some of the paintings in the collection include illustrations from *Prajñāpāramita* and *Rasikapriyā*, a leaf from *Babur-nameh* and the imperial album (*murakkas*) of Jahangir, and scenes from the Romance of Nala and Damayanti. The gallery also has a few embroidered Kashmiri shawls. In 1979, the gallery installed an exhibition, "The Brush of the Masters: Drawings from Iran and India," which included several items representing Mughal, Deccani, and Rajput schools.

4. The Freer Gallery of Art occasionally publishes illustrated catalogs and guides to its collection or special exhibitions. Some of these publications of interest include: Aschwin Lippe, *The Freer Indian Sculptures* (1970); Esin Atil, *The Brush of the Masters, Drawings from Iran and India* (1978), and *Ceramics from the World of Islam* (1973); W. Norman Brown, *K'ālikācārya: The Story of Kālaka* (1933), and *A Descriptive and Illustrated Catalogue of Miniature Paintings of the Jaina Kalpasūtras as Executed in the Early Western Indian Style* (1934). The Freer Gallery also publishes jointly with the University of Michigan, the *Ars Orientalis* (previously *Art Islamica*), a journal devoted to the arts of the Near and Far East. An illustrated booklet, the *Freer Gallery of Art,* is available free.

C4 Hirshhorn Museum and Sculpture Garden (Smithsonian Institution)

1. a. *7th Street and Independence Avenue, S.W.*
    Washington, D.C. 20560
    357-3091

    b. Exhibits:
    April 1–Labor Day:
    10:00 A.M.–9:00 P.M.   Monday–Sunday

    Day after Labor Day–March 31:
    10:00 A.M.–5:30 P.M.   Monday–Sunday
    Closed Christmas Day

    Offices:
    8:45 A.M.–5:15 P.M.   Monday–Friday

    c. Open to the public; for examination of items not on display, contact the Registrar (Douglas Robinson, 357-3281).

    d. Visitors may take photographs using hand-held cameras without flash. For reproduction facilities, contact the Photo Laboratory (John Tennant, 357-3273).

    e. Abram Lerner, Director

2-4.   The museum's more than 7,000 works concentrate on American and European painting and sculpture of the nineteenth and twentieth centuries. Items of interest include a few Islamic art works and a self-portrait of a contemporary Indian artist, Satish Gujral. The museum houses a specialized art library (Anna Brooke, Librarian, 357-3222), which may be visited by prior appointment. The museum also assists in the exchange of publications between the U.S. and foreign libraries, scientific societies, and educational institutions.

C5 National Air and Space Museum (Smithsonian Institution)

1. a. *7th Street and Independence Avenue, S.W.*
    Washington, D.C. 20560
    357-2491

    b. April 1–Sept. 1:
    10:00 A.M.–9:00 P.M.   Monday–Sunday

    September 2–March 31:
    10:00 A.M.–5:30 P.M.   Monday–Sunday

    Closed Christmas Day

    c. Exhibits are open to the public.

    d. Photoreproduction facilities are available.

    e. Noel W. Hinners, Director

2-4. Created to memorialize the development of aviation and space flight, the museum collects, displays, and preserves aeronautical and space-flight artifacts of historical significance, as well as documentary and artistic materials related to air and space. Although the museum has virtually no holdings related directly to South Asia, the exhibits, "Social Impact of Flight" (Gallery 111) and "Satelites" (Gallery 110), show how remote sensing, via space satelites, is employed to study the earth and map its resources.

The "Social Impact of Flight" exhibition contains some materials of the ATS 6 one-year test program of beaming educational television in the remote regions of India. Films screened in the Einstein Spacearium (357-1529) also contain some footage on South Asia. Scholars should contact the Center for Earth and Planetary Studies (Farouk El-Baz, 357-1424), the major center in the museum's research program. The center cooperates with the National Aeronautics and Space Administration (NASA), and several major U.S. and foreign universities in conducting geological studies based on space photos.

The National Air and Space Museum Library (Catherine D. Scott, Librarian, 357-3133) is open to the public for on-site use from 10:00 A.M. to 5:00 P.M., Monday through Friday. Photoduplication services are available. A specialized technical library, its collection consists of some 25,000 books, 5,000 bound periodicals, 500,000 technical reports, 10,000 documentary files, and 900,000 photographs covering aeronautics, astronautics, and space flights. South Asian materials in the collection are limited and scattered.

C6 National Gallery of Art (Smithsonian Institution)

1. a. *6th Street and Constitution Avenue, N.W.*
   Washington, D.C. 20560
   737-4215

   b. April 1–Labor Day:
   10:00 A.M.–9:00 P.M.   Monday–Saturday
   Noon–9:00 P.M.   Sunday

   Day after Labor Day–March 31:
   10:00 A.M.–5:00 P.M.   Monday–Saturday
   Noon–9:00 P.M.   Sunday

   Closed Christmas and New Year's Day

   c. Open to the public

   d. Exhibits may be photographed. Photographs of many items in the collection are also available on sale.

   e. J. Carter Brown, Director

2-4. One of the finest collections of European and American paintings, sculpture, and graphic arts, the National Gallery of Art also contain a few materials of interest to South Asian scholars. The Islamic carpets and tapestries in the Widner Collection contain a few Afghani and Indian rugs from the sixteenth and seventeenth centuries. For further information on this collection contact Joseph Columbus (737-4215).

The gallery also holds special exhibitions on such themes as "Asian Artists in Crystal" (1956), "Persian Miniatures" (1980), and "In Search of Alexander" (1980). Calalogs of the recent or current exhibitions are available from the gallery's gift shop. The exhibition, "Asian Artists in Crystal," represented 16 Asian countries including India and Pakistan, and an 83-page catalog was printed describing the 36 pieces in the exhibition.

C7 National Museum of American History (Smithsonian Institution)

1. a. *14th Street and Constitution Avenue, N.W.*
    Washington, D.C. 20560
    357-2510

    b. Public exhibits:
    April 1–Labor Day:
    10:00 A.M.–9:00 P.M.   Monday–Saturday
    Noon–9:00 P.M.   Sunday

    Day after Labor Day–March 31:
    10:00 A.M.–5:30 P.M.   Monday–Saturday
    Noon–9:00 P.M.   Sunday

    Closed Christmas and New Year's Day

    Departmental offices and research facilities:
    8:45 A.M.–5:15 P.M.   Monday–Friday

    c. Exhibit areas are open to the public. Prior appointments are recommended for visiting research facilities and viewing items not on display.

    d. Exhibits may be photographed, but permission is required for publication. Photoreproduction facilities are available through the departmental offices. Color transparencies and prints of some exhibits are available for sale in the museum gift shop.

    e. Roger G. Kennedy, Director

2. Being a museum of American experience, the collection primarily focuses on the growth of the United States, and therefore materials on foreign areas are limited. Materials of interest to South Asian scholars are discussed below under appropriate divisions or units. The museum's curators, specialists, and technicians have command of professional knowledge and skills that are basic to the exhibits. The staff publishes widely, and some of its exhibit catalogs and research monographs are available in the museum bookstore.

    NATIONAL PHILATELIC COLLECTIONS
    Robert G. Tillotson, Director
    357-1796

    This unit manages a philatelic collection of over 15,000,000 objects, including approximately 500,000 items from South Asia. Some of the stamps in this excellent South Asian collection date back to the late eighteenth century and contain conventional stamps issued by the British government in India, as well as stamps issued by the feudatory states of Travancore (Cochin) and Hyderabad. The bulk of the South Asian collection constitutes a part of the world-wide general collection of twentieth-century stamps. The museum's collection of recent issues from India, Pakistan, Nepal, and Sri Lanka are extensive. There are also some specialized study collections on India, Afghanistan, and Nepal. For further information on the collection, researchers may confer with Lowell S. Newman, Museum Technician (357-1796). The unit's specialized reference library contains an extensive set of catalogs, handbooks, journals, and other literature related to philately.

DEPARTMENT OF NATIONAL HISTORY
Vladimir Clain-Stefanelli, Chairman
357-2825

The Division of Numismatics (Vladimir Clain-Stefanelli, Curator, 357-1798) maintains an extensive collection of some 13,000 coins from South Asia including some from medieval times. *History of the National Numismatic Collections* (1968), prepared by Vladimir Clain-Stefanelli, is a useful guide to the collection. Also, a travel brochure on India may be found in the manuscript of Thomas Cochrane Dudley Papers (circa 1847–1864) maintained by the Division of Naval History (Philip K. Lundeberg, Curator, 357-2249). Dudley was assistant purser on the *Powhatan*, one of the ships on Matthew C. Perry's mission to Japan in 1852. Another subdivision of the department, the Division of Political History (Margaret B. Klapthor, Curator, 357-2277) maintains a collection of Indian gifts to President Eisenhower.

DEPARTMENT OF HISTORY OF SCIENCE
Bernard S. Finn, Chairman
357-1963

The collection of the Division of Mathematics (Uta C. Merzbach, Curator, 357-2392) contains a few astrolabes from the Lahore region, most likely from the medieval period. In addition, the Division of Medical Sciences (Audrey B. Davis, Curator, 357-2274) may contain some materials of interest in its Islamic or Near Eastern collection.

DEPARTMENT OF HISTORY OF TECHNOLOGY
John T. Schlebecker, Chairman
357-2095

The Division of Textiles (Rita J. Adrosko, Curator, 357-1889) within the department maintains a collection of some 30 Indian shawls woven during the eighteenth and nineteenth centuries. In addition, the Division of Photographic History (Eugene Ostroff, Curator, 357-2059) maintains a few nineteenth-century studio portraits from India. Most of these items are unidentified.

EISENHOWER INSTITUTE FOR HISTORICAL RESEARCH
Forrest D. Pogue, Historian
357-2183

This institute conducts scholarly studies into the meaning of war, its effect on civilization, and the role of the armed forces.

3.   The Dibner Library (Mary Rosenfeld, Librarian, 357-1568), which is a rare book collection of some 13,000 items, contains a few titles on South Asia, including: A. C. Carlleyle's *Letter on the Hindu Language, June 14, 1878 to April 23, 1879 to Rivett-Carnac;* and Giovanni Pietro Maffei's *Historium Indicarum* (1588). The Dibner Library is open from 8:45 A.M. to 5:15 P.M., Monday through Friday. An appointment is required for visiting the library. The 150,000-volume collection of the History and Technology Bureau Library (Frank Pietropaoli, Librarian, 357-2036) contains only a few insignificant titles on India.

4.   No comprehensive guide to the museum's collection is available. However, a project for a computerized index to the collection is being currently considered.

C8 National Museum of Natural History (NMNH) (Smithsonian Institution)

1. a. *10th Street and Constitution Avenue, N.W.*
    Washington, D.C. 20560
    357-2664

    b. Public exhibits:
    April 1–Labor Day:
    10:00 A.M.–9:00 P.M.   Monday–Saturday
    Noon–9:00 P.M.   Sunday

    Day after Labor Day–March 31:
    10:00 A.M.–5:00 P.M.   Monday–Saturday
    Noon–9:00 P.M.   Sunday

    Closed Christmas and New Year's Day

    Departmental offices and research facilities:
    8:45 A.M.–5:15 P.M.   Monday–Friday

    c. Exhibit areas are open to the public. Appointments are recommended for visiting offices and research facilities.

    d. Exhibits may be photographed, but clearance is needed for publication. Color transparencies and prints of many exhibition objects are for sale in the museum gift shop. Photoreproduction services are also available through the departmental offices.

    e. Richard S. Fiske, Director

2.   A national and international center for the natural sciences, the National Museum of Natural History contains more than 60,000,000 objects in its research collections and maintains one of the finest natural-history reference collections available to qualified researchers. The scientific staff conducts basic research on man and his artifacts, plants, animals, fossils, organisms, rocks, minerals, and materials from outer space. The museum staff participates in joint educational programs with universities by teaching courses, training graduate students, and conducting science seminars. A Scientific Event Alert Network (SEAN) notifies scientists throughout the world of

geophysical, biological, astronomical, and anthropological events such as volcanic eruptions.

In the absence of a comprehensive geographic inventory of the museum's collection, it is difficult to determine the precise strength of the holdings pertaining to South Asia. Although objects concerning Europe and the Americas dominate the collection, significant and numerous materials representing South Asia are also to be found. South Asia-related materials are discussed below briefly under the appropriate departments responsible for their custody and study.

3. DEPARTMENT OF ANTHROPOLOGY
Douglas H. Ubelaker, Chairman
357-2363

This department's extensive repository of anthropological, archaeological, and ethnographic artifacts contains a modest collection of South Asian objects. The Archaeology Section (William Trousdale, Curator, Far Eastern Archaeology, 357-2671) maintains some 2,000 specimens from South Asia, including a collection purchased in 1891 (A. C. Carlyle, Collection) of prehistoric antiquities—mostly from the caves and rock shelters from the Central Province of British India—comprising: 1,613 minute stone implements of agate, chalcedony, chert and jasper; 5 fragments of pottery; and one animal bone.

The Old World Archaeology Division also maintains a Government of Madras gift collection (1925) of 7 quartzite implements; a P. O. Bodding gift (1920) of 101 Neolithic stone implements and beads from Mohul Pahari (Santal Parganas); a National Museum of India gift of 20 Indus Valley objects; and a collection of 29 potsherds from the surface of a site at Parom, Makran area, Pakistan, collected by John Neal in 1965. Other specimens include items collected from several sites in North West Frontier Province, Madras, Bombay, Bundelkund, Pennaar River Valley, Rohri Hills, Darjeeling, Poondi, and Bahbhore.

The Ethnology Section (Robert A. Elder, 357-2483) maintains a small collection of some 4,500 objects from South Asia featuring earthenware, baskets, Khyber knives, and a rosary from Afghanistan; a model of the Tower of Silence (Bombay) and several Parsee ritual objects, including a Gujarati *Book of Verses;* jewelry, pottery, and costumes from Pakistan, Nepal, and Bangladesh; and a variety of regional and ethnic artifacts from India, including a Kashmiri shawl, a small flaked-flint stone implement, Kinnari Vina, shankha, incense holder, sandalwood, brass throne for Hindu idols, sitar, Mogul shields, batik textiles, astrological manuscripts, house models, and representations of Sri Krisha, Hanumann, Lakshmi, Ganesha, and Garuda. Physical Anthropology Section (Herman Viola, Director, 357-1986) maintains a small collection of some 50 specimens of uncolored plaster castes of fossil primate teeth and skeletal fragments from India.

Some card catalogs and inventory lists are maintained in the department's Processing Laboratory (George E. Phebus, Supervisor, 357-2483) which may be consulted by visiting scholars.

The Anthropology Branch Library (Janette K. Saquet, Librarian, 357-1819) is open to the public for on-site use from 9:00 A.M.–5:00 P.M., Monday through Friday, and maintains a specialized collection of some 53,000 volumes and 1,200 periodicals. The South Asian portion of the collection consists of approximately 300 titles on antiquities, archaeology, and description. Interesting items include Indian Archaeological Survey's *Annual Report,* 1904—; and *Epigraphic Indica* 1889—. Two separate card catalogs provide access to the collection. Interlibrary loan and photoduplication facilities are available.

DEPARTMENT OF MINERAL SCIENCES
Daniel E. Appleman, Chairman
357-2680

Within this department, the Division of Mineralogy (Paul E. Desautels, Curator, 357-2226) maintains an extensive collection of gems and mineral specimens from South Asia.

DEPARTMENT OF BOTANY
Dieter C. Wasshausen, Chairman
357-2534

Of the department's collection of approximately 3,500,000 specimens, some 150,000 are of South Asian origin. Following is a list of special collections pertaining to South Asia received by the department prior to 1965:

India: W. S. Atkinson; L. Biswas; H. F. Blanford; Bourne; C. B. Clarke; C. Curtis; J. F. Duthie; J. S. Gamble; G. A. Gammie; W. Griffith; C. W. Hope; E. K. Janaki; R. W. MacKinnon; Prain; H. N. Ridley; R. R. Stewart; G. H. K. Thwaites; N. Wallich; L. Wray. Ceylon: William Ferguson; Afghanistan: Walter Koelz. It may be noted that the department designates accession numbers to specimens by their characteristic biological classifications; e.g., family, genera, and species.

In addition, scientific staff of the department conduct field trips and research dealing with South Asian subjects. Curator D. H. Nicolson (357-2521) specializes on the flora of India. Other staff botanists in the department who have current research interest in South Asia are: Robert Faden (357-2540), Sri Lanka and India; George Russell (357-2795), India; and Thomas R. Soderstrom (357-2795), bamboos, including those of South Asia. South Asia-related staff publications include: M. D. Dassanayake and F. R. Fosberg, *Flora of Ceylon* (1980); Cecil J. Saldanha and Dan H. Nicolson, *Flora of Hassan District, Karnataka, India* (1976); and D. H. Nicolson and Tirtha Bahadur Shustha, *Keys to the Dicot Genera in Nepal* (1968). The studies on Ceylon and Hassan district were financed by the Smithsonian, using U.S. excess foreign currency under the provision of Public Law 480.

The department also provides facilities for the visiting research scholars and lends its specimens through university departments.

The following departments may also contain items of interest: Department of Entomology (Donald R. Davis, Chairman, 357-2078); Department of Invertebrate Zoology (W. Duane Hope, Chairman, 357-2030); Department of Paleobiology (Martin A. Buzas, Chairman, 357-2211); and Department of Vertebrate Zoology (George R. Zug, Chairman, 357-2740).

4. Until 1979, inventories of the museum's collection had been performed piecemeal, partially by manual means and partially by using the museum's Automatic Data Processing (ADP) facilities. But now, an accelerated ADP

program has begun with the objective of establishing computerized records of the museum's full collection. By the end of fiscal year 1979, more than 1,500,000 specimens and lot records had been extended into the computer.

C9 National Rifle Association Firearms Museum

1.   a. *1600 Rhode Island Avenue, N.W.*
Washington, D.C. 20036
828-6000

    b. 10:00 A.M.–4:00 P.M. Monday–Sunday

    c. Open to the public

    d. Permission is required for photographing any items in the collection.

    e. Dan R. Abbey, Curator

2-4.   The museum's extensive collection includes a few nineteenth-century matchlock and percussion guns from India.

C10 Renwick Gallery (Smithsonian Institution)

1.   a. *17th Street and Pennsylvania Avenue, N.W.*
Washington, D.C. 20560
357-2531

    b. 10:00 A.M.–5:30 P.M. daily except Christmas
Visiting hours are extended to 10:00 P.M. during August.

    c. Open to the public

    d. Exhibits may be photographed.

    e. Lloyd E. Herman, Director

2.   A curatorial department of the National Museum of American Art (Harry Lowe, Acting Director, 357-1959), the Renwick Gallery hosts a continuing series of visiting exhibitions from foreign countries. Two such exhibitions were: "Painting from Pakistan," January–March, 1974; and "Contemporary Painting from India," March–April 1973. Installation shots and checklists of these exhibitions are available in the gallery office. It was reported that negotiations have been initiated for holding another exhibit from India.

C11 Textile Museum

1.   a. *2320 S Street, N.W.*
Washington, D.C. 20008
667-0441

    b. 10:00 A.M.–5:00 P.M. Tuesday–Saturday

c. Open to the public; items which are not on display may be viewed by special arrangement.

d. Color transparencies and photographs of some items in the collection are on sale. Visitors may also photograph items in the collection by making prior arrangements. Limited photoduplication services are also available.

e. Andrew Oliver, Director

2-4.   The museum's excellent collection of some 10,000 textiles, rugs, and tapestries contain an extensive selection from the world of Islam, including some 300 items from Islamic India. A 1976 exhibition, "Masterpieces in the Textile Museum," included a few items from India. For further information on South Asian items call Mattiebelle Gittinger, Research Associate, specializing in the South Asian collection (667-0441.)

The Textile Museum Library (Katherine Freshley, Librarian, 667-0441) is open to the public for on-site use from 10:00 A.M. to 5:00 P.M., Wednesday, Thursday, and Friday, and from 10:00 A.M. to 1:00 P.M., Saturday. A research library of over 7,000 titles on technical and historical aspects of ancient textiles and rugs, it contains many works related to the area of our interest.

There is no published catalog on the museum's collection on South Asia. However, researchers may request to see the curator's card catalog, which is arranged by country. An annual journal and a quarterly newsletter are distributed to the museum's associate members.

D Collections of Music and Other Sound Recordings

South Asia-related collections of music and other sound recordings are rather limited in the area. A representative collection of South Asian folk songs, religious chants, classical music, ragas, and sitar recitals, are available at the Library of Congress Folk Life Center. Some examples of South Asian music are also located in the Library of Congress in the Music Division as well as in the Motion Picture Broadcasting and Recorded Sound Division. The holdings of the latter also contain voices of prominent South Asian public leaders. Other significant nonmusical audio materials, including the broadcasts of the Azad Hind Revolutionary Government during World War II, are available in the depositories of the National Archives and Records Service's Motion Picture and Sound Recordings Branch.

Collections of Music and Other Sound Recordings Entry Format (D)

1. General Information
   a. *address; telephone numbers*
   b. hours of service
   c. conditions of access
   d. name/title of director and key staff members

2. Size of Holdings Pertaining to South Asia

3. Description of Holdings Pertaining to South Asia

4. Facilities for Study and Use
   a. availability of audio equipment
   b. reservation requirements
   c. fees charged
   d. reproduction services

5. Bibliographic Aids Facilitating Use of Collection

Indian Embassy Music Collection See entry K3

D1 Indian Spice and Gift Store

1.   a. *4110 Wilson Boulevard*
Arlington, Virginia 22203
(703) 522-0149

2-3.   A commercial enterprise that caters to the South Asian ethnic community, the store carries a good assortment of South Asian music in records, tapes, and cassettes. The store's stock of music contains both the regional varieties and many of the latest hits.

D2 Indo-Pak Records Club

1.   a. *6192 Oxon Hill Road*
Oxon Hill, Maryland 20022
(301) 839-1133

     d. Ramzan Sabir, President

2-3.   A commercial enterprise, the Indo-Pak Records Club maintains a good inventory of records, tapes, and cassettes of Indian and Pakistani music of all kinds. Club members receive a discount on all purchases and also receive information on latest musical releases from India and Pakistan.

D3 Library of Congress—American Folklife Center—The Archive of Folk Song

1.   a. *Thomas Jefferson Building, Room G-152*
10 First Street, S.E.
Washington, D.C. 20540
287-5510

     b. 8:30 A.M.–5:00 P.M.   Monday–Friday except national holidays

     c. The Reading Room is open to the public during these hours: no appointment is required except for listening.

     d. Joseph C. Hickerson, Head
Gerald E. Parsons, Reference Librarian

2.   Established in 1928 as a unit within the Music Division, the archive was to be the national repository for documentary manuscripts and sound recordings of American folk music. Originally designated as the Archive of American Folk-Song, its name was changed in 1955 to the Archive of Folk Song to emphasize its growing collection of traditional music and lore from all parts of the world. In 1978 the archive ended its affiliation with the Music Division to become a part of the American Folklife Center, which was established

in the LC in 1976 by an act of the U.S. Congress. Through recent years the archive maintains and administers all LC's acquisitions, references, and reader-service activities in the broad fields of folklore and ethnomusicology. It may be noted here that commercial recordings pertaining to folklore and ethnomusicology are in the province of the LC's Motion Picture, Broadcasting, and Recorded Sound Division.

The archive currently houses over 30,000 recordings (cylinders, discs, wires, and tapes) containing over 300,000 items of American as well as exotic folk song, folk music, folk tale, oral history, and other types of folklore. In addition, the archive controls over 225,000 sheets of manuscript material. In the excellent reading room of the archive are assembled over 3,500 books and periodicals, a sizable collection of magazines, newsletters, and ephemera of interest to folklorists and ethnomusicologists as well as a variety of unpublished theses and dissertations.

Quite understandably, the archive's holdings are strong on the U.S.A., but materials on South Asia and other Asiatic regions are not negligible. At present, approximately 20 percent of the archive's recorded collection is from abroad, and an additional 20 percent from the U.S. is in languages other than English.

The archive maintains vertical files of written materials on India and Asia containing pamphlets, correspondence, reviews, and reports. An examination of these files revealed the following reports written by Richard A. Waterman apparently during the course of World War II: "Music of the Middle East and Far East (A confidential supplement): A Report on the Use of Music in Propaganda in the Orient," and "Music of the Middle East and Far East—A Bibliographic Report on Materials Available in the United States." The second report contains a description and comment on records of Indian music in the LC prepared by Horace Poleman of the LC's Orientalia Division (now Asian Division). The India file also contains a copy of an out-of-print pamphlet, also prepared by Poleman, entitled *The Music of India,* published by the LC in 1945.

Following is a selection from the field-recordings collection of the archive on South Asia: 2 12-inch records of readings from the *Bhagavad Gita,* sung by Haridas Muzumdar and recorded by Dorothy Spencer, 1946; 1 13¼-inch record of an Indian chant in the temple, 1944; 7 wire spools from the Prince Peter of Greece Project, including a Nestorian church service at Trichur, South India, and Tibetan recordings from Kalimpong, West Bengal, 1949–1950; 4 12-inch records of native music of India, Hyderabad, Deccan (Andhra Pradesh), 1948; 2 16-inch records of Amita Dutta-Mujumdar singing Hindu folk songs, 1948; 7 10-inch records of folk songs of India, Government of India, Calcutta, 1955; folk songs from Tirachi, South India, transcription service, All India Radio, 1956; 2 7-inch tapes of Indian folk music, United States Information Agency, New Delhi, 1962; Gujarati songs (chants) sung by pundits and recorded by Dorothy Spencer, 1946; 10 12-inch discs of music of India and Burma, duplication project of foreign folk music project by joint Army-Navy Committee, 1969; 1 5-inch tape of Vedic chants sung by two Vedic pundits recorded by Roland O. Olson, Rishikesh, United Province, 1966; 6 7-inch reel tapes of classical music of India, primarily ragas, from North India, Pan Orient Art Foundation, 1970; 1 10-inch reel tape of Ceylonese folk music and folk music-drama; 2 reels of 10-inch tape of Sinhalese folk music sung by Devar S. Sena and Nelun Devi, 1951; 1 10-inch tape of a sitar recital by a Pakistani artist; 1 7-inch tape of Pakistani folk music and poetry; and segments of 12 10-inch reels of folk music recorded in Pakistan by Sidney Robertson Cowell, 1959.

4.   a. Listening equipment to play library recordings is available.

     b. Appointments are required for using listening facilities. Prior appointments are advisable for lengthy reference services.

     c. There is no fee or charge for the use of the collection.

     d. In special cases duplicating or photocopying of certain materials may be arranged through the reference staff.

5.   The archive's recordings are identified and shelved by accession number. In addition to a shelflist, the collections are accessible through an alphabetical card index. Extensive field notes, many textual transcriptions, and some musical transcriptions are available in folders and bound volumes for supplementary information about the recordings. Finally, 4 card indexes analyze parts of the collection in terms of individual items: a numerical file, an alphabetical title index, an alphabetical index of informants, and a geographical index.

There is also a general alphabetical card index for collections in manuscript and microform. An indispensable, printed reference aid is the ongoing LC publication, *Music, Books on Music and Sound Recordings,* and its predecessor, *Library of Congress Catalog: Music and Phonorecords.* There is also an outdated 3-volume LC printed catalog, *Check-List of Recorded Songs in the English Language in the Archive of American Folk Song to July 1940,* 1942. The archive has also compiled more than 155 bibliographies, directories and other reference and finding aids.

Since there is no comprehensive inventory for public use of all the holdings of the archive, a prerequisite for research is to draw upon the personal knowledge of the professional staff of the archives. A person with expertise on South Asian music is Ronald Walcott of the American Folklife Center of the Library of Congress (287-6590). A mimeographed brochure prepared by the archive, "The Archive of Folk Song and a Guide to the Collection of Recorded Folk Music and Folklore in the Library of Congress," is distributed free.

D4 Library of Congress—Motion Picture Broadcasting and Recorded Sound Division—Recorded Sound Office

1.   a. *Thomas Jefferson Building, Room G-152*
10 First Street, S.E.
Washington, D.C. 20540
287-5508

     b. 8:30 A.M.–4:30 P.M.   Monday–Friday

     c. Open to the public

     d. James Smart, Reference Librarian

2-3.   Following a reorganization in 1978, the Recorded Sound Office of the Music Division was separated from the Music Division and merged with the newly created Motion Picture, Broadcasting and Recorded Sound Division. Pending the scheduled relocation of the entire division sometime during 1980–1981 to the new facilities of the James Madison Memorial Building, the Recorded Sound office is operating in the Thomas Jefferson building.

Under the jurisdiction of the new division, the Recorded Sound Section continues its responsibility for the acquisition, custody and service of all of LC's sound recordings, including commercially produced musical recordings, interviews and speeches, and recorded radio programs, in conjunction with LC's Music Division (entry A23). However, excluded from its jurisdiction are the "talking books" and the materials in the province of the Archive of Folk Song. For a description of the division's film and television collection, see entry F5.

The Recorded Sound facility holds over 850,000 items of commercial (LP and pre-LP) and noncommercial recordings. Over 80 percent of these materials are uncataloged. The available catalog for processed items is not geographically indexed, and items are retrievable only by manufacturer's trade name and catalog number. To locate material, the researcher either should know the required manufacturing data or must rely on the assistance of staff members.

In the absence of a comprehensive inventory, no thorough assessment of South Asian materials is possible. However, a gross estimate of its holdings of both commercial recordings—of mostly classical and popular songs—and nonmusical recordings will number more than 1,500 items. Examples of nonmusical recordings include: "India and Pakistan at War and the Rise of Bangladesh," phonotape by Bangladesh spokesman, A. S. Choudhury, Pakistani foreign minister, Z. A. Bhutto, and Indian foreign minister, C. Singh (1971); "Indian Pakistan Conflict" (1965); "Indian Fairy Tales;" "India Music and Bach;" "Indian Population Crisis" (1974); "Chinese vs. Indian Development" (1972); and "Indira Gandhi Speaks to the Nation" (1972).

Collections of nonmusical recordings also include Voice of America broadcasts; speeches delivered by U.S. officials and visiting dignitaries at the National Press Club; CBS and other radio network broadcasts; recordings of United Nations' proceedings; and audiotapes of U.S. House of Representatives debates. Recently NBC transferred its entire radio archive of 175,000 recordings of radio programs and events broadcast from 1933 to 1970 to the LC.

Facilities for listening to sound recordings are made available without charge to persons engaged in serious research. Because of the limitations of space, investigators whose work requires access to recordings should make appropriate arrangements at least 2 weeks in advance. Audio materials in the collections can be duplicated, provided no special restrictions are attached to the desired items. Fees for reproduction are substantial. The division offers copies of some of its holdings for sale in disc form. Research collections are not available for loan or rental.

A vast ensemble of manufacturer's published catalogs, trade catalogs, discographics, books, and periodicals on sound recordings are available in the adjacent reading room of the LC's Music Division (Main Building, Room G-146), which also serves as the reading room for the collection. Further materials of this kind are included in LC's general and periodical collections, and can be consulted in the general reading rooms.

The reading room houses the audio listening facilities and also the card catalog for sound recordings. A card index for many uncataloged recordings is kept in the reference office for sound recordings, together with some other finding-aids, reference books, subject folders, and lists.

An extremely useful, printed finding-aid for the collection is the LC publication, *Music, Books on Music and Sound Recordings,* and its earlier version, *Music and Phonorecords.* The newest addition to the record researcher's tool kit is a U.S. Copyright Office publication, *Catalog of Copyright Entries: Sound Recordings.* There are also several free brochures on the collection.

D5 Martin Luther King Memorial Library—Music Division

1. a. *901 G Street, N.W., Room 209*
       Washington, D.C. 20001
       727-1285

    b. 9:00 A.M.–9:00 P.M.   Monday–Thursday
       9:00 A.M.–5:30 P.M.   Friday–Saturday

    c. Open to the public

    d. Mary Elliott, Division Chief

2-3. This excellent international collection of music records, music scores, and music books contains some 20 albums of Indian music, including: Pannalal Ghosh (banboo flute); Bismillah Khan (shehnai); Ravi Shankar (sitar); Ustad Ali Akbar Khan (sitar); and Bade Ghulam Ali Khan (sitar). The collection also contains several books on Indian music.

4. Materials may be borrowed without charge. Audio equipment and reproduction facilities are not available.

5. Card catalogs provide access to the collection.

D6 National Archives and Records Service (NARS)—Motion Pictures and Sound Recordings Branch (Audiovisual Archives Division)

1. a. *8th Street and Pennsylvania Avenue, N.W.*
       Washington D.C. 20408
       523-3267

    b. 8:45 A.M.–5:00 P.M.   Monday–Friday

    c. Open to researchers with a National Archives identification card obtainable from the Central Reference Division, Room 200-B; first-time users are recommended to consult the reference staff before beginning any work.

    d. William T. Murphy, Chief of the Branch

2. The branch has the custody of approximately 107,000 discs, reels of magnetic tape, cartridges, and cassettes. These spoken-word recordings were received primarily from U.S. government agencies and from private, commercial, and foreign sources. Although the bulk of the material in this branch relates to the U.S., the collection is also international in scope. The

South Asian portion of the collection is not very extensive, although its size cannot be accurately determined. This entry deals only with sound recording. For a discussion of the motion-picture holdings of the branch, see entry F12.

3. The audio materials in the collection are organized into the Record Groups (RG) established by the National Archives. For an explanation of the concept of Record Groups see entry B6. Some of the South Asian audio materials are to be found in the following Record Groups:

RG 12: Records of the Office of Education (1942–1965). Selected radio broadcasts produced by the Office of Education during World War II contain the American endorsement of the independence of India (October 26, 1942). Recordings of the White House Conference on Education—Overseas Program and Foreign Students may also be relevant to the South Asianists.

RG 59: General Records of the Department of State. Sound recordings relating to South Asian interests may be found in the radio broadcasts of the secretaries of state; a special series on world history for the period 1918–1939; and memovox recordings of broadcasts of the International Broadcasting Division of the Office of Information and Educational Exchange to foreign countries, 1946–1949.

RG 200: National Archives Gift Collection (1892–1971). Recordings of speeches, interviews, and panel discussions by prominent persons include Mahatma Gandhi, Pandit Jawaharlal Nehru, Sarojini Naidu, Syed Amjad Ali, and Vijaya Lakshmi Pandit. Also included in the collection is the 83-minute recording of the Inter-Asia Relations Conference at New Delhi (1947). Excerpts of the first session include a major address by Pandit Nehru on the role of the conference in bringing about a "new day" for all Asians; a speech by conference chairperson and poet, Naidu, on Asian and Indian culture and its role in world history; and opening remarks by the leaders of the various Asian delegates. Gandhi, in his speech, the "Message of Asia," asserts the superiority of the culture of India and Asia. Another item in the collection is an address to a joint session of the Congress by Prime Minister Pandit Nehru, who discussed the common ideals shared by the United States and India, despite different cultural heritages, and pledged future friendship in the postwar era (October 13, 1949).

RG 262: Records of the Foreign Broadcast Intelligence Service (FBIS) (1940–1947). This large collection of 36,000 items of recordings of foreign broadcasts, in English and other languages, by German and Japanese radio during World War II, contains a few South Asian items of historical significance. One of the Japanese broadcasts from Saigon, monitored by the service, contains a speech in English by Subhas Chandra Bose (1945), the leader of the Azad Hind revolutionary government in exile.

The monitoring log of the foreign broadcasts, maintained by the service, recorded at least one long daily broadcast of news, announcements, messages, and music in Hindi, from Japanese radio, of unknown location (1941–1945). The collection also contains recordings of the broadcasts from Colombo (1945–1946), All India Radio (1946), Voice of Free India (1942–1943), Indian Home Service (1946), and the clandestine station Indian Freedom (1942).

RG 306: Records of the United States Information Agency (1950–1965). This group contains recordings made by or for the Voice of America for overseas release and consists of dramatizations, reports, speeches, and interviews designed to promote better understanding of the United States. South Asian material in the group includes an interview with Pandit Nehru and other South Asian visiting dignitaries.

4. a. Audio equipment is available for use in the research room.

   b. Audio equipment and recordings are to be used only in the research room and may be reserved in advance. Requests for same-day service may require some waiting.

   c. No fees are charged for the use of the facilities.

   d. Staff assistance for a fee is available for duplicating material not encumbered by copyright or other restrictions. Researchers may also make audio copies using their own equipment, provided the material is in the public domain, or prior permission has been secured.

5. A primary reference aid in facilitating the use of the collection is the *Guide to the National Archives of the United States* (1974). In addition, researchers may find it useful to consult: *Sound Recordings in the Audiovisual Archives Division of the National Archives* (1972), compiled by Mayfield S. Bray and Leslie C. Waffen; *Audiovisual Records in the National Archives Relating to World War II* (1974), compiled by Mayfield S. Bray and William T. Murphy; and a selected audiovisual record, *The Crucial Decade: Voices of the Post War Era, 1945–1954* (1976). Other finding aids include a card index and various files and preservation folders on different Record Groups maintained by the branch. The researcher should also note that staff help is indispensable in locating most material.

D7 National Audiovisual Center (National Archives and Records Service)

1. a. *8700 Edgeworth Drive*
   Capital Heights, Maryland 20027
   (301) 763-1896

   b. 8:00 A.M.–4:30 P.M.   Monday–Friday

   c. Open to the public

   d. John McLean, Director

2-3. The National Audiovisual Center is the central information and distribution source for more than 12,000 films, filmstrips, audio/slide sets, and other audiovisual materials produced by federal agencies for public use. South Asian materials in the center include 19 2-track audio-cassettes of a course in Baluchi, and 13 2-track audio-cassettes of a course in Urdu.

4. All audio-casettes are on sale. The center provides no facilities for reviewing of materials. The text for the courses in Baluchi and Urdu may be purchased from Spoken Language Services, P.O. Box 783, Ithaca, N.Y. 14850, (607) 257-0500.

5. A *List of Audiovisual Materials Produced by the United States Government*

for Foreign Language Instruction (1980) and several other catalogs and pamphlets are available free on request.

Pakistan Embassy Music Collection See entry K5

Sri Lankan Embassy Music Collection See entry K6

D8 WHFS—FM

1. a. *4853 Cordell Avenue*
Bethesda, Maryland 20014
656-0600

d. Jacob Einstein, Executive Vice President

2-3. A local radio station, WHFS sponsors an ethnic music program on Indian music. The program is broadcast from 2:00 P.M. to 4:00 P.M., on Sundays, at a frequency of 102.3 FM. For further information, contact program host Punita Bhatt (638-6825).

D9 WPFW—FM

1. a. *700 H Street, N.W.*
Washington, D.C. 20001
783-3100

d. Lorne Cress Love, General Manager

3. A noncommercial, community supported radio station, WPFW sponsors an Indian music program on the second Friday of every month, at 7:30 P.M., at a frequency of 89.3 FM. For further information, contact program host, J. K. Naidu.

E Map Collections

South Asia-related map collections in the Washington area are few but valuable. The Library of Congress Geography and Map Division's collection of maps, atlases, and charts include considerable South Asian items, including materials produced by the British Admiralty and the Indian Naval Hydrographic Office. Copies of U.S. government-produced maps of foreign areas and maps of foreign areas obtained by the U.S. government are often deposited in the Center for Cartographic and Architectural Archives of the National Archives and Records Service, or with the U.S. Geological Survey. Most maps produced by the Defense Mapping Agency Hydrographic/Topographic Center are classified. The National Geographic Society's collection, however, is available to scholars; it includes some maps for sale. Several South Asian embassies in the city may also provide maps of their countries or cities to interested individuals.

Map Collections Entry Format (E)

1. General Information
   a. *address; telephone numbers*
   b. hours of service
   c. conditions of access
   d. reproduction services
   e. name/title of director and heads of relevant divisions

2. Size of Holdings Pertaining to South Asia

3. Description of Holdings Pertaining to South Asia

4. Bibliographic Aids (inventories, calendars, etc.) Facilitating Use of Collection

E1 Defense Mapping Agency Hydrographic/Topographic Center (DMAHTC) (Defense Department)

1. a. *6500 Brookes Lane, N.W.*
   Washington, D.C. 20315
   227-2700

b. 7:30 A.M.–4:00 P.M.   Monday–Friday

c. The center is not open to the public. Researchers may, however, obtain special permission for limited access to the collection. For further assistance, contact the Public Affairs Office (J. D. Millēr, 227-2006).

d. Unclassified maps and charts may be purchased from the Customer Service and Sales Management Division of the Defense Mapping Agency Office of Distribution located at 6101 MacArthur Boulevard, N.W., Washington, D.C. 20315, (227-3048).

e. J. R. Lund, Director

2-3.   The mapping, charting, and geodesy functions of the Defense Mapping Agency are principally conducted by its two major production components. While the Aerospace Center (DMAAC) (St. Louis, Missouri) produces aeronautical charts, the Hydrographic/Topographic Center primarily produces nautical and topographical maps and charts. Aeronautical charts, published by the DMAAC that cover foreign areas and are available for public sale, are distributed by the National Ocean Survey's Distribution Division, Riverdale, Maryland 20840, (301) 436-6990.

Following some recent reorganization, the center's data facilities contain approximately 700,000 maps and some 300,000 books, periodicals, and documents on cartography, geodesy, and geography. Materials in the map collection are, for the most part, classified. The extent of the South Asian holdings is difficult to determine, but it is estimated to be significant. Unclassified maps produced by the Defense Mapping Agency are distributed to several repositories, which include the Library of Congress Geography and Map Division, The George Washington University Library, the University of Maryland Library, and, on an exchange basis, the National Geographic Society.

4.   There is no published inventory to the DMA map collection. The center maintains a 5-volume *Catalog of Maps, Charts, and Related Products* in loose-leaf form, the use of which is mostly restricted. Requests for access to the catalog may be directed to the Map Release Officer (Judy Propst, 227-2178). A copy of the *DMA Price List of Maps and Charts for Public Sale* is available free on request.

E2   Earth Satellite Corporation

1. a. *7222 47th Street
Bethesda, Maryland 20015
(301) 652-7130*

b. 8:00 A.M.–4:30 P.M.   Monday–Friday

c. Open to scholars

d. Copies of maps and imagery may be obtained for a fee.

e. J. Robert Porter, President

2-3.   The Earth Satellite Corporation is a private commercial consulting firm that provides various mapping services and natural resources inventories based upon remote sensing. Its limited inventory of South Asian materials consists of some 6 images of India (Gangetic delta and Jaipur region) and a few images of the agricultural zone in the northeastern region of Pakistan. Currently, the corporation's South Asia-related work includes supplying of processed Landsat imagery of the South Asia region to the World Bank in support of the bank's agricultural program. The corporation has also done a geological mineral study in Pakistan in 1979.

4.   The corporation does not publish a list of its holdings for public use. Requests for project reports should be made directly to the appropriate client or funding agency. The staff may assist scholars interested in locating images or maps of specific regions or countries.

E3 Geological Survey Library (Interior Department)—Map Collection

1.   a. *12201 Sunrise Valley Drive*
Reston, Virginia 22092
(703) 860-6671

b. 7:15 A.M.–4:30 P.M.   Monday–Friday

c. Maps are available for inspection in the library or they may be borrowed by interlibrary loan.

d. Researchers wishing to obtain copies of maps in the collection are directed to several local commercial photoduplication firms which provide such services for a fee.

e. George E. Goodwin, Jr., Librarian

2-3.   One of the largest earth-science libraries in the world, the U.S. Geological Survey Library's map collection exceeds 350,000 items. A shelflist measurement of maps and atlases revealed a total of approximately 450 items on South Asia: Afghanistan 59; Bangladesh 15; India 260; Pakistan 45; and Sri Lanka 50. The staff advised that the shelflist is not very comprehensive since some regional and state maps are not included in the country categories. Also, items added after 1978 are not included in the shelflist. Various subcategories include: agriculture, coral, bauxite, earthquakes, economics, engineering, geology, ground water, iron, irrigation, metamorphic metals, minerals, physical division, physiological division, relief, topography, vegetation, and others. Approximately 10,000 foreign and U.S. maps are added to the holdings annually.

4.   The library utilizes the on-line computerized cataloging system operated by the Ohio College Library Center (OCLC). At present no published catalog or inventory for the map collection is available. A bibliographic record of maps published by the Geological Survey is provided in *Publications of the Geological Survey, 1879–1961*, and *Publications of the Geological Survey, 1962–1970*. Current USGS maps are listed in the monthly (with yearly supplements) *New Publications of the Geological Survey*. These are available from the Geological Survey's Branch of Distribution, 1200 South Eads Street, Arlington, Virginia 22202 (703) 557-2751; or the survey's National Center, Room 1C-402, Reston, Virginia 22092 (703) 860-6167.

George Washington University Library Map Collection
See entry A13

E4 Library of Congress—Geography and Map Division

1. a. *James Madison Memorial Building*
    First Street and Independence Avenue, S.E.
    Washington, D.C. 20540
    287-6277

    b. 8:30 A.M.–5:00 P.M. Monday–Friday
    8:30 A.M.–12:30 P.M. Saturday

    c. Open to the public

    d. Photoduplication facilities are available.

    e. John A. Wolter, Chief

2-3.   The largest and most comprehensive cartographic collection in the world,
the division's holdings exceed 3,600,000 maps, 40,000 atlases, 8,000 reference books, 250 globes, and 2,000 3-dimensional plastic-relief models.
This outstanding collection is all inclusive, but historical maps and atlases
predominate. The massive holdings of maps, atlases, and charts cover individual continents, countries, states, and cities as well as the world, and
range in scope from comprehensive to topical. Official topographic, geologic, soil, mineral, and resource maps, and nautical and aeronautical charts
are available for most countries of the world. A vast majority of the material
in the collection is received from official sources.
   In the collection, material on the Americas and the Western hemisphere
predominate. The limited South Asian holdings consist of approximately
250 atlases, 1,150 maps (Afghanistan 60, Bangladesh 60, Bhutan 5, India
550, Nepal 190, Pakistan 110, Sri Lanka 100), and 200 reference books.
   The South Asian cartographic collection is of diverse origins and includes
items produced by the U.S., British, and Indian governments. It covers a
wide variety of subjects, namely, climate, maritime zones, administrative
divisions, electoral districts, land utilization, epidemiological status, ethnological distribution, census statistics, dietary and nutritional variations,
plantation, and irrigation. Some of the maps and atlases deal only with a
city or locality, providing such details as street names and house numbers;
a few contain texts in vernacular languages with romanized legends.
   The division holds numerous nautical charts (with catalogs) of the Indian
Ocean region, produced by the U.S. Defense Mapping Agency and Indian
Naval Hydrographic Office. Also available are the charts of the Indian
Ocean produced by the British Admiralty, the Instituto Hidrografico de la
Marina (Cádiz), Service Hydrographique et Océanographique de la Ma-
rine (Paris), and Deutsches Hydrographisches Institut (Hamburg). Sailing
directions, released by U.S. and Indian governments, containing coastal-
and port-approach information for different sectors of the Indian Ocean
region, are also maintained in the division.
   The small but selective collection of South Asian reference books consist

mostly of gazetteers, descriptions, travelogs, and history. Also available for consultation are 200 cartographic and geographic journals including: *Deccan Geographer* (Secunderabad); *Geographical Observer* (Meerut); *Geographical Review of India* (Calcutta); *Indian Geographer* (New Delhi); *National Geographical Journal of India* (Benares); *Pakistan Geographical Review* (Lahore); and *Oriental Geographer* (Dacca).

4. There is no single comprehensive catalog of the division's total holdings, but several card and book catalogs provide access to specialized segments of the collection. Separate card indexes for maps, atlases, and reference books are located in the spacious public reading room of the division.

   A useful printed bibliography to the collection is *A List of Geographical Atlases in the Library of Congress,* complied by Philip Lee Phillips, 4 vols. (1920), and the subsequent 4-vol. supplement (1974), compiled by Clara Egli LeGear. G. K. Hall's *Bibliography of Cartography,* 5 vols. (1973), with a 2-vol. supplement (1980), is a comprehensive and unique analytical index to the literature of cartography, providing author, title, and subject access to books and journal articles relating to maps, mapmakers, and the history of cartography. The bibliography contains more than 100,000 entries and includes materials published during some 500 years of map making.

   Other bibliographies and checklists published by the division describe various cartographic groups. A list of current publications is available upon request. In 1968, the division introduced computer-assisted cataloging procedures to control current receipts of single sheet maps. A free brochure, *Geography and Map Division* (1977) is available on request.

E5 National Archives and Records Service (NARS) (General Services Administration)—Center for Cartographic and Architectural Archives

1. a. *8th Street and Pennsylvania Avenue, N.W.*
   Washington, D.C. 20408
   523-3062

   b. 8:45 A.M.–5:00 P.M.   Monday–Friday

   c. Open to the public with a National Archives research card, obtainable from the Central Reference Division, Room 200-B.

   d. Reproduction facilities are available.

   e. Charles E. Taylor, Acting Chief

2. Among the records in the division are over 1,600,000 maps and 2,250,000 aerial photographs, comprising one of the world's largest accumulations of cartographic materials. South Asian maps and charts, either produced or collected by different U.S. agencies, are scattered in many record groups and, therefore, render a numerical estimate impossible. Some of the significant holdings pertaining to South Asia are described below under the Record Group (RG) numbers into which the holdings are organized. For an explanation of RG numbers see entry B6.

3.   South Asian cartographic materials include diverse basic maps; nautical charts; aeronautical charts; military maps; and various topical maps (e.g., economic resources, production and consumption, transportation and communication systems, commerce and trade routes, and religious and demographic charts). Many of these maps and other graphic records are in manuscript form, and a few date back to the 1850s. A vast majority of the cartographic documentation on South Asia belongs to the World War II period and was generated by the U.S. federal defense and security agencies.

RG 18: Records of the Army Air Forces. The compilation and production of aeronautical charts for air navigation began in 1923. The organization responsible for the cartographic activities of the Army Air Forces was the Aeronautical Chart Service and its predecessors. Among the chart series produced were the World Long Range, World Planning, World Weather, Approach Charts of Strategic Areas, and large-scale Target Charts. In addition, the Army Air Forces initiated the most extensive program of aerial photography that had been undertaken until that time. The cartographic records of the group contain an indeterminate number of maps and charts of South Asia and the Indian Ocean in small territorial segments.

RG 37: Records of the Hydrographic Office. This office conducts hydrographic surveys in foreign waters and on the high seas; collects and disseminates hydrographic and navigational data; prepares maps and charts relating to navigation, including strategic and tactical charts required for naval operations and maneuvers; and issues sailing directions, light lists, pilot charts, navigational manuals and periodicals.

Included in this record group are several items on South Aisa: a printed plan of Karachi harbor—forwarded by the U.S. consular agent in 1890—showing harbor facilities, location of the town, the government house, the hospital, railway stations, the observatory, native infantry lines, and surrounding swampland; a manuscript chart of Madras harbor, prepared by German steamship Wildnefels, showing harbor facilities; and original manuscript plotting sheets, by lieutenants Fitzerald and West, for a pilot chart of the North Indian Ocean (1855–1856).

The collection also includes several other maps of the south coast of Asia, Ceylon, the Arabian Sea, the Bay of Bengal (1948), and a pilot chart of the Indian Ocean prepared in 1916.

RG 38: Records of the Office of the Chief of Naval Operations. The office, established in 1915, directs the preparation and logistical support of the operating forces of the Navy and the coordination of the bureaus and offices of the Navy Department. The Naval Oceanographic Office (formerly the Hydrographic Office), which is attached to the office of the Chief of Naval Operations, is the official mapping agency of the Navy Department, and its records constitute the Record Group 37 described above.

Aside from the activities of the Naval Oceanographic Office, the Office of the Chief of Naval Operations has no large-scale mapping program, although some of its other component units, particularly the Office of Naval Intelligence (ONI), prepares maps as working tools or to illustrate information they have compiled. In this Records Group are to be found a few diverse maps of South Asia, including the Indian Ocean, Afghanistan, and Baluchistan.

The group also contains the following items of interest: several charts of the world showing submarine cables with principal connecting lines and little-known seacoast telegraphic stations in parts of the world (1885); map graphs showing direction and value of world trade (1923); chart of the world showing coal and fuel-oil fields, together with amount produced in each location and showing depots and supply (1923); chart of the world, annotated to show active oil fields, annual production figures, and estimated reserve in each field (1924); charts of the world's telegraphic connection (1925); charts of the world's ports (1925); chart of the world showing naval facilities (1925); chart of the world showing colonies or mandates of various countries (1925), raw materials by area throughout the world (1928), and naval bases and stations of the British Empire (1929).

RG 59: General Records of the Department of State. Cartographic records in this very large and important collection contain more than 1,600 items and primarily consist of miscellaneous maps showing the location of U.S. diplomatic and consular posts (1844–1951); maps enclosed in confidential and diplomatic inspection reports showing American and foreign consulates, embassies, and significant commercial and industrial establishments; maps and graphs from U.S. consular reports showing natural resources and economic activities in various foreign countries (1943–1949); and maps and charts of foreign countries maintained by the Office of the Geographer of the State Department.

Among the inspection reports on foreign-service posts there are at least 5 local maps of Calcutta, Bombay, Karachi, Madras, and Colombo. The numerical map file, in the records of the geographer of the Department of State, contains the following maps: Afghanistan and the Middle East; India, showing 1931 census by province; Afghanistan, Russo-Afghan frontier; India, production of milled rice 1935/36–1940/41 and 1942/43 averages; India, production of 7 food grains (milled rice, wheat, sorghum or jowar, chickpeas or gram, millet or bojra, barley, maize), averages 1935/36–1940/41; India, per-capita consumption of 7 food grains by provinces; India, total requirements and production of 7 food grains or caloric bases; Bengal and Assam, a base map of political boundaries; India, density of population (1941); India, distribution of population according to religious communities (1941); India, distribution of Muslims (1941); Bengal, literacy according to religious communities (1941); Bengal and Assam, Hindu population by caste group; the Punjab, areas with Muslim majorities (1941); the Punjab, distribution of religions (1941); Bengal and Assam, distribution of religions; India, distribution of Muslims (1941); Bengal and Assam, distribution of largest communities and Hindu-Muslim percentage (1941).

In addition, the Bowman collection in RG 59 contains a few items of interest, namely: Near and Middle East political divisions, including Pakistan, Afghanistan, and Baluchistan (1942); India (1943), giving British India, native states, and tribal states; India, states and regions (1942); and distribution of population in India (1944). Among the map studies made in the Department of State during World War II—chiefly for the use of the committee headed by Leo Pasvolsky in preparation for a peace conference after the war—may be found several maps of South Asia delineating the demographic trends and food supply.

RG 70: Records of the Bureau of Mines. Records in the Petroleum Division, 1919–1929, include a map of the world, annotated to show the distribution and relative magnitude of oil reserves, oil production, and prospective oil fields.

RG 76: Records of Boundary and Claims Commissions and Arbitration. Cartographic items in this collective record-group—established for segregated files, relating to international boundaries, claims, and arbitration received from the Department of State and international commissions—include charts of coral fisheries and pearl fisheries off the coast of India and Ceylon.

RG 77: Records of the Office of the Chief of Engineers (OCE). One of the responsibilities of the OCE (U.S. Army) is producing and distributing army maps. Cartographic records include published general and topographic maps of many land areas of the world, as well as foreign-operations and campaign maps. South Asian items include the following: a map of Hunza Nagar by Colonel R. G. Woodthrope of the Royal Engineers (1891); a map showing the seat of insurrection in the northwest border of India (1897); a map of Afghanistan, showing the seat of war in Asia, from surveys made by British and Russian officers up to 1875, and published for the information of the officers of the U.S. Army (1878); a map of Central Asia, showing Afghanistan and her relation to British and Russian territories (1885); a map showing the Bolshevik situation in Europe and Asia; and several other maps of countries between Russian and British domination in Asia (1882–1885).

In addition, the Army Map Services cartographic records (1942–1968) contain several series (approximately 100) of topographic maps on South Asia dealing with cities, states, or provincial divisions and containing demarcated and undemarcated international boundaries; roads classified according to surface, vehicular use, and importance; railroads classified according to gauge or number of tracks; vegetation and cultivated areas; and cultural features.

RG 83: Records of the Bureau of Agricultural Economics (BAE). This large collection of 4,361 items of maps, atlases, and graphs contain the following on South Aisa: 1917 "dot" maps showing production and acreages of crops and livestock in India and Ceylon; a manuscript dot-map of the world showing distribution of horses, mules, and asses and a historical chart showing numbers of these animals in British India annually from 1840 to 1923; and a base map of India with provinces (1917).

RG 120: Records of the American Expeditionary Forces, World War I (1917–1923). Included in the collection are a few topographical maps of India printed in color with altitude tint: Bombay, Godavari, Kathawar and Madras.

RG 160: Records of Headquarters Army Service Forces (ASF). Among the 2,021 cubic feet of records of the ASF—which was established in 1943 to provide services and support to meet military requirements except those unique to the Army Air Force—are cartographic records of an incomplete series of the published *Newsmap*, showing allied, axis, and neutral countries, and world strategic areas; and *An Atlas of World Maps*, showing land forms, ocean currents, climatic regions, vegetation types, soils, drainage basins, distribution of population, languages, religious groups, predominant types of economic activity, major agricultural regions, fuel and power production and consumption, iron and steel production and trade, major transportation facilities, overseas shipping routes, railroads and their relationship to population distribution, and areas controlled by the major powers.

RG 165: Records of the War Department General and Special Staffs. Cartographic records of the group include maps of theaters of operations in World War II and areas of strategic interest throughout the world. A large portion of these maps has been transferred to RG 77. South Asian items in the group consist of railway maps of Burma and Assam and a map of Nepal, all prepared by the Military Intelligence Services (1942–1945).

RG 166: Records of the Foreign Agricultural Service. The primary responsibility of the service—established in 1930 and known from 1939 to 1953 as the Office of Foreign Agricultural Relations—was to develop foreign markets for the surplus U.S. farm products. The group contains a few items of interest dealing with international supply and trade in food grains.

RG 169: Records of the Foreign Economic Administration (1943–1945). In the 42 items denoted as cartographic records of the group are included maps of India with political divisions, native states, transportation routes, and connecting roads outside of India.

RG 219: Records of the Office of Defense Transportation (ODT). This office holds a map of India showing percentages of cultivated areas growing rice (1943).

RG 226: Records of the Office of Strategic Services (OSS) (1942–1945). The OSS cartographic records consist generally of maps prepared in the Office of Coordinator of Information and maps prepared or gathered by the Divsion of Map Intelligence and Cartography of Research and Analysis Branch of the OSS. The extensive South Asian maps consist of: several maps of the Bengal and Assam region showing the number of industrial workers (1946); linguistic and religious distribution of population in India; road transport and telegraphic and telephone communications in Afghanistan (1946); several maps of Ceylon; routes between India and China; engineering establishments and electrical generating stations in India; charts showing the OSS organization in the India-Burma theater of war; and possible sites for development of a fertilizer industry in India.

RG 242: National Archives Collection of Foreign Records Seized, 1941—. This group contains several items of interest including a map of Portugal's Indian possessions and British territories in India.

RG 233: Record of the United States House of Representatives. Most of the cartographic materials in this group were prepared by the executive agencies to accompany reports or to fulfill special requests of the House. Included are maps illustrating irrigation in parts of India (1874).

RG 253: Records of the Petroleum Administration for War. The cartographic records of the Petroleum Administration for War, established in 1942 and abolished in 1946, consists of a general reference file of maps and graphs from various sources and other maps relating to petroleum-producing areas throughout the world. Among these are maps showing pipelines and other conveying facilities, production volumes, export and import volumes, and graphs showing world petroleum resources. South Asian materials include maps of the Near East, including the west coast of India, Baluchistan, and Afghanistan; India-Burma frontiers; and several others depicting the resources, production, and marketing in India.

RG 256: Records of the American Commission to Negotiate Peace. The American Commission to Negotiate Peace, the official U.S. mission to the Paris Peace Conference of 1919, included a group of geographers, historians, political scientists, and economists, known aggregately as "The Inquiry," which in 1917 and 1918 had studied the geographic, historical, ethnographic, economic, and political questions that were likely to be considered at any postwar peace settlement. When the Treaty of Versailles was signed in January 1919, the commission's work was completed. Records in this group contain a number of general, annotated maps of Asia, including India.

RG 313: Records of Naval Operating Forces. Included are published charts relating to the U.S. Atlantic Fleet's round-the-world cruise, 1907–1909.

RG 324: Records of the Office of Geography. The Office of Geography provides research and other staff services on foreign geographic nomenclature for the interdepartmental Board of Geographic Names and the Secretary of the Interior. The office inherited functions and records of earlier boards and committees engaged in similar work. Included in the records of the office are gazetteers from the Board of Geographic Names and the Central Intelligence Agency on Afhanistan, Ceylon, India, and Pakistan. These gazetteers provide geographical locations or coordinates of cities, towns, and villages.

RG 332: Records of the United States Theaters of War, World War II. Cartographic records of the group include a map of the China-Burma-India theater of war.

RG 341: Records of the Headquarters, United States Air Force. The U.S. Air Force, which succeeded the Army Air Forces in 1947, requires maps for planning purposes, for air navigation, and for the conduct of tactical operations. The Aeronautical Chart and Information Center (ACIC), which is responsible for meeting these requirements, has prepared many standard series of charts and a variety of special maps and charts, including strategic planning charts, navigational charts, and the world aeronautical charts, which have been adopted as the standard aeronautical chart series by the International Civil Aviation Organization. The mapping activities of the ACIC are world-wide in scope and include several aeronautical charts of South Asia.

In addition the following record groups may contain a few items of interest to the South Asian scholar: RG 32: Records of the United States Shipping Boards; RG 46: Records of the United States Senate; RG 94: Records of the Adjutant General's Office; RG 95: Records of the Forest Service; RG 114: Records of the Soil Conservation Service; RG 127: Records of the U.S. Marine Corps; RG 237: Records of the Federal Aviation Agency; RG 319: Records of the Army Staff; RG 331: Records of Allied Operational and Occupation Headquarters, World War II.

4. Access to the collection is provided through the lists, catalogs, and other special indexes available in the division. Most of these finding aids are maintained in manuscript or typescript form in the research room of the division; a number have also been published and are available to interested researchers without cost. Electrostatic copies of out-of-print items are obtainable for a fee.

Although outdated, the most comprehensive and useful printed guide to the holdings of the division is the *Guide to Cartographic Records in the National Archives,* compiled by Charlotte M. Ashby et al. (Washington, D.C.: Government Printing Office, 1971). Another valuable reference tool is: United States Hydrographic Office, *Manuscripts Charts in the National Archives,* 1838–1908 (1978), by William J. Heynen.

In addition, the division compiles a number of resource papers designed principally to indicate potential research topics and supporting documentation. A list of the available papers and other useful information concerning the division is provided in an informative pamphlet, *Cartographic Archives Division* (1973).

E6 National Geographic Society—Cartographic Division Map Library

1. a. *Membership Center Building*
   11555 Darnestown Road
   Gaithersburg, Maryland 20760
   (301) 857-7000, ext. 1401

   b. 7:30 A.M.–4:00 P.M.   Monday–Friday

   c. Open to the public for on-site use only; maps from this collection may also be made available to scholars through the National Geographic Society Library (see entry A27).

   d. Photoduplication facilities are available.

   e. Margery Barkdull, Map Librarian

2-3.   This excellent world-wide collection is estimated to contain some 100,000 maps, mostly of recent origin. The cartographic materials include topographic, administrative subjects, and highway maps, as well as lunar maps, nautical and aeronautical charts, and city plans. The library is the depository of all maps produced by the National Geographic Society. Library holdings also include extensive acquisitions from various foreign and national mapping agencies. A good selection of atlases, reference books and gazetteers is also available. South Asian items, although not extensive, include: Afghanistan 5; India 35; Nepal 10; Pakistan 30; and Sri Lanka 5. Most of the maps on India and Pakistan are post-1960.

4.   A card catalog arranged by geographical region and country provides access to the collection. Maps published by the Society may be purchased at the Explorers Hall sales desk located at 1145 17th Street, N.W., Washington, D.C. 20036, 857-7589.

E7 World Bank Map Library

1. a. *1919 K Street, N.W.*
   Washington, D.C. 20433
   676-0229

   b. 8:30 A.M.–4:30 P.M.   Monday–Friday

   c. Accessible to the public on the basis of previous appointment for on-site use only

   d. Reproduction facilities are available.

   e. Chris Windheuser, Librarian

2-4.   This small reference collection of some 10,000 items contains approximately 1,000 basic general maps and topographic sheets on the countries of South Asia. There is no catalog or inventory available for this collection. It may be noted that most items in this collection are also available at the Geography and Map Division of the Library of Congress (see entry E4).

F Film Collections (Still Photographs and Motion Pictures)

There is a considerable number of South Asian still photographs and motion pictures in the various depositories in the area. Notable South Asian film resources consist of the holdings of the Still Pictures Branch, and the Motion Pictures and Sound Recordings Branch of the National Archives and Records Service; and the holdings of the Prints and Photographs Division and the Motion Picture, Broadcasting, and Recorded Sound Division of the Library of Congress. In addition, examples of nineteenth-century photographs from India are to be found in the holdings of the National Anthropological Archives. Photographic collections of the Agency for International Development (AID) and the World Bank contain numerous photographic documentations of development projects and related subjects in South Asia. South Asian motion-picture documentaries are available in certain area libraries and embassies. Several local theaters also frequently organize commercial presentation of South Asian movies.

Film Collections Entry Format (F)

1. General Information
   a. *address; telephone numbers*
   b. hours of service
   c. conditions of access
   d. name/title of director and key staff members

2. Size of Holdings Pertaining to South Asia

3. Description of Holdings Pertaining to South Asia

4.   Facilities for Study and Use
   a. availability of audiovisual equipment
   b. reservation requirements
   c. fees charged
   d. reproduction services

5.   Bibliographic Aids Facilitating Use of Collection

F1 Agency for International Development (AID)—Photo Collection

1.   a. *AID Office of Public Affairs*
      State Department Building, Room 4898
      320 21st Street, N.W.
      Washington, D.C. 20532
      632-8632

      b. 8:45 A.M.–5:30 P.M.   Monday–Friday

      c. Open to researchers; appointments and clearance should be arranged in advance.

      d. Lois Devlin

2.   The AID photograph collection contains approximately 20,000 photographs (black-and-white prints and some color slides) covering such AID foreign-aid projects as the construction of dams, hospitals, schools, and documenting the living conditions and various scenes of the populations and habitats of the host countries. The South Asian portion of this collection is considerable, although a numerical estimate is not possible.

4.   A fee is charged for reproducing photos. Requests for prints must be made in person at the office.

F2 American Red Cross Photograph Collection

1.   a. *Office of Communications Resources—Photographic Services*
      18th and E Streets, N.W.
      Washington, D.C. 20006
      857-3428

      b. 8:30 A.M.–4:45 P.M.   Monday–Friday

      c. Open to the public; researchers who wish to view the collection should call ahead for an appointment.

      d. Rudolf A. Clemen, Jr., Information Research Specialist

2-3.   The total collection consists of more than 20,000 black-and-white photographs and some 1,000 color transparencies. Coverage includes nursing and relief activities of the Red Cross and the humanitarian efforts in the aftermath of natural calamities, disasters, and warfare. Most of the photographs deal with the period since 1950.

4.   Photoduplication services are available.

5.   South Asia-related prints are arranged chronologically, by country, in an International Services File.

Georgetown University Library Film Collection See entry A15

F3 Indian Embassy—Information Service

1.   a. *2107 Massachusetts Avenue, N.W.*
       Washington, D.C. 20008
       265-5050

      b. 9:30 A.M.–5:30 P.M.   Monday–Friday

      c. Open to the public by appointment

      d. L. Sailo, Film Assistant

2-4.   This collection of mostly documentary films, exceeding 150 titles, focuses on many facets of India, such as agriculture and irrigation, arts and culture, education and youth training, foreign relations, science and natural resources, geography and travel, government and citizenship, industry and energy, monuments and temples, nature and wildlife, transportation and communication, and the people. There are also biographies of Gandhi, Nehru, Tagore, Vinoba Bhave, Mirza Ghalib, Zakir Hussain, artist Nandlal Bose, and others. Archival footage includes one film on the history of the Indian film industry, 1913–1963. All films are lent without any charge, for noncommercial purposes only. The Information Division may entertain inquiries regarding the purchase of prints of films. It is sometimes possible to view films on a projector at the embassy.

5.   The periodically updated *Catalogue of Indian Documentary Films* is issued complimentarily by the embassy.

F4 Indian Film Enterprises

1.   a. *1325 18th Street, N.W.*
       Washington, D.C. 20036
       296-7697

      d. Raj Joshi, Manager

2-3.   Indian Film Enterprises is a private, commercial corporation engaged in supply and distribution of Indian movies and films in the United States. It also assists in the production of Indian films in the U.S.A.

F5 Library of Congress—Motion Picture, Broadcasting, and Recorded Sound Division

1. a. *John Adams Building, Room 1046*
    10 First Street, S.E.
    Washington, D.C. 20540
    287-5840.

    The division was scheduled to move to the first floor of the newly opened James Madison Memorial Building at the time of this writing.

    b. 8:30 A.M.–4:30 P.M. Monday–Friday

    c. Open to the public

    d. Erik Barnouw, Chief

2. Reorganized in 1978, this division is responsible for the acquisition, cataloging, preserving, and servicing of the motion picture and television collections—including items on film, videotape, and videodisc—and has the responsibility for the LC's collections of sound recordings and radio programs. For a description of the collections in the latter category see entry D4.

    The film and television collections contain over 75,000 titles, with several thousand titles being added each year through copyright deposit, purchase, gift, or exchange. The collection also includes some 300,000 stills. The Library of Congress has for a long time recognized the need to preserve motion pictures as a historical record and has made continuous efforts to enhance its studio deposits, including some selected foreign films.

3. The division's limited inventory in the area of our interest is acquired primarily through gifts to the LC by government agencies and cultural institutions and partly through the assistance of the American Libraries Book Procurement Center of the Library of Congress in New Delhi and Karachi. Approximately 75 percent of the small South Asia collection of some 200 items consists of educational documentaries on the rich antiquities of the region and on its panoramic cultural diversity. The collection also contains the entire series of classic movies produced by the internationally recognized Indian film producer and director, Satyajit Ray.

    Following is a selected list of South Asian documentaries and educational films to be found in the collections of the division:

    India: *Mahatma Gandhi: 100 Years; Rabindranath Tagore; Portrait of a City; Kumba Mela; Song of the Snows; The Last Journey; Beauty in Blossom; Cave Temples of India; A Century of Indian Archaeology; National Library; Marine Marvels; Jodhpur; Music of India (Instrumental); Music of India (Drums); Udaipur; Nalanda; Women of India; Invitation to an Indian Wedding; Kerala: Land of Lagoons; Indian Water Birds; Call of the Flute; Jaipur; Malwa; Gotama Buddha; Khajuraho; Madurai;* and *Ladakh.*

    Pakistan: *Fury of the Mighty Indus; Sind through the Ages; Folk Music of West Pakistan; Wonders of West Pakistan; Antiquities of Pakistan; Folk Songs and Folk Dances of Pakistan; Paintings in Pakistan; Cities of Pakistan.*

    In addition the division's collection includes documentaries and other footage produced by the 3 major national television networks (CBS, NBC, and ABC), which contain some coverage of South Asia. These materials are generally acquired by the division through the copyright regulations. A series-title index to the television collection is available.

4. a. The film and television research collections are not available for public projection, rental, or loan. The division provides limited viewing facilities— 35-mm and 16-mm viewing machines and videotape players—for specialized, individual research. The facilities are not open to high-school students; undergraduate college students must provide a supporting letter from a supervising professor.

     b. Advance appointments are required for the use of viewing facilities.

     c. Use of all research facilities are without any charge.

     d. Copies of works not restricted by copyright, or by provisions of gift or transfer, and in sound physical condition may be ordered through the division. The requester is responsible for any necessary search to determine copyright status of specific works. Inquiries in this matter may be obtained from the Registrar of Copyright, Library of Congress.

5.   There is no comprehensive bibliographic aid to the holdings of the division. Initial research inquiries should be directed to the professional reference staff of the division. Primary access to the materials is provided by an author/ title card catalog, located in the reading room of the division, where is also housed a basic collection of reference works on cinema and television, along with distributors' catalogs, yearbooks, reviews, and trade periodicals. The division's catalogers are in the process of computerizing the cataloging information which will eventually replace the various card catalogs with a data base from which bibliographic information can be retrieved in a variety of ways.

     A published catalog, *Motion Pictures from the Library of Congress Paper Print Collection: 1894–1912*, by Kemp R. Niver (Berkeley, Calif.: University of California Press, 1967), is available on the premises. Scheduled for publication in 1981 is an LC catalog, *Television Programs in the Library of Congress: Programs Available for Research as of December 1979.* The LC catalog, *Films and Other Materials for Projection,* and the National Union Catalog's volumes on *Motion Pictures and Film Strips* are valuable research and reference tools, but do not reflect the actual holdings of the division.

     Other relevant LC publications are: *Library of Congress Catalog— Audiovisual Material* and *Catalog of Copyright Entries: Motion Pictures.* The division distributes a printed guide, *Film and Television,* containing basic information on the division. The division also maintains a vertical file on India, which contains correspondence on acquisitions and catalogs of Indian motion pictures and educational films.

     Scholars interested in pursuing South Asian studies relevant to the division's resources will find it rewarding to consult the division's chief, Erik Barnouw, who recently collaborated with S. Krishnaswamy in producing a valuable contribution entitled *Indian Film,* the second edition of which was published in 1980 by the Oxford University Press.

F6 Library of Congress—Prints and Photographs Division

1. a. *John Adams Building, Room 1051*
     10 First Street, S.E.
     Washington, D.C. 20540
     287-6394

    b. 8:30 A.M.–5:00 P.M. Monday–Friday

    c. Open to scholars

    d. Oliver Jensen, Chief

2-3.   The Prints and Photographs Division maintains custody of LC's extensive holdings of more than 10,000,000 photographs, negatives, prints, posters, and other pictorial materials. The division's general collection of 9,000,000 photographs and negatives comprises one of the finest general historical collections in the world and provides a pictorial record of the political, social, and cultural history of America and the world from 1860 to the present.

    The division's scanty South Asian holdings of approximately 200 items contain some significant materials. To illustrate the quality of these materials, a few card numbers are noted below. A card number refers to an album, portfolio, or stereograph containing several items: Card No. 7126, Visit of Edward and Mary, Prince and Princess of Wales, to India in 1906; Card No. 2136, American Flying Squadron in India, December 1942; Card No. 2426, Gandhi after release, 1944; Card No. 6615, Bombay Presidency, groups, costumes, etc., 1883; Card No. 3855, Kanu Desai, artist, Indian decorative art, 1930; Card No. 3874, Ajanta and Ellora, 1942; Card No. 10212, erotic, painted-wood sculptures of Nepal, 1964. The division also has separate vertical portrait files on Gandhi and Nehru located with other vertical name files. A vertical country file is maintained but contains no significant items pertaining to South Asia.

4.   The division maintains the collection as a research archive and does not function as a commercial agency. Photocopies of materials in the division's collections, which are not under copyright or other restrictions, may be ordered through the library's Photoduplication Service. Photographic prints, photostats, color transparencies, microfilm, and other types of photocopying processes are available.

5.   The holdings are accessible through the divisional card catalog (arranged by subject, photographer or creator, and collector) and other reference indexes, inventories, and staff. Researchers may consult the collections in the reading room maintained by the division. The reading room houses the general and special card catalogs, files of photoprint reference copies, and a limited collection of reference books. Reference specialists and curators are available for consultation about the collections in their special fields. A list of free-lance picture searchers in the Washington, D.C., area is available upon request. A free brochure on the division, introducing the collection, is a useful first step to using the collection.

F7 Manoranjan Enterprises

1.   a. *1412 New York Avenue, N.W.*
       Washington, D.C. 20005
       638-6825

    d. Punita Bhatt

2-3.   Manoranjan Enterprises is a commercial concern that organizes presentation of South Asian movies and musical concerts and other cultural functions. Currently, it is showing a series of exceptional Indian films at the Takoma Theater (4th and Butternut Streets, N.W., Washington, D.C., 829-0001).

F8   Martin Luther King Memorial Library—Audiovisual Division

1.   a. *901 G Street N.W., Room 226*
Washington, D.C. 20001
727-1265

b. 9:00 A.M.–9:00 P.M.   Monday–Thursday
9:00 A.M.–5:30 P.M.   Friday–Saturday

c. Open to the public; all library patrons are eligible to borrow films for an overnight period during weekdays.

d. Diane Henry, Division Chief

2-3.   The entire collection of the division comprises over 3,000 film titles, some 700 filmstrips, and numerous slides covering a wide range of subjects. This growing collection includes the following films of interest on India: *India: Introduction to History; Four Families; Mahatma Gandhi; Mooti, Child of New India; Tagore;* and *Village in India: Fifty Miles from Poona.*

4.   a. Appropriate equipment for viewing is available to all library users in the Audiovisual Division.

b. Borrowers are encouraged to reserve films as far in advance as possible.

c. No fees are charged.

d. No reproduction services are available.

5.   *DC Public Library Media Catalog,* 1979, lists all the films in the collection.

F9   Middle East Institute Film Library

1.   a. *1761 N Street, N.W.*
Washington, D.C. 20036
785-1141

b. 10:30 A.M.–5:00 P.M.   Monday–Friday
10:00 A.M.–5:00 P.M.   Saturday

c. Open to the public

d. Mary Cook, Director of the Film Library

2-3.   The Film Library was established in 1970 as part of the institute's expanding educational activities. It covers both general and specific topics, focusing primarily on contemporary Middle East and North Africa, emphasizing educational and avoiding propagandistic themes. Items of interest include several films on Islam and the following films on Afghanistan: *Afghan Woman*, daily life of secluded women in a rural community of northern Afghanistan; the *Nomads of Badakhshan*, intimate view of the lifestyle, routines, and values of the nomads; *The Painted Truck*, reveals much about the lives and traditions of the people associated with the principal mode of transportation in Afghanistan; and *Stones of Eden*, documents a year in the life of a wheat farmer in central Afghanistan, showing the simplicity of the family's existence and farming methods.

4.   a. No on-site viewing facilities are available.

     b. All films are 16 mm with sound. Advanced reservations are required.

     c. A small fee is charged.

     d. All films are available for sale.

5.   *The Middle East Institute Film Library* catalog is available free on request.

National Air and Space Museum (Smithsonian Institution) Film Collection See entry C5

F10 National Anthropological Archives (Smithsonian Institution)

1.   a. *National Museum of Natural History Building, Room 60-A* ·
10th Street and Constitution Avenue, N.W.
Washington, D.C. 20560
357-1986

     b. 9:00 A.M.–5:00 P.M.   Monday–Friday

     c. Open to the public; appointments in advance are recommended.

     d. James R. Glenn, Archivist

2-4.   Although this collection primarily focuses on native Americans, the photographic collection contains some 200 nineteenth-century portrait and scenic photographs from India, taken by court or professional photographers. A few photographs from Pakistan and Sri Lanka are also to be found in the collection. For further information contact Museum Specialist Paula Fleming (357-1986).

F11 National Anthropoligical Film Center (NAFC) (Smithsonian Institution)

1.   a. *955 L'Enfant Plaza, S.W.*
Washington, D.C. 20560
287-3428

     b. 9:00 A.M.–5:00 P.M.   Monday–Friday

     c. Open to the public but prior appointment is recommended.

     d. E. Richard Sorenson, Director

2-3.   The NAFC (Center for the Study of Man) aims at developing the means to take greater advantage of the potential for visual and aural records as a means of furthering human understanding. The center deals with questions having to do with the nature of the human condition, including all aspects of the human heritage, such as behavioral development, philosophy, ethics, cultural history, aesthetics, the visual arts, and the behavioral and human sciences. Currently the NAFC is collaborating with leaders and scholars in several Third World nations on film documentation of their threatened cultural heritages. Facilities are being developed for preservation and retrieval of the visual data obtained in response to interest and invitations received by the center. NAFC's current projects include Nepal, India, and Pakistan.

The center's growing collection now exceeds 2,000,000 feet of film. In its efforts to build up a documentary collection of aspects of life throughout the world, the NAFC has been experimenting with various kinds of support to film makers and scholars interested in producing films as permanent scholarly resources. This effort includes: providing consulting services, film-making expertise, or equipment; supplying film stock, processing facilities, logistic support, training, assembly, and annotation services; helping with grant applications; and supplying preservation service and facilities for analysis. In providing such assistance, the NAFC maintains a flexible policy aimed at filling project gaps with resources not otherwise available. NAFC also supports the Ethnofilm Training Program, which is mostly participated in by trainees from non-Western cultures. South Asian students have participated in this program.

4.   Viewing equipment is available for use in the center without charge. It is advisable to make a prior appointment.

5.   A computer index is planned. The center is described in E. Richard Sorenson, "To Further Phenomenological Inquiry: The National Anthropological Film Center," *Current Anthropology* 16 (2) (June 1975): 267–69.

F12   National Archives and Records Service (NARS)—Audiovisual Archives Division—Motion Pictures and Sound Recordings Branch

1.   a. *8th Street and Pennsylvania Avenue, N.W.*
Washington, D.C. 20408
523-3267

b. 8:45 A.M.–5:10 P.M.   Monday–Friday

c. Open to all serious researchers with a National Archives identification card, obtainable from the Central Reference Division, Room 200-B; first-time visitors are advised to consult with a reference specialist before beginning work.

d. William T. Murphy, Chief of the Branch

2.   One of the three branches of the Audiovisual Archives Division (the other two being Still Pictures Branch and Stock Film Library), the Motion Picture

and Sound Recording Branch has approximately 113,000 reels of motion picture films including an indeterminable number of items related to South Asia. Sound-recording collections of the branch are discussed in entry D6. The limited but varied South Asian film depository in the branch is certainly fascinating and is illustrative of historical activities of the people of South Asia.

3.　　For custody, reference, and retrieval purposes, the film depository in the archive—as are all other materials—are organized into Record Groups (RG). For an explanation of the Record Groups system see entry B6. Some materials of interest to South Asian specialists may be found in the following Record Groups:

RG 18: Records of the Army Air Forces. Within this collection of 5,828 reels of mostly World War II motion pictures are included Air Transport Command briefing films, consisting of aerial and ground views of terrain, flight routes, and landing facilities in India and other strategic regions of the world. Animation for the briefing films shows particular flight routes, locations of landing strips, radio beams, and the principal geographic configurations of specific areas.

The motion-picture records of the group also include combat footage of the China-Burma-India theater of war, concerning the activities of the USAAF; camera records of other aspects of war such as rest and recreation activities of the air force personnel; and native peoples and their customs and their participation in the war (e.g., U.S. troops loading in Parbatipur [Eastern Bengal]); 14th Air Force Operation in India in support of the Chinese defense efforts against Japan; training and briefing of 3rd Gurkha Rifles; Indian aboriginals guiding GIs through jungles in Assam; vacationing GIs relaxing at golf courses, race tracks, and bazaars; scenes of Red-Cross girls entertaining the U.S. forces; and joy rides in the tonga. Also included in the collection is some footage of color films of activities of Indian troops in France and Italy (1944).

RG 59: General Records of the Department of State (1911–1965). This group of 206 reels includes films made by the department, its subsidiary agencies, other government departments, and private companies. Reflecting Department of State activities and policies, they illustrate the history of the U.S. role in world affairs. Some of the noteworthy films in the group are: the work of the United Nations Educational, Scientific and Cultural Organization in assisting students from all over the world (1947); those reviewing international events from 1945 to 1951; some, mostly from television shows, speeches, interviews and discussions, featuring secretaries of state, assistant secretaries of state, and others—including Dean Acheson, Christian Huber, Dean Rusk, George Ball, Douglas Dillon, and W. Averell Harriman, 1950–1965—relating to U.S. foreign policy and world conditions; and film records of world-wide war activities (1941–1944).

RG 107: Records of the Office of the Secretary of War (1941–1945). Composed of 191 reels of films from the Bureau of Public Relations that document American military activities in all theaters of operation during World War II.

RG 111: Records of the Office of the Chief Signal Officer (1905–1954). This large collection of 15,597 reels provides documentary coverage of all aspects of World War II, including the conduct of war in all theaters, mobilization and training, entertainment for the troops, and postwar problems in Asia. Motion pictures accumulated in this group include those made by the Navy Department, the Red Cross, and newsreel companies.

The wide range of South Asian film footage includes the following: surrender of Indian National Army (April 13, 1945); American Red Cross activities in Calcutta; American soldiers watching cremation at Nimtollah; presentation ceremony of Legion of Merit with the U.S. and British soldiers (September 22, 1945, New Delhi); American troops' departure from India (September 1945); Gandhi at the Aga Khan's palace (February 23, 1945); Nehru visiting the U.S.A. (October 1949); Indian infantry and paratroops' capture of Rangoon (1945); and Indian regiments in the desert during World War I. The depository of the Signal Corps also contains many bazaar scenes, historical sites, Hindu holy men, Hindu pilgrims bathing in the Ganges, untouchables, sacred cattle, wealthy princes and their retinues, street crowds, political rallies, communal violence, potitical leaders, Gandhi fasting, hospital facilities in India, and instruction in Calcutta University.

RG 131: Records of the Office of Alien Property. A 1937 reel of Ceylon, depicting street scenes, a tea plantation garden, a ballet, animals, and snakes.

RG 200: National Archives Gift Collection (1896–1969). This massive gift collection of 13,025 items contains several unbroken newsreel series of Paramount, Movietone, News of the Day, Pathé, Fox, International Telenews, and Universal Newsreels, and other commercial educational and documentary films. The depository of the Universal Newsreel, which has separate indexes, contains approximately 500 items pertaining to South Asia and covers a wide spectrum of subjects: Kumbha mela in Allahabad; Gandhi's funeral; floods; trials of Nathu Ram Vinayak Godse; hungry mobs in Calcutta (1932); Italian prisoners in Bombay (1941); India greeting Lord Linlithgow, the new Viceroy (1936); salt uprising (1930); Dalai Lama receiving asylum in India; American supplies over the "hump" to China during World War II; foreign dignitaries visiting India; Indian leaders abroad; and various other newsworthy items.

Other gift items on South Asian subjects include the National Archive of India, Sir Stafford Cripps's Mission to India, Portuguese withdrawal from Goa, Indian troops in the Congo, and the India-Pakistan conflict over Kashmir.

RG 208: Records of the Office of War Information (1941–1945). Some 661 reels of informational propaganda and documentary films covering all phases and aspects of the war years. Newsreel footage in the collection includes "Indian News" released in India in 1945. South Asian coverage in the group is varied: Indian troops in North Africa, Simla conference (1946) on Indian independence and the future of the Raj, and panoramic views of Hindu religious ceremonies.

RG 242: National Archives Collection of Foreign Records Seized (1941–). The bulk of the materials in this group is on World War II and includes Japanese propaganda, documentation, and newsreels from the Burma-India front including some footage of British and Indian prisoners of war.

RG 286: Records of the Agency for International Development. This record group contains films of the International Cooperation Administration, consisting of a report to the American people on technical cooperation and illustrating U.S. assistance to India and Afghanistan in improving educational, agricultural, medical, and other techniques. Also included are films concerning U.S. military assistance programs to the now defunct South East Asia Treaty Organization (SEATO).

RG 306: Records of the United States Information Agency (1932–1955). Of the 368 reels of documentaries produced or acquired by the agency for distribution abroad, several deal with South Asia; e.g., Soviet Presidium and Russian propaganda in India, USIS "Atom for Peace" exhibitions in India and Pakistan, several Government of India scientific documentaries depicting mining and manufacturing of nuclear fuels in India, and a few instructional films that were used in technical assistance programs.

RG 326: Records of the Atomic Energy Commission. Includes a Government of India film on the Canada-India reactor illustrating India's political, social, and scientific reasons for joining with Canada under the Colombo Plan in a joint atomic energy research venture and the specific problems associated with building a high flux nuclear reactor in Trombay, India.

RG 342: Records of the United States Air Force Command's Activities and Organizations, 1900–1964. This group consists of 4,370 reels and includes films made in all theaters of operation during World War II concerning the activities of the Army Air Forces and all other aspects of the war. South Asian footage consists of an AAF Calcutta-Kunming supply operation (1944).

4. a. Audiovisual equipment is available for viewing; basic instruction in the use of the equipment is provided, but researchers must operate the machines themselves. Researchers are expected to use reasonable care when handling archival material.

b. It is advisable to make advance reservation for the use of audiovisual equipment and films. Requests for same-day service may require a long wait.

c. No fees are charged for the use of the facilities.

d. Reproduction of audiovisual film is available at a cost and requires prior scheduling. In cases of materials encumbered by copyright or other restrictions, prior written permission is needed. Researchers using their own equipment may reproduce materials at no cost in the media research room provided the material is in the public domain or prior written permission has been secured.

5. One indispensable bibliographic aid to the collection is the *Guide to the National Archives of the United States* (1974). Researchers may also consult *Motion Pictures in the Audiovisual Archives Division of the National Archives* (1972) prepared by Mayfield S. Bray and William T. Murphy and *Audiovisual Records in the National Archives Relating to World War II* (1974) also prepared by Bray and Murphy. Additional finding aids include card catalogs and preservation folders. It is appropriate to note here that researchers should consult the archivists of the branch for identifying and retrieving materials.

Note: The Stock Film Library Branch of the Audiovisual Archives Division (National Archives and Records Service), located at 1411 South Fern Street, Arlington, Virginia 22202, (703) 557-1114 (hours: 8:00 A.M.–4:30 P.M., Monday–Friday) contains a few footages on South Asia, including a 30-minute NASA film, *Images of Life—India.*

F13 National Archives and Records Service—Still Pictures Branch (Audiovisual Archives Division)

1. a. *8th Street and Pennsylvania Avenue, N.W.*
    Washington, D.C. 20408
    523-3236

    b. 8:45 A.M.–5:10 P.M.   Monday–Friday

    c. Open to scholars with a National Archives identification card obtainable from the Central Reference Division, Room 200-B

    d. Joseph Thomas, Chief

2.   The Still Picture Branch, which is one of the three components of the Audiovisual Archives Division (the other two being Motion Picture and Sound Recording Branch and Stock Film Branch), has a collection in excess of 5,000,000 items including black and white original and copy photographs, glass and film negatives, prints, color transparencies and negatives, stenographs, posters, art work, and photographs of art work dating from the seventeenth century. The holdings include the archival photograph files of over 140 U.S. federal agencies and several gift collections. Although the bulk of the material relates to the United States, the collection is also international in scope. South Asian materials in this collection are not very extensive; an accurate assessment is not possible since some materials are widely dispersed in different Record Groups.

3.   The following Record Groups contain materials relating to South Asia. The list here is not exhaustive and other Record Groups may also hold items of interest.
    RG 18: Records of the Army Air Forces (1901–1964). This extensive collection contains approximately 3,000 aerial, ground, and miniature photographs of South Asia, illustrating the activities of the Air Transport Command bases in India and Ceylon and showing physical features for guiding pilots along military routes in the China-Burma-India theater of war during World War II. Most of these photographs, taken from different altitudes, are of military installations and aviation facilities. Some of the items are: Gwador, Mauripur airport (Karachi), Jamshedpur, Umarkot, Jodhpur, Ajmir, Agra, New Delhi, Lalmanirhat, Bhagalpur, Gaya, Bangalore, Bombay, and Sikandra. A photograph of Calcutta taken by Russell Lee decorates the research room of the branch.
    RG 59: General Records of the Department of State (1774–1955). Materials in this group include photographs received by the Department of State from U.S. consular and diplomatic representatives on the subjects of trade activities, transportation facilities, farming, living conditions, industries of all kinds, and the buildings, bridges, docks, and ruins. Among the numerous items in this category are to be found, mostly undated, photographic documentations of all major cities of South Asia, dock facilities in the coastal regions, and details about certain selected industries and trade. Other materials in this Record Group consist of photographs of war surplus and lend-lease materials (1945–1949), illustrating the scope of early U.S. postwar aid to all parts of the world including South Asia. The collection

also contains photographs of Nixon's trip to South Asia and Nehru's visit to the U.S. Materials relating to South Asia also may be found in the department's collection of UNESCO activities (1945–1951) and among its materials on foreign diplomats (1943–1956).

RG 80: General Records of the Department of Navy (1788–1958). Still photographs in the group include navy bases and yards in foreign countries and photographs of foreign navies and scenes. There are several items of interest relevant to South Asia, such as one of the U.S.S. *Princeton* being loaded in Colombo, and pictures of other major port facilities in India and Pakistan.

RG 151: Records of the Bureau of Foreign and Domestic Commerce. Pictorial records in the collection (1899–1939) consist of photographs made in more than 80 countries relating to the functions of the bureau. The photographic holdings on India portray various phases of the economic life of the country.

RG 165: Records of the War Department General and Special Staffs. Included in the pictorial records of foreign military operations are photographs of Indian troops in China during the Boxer uprising in 1900–1901.

RG 169: Records of the Foreign Economic Administration (1943–1945). Included in the record group are a small number of photographs on agriculture in South Asia.

RG 200: National Archives Gift Collection. This group may contain some scattered materials relating to South Asia.

RG 208: Records of the Office of War Information (1941–1945). This group contains approximately 1,500 photographs on South Asia, a majority of which depict Indian soldiers fighting for the cause of the allies during World War II in Italy, Singapore, Arakan, and Assam valley. One of the photographs caught the emotional moment of an Indian soldier, of the 8th Indian Division, just returning home from Italy (September 1945) with death-filled years behind him, prostrating and kissing the soil of his native land. This group contains other South Asia-related pictures of merchant marines, native music, royal navy, refugees from Burma, religious scenes, transportation facilities, farming, hospitals, harbors, and native crafts. Some items of interest may also be found in the records of foreign dignitaries' postwar visits to the U.S.

RG 306: Records of the United States Information Agency (1900–1950). A unique and valuable still-picture collection in this Record Group is the photographic file of the Paris bureau of the *New York Times* (1900–1950), containing world-wide coverage of a broad range of subject matter from sports and fashions to military operations during the world wars and postwar developments. Among the materials of the Paris bureau, there are approximately 2,000 photographs, some of them unidentified and undated, of South Asian subjects. Most of the annotation in the file is in French. A few examples of these South Asian pictorial records are: the royal palaces in Kabul and Seistan, mosques and tombs in several locations in Afghanistan, training of the military in Afghanistan, Gandhara sculptures, Indo-Afghan frontier (1935), Afghan royalty, Afghan insurgents (1936), Swastika League training camp in Bombay (1930), portraits of Gandhi, Liaquat Ali Khan, Gaffar Khan and other eminent public figures, Cabinet Mission (1946), political agitation in Calcutta (1931), and photographs of political rallies.

Other South Asian materials in this Record Group contain more than

200 miscellaneous items in the general file depicting the life and culture of the people of South Asia and various aspects of U.S. collaboration in developmental activities. Subject matter of these still pictures varies: Indian housewives demonstrating outside the New Delhi Legislative Assembly to protest the rising cost of living (1952), "atoms for peace" exhibitions, cobra dances, and a sacred thread ceremony.

4.   Various types of audiovisual equipment are available for use in the research room without charge. Reproduction facilities are also available for materials not restricted by copyright or other reasons. Researchers are also allowed to use their own equipment for duplication or enlargement purposes.

5.   Researchers should consult the *Guide to the National Archives* (1974) and *Still Pictures in the Audiovisual Archives Division of the National Archives* (1972) compiled by Mayfield S. Bray. Several other card indexes, preliminary inventories, and folders are also available for different Record Groups. None of these sources is exhaustive, and it is therefore indispensable for a researcher to consult an archivist in the branch.

F14 Embassy of Pakistan—Information Division

1.   a. *2315 Massachusetts Avenue, N.W.*
   Washington, D.C. 20008
   332-8330

   b. 9:00 A.M.–5:00 P.M.   Monday–Friday

   c. Open to the public by appointment

   d. Naseer Tareen, Film Section

2-4.   This film collection consists of some 22 documentaries showing the geography, culture, antiquity, and history of Pakistan. Specific titles include *Hunza, Kafiristan, Gilgit, The Karokorum Range, Gandhara, Moenjodaro, The Indus River,* and an account of the Islamic Summit held in Lahore in 1974. All films may be borrowed. Limited screening facilities are also available at the embassy.

5.   A film catalog, *Documentaries from Pakistan,* is available free.

Senate Historical Office Photo Archive See entry J29

F15 United Nations Information Centre—Film Collection

1.   a. *2101 L Street, N.W.*
   Washington, D.C. 20037
   296-5370

   b. 9:00 A.M.–1:00 P.M.   Monday–Friday

   c. The center makes the U.N. films available on loan to individuals and organizations for a period of one week.

d. Vera Gathright, Reference Librarian

2-3. This collection consists of some 120 16mm films. Titles of interest include *Asia: Two Thirds and Counting; India: Population 500 Million; Malaria: Images of Reality*; and several titles on human rights and socio-economic growth in the Third World.

4. Reservations for films should be made one week in advance of the date the film is required. No fees are charged for the use of films. All U.N. films are available for purchase.

5. A free catalog of the center's film collection, *Films Available for Distribution* (1980), is updated periodically. *Films of the United Nations Family* (1980–1981), which is a comprehensive catalog of all films made by the different U.N. agencies, is also available free at the center. The latter catalog has a geographic and a subject index.

F16 World Bank Photo Library

1. a. *801 19th Street, N.W.*
Washington, D.C. 20433
676-1638

b. 9:00 A.M.–5:00 P.M.   Monday–Friday

c. Open to the public by appointment only

d. Leah Suffin, Photo Librarian

2-5. The photo library contains over 40,000 35mm color slides and 12,000 black-and-white prints relating to some 70 developing countries of the world. The collection has been developed from the photographs taken in conjunction with World Bank overseas projects. Major subject areas are agriculture, industry, social services, and transportation. India, Pakistan, Sri Lanka and Bangladesh are well represented in the collection. Photographs may be freely reproduced and used for nonadvertising purposes but must be properly acknowledged.

A World Bank photo library catalog lists the countries, categories, and photo-type (color slide or black-and-white print) available, and is free upon request. The library also maintains a card catalog, organized by country, and is preparing a subject catalog which it hopes to computerize in the future.

G Data Banks

A large number of Washington area libraries, government agencies, academic institutions and research organizations maintain their own series of subscriptions to a wide variety of data banks that can be drawn upon throughout the U.S. and, in many cases, throughout the world. The listing included here is primarily of those data-base systems that are developed or prepared in Washington and contain significant resource material, which could be of interest to South Asian specialists. Due to the nature of the medium, it is not surprising that the vast majority of the collections listed below deals with scientific or economic data.

Data Banks Entry Format (G)

1. General Information
    a. *address; telephone numbers*
    b. hours of service
    c. conditions of access (including fees charged for information retrieval)
    d. name/title of director and key staff members

2. Description of Data Files (hard data and bibliographic references) Pertaining to South Asia

3. Bibliographic Aids Facilitating Use of Storage Media

G1 Agency for International Development (AID)—Economic and Social Data Services Division (ESDS)

1. a. *Room 633 Pomponio Plaza (SA—14)*
    1735 North Lynn Street
    Arlington, Virginia 22209
    (703) 235-9170

    b. 8:45 A.M.–5:30 P.M.   Monday–Friday

    c. This data bank is primarily for the use of AID personnel. Private scholars may use the facility by prior arrangement.

    d. Annette Binnendijk, Acting Chief

2. The Economic and Social Data Services Division is a service-oriented division that provides other AID offices and missions with quantitative indicators, relevant to AID's policy, program, and reporting needs, of economic and social development in less developed countries. The Division also provides analytical expertise in the use and interpretation of the data. A related responsibility is to serve as the AID management focal-point for agency-financed data collection and survey activities. For example, ESDS monitors an interagency contract with the U.S. Bureau of the Census to support regional bureaus, missions, and host governments in collecting and compiling survey data for their project development and evaluation needs.

    A major function of ESDS is the maintenance and improvement of the agency's macro Economic and Social Data Bank (ESDB), an automated system for the storage, analysis, and dissemination of country-level economic and social data relevant to AID's policy and program needs. The data available from ESDB is usually aggregate in nature, representing national averages, although occasionally it is available for breaking the information down into categories as rural-urban, sex, or age-specific data. The data bank currently includes about 450 variables for a 30-year time series (1950–1980) for up to 170 countries.

    Data is available in the following categories: social (population, living conditions, and social-service statistics); economic (labor force, national accounts, and price statistics); financial (government finance, balance of payments, trade, and debt statistics); and agricultural (production statistics by commodity). The computerized data comes mostly from international organizations, data banks of other U.S. government agencies, private institutions, and universities.

    Another area of ESDS activities is in the micro data or individual household level data. However, implementation is still in the design stage.

3. Much of the data is available in hard copy form. An informative brochure, *Briefing Paper on the Activities of the Economic and Social Data Services Division* (1980) is available on request.

G2 Agency for International Development (AID)—Office of Development Information and Utilization (DIU)

1. a. *Room 509 Pomponio Plaza (SA—14)*
    1735 North Lynn Street
    Arlington, Virginia 22209
    (703) 235-9207

    b. 8:45 A.M.–5:30 P.M.   Monday–Friday

    c. DIU's data bases are primarily maintained for the use of AID project designers, field project managers, and contract researchers. Private researchers may, however, also have access to the system with a prior appointment.

    d. Lida Allen, Director

2. DIU's computerized storage and retrieval system contains several data components. The Development Information system consists of project-specific

information on more than 2,000 AID-funded or supported projects. This data includes the project number, title, a summary of the project, some financial information, project designs, feasibility studies, evaluation documents, and task force reports.

The Research and Development Report system contains over 9,000 titles from AID-supported research. Subject and country searches may be run on the computer for the Research and Development Reports, and copies may be ordered in paper or microfiche from the AID R&D Report Distribution Center, P.O. Box 353, Norfolk, Virginia 23501.

The Economic and Social Data system maintains combined economic and social data from IBRD, IMF, USDA, and AID sources for virtually all countries covering, in most cases, a 20-year period.

The Economic and Social Data system provides data analysis services for researchers, analysts, economists, and project designers in developing areas of specific concern.

In addition, the DIU contracts—or makes other working arrangements—with the USDA, Bureau of the Census, Department of Commerce, and organizations such as Volunteers in Technical Assistance (see entry M34) to allow rapid access to additional specialized information of priority interest to AID.

3. DIU is working now on a *Ready Data Book,* which will provide selected economic and social data in policy and sectoral areas of priority interest on a regular basis, for each AID country and region.

G3 Agency for International Development (AID)—Program Data Services Division

1. a. *Room 625 Pomponio Plaza (SA—14)*
1735 North Lynn Street
Arlington, Virginia 22209
(703) 235-9167

   b. 8:45 A.M.–5:30 P.M.   Monday–Friday

   c. This data bank is primarily for the use of the AID personnel. Private scholars should call in advance for possible access to the data bank.

   d. Anna K. Lee, Chief

2. The Program Data Services Division maintains a comprehensive data bank of all bilateral and multilateral assistance abroad from the United States and international organizations. The data includes economic and military assistance from the U.S., assistance from the Export-Import Bank, PL 480 aid data from the Commodity Credit Corporation, and records of assistance provided by international organizations.

3. The data bank is also available in printed form as the AID annually updated publication, *U.S. Overseas Loans and Grants and Assistance from International Organizations: Obligations and Loan Authorization, July 1945—.* Copies of a discontinued periodical, *Operations Report,* which contains extensive data on U.S. economic assistance programs to South Asia, are available for reference use in the division.

G4 Agriculture Department—Data Services Center

1. a. *500 12th Street, S.W.*
   Washington, D.C. 20250
   447-7577

   b. 8:30 A.M.–5:00 P.M.   Monday–Friday

   c. The data base is maintained primarily for internal use; researchers should make special arrangement before visiting the center.

   d. Marge Bever, International Coordinator

2. The center's data files contain indexes of world agricultural production from 1950 to the present compiled by the United States Department of Agriculture; USDA-generated data on international grain-crop acreage and yields; international trade data compiled by the United Nations (1967–present); trade and production data (1961–1974) compiled by the United Nations Food and Agriculture Organization (FAO); and population data by country (1950–present) compiled by the U.S. Agency for International Development.

   In addition, the Data Systems Development Division (Eldon Hildebrandt, Director, 447-5255), of the department's Foreign Agricultural Service, maintains USDA-generated machine-readable data on foreign agricultural production, supply and distribution from 1960 to present; and extensive U.S. Census Bureau data on U.S. trade with foreign countries.

Census Bureau (Commerce Department) Data Base See entry G5

G5 Commerce Department Data Bases

1. a. *14th Street and Constitution Avenue, N.W.*
   Washington, D.C. 20230
   377-2000

   b. 8:30 A.M.–5:00 P.M.   Monday–Friday

   c. Most data is accessible to the public; some services are free.

   d. Listed with the appropriate units below

2. No single facility stores all of the machine-readable bases generated within the Department of Commerce. Data files containing South Asian materials are available in several departmental bureaus and offices.

   BUREAU OF THE CENSUS: The Population Division's Demographic Data Retrieval System (DDRS) contains unevaluated demographic data consisting primarily of census reports, demographic surveys, and government publications containing vital statistics for all developing countries. The data base also contains the results of selected demographic data analyzed by demographers in the Census Bureau. Some U.N. data not generally found in published sources are also included. The data base is on microfilm.

Data tables from the sources mentioned above are microfilmed, and each table is coded according to its cross classification of data variables, date of information, and country name. The basic demographic topics selected for the data base include: population composition and characteristics; population dynamics, including fertility, mortality, migration, marriage, and divorce; population projections; educational attainment and school enrollment; and labor force characteristics. Service from the DDRS is free of charge unless a large amount of photocopying is required. Researchers may contact Martha A. Barger (301/763-2834) for further information on the DDRS data bases.

The bureau's Foreign Trade Division can make available magnetic tapes containing statistics of the United States trade with South Asian countries. The division's Trade Information Branch (301/763-5140) can provide order forms and further details. Researchers may contact the division's Special Reports Branch (301/763-7700) for obtaining tapes of import and export statistics designed to meet specific research needs.

BUREAU OF ECONOMIC ANALYSIS: The bureau's Data Retrieval and Analysis Branch (523-0652) within the International Investment Division, compiles data on U.S. private investments abroad. Computer tapes of some of the crude data collected by the division are available on a commercial basis. In addition, the bureau's Balance of Payment Division (523-0621) may make available to researchers copies of tapes containing data on the balance of payments between the U.S. and South Asian countries.

BUREAU OF EXPORT DEVELOPMENT (International Trade Administration): The bureau's Trade Information Services Division (377-4532) compiles the *Foreign Traders Index,* which contains data on non-U.S. foreign business firms and products in various areas of the world including South Asia.

NATIONAL BUREAU OF STANDARDS (NBS): NBS maintains a highly technical National Standard Reference Data System (NSRDS) (301/921-2228). It assesses data reported in primary research literature on the physical and chemical properties of well-characterized materials or systems, and prepares compilations of critically evaluated data that serve as reliable standards for the scientific and technical community. Copies of the *National Standard Reference Data System Publications List, 1964–1977* are available free on request.

The bureau's Standard Information Service (SIS) (301/921-2587) maintains a reference collection of engineering and related standards, which include standards and specifications of the major foreign and international standardizing bodies. By means of a computer-produced key-word-in-context index, SIS has generated from the data in its files a publication of special interest for overseas users—the *Index of International Standards,* copies of which may be obtained from the Government Printing Office or the National Technical Information Service.

NATIONAL OCEANIC AND ATOMSPHERIC ADMINISTRATION (NOAA): The Environmental Data and Information Service (EDIS) (634-7236) maintains computer-searchable interdisciplinary files of environmental data in a system of data bases known as Environmental Data Index (ENDEX). These bases can be searched by geographic area, type of data, name of the institution holding the data, and projects. EDIS provides users with rapid, computerized referral to available environmental data files, published literature and on-going research projects in the atmospheric sciences, marine and coastal studies, and a wide range of other subjects. The *Guide to NOAA's Computerized Information Retrieval Services* (1979) is available free on request from the EDIS Publications and Media Staff (634-7305).

G6 Defense Documentation Center (Defense Department)

1. a. *Cameron Station*
    Alexandria, Virginia 22314
    (703) 274-7633

    b. 7:30 A.M.–4:00 P.M. Monday–Friday

    c. The center primarily serves the Defense Department components, research and development activities within the U.S. government, and their associated contractors, subcontractors, and grantees with current government contracts. DDC serves the general public indirectly, where unclassified or unlimited documents are concerned, through a special arrangement with the National Technical Information Service (NTIS). By this arrangement with the NTIS, DDC provides copies of these research and development reports which are sponsored, cosponsored, or generated by the Department of Defense.

    Additionally, reports which were formerly classified or limited are furnished as soon as they are declassified and made available through this program. More than half of the technical reports received in DDC are made available through this special arrangement. NTIS announces the DDC reports released to it through its *Government Reports Announcements and Indexes*. DDC responds to inquiries from individual researchers asking information concerning the availability of technical reports that are not in the public domain. If a report cannot be identified as a Defense Department-generated report, the DDC representative contacts other government and nongovernment agencies to locate and determine availability, cost, and other pertinent data to provide complete information to the requester.

    d. Hubert E. Sauter, Administrator

2. The Defense Documentation Center acts as the clearinghouse for the Defense Department's collections of research and development in virtually all fields of science and technology, including behavioral and social sciences. The four data banks in DDC are: R&D Program Planning Data Bank (R&DPP)—a repository of research and program-planning documentation at the project and task level; R&T Work Unit Information System Data Bank (WUIS)— a collection of technically oriented summaries describing research and technology projects currently in progress at the work unit level; Technical Report Data Bank (TR)—a collection of formally documented scientific and technical results of Department of Defense-sponsored research, development, test, and evaluation; Independent Research and Development Data Bank (IR&D)—a data bank of information describing the technical programs being performed by Department of Defense con-

tractors as part of their independent research and development programs. The strength of the collection is in the physical sciences, technology, and engineering as they relate to national defense and military matters. Some social-science research on international affairs, including South Asia, may also be in the facility.

3.   An unclassified *DDC digest* is distributed free, announcing plans, changes in service, new DDC publications, and other developments in the scientific and technical information field. The publications, *Users Guide* and the *Organizations which Provide, Certify, and Approve Access to Scientific and Technical Information* of the DDC, are available free on request. Additionally a DDC registration kit includes an explanation of the various forms required to request services and other informational materials concerning programs, products, and services offered by the center.

G7 Educational Resources Information Center (ERIC)

1.   a. *National Institute of Education (Department of Education)*
        1200 19th Street, N.W.
        Washington, D.C. 20208
        254-5500

      b. 8:00 A.M.–4:30 P.M.   Monday–Friday

      c. Open to the public; fee schedules vary for different services. ERIC data bases may be accessed from many university libraries, state departments of education, educational information centers, research centers, and commercial organizations. The ERIC Processing and Reference Facility is located at 4833 Rugby Avenue, Bethesda, Maryland 20014 (301/656-9723).

      d. Robert Chesley, Head

2.   ERIC is a national information system supported and operated by the National Institute of Education (NIE), for providing ready access to descriptions of exemplary programs, research and development efforts, and related information that can be used in developing more effective educational programs.

      There are 16 clearinghouses in the nationwide ERIC network. Each specializes in a different, multidiscipline, educational area. Each searches out pertinent documents: current research findings, project and technical reports, speeches and unpublished manuscripts, books, and professional journal articles. These materials are screened according to ERIC selection criteria, abstracted, and indexed. All of this information is put into the ERIC computer data base and announced in the ERIC reference publications. Through these sources any person interested in education has easy access to reports of innovative programs, conference proceedings, bibliographies, outstanding professional papers, curriculum-related materials, and reports of the most significant efforts in educational research and development regardless of where they first appeared.

3.   Useful bibliographic aids include: *A Bibliography of Publications about the Educational Resources Information Center, How to Use ERIC, Directory*

of *ERIC Microfiche Collections, Directory of ERIC Search Services,* and *ERIC Information Analysis Products.*

Note: Also see entry J10.

Energy Department Data Base See entry J11

Health and Human Services Department Data Base See entry J16

Interior Department Data Base See entry J18

G8 International Bank for Reconstruction and Development (World Bank)—Data Systems

1.   a. *1818 H Street, N.W.*
Washington, D.C. 20433
676-1811

  b. 9:00 A.M.–5:00 P.M.   Monday–Friday

  c. The World Bank maintains a variety of data systems for internal use. Copies of magnetic tapes are exchanged with U.S. government agencies and other international organizations, and are made available to private users (universities, research centers, individual scholars) upon request, at little or no charge.

  d. Ramesh Chander, Adviser, Data Systems
676-1822

2-3.   The World Bank's Economic Analysis and Projections Department transfers a broad spectrum of statistical data into machine-readable format. The Systems and Methods Division (Jean-Paul Dailly, Chief, 676-9083) manages the operation of the data systems while the following sectoral divisions develop and maintain the data sets and may provide information to scholars about the contents and utilization capabilities of the data. National accounts, social indicators, trade (prepared by GATT) and industrial development data are under the Economic and Social Data Division (Sang Eun Lee, Chief, 676-1837). Capital markets data are prepared by the International Trade and Capital Flows Division (Francis X. Colaco, Chief, 676-1901). Commodities and commodity price data are assembled and maintained by the Commodities and Export Projections Division (Choeng H. Chung, Chief, 676-0049). Data on public borrowing, external indebtedness and balance-of-payments by country are prepared by the External Debt Division (Catherine Slappey, Chief, 676-1862), with country modeling undertaken by the Comparative Analysis and Projections Division (Nicholas G. Carter, Chief, 676-1924).
The statistics and other information used to prepare these data systems are drawn from various sources including the following bank publications: *Borrowing in International Capital Markets* (quarterly); *Commodity Trade and Price Trends* (annual); *Economic and Social Indicators* (quarterly); *The*

World Bank Atlas (annual); *World Bank Commodity Working Papers* (occasional); *World Bank Country Studies* (occasional); *World Bank Staff Working Papers* (occasional); *The World Debt Tables* (annual); *The World Tables* (triennial); *The World Bank Annual Report* (annual); and the *World Development Report* (annual).

International Communication Agency Data Base See entry J19

G9 International Monetary Fund (IMF)—Data Bank

1. a. *700 19th Street, N.W.*
   Washington, D.C. 20431
   477–3207

   b. 9:00 A.M.–5:00 P.M.   Monday–Friday

   c. The IMF programs data from 4 of its statistical publications into machine-readable form. Copies of magnetic tapes are made available on a commercial-subscription basis. Each subscription consists of 12 monthly tapes, the corresponding IMF book publication that serves as a guide to the contents of the tape, and documentation and instructions on how to use the data and programs contained on the tape.

   d. Robert L. Kline, Chief, Data Fund Division

2-3.   *International Finance Statistics* tape subscriptions contain approximately 16,000 time series, including series appearing in the IMF's published *International Finance Statistics* country pages and world tables, exchange-rate series, and international liquidity series for all countries, and 14 major series on countries' relationships with the IMF. Annual entries begin in 1948, quarterly and monthly entries at later dates.
   Direction of Trade tapes subscriptions contain approximately 42,000 time series reported in the IMF's published *Direction of Trade* country pages. Data include sources of imports and destination of exports for some 150 countries. Annual entries begin in 1948 and quarterly entries in 1969. All series are expressed in millions of U.S. dollars.
   Balance of Payments tape subscriptions consist of about 35,000 time series on balance-of-payment components and aggregates covering 116 countries. Of these time series, some 33,000 correspond to data in the IMF's published *Balance of Payments Yearbook,* with annual data beginning in 1965 or later. The other 2,000 time series are long-term data series often extending back to the mid-1950's.
   Government Finance Statistics tape subscriptions contain approximately 13,000 annual time series of data reported in the IMF's published *Government Finance Statistics Yearbook.* Included are data on revenues, expenditures, grants, lending, financing, debts, and social security funds.

Joint Publications Research Service Data Base See entry P14

Library of Congress Data Base See entry A23

G10 Machine Readable Archives Division (National Archives and Records Services)

1. a. *711 14th Street, N.W.*
    Washington, D.C. 20408
    724-1080

    b. 8:45 A.M.–5:15 P.M. Monday–Friday

    c. Open to the public; substantial fees are charged for documentation and computer processing. The reproduction service for files in the division's holdings is presently limited to copying from card to card, tape to card, card to tape, tape to tape, tape to printout, extracts of specific information, and electrostatic copying of documentation. A fee schedule is available on request.

    d. Charles M. Dollar, Director

2. Originated in 1969, the Machine Readable Archives Division maintains magnetic tape records of archival value as received from various U.S. government agencies. These records may have been created for specific projects or may be part of a continuing data-collection program. Record Groups (RG) in the division, which may contain South Asia related materials, are listed below.

    RG 77: Records of the Office of the Chief of Engineers—domestic and international transportation of U.S. foreign trade. Contains records of 44,502 commodity shipments in U.S. foreign trade during 1970 by world areas, states, custom districts, and production and market areas. The survey that yielded the data contained in this file was sponsored jointly by the Department of Transportation and the U.S. Army Corps of Engineers and was conducted by the Census Bureau.

    RG 90: Records of the Public Health Service—World Health Organization—international collaborative study of medical care utilization (1968–1969). This study grew out of meetings held under World Health Organization auspices in 1963–1964. Records may contain some scattered materials on South Asia.

    RG 166: Records of the Foreign Agricultural Service—U.S. agricultural imports and exports trade history. U.S. agricultural imports and exports statistics are derived from the foreign-trade-statistics program conducted by the Bureau of the Census. The period covered is from January 1967 to June 1974.

3. *A Catalog of Machine Readable Records in the National Archives of the United States* is available without charge.

National Agricultural Library Data Base See entry A26

National Library of Medicine Data Base See entry A29

G11 National Space Science Data Center (National Aeronautics and Space Administration)

1. a. *Building 26*
    Goddard Space Flight Center
    Greenbelt, Maryland 20771
    (301) 344-7354

    b. 8:00 A.M.–4:30 P.M.   Monday–Friday

    c. Open to researchers by appointment; there is normally no charge for outside researchers to use the data bases at the center.

    d. James I. Vette, Director

2. The National Space Science Data Center maintains bibliographic information, substantive reports, technical data, and other materials on space programs of the United States and certain foreign countries including India. Information concerning Indian spacecraft launchings may be found in two files: Automated Internal Management file, and the Committee for Space Resources (COSPAR) reports file.

3. *Data and Distribution Services,* a basic guide to the center, is available on request.

National Technical Information Service (Commerce Department)
See entry J6

G12 *New York Times* Information Bank—Washington Office

1. a. *1111 19th Street North*
    Arlington, Virginia 22209
    (703) 243-7220

    b. 9:00 A.M.–5:00 P.M.   Monday–Friday

    c. Open to the public; researchers may utilize, for a fee, the Retail Service of the Information Bank.

    d. Sharon Taylor, Regional Manager

2. The *New York Times* Information Bank contains more than 2,000,000 abstracts of news stories, editorials, and other significant items published in the *New York Times* since 1959, and some 55 national and international periodicals. The bank may be searched by geographic and by a variety of other subject and name indicators. Abstracts vary in length from 3 to 50 lines.

3. An information flyer describing the bank, its services, and its sources is available free on request.

Smithsonian Science Information Exchange (Smithsonian Institution) See entry J30

Transportation Department Data Base See entry J32

G13 United Nations Environment Program (UNEP)—International Referral System (INFOTERRA)

1. a. *U.S. Environmental Protection Agency—U.S. International Environmental Referral Center (USIERC)*
    401 M Street, S.W. (PM 213)
    Washington, D.C. 20460
    755-1836

    b. 8:00 A.M.–4:30 P.M. Monday–Friday

    c. Open to the public; the services provided by INFOTERRA are free.

    d. Charlene S. Sayers, Source Coordinator

2. In 1972 the Stockholm Conference on the Human Environment set up an International Referral System to direct the flow of environmental information from those who have it to those who need it. The over-all purpose of INFOTERRA is to ensure that, in making important decisions in relation to the environment, governments and others will have access to the latest scientific and technical data and expertise. INFOTERRA neither stores information nor answers substantive questions; its task is simply to enable the potential user of environmental information to locate the most appropriate source of the information required. This it does by employing a network of government-designated National Focal Points (NFP's) which feed the names of potential sources of environmental information into the INFOTERRA international directory and assist users in their own countries to identify the sources to which they need to refer.

    Over 7,000 sources of environmental information have been classified into approximately 1,000 computer-coded subject areas, from which the required list of sources to contact can be provided to the inquirer. In 1975 USIERC was named as the U.S. National Focal Point. National Focal Points have been functioning in Bangladesh, India, Pakistan, and Sri Lanka. When an NFP receives a question, it codes the question and carries out a manual or computer search of the international directory for the relevant sources of information. NFPs without local access to a computer may also forward the question to the system's central data bank in Geneva, Switzerland. Once a computer search has identified the information sources, the user may contact the sources directly for substantive information. NFPs have enabled each cooperating nation to develop self-reliance for its information needs and to promote global cooperation for improving the flow of information about the environment.

3. Several brochures describing the INFOTERRA data base and the UNEP are available from USIERC.

ORGANIZATIONS

H Research Centers

Although a number of the nation's most prestigious research organizations are located in the area, only those research centers having programs relevant to South Aisa, or maintain staffs, consultants, and associates who are knowledgeable about South Asian matters, have been included in this section. The list here is by no means comprehensive. For locating research centers not included in this section, scholars may contact the Commerce Department, which monitors foreign contracts obtained by U.S. firms. They may also consult the lists prepared by various government agencies (particularly the State Department, Agency for International Development, International Communication Agency, and the Defense Department) for contracts awarded by the U.S. government agencies for work on or in foreign countries.

In approaching the entries in this section, scholars may be cautioned that, not unlike the federal government departments and agencies, programs and personnel in the research centers may undergo frequent changes. Many research centers introduce new research programs on the basis of current interests or availability of funds. Personnel brought into a research institution for a specific research program may leave after the conclusion of the project, thereby effecting an institutional change in the area of research emphasis.

Research Centers Entry Format (H)

1. *Address; Telephone Numbers*

2. Name and Title of Chief Official

3. Programs and Research Activities Pertaining to South Asia

4. Library and Research Facilities

5. Publications

H1 Advanced International Studies Institute (AISI) (University of Miami)

1. *East-West Towers*
    4330 East-West Highway
    Washington, D.C. 20014
    951-0818

2. Mose L. Harvey, Director and Senior Analyst

3. AISI was established in 1978 as a nonprofit research and educational organization in association with the University of Miami at Coral Gables, Florida. AISI conducts research and publishes in the area of international affairs and U.S. foreign policy, with primary focus on the Soviet Union. The institute also sponsors various workshops, conferences, and seminars dealing with international affairs. AISI's limited interest in South Asia is viewed from the perspective of the Soviet Union's goals and strategy in that region. Researchers may contact Morris Rothenberg (Senior Analyst) for information concerning the institute's research activities relevant to South Asia.

4. The institute maintains a small reference collection. Researchers may use the collection by special arrangement.

5. Publications include occasional papers and monographs on international affairs; *Research Notes* (monthly); *Soviet World Outlook* (monthly); and *Special Reports,* which provide time-sensitive responses to newly arising critical issues or developments affecting U.S. international interests and objectives.

H2 American Enterprise Institute for Public Policy Research (AEI)

1. *1150 17th Street, N.W.*
    Washington, D.C. 20036
    862-5800

2. William J. Baroody, President
    Robert J. Pranger, Director of Foreign and Defense Policy Studies

3. The AEI, established in 1943, is an independent, nonprofit, nonpartisan, research and educational organization that studies public-policy issues, both national and foreign. Through its continuing series of Public Policy Forums, the institute features scholarly discussions on major public policy problems of current interest. Proceedings of the forums are available in cassettes and films. The forum programs are also broadcast across the country. In addition, the AEI sponsors conferences on issues of vital public interest. The institute offers an associates' program and a small number of fellowships to visiting scholars for research.

4. The institute's small reference library (Evelyn Caldwell, 862-5831) of some 15,000 volumes is open to the public by appointment only.

5. AEI publications of interest include: Myron Weiner, *India at the Polls: The Parliamentary Elections of 1977* (1978); Muhammad Abdul Rauf, *The Islamic Doctrine of Economics and Contemporary Economic Thought: Highlights of a Conference.* The institute also publishes several periodicals, namely, *The AEI Economist* (monthly); *AEI Foreign Policy and Defense Review* (bimonthly); and *Memoranda* (quarterly). A catalog, *New Publications* (1980), and an informative booklet, *Public Policy Forums,* are available on request.

H3 American University—Foreign Area Studies (FAS)

1. *5010 Wisconsin Avenue, N.W.*
    Washington, D.C. 20016
    686-2769

2. William Evans-Smith, Director

3. Operating under a contract between the American University and the U.S. Department of the Army, the FAS compiles over 100 area handbooks or country studies of foreign countries including Afghanistan, Bangladesh, Sri Lanka, India, Pakistan, Nepal, Bhutan and Sikkim. The central concern of each study is the contemporary society. Particular attention is given to the various elements of that society, such as origins and traditions, dominant beliefs and values, the community of interests and forms of association, and the nature of access to economic and political power. Considerations are also focused on the expectations of the people, their affections and disaffections, and their attitudes toward each other, toward the social, political, enconomic, and national security systems under which they live, and toward the conditions of their daily life. Country studies are prepared by interdisciplinary research teams of scholars at FAS.

4. The FAS library of some 7,000 volumes of reference books and periodicals is accessible to private researchers by previous appointment.

5. A listing of the country studies is available on request. Copies of the country studies may be purchased from the sales outlets of the U.S. Government Printing Office.

H4 Aspen Institute for Humanistic Studies

1. *2010 Massachusetts Avenue, N.W.*
    Washington, D.C. 20036
    466-6410

2. Stephen P. Strickland, Vice President

3. The New York-based Aspen Institute for Humanistic Studies (717 Fifth Avenue, New York, New York 10022, 212/759-1053) is an independent, international, nonpartisan, and nonprofit organization that considers contemporary issues from a human-centered viewpoint. International affairs covers a range of concerns from arms control to concepts of basic human needs and fulfillment and the impact of the interrelationship between the industrialized countries and the developing nations. The institute's activities have included seminars on Asian thought, including South Asian themes.

5.   Inquiries concerning Aspen's publications may be addressed to the institute's Publication Office, P.O. Box 150, Queenstown, Maryland 21658.

H5 Atlantic Council of the United States

1.   *1616 H Street, N.W.*
Washington, D.C. 20006
347-9353

2.   Kenneth Rush, Chairman

3.   The Atlantic Council is a bipartisan, nonprofit, educational organization that seeks to promote closer mutually advantageous ties among the nations and individuals of the Atlantic community. It conducts its program to promote understanding of major, international security, political, and economic problems; to foster public debates on these issues; and to make substantive policy recommendations to both the executive and legislative branches of the U.S. government, as well as to appropriate key international organizations.
      The council is currently planning an extensive project on world food production and use in relation to economic development and population growth. The council's working group on development policy has conducted an investigation on the problems and opportunities shared by the countries of the Atlantic community with respect to the developing world, particular emphasis being placed on U.S. policies. In another study, the council's working group on security studies has reviewed the recent developments in Afghanistan and their implications for U.S. security problems.

4.   The council maintains a specialized working library of over 1,500 volumes, 150 periodicals and U.S. government and international documents. These materials are available for scholars and practitioners in international relations.

5.   The council's publications in the security series include: *The United States and the Developing Countries* (1977), and *After Afghanistan—The Long Haul: Safeguarding Security and Independence in the Third World* (1980). The council also publishes a monthly newsletter, *The Atlantic Community News,* and the *Atlantic Community Quarterly.*

H6 Battelle Memorial Institute—Washington Operations

1.   *2030 M Street, N.W.*
Washington, D.C. 20036
785-8400

2.   George B. Johnson, Director

3.   An independent, nonprofit, research organization with headquarters in Columbus, Ohio (614/424-4533), the Battelle Memorial Institute seeks to achieve the advancement and utilization of science through technological innovation and educational activities. Research in the metropolitan area

includes population studies. Since 1977 Battelle has become involved in demographic research and technical assistance operations through its Population and Development Policy Program (Leonard Robinson, Director). The program focuses on several social and economic issues related to the determinants of fertility, the changing status and roles of women, consequences of family size for personal and family welfare, population impact analysis, and difficulties in effective population and family planning programs. Although the institute has no definitive program involving the countries of South Asia, it is currently exploring the possibilities of doing some work in Pakistan and Sri Lanka.

4. Population and Development Policy Program is developing a library containing staff reports, working papers, policy papers, and reference books in the field of population studies. The collection may be consulted by prior arrangement.

5. Several brochures and newsletters, including one describing the Population and Development Policy Program, are available on request.

H7 Brookings Institution

1. *1775 Massachusetts Avenue, N.W.*
    Washington, D.C. 20036
    797-6000

2. Bruce K. MacLaury, President

3. The Brookings Institution is a private, nonprofit organization devoted to research, education, and publishing in economics, government, foreign policy, and the social sciences generally. Its activities are carried out through these research programs: Economic Studies, Governmental Studies, Foreign Policy Studies; an Advanced Study Program; a Social Science Computer Center; and a Publication Program.

    For identifying issues for study, the institution conducts continual reviews of its fields of interest. Subjects are selected for study on the basis of their significance and timeliness, among other criteria. With the exception of two studies on food and transportation problems in India, no other substantial South Asia-related research has been conducted at Brookings. Brookings's educational activities include fellowships and guest scholar appointments awarded to faculty members, graduate students, and others whose research is related to the purposes of the institution. Brookings's Social Science Computer Center provides computing services for Brookings and other nonprofit organizations engaged in social science research.

4. Brookings maintains a specialized library of books and periodicals designed to meet the needs of its research programs. Its current holdings include 60,000 volumes, 500 periodical titles, vertical files of pamphlets and government documents, and a selective United Nations collection. A program of on-line data-base bibliographic searching facilitates research activities in

the institution. Use of the library is restricted to resident staff members and guests.

5. Brookings has an extensive publications program. Titles of interest include: *Food Trends and Prospects in India* (1979); *Nuclear Arms in the Third World: U.S. Policy Dilemma* (1979); *Technology for Developing Nations: New Directions for U.S. Technical Assistance* (1972); *Distance and Development: Transport and Communication in India* (1968); and *World Politics and International Economics* (1975). The Brookings annual report, program description, and publications list are available on request.

H8 Business Council for International Understanding (BCIU) Institute (American University)

1. *3301 New Mexico Avenue, N.W.*
    Washington, D.C. 20016
    686-2771

2. Gary E. Lloyd, Director

3. BCIU Institute of American University conducts programs to prepare U.S. and foreign business executives and their families to effectively work and live in other cultures. The institute provides workshops monthly for personnel from international organizations. Its program consists of language instruction, intercultural communications workshops, and area studies. Programs are developed according to perceived needs. Recently a program was conducted on Afghanistan.

5. Program information kits are available on request.

H9 Carnegie Endowment for International Peace—Washington Office

1. *11 Dupont Circle, N.W.*
    Washington, D.C. 20036
    797-6400

2. Thomas L. Hughes, President

3. An operating foundation, the Carnegie Endowment for International Peace conducts its programs of research, discussion, publication, and education in international affairs and American foreign policy. Program activities change periodically; recently they have included international law and organizations and precrisis fact-finding on selected issues in South Asia. Carnegie's International Fact-Finding Center is located in New York (30 Rockefeller Plaza, New York, New York 10020, 212/572-8200). Selig H. Harrison, a senior associate of the center, is currently preparing a monographic study on Afghanistan.

5. The endowment is the publisher of the quarterly *Foreign Policy*. A list of publications and a report, *Carnegie Endowment for International Peace in the 1970's*, are available free on request.

H10 Center for Defense Information

1. *122 Maryland Avenue, N.E.*
    Washington, D.C. 20002
    543-0400

2. Gene R. La Rocque, Director

3. The Center for Defense Information is a nonprofit, nonpartisan, public-interest organization that provides objective information and analysis of U.S. national defense. The center's recent analytical focus has included demilitarization of the Indian Ocean, nuclear nonproliferation, and U.S. arms sales overseas.

4. The center's library houses a growing specialized collection of congressional documents and analyses essential to the work of its research staff. The collection is available to researchers for on-site use.

5. In addition to occasional papers, monographs, and analyses, the center also publishes a monthly newsletter, *The Defense Monitor,* which often contains material on South Asia. A copy of the annual report may be obtained from the Fund for Peace, 1995 Broadway, New York, New York 10023.

H11 Center for International Policy

1. *120 Maryland Avenue, N.E.*
    Washington, D.C. 20002
    544-4666

2. Donald L. Ranard, Director

3. A private, nonprofit, research organization, the Center for International Policy seeks to provide an independent critical perspective on current U.S. foreign policy issues. The center's primary focus is on U.S. relations with the Third World, especially the U.S. foreign aid programs. In 1978 a study was done, evaluating the World Bank and the AID assistance program in Bangladesh.

5. The center publishes an annual survey of *Human Rights and the U.S. Foreign Assistance Program* and a bimonthly *International Policy Reports* series.

H12 Center for National Security Studies (CNSS)

1. *122 Maryland Avenue, N.E.*
    Washington, D.C. 20002
    544-5380

2. Morton H. Halperin, Director

3. The Center for National Security, the activities of which are jointly sponsored by the Fund for Peace and the American Civil Liberties Union Foun-

dation, conducts research and produces information on issues of national security, and assists those seeking information under the Freedom of Information Act. The center closely monitors legislation affecting the intelligence agencies and government secrecy. Although the center does not conduct any direct studies on South Asia, some of its activities are relevant to the area.

4.   The center's library is open by appointment for use by serious researchers. Copying services are available at cost. Its holdings, cataloged and arranged by subject, focus on access to government information, terrorism, and political violence, among other topics. *From Official Files* is a catalog of materials in the library that will be of interest to people who want to examine government files for their own research. These materials have come from Freedom of Information Act releases and from discovery process in law suits.

5.   Publications include: *The 1980 Edition of Litigation Under the Federal Freedom of Information Act and Privacy Act,* and *Using the Freedom of Information Act: A Step by Step Guide.* The center also publishes a monthly newsletter, *First Principles,* and several other books and reports on various aspects of the national security establishments.

H13 Center for Naval Analysis (CNA)

1.   *200 North Beauregard Street*
      Alexandria, Viriginia 22311
      (703) 998-3500

2.   David B, Kassing, President

3.   An affiliate of the University of Rochester (Rochester, New York 14627), the Center for Naval Analysis is a nonprofit organization that conducts operations-research-systems analysis and economic studies for the U.S. Navy and other government agencies. The research staff in the Program, Plans and Policy Division of the Institute of Naval Studies monitors and conducts research on Soviet naval developments and diplomacy in the Indian Ocean. Studies have been done also on naval diplomacy during the India-Pakistan war of 1971, and on Soviet-Indian relations. For further information call Richard Remnek (998-3674), who has done several studies on naval security in the Indian Ocean region. Most of the work done by the division is classified. For access to classified materials, inquiries may be addressed to the Office of the Chief of Naval Operations, Systems Analysis Division, Navy Department, Washington, D.C. 20350.

4.   The center's library contains some 9,000 bound volumes and over 500 periodical subscriptions in the fields of political and social science, economics, weapons research, development, and other related areas. A security clearance is required for visitation privileges.

5.   Unclassified CNA materials are listed in the periodically updated *Index of Selected Publications* (1980). It is available without charge, as is the CNA's annual report.

H14 Center for Strategic and International Studies (CSIS) (Georgetown University)

1. *1800 K Street, N.W.*
   Washington, D.C. 20006
   833-8595

2. David M. Abshire, Chairman
   Michael A. Samuels, Executive Director for Third World Studies

3. The Center for Strategic and International Studies of Georgetown University is a nonprofit, nonpartisan, research institution founded in 1962 to foster scholarship and public awareness of emerging international issues on a broad interdisciplinary basis. Since 1977, the center has initiated a new program of studies on the Third World, but so far no specific program has been adopted on South Asia.

5. The center has an extensive publications program. In addition to the *Washington Quarterly*, and the *Washington Review of Strategic and International Studies* (quarterly), the center publishes several reports and monographs. Some of the titles of interest include: *Food Grain Production in India* (1977); *Seminar on World Food Supply, Health, and Nutrition* (1977); and *World Food: A Three Dimensional View of Production* (1977). Publication lists and the annual report are available on request.

H15 Committee for Economic Development (CED)

1. *1700 K Street, N.W.*
   Washington, D.C. 20006
   296-5860

2. Robert C. Holland, President

3. The Committee for Economic Development is an independent, nonpartisan, nonprofit, research and educational organization composed of approximately 200 trustees who develop specific recommendations for business and public policy. Findings and recommendations include national as well as international economics. CED is problem oriented and issue oriented. Its goal is to anticipate, identify, and attack the crucial problems that will affect business and society in the years to come. Multinational corporations and Third World development has been identified as one of the crucial issue areas for in-depth study in 1980. Although CED does not conduct any research directly on South Asia-related issues, CED's research on economic relations between industrialized and less developed countries has implications for the experience of some South Asian countries.

5. Publications include: *Assisting Development in Low Income Countries* (1969); *How Low Income Countries Can Advance their Economic Growth* (1966); *International Economic Consequences of High-Priced Energy*; and *Trade Policy Toward Low-Income Countries*. CED's annual report and a list of its publications are available free on request.

H16 Environmental Fund

1. *1302 18th Street, N.W.*
   Washington, D.C. 20036
   293-2548

2. Garrett Hardin, Executive Officer

3. An operating foundation, primarily concerned with the effect of continued population growth on the environment, the Environmental Fund conducts forums and programs of research on the relationship of population growth to such problems as resource depletion, pollution, and other social problems. The fund's main objective is to create an awareness around the world of the urgent need to stabilize the size of world population.

4. The Environmental Fund's small reference library contains several secondary materials, U.N. reports, magazines, and newspaper clippings on South Asian population problems.

5. Fund publications include an irregular newsletter, *The Other Side*, and the annual *World Population Chart* which is broken down by region and country.

H17 Foreign Policy Institute (FPI) (Johns Hopkins University—School of Advanced International Studies)(SAIS)

1. *1740 Massachusetts Avenue, N.W.*
   Washington, D.C. 20036
   785-6800

2. Lucius D. Battle, Chairman

3. The Foreign Policy Institute, a successor organization to the SAIS's Washington Center of Foreign Policy Research, was established in July 1980 to conduct research on current issues such as international security, energy, and economic policies, and to serve as a resource for policy makers, journalists, and others interested in foreign affairs. The institute continues to sponsor discussions, seminars, and meetings on current trends and issues in a variety of specialized subjects. The institute's current Asia-Pacific Forum focuses appropriately on South Asian issues. The institute has a special program for a limited number of scholars and government officials of foreign nations to participate as fellows in the activities of the institute and to pursue their own research and study projects.

5. The institute will continue to publish the monographic series, *Studies in International Affairs*. These studies, somewhat between an article and a book in length and scope, are particularly adapted to analytical essays on topical issues. Titles of interest in the series include: Shelton L. Williams, *The U.S., India, and the Bomb* (1969); and George Liska, *Alliances and the Third World* (1967).

H18 Fund for Investigative Journalism

1. *1346 Connecticut Avenue, N.W.*
    Washington, D.C. 20036
    462-1844

2. Howard Bray, Executive Director

3. The Fund for Investigative Journalism was incorporated in 1969 for the purpose of increasing public knowledge about the concealed, obscure, or complex aspects of matters significantly affecting the public. Towards that end, the fund makes grants to writers to enable them to probe abuses of authority or the malfunctioning of institutions and systems that harm the public. The fund has awarded more than 450 grants to writers since 1969. Lawrence Lifschultz, for his work entitled *Bangladesh: The Unfinished Revolution* (London: Zed Press, 1979) received support from the fund.

H19 General Research Corporation (GRC)

1. *7655 Old Springhouse Road*
    McLean, Virginia 22101
    893-5900

2. John L. Allen, President

3. A subsidiary of the Flow General, the General Research Corporation is a private, research corporation that performs defense research, analysis, and simulation. Its activities also include research and analysis of foreign-aid programs, and urban and transportation problems. GRC's South Asia-related activities include a recent study on rural development in Bangladesh.

4. The GRC library, which is not open to the general public, contains some 28,000 books, 500 periodical subscriptions, and some 30,000 documents.

5. GRC publications are restricted.

H20 Heritage Foundation

1. *513 C Street, N.E.*
    Washington, D.C. 20002
    546-4400

2. Edwin J. Feulner, President

3. The Heritage Foundation is a nonprofit research organization that analyzes and disseminates information on a variety of public policy issues both domestic and foreign. The foundation sponsors a continuing series of congressional briefings, lectures, symposia, and conferences to facilitate the exchange of ideas on public-policy issues. The foundation's research interest in South Asia has been recently focused on Afghanistan.
    Through its Resource Bank program, the foundation works to keep ac-

ademics and organizations across the country in constant touch with Washington. Over 1,000 scholars and 300 organizations are linked to the bank. Another Resource Bank activity, the International Visitor's Center, gives foreign dignitaries a unique opportunity to observe and contribute to the Washington policy-making scene. For further information contact Willa Ann Johnson (Director, Resource Bank).

4. The foundation's small reference library of secondary materials and periodicals is primarily for the use of the staff.

5. South Asia-related publications include two *Backgrounder* series reports on Afghanistan: *The Soviet Invasion of Afghanistan* and *Afghanistan: The Soviet Quagmire*; and another *National Security Record* series report, *Afghanistan: The U.S. Response.* A publication list and an annual report are available free on request.

H21 Institute for Defense Analysis (IDA)

1. *400 Army-Navy Drive*
   Arlington, Virginia 22202
   (703) 558-1000

2. Alexander H. Flax, President

3. The Institute for Defense Analysis, a nonprofit, research advisory corporation, performs studies for the U.S. government, primarily for the Defense Department. The International Security Assessment Division (William J. Schultis, Director) conducts research on military strategy world wide, and on the balance of power and stability at a regional and local level. Recently no specific South Asia-related research has been performed by the division. Much of the work done by the IDA is restricted.

4. The IDA library is primarily for staff use. Requests for using the library and the IDA computer facilities may be addressed to Frederick G. Latreille, Vice President.

5. IDA does not provide a list of its publications to outsiders. Most of its publicly released studies, however, are available from the National Technical Information Service.

H22 Institute for International and Foreign Trade Law (Georgetown University Law Center)

1. *600 New Jersey Avenue, N.W.*
   Washington, D.C. 20001
   624-8330

2. Don Wallace, Director

3. Georgetown University Law Center's Institute for International and Foreign Trade Law is an academic center serving law students, lawyers, officials, and the business community of America, Europe, and developing

countries. The institute offers a combination of research and practical training that focuses on the legal aspects of international trade and investment. The institute sponsors an annual 3-week orientation to the U.S. legal system for foreign lawyers about to begin graduate law studies in the United States. The institute also organizes conferences and colloquia, and awards limited fellowships to foreign students and officials.

The institute's Investment Negotiation Center (INC) was established in 1974. It provides research and training services for government officials from developing countries to enable them to negotiate more effectively with foreign direct investors and contractors. The INC is cosponsored by the Parker School of Foreign and Comparative Law of Columbia University. In addition to conducting seminars in Washington, D.C., and abroad, the INC also serves as consultant to international organizations. Among the recent research projects undertaken by INC personnel have been a study of procurement contracts for the World Bank, a feasibility and design study on a comprehensive, investment-information system for the United Nations Centre on Transnational Corporations, and a procurement-training design project for the Asian Development Bank. To date, Afghanistan, Bangladesh, and Pakistan have sent their officials to participate in INC programs.

4.   For the Georgetown University Law Center Library, see entry A14.

5.   *Law and Policy in International Business*, the quarterly international law journal of the Law Center, analyzes legal aspects of transnational trade and investment. The institute's publications include *Career Opportunities in International Law*, and *A Lawyer's Guide to International Business Transactions* (in 2 parts). A list, *Recent Publications*, and several brochures on the institute and the INC are available on request. The INC periodically publishes a newsletter, *Foreign Exchange*.

H23 Institute for Policy Studies (IPS)

1.   *1901 Q Street, N.W.*
      Washington, D.C. 20009
      234-9382

2.   Robert Borosage, Director

3.   The Institute for Policy Studies is an independent, nonprofit, transnational center of research and education on domestic and international public-policy problems. The IPS sponsors critical examination of the assumptions and policies that define American posture on domestic and international issues and offers alternative strategies and visions.

The Militarism and Disarmament Project of the institute conducts research, writing, and educational work on the issues of arms sales, nuclear disarmament, and U.S. military policy. The IPS Transnational Institute, with centers in London and Amsterdam, addresses the fundamental disparity between the rich and the poor peoples and nations of the world, investigates the causes for the disparity, and develops remedial alternatives. Although currently the institute has no specific research program on South Asia, several fellows at the institute have expertise on the region and have made published contributions and analyses on South Asian subjects. From time to time, the institute organizes lectures and discussions on subjects of timely interest.

5. IPS publishes approximately 20 books, and issues papers and reports each year. A catalog of its publications is available free.

H24 International Center for Research on Women (ICRW)

1. *1010 16th Street, N.W.*
    Washington, D.C. 20036
    293-3154

2. Mayra Buvinic, Director

3. ICRW is a nonprofit, research-oriented policy and educational organization. The center's current research, training and information-dissemination programs, and technical assistance offered in program design and evaluation, emphasize the productive roles of women, especially the economic condition of landless women in rural areas and low-income women in urban settings. The center's primary focus is the Third World nations, and its research emphasis is on selected issues rather than regional studies. The center is recently exploring the possibility of undertaking specific studies on South Asia under AID or other U.S. government-agency contracts. One such example is a proposal submitted to AID for an evaluation of the impact of women's education and labor-force participation on decision making, regarding marriage and fertility in Sri Lanka. The Center's Research Director, Nadia Haggag Youssef, is working on a study of women's status and fertility in Muslim and non-Muslim Asia.

    ICRW maintains an international network of contacts, which includes national research institutes, women's organizations, researchers, and practitioners. The center also has on file the vitae of more than 100 experts, on women and development, who are available as consultants. The center also organizes informal seminars and workshops.

4. ICRW maintains a collection of some 1,000 reports and studies, some of which are unpublished, on women and development by an international group of social scientists and development practitioners. The library is available to scholars.

5. ICRW's quarterly newsletter, now discontinued, is expected to resume publication in 1981. An ICRW brochure containing a list of its publications is available on request.

H25 International Economic Policy Associates (IEPA)

1. *1625 Eye Street, N.W.*
    Washington, D.C. 20006
    331-1974

2. Timothy W. Stanley, President

3. IEPA is a nonprofit, research organization founded for the purpose of

developing and fostering an inclusive and consistent international economic policy, and for promoting the advancement and diffusion of knowledge and understanding of international economics. The association has made a speciality of analyzing U.S. balance of payments, foreign investments, and raw-materials problems. It has an affiliated Center for Multinational Studies, which conducts a research program in conjunction with academic scholars. Another affiliate of the IEPA is the International Economic Studies Institute (IESI), which conducts interdisciplinary research in international economic problems of concern to America, such as raw materials and foreign policy, technology transfer, and international economics and security. Both affiliates are located at the IEPA address. Although no special research or study has been done by the IEPA on South Asia, much of IEPA's work is relevant to the region.

5. IEPA publications include a monograph series and research reports on the U.S. foreign economic policy issues. The Center for Multinational Studies publishes an *Occasional Paper Series*, while the IESI publishes a *Contemporary Issue Series* and *Conference Papers*. A list of IEPA publications is available on request.

H26 International Food Policy Research Institute (IFPRI)

1. *1776 Massachusetts Avenue, N.W.*
Washington, D.C. 20036
862-5600

2. John W. Mellor, Director

3. A nonprofit, research and educational institution, the IFPRI's purpose is to analyze the world food situation, especially as it affects developing countries, and conduct research on major policies to increase the availability of food in developing countries. The primary target audience of IFPRI is the policy makers; research results are distributed to those involved in making food-policy decisions at national and international levels. IFPRI relies on data collected by the FAO, the World Bank, and regional and national organizations dealing with food and related issues. IFPRI sponsors seminars and workshops in collaboration with other organizations when possible. It also enjoys observer status in UN organizations that deal with food policies.

Research programs of the institute include: analysis of trends in the production, exchange, and consumption of food in developing countries; policies that affect agricultural production in developing countries; programs and policies to improve distribution of available food stuffs, with special attention to populations having inadequate diets; and policies that will increase the ability of developing countries to make effective use of international trade.

The institute has a number of South Asia-related programs of research. In addition to the study involving linkages between agricultural and industrial growth in Bangladesh and India, the institute's South Asia project for food-distribution policies examined the operation of the comprehensive, public food-distribution schemes functioning in several countries of that region. These resulting country studies include 2 on Kerala (India), 1 on Bangladesh, and 1 on Sri Lanka.

4. The institute's small, specialized library contains representative collections on general food policy, agricultural economics and statistics, development economics, and specialized periodicals. Country-level field data from some developing countries are also available at the library. The library is open to private researchers for on-site use. Interlibrary loan facilities are available.

5. Publications include: Timothy Josling, *Developed-Country Agricultural Policies and Developing-Country Supplies: The Case of Wheat* (1980); Peter Oram et al., *Investment and Input Requirements for Accelerating Food Production in Low-Income Countries by 1990* (1979); Shubh Kumar, *Impact of Subsidized Rice on Food Consumption and Nutrition in Kerala* (1979); P. S. George, *Public Distribution of Foodgrains in Kerala—Income Distribution Implications and Effectiveness* (1979); Raisuddin Ahmed, *Foodgrain Supply, Distribution and Consumption Policies within a Dual Pricing Mechanism: A Case Study of Bangladesh* (1979); James Gavan, *The Impact of the Public Foodgrain Distribution on Food and Welfare in Sri Lanka* (1980). In addition, research papers, "Consumer Demand for Foodgrains in India from 1961/62 to 1973/74," by P. S. George, and "Behavior of Foodgrain Production and Consumption in India, 1960–77," by J. S. Sarma and Shyamal Ray, have been completed and are in the process of being reviewed for publication. The IFPRI annual report and publication list are available on request.

H27 International Institute for Environment and Development (IIED)— Washington Office

1. *1302 18th Street, N.W.*
    Washington, D.C. 20036
    462-0900

2. Robert T. Hoffmann, Director

3. IIED is a nonprofit, privately operated foundation with its headquarters located in London (27 Mortimer Street, London WIN 8DE, tel.: 01-580-7656).Currently its concern includes the issues of future energy and food supply, the development of sufficient shelter and clean water for mankind, and environmental consequences of major aid programs, especially in the Third World countries. The institute runs an environmental information unit, called Earthscan, for the press and maintains close working contact with many nongovernmental organizations working in similar fields around the world. In 1977–1978 the institute collaborated with the University of Mysore (India) in preparing a series of assessments of national human settlement policies in Nepal and India. Most IIED research and publications contain material pertinent to South Asian studies.

4. The Washington office library contains a collection of specialized United Nations' conference documents relating to environmental issues. The collection is open to scholars with a prior appointment.

5. IIED publications include: Anil Agarwal, *Drugs and the Third World*; *International Directory of Environment Film Sources* (1977); Arjun Makhijani, *Energy Policy for the Rural Third World* (1976); B. S. Bhooshan,

The Development Experience of Nepal (1979); R. P. Misra (ed.), *Habitat Asia: Issues and Responses*, 3 vols. (1979); and Stuart Donelson et al., *Aid for Human Settlements in the Third World: A Summary of the Activities of the Multilateral Agencies* (1979). IIED *Annual Report* and a list of publications are available on request.

H28 National Association of Manufacturers (NAM)—International Economic Affairs Department

1. *1776 F Street, N.W.*
    Washington, D.C. 20006
    626-3700

2. Lawrence A. Fox, Vice President

3. The International Economic Affairs Department conducts research on international trade, investment, and finance for NAM member companies. It evaluates policy implications of interrelated domestic and international economic factors—such as inflation, productivity, and capital investment in regard to long-term U.S. industrial competitiveness—among other data. The department collects data on global balance of payments, exchange rates, U.S. trade with world areas, international investments, and international financial institutions.

5. Publications include an annual review and perspective, *International Economic Issues*; a monthly newsletter, *International Economic Report*; and special research reports, such as *LDC External Debt: Facts, Figures, Perspectives*, and *Indicators of International Economic Performance*. A list of publications is available on request.

H29 National Planning Association (NPA)

1. *1606 New Hampshire Avenue, N.W.*
    Washington, D.C. 20009
    265-7685

2. Neil J. McMullen, Executive Director

3. NPA is a nonprofit association of businessmen, trade unionists, and professionals that conducts studies of national economic problems and makes long-range economic projections available to subscribing organizations. The staff also undertakes approved economic research, sometimes funded by outside sources. A large number of its research projects are relevant to South Asian studies.

5. NPA prepares a quarterly, *Development Digest*, under contract for the U.S. Agency for International Development. The *New International Realities* is an in-house magazine that is published 3 times a year. A list of NPA publications is available on request.

H30 Overseas Development Council (ODC)

1. *1717 Massachusetts Avenue, N.W.*
   Washington, D.C. 20036
   234-8701

2. John W. Sewell, President

3. ODC is an independent nonprofit center for study and research that is concerned with increasing the American understanding of the economic and social problems confronting the developing countries and advocating the importance of these countries to the U.S. in an increasingly interdependent world. The council pursues its objectives through research, conferences, publications, and liaison with mass-membership organizations interested in U.S. relations with the developing world. Prominent emphasis in the council's current work program include: analysis of the implications of the increasing interdependence of economic growth or stagnation in the industrialized and developing countries; assessment of the costs and benefits, for all countries, of the major proposals for a new international economic order being debated in the North-South dialogue; identification of improved ways to achieve Third World population and health goals, including analysis of how development can affect health and fertility; continued study of alternative development strategies; and refinement of a new tool for measuring development achievement. Most council studies are done from a global, rather than a regional perspective.

4. ODC has a small research library primarily for the use of the staff.

5. ODC has an extensive publication program of monographic studies, occasional papers, and communiques. Recent publications include: Martin M. McLaughlin, *The United States and the World Development Agenda 1979*, (1979); William R. Cline, *Policy Alternatives for a New International Economic Order: An Economic Analysis* (1979); Morris David Morris, *Measuring the Condition of the World's Poor: The Physical Quality of Life Index* (1979); Jairam Ramesh and Charles Weiss, *Mobilizing Technology for World Development* (1979); Godfrey Gunatilleke, *Participatory Development and Dependence—The Case of Sri Lanka* (1979); and Ronald Ridker, *Employment in South Asia: Problems, Prospects, and Prescriptions* (1979). The ODC annual report and a catalog of publications are available free.

H31 Population Reference Bureau (PRB)

1. *1337 Connecticut Avenue, N.W.*
   Washington, D.C. 20036
   785-4664

2. Robert Worrall, President

3. The Population Reference Bureau is a nonprofit, educational organization established to gather, analyze, and interpret the facts of population dy-

namics and relate them to the world's economic and social problems. Bureau staff may provide statistical information on population trends in South Asian countries.

4. The Population Reference Bureau Library is open to the public from 8:30 A.M. to 4:30 P.M., Monday through Friday. The collection consists of some 12,000 monographs; about 450 journals and newsletters; United Nations' statistical materials; and newspaper clippings, reprints, and papers on various aspects of population, family planning, and demography.

5. The bureau publishes an international newsletter, *Intercom*, on population; the bimonthly *Population Bulletin*; the annual *World Population Data Sheet*, with data on population, birth rates, death rates, life expectancy, and infant mortality; and special publications including *World Population Growth and Response, 1965–1975: A Decade of Global Action, Population Handbook*, and *Source Book on Population, 1970–1976*. The bureau's annual report and a publication list are available on request.

H32 Rand Corporation—Washington Office

1. *2100 M Street, N.W.*
   Washington, D.C. 20037
   296-5000

2. George K. Tanham, Director

3. The Rand Corporation, headquartered in Santa Monica, California, is a private, nonprofit, research organization that analyzes domestic and international issues affecting the public welfare and national security. Currently, Rand's National Security Research Division—which focuses on the planning, development, acquisition, deployment, support, and protection of military forces, and includes international affairs that may affect U.S. defense policy and strategy—has intensified its research program related to South Asia.

4. The Washington Office library contains over 7,000 volumes in social sciences, some 12,000 technical reports, a good collection of congressional hearings, and some 200 newspaper and periodical subscriptions. Although the library is not open to the public, some materials may be obtained through interlibrary loan.

5. Much of Rand's strategic research is produced under contract for U.S. Government agencies and is therefore classified. Unclassified Rand publications are disseminated to some 350 U.S. libraries on a subscription basis. In the Washington area, these repositories include the Library of Congress, George Washington University Library, and the Army Library. In South Asia, Rand publications are available at the National Institute of Bank Management Library (Bombay), Defense Science Library (New Delhi), Indian Council of Social Science Research (New Delhi), and Institute of Defense Studies and Analysis Library (New Delhi).

   Rand Corporation's South Asia-related, unclassified publications are listed in the periodically updated *A Bibliography of Selected Rand Publications: Asia*. There are also specialized Rand bibliographies on *Middle East, For-*

eign Aid, Foreign Policy, and dozens of other topics. A list of bibliographies and the corporation's annual report are available on request. *Rand Research Review*, issued 3 times a year, reports on selected developments of general interest in Rand's research programs.

H33 Resources for the Future (RFF)

1.   *1755 Massachusetts Avenue, N.W.*
     Washington, D.C. 20036
     328-5000

2.   Emery N. Castle, President

3.   RFF is a nonprofit corporation the purpose of which is to advance research and education in the areas of domestic and international policy issues relating to natural resources, environmental quality, population, and energy. A majority of its programs are carried out by resident staff but a few are supported through grants to universities and other nonprofit organizations. RFF's research and other work are supported by grants and contracts from foundations, the government, and private industry.

     Most of its studies are in the social sciences and are broadly concerned with the relationships of people to the natural environment. RFF's South Asia-related research, in the context of the developing world, is carried out by its Center for Energy Policy and the Renewable Resources Division. Recently the Renewable Resource Division conducted a 3-country study (India, Colombia, Indonesia) that focused on problems of the environment and nuclear power; energy transition; migration and urbanization; application and development of managerial skills and technological know-how; long-term planning; and long-run social, institutional, and political factors. RFF's Wednesday seminars includes such themes as Energy Aspects of Poverty in Developing Countries, and Material Requirements and Economic Growth.

5.   The results of RFF research are disseminated primarily through books and monographs published and distributed by Johns Hopkins University Press. Relevant publications include: *Household Energy and the Poor in the Third World* (1979); *Economic Equality and Fertility in Developing Countries* (1979); and *Rural Women at Work: Strategies for Development in South Asia* (1978). RFF's *Annual Report* and a publication list are available free on request.

H34 United Nations Information Centre

1.   *2101 L Street, N.W.*
     Washington, D.C. 20037
     296-5370

2.   Marcial Tamayo, Director

3.   The United Nations Information Centre is the Washington branch of the UN Office of Public Information, which supplies public information on the activities of the UN. Besides being a depository for UN documents and

publications, the center provides a complete range of reference services and utilizes a variety of public media, including films and exhibitions, to disseminate information about the work and activities of the UN and its various specialized agencies. The center maintains ties with the press and other information media, educational institutions, government, and private organizations.

4.   The center's library is described in entry A33.

Note: Also see entry F15.

H35 Woodrow Wilson International Center for Scholars (WWICS)

1.   *Smithsonian Institution Building*
1000 Jefferson Drive, S.W.
Washington, D.C. 20560
357-2429

2.   James H. Billington, Director

3.   The Woodrow Wilson International Center for Scholars was created by the United States Congress in 1968 as the nation's official living memorial to its twenty-eighth president. As a national institution with international interests, the center seeks to encourage the creative use of the unique human, archival, and institutional resources in the nation's capital for studies illuminating our understanding of the past and present.

Through its residential fellowship program of advanced research, the center seeks to commemorate both the scholarly depth and the public concerns of Woodrow Wilson. The center welcomes outstanding project proposals representing a wide diversity of scholarly interests and approaches from individuals throughout the world. It has no permanent or tenured fellows. Its fellowships are awarded, for periods ranging from four months to one year or more, in one broadly defined division and five more focused programs of research. The broadly defined division—History, Culture, and Society—enables the center to attract superior projects from the entire range of scholarship in the humanities and social sciences that fall outside one of the more focused programs. The five designated programs are the Kennan Institute for Advanced Russian Studies, the Latin American Program, the International Security Studies Program, the East Asia Program, and the Program in American Society and Politics. The center also operates a Guest Scholar Program for the short-term use of the center's facilities by a small number of visiting scholars and specialists.

Through these programs, and particularly through the division of History, Culture, and Society, scholars specializing in South Asian affairs—from South Asia, the United States, and elsewhere—are brought into the center to carry out research. The number varies from year to year. Since 1973, center fellows and guest scholars with South Asian specialities, and their respective projects, have included: Rajeshwar Dayal, "United Nations Peace-Keeping Mission"; Raja Rao, "Wisdom, Power, and the State"; K. P. Misra, "International Politics in the Indian Ocean Area"; Muhammad Shamsul Huq, "Alternative Patterns of Growth in Developing Countries: South and Southeast Asia"; Rishikesh Shaha, "Political Developments in Nepal Since

1951"; John Cobb, "The Western Experience of Time and Divinity in Light of Buddhist Thought"; Manakkal Venkataramani, "The State of United States-Indian Relations: a Critical Inquiry"; Martin Green, "Tolstoi and Gandhi: An Essay in World History"; and Henry S. Bradsher, "Soviet-Afghan Relations".

The center's activities include frequent colloquia, evening seminars, and other discussions designed to foster intellectual community among the participants. Since 1973, the center has organized major meetings on the following South Asian topics: "Perspectives on Developing Countries, Particularly India, on Long-Term Issues of Sustainable Growth;" "Nepal As a Zone of Peace: Non-Alignment between India and China;" "Present and Future Importance of Islam in World Affairs;" and "Perspectives on the Afghanistan Crisis." The scheduled events are announced in the monthly *Calender of Events*.

4.   The Wilson Center has a working library containing 16,000 volumes of basic reference works, bibliographies, and essential monographs in the social sciences and humanities, with an emphasis on the areas covered by the center's programs. The library subscribes to, and maintains, the back files of about 300 scholarly journals and periodicals. As part of a National Presidential Memorial, the library has special access to the collections of the Library of Congress and other government libraries. The librarian is Zdeněk V. David (357-2567).

5.   The *Wilson Quarterly* (circulation 105,000) carries occasional articles on South Asia. The Autumn 1978 issue, in particular, included four articles on post-World War II political and economic trends in India and a bibliographic essay. The Center also sponsors the preparation and publication of the series, *Scholars' Guides to Washington, D.C.* Available from the Smithsonian Institution Press (P.O. Box 1579, Washington, D.C. 20013), the *Guides* survey the collections, institutions, and organizations pertinent to the study of particular geographic areas, such as Africa, Central and Eastern Europe, East Asia, Latin American and the Caribbean, the Middle East, Russia/Soviet Union, and other world regions. A separate *Guide* covers film and video collections in the Washington, D.C., area. The center's programs (Kennan Institute, Latin American, International Security Studies, and East Asia) publish *Occasional/Working Papers*, distributed free of charge to interested parties upon request. Lists are available from the Publications Office or individual program offices. The *Annual Report* and an occasional bulletin, the *Newsletter*, are sent to former fellows and other friends of the Wilson Center.

H36 World Peace Through Law Center (WPTLC)

1.   *1000 Connecticut Avenue, N.W.*
      Washington, D.C. 20006
      466-5420

2.   Charles S. Rhyne, President

3.   Dedicated to the replacement of force by law in international affairs, the World Peace Through Law Center is a world-wide organization of judges,

lawyers, law professors, and law students representing 151 nations, including Afghanistan, Bangladesh, Nepal, Pakistan, India, and Sri Lanka. A nonprofit and nonpolitical organization, the center draws its members from its constituent professional associations: World Association of Judges, World Association of Lawyers, World Association of Law Professors, and World Association of Law Students. WPTLC maintains separate, specialized sections for dealing with issues such as Human Rights and International Legal Education.

The center sponsors World Law Day, and biennial World Law Conferences, featuring demonstration trials on such themes as human rights and law of the sea, at different locations throughout the world. Within the vast spectrum of law, the council's widespread concern includes investment disputes, human rights, refugee rights, and many other international issues. The center has consultative status as a nongovernmental organization with the United Nations, and through its computer list of over 150,000 judges, lawyers, law professors, and law students from 151 nations, WPTLC reaches the legal profession of the world.

5.   WPTLC's extensive publications include: *The Law and Woman; Model Code of Conduct for Transnational Corporations; International Legal Protection for Human Rights: The Handbook for World Law Day, August 21, 1977; Peace with Justice under World Rules of Law; Law and Judicial Systems of Nations*; and *World Legal Directory*. The center also publishes a monthly newsletter, *The World Jurist*; and *World Law Review*, which contains the proceedings of the biennial conferences. A list of the center's publications and *A Report on the Activities of the World Peace Through Law Center* are available on request.

H37   Worldwatch Institute

1.   *1776 Massachusetts Avenue, N.W.*
     Washington, D.C. 20036
     452-1999

2.   Lester Brown, President

3.   The Worldwatch Institute is a nonprofit, research organization which studies, from a global perspective, issues of population, energy, food, environment, and the changing roles of women.

5.   The institute's *Worldwatch Paper* series includes such titles of interest as *Women in Politics: A Global Review; World Population Trends: Signs of Hope, Signs of Stress; The Two Faces of Malnutrition*; and *Energy and Development: Third World Options*. A publication list is available on request.

I Academic Programs and Departments

Washington is the home of a host of fine academic institutions. Limited specialization on South Asian fields or area studies are offered by individual institutions independently or in cooperation with other area institutions through the instrumentality of the Consortium of Universities of the Washington metropolitan area. It may be noted that institutions or departments without any specific South Asia-related programs or courses may yet have faculty members or research associates with interest and expertise in South Asian studies. For further information on academic programs and faculty interests, and on-campus international activities, scholars may contact the departmental chairperson or the international student office.

Academic Programs and Departments Entry Format (I)

1. *Address; Telephone Numbers*

2. Chief Official and Title

3. Degrees and Subjects Offered; Program Activities

4. Libraries and Research Facilities

I 1 American University (AU)

1. *Massachusetts and Nebraska Avenues, N.W.*
   Washington, D.C. 20016
   686-2000

2. Richard Berendzen, President

3.　The American University, established in 1893, is an independent Methodist-related university. Originally founded as a graduate school of history and public affairs, it currently provides a wide range of undergraduate and graduate programs in almost every academic discipline in its five colleges and schools. Current enrollment includes foreign students from 117 countries. The Office of International Programs (686-2077) is responsible for all international programs offered by the university. It ascertains the needs and problems of the international students, and maintains the International Student Center.

In the Washington metropolitan area, the American University offers the most in South Asian studies. The courses of studies in the Department of History (James A. Malloy, Chairman, 686-2401), which offers several undergraduate and graduate programs, includes two courses in Indian history. The Department of Language and Foreign Studies (Bruno F. Steinbruckner, Chairman, 686-2280), which offers a variety of fields of study dealing with foreign languages and culture, offers a Hindi studies program consisting of elementary and intermediate Hindi. Within the Department of Philosophy and Religion (Charley D. Hardwick, Chairman, 686-2425) courses are offered in Eastern thought, philosophy, literature, Islam, and Hinduism. South Asian materials are also included in several courses in Third World and comparative politics listed by the School of Government and Public Administration (Dorothy James, Dean, 686-2372). Materials on South Asia are also covered in courses on international communication systems offered by the School of Communication (Lincoln Furber, Chairman, 686-2055).

The School of International Service (Gregory Wolfe, Dean, 686-2468) offers several undergraduate and graduate programs including international affairs, international relations, and languages and area studies. The school's Center for Asian Studies coordinates Asian studies throughout the university and administers those programs on Asia offered by the school. Programs are available at the undergraduate, master's, and doctoral levels with emphasis on South Asia along with other areas. The program of the Center for Asian Studies utilizes not only the resources of the American University but also those of the other members of the consortium of universities. Courses offered through the center include: Civilization of Asia; Islamic Civilization; Contemporary South Asia; Asian Power Rivalries; Selected Topics in Regional International Systems; an Interdisciplinary Seminar: Selected Foreign Areas; and International Relations of South Asia. Charles H. Heimsath is the South Asian area specialist of the school.

4.　The American University Library is described in entry A2.

Note:　Also see entries H3 and H8.

I2 Catholic University of America

1.　*620 Michigan Avenue, N.E.*
Washington, D.C. 20017
635-5000

2.　Edmund D. Pellegrino, President

3. The Catholic University of America, founded in 1789, is the national university of the Catholic Church in the United States. The university offers undergraduate and graduate programs in numerous disciplines, but with the exception of a graduate course in the Department of Religion and Religious Education, no other courses or programs of studies on South Asian studies are currently available in the campus. A faculty member in the Department of Modern Languages, Siegfried Schulz, has expertise in Hindi and Sanskrit. The campus has a significant number of international students. Information and other assistance for international students may be obtained from the Office of International Studies (635-5630).

4. University library facilities are described in entry A4.

I3 Consortium of Universities of the Washington Metropolitan Area

3. The universities in Washington, D.C.—namely, American University, Catholic University of America, George Washington University, Georgetown University, Howard University, and the University of the District of Columbia—are associated in a consortium through which they coordinate the use of their respective facilities. Gallaudet College, Mount Vernon College, and Trinity College are associate members of the consortium. Students in approved programs leading to degrees in any one of these institutions have the opportunity to select from the combined offerings of all the cooperating universities to meet their needs. Students register and pay tuition at their own institutions for all consortium courses. Since there is no comprehensive South Asia program offered in any one institution in the area, the consortium may be particularly helpful to a student wishing to pursue area studies on South Asia.

I4 George Mason University

1. *4400 University Drive*
    Fairfax, Virginia 22030
    (703) 323-2000

2. George W. Johnson, President

3. Founded in 1957, George Mason University gained independent university status in 1972. An independent, state-operated institution, it offers more than 40 undergraduate and 19 graduate programs. In addition to the courses in ancient and modern India and Pakistan and cultural history of Islam offered by the Department of History (Joseph L. Harsh, Chairman, 703/323-2242) and a course in Hindu religion and philosophy listed by the Department of Philosophy and Religion (Debra Bergoffen, Chairman, 703/323-2252), the Department of Public Affairs (Robert P. Clark, Chairman, 703/323-2272) offers an interdisciplinary program of study in International Studies leading to BA and MA degrees, within which a limited concentration on South Asia is possible. For further information on the program,

contact Nguyen Hung (703/223-2065). George Gangloff in the Admissions Office (703/323-2108) provides information and counseling to the international students on the campus.

4.   The university's Fenwick Library (John G. Veenstra, Library Director, 703/ 323-2391) is open to the public for on-site use from 7:30 A.M.. to 11:00 P.M., Monday through Thursday; 7:30 A.M. to 5:00 P.M., Friday; 9:00 A.M. to 7:00 P.M., Saturday; and 11:00 A.M. to 9:00 P.M., Sunday, when classes are in session.

Interlibrary loan and photoduplication services are available. The library contains some 180,000 volumes, 230,000 microfilm units, and 2,660 current periodical subscriptions. South Asia-related materials in the collection consist of some 300 items of monographic studies and reference works. The library follows the LC classification schedule.

I5 George Washington University

1.   *2121 Eye Street, N.W.*
Washington, D.C. 20052
676-6000

2.   Lloyd Hartman Elliott, President

3.   Established in 1821, the George Washington University is a private nonsectarian institution that now offers undergraduate, graduate, and professional programs in its 12 schools and divisions. As a service to the university's large international population, the school maintains an International Student Advising Office (676-6860) which serves as a consultation, information, and resource center for the foreign students on campus. South Asia-related courses and programs currently available at the university include the following:

The School of Public and International Affairs (B. M. Sapin, Dean, 676-6240)—an interdisciplinary, policy-oriented school that emphasizes both domestic and foreign governmental policy—offers a graduate program in international affairs, which allows geographic concentration on South Asia. Also within the framework of a doctoral program in International Relations, which is directed by a committee the members of which are drawn from the Economics, Political Science, and History Departments, a limited concentration on South Asia is possible.

The Department of Religion (H. E. Yeide, Chairman, 676-6325), through the Consortium of Universities program, offers a Master of Arts degree in the field of History of Religions—Hinduism. Information regarding courses and requirements is available from the program advisor, A. J. Hiltebeitel (676-6326).

First- and second-year Sanskrit is available in the Department of Germanic Languages and Literatures (C. Steiner, Chairman, 676-6195).

Additionally, the Department of Political Science (B. Reich, Chairman, 676-6290) lists courses in government and politics of South Asia and Southeast Asia.

4.   George Washington University Library is described in entry A13.

I 6 Georgetown University

1. *37th and O Streets, N.W.*
    Washington, D.C. 20057
    625-0100

2. T. S. Healy, President

3. Established in 1789, Georgetown is the oldest Catholic university in the United States. Composed of four graduate and professional schools and five undergraduate schools, the university offers a wide variety of academic programs, both at the undergraduate and graduate levels. The university attracts a good number of foreign students. Information and counseling for the international students are provided through the International Student Center (Eric Heiberg, Foreign Student Advisor, 625-4386).

    The university does not offer any special program of studies on South Asia, but South Asia-related courses offered by different schools or departments include: courses in Sanskrit, available in the School of Languages and Linguistics (625-4301); courses in South Asian history, offered from time to time by the Department of History (625-4007); and courses in Asian governments and politics in the Department of Government (625-4941).In addition, through the interdisciplinary Master of Science program in the Edmund A. Walsh School of Foreign Service (625-4225), it is possible to develop a course of studies with regional emphasis on South Asia. For information on the school's Asian Studies Program, which is in the planning stage, contact Associate Dean Matthew M. Gardner (625-4216).

4. Georgetown University library is described in entry A15.

Note: Also see entries A14, A16, H14, and H22.

I 7 Howard University

1. *2400 6th Street, N.W.*
    Washington, D.C. 20059
    636-6100

2. James E. Cheek, President

3. Jointly supported by congressional appropriations and private funds, Howard University was established in 1867. Through its 17 schools and colleges, the university offers undergraduate and graduate instruction in a wide variety of fields and disciplines. The university has a large enrollment of foreign students. International students may contact the International Students Services (Barry Bem, Director, 636-7517) for information and counselling.

    As far as could be ascertained, with the exception of a course listed in the Department of Political Science (Vincent J. Brown, Chairman, 636-6720), no other courses or programs on South Asian studies are available on the campus.

4. The university library facilities are discussed in entry A19.

18 School of Advanced International Studies (SAIS) (Johns Hopkins University)

1. *1740 Massachesetts Avenue, N.W.*
   Washington, D.C. 20036
   785-6200

2. George R. Packard, Dean of SAIS

3. The School of Advanced International Studies is a graduate division of the Johns Hopkins University. SAIS offers a two-year course of study leading to the degree of Master of Arts and, to a smaller number of students, it offers a program of studies leading to the Doctor of Philosophy degree. To a group of students chosen from mid-career government and business positions in the U.S. and foreign countries, it offers a year of study leading to a Master of International Public Policy.

   Amid the profusion of international studies, the school offers a broad array of courses in an interdisciplinary setting. Besides courses in comparative politics and modernization, international economics, and international relations, two courses on South Asia (South Asia and the World, and Seminar on South Asian Politics and Economics) are offered with the Asian geographical areas studies program. Through the geographic areas studies program on the Middle East, courses in Islamic institutions and political theory and Islamic law are available. Students can also arrange reading courses with faculty where regular courses do not adequately cover special needs. The center sponsors numerous public and private lectures and symposia, in which visiting scholars, SAIS faculty members, and members of the local diplomatic and foreign-policy community participate.

4. The SAIS library is described in entry A30.

19 University of Maryland

1. *College Park, Maryland 209742*
   (301) 454-0100

2. John S. Toll, President

3. A land-grant institution established in 1859, the University of Maryland administers a number of undergraduate and graduate programs through its five campuses. The university is a member of the South-East Consortium for International Development, a concern of which is the economic and social needs of less developed countries. The campus attracts a large number of foreign students. The Office of International Education Services (301/454-3043) provides information and consulting services to the international students on the campus. Although, currently, no specific courses are offered on South Asia, selected South Asian materials are covered in several courses in the departments of Government and Politics, History, German Literature and Language, Music, and Economics.

4. The university library is described in entry A34.

I10 University of the District of Columbia (UDC)

1. *4200 Connecticut Avenue, N.W.*
    Washington, D.C. 20008
    282-7300

2. Lisle C. Carter, President

3. Established in 1977 from the merger of D.C. Teacher's College, Federal City College, and Washington Technical Institute, UDC serves as the only public, land-grant university in the District of Columbia. Courses are offered in its recently consolidated colleges at three locations: Georgia Avenue-Harvard Street Campus, Mount Vernon Square Campus, and Van Ness Campus. The university offers hardly any courses or programs in South Asian studies. An introductory course in Asian civilization offered by the Department of History (Ali Bakri, Chairman, 727-2534) deals selectively with South Asian themes. In addition, the Department of Political Science (727-2292) may offer, from time to time, a South Asia-related course. The university accepts a limited number of students who are citizens of other countries. Selection of international students for admission is competitive and is based on grade-point average or its equivalent.

4. UDC's Library and Media Services (727-2500) contains a combined collection of some 400,000 items. The library's South Asia-related materials are insignificant. The library is open to the public.

J United States Government Agencies

Particularly for scholars investigating various aspects of contemporary South Asia, the enormous resources in the agencies and departments of the United States Government in the Washington area may prove to be of tremendous help. Most government officials and analysts are willing, within the constraints imposed by their work schedules and security restrictions, to discuss research projects with visiting scholars, to provide them with information and materials, and to direct them to appropriate organizations or persons having expertise on the subject. In addition, most U.S. government agencies and departments, subject to certain restrictions, allow private scholars to examine their libraries, reference collections, data banks, and other facilities, which contain records and documents not generally available elsewhere.

In obtaining access to those internal records and documents that are not publicly available, either from the agencies or departments generating the materials, or from the National Archives and Records Service, researchers may find it advantageous to familiarize themselves with the Freedom of Information Act processes. The Freedom of Information Act (Public Law 89-487 of 1966, as amended by Public Law 93-502 of 1974) provides that any person has the right of access to, and can obtain copies of, any document, file, or other record in the possession of any federal agency or department, with certain exceptions, including certain personnel records and classified documents, the classification of which can be justified as essential to national security.

Most government agencies have a Freedom of Information office or officer available to process requests for internal agency documents. In contacting them, whether in writing or by telephone, researchers should cite the Freedom of Information Act, and should make their requests as detailed and specific as possible. Researchers are not required to explain or justify their requests. Denials of requests may be appealed to the director of the agency; such appeals are often successful. Rejected appeals may be challenged through court litigation. By law, agencies have ten working days in which to respond to an initial Freedom of Information Act request and twenty days in which to respond to an appeal.

Researchers should note that agencies are permitted to charge rather substantial fees for document searches and photoduplication of released documents. Information on such fees should be requested when filing an initial Freedom of Information Act request. In most cases, researchers are permitted to examine the released records in person at the agency.

Several organizations in Washington can assist researchers in using the Freedom of Information Act processes. They include: the Freedom of Information Clearinghouse, P.O. Box 19367 (2000 P Street, N.W., Suite 700), Washington, D.C. 20036 (785-3704), a project of Ralph Nader's Center for the Study of Responsive Law; and the Project on National Security and Civil Liberties, 122 Maryland Avenue, N.E., Washington, D.C. 20002 (544-5380), an organization sponsored by the American Civil Liberties Union and the Center for National Security Studies (see entry H12). Both organizations distribute, without charge, guides to Freedom of Information Act processes. Another useful guide can be found in the October 1975 issue of the American Historical Association *Newsletter*. A particularly useful source of information on declassified government documents is provided by Carrollton Press (see entry P5).

Researchers should be aware that in Washington, bureaucratically inspired reorganizations of government departments and agencies are frequent; indeed, various agencies within the national intelligence community regularly reorganize their internal structures in order to disguise their functional activities and to confuse foreign observers. Reorganizations often entail relocating or shifting offices, as well as changes in titles, personnel, and telephone numbers. Presidential elections also often lead to major administrative reorganizations within the federal bureaucracy. As a result, many of the names and telephone numbers listed in the entries below are subject to change and should be considered somewhat transitory.

Researchers would be well advised to obtain the latest telephone numbers for various offices by consulting the latest edition of each government department's telephone directory. Some are updated on a quarterly basis. Most are available for purchase from the Government Printing Office. If all else fails, contact the Federal Information Center (755-8660).

United States Government Agencies Entry Format (J)*

1. General Information
    a. *address; telephone numbers*
    b. conditions of access
    c. name/title of director and heads of relevant divisions

2. Functions, Programs, and Research Activities (including in-house research, contract programs, research grants, employment of outside consultants, and international exchange programs)

3. Libraries and Reference Facilities

4. Publications and Records (including unpublished materials, indexes, and vertical files, among other data)

    *In the case of large, structurally complex agencies, each relevant division or bureau is described separately in accordance with the above entry format.

J1 Agency for International Development (AID) (International Development Corporation Agency)

1. a. *320 21st Street, N.W.*
    Washington, D.C. 20523
    632-9620

b. Open to the public with prior appointment

c. Douglas J. Bennet, Jr., Administrator

2.   The Agency for International Development administers most of the foreign economic-assistance programs of the U.S. government. Designed to help the people of certain less-developed countries advance their human and economic resources, increase productive capacities, and improve the quality of human life, these programs also promote economic or political stability in friendly countries. As of October 1, 1979, AID is no longer part of the State Department, but instead has been shifted to the newly created International Development Cooperation Agency (IDCA), the director of which is now the principal international development adviser to the president of the United States and the secretary of state.

   AID programs, as authorized by the Congress under the Foreign Assistance Act of 1961, provide two kinds of economic assistance: development assistance and security-supporting assistance. The agency implements its economic-assistance programs by means of concessional loans, technical cooperation, and development grants, including specific grant authorities for U.S. research and educational institutions. The agency, in cooperation with the Department of Agriculture, also implements Public Law 480 (The Agricultural Trade Development and Assistance Act of 1954, popularly known as Food for Peace Program, as amended).

   The AID focuses its development-assistance programs in those functional sectors that affect the lives of the majority of the people in developing countries: food, nutrition, and rural development; population, planning, and health; education and human-resources development; and technical assistance, energy, research reconstruction, and selected development problems. In addition, AID is also concerned with several specific programs, including the international disaster-assistance program. Most AID programs in South Asia concentrate on development assistance and food for peace.

   The vast bulk of AID research, including those projects related to South Asia, is produced under contract or through research grants to educational institutions and research centers. South Asian specialists are also periodically engaged as consultants. It is also AID policy to encourage, in its work, the collaboration of research bodies in the developing countries. A large number of research institutions in South Asian countries are involved with several AID programs.

   The agency's retired files and unpublished reports are transferred to the custody of the National Archives and Records Service. Both the AID Records Management Staff (632-8518) and the originating-agency offices maintain indexes to retired documents. For access to AID's classified materials, researchers may contact Arnold H. Dadian, the agency's Freedom of Information Officer (632-1850).

3.   For AID library and reference facilities, see entry A7.

4.   Of the massive literature generated by the agency, a selected few, considered to be germane to South Asian research, are noted below. Bibliographic control of AID publications has until recently been difficult; the great majority do not appear in the *Monthly Catalog*. Also, the *Catalog of Selected AID Publications* (1974), as the title indicates, is neither comprehensive nor up-to-date. *AID Memory Documents*, a restricted, comprehensive,

quarterly catalog of AID-generated documents, was published for only a
short period during 1972–1974.

The series of AID newsletters, pamphlets, and brochures, produced for
popular use, include: *Agenda,* a monthly devoted to international development; *Front Lines,* a weekly newsletter; *A.I.D. Forum,* a monthly exchange of views about AID and development; *A.I.D. News,* frequently
used for brief announcements; *World Development Letter,* a biweekly report
of facts, trends, and opinion in international development; *AID's Challenge,*
a pamphlet explaining the agency's purpose; *AID's Work in Nutrition,* one
of several informative and educational pamphlets; and *AID in the Third
World,* a series of fliers on different aspects of AID programs in the less-
developed countries.

More substantial publications include:

*U.S. Overseas Loans and Grants and Assistance from International Or-
ganizations, Obligations and Loan Authorizations, July 1, 1945–September
30, 1979,* a report prepared, on request, for the use of congressional committees primarily concerned with foreign aid that includes all countries
receiving any type of loans or grants (economic, military, and others) since
July 1945, regardless of whether or not the particular country received
assistance under the Foreign Assistance Act and antecedent legislations.

*AID—Financed University Contracts and Grants Active During the Period
October 1, 1978 Through September 30, 1979.*

*Current Technical Service Contracts and Grants Active During the Period
October 1, 1978 Through September 30, 1979.*

A.I.D. Research and Development Abstracts, a quarterly abstract of materials from AID-funded projects through contracts or grants.

Directory of Development Resources (1979), which lists on-call, technical-
support services, information clearinghouses, field research facilities, newsletters, data banks, and training currently available to less-developed countries.

Research Literature for Development, 2 vols. (1976–1977), in which titles
collected and arranged represent findings and results produced in the search
for expanded knowledge and new approaches to developmental problems
covering the period from 1962 to 1976.

Asia Economic Growth Trends (1977), a summary of basic data of rate
of population growth, density, urbanization, labor forces in agriculture,
agricultural land, gross national product per capita, and power per capita.

The agency also publishes from time to time a series of *Policy Papers* on
significant themes, such as *A Strategy for a More Effective Bilateral Development Assistance Program* (1978), and *Agricultural Development* (1978).
In addition, the agency compiles the *AID Bibliographic Series,* consisting
of 28 subject bibliographies on development-related fields. *Fiscal Year Submission to the Congress* is the agency's annual budget presentation and
program review to the Congress.

Of the several publications of the AID missions abroad, the following
may be useful: *Decade of Development* (Ankara, 1970), focusing on CENTO
(the Central Treaty Organization), of which Pakistan was a member; *Statistical Information on Agriculture in India,* a voluminous and substantial
work published in 1963; *The USAID Contribution to Economic Development of Mysore* (1968); *Economic Data Papers, Nepal; Statistical Fact Book:
Selected Economic and Social Data on Pakistan;* and *Action,* a quarterly

journal published by the AID mission in Pakistan.

For further information concerning AID publications contact Press and Publications Division (Edward Caplan, Chief, 632-8632) and see J. A. Downey, *U.S. Federal Official Publications* (1978).

BUREAU FOR ASIA (ASIA)
John H. Sullivan, Assistant Administrator
632-9223

OFFICE OF BANGLADESH AND INDIA AFFAIRS (ASIA/BI)
Joan Gayoso, Director (acting)
632-9064
William Erdahl, Country Officer, Bangladesh
632-9064
David J. Garms, Country Officer, India
632-0212

OFFICE OF PAKISTAN, NEPAL AND SRI LANKA AFFAIRS (ASIA/PNS)
Bryant George, Director
632-8226
Robert Thompson, Country Officer, Pakistan
632-8226
Howard Thomas, Country Officer, Nepal
632-8226
John M. Miller, Country Officer, Sri Lanka
632-0212

Afghanistan is the responsibility of the Office of Near Eastern/North African Affairs (NE/NENA) of the Bureau for Near East (NE). Country Officer for Afghanistan and Iran is Anne Dammarell (632-9142).

One of the four geographic bureaus, the Bureau for Asia is the principal AID office with responsibility for the planning, formulation, and management of U.S. economic development and supporting assistance programs in South Asia. The bureau assures necessary liaison with other AID offices, the Department of State, other U.S. bilateral and multilateral agencies, and officials of recipient countries; and represents AID at country consortia or consultative group meetings. AID overseas field missions and offices— located in South Asia—for carrying out bilateral economic assistance programs, report to this bureau. Currently AID missions are located in Kabul, Dacca, New Delhi, Kathmandu, Islamabad, and Colombo.

The country directors and desk officers have accumulated expertise on the AID programs in the countries under their charge and, therefore, researchers will find it extremely helpful to consult these officials who can also refer the researchers to the appropriate sectoral specialists within the agency.

Other sub-units of the bureau that may provide researchers with valuable information are: Office of Development Planning (Robert Halligan, 632-9044), which reviews and approves research proposals from within the agency and from outside researchers; Office of the Project Development (Edward Sharlach, South Asia Division Chief, 235-8450), which designs and implements bureau programs and projects and monitors performance; and the Office of Technical Resources (Thomas M. Arndt, Director, 235-

8880), which is responsible for social and human resources, population, health and nutrition, agriculture and rural development, and scientific, technical, and environmental problems.

BUREAU FOR DEVELOPMENT SUPPORT (DS)
Sander M. Levin, Assistant Administrator
632-8614

This bureau administers the agency's international training program (235-1853) and provides professional leadership and technical support to agency activities through the unit offices of: Agriculture (235-8945), Nutrition (235-9779), Education (235-9015), Health (235-8929), Urban Development (235-8902), Rural Development and Development Administration (235-8918), Science and Technology (235-9046), Population (235-8117), Engineering (235-9827), and Energy (235-9090). The bureau's numerous offices, located in the Rosslyn Plaza Building, 1601 Kent Street, Arlington, Virginia 22209, are structured along with the above-mentioned sectors of development assistance in which the agency is active. Each office administers AID contract research projects in its field of specialization. Usually within each office, persons with expertise in South Asian matters are available. The bureau's Office of Development Information Utilization (235-9207), a memory bank for AID missions and project designers, administers its Development Information Centers (see entry A7).

BUREAU OF INTERGOVERNMENTAL AND INTERNATIONAL AFFAIRS (IIA)
David Bronheim, Assistant Administrator
632-9421

This bureau serves as the focal point within AID for coordination with other U.S. government agencies on U.S. economic-policy issues that affect the development process in the less-developed countries, and for coordination of U.S. economic-assistance policies and programs with those of other bilateral and multilateral assistance donors.

The bureau provides support to the Development Coordinating Committee, which is chaired by the Administrator of the AID, by identifying problems of interagency coordination, developing alternatives for resolution of these issues, and preparing or coordinating analysis for committee discussions. It formulates AID short-term policy on major international financial, trade, and other issues which affect U.S. development objectives and activities, and analyzes and plans AID policy on long-range issues affecting development. It also develops and recommends AID policy toward other development assistance donors, international financial institutions, and other international organizations having an impact on development.

OFFICE OF PUBLIC AFFAIRS
James W. McCulla, Director
632-9170
Arnold H. Dadian, Freedom of Information Officer
632-1850
Rhea Johnson, Privacy Act Coordinator
632-8639
Edward Caplan, Chief, Press and Publication Division
632-8632

This office has responsibility for information policy leadership and coordination to ensure that information about AID policies, objectives, and operations is disseminated fully and freely to the Congress and to the public. This office also prepares and distributes certain informational materials; responds to public inquiries and to requests for information filed under the Freedom of Information Act and the Privacy Act; and has responsibility for declassification of AID documents.

BUREAU FOR PRIVATE AND DEVELOPMENT COOPERATION (PDC)
Calvin H. Raullerson, Assistant Administrator
632-8298

This newly created, functional bureau with jurisdiction over several offices has a vast array of responsibilities that include encouraging and strengthening the effective participation of nongovernmental organizations in support of humanitarian objectives; performing designated responsibilities for the Food for Peace program; coordinating internal AID and U.S. government responses to foreign disasters with those of other private and international organizations; and providing leadership and policy guidance for agency activities in the development-related labor and manpower fields. Some of the bureau offices with South Asian involvement are discussed below. Staff members dealing with South Asia are willing to confer with researchers:

OFFICE OF PRIVATE AND VOLUNTARY COOPERATION
Thomas Fox, Director
235-1623

This office creates and explores approaches to enlarging the role of volunteerism in the development process; maintains liaison with the American Council on Foreign Aid, the Advisory Committee on Overseas Cooperative Development, and the community of voluntary agencies generally; and provides staff support to the Advisory Committee on Voluntary Foreign Aid. Steve Bergen (235-8420) deals with Asia-related matters.

OFFICE OF FOOD FOR PEACE
1735 North Lynn Street,
Arlington, Virginia 22209
Kathleen S. Bittermann, Coordinator
235-9220

In cooperation with the Department of Agriculture, this office administers U.S. food-aid programs in South Asia under Public Law 480 (Agricultural Trade Development and Assistance Act of 1954, as amended). AID supports the use of food aid in ways that promote, rather than hinder, the growth of food production and associated policy and program initiatives in the host country. Until recently, the Food for Peace program extended to all the countries of South Asia.

OFFICE OF UNITED STATES FOREIGN DISASTER ASSISTANCE
Joseph A. Mitchell, Director
632-8924

This office serves as the national coordinating center to provide both public and private international emergency relief, or technical assistance, to foreign disasters resulting from earthquakes, droughts, famines, epidemics, floods and storms, civil strife, power shortages, and accidents. In addition to emergency responses to disasters, programs in disaster preparedness, prediction, and prevention are also supported. The office publishes an annual report entitled *Foreign Disaster Relief.*

OFFICE OF LABOR AFFAIRS
Dale E. Good, Director
632-3662

This office serves as the principal agency office for liaison with the AFL-CIO in its Asian activities (see entry M5).

BUREAU FOR PROGRAM AND MANAGEMENT SERVICES (SER)
Donald G. MacDonald, Assistant Administrator
632-9888

The bureau provides centralized services in the areas of management planning, management operations, data management, direct contracting and commodity management. It establishes and monitors AID policies, regulations, and procedures in all of these areas.

BUREAU FOR PROGRAM AND POLICY COORDINATION (PPC)
Alexander Shakow, Assistant Administrator
632-0482

This functional bureau is responsible for the agency's over-all program-policy formulation, planning, coordination, resources allocation and evaluation, and the program management-information systems which support them. The bureau develops economic-assistance policies, provides guidance on long-range program planning, economic analysis, sector assistance strategies, and project analysis and design. The bureau reviews and monitors all country program strategies and project proposals and selectively reviews project papers from other AID bureaus. The bureau also seeks to encourage and develop democratic institutions and human rights in the developing countries, in accordance with the federal government guidelines.

Through its automated and manual systems, the bureau also provides statistical services to the agency. The Economic and Social Data Services Division, located at 1735 North Lynn Street, Arlington, Virginia 22209 (Annette Binnendijk, Acting Chief, 235-9170), maintains a computerized Economic and Social Data Bank (ESDB) containing country information and some microdata components of household surveys. The data bases are accessible to the public. Another automated system, the Program Data Services Division (235-9167), located at the same address in Rosslyn, compiles *U.S. Overseas Loans and Grants.* The bureau also compiles *Selected Economic Data for the Less Developed Countries, Food and Total Agricultural Production in Less Developed Countries, Economic Growth Trends,* and *Operations Report* which ceased publication in 1973.

OFFICE OF WOMEN IN DEVELOPMENT (WID)
Arvonne Fraser, Coordinator
632-3992

In recognition of the fact that women in developing countries play a significant role in economic production, family support, and the over-all development process of the national economies of such countries, the AID is under statutory obligation to give particular attention to those projects and activities that tend to integrate women into the national economies of developing countries, thus improving their station and assisting the total development effort. In carrying out this responsibility, the office conducts research and oversees contract grants on the role of women in the development process, including that in South Asia, both from regional and comparative perspectives.

The office has a resource center that distributes some 100 publications. Mostly these are current WID reports, conference proceedings, research papers, and project reports from AID as well as from other institutions. These publications cover a variety of topics involving rural women and the development process: agriculture and food production, appropriate technology, employment and income-generating activities, formal and nonformal education, and the status of women in specific developing countries. Limited copies are available to those working in the area of women in development. *An Annotated Bibliography of Available Materials* may be obtained free from the resource center.

Some of the WID reports of interest include: University of Colombo, *Status of Women in Sri Lanka* (1979); Lynn Bennett, *Tradition and Change in the Legal Status of Nepalese Women* (1979); Susan Fuller Alamgir, *Profile of Bangladeshi Women* (1977); *International Conference on Women and Food* (1978), background papers and proceedings of a WID sponsored conference held at the University of Arizona on the role of women in meeting basic food and water needs in developing countries; and *Progress Towards an A.I.D. Data Base on Women in Development* (1977), a study of the establishment of data bases on women in AID recipient countries. Other useful publications prepared by the office are: *International Directory of Women's Development Organizations* (1977), and *Women in Development*.

Note: Also see entries A7, F1, G1, G2, and G3.

J2 Agriculture Department (USDA)

1.   a. *Independence Avenue between 12th and 14th Streets, S.W.*
     Washington, D.C. 20250
     447-2791

     b. Open to the public; previous appointment recommended

2.   The Department of Agriculture, in addition to its numerous domestic services and programs, also develops and expands markets abroad for agricultural products, and assumes global responsibilities for food and agricultural technical assistance. Most research is done within the department.

3.   For the department's libraries and reference facilities, see entry A26.

Numerous USDA popular publications for farmers, suburbanites, home-makers, and consumers, on a wide variety of subjects, are available free from the Office of Governmental and Public Affairs (447-4894). While most of the significant publications and documents are noted with descriptions of the concerned units, a selected list of other useful publications follows:

World Fertilizer Review and Prospects (1976); *The World Food Situation and Prospects* (1974); *World Population Growth: Analysis and New Projections of the United Nations* (1977); *Foreign and Domestic Prospects for the U.S. Fast Food Franchise Industry* (1976); *An Analysis of the UNCTAD Integrated Programme for Commodities* (1978); *Development and Spread of High Yielding Varieties of Wheat and Rice in the Less Developed Nations* (1974); *World Economic Conditions in Relation to Agricultural Trade* (published twice a year); *Foreign Agricultural Trade of the United States* (published monthly); and the annual *Report of the Secretary of Agriculture,* which also summarizes the condition of agriculture in the U.S. and in the world during the year. For bibliographic control of the USDA publications consult *List of Available Publications of the United States Department of Agriculture* (1979) and *Fact Book of U.S. Agriculture* (1979).

The department's principal Freedom of Information Act contact is Hal R. Taylor, Deputy Director, Information, Office of Governmental and Public Affairs, 447-7903. For information concerning retired or inactive files, which are stored in the Federal Record Center in Suitland, Maryland, contact Roxanne R. Williams, Chief, Information Systems and Planning Division (Administration), 447-2118. It may be pointed out that most records and documents of the department are open to the public.

INTERNATIONAL AFFAIRS AND COMMODITY PROGRAMS
Dale E. Hathaway, Under Secretary
447-3111

The bulk of the international activities of the department are carried on by this unit. The responsibilities of the International Affairs and Commodity Programs cover several broad areas including the following:

FOREIGN AGRICULTURAL SERVICE (FAS)
Thomas R. Hughes, Administrator
447-3935

The FAS is an export promotion and service agency for U.S. agriculture. FAS also provides staff support for the department's participation in international organizations and in international conferences and meetings held to consider policy and operating programs that deal with agriculture, the trade in agricultural products, the over-all economic problems, and technical and scientific activities related to agriculture.

Foreign Market Development
Jimmy D. Minyard, Assistant Administrator
447-4761

This section works to maintain and expand export sales by cooperating with domestic, nonprofit trade associations, agriculture departments of the 50

U.S. state governments, and others on jointly financed market-development projects abroad; by appraising overseas marketing opportunities and communicating them to the U.S. agricultural trade; and by encouraging and cooperating with state and regional groups involved in export promotion.

International Trade Policy
Vernon L. Sorenson, Assistant Administrator
447-6887

This section is concerned with improving access to foreign markets for U.S. farm products through representations to foreign governments and through participation in formal negotiations. This section also acts as the department's liaison with the General Agreement on Tariffs and Trade (GATT), Food and Agricultural Organization (FAO), and other international organizations to reduce international trade barriers, increase world trade in agricultural products, and further trade policies advantageous to U.S. agriculture. Inquiries concerning South Asia may be addressed to the South and East Asia Group (Dewey Pritchard, Chief, 447-7225) of the Developing Countries Division (447-4083).

Commodity Programs
Turner L. Oyloe, Assistant Administrator
447-5404

By conducting foreign commodity analyses on worldwide production competition, trade, marketing, prices, consumption, and other factors affecting U.S. exports and imports of agricultural commodities, the Commodity Programs unit provides vital data on the development of U.S. foreign-market plans and programs. Analysts of different divisions—Oilseeds and Products, 447-5635; Horticultural and Tropical Products, 447-5330; Grain and Feed, 447-6219; Dairy, Livestock and Poultry, 447-8031—are knowledgeable about South Asian commodities and related matters.

Agricultural Attachés
Larry F. Thomasson, Assistant Administrator
447-6138

The department's global reporting and analysis network, covering world agricultural production, trade, competition, and policy situations affecting U.S. agriculture, are managed by this section. This service is made possible through the agricultural attachés and officers stationed at 65 key posts, covering more than 100 countries, and through specialists who make surveys abroad. In addition to reporting and analysis, the attachés engage in efforts to open markets for U.S. agricultural products in the country of assignment and to eliminate trade barriers. Currently, agricultural attachés are stationed in New Delhi, Islamabad, and Dacca. Stanley W. Phillips (447-6472) is the Area Officer for South Asia. Unclassified attaché reports may be obtained from the Records and Communications Office (447-6135). An informative pamphlet, *The Agricultural Attaché*, is available on request.

Office of the General Sales Manager (OGSM)
Kelly Harrison, General Sales Manager and Associate Administrator
447-5173

This office works to improve the department's ability to develop export policy and assist in orderly export marketing of agricultural commodities in ample supply in the U.S. In addition to its numerous responsibilities concerning commercial exports, the OGSM also administers Public Law 480 (Agricultural Trade Development and Assistance Act of 1954, as amended), which aims to "use the abundant agricultural productivity of the United States to combat hunger and malnutrition and to encourage economic development in developing countries."

PL 480, also known as the Food for Peace program, includes concessional sales (Title I); donation and disaster relief (Title II); and food for development and barter (Title III). Title III aims to assist the developing countries in their efforts to increase the availability of food for the poor, and to improve the quality of their lives by permitting the funds accumulated from the local sale of PL 480 Title I commodities to be applied against the repayment obligations of these countries to the U.S. Currently, PL 480 programs are active in Pakistan, Sri Lanka, and Bangladesh; the program has an earlier history in Afghanistan and India. Harold L. Norton (447-7763) is the Title I Program Coordinator for South Asia of the Public Law 480 Programs.

An annual review of the department's export activities, carried out under the PL 480 program, is to be found in the secretary of agriculture's annual report to the Congress entitled *Food for Peace*. Another annual report, *Title I Public Law 480*, prepared by the Foreign Agricultural Service, shows statistical information about total quantity and value of exports under PL 480, by country and commodity, from the beginning of the program to the date of the publication. The OGSM also collects information from private exporters of agricultural commodities on their export sales and related transactions, and it publishes a weekly compilation, *US Export Sales*.

Foreign Agricultural Service publications related to South Asia include: *Foreign Agriculture*, a weekly, containing summary reports on world agriculture and its incidence on the U.S. farmers; *Foreign Agriculture Circulars*, available only to U.S. residents, an irregular series, each issue of which provides statistical information on such items as canned deciduous fruits, coffee, and cocoa; *World Agricultural Production and Trade, Statistical Report*, a monthly, also restricted to U.S. residents, contains statistical data and comments; *Weekly Roundup of World Food Production and Trade*, a news release summarizing global agricultural developments; and the miscellaneous, *Special Reports*, such as *Pakistan's Cotton Industry* (1980), and *Peanut Industry in India* (1975). For information concerning FAS publications, contact the FAS Information Division (J. Don Looper, Director, 447-3448).

OFFICE OF INTERNATIONAL COOPERATION AND DEVELOPMENT (OICD)
Quentin M. West, Director
447-3157

The USDA is the largest single source of agricultural expertise in the world. The OICD coordinates, plans, and directs the department's efforts in international development and technical cooperation in food and agriculture. It also coordinates international organization affairs and scientific exchange programs for the department. In carrying out its responsibilities, OICD works closely with other U.S. international organizations to assist them in utilizing the scientific and institutional resources of American agriculture in carrying out development-assistance programs. In addition, it develops and maintains effective relationships with international and U.S. organizations in planning and coordinating departmental activities that are designed to support U.S. programs to reduce world hunger and malnutrition. An information brochure, *Sharing Agricultural Knowledge with Other Nations,* outlines the activities of this agency.

International Organization Affairs
Martin Kriesberg, Coordinator
447-4493

This unit is responsible for liaison between the department and international organizations dealing with agricultural development: Food and Agriculture Organization (FAO), the World Bank (IBRD), and the U.N. World Food Council, among others. Together with the Foreign Agricultural Service, the division also helps in liaison work with the United Nations Conference on Trade and Development.

Interagency and Congressional Affairs
George Waldman, Assistant Director
447-7143

This unit coordinates agricultural development activities with other U.S. departments and agencies, such as the Department of State and the Agency for International Development.

International Training Division
Robert I. Ayling, Deputy Director
447-4711

A series of technical short courses is conducted by this division that also coordinates academic programs in a wide range of topics—agricultural, nutritional, managerial, and rural development skills—for foreign participants in the U.S. and overseas. Following is a breakdown of South Asian participants for the fiscal year 1978–79: India, 38; Pakistan, 38; Sri Lanka, 28; and Bangladesh, 49. Most of these training programs are funded by AID or the World Bank. For further information, contact Gloria McCaskill, Head of the Participant Services Unit (447-7203) of the division.

Technical Assistance Division
William S. Hoofnagle, Director
235-2285

Providing technical-assistance personnel to various agriculture-development projects funded by other U.S. agencies, particularly AID, the division is currently assisting AID-sponsored agricultural research and farm water-management projects in Pakistan, and soil- and water-conservation projects in Nepal. Jerome Hammond (235-2290) is the leader of the Asia Program of the division. Useful annual project data and information on the program of the division are provided in the booklet entitled *Summary of USDA International Technical Assistance Activities.*

Scientific and Technical Exchange Division
Roger E. Neetz, Deputy Director
447-4445

This division coordinates all overseas agriculture-related, scientific and technical activities of the department. The limited activities of the division are currently confined to fertilizer, fisheries, and a few other sectors in India. As of this writing, negotiations are in progress for an extensive, agricultural exchange program in India through the aegis of the proposed Indo-U.S. joint subcommission on agriculture.

Development Project Management Center
Morris J. Solomon, Coordinator
447-5804

By providing training, materials, and technical assistance, this AID-funded unit helps developing countries improve their project-management capabilities. However, with the exception of some limited activities concerning agricultural management training in Nepal, this unit's South Asia-related activities are marginal.

Reports and Technical Inquiries Group
Patricia Wetmore, Technical Information Officer
447-2893

This AID-funded unit provides agricultural information needed for the design and implementation of AID's agricultural programs overseas. Its small reference collection of monographs, OICD reports and studies, and country vertical files may be reviewed by researchers with prior appointments.

AGRICULTURAL STABILIZATION AND CONSERVATION SERVICE (ASCS)
Ray Fitzgerald, Administrator
447-3467

ASCS provides accounting, budget, personnel, and other administrative and management support necessary for the Office of General Sales Manager to administer the department's Commodity Credit Corporation's export credit sales and the Public Law 480 (Food for Peace) programs.

COMMODITY CREDIT CORPORATION (CCC)
Bob Bergland, Chairman
447-3631

With a huge borrowing authority, CCC finances farm programs, domestic and export surplus-commodity disposal, foreign assistance, storage, and related programs and operations of the department, utilizing ASCS personnel.

ECONOMICS, POLICY ANALYSIS AND BUDGET
Howard W. Hjort, Director
447-5681

WORLD FOOD AND AGRICULTURAL OUTLOOK AND SITUATION BOARD (WFAOSB)
Dawson Ahalt, Chairman
447-8651

Created in 1977 when an era of stable world-food prices and supplies gave way to extreme price fluctuations and food shortages, the board primarily coordinates USDA analyses related to the agricultural situation in the United States and throughout the world. The board ensures a constant flow of vital information to the policy makers and the public. In carrying out its responsibilities, the board oversees and clears for consistency of analytical assumptions and results, all estimates and analysis that relate significantly to international and domestic commodity supply and demand.

Among the board's responsibilities is the leadership of USDA interagency committees on each of the major commodities. Also, in cooperation with the Department of Commerce, the board maintains a Joint Agricultural Weather Facility to participate and monitor global weather patterns which aid experts in interpreting the probable impact of weather on crop production. Publications of the office include the monthly *World Crop Production, Agricultural Supply and Demand Estimate* (monthly), and *Weekly Weather and Crop Bulletin.*

ECONOMICS, STATISTICS, AND COOPERATIVE SERVICE
Kenneth R. Farrell, Administrator
447-8104

This service analyzes and collects domestic and international information on agriculture, and develops and administers a program of economic, statistical, and other social-science research related to food and agriculture, nationally and internationally. The results of these activities are made available to users through research and statistical reports and through outlook and situation reports on major commodities and areas.

International Economic Division
J. B. Penn, Director
447-8710

Within this division, the Asia Branch (Carmen O. Nohre, Chief, 447-8860) conducts research on South Asian agricultural and economic situations, market developments, monetary and trade conditions, and governmental policies affecting the export of U.S. farm products. Whereas the Foreign Agricultural Service (FAS) is primarily commodity oriented, this division focuses on countries; therefore, the division's economists, who are specialists on South Asia, may be able to provide researchers with statistics and outlook analyses for agriculture in that region.

Agricultural History Branch (National Economic Division)
Wayne D. Rasmussen, Chief
447-8183

A reference center composed primarily of key USDA documents and U.S. agricultural history and related materials, the Agricultural History Branch also contains a small amount of materials related to South Asia and U.S. bilateral relations with the region. The American Agricultural Economics Documentation Center (Cynthia Kenyon, Director, 447-4383) of the branch, although concentrating on American and Canadian agricultural literature and documentation, also contains some materials pertaining to South Asia.

The center's on-line retrieval facilities include USDA's AGRICOLA. The center also has access to the bibliographic-data files of the American Agricultural Economics Association. Both the Agricultural History Branch and the Documentation Center are accessible to the public.

Economics, Statistics and Cooperative Service prepares a number of useful publications that may be obtained from the Publication Division (447-7255). Some of the South Asia-related publications include:

Martin Kriesberg, *International Organizations and Agricultural Development* (1977), a report describing major international organizations with programs to help low income countries improve their agriculture and rural sectors.

Report Assessing Global Food Production and Needs, an annual report to the U.S. Congress that fulfills the requirements of Public Law 480, and responds to congressional wishes for a report that assesses world food production and needs, to serve as a reference document for future program-planning under Title I of the law.

Asia Agricultural Situation, an annual review and outlook for agricultural production, agricultural trade, and the economic situation of Asiatic countries, including the countries of South Asia.

World Agricultural Situation, published 3 times a year, containing summaries of comparative prices, agricultural developments, and international trade agreements.

Note: Also see entries A26 and G4.

J3 Arms Control and Disarmament Agency (ACDA)

1.   a. *State Department Building*
320 21st Street, N.W.
Washington, D.C. 20451
632-9610

b. Open to the public but visits should be arranged in advance.

c. George Seignious II, Director
Thomas A. Halsted, Public Affairs Adviser
632-0392

2.   ACDA formulates and implements arms control and disarmament policies for promoting the national security of the United States and its relations with other countries. Although at present, the agency's primary concern centers on the negotiations with the Soviet Union on strategic arms-limitation issues, the agency is also responsible for preventing the spread of nuclear weapons to countries that do not possess them, and monitoring the flow of arms trade throughout the world. Thomas Graham (632-1107), of the Non-Proliferation Bureau, is the agency's expert on South Asia who may be consulted by researchers. Scholars may also contact the International Security Programs Bureau (John Newhouse, 632-3612).

Research opportunities available in the agency are announced in the *Commerce Business Daily* of the U.S. Department of Commerce. For information on unsolicited research proposals, contact Evalyn W. Dexter (235-8248) of the Contract Office. Information concerning the agency's recently instituted graduate fellowship program in social sciences may also be obtained from the Contract Office.

3. The Arms Control and Disarmament Agency Library is located in Room 804, 1700 North Lynn Street, Arlington, Virginia 22209. The library is open to qualified researchers, but prior permission should be obtained from the librarian, Diane Ferguson (235-9550). The library is open from 9:00 A.M. to 4:45 P.M., Monday through Friday. Its small collection of approximately 5,500 volumes includes unclassified ACDA publications and contract research reports, as well as a few selected titles on Third World arms trade, nuclear proliferation, and other related subjects.

4. An extremely useful agency publication, *World Military Expenditures and Arms Transfers, 1968–1977,* presents data on military expenditures, armed forces, and arms transfers for 145 countries over a 10-year period. In order to have a backdrop against which to evaluate this military data, the report also presents information for each country on gross national product, central government expenditures, total exports and imports, public health, and educational expenditures, as well as total population and numbers of teachers and physicians. The data used in this publication is provided by official U.S. or foreign government sources, or by international organizations; some data is more reliable or complete than others.

   Other publications include: *Arms Control Report to the Congress,* an annual; *ACDA External Research Reports,* an irregular unclassified series resulting from external research sponsored by the agency; and *Official Publications of the United States Arms Control and Disarmament Agency.* The agency's internal records, including classified research reports, are maintained by the Communications and Services Section (632-0931) of the Office of Administration. For access to the agency's classified records through the Freedom of Information Act, scholars should contact ACDA's Freedom of Information Officer, Charles Oleszycki (632-0760).

J4 Central Intelligence Agency (CIA)

1. a. *Washington, D.C. 20505*
      351-7676

   b. Open to persons with security clearance

   c. Stansfield Turner, Director

2. Established under the National Security Council by the National Security Act of 1947, as amended, the CIA coordinates intelligence activities of the U.S. government departments and agencies as they relate to national security. The CIA, among other responsibilities, collects foreign intelligence, including information not otherwise obtainable; disseminates, as needed for national security, foreign political, economic, scientific, technical, military, geographic, and sociological intelligence; conducts and coordinates counterintelligence activities outside the U.S.; and produces and disseminates counterintelligence studies and reports.

   The CIA occasionally carries out authorized research contracts, primarily for technical studies and for research on aspects of methodology and model building. The agency also engages foreign-area specialists as outside consultants. Inquiries for contract research and consulting possibilities should be addressed to the Coordinator for Academic Relations and External Analytical Support (James King, 351-7848).

Area specialists in the Office of Political Research and Analysis of the National Foreign Assessment Center (Bruce C. Clarke, Deputy Director, 351-5151) and other units monitor and analyze developments in different regions and countries of the world, including South Asia. Most of the reports and analyses produced by the agency, however, are not available to the public. Scholars may contact the Public Affairs Office (Herbert Hetu, Chief, 351-7676) about information concerning access to materials and other research assistance. Requests for release of CIA internal documents, under the provision of the Freedom of Information Act, are processed by the agency's Information and Privacy Coordinator (John Bacon, 351-7486).

Declassified CIA records and documents are listed in the *Declassified Documents Quarterly Catalog* published commercially by Carrollton Press (1911 N. Fort Myer Drive, Arlington, Virginia 22209, 703/523-5940). Although, as of this writing, there are no significant materials in the CIA record group (RG 263) at the National Archives, a few selected, declassified CIA studies are available in its Modern Military Branch, within the Military Archives Division. Also CIA-declassified documents are available at the Center for National Security Studies (see entry H12).

3. The Central Intelligence Agency Library is not accessible to private researchers. Limited, interlibrary loan facilities are available however. Bibliographic access to the library's unclassified titles is provided through the automated Ohio College Library Catalog (OCLC) system.

4. In addition to numerous, confidential series of documents, such as the *National Intelligence Estimates* and *Special National Intelligence Estimates,* the CIA also produces a number of unclassified publications. Following is a selection of CIA publications considered to be significant to South Asian scholars: *National Basic Intelligence Factbook,* a semiannual compilation, giving outline data on land, water, government, economy, communications, and defense forces of all nations; *Potential Implications of Trends in World Population, Food Production and Climate* (irregular); *Chiefs of State and Cabinet Members of Foreign Governments) (monthly); Economic Indicators* (weekly); *International Energy Biweekly Statistical Review; Communist Aid to the Less Developed Countries of the Free World* (annual); *Annotated Bibliography on Transnational and International Terrorism* (1976); *Arms Flow to LDCS: U.S.-Soviet Comparisons, 1974–1977* (1978).

The CIA unclassified "Reference Aid Series" is released to the public through the Document Expediting Project (DOCEX) (287-5253), of the Exchange and Gift Division of the Library of Congress. DOCEX staff maintains a card index of all CIA publications received since the program's inception in 1973. These publications are also entered into LC's main collection. A list of the CIA publications is provided in the annually updated catalog, *CIA Publications Released to the Public through Library of Congress DOCEX.* The agency also produces a series of unclassified maps and atlases, on most countries of the world, which are available through the U.S. Government Printing Office sales outlets.

J5 Civil Aeronautics Board (CAB)

1.　a. *1825 Connecticut Avenue, N.W.*
Washington, D.C. 20428
673-5990

　　c. Marvin S. Cohen, Chairman

2.　The CAB promotes and regulates the civil air transport industry within the United States and between the United States and foreign countries in the interests of the foreign and domestic commerce of the U.S., the postal service and the national defense.

BUREAU OF INTERNATIONAL AVIATION
Stanford Rederer
673-5417

Air transportation between the U.S. and foreign countries is conducted pursuant to international agreements. The bureau, on behalf of the CAB, advises and assists the Department of State in the negotiations of these agreements and participates in the formulation of U.S. positions for international civil aviation conferences. James McMahon (673-5007) is the Desk Officer for Pakistan; Mary Pett (673-5416) is the Desk Officer for India.

J6 Commerce Department

1.　a. *Main Commerce Building*
14th Street and Constitution Avenue, N.W.
Washington, D.C. 20230
377-2000

　　b. Open to the public

2.　The primary mission of the Department of Commerce, a very large and complex organization, is to encourage, serve, and promote the U.S. economic development and technological advancement. Within this framework—and together with a policy of promoting the U.S. national interest through the encouragement of the competitive free-enterprise system—some of the operating units of the department are directly concerned with development abroad, while others, such as the Bureau of the Census, utilize the resources accumulated through U.S. work in promoting development overseas. Research concerning South Asia is mostly in-house, and very few opportunities are available for South Asian specialists to do research and consulting on a contract basis.

3.　The main Commerce Department Library and the Census Bureau Library are described in entries A6 and A5, respectively. Other smaller libraries and reference collections are described under the departmental sub-units to which they are attached.

4.　The department compiles a biweekly periodical, *Commerce America,* available for sale, which is primarily oriented to aiding exporters by providing data on international trade, economic growth, technological development, and business services. A useful, key-business indicator and guide to the department's publications is the weekly, *The Business Service Checklist,* also for sale, and researchers will find the annual, *The United States Department of Commerce Publication Catalog and Index,* very useful. These departmental publications also refer to entries from the *Monthly Catalog of United States Government Publications* and *Government Reports Announcement and Index.* The department's Office of Publications (377-3721) may be contacted for information on publications and sales. Other relevant publications are described below under the sub-units responsible for originating them.

Each major departmental sub-unit contains a records-management facility for storing internal records until they are transferred to the National Archives. Inventories of retired office files are maintained. The Records Management Division (Ivy Parr, Chief, 377-3630) can assist researchers in finding appropriate records-management offices and in locating retired files. Scholars, desiring to invoke the Freedom of Information Act, may contact the Central Reference and Records Inspection Facility (John Boyd, Head, 377-4217) of the Information Management Division. Most departmental sub-units maintain a desk for providing assistance to requests for Freedom of Information.

CENSUS BUREAU
Federal Office Building
3 Silver Hill and Suitland Roads
Suitland, Maryland 20233
Vincent P. Barabba, Director
(301) 763-5190

There is a daily shuttle-bus service between the Main Commerce Building and the Bureau of the Census office in Suitland.

The bureau is a general-purpose statistical agency that collects, tabulates, and publishes a wide variety of statistical data primarily about the people, economy, and foreign trade of the United States. The bureau is also involved in a wide variety of international activities, including the collection and analysis of selected demographic and economic data on South Asian countries. The following sub-units of the bureau are concerned with South Asia:

INTERNATIONAL STATISTICAL PROGRAM CENTER (ISPC)
Robert O. Bartram, Chief
(301) 763-2832

The ISPC is responsible for collecting and compiling most of the international statistics of the bureau. Although the center's extensive program includes economic and social subjects, systems analysis, data processing, methodology, and sampling, its principal focus is on population.

The center's accumulated international demographic statistics and information provide planners and researchers with readily available source materials for studies and analyses. They provide data bases to the Agency for International Development (AID) in evaluating programs and determining policies—particularly in the population field, and in constructing mathematical models to help developing nations project trends and quantify the results of alternative demographic, economic, education, and health policies.

The center's aim also is to assist the developing nations of the world achieve improvements in their statistics and statistical systems through training courses, given both in its own classrooms and by correspondence, through overseas workshops and consultation, and through the development of methodological materials. Since 1975, the center, in collaboration with George Washington University, the United Nations, and the Office of Population (AID), has established a Masters of Science program in social and economic statistics for visiting foreign statisticians, demographers, economists, and computer specialists. For further details see the free pamphlet, *International Statistical Programs of the Bureau of the Census* and the offprint of Beulah Washabaugh's *Summary Report U.S. Bureau of the Census International Statistical Training* (1974) available at the center. The center's Overseas Consultation, Training and Information Services, which provides the training programs of the center, distributes a free *Training Branch Newsletter* and a syllabus of courses offered.

ISPC publications include several irregular series, such as *Demographic Reports for Foreign Countries, Country Demographic Profiles, Research Documents*, the *World Mortality Pattern*, and *Current Publications of the ISPC*. Also available is the monthly, *Acquisition List*, compiled by the center's Documentation Branch. The center is equipped with an automated microfilm storage and retrieval system that covers a wide range of global, demographic, and family planning statistics, with concentration on developing countries. Census reports, statistical publications, sample surveys, family-planning-program reports, U.N. documents, professional journals, and the center's internal working papers and publications provide the data bases.

INTERNATIONAL DEMOGRAPHIC DATA CENTER (IDDC)
(POPULATION DIVISION)
Samuel Baum, Chief
(301) 763-2870

The IDDC collects, compiles and analyses in-depth data on all developing countries of the world, particularly countries with AID programs, since IDDC is funded by the AID's Office of Population. The division's annual publication, *World Population*, contains basic vital statistics of birth, mortality, and growth rates arranged by country. IDDC staff analysts also compile the series, *Country Demographic Profiles*, which present detailed data on individual countries, both adjusted and unadjusted, including urban-rural and age-sex distribution of population, marital status, fertility, family planning, mortality, migration, education, land use, labor force, occupation, and other selected indicators. So far, demographic profiles have been published on India, Pakistan, Nepal, and Sri Lanka; one on Bangladesh is under preparation.

Staff analysts, Roger Kramer and Frank Hobbs (301/763-2834) monitor South Asia and maintain notebooks and files of background information on South Asian countries. The staff analysts may be consulted by researchers for additional information and data. The division's Demographic Data Retrieval System (DDRS) is a data bank of microfilm with unevaluated data for all developing countries including some family-planning data on South Asia. Researchers may contact Martha A. Bargar (301/763-2834) for further information on DDRS data. The division also occasionally compiles *Information Research Documents*, focusing on methodology and other specialized topics in demographic studies. The Population Division's recent publication, *A Compilation of Age Specific Fertility Rates for Developing Countries* (1980), may be of interest to those engaged in South Asian demographic studies.

Researchers may also benefit by contacting: Bureau's International Programs Staff (Anthony Turner, Chief, 301/763-1121) of the Statistical Methods Division (Charles D. Jones, Chief, 301/763-2672); Foreign Demographic Analysis Division (John S. Aird, Chief, 301/376-7692); and Foreign Trade Division (Emanuel A. Lipscomb, Chief, 301/763-5342). The last named division publishes a number of technical and statistical reports and classifications of foreign trade, both waterborne and airborne, by commodity, country, and region. Most of these materials are also available in microform and on computer tape. For further information, contact Trade Information Branch (301/763-5140).

BUREAU OF ECONOMIC ANALYSIS
Tower Building
1401 K Street, N.W.
Washington, D.C. 20230
George Jaszi, Director
523-0777

The Bureau of Economic Analysis prepares, develops, and interprets the economic accounts of the United States, including balance-of-payments accounts, which give details on U.S. transactions with foreign countries. The bureau's monthly *Survey of Current Business* occasionally contains data of interest for South Asianists. Its public-information office maintains a small reference room (523-0595), which contains a collection of the bureau's periodicals and staff papers.

INTERNATIONAL INVESTMENT DIVISION
George R. Kruer, Chief
523-0657

This unit monitors U.S. direct investment overseas and analyses the economic impact of multinational corporations. The division publishes several annual statistical aggregates on foreign investments in the bureau's *Survey of Current Business*. Other publications include *U.S. Direct Investment Abroad* (1966–1977), containing data arranged by industry and region on the value of U.S. overseas investments and the involvement of foreign affiliates in those investments; *Revised Data Series on U.S. Direct Investment Abroad, 1966–1974* (1976), containing data on net capital outflow, reinvestment earnings, balance of payment income, and other earnings, fees, and royalties; *Special Survey of U.S. Multinational Companies, 1970* (1972), presenting the activities of the U.S. multinationals and their foreign affiliates from 1966 to 1970. Aggregate data on U.S. private investments in South Asia may be obtained by researchers from the staff; however, for reasons of confidentiality, information concerning the investment of individual companies is not accessible. Computer tapes of some of the crude data collected by the division are available at cost from the division's Data Retrieval and Analysis Branch (523-0652).

BALANCE OF PAYMENT DIVISION
Christopher L. Bach, Chief
523-0621

This division computes statistics and prepares analyses of quarterly U.S. balance of payments and annual analyses of the international investment position in the U.S. These studies are announced in the bureau's *Survey of Current Business.*

INTERNATIONAL TRADE ADMINISTRATION (ITA) (formerly Industry and Trade Administration)
Main Commerce Building
Robert E. Herzstein, Under Secretary
337-3808

The administration's objectives include promoting progressive business practices and world trade, strengthening the international trade and investment position of the United States, supporting a vital, private economic sector, and assisting in adapting to changes within the U.S. economic system. The sub-units, which are more directly involved with South Asia, are discussed below. For ITA publications, consult *Publications for Business from ITA* (1980), which is available free from the Publications and Sales Branch (Room 1617), located in the Main Commerce Building.

BUREAU OF EXPORT DEVELOPMENT (BED)
Peter G. Gould, Deputy Assistant Secretary
377-5261

The bureau assists U.S. business in securing international markets by a variety of means, such as providing counseling and marketing information-services, organizing and conducting overseas sales and trade missions, and other promotional activities.

Office of Country Marketing
Peter B. Hale, Director
377-5341

This office is organized into several geographical divisions; South Asia is included in the Asia/Africa Division (James A. Moorhouse, Director, 377-5655). Each division is further organized into regions and placed in charge of regional marketing managers who are required to collect, compile, and analyze relevant economic data for the countries under their charge. As desk officers, these managers also serve as contacts with the U.S. diplomatic missions abroad and foreign missions in the U.S. Robert S. Kelly (377-3893) is the regional manager for the countries of our interest.
     The office is responsible for compilation and publication of international marketing information. The annual or semiannual reports, *Foreign Economic Trends and their Implications for the United States* (FET), are prepared with the assistance of U.S. embassies and consulates abroad. This series of approximately 150 reports a year, available for sale, presents current business and economic developments in nearly every country and analyzes the market for U.S. goods. There are separate FET reports on Afghanistan (79–51), Bangladesh (79–138), India (79–91), Nepal (79–124), Pakistan (79–133), Sri Lanka (79–169).
     Another publication for sale, the *Overseas Business Report* (OBR), presents basic, authoritative information for exporters, importers, manufacturers, researchers, and those concerned with international trade and economic conditions. These reports are also prepared by the bureau substantially on

information furnished by the U.S. missions abroad. OBRs on South Asia include *World Trade Outlook for the Far East and South Asia* (80–10), *Market Profiles for Asia and Oceania* (79–14), *Marketing in Pakistan* (77–07), and *Marketing in India* (75–54).

Office of Export Planning and Evaluation
Jonathan C. Menes, Acting Director
377-5055

Another organ of the bureau for export promotion operation, this office is reponsible for the publication, *Country Market Sectoral Surveys*, which pinpoints the best U.S. export opportunities in a single foreign country; and the *Global Market Surveys* (GMS) which provides detailed information on 15–20 of the best foreign markets for the products of a single U.S. industry or a group of related industries. The two GMS series on South Asia are *Metalworking and Finishing Equipment in India* (1975) and *Machine Tools in India* (1980).

Office of Export Marketing Assistance
Richard Garnitz, Acting Director
377-5131

This office is also responsible for stimulating U.S. exports and investments abroad. Its *Foreign Market Reports* series contains data on foreign economic conditions by country. A monthly index is available. This office also prepares, on request, World Traders Data Reports describing the history, operation, sale, territories, business connections, and chief executives of individual foreign business firms. This unit's Trade Facilities Information and Services Division (Brooks Ryno, Director, 377-4992) maintains a reference room (Room 1063, 377-2997) that contains a variety of World Bank (IBRD) reports and research papers. Included are monthly operational summaries of loans under consideration by the World Bank, appraisal reports on bank-funded projects, and World Bank economic and country studies. This facility is open to the public.

In addition, researchers may find it useful to contact the bureau's Office of Export Promotion (John Roose, Director, 377-4231) and the Office of International Commercial Representation (Betty D. Neuhart, Director, 377-5777).

BUREAU OF INTERNATIONAL ECONOMIC POLICY AND RESEARCH (BIEPR)
Main Commerce Building
Abraham Katz, Assistant Secretary
377-3022

The BIEPR is responsible for coordinating activities involving the research, analysis, and formulation of international economic and commercial programs and policies relating to trade, finance, and investment as well as those of a bilateral, multilateral, or regional nature. The bureau's activities also include initiating and reviewing research studies on developments affecting U.S. foreign trade and commercial interests abroad; representing the department in international trade and related negotiations; and carrying out the department's interagency policy role in such organizations as the National Security Council and the National Advisory Council on International Monetary and Financial Policies.

Office of Country Affairs
David E. Bitchick, Director
377-5820

For South Asian researchers, this office may constitute a very useful primary contact and referral point. The desk officers or country specialists monitor trade and economic trends in the countries under their charge and advise U.S. business and government in matters of foreign trade and investments. South Asia is the assigned responsibility of a Senior Desk Office for Near East/South Asia (Marion Thompson, 377-4528) of the Developing Nations Division (James R. Johnston, Director, 377-2954).

Office of International Economic Research
Franklin J. Vargo, Director
377-5638

This office has little direct involvement in South Asia and generally conducts research on international economic policy issues, sector analysis, export projections, and world-wide trade developments and trends. However, several of its published and unpublished reports contain South Asian regional information.

The *Staff Economic Report* series includes *U.S. Trade with Developing Economies: The Growing Importance of Manufactured Goods* (1975); *Capital Requirements of the Non-OPEC Less Developed Countries* (1976); *Selected Basic Reference on Trade Barriers and International Trade Flows* (1976); and an annotated bibliography, *Survey of Current International Economic Research*, updated periodically.

Other publications of the unit include: *Trends in U.S. Foreign Trade*, containing data by country and commodity; *International Economic Indicators*, a quarterly, presenting a wide variety of comparative economic statistics; the monthly *Current Price Development in the U.S. and Major Foreign Countries*, which provides information on consumer and wholesale world commodity, export and import prices, and nonfarm wages and currency shifts; and the annual *Market Share Reports* (MSR) (with data for 5 years, 1973–1977), issued in 2 series—the Country Series, which includes reports on 88 import markets, comparing U.S. performance in 880 manufactured products with those of 8 other principal suppliers, and the Commodity Series, which includes individual reports on 880 manufactured products comparing the U.S. export performance in 92 foreign markets with those of 13 other major exporting countries. MSRs on Bangladesh, India and Pakistan, and other countries are available from the National Technical Information Service, Springfield, Virginia 22161 (703/559-4788).

Office of International Finance and Investment
Vincent D. Travaglini, Director
377-4925

This unit monitors and analyzes global activities in the fields of international lending, taxation, transfer of technology, antitrust matters, expropriations, and other investment disputes. Its publications include the 2 volume report, *The Multinational Corporation: Studies on U.S. Foreign Investments* (1972–1973), which is for sale.

Office of International Trade Policy
Frederick L. Montgomery, Director
377-5327

Primarily concerned with unfair trade practices, this office assists in the development of U.S. positions in international trade negotiations and monitors and analyzes developments relating to foreign tariffs, import quota systems, and international commodity agreements. The office publishes progress reports, concerning multinational trade negotiations, in the department's biweekly, *Commerce America.*

Office of Foreign Investments in the United States
Milton Berger, Director
377-2175

This unit is responsible for monitoring individual foreign investments and analyzing their impact on the U.S. economy. The office also conducts in-house and contract research on foreign investments and their ramifications; summaries of the findings are released in the ITA-prepared *Commerce News.* However, because investment from South Asian nations is very insignificant, there are, in this office, few materials of direct interest to South Asian investigators.

Additional South Asia-related information and materials may be available from the International Marketing Services Staff (Bruce Strong, Director, 377-3922), of the Bureau of Field Operations, and the Foreign Trade Zones Staff (John J. DaPonte, Director, 377-2862) and the Office of Export Administration (Kent N. Knowles, Director, 377-4293), of the Bureau of Trade Regulation.

MARITIME ADMINISTRATION
Main Commerce Building
Samuel B. Nemirow
377-2746

The Maritime Administration administers programs to aid in the development, promotion, and operation of the U.S. merchant marine and to organize and direct emergency merchant-ship operations. In conducting these basic objectives, the administration also manages U.S. maritime relations with foreign countries. Researchers may confer with the staff of the International Activities Office (Reginald A. Bourdon, 377-5685) concerning the administration's South Asia activities, such as commercial shipment of grains and other commodities, trade studies, and participation in international programs in the countries of South Asia.

OFFICE OF TRADE STUDIES AND STATISTICS
Joe Bill Young, Director
377-4758

This office compiles statistical data on U.S. water-borne trade with foreign countries and foreign merchant shipping with the U.S. Publications of the office include: *New Ship Construction; Merchant Fleets of the World; A Statistical Analysis of the World's Merchant Fleets;* and *Essential U.S. Trade Routes.* Useful statistical information may also be obtained from the Foreign

Trade Information System Division (Edward L. Adams, Chief, 377-3239),
a sub-unit of the office of Management Information System.

NATIONAL BUREAU OF STANDARDS
Gaithersburg, Maryland
Mailing address: Washington, D.C. 20234
Ernest Ambler, Director
(301) 921-2411

OFFICE OF INTERNATIONAL AFFAIRS
Edward L. Brady, Associate Director
(301) 921-3641

In the pursuit of the bureau's over-all goal of strengthening and advancing
U.S. science and technology and in facilitating their effective application
for public benefit, the Office of International Affairs maintains contact and
working relationships with various foreign countries. This office is also
responsible for exchanging information and providing scientific and technological assistance to several South Asian countries. An information brochure, *National Bureau of Standards at a Glance,* is available free. Also
free are copies of *National Standard Reference Data System Publication
List, 1964–1977.*

NATIONAL OCEANIC AND ATMOSPHERIC ADMINISTRATION (NOAA)
Washington Science Center
6010 Executive Boulevard
Rockville, Maryland 20850
Richard A. Frank, Administrator
(301) 377-4190

The mission of the NOAA is to explore, map, and chart the global ocean
and its living resources; to manage, use, and conserve those resources; to
describe, monitor, and predict conditions in the atmosphere, ocean, sun,
and space environment; to issue warnings against impending destructive
natural events; to develop beneficial methods of environmental modification, and to assess the consequences of inadvertent environmental modification over several scales of time.

NATIONAL MARINE FISHERIES SERVICE
3300 Whitehaven Street, N.W.
Washington, D.C. 20235
Terry Leitzell, Assistant Administrator
634-7283

Office of International Fisheries Affairs
David Wallace, Director
634-7514

This office has three separate divisions dealing with international fisheries
affairs: Foreign Fisheries Analysis Division (Milan A. Kravanja, Chief,
634-7307); International Fisheries Development and Services Division
(Clarence P. Idyll, Chief, 634-7263); and International Organization and
Agreements Division (Henry Beasley, Chief, 634-7257).
The office maintains country and subject files which also contain maps

and photographs. On the basis of information primarily available through foreign and U.S. government publications as well as trade journals, this office prepares extensive data on several aspects of international fisheries: economics of fishing, trade, marketing, government policies and regulation, the activities of government agencies, and international disputes.

OCEANIC AND ATMOSPHERIC SERVICES
Thomas B. Owen, Assistant Administrator
(301) 443-8110

International Affairs Office
Nels Johnson, Director
(301) 443-8761

Researchers may obtain advice from the staff pertaining to NOAA's worldwide technical, climatological, meteorological, oceanographic, and marine resources data-gathering activities.

NATIONAL OCEAN SURVEY
Herbert R. Lippold, Jr., Director
(301) 443-8204

Aeronautical Charting and Cartography
Walter J. Chappas, Chief
(301) 443-8189

A few maps and charts of interest may be found in this unit. A *Catalog of Aeronautical Charts and Related Publications* (1979) is available. It may be noted that most U.S. government charting and mapping activities are handled by the Defense Mapping Agency (See entry E1).

ENVIRONMENTAL SCIENCE INFORMATION CENTER (ENVIRONMENTAL DATA AND INFORMATION SERVICE)—LIBRARY AND INFORMATION SERVICES DIVISION
6009 Executive Boulevard
Rockville, Maryland 20852
Elizabeth J. Yeates, Chief
(301) 443-8330

The NOAA library collection, which is international in scope, contains extensive literature on atmospheric sciences, fisheries, marine biology, oceanography, and the law of the sea. The collection is dispersed among several library centers throughout the metropolitan area; however, through an NOAA automated library and information system, researchers have access to an integrated processing and retrieval system for all NOAA library resources and information centers. Information on the NOAA-supported computer bases is provided in the *Guide to NOAA's Computerized Information Retrieval Services*. NOAA's Atmospheric Sciences Library, located at 8060 13th Street, Silver Spring, Maryland (301/427-8000) maintains selected research reports on microfilm, drawn from government agencies and from in-house searches. The division, from time to time, also prepares "packaged literature searches" on particular topics of interest.

NATIONAL TECHNICAL INFORMATION SERVICE (NTIS)
Sills Building
5285 Port Royal Road
Springfield, Virginia 22161
Melvin S. Day, Director
(703) 557-4788

The National Technical Information Service's aim is to simplify and improve public access to Department of Commerce publications, as well as data files and scientific and technical reports sponsored by federal agencies. The NTIS is the central point in the United States for the public sale of government-funded research and development reports and other analyses prepared by federal agencies, their contractors, or grantees.

Through agreements with more than 300 organizations, NTIS adds about 70,000 new reports a year to its collection, which now exceeds 1,000,000 titles. The agency also coordinates the publishing and technical-inquiries of various special technology groups.

Researchers may conveniently locate abstracts of interest from among the 680,000 federally sponsored research reports completed and published from 1964 by using the agency's on-line computer-search service, NTISearch (557-4640). Copies of the research reports are sold in paper or on microfiche. The NTIS Bibliographic Data File on magnetic tape, which includes published and unpublished abstracts, is available for lease. A reference guide for the *NTIS Bibliographic Data File* (1978), is available on request.

Current abstracts of new research reports and other specialized technical information in various catagories of interest are published in some 33 weekly *Abstract Newsletters.* A comprehensive biweekly journal, *Government Reports Announcements and Index,* is published for libraries, technical information specialists, and those requiring such all-inclusive volumes. A standard-order microfiche service (SRIM) automatically provides subscribers with the full texts of research reports selected to satisfy individual requirements. Scholars may also note that over 1,000 published searches on various topics are available from computer searches already conducted by the NTIS. The *NTIS Search Catalog* provides a subject index to the materials. The staff will perform, for a fee, an on-line custom search on topics requested by individual researchers.

NTIS publications of interest include monthly foreign trade reports: *Foreign Market Reports; Foreign Market Airgrams;* and Foreign Broadcast Information Service's *Daily Reports* (Vol. V includes South Asia). NTIS also distributes various reports, abstracts, and translations of the Joint Publications Research Service (JPRS), some of which are listed in the annual *Reference Aid Directory of JPRS Ad Hoc Publications* and in the biweekly *Government Reports Announcement and Index.* For general information about the services and resources of NTIS, researchers may consult *NTIS Information Services* (1979) and *Subject Guide to NTIS Information Collection.* The Information and Sales Center for the NTIS services and publications is located at 425 13th Street, N.W., Washington, D.C., 20004 (724-3509).

OFFICE OF INTERNATIONAL AFFAIRS
Terrance L. Lindemann, Chief
724-3374

This office, formerly known as the Developing Countries Staff, acting for the U.S. Agency for International Development (AID), has an on-going expanding program, through which U.S. scientific and technological information is made available to developing countries through local cooperative agencies. Currently, this program includes India, Pakistan, Sri Lanka, and Nepal; negotiations are in progress for the inclusion of Bangladesh. John Hounsell (724-3386) is the Desk Officer dealing with South Asian countries. The office is responsible for publishing the two AID bulletins: *ACCESS to Information for International Development* and *AMTID, Application of Modern Technology to International Development,* both of which contain valuable materials on South Asia. An informative pamphlet, *Technical Information for Development,* describes the program of the office and lists the foreign cooperative agencies.

PATENT AND TRADEMARK OFFICE (PTO)
Crystal Plaza
2201 Jefferson Davis Highway
Arlington, Virginia 22202
Sidney A. Diamond, Commissioner
(703) 557-3428

The PTO, in addition to its responsibility for examining all U.S. applications for patents, also processes international applications for patents under the provisions of the Patent Cooperation Treaty.

OFFICE OF LEGISLATION AND INTERNATIONAL AFFAIRS
Michael Kirk, Director
(703) 557-3065

OFFICE OF INTERNATIONAL PATENT CLASSIFICATION
Thomas Lomont, Director
(703) 557-0667

The staff of these offices may be consulted for information and publications on patent laws and regulations for South Asian countries.

SCIENTIFIC LIBRARY (PATENT DOCUMENTATION ORGANIZATION)—FOREIGN PATENT BRANCH
Barrington Balthrop, Chief
(703) 557-2970

The library collects materials on international patents and trademarks including South Asia. A card catalog and separate inventories of holdings by country are available. The collection may be useful for studies in South Asian science and technology.

Note: Also see entries A5, A6, and G5.

J7 Congress

1.   a. *The Capitol*
Washington, D.C. 20510
224-3121

b. The galleries of the Senate and the House of Representatives, as well as most committee hearings, are open to the public.

2. The work of preparing and considering legislation is done largely by committees of both houses of Congress. There are 15 standing committees in the Senate and 22 in the House of Representatives. Those committees and subcommittees, concerned with South Asian affairs, are listed below, and their staff members may be consulted by interested scholars for information concerning legislative processes and committee operations.

Committee hearings are frequently attended by academic and other professional experts for providing oral or written testimony. Proceedings of public hearings are eventually published and are available from the committee conducting the hearing or from the Government Printing Office.

Although committee schedules are subject to frequent alterations, legislative calendars are available. The *Congressional Record*'s Daily Digest section announces the legislative program for each day, and at the end of the week gives the program for the following week. In addition, the *Washington Post*, a local daily, publishes the schedules of congressional activities each day.

The Congressional Research Service (CRS) serves as the principal research arm of the Congress (see entry J8). CRS, it may be noted, works exclusively for the members of Congress, and its analyses and reports are not available to the public unless made available by a member of the Congress to a constituent. South Asian-area specialists, however, may be willing to confer with researchers for information on congressional activities related to South Asia.

3. The Library of Congress is discussed in entry A23.

4. Proceedings of the Congress are published in the *Congressional Record*, which is issued daily when the Congress is in session. A permanent, bound edition of the *Record*—the pagination of which differs from the daily issues since the text is revised, rearranged, and printed in sequence—is also issued. XEROX University Microfilms publishes the *Congressional Record* in microfiche with a *Monthly Index* and a *Guide to the Congressional Record*. Each house of Congress also publishes a *Journal* at the end of each session. The *Offiicial Congressional Directory* is very useful for locating the members of Congress, the staff, and the committees. Other publications of interest are: the Senate Foreign Relations Committee's occasional compilation, *Legislation of Foreign Relations;* the House and Senate hearings on foreign aid authorization (titles vary); *Foreign Aid Appropriation* (titles vary); *Department of State Appropriations;* the series, *Required Reports to Congress in the Foreign Affairs Field;* Senate Committee on the Judiciary, *Relief Problems in Bangladesh* (1972) and *Relief Problems in East Pakistan and India* (3 vols., 1971); and *Recognition of Bangladesh* (1972), a hearing before the Senate Committee on Foreign Relations. Several useful checklists of congresssional hearings are also commercially available. Bibliographies of congressional publications on foreign affairs, U.S. intelligence activities, and other topics are available from the Government Printing Office.

STANDING COMMITTEES OF THE SENATE

FOREIGN RELATIONS COMMITTEE
Dirksen Senate Office Building, Room 4229
224-4651

Specializing in matters relating to all U.S. treaties and agreements with foreign countries, this committee deals with South Asia-related issues through several of its subcommittees, such as Near Eastern and South Asian Affairs, International Economic Policy and Arms Control, and Oceans and International Operations and Environment.

AGRICULTURE, NUTRITION AND FORESTRY COMMITTEE
Russell Senate Office Building, Room 322
224-2035

South Asia-related issues are one of the concerns of the subcommittee on Foreign Agricultural Policy.

APPROPRIATIONS COMMITTEE
Russell Senate Office Building, Room 132
224-3471

This important committee has jurisdiction over funding of all government programs. Of particular interest to the South Asian scholar are the subcommittees on defense and foreign operations.

ARMED SERVICES COMMITTEE
Russell Senate Office Building, Room 212
224-3871

This committee has jurisdiction over matters relating to the national military establishment including research and development. Subcommittees include Arms Control.

BANKING, HOUSING AND URBAN AFFAIRS COMMITTEE
Dirksen Sentate Office Building, Room 5300
224-7391

Of special interest are the activities of the Subcommittee on International Finance, relating to international economic affairs as they affect U.S. monetary policy, credit, financial institutions, economic growth, and urban affairs.

FINANCE COMMITTEE
Dirksen Senate Office Building, Room 2227
224-4515

This committee has jurisdiction over revenue and tax matters. A Subcommittee on International Trade is concerned with South Asian affairs in the areas of customs, tariffs, and import quotas.

COMMERCE, SCIENCE AND TRANSPORTATION COMMITTEE
Dirksen Senate Office Building, Room 5202
224-5115

Foreign commerce, science, transportation, communication, and transfer of technology to developing nations are among this committee's concerns.

JUDICIARY COMMITTEE
Dirksen Senate Office Building, Room 2226
224-5225

Responsibilities of this committee include refugees, escapees, immigration, naturalization, and espionage.

STANDING COMMITTEES OF THE HOUSE OF REPRESENTATIVES

COMMITTEE ON AGRICULTURE
Longworth House Office Building, Room 1301
225-2171

COMMITTEE ON APPROPRIATIONS
The Capitol, Room H-218
225-2771

Subcommittee on Defense
The Capitol, Room H-144
225-2847

Subcommittee on Foreign Operations
The Capitol, Room H-308
225-2041

COMMITTEE ON ARMED SERVICES
Rayburn House Office Building, Room 2120
225-4151

COMMITTEE ON BANKING, FINANCE, AND URBAN AFFAIRS
Rayburn House Office Building, Room 2129
225-4247

Subcommittee on International Development, Institutions and Finance
Rayburn House Office Building, Room 2252
225-3236

Subcommittee on International Trade, Investment, and Monetary Policy
House Office Building, Annex 2, Room 3107
225-1271

COMMITTEE ON THE BUDGET
House Office Building, Annex 1, Room A-214
225-7200

Task Force on Defense and International Affairs
House Office Building, Annex 1, Room A-214
225-8506

COMMITTEE ON FOREIGN AFFAIRS
Rayburn House Office Building, Room 2170
225-5021

Subcommittee on Asian and Pacific Affairs
House Office Building, Annex 1, Room A-704
225-3044

Subcommittee on International Economic Policy and Trade
House Office Building, Annex 1, Room A-707
225-3246

Subcommittee on International Organizations
House Office Building, Annex 1, Room A-703
225-5318

Subcommittee on International Operations
Rayburn House Office Building, Room B-358
225-3424

Subcommittee on International Security and Scientific Affairs
Rayburn House Office Building, Room B-301B
225-8926

COMMITTEE ON INTERSTATE AND FOREIGN COMMERCE
Rayburn House Office Building, Room 2125
225-2927

COMMITTEE ON THE JUDICIARY
Rayburn House Office Building, Room 2137
225-3951

Subcommittee on Immigration, Refugees, and International Law
Rayburn House Office Building, Room 2137
225-5727

COMMITTEE ON SCIENCE AND TECHNOLOGY
Rayburn House Office Building, Room 2321
225-6371

Committee concerns relate in part to environmental and energy research
and production, as well as domestic and international scientific planning,
analysis, and cooperation.

COMMITTEE ON WAYS AND MEANS
Longworth House Office Building, Room 1102
225-3625

Subcommitee on Trade
Cannon House Office Building, Room 233
225-3943

JOINT COMMITTEES

JOINT ECONOMIC COMMITTEE
Dirksen Senate Office Building, Room G-133
224-5171

This committee is concerned with economic growth, fiscal policy, and international economics.

SELECT COMMITTEES

HOUSE PERMANENT SELECT COMMITTEE ON INTELLIGENCE
Capitol, Room H-405
225-4121

HOUSE SELECT COMMITTEE ON NARCOTIC ABUSE AND CONTROL
House Office Building, Annex 2, Room 3287
225-1753

HOUSE SELECT COMMITTEE ON THE OUTER CONTINENTAL SHELF
House Office Building, Annex 2, Room 3587
225-3426

SENATE SELECT COMMITTEE ON INTELLIGENCE
Dirksen Senate Office Building, Room G-308
224-1700

Note: Also see entries A18, A31, J8, and J29.

J8   Congressional Research Service (CRS)

1.   a. *Library of Congress*
James Madison Memorial Building
First Street and Independence Avenue, S.E.
Washington, D.C. 20540
287-5775

b. Not open to the public

c. Gilbert Gude, Director

2.   The Congressional Research Service works exclusively for the Congress, conducting research, analyzing legislation, and providing information at the request of members, committees, and their staffs. South Asian-area specialists (David Lockwood, 287-7645; Richard Cronin, 287-7627; and Larry Niksch, 287-7678), in the Foreign Affairs and National Defense Division (Stanley Heginbotham, Chief, 287-5064), upon request and without partisan bias, prepare studies, reports, compilations, digests, and background briefings on South Asian issues of current concern to the Congress. These research and reference services are not available to the public.

3.   See Library of Congress, entry A23.

4.   All CRS research is restricted to the use of the Congress and is not for general distribution. However, private researchers may often obtain copies from Congress, either through the office of a member or a committee. Also,

from time to time CRS studies are read into the *Congressional Record* or are published in congressional committee reports. CRS *Issue Briefs,* which are distributed only to the members of Congress, review major policy topics, summarize the pertinent legislative history, and provide reference lists for further readings. In addition, the *Congressional Research Service Review,* the *UPDATE from CRS,* and the cumulative *Subject Catalog of CRS Reports in Print* (1980) are all exclusive publications for the members of Congress. Researchers may note that the CRS indexes current periodical articles on public policy issues—including foreign affairs by country—from some 3,000 U.S. and foreign journals and magazines. The "Bibliographic Citation" file is accessible to researchers in machine-readable format in the LC's SCORPIO automated data base.

J9 Defense Department (DOD)

1. a. *The Pentagon*
    Washington, D.C. 20301
    545-6700

    b. Access is restricted to persons with prearranged appointments or with security clearance.

2. Established in 1949, the Department of Defense integrates policies, procedures, and functions of the departments of the Army, Navy, and Air Force, and other agencies concerned with the national security of the United States. Limited South Asia-related research is conducted mostly within the department. The great bulk of the activities of the department are classified and are operational in nature.

3. Libraries and reference facilities are discussed below with the constituent departments. For the Army Library, see entry A3.

4. A good review of the Defense Department's activities is provided in the *Annual Defense Department Report* to the Congress on the military budget, which also contains the secretary of defense's reflections on the military position in the U.S. Statistical financial data on U.S. overseas military sales and assistance are published in the annual *Foreign Military Sales and Military Assistance Facts.* Publications of the other component departments and agencies are described below, together with the appropriate department or agency.

    The Defense Documentation Center (see entry G6), which does not supply any of its publications to the public, is the repository of all research reports produced under DOD contracts. However, the unclassified reports received at the center are made available to the National Technical Information Service (see entry J6), which lists them in its own indexes and makes them available to the public.

    Each major component of the Department of Defense controls its own records until they are retired to the custody of the National Archives. DOD's Record Division (E. E. Lowry, 695-5363), under the Office of the Joint Chiefs of Staff, can assist researchers with the various record-control facilities in the department. The Record Division's sub-units consist of: Information Release and Safeguards Branch (Brian V. Kinney, 697-9660); Records and Information Retrieval Branch (S. W. Musinski, 697-6906);

and Records and Information Management Branch (V. D. Moss, 695-2693).

Directorate for Freedom of Information and Security Review (Charles W. Hinkle, Director, 697-4325), in the Office of the Assistant Secretary for Defense (Public Affairs), processes all requests under the Freedom of Information Act for the records of the Office of the Secretary of Defense and the Joint Chiefs of Staff. The directorate's Freedom of Information Specialist (Arthur E. Fajans, 697-1160) can refer researchers to other appropriate departmental branch offices that deal with the Freedom of Information applications and inquiries.

PUBLIC AFFAIRS
Thomas B. Ross, Assistant Secretary
697-9312

Various sub-units of the Directorate for Management (Robert C. Kinkor, 697-0792) and Defense Information (William M. Taylor, 695-9082), both within the Office of Public Affairs, respond to written and telephone inquiries from the public. This office, therefore, is a useful initial contact point for researchers seeking to locate appropriate divisions and personnel of the department.

HISTORICAL STAFF (Deputy Assistant Secretary, Administration)
Alfred Goldberg, Historian
697-4216

The Historical Staff conducts and prepares historical studies of the department. It maintains a reference file of unclassified materials of departmental publications and documents and press clippings related to the structural evolution of the department and the military services. Researchers may visit this facility with a prior appointment.

OFFICE OF THE ASSISTANT SECRETARY OF DEFENSE FOR INTERNATIONAL SECURITY AFFAIRS (ISA)
Robert H. Pelletreau, Jr., Deputy Assistant Secretary for Near Eastern and South Asian Affairs
697-1335
Henry H. Gaffney, Director, Near Eastern and South Asian Affairs
697-1335
Ronald P. Zwart, Desk Officer, South Asia
695-9897

The ISA develops and coordinates Department of Defense policies and procedures in the fields of international political, military, and foreign economic affairs. This responsibility encompasses general problems of international security as well as arms control and disarmament questions, military-assistance-program administration, military sales to foreign governments, policy guidance for both U.S. missions and U.S. representatives to international organizations and conferences, as well as the negotiations and monitoring of agreements with foreign governments with respect to equipment, facilities, operating rights, and status of forces.

Continuous ISA external research programs focus on identifying and analyzing alternative defense policies for dealing with emerging international problems relevant to the security of the United States. Research for ISA is performed by federal contract research centers, other nonprofit analytical centers, commercial research firms, and university-based study centers. Research proposals are accepted from these and other research organizations if they meet ISA requirements. For the past few years, no research has been conducted on South Asia-related topics. ISA does not provide any recurring research publications. ISA-funded, unclassified research studies may be purchased from the National Technical Information Service.

DEFENSE INTELLIGENCE AGENCY (DIA)
Eugene F. Tighe, Jr., Director
695-7353
E. M. Collins, Vice Director for Foreign Intelligence
697-7695
Robert B. Patrick, Defense Intelligence Officer for Middle East and South Asia
695-0198

DIA coordinates the overseas military intelligence-gathering operations of the 3 branches of the U.S. armed forces: The Army's Assistant Chief of Staff for Intelligence (ACSI); the Office of Naval Intelligence (ONI); and the Air Force Intelligence Service (AFIS). A network of defense attachés from the 3 services are stationed in the U.S. embassies abroad. They report to the DIA analysts concerning various aspects of the armed forces of the countries under their charge. These attaché reports remain classified.

Although the DIA Reference Library (692-5311) is closed to outside researchers, the library does entertain written requests for information on specific topics. Limited interlibrary loan and photoduplication facilities are also available. Neither the facilities nor the materials generated by the DIA's Defense Intelligence School (433-4250) is accessible to private scholars. Most of the documents and records assembled in the office of the Assistant Vice Director for Attachés and Training (694-5657)—which manages the defense attaché program, including selection, training, and evaluation of personnel—are restricted materials.

NATIONAL SECURITY AGENCY (NSA)
Fort George G. Meade
Maryland 20755
(301) 688-6524
(301) 688-6964 (Freedom of Information)

NSA is perhaps the most secretive U.S. intelligence agency. It conducts highly technical, communication intelligence-gathering activities throughout the world. Its organizational structure remains classified.

DEFENSE SECURITY ASSISTANCE AGENCY
Ernest Graves, Director
695-3291

This agency administers U.S. military-assistance programs in foreign countries. Ron J. Malachowski (695-2720) is the chief of the Middle East/South Asia Division. The agency issues an annual unclassified publication, *Foreign*

Military Sales and Military Asisstance Facts, containing tabular data on U.S. military-assistance programs and arms sales abroad by country and by year for the last 10 years, as well as cumulative data in some instances from 1950. This publication may be obtained from the agency's Data Management Division (Stanley Stack, 697-3574).

JOINT CHIEFS OF STAFF
Policy Directorate
R. L. Lawson, Director
695-5618

The directorate's Far East/South Asia Division (D. M. Murane, 697-8830) prepares classified policy papers and estimates, relating to U.S. security interests, security assistance, and military relations in South Asia, for the Joint Chiefs of Staff.

HISTORICAL DIVISION
Robert J. Watson
697-3088

This division prepares histories and special background studies, most of which are classified. Some declassified documents from the 1940s are available to researchers in the Modern Military Branch of the National Archives.

DEFENSE ADVANCED RESEARCH PROJECTS AGENCY (DARPA)
1400 Wilson Boulevard
Arlington, Virginia 22209
Robert F. Fossum, Director
694-3077

A separately organized research and development agency in the Defense Department, the DARPA supplements the research program of the 3 military services. Its assigned research responsibilities include strategic technology, tactical technology, nuclear monitoring, materials sciences, information-processing techniques, and cybernetics technology.

Within the Cybernetics Technology Division (Craig I. Fields, 694-1303), research related to foreign and national security affairs is carried out at both the basic and exploratory research levels. Specific areas of emphasis include the development of prototype systems for early warning of crises; development of prototype systems for defining and measuring U.S. national interests abroad; development of quantitative methods for assessing and forecasting strategic threats; development and application of advanced analytic and computerized approaches to strategic planning and forecasting in short, medium, and long-run time frames.

A large majority of the research conducted in these areas is unclassified, and the results are published in professional literature. Inquiries concerning research proposals should be addressed to the Director of the DARPA. The National Technical Information Service furnishes the public with those agency reports that are available for general release. An informative brochure, *Defense Advanced Research Projects Agency*, is available on request.

ARMY DEPARTMENT
Pentagon Building
Washington, D.C. 20310
697-7589

OFFICE OF PUBLIC INFORMATION DIVISION HQDA (SAPA-PID)
Room 2E 641
Pentagon Building
Washington, D.C. 20310
Robert A. Sullivan, Chief of Public Affairs
695-5135

Since public access is restricted to many of the work areas and records and documents of the department, researchers may find it convenient to contact this unit first. Public Information Division (Gary Werner, Chief, 697-8719) may assist scholars in locating appropriate personnel and offices related to their specific inquiries. The Office of Freedom of Information (William J. Donohoe, Chief, 697-4122) processes all requests for declassification provided under the law.

RECORDS MANAGEMENT DIVISION (THE ADJUTANT GENERAL)
Forrestal Building
1000 Independence Avenue, S.W.
Washington, D.C. 20314
Guy B. Oldaker, Chief
693-7831

This division with its 4 components: Access and Release Branch (W. Anderson, Chief, 693-1847); Programs Branch (Wendell R. Boardman, Chief, 693-1937); Declassification Operations Branch (John Hatcher, Chief, 763-2742); and Privacy and Rule Making Branch (Cyrus H. Fraker, 693-0973) play an important role in providing access to U.S. historical records. The division decides on the maintenance and disposition of records, grants clearance and access to materials, determines what has been declassified, and assists the National Archives in processing army documents and records.

DEPUTY CHIEF OF STAFF FOR OPERATIONS AND PLANS
Pentagon Building
G. K. Otis
695-2904

The Office of the Deputy Chief of Staff for Operations and Plans supports foreign affairs research through an annual contract with Foreign Area Studies of the American University (Washington, D.C. 20016, 686-2769) for the preparation of area handbooks about the peoples and societies of foreign countries. Area handbooks are studies of a country's social, economic, political, and military institutions. Each area handbook depicts cultural and historical origins and the role these play in the country's present-day society. In 1980, area handbooks were available on 108 countries and areas. Area handbooks on South Asian countries include: Afghanistan (1973), Bangladesh (1975), Sri Lanka (Ceylon) (1971), India (1975), Pakistan (1975), and Nepal, Bhutan, and Sikkim (1973).

Intended to provide insights into general patterns, the area handbooks—

which vary from 300 to 800 pages—make optimum use of figures and tables for presentation of maps and statistical material. Research and writing are also conducted for the continued maintenance of existing area handbooks, for reducing obsolescence of information contained therein, and for supplying updated material. These handbooks may be purchased through the sales outlets of the U.S. Government Printing Office.

Strategy Plans and Policy Directorate
R. L. Schweitzer, Director
695-5032

The South Asia Regional Desk (A. Husnian, 695-6454), of the Politico Military Division (W. M. Stokes III, 695-2283), prepares memoranda and position papers, some of which are unclassified, that contribute to the formulation of U.S. Army policy objectives on strategy and security issues in South Asia.

ASSISTANT CHIEF OF STAFF FOR INTELLIGENCE (ACSI)
Pentagon Building
E. R. Thompson
695-3033

Foreign Intelligence Directorate (J. B. Churchill, 697-3398) of the ACSI monitors overseas developments, prepares information papers, and contributes to U.S. intelligence estimates.

CHIEF OF ENGINEERS
20 Massachusetts Avenue, N.W.
Washington, D.C. 20314
693-6456

Historical Division
J. T. Greenwood, Director
272-0237

Consisting of 8 professional historians, this division is responsible for preserving the historical records of the Corps of Engineers. The division's records on South Asian activities of the Corps of Engineers are maintained by the Trans East District branch of the Mediterranean Division. The records include reports on various feasibility studies and project-completion studies on highway construction in Afghanistan, construction of the Karachi International Airport under the AID program, and construction of several military facilities in Pakistan under the U.S.-Pakistan bilateral military-assistance program. While some of the reports and records are classified, researchers may find much useful information from the unclassified, published *District History* series which contains valuable technical data and charts.

Available for consultation in the division's study facilities is an unpublished study, prepared under contract by Richard T. Farrell, entitled, "History of the Mediterranean Division" (1978), which contains several references to the activities of the Corps of Engineers in Afghanistan and Pakistan. Researchers should also inquire about the division's oral-history project. A recently published volume, *Engineer Memoirs, Lieutenant General Frederick J. Clarke* (1980), contains many useful personal observations and facts about the activities of the corps in Pakistan and Afghanistan. The division also maintains card indexes to the retired military construction files in Afghanistan and Pakistan.

Current and retrospective volumes of the *Military Engineer*, a journal of the Society of American Military Engineers (dedicated to national defense) are maintained in the division. Some of the articles of interest in this journal include: Emerson C. Itschner, "Indus Basin Plan," 55 (March–April 1963); C. M. Messall, "Modern Highways for Afghanistan," 55 (November–December 1963); Phillip D. Weinert, "Suspension Bridges in Afghanistan," 59 (March–April 1967); W. K. Wilson, "Overseas Military Construction," 50 (September–October 1958).

The Chief of Engineers Library, located in Room 3119 of the Pulaski Building (Penny Crumpler, Acting Librarian, 272-0455), is open 8:00 A.M. through 4:00 P.M., Monday through Friday and is accessible to the public on the basis of prior appointment. The library's collection of 55,000 monographs, 22,000 technical reports, and 800 periodical subscriptions focuses on technology, management, and environment. The library follows the LC classification system. Reference assistance, photoduplication services, and interlibrary loans are available. A card catalog and a published monthly cumulation, *Current Acquisitions*, provide access to the collection.

The library's holdings contain many significant reports and studies, produced by the Army Corps of Engineers, not available elsewhere. Following is a sample selection of materials considered important to South Asian studies: *Transportation Survey of East Pakistan*, 3 vols. (1961), Vol. I *Summary Report*, Vol. II *Detailed Report*, Vol. III *Annexes and Maps; Transportation Survey of West Pakistan* (1962), 3 vols., titled as in preceding entry; *Feasibility Study Herat-Islam-Qala Highway Afghanistan* (1963); *Kandahar Spin Baldak Highway—Afghanistan—Special Investigation* (1962); and *Technical Assistance Project, History and Analysis Report, Afghanistan* (1967 and 1968).

Additional, significant items in the collection include a photographic album presented to H. D. Vogel by the Indus Basin Project Division of the West Pakistan Water Power Development Authority (WAPDA). A retired general of the Corps of Engineers, Vogel served as the Engineer Advisor of the World Bank and as the Engineer Member of the Bank's Working Party for the Indus Basin Project. A collection of articles, speeches, and statements by Vogel are also available in the library.

CENTER OF MILITARY HISTORY
Pulaski Building
20 Massachusetts Avenue, N.W.
Washington, D.C. 20314
272-0291
Maurice Matloff, Historian
693-0293

The U.S. Army Center of Military History provides advisory and coordination services on historical matters, including historical properties, formulation and execution of the Army Historical Program, and preparation and publication of histories required by the Department of the Army. All of the center's research is produced in-house, and a substantial portion of the unpublished items remain restricted. The center is open from 8:00 A.M.

through 4:30 P.M., Monday through Friday. Unclassified materials may be used on-site. It is advisable that researchers make prior appointments before visiting the center. Photoduplication services are available.

The center is the repository of U.S. Army unit histories and contains a collection of some 6,000 published, and an equal number of unpublished, historical studies prepared by the army unit historians. Of the several multivolume, published, historical series, the 80-volume *United States Army in World War II* includes the following titles prepared by Charles F. Romanus and Riley Sunderland: *China-Burma-India Theater, Stilwell's Mission to China* (1953); *China-Burma-India Theater* (1959); *China-Burma-India Theater, Stilwell's Command Problems* (1956); *China-Burma-India Theater, Time Runs out in CBI* (1959). Another volume prepared by Joseph Bykofsky and Harold Larson, *The Technical Services, The Transportation Corps Operation Overseas* (1957), contains a chapter (XII, pp. 547–604) on the China-Burma-India Theater. A catalog, *Publications of the U.S. Army Center of Military History*, can be obtained free upon request.

Among the center's collection of records and unpublished historical manuscripts may be located several items of interest related to South Asia, namely: copies of General Stilwell's final report, entitled "History of China-Burma-India Theater, 21 May to 25 October 1944" (3 vols., 1 with 31 vols. of annexes); "History of Service of Supply China-Burma-India, 11 June 1942 to 24 October 1944" (38 vols), contains activities of bases located at Karachi, Calcutta, Ledo, Gaya, Diburugarh, and Chabua (Assam); "History of India-Burma Theater, 25 October 1944 to 23 June 1945 and 24 June 1945 to 31 May 1946" (28 vols.); and 3 albums of photographs of the India-Burma Theater.

Some of the resources used in the preparation of these studies are to be found in the set of some 100 geographically arranged Historian's Background Materials Files. The interesting array of materials in these files include copies of war diaries, dispatches, telegrams, press releases, radio newsbroadcasts, and operations reports and statistics. There is no catalog of the Center's manuscript holdings, but researchers may obtain assistance from Hannah M. Zeidlik (693-1545), Chief of the Historical Records Branch. Staff historians can also assist the researchers in locating and retrieving materials in the National Archives and other depositories of U.S. Army records.

The center's 35,000-volume reference library contains a comprehensive collection of army publications, regulations, and directories. A card catalog provides access to the collection. South Asia-related materials in the collection are insignificant.

NAVY DEPARTMENT
The Pentagon
Washington, D.C. 20310
697-4627

OFFICE OF INFORMATION
D. M. Cooney, Chief
697-7391

This office may provide valuable assistance to researchers in locating appropriate offices and personnel.

NAVAL RECORDS MANAGEMENT AND ADMINISTRATION SERVICES DIVISION
(OFFICE OF THE CHIEF OF NAVAL OPERATIONS)
W. D. Paschall, Chief
697-2330

This division is responsible for management, disposal, declassification, and access to all records of the department. Some of the useful contacts are: Freedom of Information (D. Carr, 697-1459), Privacy Act (G. Rhoads, 694-2817), and Records Disposal (L. A. Kelley, 695-1921).

OFFICE OF NAVAL RESEARCH (ONR)
800 North Quincy Street
Arlington, Virginia 22217
A. J. Baciocco, Jr.
696-4258

The ONR is engaged in a wide variety of naval research, much of which is international in dimension, including several branches of physical, mathematical, biological, and psychological sciences. No indexes to the research projects or completed reports are available, but the staff will assist in locating materials. Most research is done through external research contracts. Currently there are no on-going research projects related to South Asia, but several cooperative research programs—especially in the field of microbiology (marine plant-life, natural antiviral substances, diarrheal diseases, and malaria control)—are under consideration. For further information contact A. J. Emery (696-4056). In addition, researchers may note the following contact numbers: Physical Sciences Division (T. G. Berlincourt, 696-4212); Mathematical and Information Sciences Division (R. E. James, 696-4310); Biological Sciences (Ronald Oshlund, 696-4051); and Psychological Sciences Division (G. L. Bryan, 696-4425).

OFFICE OF NAVAL INTELLIGENCE (ONI)
S. Shapiro, Director
695-3944

ONI monitors developments and collects data on global naval activities. However, most of its works are classified. A. S. Button (695-3974), of the Politico Military Affairs unit (697-3671) is responsible for South Asian matters. An informative book, *Naval Intelligence Command* (1975), and an organizational chart are available free. A study, "History of Naval Intelligence," is under preparation by Wyman Packard (433-3170).

DEPUTY CHIEF OF NAVAL OPERATIONS (PLANS, POLICY AND OPERATIONS)
S. R. Foley
695-3707

Politico Military Policy and Current Plans Division
R. T. Gaskill, Director
695-2453

The division's South Asia Plans and Political Branch (F. N. Hannigan, 695-9406) monitors political and military developments in South Asia and prepares policy papers on issues of special interest to the U.S. Navy, including arms transfer and security assistance.

NAVAL HISTORICAL CENTER
Washington Navy Yard
9th and M Streets, S.E.
Washington, D.C. 20374
J. K. Kane, Jr., Director
433-2210

The Naval Historical Center undertakes research, writing, and publication programs in the fields of U.S. naval history. It additionally operates a library, an archive, and a museum and provides a number of historical services to naval officials, research organizations, scholars, and the general public.

Navy Department Library
S. Kalkus, Director
433-2386

The Navy Department Library is open to the public for on-site use from 8:00 A.M. through 4:30 P.M., Monday through Friday. Interlibrary loan and photoduplication services are available. Its collection exceeds 125,000 volumes and bound periodicals covering all aspects and periods of the U.S. Navy. The library also includes materials on foreign navies and some nineteenth-century travels and descriptions. South Asian holdings of the library consist of approximately 500 secondary English-language reference titles, focusing on history, geography, government, and international relations.

   Among the library's special collections are a group of manuscript histories covering naval administration in World War II, unpublished journals, graduate dissertations, and microfilm copies of many of the navy's basic nineteenth-century records. The library also owns available microfilm copies of naval documents deposited in the National Archives. Principal reference source to the collection is the card catalog. An informative brochure, *The Navy Department Library: A Brief Description*, is available free. Scholars may also find it useful to examine *United States Naval History: A Bibliography* (1972), prepared by the library.

Historical Research Branch
W. J. Morgan
433-3459

A comprehensive collection of photocopied naval and maritime documents, dating from the era of the American Revolution, gathered from archives and libraries in the U.S. and abroad, is held in this branch.

Ships Histories Branch
R. T. Speer
433-2585

Extensive source materials on the histories of individual ships are maintained here to support the activities of the branch. *The Dictionary of American Naval Fighting Ships* (6 vols.) contains capsule histories of ships based on these materials and other sources.

Operational Archives
D. C. Allard
433-3170

The center's Operational Archives holds selected archival and manuscript collections relating to fleet operations over the last 40 years, materials on the formulation of naval policy and strategy during the same period, the papers of some senior naval officers, and bibliographic reference files on many naval officers who have served since the early part of the nineteenth century.

Naval History Division
H. A. Vadnais, Jr., Curator
433-2220

This division has published a number of works on the history of the U.S. Navy which may be of some interest to a South Asianist. Examples are: *Guide to United States Naval Administrative Histories of World War II* (1976); *U.S. Naval History Sources in the Washington Area and Suggested Research Subjects;* and *Naval Historical Publications in Print.*

Navy Department Declassification Team
K. L. Coskey, Officer in Charge
433-4071

This team is responsible for declassifying of and providing access to naval documents.

MARINE CORPS HISTORICAL CENTER
Washington Navy Yard
9th and M Streets, S.E.
Washington, D.C. 20374
433-3840

The center maintains a comprehensive research, writing, archival, and museum program related to the study and exploitation of United States Marine Corps historical materials. The division has extensive subject, geographical, and personality files. There is a large photographic collection covering Marine activities overseas. The center has a 25,000-volume historical reference library section (E. A. Englander, Librarian, 433-3447), which concentrates on Marine Corps activities.

AIR FORCE DEPARTMENT
The Pentagon
Washington, D.C. 20310
697-7376

OFFICE OF PUBLIC AFFAIRS
H. J. Dalton, Director
697-6061

The Security Review Branch (William B. Allison, 697-3222) of this office reviews all research involving classified materials. The staff can assist researchers in locating needed materials and in obtaining limited clearance.

INFORMATION MANAGEMENT AND RESOURCES DIVISION (DIRECTORATE OF ADMINISTRATION)
H. G. Geiger
697-3491

Two components of this division: the Air Force Freedom of Information Act Office (C. C. Ratcliffe, 694-3488) and the Air Force Privacy Act Office (L. Behrens, 694-3431) receive all requests for declassification as provided by law. The staff can also be of assistance in identifying and locating materials.

AIR FORCE INTELLIGENCE SERVICE
J. L. Brown
695-5613

Analysts of the various units monitor overseas current events and collect data on foreign aircraft and other matters of interest to the U.S. Air Force. It is also responsible for the department's Air Attaché affairs.

DEPUTY CHIEF OF STAFF OPERATIONS PLANS AND READINESS
A. Gabriel
697-9991

Various analysts in this unit assist in the formulation of U.S. Air Force policies on international political and military issues such as U.S. foreign military sales.

INTERNATIONAL AFFAIRS DIVISION (OFFICE OF THE CHIEF OF STAFF)
Donald L. Helliger
695-2251

Activities of the division include protocol affairs, disclosure policy, and matters related to munitions and exports.

OFFICE OF AIR FORCE HISTORY
Bolling Air Force Base
Washington, D.C. 20332
Stanley L. Falk, Historian
767-5764

Staff historians prepare historical studies of the U.S. Air Force, much of which, however, is classified. The staff may be of assistance in locating Air Force records and the office possesses microfilm copies of Air Force archival materials located at the Albert F. Simpson Historical Research Center, Maxwell Air Force Base, Alabama. The bulk of these materials are classified. The office also maintains a small reference library that contains a collection of mostly classified Air Force historical studies and a collection of selected statements by principal Air Force and Defense Department officials since 1958. Two publications by the office may be of interest to researchers: *United States Air Force History: A Guide to Documentary Sources* (1973) and *United States Air Force History: An Annotated Bibliography*, which is periodically updated. Also useful in working with classified materials is the *Air Force Historical Archives Documentation Classification Guide* (1971).

NATIONAL DEFENSE UNIVERSITY (NDU)
Fort Lesley J. McNair
4th and P Streets, S.W.
Washington, D.C. 20319

Robert G. Gard, Jr., President
693-1076

NATIONAL WAR COLLEGE (NWC)
John C. Barrow, Commandant
693-8318

INDUSTRIAL COLLEGE OF THE ARMED FORCES (ICAF)
John E. Ralph, Commandant
693-8305

Established in 1976, the NDU consists of 2 senior-service constituent institutions: The National War College and the Industrial College of the Armed Forces, both located at Fort McNair. The NDU's mission is to insure excellence in professional military education. Essential elements of national security—and their interrelationships—are stressed to enhance the preparation of selected personnel from the departments of Defense and State, as well as other government agencies, in the exercise of senior policy, command, and staff functions, the planning of national strategy, and the management of national-security resources.

A graduate-level school in the field of politico-military affairs, the NWC enrolls 160 selected senior military and civilian officers for a 10-month, full-time study program that focuses specifically on national security policy formulation, and implementation. The curriculum is broadly divided into a Core Program, taken by all students, and an Elective Studies Program (ESP). Within the latter category, a seminar on South Asia is occasionally offered. International studies, domestic studies, and national security studies constitute the 3 academic departments of NWC. The NWC faculty and guest lecturers are drawn from the services and civilian sectors, including the State Department, AID, ICA, the CIA, and the professional academic community. An information brochure, *The National War College,* is available on request.

In addition to the resident courses taught at the NWC, the university conducts a defense-strategy seminar, a reserve-components national-security seminar, and a correspondence course. The ICAF, which enrolls 218 selected students annually from any of the defense and civilian branches of the government, concentrates its curriculum on the management of resources for national security.

The NDU Library (693-8437) consists of 50,000 monographs and 750 journal subscriptions. The principal focus of the collection is in history, economics, government, international relations, and security studies. The library is open from 8:00 A.M. to 4:30 P.M., Monday through Friday (closed every alternate Friday). Interlibrary loan and photoduplication facilities are available. The library may be used by the public on the basis of prior appointment.

Note: Also see entries A3 and G6.

J10 Education Department

1. a. *400 Maryland Avenue, S.W.*
    Washington, D.C. 20202
    245-3192

    b. Open to the public; previous appointment recommended

2. Under the provision of the Department of Education Act (October 17, 1979), this newly created thirteenth cabinet-level department was inaugurated on May 4, 1980. Currently, the department administers some 162 programs from the departments of Health, Education and Welfare—of which it constituted a division before the reorganization—Defense, Justice, Housing and Urban Development, Labor, and the National Science Foundation. Responsibilities of the department include: insuring equal educational opportunity for all; promoting improvement in the quality of education through research, evaluation, and management; and accountability of federal educational programs.

    Most research is conducted in-house, but occasional outside consultant and contract research is available. The department also participates in several international exchange programs that are noted below.

    Currently, the department is being reorganized; some telephone numbers, offices, and titles were not available at the time of this writing, and information given here may vary later when the reorganization is completed.

3. For National Institute of Education Library see entry A28.

4. The department's publications are described below with the appropriate units. Other popular publications include: *Daily Education News; American Education; Study Abroad; Opportunities Abroad for Teachers; Inventory of Federal Programs Involving Education Activities Concerned with Improving International Understanding and Cooperation;* and *Asian Studies in American Secondary Education.*

OFFICE OF INTERNATIONAL EDUCATION
7th and D Streets, S.W.
Washington, D.C. 20202
Edward L. Meader, Director
245-9692

The Office of International Education is responsible for expanding the international and global dimensions of the U.S. education system and for promoting awareness of other cultures. Its activities include training, curriculum development, research, exchange, and a wide range of services in the field of international education.

INTERNATIONAL SERVICES AND RESEARCH BRANCH
Stewart Tinsman, Chief
245-7401

This branch conducts research and studies on the educational systems of other countries. Its Comparative Education Staff (Seymour Rosen, 245-

9425), often aided by outside consultants, prepares and publishes educational material on foreign countries. South Asia-related publications include: *Bibliographic Resources About India: An Annotated List of English Language Reference Works Published in India, 1965–70* (1972); *Higher and Professional Education in India* (1969); *Selected Bibliography and Abstracts of Educational Materials in Pakistan;* and *Historical and Political Gazetteer of Afghanistan.* A list, *Publications of Comparative Education* (1978), is available on request.

The Comparative Education staff also provides U.S. educational institutions, agencies, organizations, and individuals with consultative and technical assistance on education systems abroad. Staff reference files on South Asian countries, containing reports and documents of U.S. embassies, international organizations, education ministries, and universities, may be used by researchers.

The International Organization Staff (245-2761) works with international organizations, including UNESCO, UNICEF, WHO, and UNDP, on educational programs and conferences. The staff assists in developing U.S. policy and position papers for use in international conferences, nominates American educators to serve on U.S. delegations to international meetings, and recruits American educators for field positions abroad.

INTERNATIONAL STUDIES BRANCH
Richard Thompson, Director
245-2356

This office administers domestic and overseas programs in foreign language and area studies as authorized by Title VI of the National Defense Education Act of 1958 (NDA), as amended, and the National Defense Education Act of 1961 (Fulbright-Hays). For statistical information on these programs, see the annual *Fact Book* of the Bureau of Higher and Continuing Education.

Centers and Research Section (Joseph Belmonte, 245-9588) provides grants to higher-education institutions, or consortia of such institutions, to establish and operate multidisciplinary problem- or topic-oriented, international-studies programs and centers for foreign-language and area studies at the undergraduate and graduate levels. Currently, there are 8 such centers for South Asian studies: University of California, Berkeley (Bruce Pray, 415/642-3608); University of Chicago (Edward Dimock, 312/753-4350); Columbia University (Theodore Riccardi, 212/280-4662); University of Pennsylvania (Ludo Rocher, 215/243-7475); University of Texas (F. Tomasson Jannuzi, 512/471-5811); University of Virginia (Walter Hauser, 804/924-7146); University of Washington (Karl Potter, 206/543-4964); and University of Wisconsin (Manindra K. Verma, 608/262-3012). For further information call Marian Kane, Centers Program Specialist (245-9588).

The Centers and Research Section's Research Program (245-9819) also provides grants to higher-education institutions, organizations, and individuals in support of surveys and studies to determine the need for increased or improved instruction in modern foreign-language, area, and international studies. The grants are also to develop more effective methods or specialized materials for such training. A useful publication compiled by Julia A. Petrov (Research Program), *Foreign Language Area and Other International Studies, A Bibliography of Research and Instructional Materials,* lists and summarizes, in the form of an annotated bibliography, the results of all activities carried out under the research authority of NDEA Title VI to the date of publication.

Fellowships and Overseas Projects Section (John Paul, 245-2356) administers several programs, including: the Foreign Language and Area Studies Fellowship (FLAS) program for graduate students (245-9808); the Doctoral Dissertation Research Abroad program, providing assistance for graduate students to engage in full-time dissertation research abroad in modern, foreign-language and area studies; the Faculty Research Abroad program (245-2794), designed to assist higher-education institutions in strengthening their international-studies programs; the Group Projects Abroad program (245-2794), which provides grants to U.S. educational institutions or nonprofit educational organizations for training, research, advanced foreign-language training, curriculum development, and instructional materials acquisitions in the fields of international and intercultural studies. In addition, the Foreign Curriculum Consultant program (245-2794) brings experts from other countries to the U.S. for an academic year to help selected American educators plan and develop curricula in foreign-language and area studies.

ETHNIC HERITAGE STUDIES BRANCH
Stanley Wilcox, Chief
245-9506

This program provides grants to nonprofit educational institutions and organizations to promote a better understanding of the ethnic heritage of the United States. So far, no South Asia-related grant has been awarded. A useful publication is *Ethnic Heritage Studies Program Grants 1974 through 1978*.

INTERNATIONAL EXCHANGE BRANCH
Nathan Pitts, Director
245-2454

International Exchange Branch administers teacher exchange and visitor programs. The Teacher Exchange Section (Dorothy Stewart, 245-9700) provides opportunities for elementary and secondary school teachers and, in some cases, for college instructors and assistant professors to teach outside the United States. Various arrangements are made by the U.S. government with other countries to provide a direct exchange of teachers. Similarly, the Seminars Abroad program affords opportunities for teachers at elementary, secondary, and college levels to participate in a variety of short-term seminars abroad on a selection of topics.

The International Visitors Program (Timothy King, 245-9481) plans itineraries and provides educational counseling for visiting foreign educators who are not on U.S. government grants. The staff arranges appointments for individual foreign educators to consult with department specialists. The Educational Development Program (William Shamblin, 245-9451) arranges educational training programs for teachers and administrators from other countries; training includes regular courses, special seminars, and site visits to demonstration and research centers.

CLEARINGHOUSE
David Levin, Education Program Specialist
245-7804

The Clearinghouse staff responds to inquiries about student-exchange programs, regular academic-year-abroad programs, general educational tours for teachers and students, overseas employment, and programs of financial assistance to foreign students—activities that fall outside the department's international educational programs and services. The Clearinghouse also prepares and distributes brochures, pamphlets, and other reference material describing the department's programs and services, as well as activities in the field of international education in general. Some of the useful publications available in the Clearinghouse include: *International Education Programs and Services* (1980); *Study and Teaching Abroad* (1980); *International Teacher Exchange* (1975); *Foreign Students in the United States;* and *Selected U.S. Office of Education Publications to Further International Education* (1977).

DISSEMINATION SPECIALIST
Richard Jorgensen
245-9434

A Dissemination Specialist in the office of the director coordinates an information-sharing network for the advancement of international and global education among the states, local education agencies, institutions of higher education, and international organizations; and facilitates communication between the department-supported programs and activities sponsored by other agencies, both public and private.

NATIONAL INSTITUTE OF EDUCATION (NIE)
1200 19th Street, N.W.
Washington, D.C. 20208
P. Michael Timpane, Director
254-5500

The NIE was created to provide leadership in the conduct and support of scientific inquiry into the educational process, to provide more dependable knowledge about educational quality, and to improve education—including career education. The principal focus of NIE activities is domestic. However, the computerized Educational Resources Information Center (ERIC) (254-5500) data bases contain some bibliographic information on international education. Two useful NIE publications provide access to the ERIC data bases: *Survey of ERIC Data Base Search Services* and *Directory of ERIC Collections in the Washington, D.C. Area.* Researchers working with ERIC data bases may also find it useful to examine *Resources in Education* (a monthly index); *Current Index to Journals in Education* (a monthly index); *Thesaurus of ERIC Descriptors;* and *ERIC Identifiers: Term Posting and Statistics for Research in Education.*

NATIONAL CENTER FOR EDUCATION STATISTICS (NCES)
200 Independence Avenue, S.W.
Washington, D.C. 20201
Marie D. Eldridge, Administrator
245-8352

The National Center for Education Statistics collects and disseminates statistics and other data related to education in the United States and in other nations. The center coordinates the information-gathering activities for education programs, performs special analyses and disseminates the statistical data gathered. For international data, contact Mary Golladay (245-7025) of Educational Indicators and Foreign Statistics Branch. An annual report, *The Condition of Education,* provides an overview of the major program activities of NCES.

Note: Also see entry A28.

J11 Energy Department (DOE)

1. a. *Forrestal Building*
    1000 Independence Avenue, S.W.
    Washington, D.C. 20545
    252-5565

    b. Limited access to the public, on the basis of previous appointment. Scholars may note that many DOE files and documents are classified. Inquiries for access to the restricted materials should be directed to the Freedom of Information and Privacy Activities Division (Milton Jordan, 252-5955).

2. The Department of Energy was established in 1977 to provide the framework for a comprehensive and balanced, national energy plan through the coordination and administration of the federal government's energy functions. DOE's responsibilities include: research, development, and demonstration of energy technology; energy conservation; nuclear weapons program; regulation of energy production and use; and a central, energy-data collection and analysis program. Many of the activities of the department are international in dimension. DOE research is done internally as well as by outside contract. However, outside-contract research opportunities, related to South Asia, are extremely rare.

3. LIBRARY SERVICES DIVISION
    C. Neil Sherman, Director
    (301) 353-4301

    The U.S. Department of Energy Library, which functions as a major repository of energy-related information, consists of the 3 separate facilities described below.

    Germantown Library
    Germantown, Maryland 20545
    Ruth E. Parks, Chief
    (301) 353-2855

    Largest of the 3 branches, the Germantown collection consists of approximately 85,000 cataloged and 20,000 uncataloged volumes. In addition, the holdings include some 2,000 International Atomic Energy Agency (IAEA) publications, 2,500 current professional-journal subscriptions, approximately 650,000 uncataloged technical reports, and a large collection of congressional reports and documents. The library has access to some 100 data bases available only to agency personnel. The principal focus of the collection is in: energy resources and management; economic, environmental, and social effects of energy; and water resources.

Interlibrary loan and photoduplication facilities are available. Most of the collection is accessible to the public. It is, however, recommended that visitors make advance appointments. The library hours are 8:30 A.M. to 5:00 P.M., Monday through Friday. Published bibliographies include the weekly *Library Accessions*, the monthly *Selected DOE Headquarters Publications*, and the *Energy Library Journals Available*. Other computer-produced catalogs and indexes are also available. An information booklet, *Energy Library* (1978), which contains a selected list of the data bases accessed by the library, may be obtained free.

Federal Energy Regulatory Commission (FERC) Library
825 North Capitol Street, N.E.
Washington, D.C. 20426
Robert Kimberlin, Chief
275-4303

This small reference collection of approximately 55,000 volumes mostly on electric power, natural gas, and energy regulations and law, is open from 8:30 A.M. to 5:00 P.M., Monday through Friday. Private researchers may use the collection on the basis of prior appointment. Interlibrary loan and photoduplicating services are available.

D.C. Library
Room GA-138
1000 Independence Avenue, N.W.
Washington, D.C. 20585
Denise Diggin, Chief
252-9534

This library contains a small reference collection of 6,000 volumes on the general subject of energy. The library is open from 8:30 A.M. to 5:00 P.M., Monday through Friday, and is accessible to the public on the basis of prior appointment. Interlibrary loan and photoduplicating facilities are available.

4.   In addition to several DOE publications to be mentioned later, other publications of interest include: *Guide for the Submission of Unsolicited Proposals* (1980); *The DOE Program Guide for Universities and Other Research Groups* (1980); *Energy Abstracts for Policy Analysis* (monthly), which contains world-wide abstracts of journal articles and books on energy analysis of a nontechnological or quasi-technological nature; *Annual Report to Congress*, which contains a compendium of statistical charts and tables on Afghanistan, Bangladesh, India, and Pakistan; *Energy Meetings*, a listing of conferences, symposia, workshops, congresses, and other formal meetings pertaining to DOE's programmatic interests; and the *First Annual Report on Nuclear Non-Proliferation* (1979), a document submitted to the Congress in accordance with the requirements of law. Free copies of most of these publications are available in the Office of Public Information Administration (Forrestal Building, Room GA-343, 653-4055).

INTERNATIONAL AFFAIRS (IA)
1000 Independence Avenue, S.W.
Washington, D.C. 20585
Leslie Goldman, Assistant Secretary
252-5800

Charged with formulating U.S. international energy policy, this office is responsible for developing, managing, and directing programs and activities that implement and support energy policy and U.S. foreign policy. The office assesses trends and technological developments in world prices and supplies; it also studies the effects of international actions on U.S. energy supplies. In addition to supporting U.S. policies on international nuclear nonproliferation and international fuel cycle, the office also coordinates cooperative international energy programs and maintains relationships with foreign governments and international organizations. This office prepares the periodically updated, unclassified report, *International Bilateral and Multilateral Arrangements in Energy Technology.*

INTERNATIONAL NUCLEAR AND TECHNICAL PROGRAMS
Holsey G. Handyside, Deputy Assistant Secretary
252-5921

This office is required to establish and maintain relationships with foreign governments, agencies, and international organizations concerned with energy-technology programs and issues. It also develops, negotiates, implements, coordinates, and evaluates bilateral and multilateral cooperative arrangements to this end. A third responsibility it has is to formulate and implement nuclear nonproliferation policy, as well as coordinate nuclear and nuclear-related export control.

Office of Nuclear Affairs
Harold D. Bengelsdorf, Director
252-6175

Maintaining current information on energy sources and nuclear technology in various foreign countries, this office develops and implements the department's nuclear energy policy, negotiates bilateral and multilateral cooperative nuclear agreements, and monitors nuclear proliferation and nuclear fuel-export transactions. The U.S. currently has an agreement with India, signed in 1963, for cooperation concerning civil uses of atomic energy.

Office of Technical Cooperation
Jack Vanderryn, Director
252-6140

This office negotiates, implements, coordinates, and evaluates international cooperation in energy technology. It also identifies relevant foreign technology of potential benefit to the U.S. South Asian matters are dealt with by John Leech of Team B (252-6144). Currently, there are several on-going programs in India, including those on solar energy and grain drying.

Office of Country Energy Assessments
Robert Summers, Director
252-6383

The mission of this unit is to plan, negotiate, direct, implement, and co-ordinate U.S. energy-planning cooperation with developing nations. This office prepares energy-assessment reports of a few selected countries. So far, no such reports have been produced on any South Asian countries; however, classified files on most of the South Asian countries are maintained by this office. A computerized World Energy Data System (WENDS), produced by this office, contains energy-related data on some 60 countries, including India, Pakistan, and Bangladesh. WENDS is currently managed by ARGONNE National Laboratory in Argonne, Illinois 60439. WENDS data bases were published in 1979, in 11 volumes, by ARGONNE. It is an extremely useful publication and is organized by country and by energy technology of 15 selected countries—including India—in addition to the 60 country data. For further information contact Martha Strong of the ARGONNE local office at 1111 20th Street, N.W., Washington, D.C. 20461 (254-9702).

INTERNATIONAL ENERGY ANALYSIS
James Moose, Deputy Assistant Secretary
252-5890

To analyze international energy developments and forecasts that concern policy formulation is the purpose of this office, which serves as a focal point for substantive matters with Congress. Its major functions are divided between its 2 following components.

International Market Analysis Office
Herman Franssen, Director
252-5893

Responsibilities of this office include collecting and analyzing data and information in support of other IA offices; evaluating and analyzing substance and methodology of world energy forecasts; developing world energy-balance estimates; analyzing current oil-market activity trends; and administering the Foreign Energy Supply Assessment Program (FESAP), which is called upon to confirm proven reserves, estimate ultimate resource recovery, and develop production scenarios for oil- and gas-producing countries.

Office of Special Projects
James A. Geocaris, Director
252-8355

The mission of the Office of Special Projects is to coordinate and provide analytical support for the DOE's special programs and projects having international implications; and to supply Congress with information regarding legislative initiatives that affect international energy matters.

INTERNATIONAL INTELLIGENCE ANALYSIS
Milton Iredell, Deputy Assistant Secretary
252-5915

This unit provides intelligence support to the DOE, coordinates DOE participation in the intelligence community, and analyzes economic, political, and technical intelligence as it relates to energy production and consumption in foreign countries.

Current Reporting Office
John LaBarre, Director
252-5174

From U.S. intelligence sources, primarily, this office monitors energy resource developments in foreign countries and produces short-term analysis and policy recommendations. The staff analyst concerned with South Asian matters is Roseanne Bartholomew (252-5162). Most records and documents here are classified.

Office of Strategic Assessments
J. Despres, Director
252-8355

This office conducts analysis of economic, political, and technical intelligence to assess the factors underlying energy production and consumption in foreign countries. It also represents DOE on interagency working groups developing National Intelligence Estimates (NIE).

INTERNATIONAL ENERGY RESOURCES
John E. Treat, Deputy Assistant Secretary
252-5918

Responsibilities of this office include developing comprehensive policies, strategies, and options for bilateral, multilateral, and regional energy relations, negotiations, and developments. Its 2 sub-units are: Office of Energy Producing Nations (F. Verrastro, Director, 252-5924) and Office of Energy Consuming Nations (Daniel I. Hickey, Director, 252-6777). A staff member dealing with South Asia is William Carter (252-6380).

ENERGY INFORMATION ADMINISTRATION (EIA)
12th and Pennsylvania Avenue, N.W.
Washington, D.C. 20461
Albert H. Lunden, Acting Administrator
633-9085

The principal data collection and analysis arm of the DOE, the Energy Information Administration is responsible for the timely and accurate collection, processing, and publication of data on energy reserves, the financial status of energy-producing companies, and the production demand and consumption of energy in the U.S. and abroad.

ENERGY DATA OPERATIONS
1000 Independence Avenue, S.W.
Washington, D.C. 20585
Jimmie Peterson, Assistant Administrator
252-6401

The unit is responsible for 2 publications of interest: *International Petroleum Annual* and a *Monthly Energy Review.* Of the 5 constituent offices of this unit, the following office may provide useful information to the South Asianist.

Interfuel, International and Emerging Energies Statistics Office
Frank H. Lalley, Director
633-8500

International Statistics Division (Louis DeMouy, Chief, 633-9364) maintains statistical data and other records on world-wide energy production, consumption, imports, exports, and price. This data may be consulted by researchers through arrangements with this office.

APPLIED ANALYSIS
12th and Pennsylvania Avenue, N.W.
Washington, D.C. 20461
C. Roger Glassey, Assistant Administrator
633-8543

International Energy Analysis Division
W. Calvin Kilgore, Director
633-9721

This division, utilizing various automated systems, is concerned with econometric forecasting and modeling. Its computer files include United Nations' data on world energy consumption from 1950 to 1975, and DOE's country profiles of nuclear plants and capacity. Computer printouts are supplied to researchers on request. A number of the energy analyses of this office have been published: *An Evaluation of Future World Prices; International Energy Assessment* (1979); and the *International Energy Evaluation System* (1978), 2 vols.

ENERGY INFORMATION SERVICES
1726 M Street, N.W.
Washington, D.C. 20461
John Daniels, Director
634-5602

Energy Information Administration Clearinghouse
B. Somers, Chief
634-2151

The clearinghouse disseminates several publications and popular handouts of potential interest to South Asianists: *International Petroleum Annual*, containing data on oil production, trade, consumption, and prices by country; the annual *World Natural Gas Production and Consumption; World Petroleum Production*, an annual report focusing on OPEC member nations; and the *Monthly Energy Review*, providing international statistics based on published CIA data.

National Energy Information Center
W. Neal Moerschel, Chief
634-5583

This unit distributes many useful printed materials including the *EIA Publications* and the *EIA Publications Directory*.

DEFENSE PROGRAMS
1000 Independence Avenue, S.W.
Washington, D.C. 20585
Duane C. Sewell, Assistant Secretary
252-2177

INTERNATIONAL SECURITY AFFAIRS OFFICE
Ray E. Chapman, Director
252-2100

Politico-Military Security Affairs Division
Vance H. Hudgins
252-2127

Primarily concerned with issues related to nuclear energy and nonproliferation, this office also collaborates with the CIA and the Departments of State and Defense on international policy questions, including security of foreign oil production and its availability to the U.S.

J12 Environmental Protection Agency (EPA)

1.   a. *401 M Street, S.W.*
     Washington, D.C. 20460
     755-0707

     b. Open to the public but previous appointment is recommended

     c. Douglas M. Costle, Administrator

2.   Established in 1970, the EPA's mission is to abate pollution of air and water, and control solid waste, noise, radiation, and toxic substances. In order to carry out its mission, the EPA conducts a variety of integrated monitorings and research, and participates in international, cooperative environmental research. The agency supports both in-house and contract research.

     INTERNATIONAL ACTIVITIES
     Donald T. Oakley, Director
     755-2780

     This office coordinates various international programs that are designed to maximize international cooperation in improving the environment.

     BILATERAL DIVISION
     Thomas J. LePine, Chief
     755-0523

     Bilateral activities include exchanging environmental documents and supplying U.S. experts to provide training and support for environmental research programs abroad. Currently, there are 4 EPA projects in India and 3 in Pakistan in the fields of toxic substances, virus bacteria, air pollution, water reclamation, and other related areas. An EPA publication, *Scientific Activities Overseas Programs* (1979), provides a cumulative listing of projects in India and Pakistan funded from the excess foreign-currency program. EPA international activities are briefly summarized in a series of pamphlets, such as *EPA and the World Health Organization*, and *EPA and the United Nations Environmental Program*. A folder, *International Activities of the United States Environmental Protection Agency*, containing much useful information, may be obtained free from Linda L. Clawson, International Visitor Coordinator in the Office of International Activities (755-2780).

3.   The EPA Headquarters Library (Sami Klein, Librarian, 755-0308) contains over 7,000 monographs, 180,000 documents and reports, and 1,000 periodical subscriptions. The collection is predominantly technical in nature, with focus on pollution and ecology. The facility is open to the public for on-site use from 8:00 A.M. to 5:00 P.M., Monday through Friday. Reference tools include card catalogs and the quarterly *EPA Reports Bibliography*, available at the National Technical Information Center (see entry J6). There is also the *Guide to EPA Libraries*, available free.

   EPA's International Environment Referral Center (Carol Alexander, Director, 755-1836) has a collection of miscellaneous, foreign environmental documents acquired during the years 1972 to 1976, through bilateral, information-exchange programs. The collection may be examined by outside researchers through prior arrangement. A country index to this collection is available. The center also maintains an international directory—*International Referral System*—of environmental information for some 70 participating countries of the U.N. Environment Program.

4.   A monthly EPA publication on its overseas activities, *Summaries of Foreign Government Environmental Reports*, is distributed by the National Technical Information Service. Other publications of interest include: *Air Pollution Translations Bibliography with Abstracts*, which provides an indexed English rendering of technical air-pollution literature; the annual *Environmental Protection Research Catalog*, which lists all projects funded by the EPA; and the monthly *Air Pollution Abstracts*, which catalogs all journal articles and technical reports on the subject of air pollution.

J13 Export-Import Bank of the United States (EXIMBANK)

1.   a. *811 Vermont Avenue, N.W.*
        Washington, D.C. 20571
        566-8990

   b. Open to the public but internal records are restricted.

   c. John L. Moore, Jr., President and Chairman

2.   An independent agency, the Export-Import Bank of the United States facilitates and aids in financing exports of U.S. goods and services. In liaison with the departments of State and Commerce, the EXIMBANK prepares confidential assessments on the capability of foreign countries to pay for U.S. imports.

   DIRECT CREDIT AND FINANCIAL GUARANTEES
   Charles E. Houston, Vice President, Asia Division
   566-8885

   Economists and loan officers of the Asia Division maintain confidential, loan project files and prepare country and regional studies on the economic conditions and credit worthiness of the Asian countries. For outstanding loans and guarantees to South Asian countries, contact economist Alice Mayo (566-8949). Philip Dunton (566-4779), of the Africa and Middle East Division (566-8919), is the loan officer for Afghanistan and Pakistan. The loan officer for India, Bangladesh, Nepal, and Sri Lanka is David K. Peacock (566-8097) of the Asia Division.

POLICY ANALYSIS AND COMMUNICATION DIVISION
James Cruse, Vice President
566-8861

A team of Policy Analysis Economists prepares studies on the international economic developments and their impact on the EXIMBANK and its programs. Research fields include methodologies for economic analysis and reviews of bank programs, export financing activities in the U.S. and abroad, world-wide trend in individual industries and commodities, international and domestic capital-market developments, and fluctuations in interest rates, prices, and other economic indicators. Most of these studies are restricted.

INTERNATIONAL RELATIONS OFFICE
L. Lauredo, Senior Vice President
566-8873

This office is responsible for the bank's international market development and relations with the foreign commercial, economic, and official representatives posted in the United States.

3. EXIMBANK Library (Theodora McGill, Librarian, 566-8320) is open to the public from 7:30 A.M. to 5:30 P.M., Monday through Friday. Library facilities include photoduplication and interlibrary loan services. The library's small but specialized holdings, of approximately 15,000 books and 950 current periodical subscriptions, concentrate on international banking, finance, commerce, trade, and developmental economics. A periodical list is available upon request, and a card catalog, arranged alphabetically by country, provides access to the collection.

4. An annual publication, *Report to Congress*, is for sale; it lists credits, guarantees, and insurance authorized for each country in the previous year. Other publications include: *Export-Import Bank of the United States*, which describes its history, operations, and programs; *Eximbank Record*, a monthly newsletter; *Eximbank-Export Financing for: American Exporters, Overseas Buyers, Banks* (1978); and *Businessman's Guide to the Cooperative Financing Facility* (1978).

    Most of EXIMBANK's internal records, research reports, and loan project files are restricted from public use. Researchers, however, may request access to those documents under the provisions of the Freedom of Information Act (566-8864). Most of EXIMBANK's internal records are under the custody of the Records and Central Files Manager (Helene H. Wall, 566-8815) in the Administration Office. The EXIMBANK is currently reproducing its records from 1937 to 1967 in microforms, with the originals being transferred to the custody of the National Archives. It is also developing an automated indexing system for its project records of active loans.

J14 Federal Reserve System

1. a. *20th Street and Constitution Avenue, N.W.*
    Washington, D.C. 20551
    452-3000

    b. Open to the public; previous appointments are recommended.

    c. Paul A. Volcker, Chairman

2. The Federal Reserve System, the central bank of the United States, is charged with administering and making policy for the nation's credit and monetary policy. Since the U.S. economy is an important and interdependent part of the world economy, the operations and activities of the Federal Reserve also incorporate several international economic and financial spheres.

Most analytical activities are carried out by staff economists, but occasionally outside consultants are also contracted to prepare special studies or to lead or participate in staff seminars.

INTERNATIONAL FINANCE DIVISION
Edwin M. Truman, Director
452-3614

This division monitors U.S. balance of payments, movements in exchange rates and transactions in foreign-exchange markets, flow of capital between the U.S. and foreign financial centers, and other economic and financial developments abroad that may have an impact on U.S. monetary policy. In addition, this division assists the Federal Reserve in its advisory and consultative role within the U.S. government in discussions of international financial matters; in directing U.S. participation in various international, financial and monetary organizations; and in maintaining informational contacts with the central banks of other countries. The division also collects and analyzes information and data relating to the activities of U.S. banks abroad and foreign banks in the U.S.

Within the division, basic research and analysis are conducted by staff economists, who are organized into several functional sections: International Development Section (David Dod, Chief, 452-3784) deals with economic and financial problems and policies of the developing countries; International Banking Section (Henry Terrell, Chief, 452-3768) monitors activities of U.S. banks abroad and foreign banks in the U.S.; U.S. International Transactions Section (Michael Dooley, Chief, 452-3728) collects data on international trade and capital movements and their influence on the U.S. economy; International Trade and Financial Studies Section (Bill Henderson, Chief, 452-4708) prepares long-range, theoretical research studies on international economic problems; and Quantitative Studies Section (Guy Stevens, Chief, 452-3775) develops and maintains econometric models on U.S.-foreign economic interdependence.

The International Information Center (Cynthia Sutton, Supervisor, 452-3411) of the division maintains a collection of research reports, briefing papers, and internal records produced by the division, and microfiche copies of documents from other U.S. government agencies and international organizations. Some of these materials are, however, classified. Access to the center is based on advance appointments.

3. The Federal Reserve System's Research Library of the Board of Governors (Ann Roane Clary, Chief Librarian, 452-3398) is open to the public from 8:45 A.M. to 5:15 P.M., Monday through Friday. Interlibrary loan and limited photocopying facilities are available. The collection consists of some 90,000 monographic volumes and 2,300 current periodical subscriptions. The subject strengths in the collection are in the areas of banking, monetary policy, and economic conditions in the United States and abroad. Researchers may note that the library's holdings contain a good number of foreign monetary

and banking laws, publications of the foreign central banks, and official statistical releases of more than 100 foreign countries. A biweekly publication, *Research Library Recent Acquisitions*, and a computer-generated printout of the library's periodicals are available.

4. *Federal Reserve Board Publications* lists all major publications and staff studies of the Federal Reserve System. *Federal Reserve System Purposes and Functions* (1979) is a handbook, presenting a concise account of the responsibilities and operating techniques of the system in the areas of monetary policy, banking and financial regulations, and international finance. Statistical releases and staff studies are published from time to time in the monthly *Federal Reserve Bulletin*. The system's *Annual Report* provides useful summaries of its activities.

All requests for access to classified records and documents should be directed to Rose Arnold (452-3684), the system's Freedom of Information Officer.

J15 General Accounting Office (GAO)

1. a. *441 G Street, N.W.*
   Washington, D.C. 20548
   275-2812

   b. Open to the public; previous appointment is recommended.

   c. Elmer B. Staats, Comptroller General

2. An independent, nonpolitical agency in the legislative branch of the government, the GAO assists the Congress, its committees, and its members in carrying out their legislative and supervisory responsibilities. Most GAO research is conducted in-house; however, limited consulting opportunities are also available.

   INTERNATIONAL DIVISION
   J. Kenneth Fasick, Director
   275-5518

   This division's resources are very valuable to the South Asianist. Several groups in this division evaluate the effectiveness of U.S. foreign aid and military-assistance programs, study the impact of U.S. policy on U.S. trade and international financial status, and review all bilateral and multilateral programs and aggreements to determine if the intended objectives and purposes—as laid down in those programs and agreements—have been realized. Evaluation reports on South Asia include an overview of the U.S. presence in Afghanistan (1971), economic assistance to India (1969), a review of the U.S. AID program in Pakistan (1976), and a study on the Bangladesh refugee relief program (1973). Most of these reports are unclassified and are available upon request. For further information, contact Samuel Bowlin (Development Assistance Group, 275-5790); Harry R. Finley (Security and International Relations Group, 275-5857); and Melvin Berngartt (Trade and Finance Group, 275-5889).

3. The General Accounting Office Library (Marju Parming, Library Director, 275-3691), including its two constituents, the Technical Library (275-5030) and the Law Library (275-2972), is open to the public for on-site use from 8:15 A.M. to 5:00 P.M., Monday through Friday. Interlibrary loan and photoduplication facilities are available. The collection consists primarily of materials in the areas of program evaluation, policy analysis, energy, accounting, law, and civilian and military regulatory materials. The library maintains current and retrospective files of most GAO special reports and annual reports.

4. GAO's principal publication is its annual *Report to the Congress*, which includes comments on the financial administration of U.S. programs for developing countries. Also available free is the semiannual *Publication List*, which contains information about other special country reports and program target evaluations.

    GAO's Freedom of Information officer is Nola Casieri (275-6172). For information concerning retired and inactive files, contact Edmond Sawyer, Technical Information Specialist (275-5042), in the Information Management Office. Microfilm copies of some of the documents transferred to the National Archives are available in the library.

J16 Health and Human Services Department

1. a. *200 Independence Avenue, S.W.*
    Washington, D.C. 20201
    245-1850

    b. Open to the public

2. The Department of Health and Human Services, formerly the Department of Health, Education and Welfare, works to protect and advance the health of the American people and provides essential human services to improve the quality of life for all Americans. Carrying out this mission involves a complex and diverse set of interrelated activities, some of which are international in dimension. Currently, the department administers more than 300 programs. In spite of the magnitude of its own in-house research, the department finances many outside research, consulting, and exchange programs.

3. The National Library of Medicine is described in entry A29. Health and Human Services Department Library is described in entry A17.

4. Selected publications are noted under the concerned units. Additional information is available in the annually updated *Publications Catalog of the U.S. Department of Health, Education and Welfare*. Most of the documents and records are open to the public. The department's Privacy Act Officer is Hugh O'Neill (245-6478), and Russell M. Roberts is the Freedom of Information Officer (472-7453).

PUBLIC HEALTH SERVICE
Julius B. Richmond, Assistant Secretary
245-7694

The Public Health Service, which is charged by law to promote and assure the highest level of health attainable for every individual and family in America, is also responsible for developing cooperation in health projects with other nations.

OFFICE OF INTERNATIONAL HEALTH
John H. Bryant, Deputy Assistant Secretary
Parklawn Building
Room 1887
5600 Fishers Lane
Rockville, Maryland 20857
(301) 443-1774

This office is the focal point for the over-all coordination and support of the international health activities of the Public Health Service. It has a continuing interest in research activities, which provide background information for the appraisal of health conditions in foreign countries and the evaluation of national and international efforts directed toward improving those conditions. In cooperation with the Agency for International Development, the Program and Policy Analysis Division (Howard Minners, Acting Director, 301/443-1776) prepares for sale a series of intermittent monographic studies, *Syncrises: the Dynamics of Health,* on the interactions of health and socio-economic development in various countries. So far, *Syncrises* have been compiled on Pakistan (1976), Afghanistan (1979), and Bangladesh (1976).

The Bilateral Organizations Division (Rose Belmont, 301/443-6278) is the official liaison office with the international organizations. Of particular interest is the Bilateral Programs Division (Robert D. Fischer, 301/443-4010), which is responsible for all U.S. bilateral programs in South Asia. For further information, contact Linda Vogel (301/443-4130) of the Asia and Western Pacific Office. The annual publication, *Report on the Health, Population and Nutrition Activities of the Agency of International Development,* prepared by the Office of International Health, is available free.

NATIONAL CENTER FOR HEALTH STATISTICS
3700 East-West Highway
Hyattsville, Maryland 20782
Dorothy P. Rice, Deputy Director
(301) 436-7016

The center was established in 1960, primarily to collect and disseminate data on health in the U.S., but it also fosters research, consultations, and training programs in international health. Robert M. Thorner (301/436-7039) is the Associate Director of the International Statistical Office. The center has occasionally introduced various publications of foreign countries. There is, for instance, an analytical study, *Height and Weight of Children in the United States, India and the United Arab Republic.* Another useful publication is the *Current Listing and Topical Index to the Vital and Health Statistics Series, 1962–1973.* The annual *Catalog of Publications of the National Center for Health Statistics* is also available free.

ALCOHOL, DRUG ABUSE, AND MENTAL HEALTH ADMINISTRATION (ADAMHA)
3700 East-West Highway
Hyattsville, Maryland 20782

Gerald Klerman, Administrator
(301) 443-4797

Through its three institutes (located at 5600 Fishers Lane, Rockville, Maryland 20852), the National Institute of Alcohol Abuse and Alcoholism (301/443-3885), the National Institute of Drug Abuse (301/443-6480), and the National Institute of Mental Health (301/443-3673), the administration spearheads the federal effort to prevent and treat problems related to alchol, drug abuse, and mental and emotional illness. Through its international activities office, the ADAMHA carries on extensive, health-related social- and behavioral-science research programs in many foreign countries. However, the administration's current South Asia program is limited to a Karachi social-psychology project on the role of women, and a bio-feedback project in Madras. In the past, the administration had participated—in a limited way—in the Indian Council of Medical Research project on drug abuse on campus and other similar studies.

The International Activities Office maintains contract-research project files and can provide assistance to researchers seeking access to pertinent sources of information. For information on ADAMHA-funded research projects, see the annual *Alcohol, Drug Abuse, Mental Health Research Grant Awards*. It may also be noted that each of the 3 component institutes of the administration mentioned above has its own information clearinghouse equipped with automated, bibliographic data files. Courtesy services are provided to serious researchers in these clearinghouses: National Clearinghouse for Mental Health Information (301/443-4517); National Clearinghouse for Drug Abuse Information (301/443-6500); and National Clearinghouse for Alcohol Information (301/468-2600).

NATIONAL INSTITUTES OF HEALTH (NIH)
900 Rockville Pike
Bethesda, Maryland 20014
Donald Fredrickson, Director
(301) 496-4461

A leading biomedical research facility in the world, the NIH also encourages international contacts and exchange of scientific knowledge.

Fogarty International Center
Edwin D. Becker, Director
(301) 496-1415

Established in 1968, the center is the focal point for coordinating the agency's over-all participation in international biomedical and behavioral research. The center's International Research Fellowship Section (Marcus Hairstone, 301/496-1653) administers a competitive postdoctoral fellowships program. Currently, the program is limited to India. Up to fiscal year 1980, a total of 36 fellowships have been awarded to applicants from India. Currently, negotiations are underway on programs for the establishment of a national nominating committee in Bangladesh. The International Cooperation and Geographic Studies Branch (Joseph R. Quinn, 301/496-5903) has published a number of important studies on the subject of health in individual foreign countries, but none on South Asian countries. Funds for short projects and travel grants to U.S. scientists are administered through the Special Foreign Currency Program Branch (Morris T. Jones, 301/496-6688).

Following is a selected list of publications of interest produced by the center: *Annual Report of International Activities* contains a description of various international programs and a list of research grants and contracts to foreign institutions and fellowships to foreign scientists; the annual *National Institutes of Health: International Awards for Biomedical Research and Research Training* includes information on international conferences fully or partially funded by NIH; and *National Institutes of Health: Statistical Reference Book of International Activities* gives summaries of activities and tabulates research grants and contracts.

Research Grants Division
Carl D. Douglass, Director
(301) 496-7211

This division serves as the central research-fund-granting agency of the department in the health-related projects. Research proposals, from American scholars interested in conducting research abroad in the health sciences, are processed by this office. The division's Research Documentation Section (John C. James, 301/496-7543), in addition to publishing the annual *Research Grants Index*, maintains CRISP, a computerized search service that gives information about the scientific and fiscal aspects of research projects supported by the various research-grants programs of the NIH and other components of the Department of Health and Human Services.

The institute's National Library of Medicine (see entry A29), in cooperation with the Educational Commission for Foreign Medical Graduates, compiles the publication *Foreign Medical Graduates in the United States*, which deals with the subject from several perspectives, including education of the foreign medical graduates abroad, the flow of foreign medical graduates to the U.S., and their training and utilization in American medicine. The library's International Program (Mary E. Corning, 301/496-6481) is also responsible for various cooperative undertakings in the developing world to improve library and health information services.

HEALTH RESOURCES ADMINISTRATION
3700 East-West Highway
Hyattsville, Maryland 20782
Henry A. Foley, Administrator
(301) 436-7200

The Office of International Affairs (Darl Stephens, 301/436-7179) is currently negotiating 2 programs in India relating to health, manpower planning, and health information assistance. The office also organizes workshops in New Delhi. No activities of the office are reported in other countries of South Asia.

HEALTH SERVICES ADMINISTRATION
5600 Fishers Lane
Rockville, Maryland 20857
George I. Lythcott
(301) 443-2216

For information concerning the administration's international activities, contact William R. Gemma (301/443-6152) of International Health Affairs. Current programs in South Asia include: investigation of hearing and speech disorders (Benares, India); investigation of medical and reconstructive procedures in otolaryngological disorders (India); epilepsy and leprosy control (India); rehabilitation of pregnant diabetic women (Pakistan); and study of the control of soil treatment helminths. Reports of all completed studies are available from the unit.

FOOD AND DRUG ADMINISTRATION
5600 Fishers Lane
Rockville, Maryland 20857
Jere E. Goyan, Commissioner
(301) 443-2410

The International Affairs Staff (Irvin M. Asher, 301/443-4480) and PL 480 Research Coordinator (B. H. Van Schoick, 301/443-1357) may be contacted for the division's activities in South Asia. Also contact Robert W. Week (426-8998), International Studies Assistant to the Director of the Bureau of Food (200 C Street, S.W., Washington, D.C. 20204). The limited South Asia program includes a foreign-currency research project on mycotoxin in India.

HUMAN DEVELOPMENT SERVICES
200 Indepencence Avenue, S.W.
Washington, D.C. 20201
Cesar A. Perales, Assistant Secretary
245-7246

The International Activities Group (Stanley Bendet, 245-6436), of the Office of Planning, Research and Evaluation, is responsible for all overseas programs and research projects. Currently, the Human Development Services' South Asian programs are limited to several research and demonstration projects in social welfare and rehabilitation programs in Pakistan and India. A list of the international projects, and a descriptive brochure of the international activities of the division, are available.

SOCIAL SECURITY ADMINISTRATION
Office of Research and Statistics
1875 Connecticut Avenue, N.W.
Washington, D.C. 20009
John J. Carroll, Director
673-5602

The Social Security Administration operates the world's largest social insurance program. The administration acquires through its Comparative International Studies Staff (Max Horlick, 673-5714) comparative data from other countries concerning unemployment insurance, health care systems, workmen's compensation and other similar programs. The staff also prepares analytical studies on selected aspects of social security systems in individual foreign countries. A forthcoming publication on international studies, by the Social Security Administration, will list these country studies. A comprehensive review of social security programs in some 130 nations is reported in the biennial publication, *Social Security Programs Throughout the World,* which is supplemented by monthly items in the *Social Security Bulletin* and in occasional research notes.

The administration also published *The Role of Social Security in Eco-*

nomic Development, a special report of a 1967 seminar sponsored by the administration; and the *Role of Social Security in Developing Countries* (1963, reprint 1967), a study prepared by the Social Security Administration for the Agency of International Development. A reference room open to the public is maintained by the Comparative Studies Staff (Ilene Zeitzer, 673-5713) and contains a good collection of books, periodicals, and country files.

Note: Also see entry A17.

J17 Housing and Urban Development Department (HUD)

1.   a. *451 7th Street, S.W.*
      Washington, D.C. 20410
      755-5111

      b. Open to the public

2.   In addition to its domestic responsibilities for programs concerned with housing needs, fair housing opportunities, and urban development, the department is also involved in cooperative activities with many foreign countries and international organizations. Its Office of International Affairs (Tila Maria de Hancock, Assistant to the Secretary for International Affairs, 755-7058) is responsible for all overseas activities of the department and manages its foreign visitors program. The office also recruits technical advisors to serve overseas for the USAID and other U.S. government departments and agencies, and coordinates U.S. activities in the areas of housing and urban development in international organizations. There has been a recent slowdown of international activities within the department. A pamphlet, *HUD International Program and Activities,* describes its works.
      Information and Technology Division (Susan Judd, 755-5770) maintains an automated Foreign Information Retrieval System (FIRS) of bibliographic references on the subjects of housing and urban affairs. Indexed by subject, country, and author, the system may be searched without fee. *Foreign Publications Accessions List* is an irregular computer-generated printout of new publications received by the division on such subjects as architecture, building, environment, urban renewal, and planning.

3.   The HUD Library is located in Room 8141 (Elsa Freeman, Director, 755-6370) and is open Monday through Friday, 8:30 A.M. to 5:15 P.M. The library is open to the public, and interlibrary loan and photoduplication services are available. The library contains nearly 500,000 items including some 2,000 periodical titles. Principal focus of the collection is on American housing, urban planning and development, and related socio-economic issues. South Asia-related material in the collection is insignificant. The library's holdings are published in the 19-volume *Dictionary Catalog of the United States Department of Housing and Urban Development Library and Information Division* (G. K. Hall, 1972). The catalog's first supplement appeared in 1974. In addition, researchers may consult the bimonthly, *Housing and Planning Reference,* which indexes current literature on the subject, and the semimonthly, *HUD Library Recent Acquisitions.* The library also prepares a reference guide entitled *Bibliography on Housing,*

Building and Planning for Use of Overseas Missions of the United States Agency for International Development.

4. The Office of International Affairs publishes a series of reports on housing and related subjects in developing countries. *HUD International Country Reports*, which cover all countries, are issued at irregular intervals and are designed to assist in the orientation of AID personnel and American business personnel interested in foreign investments. Other publications include the *HUD International Review*, a quarterly; *Hud International Newsletter;* and *International Information Sources*. HUD's Freedom of Information Officer is Louise C. North (755-6420).

J18 Interior Department

1. a. *18th and C Streets, N.W.*
    Washington, D.C. 20240
    343-3171

    b. Open to the public; previous appointment recommended

2. Although primarily a home affairs department and the nation's principal conservation agency, the Department of the Interior also participates in a wide variety of international activities. Most research is conducted within the department, but occasionally outside scholars are contracted as con-·sultants.

3. The Natural Resources Library (Mary A. Huffer, Director, 343-5815) of the U.S. Department of the Interior is located at 18th and C Streets, N.W., Washington, D.C. 20240. Open from 7:45 A.M. to 5:00 P.M., Monday through Friday, the library is accessible to the public for on-site use. Interlibrary loan and photoduplication services are available. The library's holdings consist of over 1,000,000 bound volumes, 21,000 serial titles, 250,000 microfiche, and 8,000 reels of microfilm. Special collections include the departmental archives, a depository collection of U.S. documents, and some 20,000 doctoral dissertations in the general area of natural resources.
    Approximately 1,000 items on South Asia in the collection include: a selection of governmental publications related to natural resources; codes and regulations concerning exploitation of natural resources; and geological and hydrological journals and magazines. A subject/author/title dictionary catalog and the published *Dictionary Catalog of the Departmental Library*, 37 vols. (G. K. Hall, 1967), and 4 supplements (1969–1975), provide access to the collection.

POLICY, BUDGET AND ADMINISTRATION
Larry E. Meierotto, Assistant Secretary
343-6181

INTERNATIONAL PROGRAMS OFFICE
James A. Slater
343-3101

Although this office has no current involvement in any South Asia-related activities, it may direct researchers to appropriate units of the department. Researchers may find it useful to contact James A. Slater who is knowledgeable about past and current departmental programs on South Asia.

U.S. GEOLOGICAL SURVEY (USGS)
National Center
12201 Sunrise Valley Drive
Reston, Virginia 22092
H. William Menard, Director
(703) 860-6118

In addition to its primary responsibilities concerning determination, appraisal, conservation, and delineation of the nation's territory, the USGS— under the auspices of AID, international organizations, or sometimes a foreign government—plays an important role in foreign assistance programs. These programs include training of foreign geologists and hydrologists both in their own countries and in the United States; the development of geological and hydrological services in selected foreign countries; and other special projects adopted through bilateral or international arrangements. The USGS staff members also seek to collaborate with their foreign counterparts in obtaining information needed to prepare comprehensive geological and resource maps of the less-developed countries.

GEOLOGIC DIVISION
Dallas L. Peck, Chief Geologist
(703) 860-6531

International Geology Office
John A. Reinemund, Chief
(703) 860-6418

The following current activities and programs in South Asia are reported. Two staff members of the division participated in the AID-sponsored Disaster Relief Preparedness Seminar held in 1979 in India. In 1981, the division will organize a proposed Indo-U.S. workshop in mineral resources evaluation. Under negotiation, at the time of this writing, is a request by the Geological Survey of India and the Center for Earth Science Studies for technical assistance and training in marine biology programs. Also, the Oil and Natural Gas Commission of India has requested assistance in the use of magnetic gravity and LANDSAT data for basement geology interpretation and the preparation of a manual dealing with regulations for the use of off-shore exploration and production.

Subsequent to the ratification of a memorandum of understanding between the USGS and the Royal Nepalese government's Department of Mines and Geology—for technical cooperation in earth sciences—negotiations are being conducted for USGS assistance in Nepalese studies of salt, phosphate, and potash deposits, and engineering geology. The government of Bangladesh is negotiating for USGS assistance in coal assessment and mining technology, as well as technical support in developing the geological survey of Bangladesh. Similarly, in Pakistan—where the USGS had provided assistance in coal mining and coal research, as well as energy-resources assessment programs, sponsored by the Department of Energy— the USGS is currently exploring new avenues for technical cooperation, including studies of phosphate and lead-zinc deposits, inland use of ultra-mafic rocks, and laboratory reviews and training. For further information on the division's South Asia programs, contact Steven J. Gawarecki (703/860-6555).

NATIONAL MAPPING DIVISION
Rupert B. Southard, Chief
(703) 860-6231

International Activities Board
Charles D. Zeigler, Chief
(703) 860-6241

With the exception of a completed training program in Pakistan and a proposed one for Sri Lanka, the division has no other involvement in South Asia.

WATER RESOURCES DIVISION
Philip Cohen, Chief Hydrologist
(703) 860-6921

International Hydrology
James R. Jones, Jr., Chief
(703) 860-6548

Although no current South Asian activities are reported, the division has, in the past, provided support to a published study, *Water Resources and Related Geology of Dera Ismail Khan District, West Pakistan, with Reference to the Availability of Ground Water for Development* (1970).

PUBLICATIONS DIVISION
Gary W. North, Chief
(703) 860-7181

International Activities Special Assistant
James R. Jones, Jr., Acting Chief
(703) 860-7186

The international program of this division is designed to provide training support to personnel in foreign government agencies responsible for publishing geologic maps and cartographic charts. Currently, the division has no activities in South Asia.

USGS publications on foreign assistance include: *Bibliography of Reports Resulting from U.S. Geological Survey Participation in the United States Technical Assistance Program 1940–1967* (1968); *Bibliography of Reports Resulting from U.S. Geological Survey Technical Cooperation with other Countries, 1967–1974* (1975); *U.S. Geological Survey International Activities* (annual); *Historical Review of the International Water Resources Program of the U.S. Geological Survey, 1940–1970* (1976); and *Worldwide Directory of National Earth-Science Agencies*. A monthly bibliography, *New Publications of the Geological Survey*, is available free from the survey. These and other USGS publications may be obtained from the Distribution Branch, Geological Survey, 1200 South Eads Street, Arlington, Virginia 22202 (703/557-2751).

EARTH RESOURCES OBSERVATION SYSTEMS PROGRAM (EROS)
Gene Thorley, Acting Chief
(703) 860-7881

The EROS Data Center (Sioux Falls, South Dakota 57198, 605/594-6511), which is a part of the EROS program, gathers remotely sensed data on natural and man-made features of the earth's surface collected by satellite and aircraft. A technical and scientific facility, the center reproduces as sales items photos, images, and electronic data on the earth acquired by spacecraft and aircraft, and provides professional service to further the understanding and use of the data. The Agency for International Development has compiled a series of *Developing Country Coverage of Earth-Resources Technology Satellite* (ERTS, renamed LANDSAT since 1975), which lists the identification number, location, acquisition date, cloud cover, and other related information for each image acquired of the subject country.

The National Cartographic Information Center (NCIC), located in Reston, Virginia 22092 (703/860-6187) and open to the public, is a clearinghouse for information about domestically produced maps and charts, mapping materials, aerial and space photographs, satellite imagery—including LANDSAT and *Skylab* data—map-related data in digital form, and geodetic control data. There are also cumulative records on approximately 12,000,000 aerial photographs.

For information on the Geological Survey Library, see entry A12.

NATIONAL PARK SERVICE
18th and C Streets, N.W.
Washington, D.C. 20240
William J. Whalen, Director
343-4621

Although this service primarily administers, for the American people, an extensive system of national parks, monuments, historic sites, and recreation areas, it is also involved in some international programs.

INTERNATIONAL PARK AFFAIRS
Robert Milne, Chief
523-5260

The activities of this office in South Asia are usually limited to consultative or advisory assistance to the programs developed and funded by other U.S. agencies, international organizations, or foreign governments. In India, the service is involved in a biospheric reserve project under a UNESCO ecological program. The National Park Service has also compiled environmental profiles on India, Pakistan, Bangladesh, and Sri Lanka under AID contracts. Negotiations are also in progress for exploring new areas of cooperation and assistance in India under the PL 480 excess-currency program.

U.S. FISH AND WILDLIFE SERVICE
18th and C Streets, N.W.
Washington, D.C. 20240
Lynn A. Greenwalt, Director
343-4717

Charged with protecting and preserving the fish and wildlife resources in the U.S., the service also assists in the development of an environmental stewardship ethic based on ecological principles, scientific knowledge of wildlife, and a sense of moral responsibility.

INTERNATIONAL AFFAIRS
Lawrence Mason, Acting Chief
343-5188

This office provides international leadership in protecting endangered fish and wildlife by restoring and preventing further disappearance of threatened species. The program includes coordination of international efforts to this end, foreign importation enforcement, and consultant services to foreign countries.

Current programs of the U.S. Fish and Wildlife Service to promote conservation and determine the status of the endangered and threatened species in South Asia are limited to the following three 5-year contracts in India, financed by the PL 480 excess-foreign currency funds; an avifauna survey of the Bombay Natural History Society; development of a hydro-biological sanctuary in Barrackpore; and a floral survey by the Botanical Survey of India. In addition several short term projects, workshops, and seminars on the subjects of conservation and ecology are sponsored from time to time both in India and Pakistan.

Negotiations are in progress with the Pakistan National Council for Conservation concerning several programs for management research and training. Although there is no on-going program in Sri Lanka, the International Affairs staff is monitoring the ecological impact of the massive Mahaweli irrigation project in Sri Lanka. The staff also collects data on other South Asian countries. For further information contact David Ferguson (International Specialist, 343-4491).

BUREAU OF MINES
2401 E Street, N.W.
Washington, D.C. 20240
Lindsay D. Norman, Director
634-1300

A research and fact-finding agency, this bureau insures adequate mineral supplies for U.S. security and other needs.

PRODUCTION, CONSUMPTION DATA COLLECTION AND INTERPRETATION
Frances E. Brantley, Director
634-1187

Foreign Data Branch
Don Colby, Chief
632-8970

Area specialists in this branch collect data on mineral production, processing, and consumption in foreign countries. It also prepares the annual reviews of mineral developments in each country in the *Minerals Yearbook* and other specical area reports. *Mineral Perspectives, Far East and South Asia* (1977), prepared by K. P. Wang, a staff member of the branch, presents a concise summary and a map of the mineral industries of Afghanistan,

Bangladesh, Bhutan, India, Nepal, and Pakistan. This useful study analyzes reserve, production, mineral trade, consumption, role of minerals domestically and in world supply, country attitudes and plans, and developments in specific mineral industries. This publication also contains base maps showing mineral deposits and mineral-processing plant locations and transport facilities for each country. A summary review describes the relative importance of the region as a mineral producer, consumer, importer, and exporter.

Note: Also see entries A12 and E3.

J19 International Communication Agency (ICA)

1. a. *1750 Pennyslvania Avenue, N.W.*
   Washington, D.C. 20547
   724-9103

   b. Open to the public; advance appointment is recommended.

   c. John E. Reinhardt, Director
   724-9042

2. The International Communication Agency, which maintains 203 posts in 125 countries, came into being in 1978 with the consolidation of the former U.S. Information Agency and the former Bureau of Educational and Cultural Affairs of the Department of State. The fundamental premise of the agency is that it is in the U.S. national interest to encourage the sharing of ideas and cultural activities among the people of the U.S. and those of other nations. The wide variety of ICA communication activities—for dissemination abroad of information about the people, culture, and policies of the U.S.—include international academic and cultural exchanges, international broadcasting, and cultural center programs abroad. The ICA also has the responsibility for reporting to the president and the secretary of state, as well as advising the National Security Council on world-wide public opinion as it is relevant to the formulation and conduct of U.S. foreign policy.

   Most research is done in-house; occasional contract research, primarily in the fields of international public opinion and media affairs is available.

3. The agency library is discussed in entry A20.

4. ICA's legislative mandate prohibits dissemination within the United States of materials produced for distribution overseas. The agency publishes 14 magazines in 16 languages, most of them printed at overseas Regional Service Centers and major posts. The contents consist largely of reprints from the best American periodicals. Pamphlets, leaflets, printed exhibits, and posters are also distributed in more than 100 countries. The principal publications of interest from the Washington, D.C., headquarters are: *Horizons USA*, a bimonthly in English; *Dialogue*, a scholarly quarterly in English; and *Economic Impact*, another English quarterly. All ICA publications are free.

   An agency automated Document Index System (DIS) (724-9968) lists all agency documents generated since 1973, when the system went into operation; earlier materials are also being added to the system gradually. These documents, some of which are classified, deal with a variety of subjects including message communications, internal memoranda, country assessments, and research studies. DIS could be searched by date, subject, or geographic area. An annual computer-generated listing of documents declassified by the agency is available. Matters concerning Freedom of Information requests are handled by the Access to Information Officer (Charles Jones, 724-9089), attached to the Office of Congressional and Public Liaison.

OFFICE OF NORTH AFRICAN, NEAR EASTERN AND SOUTH ASIAN (NEA) AFFAIRS
R. T. Curran, Director
724-9090
Louise Taylor, Country Affairs Officer, Afghanistan, Bangladesh, Pakistan, and Iran
724-9098
Dorothy Robins Mowry, Country Affairs Officer, India, Nepal and Sri Lanka
724-9199

This geographic area office is the principal agency contact with the overseas posts in South Asia. The office provides broad managerial oversight of the posts and programs in South Asia and conveys post needs and perspectives both to the core management and to functional offices of the agency. ICA posts in South Asia conduct exchange activities on behalf of the U.S. government—except for the Department of Defense—in the areas of communication, culture, and education. Country Affairs Officers, who are knowledgeable about ICA activities in their respective countries, are accessible to researchers.

ASSOCIATE DIRECTORATE FOR PROGRAMS (PGM)
Harold F. Schneidman, Associate Director
724-9349

A functional element of the ICA, the Associate Directorate for Programs is comprised of several units. In the Office of Research (Stanton H. Burnett, Director, 724-9545), the Near East and South Asia Research Staff (Robert Hartland, Chief, 724-9220), in conjunction with the Media Reaction Staff (James Schein, Deputy Chief, 724-9057), prepares assessments and surveys of South Asian attitudes and media reports for the White House, the Department of State, other departments and agencies of the government, and for the agency's own use. These research reports are available at 43 depository libraries in universities and other institutions throughout the country.

The Office of Research is also responsible for the USICA Library (see entry A20) and the USICA Archives (724-9156), the latter of which contains a comprehensive collection of agency records, records of the predecessor agencies, minutes of interagency meetings, cultural-exchange grant records, and files of agency publications. Materials deposited in the archives since 1973 can be retrieved through the computerized Document Index System.

A vast amount of materials in the archives are restricted.

International Communication Policy Staff (Ronald Homet, Chief, 724-9300) is especially concerned with matters related to the process of international communications; it works with other government and private bodies dealing with this significant area in helping to establish the main lines of U.S. policy for such major international negotiations as the World Administrative Radio Conference (WARC). The Foreign Press Center (Henry W. Grady, Coordinator, 724-1643, Room 225, National Press Building, 529 14th Street, N.W., Washington, D.C. 20547) provides facilitative services to foreign journalists working in Washington.

The Office of Program Coordination and Development (Edward Schulick, Director, 724-1900) analyzes field program-support requests, develops and maintains relevant program materials, coordinates the acquisition and production of agency media products, and identifies and recruits speakers for ICA posts overseas, insuring that these speakers will have the opportunity to acquire foreign perspectives while abroad. Acquisition and production of a variety of media products for use by agency posts abroad are the responsibility of the media offices; e.g., Press and Publication Service (Adelaide Kummer, Chief, Near East and South Asia Branch, 724-9496) and Television and Film Service (Stanley D. Moss, Director, 376-7806).

VOICE OF AMERICA (VOA) (Associate Directorate for Broadcasting)
330 Independence Avenue, S.W.
Washington, D.C. 20201
Allen Baker, Chief, Near East and South Asia Division
755-4784

The Voice of America is the global radio network of the International Communication Agency, which seeks to promote understanding abroad of the United States, its people, culture, and policies. Currently, VOA broadcasts 3½ hours a day in Bengali, Hindi, and Urdu via short and medium wave to an estimated 14,000,000 listeners in South Asia. A South Asia Correspondence Bureau is located in New Delhi. A half-hour program in Dari commenced in the summer of 1980. VOA claims to serve as "a consistently reliable and authoritative source of news," and its news broadcasts include extensive coverage of economic, social, and cultural ties between South Asia and the United States (see also entry P26).

The daily *Current Report* provides program titles, newscast subject matter, and sources of information for VOA broadcasts. Some annual VOA braodcast schedules for each geographical area are available. The News Division (Bernard Kamenske, Chief, 755-5781) and Current Affairs Division (Michael Hanu, Chief, 755-3690) monitors current events in South Asia. Further information on VOA programs may be obtained from its Public Affairs Chief (Diane Conklin, 755-4744).

OFFICE OF CONGRESSIONAL AND PUBLIC LIAISON
Michael Pistor, Director
724-9103

The responsibility of this office is to provide information about the activities of the agency to the public, the media, and the Congress.

ASSOCIATE DIRECTORATE FOR EDUCATIONAL AND CULTURAL AFFAIRS (ECA)
Alice S. Ilchman, Associate Director
724-9032

Three major offices constitute the Associate Directorate for Educational and Cultural Affairs. The Office of Culture Centers and Resources (632-6700) is responsible for providing policy direction, program support, and professional guidance and materials to ICA libraries, cultural centers, and binational centers overseas. It also promotes the teaching of English and distributes American books—both in English and translation—abroad. In addition to several cultural and information centers in India, Pakistan, Bangladesh, Nepal, and Sri Lanka, several binational centers in Pakistan (Pakistan American Cultural Centers or PACE) and Nepal also operate on a cooperative basis. The cultural center in Afghanistan has recently closed. A limited number of book presentation programs also continue in several countries of South Asia. Frank Walton, Chief, Center's Management Staff (632-6701) may be consulted for further information.

The Office of Institutional Relations (Mildred Marcy, Director, 724-9442) develops and implements the exchange of cultural presentations, including art and museum exhibits; arranges travel plans for international visitors; maintains liaison with a wide range of private institutions to encourage and support private exchange programs and foster institutional linkages across national boundaries; and coordinates international information, educational, cultural, and exchange programs conducted by other departments and agencies of the U.S. government. Joanne Rinehart (724-9308), of the International Visitor's Division (724-9984), and Robert D. Persiko (724-9796), in the Special Projects Coordination Section of the Private Sector Program Division (724-9444), may be consulted for South Asia-related activities conducted by the office. The private-sector institutions currently supported by the office include the Coordinating Council for International Issues (1900 L Street, N.W., Washington, D.C. 20036, 659-9383) (see entry L31)—a private, nonprofit organization dealing with human rights and economic developments in developing countries—and the Indo-U.S. Sub-Commission on Education and Culture (see entry L37).

The Office of Academic Programs (Stanley Nicholson, Director, 724-9941) is responsible for organizing and assisting academic exchanges between the U.S. and other countries (including the Fulbright program); facilitating the establishment and maintenance of close ties between the American academic community and those abroad; encouraging and supporting American studies at foreign universities and other institutions of higher learning; and providing staff support to the presidentially appointed Board of Foreign Scholarship, which supervises the academic exchange program. Near Eastern and South Asian Programs Branch (Robert Coonrod, Chief, 724-9715) is responsible for South Asian academic-exchange programs and for supporting the specialized institutions in the area, such as the American Institute of Indian Studies in New Delhi and American studies centers in Hyderabad (India), Calcutta, and Islamabad. Currently, Fulbright programs are available for India, Pakistan, Nepal, and Sri Lanka. The Fulbright program in Afghanistan has been recently terminated. Although there is no Fulbright program in Bangladesh, several other U.S. government-supported exchange programs, including travel-only grants, are available.

The East-West Center Liaison Officer (Carol Owens, 724-9333), of the Office of Academic Programs, serves a coordinating function with the Center for Cultural and Technical Interchange between East and West in Hawaii. This autonomous institution of learning for Americans and for the people of Asia and the Pacific promotes better understanding through cooperative programs of research, study, and training.

Note: Also see entries A20 and P26.

J20 International Trade Commission (ITC)

1. a. *701 E Street, N.W.*
    Washington, D.C. 20436
    523-0173

    b. Open to the public

    c. Joseph O. Parker, Chairman

2. An independent agency, the ITC is charged with furnishing studies, reports, and recommendations involving international trade and tariffs to the president, the Congress, and other government agencies. In order to carry out its responsibilities, the commission is required to engage in extensive research, conduct specialized studies, and maintain a high degree of expertise in all matters relating to commercial and international trade policies of the U.S.

    International economists in the Office of Economic Research (Norman S. Fieleke, Director, 724-0084) conduct research and analysis on international trade trends, economic conditions, and the impact of foreign exports on the United States. It also prepares an annual report on the operations of trade agreements and participates in investigations of unfair trade practices. Shafik M. Youssef (724-0075) is the economic analyst for South Asia.

    The Office of Trade Agreements (William T. Hart, Director, 523-0232) monitors the Generalized Systems of Preference (GSP), which allows the U.S. to extend duty-free treatment for certain articles to be imported into the U.S. from qualified underdeveloped countries. The GSP, as approved by the General Agreements for Trade and Tariff (GATT), has been in effect since 1976. India, Pakistan, Sri Lanka, and Bangladesh are among the eligible countries for GSP benefits. For further information, contact John G. Boyd (523-0428). All research is done in-house.

3. The International Trade Commission Library (Dorothy J. Berkowitz, Chief, Library Division, 523-0013) is open to the public from 8:45 A.M. to 5:15 P.M., Monday through Friday. Interlibrary loan and photoduplication facilities are available. The collection consists of approximately 77,000 volumes, and 1,200 current serial subscriptions, the primary focus of which is on international tariff and custom regulations, foreign trade serials, statistical year books, and economics and finance. The library also maintains vertical files of pamphlets and newspaper clippings on some countries of South Asia. Bibliographic tools consist of a dictionary card catalog and the *Selected Current Acquisitions List*.

4.   Publications include the ITC *Annual Report,* and its annual *Operations of the Trade Agreements,* which contains data on U.S.–South Asia trade and changes in South Asian foreign-investment policies. The ITC also publishes *Summaries of Trade and Tariff Information* and results of investigations concerning various commodities and subjects. Specific information regarding these publications may be obtained from the Office of the Secretary (Kenneth R. Mason, 523-0161).

   For information concerning retired and inactive files, contact the Director of Administration (Charles Ramsdale, 523-0187). ITC Secretary Kenneth R. Mason serves as the Freedom of Information Officer.

J21 Justice Department

1.   a. *10th Street and Constitution Avenue, N.W.*
        Washington, D.C. 20530
        633-2000

     b. Most departmental agencies discussed below are open to the public. Researchers may, however, contact each office for conditions of public access.

2.   A few departmental agencies contain interesting resources for South Asia-related research. In its responsibility for enforcing the law in the public interest, the Justice Department also enforces the Foreign Agents Registration Act of 1938, as amended, and related statutes; the immigration and naturalization laws; the extradition proceedings as provided by law; and the protocol relating to political asylum.

3.   The Justice Department Library (Maureen Moore, Library Director, 633-2133), open from 9:00 A.M. to 5:30 P.M., Monday through Friday, contains approximately 150,000 volumes of legal as well as general reference works. The collection is restricted to internal use, although interlibrary loans are available.

4.   For access to the Justice Department's restricted internal records, contact its Freedom of Information referral staff (Patricia Neely, 633-3452).

CRIMINAL DIVISION
Philip Heyman, Assistant Attorney General
633-2601

With the exception of the duly accredited diplomats and commercial agents, all foreign agents and representatives of foreign political parties are required to register with the division's Foreign Agent's Registration Unit (Joel Liska, Chief, 724-6922) and provide it with a detailed description of their activities and sources of support. They are also required to file a copy of any material they disseminate in the United States. These records are accessible to the researchers at the Public Office (Federal Triangle Building, 315 9th Street, N.W., Washington, D.C. 20530, 724-2332). The *Annual Report of the Attorney General* provides a list of foreign agents registered with this unit.

   The International Affairs Office (Michael A. Abbell, Director, 724-7600), another unit of the Criminal Division, is charged with formulating and executing transnational, criminal-justice enforcement policies, including international extradition proceedings and political asylum. General Litigation and Legal Advice Section (Lawrence Lippe, Chief, 724-6948) deals with criminal matters relating to immigration.

IMMIGRATION AND NATURALIZATION SERVICE (INS)
425 Eye Street, N.W.
Washington, D.C. 20536
David W. Crosland, Acting Commissioner
633-6900

This INS is responsible for administering the immigration and naturalization laws relating to the admission, exclusion, deportation, and naturalization of aliens.

INFORMATION SERVICES DIVISION
Irvin Klavan, Assistant Commissioner
633-2989

The Statistical Branch (Stephen Schroffel, Chief, 633-3069) of the Information Services Division collects statistical data pertaining to immigration, naturalization, nonimmigrants, passenger travel, alien annual address reports, and service actions relating to aliens. These records are maintained according to the entering alien's country of origin, sex, age, and occupation. Tables compiled from these data bases are contained in the *Annual Report: Immigration and Naturalization Service,* which is the principal publication of the INS. Additionally, the *Report of Passenger Travel Between the United States and Foreign Countries,* issued monthly, semiannually, and annually, is a compilation of data on sea and air travel by aliens and U.S. citizens. Statistical data maintained by the branch are available to the public. Private researchers may also obtain access to the branch's small reference collection of historical literature and statistical data. The INS Freedom of Information Officer is Russell A. Powell (633-3278).

DRUG ENFORCEMENT ADMINISTRATION (DEA)
1405 Eye Street, N.W.
Washington, D.C. 20537
Peter B. Bensinger, Administrator
633-1249

The lead agency in the federal narcotic and dangerous drug suppression program, the DEA operates both at the national and international levels. It conducts domestic and international investigations of major drug traffickers, concentrating efforts at the illicit sources of supply or diversion. DEA's quarterly magazine, *Drug Enforcement,* features articles relating to international activities. Most DEA files are classified. DEA's Freedom of Information officer is Russ Aruslan (633-1396).

J22 Labor Department

1. a. *200 Constitution Avenue, N.W.*
   Washington, D.C. 20210
   523-8165

   b. Open to the public

2. In carrying out its mission of fostering, promoting, and developing the welfare of the wage earners of the United States, the Department of Labor also participates in various international activities involving the interests of American labor.

    Research is conducted in-house, but contract research opportunities are also available. Requests for proposals are announced in the *Commerce Business Daily* published by the Department of Commerce. Some internal records of the department are classified, and available only through the Freedom of Information Act processes. Sofia Petters (523-6807) is the department's Freedom of Information Officer.

3. The Labor Department Library (Andre C. Whisenton, Library Director, 523-6988), open from 8:15 A.M. to 4:45 P.M., Monday through Friday, is accessible to the public for reference use only. Limited interlibrary loan and photoduplication facilities are available. This library of approximately 535,000 volumes and 3,200 current periodical subscriptions is one of the most extensive collections in the fields of labor and economics, including a considerable collection of foreign labor-union materials. The collection also contains foreign official documents, and publications of the International Labor Organization (ILO). South Asia-related materials in the collection consist of some 1,000 monographs, government serials, and periodicals.

    Besides 2 dictionary card catalogs for pre- and post-1975 acquisitions, respectively, a 38-volume *United States Department of Labor Library Catalog*, published by G. K. Hall in 1975, provides access to the collection. The library has also published a new list of *Periodicals Currently Received by the U.S. Department of Labor Library* (1980). Also useful is the biweekly *Labor Literature,* which announces new acquisitions of the library.

4. Departmental publications are discussed below along with the units generating them.

BUREAU OF INTERNATIONAL AFFAIRS
Dean K. Clowes, Deputy Under Secretary
523-6043

The bureau which assists in formulating international economic and trade policies that affect American workers, helps represent the U.S. in multilateral and bilateral trade negotiations on such international bodies as the General Agreement on Tariffs and Trade (GATT), and various other U.N. organizations. The bureau also helps administer the U.S. labor attaché program at U.S. embassies abroad, carries out overseas technical-assistance projects, and arranges trade-union exchanges and other programs for foreign visitors to the U.S.

OFFICE OF FOREIGN LABOR AFFAIRS
Gerald P. Holmes, Director
523-7571

This office monitors labor and employment trends in foreign countries and assists in administering the foreign labor attaché program. At present, a full-time labor attaché is posted in New Delhi. In the U.S. embassies in other South Asian countries, generally, an officer is designated for dealing with labor-related matters. For access to labor-attaché reports and other dispatches, consult the South Asian Area Advisor (Robert Senser, 523-6234). Researchers may also note that the Foreign Publications Group (Pat Underwood, 523-6377) of this office compiles *Country Labor Profiles* on selected foreign countries. Currently, such a profile is available on India.

OFFICE OF FOREIGN ECONOMIC POLICY
Gloria G. Pratt, Director
523-6171

This office helps the Labor Department participate in U.S. interagency teams that negotiate bilateral and multilateral agreements. Currently, the office is involved in the negotiations with Pakistan and India on an Export Subsidies Code Agreement.

OFFICE OF INTERNATIONAL VISITORS PROGRAMS
Ron Smith, Director
523-6315

This office assists the department's exchange-visitors program. Recent participants in the program include trade union leaders and other professional and governmental personnel from several South Asian countries.

BUREAU OF LABOR STATISTICS (BLS)
441 G Street, N.W.
Washington, D.C. 20212
Janet Norwood, Commissioner
523-1913

The BLS has responsibility for the department's economic and statistical research, including certain international aspects. It has no enforcement or administrative functions, and practically all of the basic data it collects are supplied by voluntary cooperation. The information collected is issued in monthly press releases and in special publications—the *Monthly Labor Review* and *Handbook of Labor Statistics*—which contain international sections.

OFFICE OF PRICES AND LIVING CONDITIONS
W. John Layng, Assistant Commissioner
523-1121

The Division of International Price Indexes (Edward E. Murphy, Chief, 523-9724) measures and analyzes price trends for U.S. exports by commodities.

OFFICE OF ADMINISTRATIVE MANAGEMENT
Donald J. Keuch Jr., Deputy Assistant Commissioner
523-1017

The Training Division (Juliet F. Kidney, Chief, 523-1028) within this office conducts several technical seminars each year, which include participants from India, Pakistan, Bangladesh, and Sri Lanka.

OFFICE OF PRODUCTIVITY AND TECHNOLOGY
Jerome A. Mark, Assistant Commissioner
523-9294

Within this office, the Division of Foreign Labor Statistics and Trade (Arthur F. Neef, Chief, 523-9291) collects foreign labor and trade statistics and analyzes foreign labor conditions, including wage levels, benefits, and productivity.

Of the several BLS publications pertaining to international labor statistics, the following may be particularly useful to South Asian scholars. While most of these publications are discontinued, they may be examined in the Labor Department Library: *Labor Development Abroad,* a discontinued monthly; *Labor Law and Practice,* an irregular series describing conditions in individual countries including Afghanistan, Pakistan, Sri Lanka, and India; *Labor Development Abroad,* a quarterly that contained tables and articles on South Asian countries; *Foreign Labor Digests,* a discontinued irregular, containing country briefs; and *Directory of Labor Organizations* in various countries. Publications in the BLS report series include: *The Forecasting of Manpower Requirements* (1963); *Conducting a Labor Force Survey in Developing Countries* (1964); and *How to Make an Inventory of High-Level and Skilled Manpower in Developing Countries* (1964). The bureau also issues quarterly releases on the *U.S. Department of State Indexes of Living Costs Abroad and Living Quarters Allowances.*

J23 National Aeronautics and Space Administration (NASA)

1.   a. *400 Maryland Avenue, S.W.*
Washington, D.C. 20546
755-8364

   b. Open to the public on the basis of advanced appointment

   c. Robert A. Frosch, Director

2.   In carrying out its mandate that activities in space should be devoted to peaceful purposes for the benefit of all mankind, NASA arranges for the most effective utilization of scientific and engineering resources of the U.S. with other nations engaged in aeronautical and space activities for peaceful purposes. It also provides for the widest practicable and appropriate dissemination of information concerning NASA's activities and their results. In addition to in-house research, NASA contracts with outside researchers and consultants.

   The International Affairs Division (Kenneth Pedersen, Director, 755-3868), within the Office of External Relations, coordinates all foreign activities and international exchanges involving foreign activities of the agency. Current activities in South Asia include, in addition to personnel exchanges, several communication and meteorogical satellite programs, and ground-based remote sensing programs. For further information on NASA activities in South Asia, contact Projects Officer Lyn Hanold (755-3880), who is knowledgeable about NASA's current South Asian projects. An informative booklet, *International Program,* briefly outlines NASA's international activities. A pamphlet, *India Space Activity Summary,* lists Indian cooperation with NASA.

3. NASA Headquarter's Library (Alfred C. String, Head Librarian, 755-2210) is open from 8:00 A.M. to 4:30 P.M., Monday through Friday. Subject to security regulations, the library facilities and all collections are accessible to the public for reference use. Limited interlibrary loan and photoduplication facilities are available. This reference collection is technical in nature with primary concentration on current aerospace development.

    The library's holdings also contain a comprehensive collection of NASA publications and publications of its predecessor, the National Advisory Committee on Aeronautics (NACA). Also available in microfiche are 5-year retrospective runs of *International Aerospace Abstracts* and other scientific and technical information generated by NASA. The library has access to RECON data bases, an automated system that yields citations and abstracts on NASA aerospace technology and developments. Primarily restricted to agency use, RECON could be searched geographically.

    NASA's Goddard Space Flight Center Library (Greenbelt, Maryland 20771, 301/344-6244) is open to the public on the basis of previous appointment from 8:00 A.M. to 4:30 P.M., Monday through Friday. This is also a technical collection in the fields of astronomy, space science, and physics, and contains some 58,000 books and 37,000 journals, including 700 current subscriptions.

    NASA's Audio Visual Services (Les Gaver, Head, 755-8366), open from 8:30 A.M. to 4:30 P.M., Monday through Friday, maintains a photolibrary of over 500,000 items, including a selection of LANDSAT photos organized on a geographical basis. Two brief catalogs, *NASA/1980 Photography Index* and *NASA Films* (1979), are available on request.

4. NASA publications are announced in *NASA Publications* and in its biweekly *Scientific and Technical Aerospace Reports* (STAR). All NASA publications should be ordered from the Superintendent of Documents, U.S. Printing Office, Washington, D.C. 20402. Many popular materials are available free from the Public Information Services (Room 6027, 755-8341).

Note: Also see entry G11.

___

J24 National Endowment for the Humanities (NEH)

1. a. *806 15th Street, N.W.*
       Washington, D.C. 20506
       724-0386

    b. Open to the public

    c. Joseph D. Duffey, Chairman

2. The activities of the National Endowment for the Humanities are designed to promote and support the production and dissemination of knowledge in the humanities, especially as it relates to the serious study and discussion of contemporary values and public issues. The NEH makes grants to individuals, groups, or institutions in support of research and other activities productive of humanistic knowledge of value to the scholarly and general public.

    The scope of NEH support is defined by law as including, but not being limited to: the study of languages, both modern and classical; linguistics;

literature; history; jurisprudence; philosophy; archaeology; criticism, theory, and practice of the arts; those aspects of the social sciences that have humanistic content and employ humanistic methods; and the study and application of the humanities to the environment. Those interested in applying for a grant in the humanities should contact the appropriate division.

NEH has no specific program for the support of foreign-affairs research. However, through its Division of Research Grants and its Division of Fellowships, the endowment does support research projects and individual study dealing with foreign affairs and foreign areas, other than research for study by degree candidates applicable toward their degrees.

DIVISION OF RESEARCH GRANTS
Harold Cannon, Director
724-0226

This division provides support to group projects of research in the humanities, to centers for research, to preparation of important research tools, and to the editing of significant humanistic texts. Through the division's 3 programs in the areas of General Research, Research Resources, and Research Materials, the division provided support for 400 collaborative and long-range projects in fiscal year 1979.

DIVISION OF FELLOWSHIPS
James Blessing, Director
724-0238

The Fellowship Division, through several programs, provides stipends that enable individual scholars, teachers, and members of nonacademic professions to study areas of the humanities that may be directly and fruitfully related to the work they characteristically perform. Through this division, in 1979, the endowment awarded 2,620 stipends for periods ranging from 2 months to 1 year.

3.   The National Endowment for the Humanities Library (Jeannette D. Coletti, Librarian, 724-0360) is a small reference collection of some 6,000 volumes and 500 current periodical subscriptions in the areas of history, philosophy, education, and humanities. The collection also contains all publications that have resulted from NEH grants, and NEH annual reports. The library is open to the public for reference use only from 9:00 A.M. to 5:30 P.M., Monday through Friday. Interlibrary loan and photoduplication facilities are available.

4.   In addition to the *Annual Report for the National Endowment for the Humanities,* the NEH disseminates free several brochures and pamphlets concerning its program announcements and deadlines for grant applications. Two NEH newsletters, *Humanities* and *NEH News,* are also available free.

J25 National Science Foundation (NSF)

1.   a. *1800 G Street, N.W.*
Washington, D.C. 20550
357-9498

b. Open to the public; prior appointments advisable

    c. Norman Hackerman, Chairman

2.   The NSF initiates and supports fundamental and applied research in all the scientific disciplines. This support is made through grants, contracts, and other agreements awarded to universities, nonprofit, and other organizations. Most of this research is directed to the resolution of scientific questions concerning fundamental life processes, natural laws and phenomena, fundamental processes influencing man's environment, and the impact of scientific forces on people as members of society as well as on the behavior of that society itself. Additional research is focused on selected societal problems.

    To NSF, science is an international enterprise. Research with South Asian implications, therefore, could be supported by any one of the following directorates: Directorate for Mathematical and Physical Sciences (William Klemperer, Assistant Director, 357-9742); Directorate for Astronomical, Atmospheric, Earth and Ocean Sciences (Francis S. Johnson, Assistant Director, 357-9715); Directorate for Engineering and Applied Science (Jack T. Sanderson, Assistant Director, 357-9832); Directorate for Science Education (F. James Rutherford, Assistant Director, 282-7922, 5225 Wisconsin Avenue, N.W., Washington, D.C. 20550); Directorate for Biological, Behavioral, and Social Sciences (Eloise E. Clark, Assistant Director, 357-9854); and Directorate for Scientific, Technological, and International Affairs (Harvey Averch, Assistant Director, 357-7631). The last 2 of the above directorates may be more useful to the South Asianist and are described later in the entry.

3.   The National Science Foundation Library (Herman Fleming, Chief, Reference and Record Management Section, 357-7811) is open to the public from 8:30 A.M. to 5:00 P.M., Monday through Friday. Interlibrary loan and photoduplication facilities are available. This small reference collection of approximately 16,000 volumes and 500 periodicals includes general works and recent research developments in the fields of environmental, biological and social sciences, and national and international science policy.

4.   *Publications of the National Science Foundation* (1979) lists all annual reports, publications of the National Science Board, descriptive brochures, and program announcements. Some of the useful publications include: *National Science Foundation Guide to Programs* (1980); *A Comprehensive Approach to the National Science Foundation Support for Human Origins Research* (1979); *National Science Foundation Films* (1978); *Applied Research Summary of Awards* (1979); *Federal Funds for Research and Development* (1979); *National Science Foundation Grants and Awards* (annual); and *National Science Foundation Report.* Both *Mosaic,* the official bimonthly magazine of the NSF and the *NSF Bulletin* provide news about programs, program deadlines, and meetings. Some of these publications may be obtained gratis from the NSF's Forms and Publications Section (Laura Harrington, Chief, 357-7811).

DIVISION OF INTERNATIONAL PROGRAMS (INT)
Bodo Bartocha, Director
357-9552

A division within the Directorate for Scientific, Technological, and International Affairs, INT carries out NSF's statutory responsibilities for international scientific activities. Established in the International Geophysical Year (1958), the division supports the U.S. side of about 300 cooperative science projects, annually, with some 40 countries, including India and Pakistan.

International programs, including cooperative scientific research activities, are supported through the exchange of American and foreign scientists and engineers, the execution of jointly designed research projects, participation in the activities of international science organizations, and travel to international conferences. At the core of INT's various programs is the acquisition of scientific information to enhance the value of U.S. scientific and technological enterprise as both a national and an international resource.

Currently, the NSF is involved in several activities in South Asia. As of October 1979, U.S.-owned Special Foreign Currency (SFC), through the PL 480 program, was available to support cooperative science activities in India and Pakistan. Both in India and Pakistan, INT has been actively involved using SFC to support collaborative research projects, joint seminars, and travel related to collaborative activities. An example of this use of SFC is the Geodynamics of Pakistan project, in which scientists from the University of Cincinnati (Ohio) and the Geological Survey of Pakistan are studying geodynamic evolution in Baluchistan. This subject is of great interest because of the location in Pakistan of an active plate boundary, the Chaman fault, which is similar to the San Andreas fault in California. Plate tectonics models, such as the one being developed in this project, promise an explanation of global geodynamics, including origins of earthquakes, volcanoes, mountains, and deposits of minerals and hydrocarbons. A volume of findings of the Geodynamics of Pakistan project was published in 1979.

SFC is also used to supplement dollar support of U.S. participation in major international research projects. One such project is the International Monsoon Experiment (MONEX) to determine what causes the erratic behavior of the monsoons in Asia and the resultant effects on global atmospheric circulation. SFC is also used for English translations of foreign scientific and technical literature in Russian, German, French, or Japanese, by contractors in India and Pakistan.

In addition, INT also cooperates with the Indian Council of Scientific and Industrial Research (CSIR) to sponsor a program of exchanges between senior-level scientists in the U.S. and India. Under the program, each country pays the international travel costs of its own scientists and provides travel and other expenses within its own borders for foreign participants. U.S. scientists interested in participating in the U.S.-India Exchange of Scientists Program are advised to discuss their plans with INT.

In the countries of Afghanistan, Sri Lanka, and Bangladesh, some limited INT programs are available through the Science in Developing Countries Program, which occasionally provides funding to American institutions for cooperative research on topics that will benefit the underdeveloped countries. For further information on INT South Asian activities, contact Osman Shinaishin (357-9402), Program Manager, U.S.-India, Pakistan, Burma, and Iran Programs. Also contact Eugene Pronko (357-9550), Senior Programs Manager, Science Information Activities and Joint Commissions, for information concerning the activities of the Indo-U.S. Subcommission on Science and Technology, which recommends programs for scientific and technological cooperation. The publication, *U.S.-India Exchange of Scientists* (1978), discusses NSF cooperative activities in India since its inception in 1967. An informative booklet, *Division of International Programs* (1979), provides a succinct outline of NSF's international activities. Another useful INT program announcement booklet is *Science in Developing Countries Program* (1980).

Behavioral and social scientists may note that within the Directorate for Biological, Behavioral, and Social Sciences, mentioned earlier, several research potentials are available. Programs in the Division of Behavioral and Neural Sciences (Richard T. Louttit, Director, 357-7564) include neurosciences, psychological sciences, and anthropological and linguistic sciences. The Division of Social and Economic Sciences (Bertha W. Rubinstein, Acting Director, 357-7966) supports programs in economics, geography, and political science, as well as social measurement and analysis, including history and philosophy of science, law, and social sciences.

J26 National Security Council (NSC)

1. a. *Executive Office Building*
    17th Street and Pennsylvania Avenue, N.W.
    Washington, D.C. 20506
    395-3440

    b. No public access

2. The statutory function of the NSC is to advise the president with respect to the integration of domestic, foreign, and military policies relating to national security. NSC staff members are not normally accessible to private researchers. Occasionally, academic specialists are contracted as consultants.

4. Most internal records of the National Security Council are classified and restricted to a small number of authorized government personnel. The NSC Freedom of Information Officer is Brenda Reger (395-3116). Some declassified NSC policy papers, intelligence directives and other internal records, together with an updated list of all such materials released are available at the Modern Military Branch (Military Archives Division) of the National Archives and Records Service (see entry B6).

J27 Overseas Private Investment Corporation (OPIC)

1. a. *Board of Trade Building*
    1129 20th Street, N.W.
    Washington, D.C. 20527
    632-8584

    b. Open to the public; prior appointment is recommended.

    c. J. Bruce Llewellyn, President

2.	A government corporation with majority private-sector representation on its Board of Directors, OPIC assists U.S. private investors in making profitable investments in developing countries, including the countries of South Asia. To mobilize and facilitate the participation of U.S. private capital and skill in the economic and social development of less-developed countries, the corporation provides financial assistance, investment information, and counseling to U.S. investors; insures U.S. investors against political risks of expropriation, inconvertibility of local currency holdings, and damages from war, revolution, or insurrection; and offers U.S. lenders other protection against both commercial and political risks. OPIC has assisted U.S. investors in 80 developing countries.

For information on business opportunities and the investment climate in South Asia, researchers may confer with Arvin M. Kramish (Senior Director for Asia in the Insurance Department, 632-9646) and Brooks H. Browne (Investment Officer for Asia, Finance Department, 254-3227). Related information may also be obtained from Melody Dill (Public Information Specialist, 632-1854).

3.	OPIC's small library (Elizabeth D. Goldberg, Librarian, 632-9408) of approximately 5,000 selected volumes of monographs and documents and 350 current periodicals focuses on international economics, business and finance, and other related subjects. The library maintains country files of miscellaneous data on some 90 developing nations, including all South Asian countries. The collection also contains records and documents of OPIC activities in overseas investment disputes and settlements; World Bank country reports and project assessments; publications of U.S. government agencies, including the departments of state, commerce, agriculture and treasury; and reports from private U.S. corporations having interests in South Asia. The library is open to the public by appointment. A card catalog facilitates access to the collection.

4.	OPIC publications include its *Annual Report*; *A Guide for Executives of Smaller Companies*; *Investment Financing Handbook*; *Investment Insurance Handbook*; and *Topics*, a bimonthly newsletter. All publications are available free. For access to OPIC's confidential internal records, researchers should address inquiries to the corporation's Freedom of Information Officer (Robert Jordan, 632-1854).

J28 Peace Corps (ACTION)

1.	a. *806 Connecticut Avenue, N.W.*
	Washington, D.C. 20526
	254-7526

	b. Open to the public; previous appointment is recommended.

	c. Richard Celeste, Director

2.	The Peace Corps Program, which administers ACTION's overseas program, is designed to promote world peace and friendship by helping the peoples of other countries meet their needs for trained manpower. The Peace Corp's South Asian activities are directed by the North Africa, Near East, Asia, and Pacific Regional Office (Perdita Huston, Director, 254-

9862). The once flourishing Peace Corps program in South Asia is now limited to Nepal (Melanie Williams, Desk Officer, 254-9832). An agreement was signed with Bangladesh in 1978 for introducing the program there, but it has not yet been implemented. Country desk officers, who act as the liaisons between Washington and the field volunteers, are accessible to researchers and can provide information on past and present Peace Corps activities in the countries of their charge. In addition, the Evaluation Co-ordinator (Rick Williams, 254-7983) of the Planning and Evaluation Division (254-7990) can provide information on specific country programs. The division occasionally engages language and area specialists as consult-ants. The division also publishes the annual *Volunteer Activity Survey*, several secondary activity reports, and *Peace Corps Overview to the Activity Surveys*. Researchers may also contact the Program and Training Office (David Levine, 254-8890) for information concerning orientation and train-ing programs.

3.   The ACTION library is discussed in entry A1.

4.   Peace Corps publications include several reports, newsletters, and direc-tories, such as *Annual Reports: Bi-Annual Statistical Summary*, giving de-tails of the volunteers and trainees of the corps; *Peace Corps Volunteer*; and *Peace Corps Program and Training Journal*, a monthly the purpose of which is to support the "Peace Corps goal of encouraging program feedback and cross fertilization by providing a forum for exchange of significant ideas, experiences, problems, successes and experimental efforts in programming and training volunteers." *Guidelines for Peace Corps Cross-Cultural Train-ing* (4 vols., 1970) is a training manual prepared for the Peace Corps Office of Training Support by the Center for Research and Evaluation (Estes Park, Colorado 80517). There is no comprehensive bibliography of all Peace Corps publications. For information concerning retired and inactive files, contact Peace Corps Freedom of Information Officer (John Nolan, 254-8105).

Note: Also see entry A1.

J29 Senate Historical Office

1.   a. *The Capitol, Room S-413*
      Washington, D.C. 20510
      224-6900

      b. Open to the public on the basis of prior appointment

      c. Richard A. Baker, Senate Historian

2–4.   A clearinghouse for Senate-related research activities, this office provides bibliographic and research assistance to scholars in locating and gaining access to the documents and records of the Senate. Recently, the staff has compiled for publication a catalog of collections of senators' papers. Also under preparation is a checklist of unpublished hearings. Both of these compilations contain materials of interest to South Asian studies. South Asia-related materials may be also found in *The Executive Sessions of the Senate Foreign Relations Committee*, a historical series edited by the Senate

Historical Office. Volume 10, covering the activities in 1958, is being processed for publication. A newsletter, *Senate History*, contains many useful research notes.

The Senate Historical Office maintains an extensive photo archive of some 20,000 items providing photographic documentation of the activities of the Senate. An oral history project is also underway for recording the recollections of retired Senate staff members.

J30 Smithsonian Institution (SI)

1. a. *1000 Jefferson Drive, S.W.*
   Washington, D.C. 20560
   357-2411

   b. Open to the public

   c. S. Dillon Ripley, The Secretary

2. An independent, federal-trust establishment, the Smithsonian Institution, the world's largest museum complex, performs fundamental research, publishes the results of studies, explorations, and investigations, preserves for study, exhibition, and reference over 70,000,000 items of scientific, cultural, and historical interest—including technology, aeronautics, space exploration, and natural history—participates in the international exchange of learned publications, and engages in programs of education and cooperative research and training nationally and internationally.

3. Smithsonian Institution libraries are described later in the entry.

4. The Smithsonian Institution Press (Felix C. Lowe, Director, 357-1912) publishes books and studies related to science, technology, history, and the arts. A book catalog and a list of studies are available from the Publication Distribution Section (Frederick H. MacVicar, Chief, 357-1793). The press also publishes *Smithsonian Year*, the institution's annual report that includes a complete listing of current titles. *Smithsonian Research Reports*, leaflets concerning various bureaus, and a brief guide to the *Smithsonian Institution* are available from the Office of Public Affairs (Alvin Rosenfeld, Director, 357-2627). The *Smithsonian Magazine* is a monthly journal of general interest published by the institution. The journal occasionally publishes articles on South Asian subjects; e.g., "Tiger Ecology Project: Royal Chitawan National Park" (Nepal), by Peter F. R. Jackson, July 1980. Other publications are discussed under the appropriate units.

OFFICE OF INTERNATIONAL ACTIVITIES
Kennedy B. Schmertz, Director
357-2519

This office supports Smithsonian programs by advising on foreign affairs affecting Smithsonian museological, cultural, and research programs. It assists in communications with foreign governments and institutions and reviews opportunities for cooperation in international projects important to the Smithsonian professional staff. This office also maintains liaison with the Department of State, the International Communication Agency, embassies in Washington, international organizations, and Smithsonian-related missions abroad, as well as with private institutions concerned with cooperative international programs. Currently the office coordinates and fosters several research- and cultural-exchange programs in India, Pakistan, and Nepal.

OFFICE OF FELLOWSHIPS AND GRANTS
Gretchen Gayle Ellsworth, Director
287-3271

In its role as a leader in the international scholarly community, the SI maintains close scholarly ties with academic and research institutions throughout the world. This office has the central management and administrative responsibility for the Smithsonian's programs of research grants, fellowships, and other visiting academic appointments. While the Fellowship Program and other academic offerings for research visitors are designed to bring scholars to the Smithsonian for the benefit of specialized work with staff researchers, the Smithsonian Special Foreign Currency Program (SFCP) awards research grants to American institutions of higher learning for studies in countries where the U.S. holds excess foreign currencies derived largely from the sale of agricultural commodities under Public Law 480. The authority that the Smithsonian has received from the Congress for the use of excess foreign currencies allows grants to be awarded in the disciplines of archaeology, physical and cultural anthropology, ethnology, and linguistics; systematic and environmental biology; astrophysics and earth sciences; and museum programs.

Currently, grants for new projects under SFCP are available in India and Pakistan. Research projects are moving towards conclusion under program support in Sri Lanka, a former excess currency country. For further information on SFCP, contact the Foreign Currency Program Office (Francine C. Berkowitz, Program Specialist, 287-3271) in the Office of Fellowships and Grants. An informative booklet, *Smithsonian Opportunities for Research and Study in History, Art and Science* (1979), and the SFCP *Program Announcement* (1979) are available free from the Office of Fellowships and Grants.

Following is a selected list of Smithsonian Special Foreign Currency Program awards related to South Asia, made from October 1, 1978, to September 30, 1979.

American Institute of Indian Studies (AIIS) (University of Chicago): continued support for administration; research fellowships; Center for Art and Archaeology; photo history of India from nineteenth- and twentieth-century photographs; production of AIIS volume on anthropology; and translation program and participation in the International Congress of Anthropological and Ethnological Sciences.

Columbia University (New York): Sayed Shah, Islam in a Punjabi village in Pakistan; the sacred year, a village temple in South India and its functions as a focus of art and ritual performance in traditional society.

Indiana University (Bloomington): preparation for publication of *Folktales of India.*

Indo-U.S. Subcommission on Education and Culture (Asia Society, New York): Indo-American fellowship program.

Lawrence University (Appleton, Wisconsin): Marathi folk songs in Maharashtra and northern Mysore (India).

National Anthropological Film Center (SI): filmic inquiry into the process of ecological adaptation and social integration in India of the Pashtoon nomads of Afghanistan.

National Museum of Natural History (SI): a metallurgical site survey of the western Chagai district in Pakistan.

Southern Methodist University (Dallas, Texas): publication of *The Afian; A Study of Stylistic Variation in a Nilotic Industry* (India).

University of California (Berkeley): conducting, recording, and filming the last performance of an Agnicayana ritual in India.

University of Connecticut (Storrs): comparative field study of socialization in three communities in India.

University of Hawaii (Manoa): U.S. participation in the Indo-Pacific Prehistory Association meeting (India).

University of Pennsylvania (Philadelphia): publication of the proceedings of a symposium on desertification (India).

University of Wisconsin (Madison): changing patterns of production in an Indian village, with a view to introducing use and local construction of solar-energy devices.

Thirteen additional study awards were given in the fields of systematic and environmental biology and paleobiology in Sri Lanka, Pakistan, and India, and 4 other awards for studies in astrophysics and earth sciences to be conducted in India.

SMITHSONIAN SCIENCE INFORMATION EXCHANGE (SSIE)
1730 M Street, N.W.
Washington, D.C. 20036
David F. Hersey, President
673-4600

SSIE serves the research community as a primary source for information on research in progress. The exchange collects, indexes, stores, and disseminates data about basic and applied work in all areas of the life, physical, and social sciences. Its active file, which covers materials collected during the past 2 fiscal years, contains information on more than 200,000 current and recently completed research projects, including 20,000 projects in all areas of research in the social-sciences. A computer search reveals the following numbers of on-going research in all fields in South Asia: India 470, Pakistan 22, Afghanistan 6, Sri Lanka 4, Bangladesh 1, and Nepal 1.

SSIE works closely with more than 11,300 supporting organizations to assure the timely registration of project descriptions of high scientific quality. Project information, normally registered at the time work is funded, is supplied to the exchange by federal agencies as well as nonprofit associations and foundations, individual research investigators, universities and colleges, and foreign organizations. Projects registered with the exchange are indexed using a comprehensive and flexible classification system, as well as a conceptual indexing process, in order to provide the capability to retrieve projects in subject categories as broad or specific as required. Researchers may request a custom search for a fee. Research information packages on subjects of high current interest are also available at cost. For further information on the SSIE search services, consult *Research Information Services for the Social Sciences* and the *SSIE Newsletter*.

The SSIE in cooperation with UNESCO has recently published the first world-wide inventory of *Information Services on Research* (1979). A study is currently being conducted on the feasibility of integrating the SSIE program with the National Technical Information Services (NTIS) of the Department of Commerce.

INTERNATIONAL EXCHANGE SERVICE (IES)
John Estes, Director
357-2073

The IES provides the means whereby learned societies in the U.S. as well as the Smithsonian Institution are able to exchange their scholarly publications for those of foreign institutions.

OFFICE OF MEMBERSHIP AND DEVELOPMENT
James M. Symington, Director
357-2359

Under the auspices of this office, the SI offers a Resident Associate Program (Janet W. Solinger, Director, 357-2696) and a National Associate Program (Robert H. Angle, Director, 357-1350). Participants in these programs are entitled to numerous benefits including exhibition previews, films, behind-the-scenes museum tours, lectures, symposia, seminars, domestic and international study tours, and free subscription services for the monthly *Smithsonian Magazine* and the monthly *Smithsonian Associate*. Barbara Schneider (357-2477) is the Foreign Study Tour Coordinator of the National Associate Program.

SMITHSONIAN INSTITUTION LIBRARIES
Natural History Building
10th Street and Constitution Avenue, N.W.
Washington, D.C. 20560
Robert M. Maloy, Director
357-2240

The collection contains more than 950,000 volumes and covers all subjects pertinent to the work of the institution. The collection is divided among the general reference and circulation service (also known as the Main Library, 357-2139), located in the Natural History Building, and the 13 bureau libraries located in each of the major museums and research bureaus. All the libraries are open to the public from 8:45 A.M. to 5:15 P.M., Monday through Friday. Photoduplication facilities are available.

South Asia-related materials in the collection consist of some 1,400 volumes with a primary focus on art, antiquities, anthropology, ethnology, numismatics, demography, and physical and natural sciences. The collection also contains an extensive collection of periodical and serial literature generated by learned and scientific societies, including the *Proceedings of the Indian Academy of Sciences* (1934–1978), *Ancient India* (1946—), *National Museum of India Bulletin* (1966—), *New Indian Antiquary* (1938—), and several publications of the Indian Museum in Calcutta. A complete set of the now rare 1903 imprint of the *Linguistic Survey of India* is also available in the library.

A dictionary card catalog in the Main Library, which combines the Dewey Decimal and the Library of Congress classification schedules, provides access to the majority of the accessioned materials in the collections. Bureau and branch libraries maintain their own card catalogs.

Note: Also see entries B2, B7, C1, C2, C3, C4, C5, C6, C7, C8, C10, F10, and F11.

J31 State Department

1. a. *2201 C Street, N.W.*
       Washington, D.C. 20520
       632-6575

    b. Access to the Department of State building is restricted. It is recommended that appointments with departmental officials be arranged in advance.

2. The oldest executive department, the Department of State advises the president in the formulation and execution of foreign policy. In promoting long-range security and well-being of the United States, the department determines and analyzes the facts relating to American overseas interests, makes recommendations on policy and future action, and takes the necessary steps in carrying out established policy. Described later in the entry are the various geographic and functional bureaus that monitor, research, and prepare policy papers on South Asian affairs. Within the limits imposed by security restrictions and time constraints, the departmental personnel are willing to assist researchers. Most South Asia-related research is carried on in-house, but occasionally both the Bureau of Near Eastern and South Asia Affairs and the Bureau of Intelligence and Research engage South Asianists as consultants.

3. For a description of the department's library and reference facility, see entry A32.

4. General foreign-policy publications issued by the department include: the *Department of State Bulletin* (for sale), a weekly serving as an official U.S. foreign policy record, with policy statements, texts of treaties, special articles, and selected press releases; *Background Notes*, continuously updated, short country summaries which describe the people, history, government, economy, and foreign relations of each country; *Department of State Newsletter* (for sale), monthly containing various articles, biographic descriptions, news, notes, and other information primarily for foreign-service personnel serving abroad; *Special Reports, Selected Documents* and *Current Policy*, pamphlets issued at irregular frequencies, containing verbatim and excerpted statements by senior departmental officials; *Gist*, a series of brief reference aids on current international issues; and *Digest of International Law*, which covers all sources of international law including materials from treaties, executive agreements, legislation, testimony and statements before congressional and international bodies, and diplomatic notes.

    In addition, the department publishes a number of useful directories and pamphlets, such as; *Diplomatic List*, a quarterly list of foreign diplomats in Washington; *Employees of Diplomatic Mission*, a quarterly companion to the *Diplomatic List,* which gives names and addresses for mission employees; *Foreign Consular Offices in the United States,* an annual listing of offices, their jurisdiction, and personnel; the recently classified Biographic Register of U.S. foreign-service officials; *Key Officers of Foreign Service Posts: Guide for Businessmen,* a quarterly directory prepared to aid Americans with business interests abroad; *Memorandum to: U.S. Business Community, From: Department of State, Subject: Assistance in International Trade* (1975), another directory to assist U.S. businessmen; periodically revised *Lists of Visits of Presidents of the United States to Foreign Countries* and *Lists of Visits of Foreign Chiefs of State and Heads of Government;* and *United States Chiefs of Mission 1778–1973.*

Other publications are issued in several named series such as: *General Foreign Policy Series; Commercial Policy Series; International Information and Cultural Series; International Organization Series;* and *Treaties and Other International Act Series.* The department also prepares the *Report Required by Section 657 Foreign Assistance Act,* which is submitted to the U.S. Congress and contains a myriad of information on U.S. foreign assistance and other transactions; and the annual *Country Reports on Human Rights,* which is also submitted to the U.S. Congress for its consideration of legislation on human rights and U.S. foreign policy. Another major publication is the set of substantial volumes entitled *Foreign Relations of the United States. Foreign Policy and the State Department* is a useful, but outdated, pamphlet on the organization of the department and its overseas posts.

Publications of the American embassies include an irregular *Commercial Newsletter,* designed to help both American and Pakistani exporters, published by the American consulate general in Karachi; and a periodic pamphlet, *Brief of Indian Agriculture,* issued by the agricultural attaché in New Delhi.

For bibliographic access to the department's publications, scholars may consult: *Major Publications of the Department of State: An Annotated Bibliography* (rev. ed., 1977); issues of *Publications of the Department of State,* 1929–1952, 1953–1957, and 1958–1960; *Selected Publications and Audio-Visual Materials of the Department of State;* and a *Pocket Guide to Foreign Policy Information Materials and Services of the Department of State.* Other useful reference guides to the department's publications are Frederic O'Hara's *Government Publications Review* (3) (1976):143–149, and *U.S. Federal Official Publications* (1978), by J. A. Downey. All publications of the department are also listed in the *Monthly Catalog.*

For information on specific publications, scholars may contact the Office of Public Communications (Room 5821) of the Bureau of Public Affairs (632-2159). Scholars interested in being included in the department's mailing list may contact Dorothy S. Gregory (632-9859) of the Publication Distribution unit of the Office of Plans and Opinion Analysis (Bureau of Public Affairs). Other relevant publications of the department will be discussed under the name of the bureau generating them.

The Department of State's internal classified records—dispatches, telegrams, and other communications between Washington and the department's diplomatic posts abroad, inter-and intraoffice memoranda, research studies and policy papers—are filed with the Foreign Affairs Information and Management Center (632-0394) of the Bureau of Administration. When these documents are retired from the department's active files, they are transferred to the Diplomatic Branch (Civil Archives Division) of the National Archives and Records Service (see entry B6). Computerized indexes are maintained for all documents processed by the center since 1973.

Classified documents are usually declassified 25 to 30 years after their origin and often coincide with the latest year for which the department's documentary volume, *Foreign Relations of the United States*, has been published. Currently, most documents through 1949 in the National Archives are open to the public. Requests for reviews of the classified records, as provided by the Freedom of Information Act (FOIA) and the Privacy Act, may be directed to Sharon B. Kotok, Chief of the Information Access Branch (632-1267) of the Bureau of Administration. FOIA requests should provide as much identifying information as possible about the document to assist the department in locating it; include subject matter, time frame, originator of the information, or any other helpful data.

Only U.S. citizens or aliens, who are lawfully admitted to the U.S. for permanent residence, can request information under the Privacy Act. Under this act, individuals may request access to records that are maintained under the individual's name or some other personally identifiable symbol. Description of record systems, from which documents can be retrieved by the individual's name, are published in the *Federal Register*.

BUREAU OF NEAR EASTERN AND SOUTH ASIAN AFFAIRS (NEA)
Harold H. Saunders, Assistant Secretary
632-9588
Jane A. Coon, Deputy Assistant Secretary
632-1030
Howard B. Schaffer, Director, Bhutan, India, Maldives, Nepal, Sri Lanka (NEA/INS)
632-2141
Robert A. Peck, Director Pakistan, Afghanistan, Bangladesh (NEA/PAB)
632-0353
  Ronald D. Lorton, Desk Officer, Afghanistan
  632-9552
  Lawrence N. Benedict, Desk Officer, Bangladesh
  632-0466
  Donald Paalberg Jr., Desk Officer, Bhutan and Nepal
  632-0653
  John R. Malott, Desk Officer, India
  632-1289
  Lee O. Coldren, Desk Officer, Maldives and Sri Lanka
  632-2351
  Teresita Schaffer, Desk Officer, Pakistan
  632-9823
Henry A. Engelbrecht Jr., Coordinator and Senior Economic Advisor (NEA/ECON)
632-6986
George B. Lambrakis, Director, Regional Affairs (NEA/RA)
632-1154
  James F. Collins, Regional Policy Advisor (NEA/RA)
  632-0574

Woolf P. Gross, Politico-Military Advisor (NEA/RA)
632-3014
George E. Lichtblau, Regional Labor Attaché and Regional Labor Advisor
(NEA/RA)
632-1278
George F. Sherman, Jr., Public Affairs Advisor
632-5150

One of the five geographic bureaus, the Bureau of Near Eastern and South Asian Affairs is responsible for U.S. foreign affairs activities in South Asia. The assistant secretary of the NEA is responsible for advising the Secretary of State in the formulation of U.S. policies toward the South Asian countries and for guiding the operation of the U.S. diplomatic establishments in those countries. The bureau's assistant secretary also directs, coordinates, and supervises interdepartmental and interagency matters involving South Asia. In these duties, the assistant secretary is assisted by directors within the bureau who are responsible for over-all guidance and interdepartmental coordination with respect to their assigned countries. These directors are the single focal point in Washington for serving the needs of U.S. diplomatic missions in South Asia. They also insure that all elements of a mission in a given country jointly pursue U.S. foreign policy directives.

At the base of the bureau's pyramidal structure are the country desk officers, at least one of whom is assigned to every country in South Asia. As a junior officer, the desk officer is responsible for following the affairs of the country under his observation and suggesting the U.S.'s course of action in respect to that country. Country desk officers serve as initial contacts in the department for South Asian scholars and are willing to confer with researchers about developments in the countries under their jurisdiction. They can also assist scholars by making unclassified documents available to them.

Other important offices of the bureau include the Economic Affairs Office (NEA/ECON), which handles general economic relations and activities, including aid, trade, and commodities and commercial affairs in the region; the Regional Affairs Office (NEA/RA), which handles politico-military activities, U.N., refugees, labor, and other related affairs pertaining to South Asia; and the Public Affairs Office, which assists with public inquiries, prepares congressional testimony, and works with the press and other media representatives. The Public Affairs Office can assist researchers who wish to identify and contact departmental specialists. The department's *Background Notes* for the countries of South Asia, as well as transcripts of public statements and congressional testimony, are prepared by this bureau.

BUREAU OF CONGRESSIONAL RELATIONS (H)
J. Brian Atwood, Assistant Secretary
632-8774

This bureau works to insure effective and continuing communication between, on the one hand, the members and committees of the Congress and the staff and, on the other hand, all the various bureaus and offices of the department. It actively seeks the views of Congress on major foreign-policy issues, represents the department in explaining U.S. foreign policy initiatives, and arranges numerous formal and informal meetings, briefings, and appearances before committees. This office also plays an important role in drafting and monitoring legislation affecting foreign policy and the Department of State. Legislative Management Officer, Peter Burleigh (632-8728), serves as the coordinator for South Asian affairs (NEA). There are also separate Legislative Management Officers for Human Rights (David Kenney, 632-8802) and Refugees (Eugene Krizek, 632-8696).

BUREAU OF POLITICO-MILITARY AFFAIRS (PM)
Reginald Bartholomew, Director
632-9022

The Bureau of Politico-Military Affairs originates and developes policy guidance and provides general direction within the department on issues that affect U.S. security policies, military assistance, nuclear policy, and arms control and disarmament matters. In addition, the bureau maintains liaison with the Department of Defense and other federal agencies on a wide range of political and military affairs. Most of the records and documents produced by the bureau are classified. Various administrative units of the bureau include: Office of International Security Policy (William Rope, Director, 632-2056) analyzes broad regional problems such as arms buildups, border tensions, and revolutionary activities from a long-range strategic perspective; Office of International Security Operations (George T. Churchill, Director, 632-1616) is concerned with visits of South Asian military officers to the U.S. and monitors all U.S. military aircraft and ship movements in the region; Office of Munitions Control (William B. Robinson, Director, 235-9755) licenses private U.S. arms exporters; Office of Security Assistance and Sales (James P. Farber, 632-3882) monitors U.S. and other international arms transfers to South Asia. Other important units are: Office of Nuclear Policy and Operations (Marvin W. Humphreys, Director, 632-1835); Office of Disarmament and Arms Control (Mark Palmer, Director, 632-1862); and Office of Security Assistance—Special Projects (Robert B. Mantel, Director 632-5104).

BUREAU OF HUMAN RIGHTS AND HUMANITARIAN AFFAIRS (HA)
Mary F. Hanley, Public Affairs Advisor
632-0855
Jessie Clear, Regional Affairs Officer for South Asia (HA/NEA)
363-2264
Lawrence L. Arthur, Asylum Officer
632-2551
Frank A. Sieverts, Country Reports Director
632-9454

This small bureau monitors conditions of human-rights in South Asian countries, as reported by U.S. embassies and other sources, and makes policy recommendations on U.S. economic- and military-assistance programs to South Asia. It also coordinates the compilation of the department's unclassified annual *Country Reports on Human Rights Practices*, concerning every country in South Asia that receives U.S. military or economic aid.

BUREAU OF INTELLIGENCE AND RESEARCH (INR)
Ronald Spiers, Director
632-0342

The Bureau of Intelligence and Research coordinates programs of intelligence, research, and analysis for the department and other federal agencies and produces intelligence studies and current intelligence analyses essential to foreign policy determination and execution. The work and publications of the INR are discussed in the State Department's *Research in Action* (1968) and *Intelligence and Research in the Department of State* (1973). Publications of the Bureau, most of which are classified, include: *External Research Studies Intelligence Brief; Intelligence Notes; Research Studies; INR Daily Summary; Communist States and Developing Countries: Aid and Trade;* and *World Strength of the Communist Party Organizations.*

OFFICE OF EXTERNAL RESEARCH
E. Raymond Platig, Director
632-1342
Daniel Fendrick, Chairman, Third World Research Group
632-2758
Edward.G. Griffin, Senior Program Officer for Middle East and South Asia
632-3968

The office maintains liaison with cultural and educational institutions and with other federal agencies on a wide range of matters relating to government contractual and private, foreign-affairs research. From time to time, the office invites South Asian experts as consultants or speakers for official conferences, colloquia, roundtable discussions, and ambassadorial briefings. This office also acts as the coordinator and information clearinghouse for all interagency government-supported research on foreign affairs. The staff does not engage in research, but can provide researchers with copies of unclassified departmental in-house and contract research studies and bibliographies.

The office publishes a quarterly and annual inventory of *Government-Supported Research on Foreign Affairs: Current Project Information*, which lists research contracts and grants supported by the various departments and agencies of the executive branch that involve the application or advancement of the social-behavioral sciences and humanities as these bear substantively on foreign areas and international relations and *A Directory of Government Resources*, which describes activities within the federal government that are related to foreign affairs research.

The Foreign Affairs Research Documentation Center, administered by the Office of External Research, has been abolished as of September 30, 1979. The center's collection of some 15,000 government-supported and privately funded research papers on foreign affairs have now been transferred to the Defense Technical Information Center (274-6871) and the National Technical Information Center (703/557-4788). For bibliographic access to the collection, the Documentation Center published 2 inventories: *Foreign Affairs Research Papers Available*, and *Special Papers Available*, with a separate volume devoted to Near East and South Asia. Copies of these inventories are available on request from B. W. Morlet (235-8079).

OFFICE OF RESEARCH AND ANALYSIS FOR NEAR EAST AND SOUTH ASIA
(INR/DDR/RNA)
Myles L. Greene, Chief, South Asia Division
632-2757

This office is the principal research arm of the department for South Asian affairs. It produces numerous, mostly classified, research papers, reports, studies, and memoranda covering short- and medium-term policy issues for the Bureau of Near Eastern and South Asian Affairs.

OFFICE OF ECONOMIC RESEARCH AND ANALYSIS (INR/DDR/REC)
David H. Cohn, Director
632-2186

This office studies global economic issues including U.S.-South Asian economic relations. The Commodity and Developing Country Division (George W. Ogg, Chief, 632-0453) analyzes the North South dialogue, trade, and commodities. The Trade Investment and Payments Division (Russell D. Prickett, Chief, 632-0090) is concerned with studies on South Asian balance of payments, foreign exchange, debt problems, and investment disputes involving private U.S. companies in South Asia. Economic research on specific geographic regions, including South Asia, is conducted by the Regional Economic Division (Dennis P. Murphy, Chief, 632-9348). Researchers may obtain copies of the CIA's unclassified annual publication, *Communist Aid to the Less Developed Countries of the Free World* through the Communist Economic Relations Division (John Danylyk, Chief, 632-9128). A classified irregular series of *Intelligence Reports* for interagency use is also assembled by this office.

OFFICE OF THE GEOGRAPHER (INR/DDR/RGE)
Lewis M. Alexander, Director
632-1428

This office monitors international affairs involving boundaries, the law of the sea, and related topics. The office publishes the following series, most of which are intended for government use: *Geographic Bulletin*, an irregular reference booklet on world or specific areas; *Geographic Note*, another irregular bulletin describing significant changes of sovereignty; *Geographical Reports* gives details on geo-administrative divisions; and *International Boundary Studies* provides intermittent discussions of border areas.

OFFICE OF POLITICAL-MILITARY ANALYSIS (INR/DDR/PMT)
Robert A. Martin, Director
632-2043

This office conducts studies, some pertaining to South Asia, on international arms sales, national military production and military capabilities, international security issues, nuclear capabilities, and potential global confrontations. The activities of the former Office of Strategic Affairs have been incorporated into this office.

BUREAU OF INTERNATIONAL ORGANIZATION AFFAIRS (IO)
Charles William Maynes, Assistant Secretary
632-9600

This bureau coordinates and develops policy guidance and support for United States participation in the activities of the U.N., the U.N. specialized agencies, and other international organizations. The bureau's staff in the various functional offices monitors the activities of the South Asian representatives to the U.N. and its specialized agencies and the repercussions of the South Asian representatives on the U.S. policy positions. Various functional offices of the bureau include: U.N. Political Affairs (Peter Bridges, Director, 632-2392); Multilateral Affairs (Philip Kaplan, Director, 632-8603); Human Rights Affairs (Warren Hewitt, Director, 632-0572); Health and Narcotic Programs (Neil Boyer, Agency Director, 632-0590); UNESCO Affairs (David Rowe, Agency Director, 632-3619); International Women's Program (Barbara Good, Agency Director, 632-6906); International Economic Policy (William Edgar, Director, 632-2506); Science and Technology (John Trevithick, Agency Director, 632-3511); Agriculture (Roger Brewin, Agency Director, 632-2525); and Office of International Conferences (Paul J. Byrnes, Director, 632-0384).

A useful publication is the *U.S. Participation in the U. N.: Report by the President to the Congress*, which is transmitted annually under provision of the United States Participation Act of 1945. Researchers may examine the bureau's collection of U.N. documents through its U.N. Documents and Reference Staff (Mary Rita Jones, Chief, 632-7992).

BUREAU OF OCEANS AND INTERNATIONAL ENVIRONMENTAL AND SCIENTIFIC AFFAIRS (OES)
Thomas R. Pickering, Assistant Secretary
632-1554

This functional bureau is responsible for the formulation and implementation of policies and proposals for the scientific and technological aspects of U.S. relations with other countries and international organizations. It also has the management responsibility for a broad range of foreign-policy issues and significant global problems related to oceans, fisheries, environment, population, nuclear technology, new energy technology, space, and other fields of advanced technology, and for cooperative efforts dealing with the application and transfer of technology.

In addition, the bureau directs the science and technology and fisheries attaché programs. Currently, there is a science attaché in the U.S. embassy in New Delhi. The bureau's activities related to South Asia include most areas of its responsibility. The units involved with South Asian affairs are listed below: Population Affairs (Richard Benedick, Coordinator, 632-3472) monitors demographic trends and population control programs in South Asia; Environment, Health and Natural Resources (William A. Hayne, Deputy Assistant Secretary, 632-7964) deals with a broad range of global environmental isues, such as natural resources depletion, land and sea pollution, endangered species, and weather modification; Nuclear Energy and Energy Technology Affairs (Louis V. Nosenzo, Deputy Assistant Secretary, 632-4360) is concerned with nuclear nonproliferation and safeguards, export and import control, and technology cooperation; Oceans and Fisheries Affairs (John D. Negroponte, Deputy Assistant Secretary, 632-2396) is concerned with maritime boundaries, marine pollution and resources, law-of-the-sea issues, and represents the U.S. in the International Fisheries Commission; Science and Technology (Norman Terrell, Deputy Assistant Secretary, 632-3004) deals with transfer of technology and science attaché programs.

BUREAU OF ECONOMIC AND BUSINESS AFFAIRS (EB)
Julius L. Katz, Assistant Secretary
632-0396
Alvin P. Adam, Special Assistant for Public Affairs
632-9310

This bureau has over-all responsibility for formulating and implementing policy regarding foreign economic matters, trade promotion, business services of an international nature, and coordinating regional economic policy with the other concerned bureaus. The bureau is organized on a functional basis, and many of its offices are concerned with various economic issues of the region of South Asia. Following is an organizational breakdown of the bureau, with a brief description of the component units.

INTERNATIONAL FINANCE AND DEVELOPMENT
Charles F. Meissner, Deputy Assistant Secretary
632-9496

Office of Business Practices
Harvey J. Winter, Director
632-0786

The Office of Business Practices deals with the legal aspects of technology transfer, copyright laws, and antitrust matters.

Office of Development Finance
David J. Dunford, Director
632-9426

This office represents the department in interagency discussions on U.S. loan policies and contributions to international financial institutions, and acts as the department's liaison with the World Bank and other international lending institutions.

Office of Monetary Affairs
Michael E.C. Ely, Director
632-1114

In addition to monitoring international monetary affairs, the Monitary Affairs office has primary responsibility for the department's relations with the International Monetary Fund (IMF) and the U.S. Treasury Department.

Office of Investment Affairs
Elinor Constable, Director
632-1128

Responsibilities of this office include investment policy, investment disputes, expropriation cases, and problems involving multinational corporations.

INTERNATIONAL TRADE POLICY
Ernest Johnston, Deputy Assistant Secretary
632-2532

Office of International Trade
Harry Kopp, Director
632-2534

This office drafts commercial treaties and trade agreements for conducting bilateral and multilateral international trade negotiations, and reviews South Asian participation in various international economic forums.

INTERNATIONAL RESOURCES AND FOOD POLICY
Michael Calingaert, Deputy Assistant Secretary
632-1625

Office of Fuels and Energy
Gerald A. Rosen, Director
632-1420

The Office of Fuels and Energy formulates the department's energy policy and represents the U.S. in international conferences.

Office of International Commodities
John P. Ferriter, Director
632-7952

This office is involved in the negotiation of international commodities agreements.

Office of Food Policy and Programs
Donald F. Hart, Director
632-3090

The responsibility of this office includes coordination of U.S. food-aid programs with the U.S. Department of Agriculture.

COMMERCIAL AND TELECOMMUNICATION AFFAIRS
Ruth H. Phillips, Deputy Assistant Secretary
632-1498

Office of International Communications Policy
Arthur L. Freeman, Director
632-3405

Primary responsibilities of this unit are in the areas of radio, telephone, telegraph, undersea cable and satellite communications, and related international agreements and regulations.

Office of Commercial Affairs
Albert L. Zucca, Director
632-8097

In cooperation with the Commerce Department, the Commercial Affairs unit works in U.S. trade promotional activities.

TRANSPORTATION AFFAIRS
James R. Atwood, Deputy Assistant Secretary
632-4045

Office of Maritime Affairs
John T. Stewart, Director
632-0704

Primarily involved in questions relating to maritime trade and commerce, this office monitors international shipping regulations and cargo-preference laws and endeavors to discourage discrimination against U.S. commercial shipping.

Office of Aviation
James Ferrer, Director
632-0316

U.S. bilateral commercial aviation negotiations are conducted through this office.

BUREAU OF PUBLIC AFFAIRS (PA)
William J. Dyess, Assistant Secretary-Spokesman
632-6575

Concerned with effective exchange of information and views on U.S. foreign relations between the department and the public, the bureau advises other elements of the department on public opinion and arranges continuing public contact between departmental officials, private citizens, and groups through conferences, briefings, speeches, media engagements, publications, films, and other means.

OFFICE OF PLANS AND OPINION ANALYSIS
Bernard Roshco, Director
632-0474

This office coordinates public-affairs guidance on foreign policy within the department and with other agencies, reviews and guides public statements, prepares analysis of public opinion, and develops plans for public information.

OFFICE OF PRESS RELATIONS
Tom Reston, Deputy Spokesman
632-2492

The Press Relations Office provides information services concerning foreign policy and the operation of the department to the press and others who are interested.

OFFICE OF THE HISTORIAN
John P. Glennon, Associate Historian for Asia
632-9477
M. Paul Claussen, African and Southwest Asian Group Chief
632-8517

The primary responsibility of this office is to prepare the official record of U.S. diplomacy, a series of volumes entitled *Foreign Relations of the United States* (1861—). In addition, the publications of this office include: *American Foreign Policy—1950–1955; Basic Documents* (2 vols.); and *American Foreign Policy: Current Documents* (12 annual vols., 1956–1967). The office also publishes a useful reference guide, *Major Publications of the Department of State: An Annotated Bibliography*, as well as occasional historical studies on selected topics of U.S. diplomatic history. Information concerning retrospective and current record-filing systems of the department, and the retrieving of diplomatic records and documents may be obtained from the staff, who are available for consultation and research guidance. The staff maintains close contact with the department's Information Management Center (632-0394), the Diplomatic Branch of the National Archives, and the presidential libraries throughout the country.

OFFICE OF PUBLIC COMMUNICATION
Paul E. Auerswald, Director
632-3656

This office is the principal public-information outlet of the department. It publishes and disseminates *Current Policy, Background Notes,* and other documents on foreign policy issues, responds to public inquiries on current and crucial international events, and directs individuals to appropriate bureaus and offices for further assistance.

OFFICE OF PUBLIC PROGRAMS
David J. Fisher, Director
632-1433

The Office of Public Programs arranges speaking engagements for department officials; sponsors conferences and special briefings on U.S. foreign policy; and organizes the department's Scholar-Diplomat, Media-Diplomat, and Executive-Diplomat Seminars. South Asian seminars are held approximately once a year. Information pamphlets describing the services provided by this office are available on request.

BUREAU OF ADMINISTRATION (A)
Thomas M. Tracy, Assistant Secretary
632-1492

In addition to its responsibilities for preparing and administering the department's budget, directing its world-wide communication network and computer center, managing its overseas real estate, providing security protection to departmental personnel and installations abroad—as well as foreign dignitaries visiting the U.S.—the bureau also operates the department's automated foreign-affairs data-processing center and the library. It provides interpretations, translations, reproduction and audiovisual services; and processes records and documents of the department.

FOREIGN AFFAIRS INFORMATION MANAGEMENT CENTER
William Price, Director
632-0394

The center administers the central file of the department's documents and records until they are transferred to the National Archives. Records received by the center from July 1973 have been computer-indexed. Most of the materials in the custody of the center are classified, and access is usually possible only through the Freedom of Information Act. Requests under the Freedom of Information Act may be directed to the center's Information Access Branch (632-1267). The center compiles an unclassified series of *Country Fact Sheets* and the classified *Monthly Highlights Reports*.

POLICY PLANNING STAFF (S/P)
Anthony Lake, Director
632-2372

The Policy Planning Staff advises the Secretary of State with broad, long-range global policy recommendations and perspectives independent of the viewpoints of the geographic bureaus. The staff includes functional as well as area specialists who are accessible to researchers. Most of its works, however, are classified, including its publication entitled *Open Forum*, which deals with foreign-policy issues and analyses.

OFFICE OF THE LEGAL ADVISER (L)—Near Eastern and South Asian Affairs
David H. Small, Assistant Legal Advisor
632-9501

The Legal Adviser is the principal adviser to the secretary and the department on all legal matters with which the department and overseas posts are concerned. Researchers may consult the staff of the Near Eastern and South Asian Affairs branch for information on South Asian legal matters, including the status of treaties and other international agreements. The following other branches of the office, which deal with various functional issues and are headed by assistant legal advisers, often deal with specific South Asian questions and issues: Economic and Business Affairs (Franklin K. Willis, 632-0242); Public Affairs (Ely Maurer, 632-2682); Human Rights (Charles Runyon, III, 632-3044); Ocean, Environment and Scientific Affairs (Mary E. Hoinkes, 632-1700); Politico-Military (Michael J. Matheson, 632-7838); Treaty Affairs (Arthur W. Rovine, 632-1074); and United Nations Affairs (Stephen R. Bond, 632-1320).

The office's publications on international law include: *Digest of United States Practice in International Law*, an annual, containing policy statement of the official U.S. position on all major questions of international law, including human rights and the law of the sea; *Treaties in Force* (TIS), an annual list of all U.S. international agreements in force as of January 1 of each publication year; the annual *United States Treaties and Other International Agreements* (1950—); *Treaties and Other International Agreements of the United States of America, 1776–1949*, 15 vols.; and *Whitman's Digest of International Law*, 15 vols. For further information on publications, contact Marian L. Nash, Editor of *U.S. Practice in International Law* (632-2628).

FOREIGN SERVICE INSTITUTE (FSI)
1400 Key Boulevard
Arlington, Virginia 22209
George S. Springsteem, Director
(703) 235-8750

The FSI is responsible for area and language training and instruction of foreign service and other personnel of the department, as well as personnel of other government departments and agencies involved in foreign affairs. The FSI library is described in entry A10.

OFFICE OF ACADEMIC AFFAIRS
Jack R. Matlock, Jr., Deputy Director
(703) 235-8714

This office develops and maintains close relations with the academic community and with learned and professional societies. It coordinates assignments of foreign service officers to universities, armed services colleges, and other educational institutions.

SCHOOL OF LANGUAGE STUDIES
James R. Frith, Dean
(703) 235-8816

The school provides intensive and part-time language instruction in support of the department's policies on language proficiency among its personnel, and to meet the needs of other government agencies with similar language requirements. Language instruction is available for several South Asian languages, including Bengali, Dari, Nepalese, Hindi, Sinhalese, Punjabi, and Urdu. Each intensive class is conducted by a native-speaking language instructor and is supervised by a scientific linguist.

The school has developed techniques and standards, widely used throughout the federal government, for testing language competence. An active program of research and development has resulted in published courses in more than 30 languages, plus a wealth of as yet unpublished and experimental material. The school maintains extensive recordings and language-laboratory facilities. Complementary tape recordings of the courses may be obtained from the National Audiovisual Center (301/763-1896) of the National Archives and Records Service.

SCHOOL OF AREA STUDIES
James F. Relph, Dean
(703) 235-8839

The School of Area Studies is a focal point for promotion of area and country knowledge within the executive branch of the U.S. government. It provides training to personnel from the department and other foreign-service agencies to meet their requirements for broad interdisciplinary knowledge of a geographic region or country. The school's South Asian Studies Branch (703/235-8845) is responsible for organizing and administering several introductory and advanced courses on the area. The center prepares annual, unannotated area bibliographies, most of which are commercially published monographs for use in its training programs.

SCHOOL OF PROFESSIONAL STUDIES
John T. Sprott, Dean
(703) 235-8779

This school provides general courses in economics, science, human rights, political analysis, politico-military affairs, multilateral diplomacy, and other related fields. The school also conducts the Foreign Affairs Interdepartmental Seminar attended by senior mid-career officers from the departments and agencies concerned with foreign affairs. The seminar provides an advanced intensive look at the major elements of U.S. foreign policy, including its formulation and conduct. Emphasis is placed on domestic factors affecting policy; current, major, foreign and national security problems; and such critical international issues as food, population, and energy.

EXECUTIVE SEMINAR IN NATIONAL AND INTERNATIONAL AFFAIRS
James J. Blake, Coordinator
(703) 235-8766

This 10-month program provides senior U.S. government officials with the most advanced training available, concerning contemporary political, economic, social, and cultural trends in the U.S., and the ways these domestic trends interact with U.S. interests abroad.

Note: Also see entries A10 and A32.

J32 Transportation Department (DOT)

1.   a. *400 7th Street, S.W.*
      Washington, D.C. 20590
      426-4570

      b. Open to the public

2.   Established in 1966 to develop an over-all national transportation policy, the Department of Transportation also participates in international technical-assistance projects. Most research is done in-house; opportunities for contract research occasionally develop.

3.   The DOT Library (Lucile E. Beaver, 426-2565), located in Room 2200, open 7:30 A.M. to 5:30 P.M., Monday through Friday, is accessible to the public for on-site use. Interlibrary loan and photoduplication facilities are available. Its collection, exceeding 500,000 volumes arranged geographically by country, concentrates on the history of transportation and on technical studies of roads, highways, railroads, and urban mass-transit. The library also maintains an extensive collection of periodical literature on the subject of transportation. An estimated 500 items deal with South Asia, and include monographs as well as various government reports and documents related to the transportation systems of India, Pakistan, Afghanistan, and Bangladesh. A dictionary card catalog, based on LC classification schedules, slightly modified, provides access to the collection.

4.   The Information Management Division (James L. Duda, Chief, 426-0975),
of the Office of Policy, Plans and Program Management (John D. Hodge,
Associate Administrator, 426-9676), has developed—in conjunction with
the Transportation Research Board (TRB) of the National Academy of
Science's National Research Council, and numerous other organizations—
a computerized bibliographic data base known by its acronym TRISNET
(Transportation Research Information Services Network). Indexed by country
and transportation mode, the system is accessible to private researchers for
a fee through the TRB computer terminal. TRB's Special Technical Activities Office (Paul E. Irick, 389-6611) may be contacted for further information. Two useful brochures describing the system are: *TRISNET:
Directory to Transportation Research Information Service* (1976) and *TRIS-
NET: A Network of Transportation Information Services and Activities* (1978).
The department sponsors the annual *World Survey of Current Research
and Development on Roads and Road Transport* prepared and distributed
by the International Road Federation. The department's collection of more
than 700,000 abstracts and annotated index entries to the periodical literature on the subject of transportation is available on 140 reels of microfilm.
Transportation Master File, 1921–1970, and a hard cover volume, *Transportation Serials,* published by the U.S. Historical Documents Institute,
and *Investment Strategies for Developing Areas: Highway Cost Model Operating Instructions and Program Documentation* (1973) prepared under
DOT contract by the Massachusetts Institute of Technology may be of
interest to the South Asianist. The department's Freedom of Information
officer is Rebecca Lima Daley (426-4542)

POLICY AND INTERNATIONAL AFFAIRS
William Johnston, Assistant Secretary
426-4544

The Bureau of Policy and International Affairs is responsible for the coordination of U.S. interests in international transportation affairs. Activities
carried on by the bureau include analysis, development, articulation, and
review of department-wide policies and programs for domestic and international transportation; analysis of the social, economic, and energy aspects
of transport systems; promotion and coordination of international research
cooperation; and technical assistance to developing countries.

INTERNATIONAL TRANSPORTATION PROGRAMS
Voyce J. Mack, Director
426-4368

International Transportation Division
Harold Handerson, Chief
755-7684

This division is the central coordinating unit for the department's international technical assistance programs. The division maintains geographic
files of transportation data for foreign countries including Afghanistan,
Pakistan, Bangladesh and India. Most of this data, supplied by U.S. embassies overseas, is accessible to researchers. The division's specialist on
South Asia is Diane Roberts (755-7684).

Technical Assistance Division
Richard Braida, Chief
426-4197

Cooperating with the Agency for International Development, the division provides technical assistance support in planning, management, and evaluation of foreign transportation projects sponsored and funded by AID. In the past, the division has been involved in projects in Afghanistan, but currently no activities are reported in South Asia.

FEDERAL AVIATION ADMINISTRATION (FAA)
800 Independence Avenue, S.W.
Washington, D.C. 20591
Langhorne M. Bond, Administrator
426-3111

The FAA, formerly known as the Federal Aviation Agency, became a part of DOT under its new name in 1967. The Federal Aviation Administration is primarily charged with regulating air commerce to foster aviation safety, but it is also called upon to make air transport studies in foreign countries.

POLICY AND INTERNATIONAL AFFAIRS
William Wilkins, Associate Administrator
426-3030

International Aviation Affairs
Norman H. Plummer, Acting Director
426-3213

Analysis and Evaluation Branch (Robert Toenniessen, 426-3231) of the International Analysis and Coordination Division (Kathleen W. Gorman, 426-3230) maintains filebooks known as "Country Profiles," which contain general and statistical information on current aviation activities in various foreign countries, including Afghanistan, Bangladesh, India, Nepal, Pakistan, and Sri Lanka. This branch also maintains separate internal country files on many foreign countries, containing in-house research reports and other agency memos and documents. International Civil Aviation Organization's statistical data on different countries is also available in this branch. All these materials are available to researchers.

The Interagency Group on International Aviation (IGIA) Secretariat (Milton Myers, 426-3180) is an administrative group within the International Analysis and Coordination Division, which monitors and coordinates the international aviation activities of U.S. government agencies and serves as the U.S. depository of all documents produced by the International Civil Aviation Organization (ICAO). The secretariat also maintains a small reference library accessible to the public containing all ICAO documents since 1945 and IGIA documents.

The Technical Assistance Division (Stuart Jamison, Chief, 426-3173), of the International Aviation Affairs, provides technical experts, when requested, to AID-sponsored overseas projects. FAA activities in South Asia include procurement of equipment for Pakistan and flight-inspection services in Sri Lanka, Bangladesh, and Afghanistan. For further information, call Stanley W. Fink, Chief, Eastern Area Operations (426-3175).

Another unit of the International Aviation Affairs, International Liaison and Policy Division (Michael Casey, Chief, 426-3057), deals with operational matters related to U.S. airmen and aircraft in foreign countries and foreign airmen and aircraft in the U.S. The division also acts as the agency liaison in coordinating the technical aspects of international civil aviation policy.

The FAA maintains a reference library (Dorothy Poehlman, Librarian, 426-3611) containing some 50,000 monographs, 50,000 technical reports, 150,000 microforms and 700 periodical subscriptions. The primary focus of the collection is in the following areas: aeronautics, aviation safety, and various facets of civil aviation, such as navigation, airports, air-traffic control, air transportation, aviation medicine, and aviation law. International in scope, the collection is accessible to the public for on-site use, except for documents restricted to agency use. Interlibrary loan and limited photoduplication services are available. The library is open from 8:30 A.M. to 5:00 P.M., Monday through Friday. A card index is the principal reference tool to the collection. The library issues bibliographies and other announcement bulletins from time to time.

FAA's Freedom of Information officer is Ben S. Lee (426-3485). The FAA's Office of the Historian (Nick A. Komons, 755-7234), within the Public Affairs Bureau, maintains a small archive of indexed key documents that reflect the evolution of the U.S. civil-aviation policy from 1926 to the present, which may include some materials of interest. The office is currently compiling a 3-volume narrative history of federal civil aviation policies. A catalog of *FAA Publications* is available free on request.

FEDERAL HIGHWAY ADMINISTRATION (FHWA)
400 7th Street, N.W.
Washington, D.C. 20590
John S. Hassell, Jr., Administrator
426-0650

A component of DOT since 1966, the FHWA, which carries out the highway transportation programs of the department, is also engaged in some limited international activities. Its Foreign Project Division (Hal Brown, Acting Chief, 426-0380) provides technical-assistance advisors for AID-sponsored overseas projects. Currently, the division reports no activities in South Asia.

J33 Treasury Department

1.   a. *15th Street and Pennsylvania Avenue, N.W.*
     Washington, D.C. 20220
     566-5252

     b. Open to the public on the basis of advance appointment

2.   The Department of the Treasury's primary responsibilities include formulating and recommending domestic and international financial, economic, and tax policies. Most research is conducted in-house although, from time to time, contract-research opportunities develop.

3. The Treasury Department Library, within the Administration's Management Information Services Division (Elizabeth Knauff, Chief, 566-2069), is open to the public from 9:00 A.M. to 5:00 P.M., Monday through Friday. Photoduplication facilities and interlibrary loan services are available. The collection consists of 125,000 monographic items, 200,000 microfiche, and 8,000 microfilms. The areas of emphasis include taxation and public finance; money and banking; and international law and economics. The library is also a depository for Congressional records and documents. The holdings contain a number of government statistical publications from South Asia, as well as documents and records produced by the Asian Development Bank. *Treasury Notes* lists the library's monthly bibliographic acquisitions.

4. Publications of interest include: *Foreign Credit by the United States Government: Status of Active Foreign Credits of the United States Government and of International Organizations* (semiannual), records the debts owed to the Government of the United States and international organizations; *Annual Report of the National Advisory Council on International Monetary Policies; Report on Developing Countries External Debt and Debt Relief Provided by the United States* (annual); and *Treasury Bulletin,* a monthly, providing statistical data on receipts and expenditures, public debt, and movement of capital between the U.S. and foreign countries. A *Selected List of Treasury Publications* is revised periodically and can be obtained free from the Office of Public Affairs (Robert Nipp, Chief, International Affairs, 566-5328).

    Inactive and retired records and documents of the department are managed by the Administration's Record Management Branch (Sarah J. Allen, Chief, 566-2010). All Freedom of Information requests should be addressed to the Disclosure Operation's Freedom of Information Branch (Linda Zannetti, Chief, 566-4441).

OFFICE OF ECONOMIC POLICY
Daniel H. Brill, Assistant Secretary
566-2551

Within this office, the Deputy Assistant Secretary for International Economic Analysis (John R. Karlik, 566-5828) is responsible for international economic issues that include developing forecasts of U.S. trade and current-account balances for use by the officials of the department in formulating international economic policy; conducting research and analysis of major policy issues in the international trade, monetary, and energy areas; and producing information on the flow of banking and corporate capital into and out of the U.S., and on the extent of portfolio investment by foreigners in the U.S. and by U.S. residents abroad. This unit also maintains the Developing Countries Data Bank, which contains information since 1960 on national income, balance of payments, and foreign debts of developing nations. This data bank, however, is not accessible to the public.

OFFICE OF INTERNATIONAL AFFAIRS
C. Fred Bergsten, Assistant Secretary
566-5363

This office advises and assists the department in the formulation and execution of policies dealing with international monetary, financial, commercial, energy, and trade policies and programs. The work of the office is organized into groups responsible for developing nations, monetary affairs, trade and investment policy, and commodities and natural resources.

DEVELOPING NATIONS
Arnold Nachmanoff, Deputy Assistant Secretary
566-8243

Office of International Development Banks
Frank Maresca, Director
566-8171

An important element within the department in conducting financial diplomacy with the developing nations, this office monitors the operations of the Asian Development Bank and the World Bank Group and makes recommendations for U.S. policy. Researchers may confer with staff members in this office for information relating to South Asia.

Office of Developing Nations Finance
Donald C. Templeman, Director
566-2373

Organized on a geographical basis, this office monitors South Asian monetary and financial conditions, including balance of payments, debt levels, and general fiscal and developmental conditions. The South Asia Desk Officer in this office (Robert Anderson, 566-8521) is the best contact person in the department for researchers seeking information on South Asian countries.

K South Asian Embassies and International Organizations

With the exception of Bhutan and the Maldive Islands, all other countries in South Asia maintain their diplomatic presence in Washington, D.C. In the entries below, each embassy is identified by its official name as presented in the Diplomatic List (August 1980) but is listed alphabetically according to its geographical designation. In addition to providing general information and current developments, the embassies may assist scholars by putting them in contact with organizations and individuals in their respective countries that have information and data otherwise difficult to obtain in the United States. The embassies often sponsor cultural events, film showings, musical or dance troupes, or lecture programs, to which the public may be invited. The embassies also disseminate various newsletters, pamphlets, statistics, and posters, projecting the historical, cultural, and development programs in their countries. The embassies are also the best sources for current South Asian newspaper files.

The presence of international organizations—especially the World Bank and its affiliates, and the International Monetary Fund—yield additional valuable resources for scholars. The personnel of the international organizations described in this section may provide useful South Asia-related information and materials within the limits imposed by their schedules and official regulations.

South Asian Embassies and International Organizations Entry Format (K)*

1. General Information
   a. *address; telephone numbers*
   b. hours and conditions of access
   c. names and titles of chief officials

2.   Organization Functions, Programs, Research Activities (including in-house research, contract research, research grants, and employment of outside consultants)

3.   Library and Reference Facilities

4.   Publications and Internal Records (including unpublished research projects)

*In the case of large, structurally complex international organizations, each relevant division or sub-unit is described separately in accordance with the above entry format.

K1 Embassy of the Democratic Republic of Afghanistan

1.   a. *2341 Wyoming Avenue, N.W.*
      Washington, D.C. 20008
      234-3770

      b. 9:00 A.M.–3:00 P.M.   Monday–Friday

2-4.   The embassy issues an irregular *Newsletter* containing excerpts from the *Kabul Time* and government regulations.

K2 Embassy of the People's Republic of Bangladesh

1.   a. *3421 Massachusetts Avenue, N.W.*
      Washington, D.C. 20007
      337-6644

      b. 9:30 A.M.–5:30 P.M.   Monday–Friday

2-4.   Back issues of the discontinued *Bangladesh A Fortnightly News Bulletin,* published by the embassy in Washington, may be available in the embassy. From time to time the embassy distributes free a news bulletin prepared by the Bangladesh Ministry of Foreign Affairs in Dacca, entitled *Bangladesh, A Fortnightly Journal.* The embassy participates occasionally in art and craft exhibits and cooperates with ethnic and cultural institutions. Scholars researching Bangladesh-related topics may confer with the staff. A few documentary films on Bangladesh are available and may be borrowed, without charge, by institutions.

K3 Embassy of India

1.   a. *2107 Massachusetts Avenue, N.W.*
      Washington, D.C. 20008
      265-5050

      b. 9:30 A.M.–5:30 P.M.   Monday–Friday

2.   The embassy cooperates with several ethnic, academic, and cultural institutions and associations in the United States. The embassy staff is willing to confer with researchers. It is advisable to make appointments.

3.   The Indian Embassy Library (Babu Raj Stephen, Librarian, 265-5050, extension 210) is open to the public from 9:30 A.M. to 5:30 P.M., Monday through Friday. Its total collection of approximately 10,000 items consists of historical and biographical monographs in English and in Indian national languages; popular literature and poetry; government publications including census reports, maps, and charts; and dictionaries, directories, and yearbooks. The library also receives some 45 current periodicals from India and 18 newspapers representing most major national languages. Newspaper files are maintained for a 3-month period. The library provides limited interlibrary loan and photoduplication services.

4.   *The United States and India 1776–1976*, was issued by the embassy to celebrate the U.S. bicentennial. The Information Service issues *India News*, available for sale. There is no subscription fee for academic institutions, libraries, registered societies, or associations. The Information Service also maintains a collection of some 50 tapes and many more long-playing records of Indian classical music, which may be lent to institutions without charge. For the Indian Embassy's film collection, see entry F3.

K4 Royal Nepalese Embassy

1.   **a.** *2131 Leroy Place, N.W.*
Washington, D.C. 20008
667-4550

    b. 9:00 A.M.–5:00 P.M. Monday–Friday.

2-4.   The embassy publishes no newsletters, and maintains a small reference collection for internal use only. The staff cooperates with ethnic and cultural groups and may confer with scholars on the basis of previous appointments.

K5 Embassy of Pakistan

1.   **a.** *2315 Massachusetts Avenue, N.W.*
Washington, D.C. 20008
332-8330

    b. 9:00 A.M.–5:00 P.M. Monday–Friday

2.   The embassy cooperates with various ethnic associations and cultural institutions.

3.   It maintains a small reference collection of approximately 2,500 volumes with primary emphasis on the history and foreign policy of Pakistan and the history of Islam. Most of the collection is in English, although a few works in Arabic and Urdu are also to be found. Current newspapers from Pakistan are available in the Information Division. Newspaper files are maintained for 3 months. The library will lend materials to institutions, scholars, and students with proper identification.

    The Information Division maintains a film collection (see entry F14) and a small collection of classical, tribal, regional, and modern music. Requests for borrowing these materials may be directed to the Information Division.

4.   The Information Division publishes and disseminates, without charge, a

fortnightly news bulletin, *Pakistan Affairs*, which sometimes contains feature articles and abstracts from newspapers in Pakistan.

K6 Embassy of the Democratic Socialist Republic of Sri Lanka

1. a. *2148 Wyoming Avenue, N.W.*
   Washington, D.C. 20008
   483-4025

   b. 9:00 A.M.–5:15 P.M.   Monday–Friday

2-4. The embassy cooperates with ethnic and cultural bodies. It publishes a monthly newsletter—which may be obtained free—and maintains a small reference collection, mostly for official use, of government publications and works on history. A few tapes on the music of Sri Lanka are also available from the Information Section. The staff will confer with scholars researching Sri Lanka studies.

K7 Food and Agricultural Organization (FAO) of the United Nations—Liaison Office for North America

1. a. *1776 F. Street, N.W.*
   Washington, D.C. 20437
   376-2306

   b. Open to the public

   c. Don C. Kimmel, North American Representative

2. An autonomous, specialized agency of the United Nations, the FAO's mission is to raise the levels of nutrition and standard of living of the peoples under its respective jurisdictions; secure improvements in the efficiency of the production and distribution of all food and agricultural products; better the conditions of rural populations; and, thus, contribute toward an expanding economy. The FAO administers its own technical cooperation program for agricultural development and works closely with a number of international and national finance institutions, including the World Bank, regional development banks, and national development banks, for the purpose of securing capital for agricultural-development projects in the developing countries. With 144 nations as members, FAO activities touch most nations in the Third World.

   FAO's Washington office serves essentially as a liaison for coordinating FAO-administered programs in the U.S. and Canada, which include, in part, administering a fellowship program (Theresa Clark, 376-2226) in North America for trainees from developing countries. Several participants are selected each year from South Asian countries.

3. The Washington office maintains a small reference collection that is open to the public weekdays and offers interlibrary loan and photoduplicating services. This collection contains selected FAO documents and publications, including budgets and conference reports, FAO statistical yearbooks on world agricultural production and trade, fisheries, forest products, animal

health, world agricultural commodity reviews and projections, and FAO nutritional and agricultural studies. In addition, the collection also includes FAO's international *Food and Agricultural Legislation series*, the *Monthly Bulletin of Agricultural and Economic Statistics*, the bimonthly *Ceres: FAO Review on Agriculture and Development*, and the Washington office's *Notes for North America*.

4.   FAO is a central point for studies of agricultural questions on a world scale. FAO collects the latest information on food, agriculture, forestry, and fisheries from all over the world and makes it available to all its member countries for the use of government planners, research workers, business-men, students and the general public. In addition to the statistical yearbooks and regular reviews of the situation and outlook for world food supplies and agriculture, scientific monographs bring together the result of research carried out in many countries. Special international catalogs list such in-formation as manufacturers of tractors, institutes of agricultural engineer-ing, genetic stocks of cereal available to plant breeders and forest-seed suppliers. Every 10 years FAO coordinates and publishes the results of a census of world agricultural resources. *FAO Books in Print*, and *FAO Periodicals* are available on request.

K8 International Bank for Reconstruction and Development (IBRD) (World Bank)

1.   a. *1818 H Street, N.W.*
        Washington, D.C. 20433
        477-1234

        b. Visitors are received by appointment.

        c. Robert S. McNamara, President

2.   For South Asian scholars, the World Bank provides valuable and extensive research resources. Established in 1945, and with a current membership of 134 countries, the World Bank is a group of three institutions: the Inter-national Bank for Reconstruction and Development (IBRD), the Inter-national Development Association (IDA), and the International Finance Corporation (see entry K9). The common objective of these institutions is to help raise standards of living in developing countries by channeling financial resources from developed countries to the developing world. The World Bank, the capital of which is subscribed by its member countries, finances its lending operations primarily from its own borrowings in the world-capital markets. As spelled out in its charter, the bank must lend only for productive purposes and must stimulate economic growth in the developing countries where it lends. In the fiscal year 1979, the World Bank, with its affiliates, made lending and investment commitments ag-gregating $10,435.9 million.
        The bank has traditionally financed all kinds of capital infrastructure; i.e., roads and railways, telecommunications, and ports and power facilities. Its present development strategy, however, places a greatly increased em-phasis on investments that can directly affect the well-being of the masses of poor people in developing countries by making them more productive

and by integrating them as active partners in the development process. This new strategy is reflected in the increasing number of bank-funded projects in agriculture, rural development, education, family planning, nutrition, water and sewerage, and low-cost housing. In addition to projects funded independently, the bank also cofinances a number of other projects together with other national or multinational development-assistance agencies.

Credit terms differentiate the IBRD from its affiliate, the IDA, which came into existence in 1960 with membership open to all member-countries of the IBRD. IDA's resources consist of subscriptions and supplementary resources in the form of: general replenishments mostly from its 21 more industrialized and developed members; special contributions by its richer members; and transfers from the net earnings of the IBRD. IDA provides finances to the developing nations on concessionary terms and are more flexible and bear less heavily on the balance of payments than those of the conventional loans, thereby furthering the objectives of the World Bank and supplementing its activities.

Following is a breakdown of the IDA cumulative lending operations in South Asia, in U.S. dollars, in the millions: Afghanistan, $230.1; Bangladesh, $1,187.2; India, $6,750.2; Maldives, $3.2; Nepal, $207.7; Pakistan, $1,079.9; Sri Lanka, $218.1. Of the total World Bank lending to South Asia in fiscal year 1979, 86 percent was on IDA terms, reflecting the poverty of South Asian countries and their very limited capacity to borrow on IBRD terms.

Research has always been an integral part of the bank's economic work, and the growing diversification of the bank's lending operations has induced further expansion of research into various economic and social aspects of the developing countries. Outside scholars are frequently contracted as research consultants. Increasingly, World Bank research is conducted in collaboration with researchers and research institutions in developing countries. The objective is to develop a network of mutually supportive studies dealing with general issues of development policy, as well as with specific sectoral problems of particular concern to the bank's operations in developing countries. The bank has designed its research program in the light of four major goals: to support all aspects of the bank's operations, including the assessment of development progress in member countries; to broaden understanding of the development process; to improve the bank's capacity to provide advice to member countries; and to assist in developing indigenous research capacity in member countries.

In view of these stated goals, the World Bank supports research projects that develop the data base, construct analytical tools, and extend the bank's understanding of rural and urban development, industry, trade, economic growth, and social condition. Two free, brief publications, *World Bank Research Program Abstracts of Current Studies* (1979) and *Uses of Consultants by the World Bank and its Borrowers* (1974), provide additional information on the research activities and availability of consultancy assignments in the World Bank.

SOUTH ASIA REGIONAL OFFICE (ASN)
W. David Hopper, Vice President
477-2395

This office is the focal point for planning and coordinating all South Asia-related activities. Afghanistan, however, falls within the jurisdiction of the Europe, Middle East and North Africa Regional Office (EMN) (Roger Chaufournier, Vice President, 477-4261). Excluding Afghanistan, in the fiscal year 1979, IBRD and IDA-lending to the region reached $2,077 million assisting 36 different projects. Afghanistan received $16.5 million IDA credit for agriculture and rural development which aimed at restructuring society through land reform and more equitable distribution. Following is a table of the bank's lending activities for fiscal year 1979 in South Asia, excluding Afghanistan; the figures are U.S. dollars, in millions.

Agriculture and rural development	$541.7
Education	35.0
Energy	30.0
Industrial development and finance (including lending to development finance companies and small enterprises)	16.0
Industry	334.0
Nonproject	100.0
Population and nutrition	32.0
Power	467.8
Technical assistance	10.0
Telecommunications	—
Tourism	—
Transportation	206.5
Urban development	—
Water supply and sewerage	304.0
Total	2,077.0
Of which: IBRD	300.0
IDA	1,777.0

Administratively, the regional offices are divided along sectoral lines (Projects Department, Robert Picciotto, Director, ASN, 477-2657; A. David Knox, Director, EMN, 477-4261) and geographic lines (Country Program Department, Michael H. Wiehen, Director, ASN, 477-4945; Attila Karaosmanoglu, Director, EMN, 477-4503). Staff economists, analysts, and technical specialists in the directorates are in frequent contact with the countries in South Asia. They negotiate loans, handle project liaison matters, collect field data, and prepare reports and studies. Following is a list of country officers within the Country Program Department. Afghanistan: William S. Humphrey (477-6061); Pakistan: Richard L. Clements (477-4935); India: Ann O. Hamilton (477-5027); Maldives, Nepal, Sri Lanka: Alphonse Shibusawa (477-3568); and Bangladesh: David A. Dunn (477-4076).

INFORMATION AND PUBLIC AFFAIRS DEPARTMENT
John E. Merriam, Director
477-2468

Regional specialists in the department should be the initial contact point for scholars seeking information concerning World Bank activities in South Asia. They may direct the scholars to the appropriate functional and geographical offices or departments.

This department also maintains an extensive collection of still photographs, slides, and motion pictures of projects supported by the bank in the member countries. For further information contact the Audio Visual Unit (Pastor B. Sison, 676-1632).

ECONOMIC DEVELOPMENT INSTITUTE (EDI)
Ajit Mozoomdar, Director
477-2203

The EDI trains officials from developing countries in the areas of economic management, development programs, and projects. A recently initiated EDI 5-year program (1979–1983) envisages: increased support for training institutions overseas through teaching, advice on training methods, course planning and administration, and the supply of training materials prepared by EDI staff; an increased number of national and regional courses; the introduction, testing, and development in its Washington teaching program of new courses and short innovative seminars.

During fiscal 1979, EDI offered 11 courses and 3 seminars for about 400 participants in Washington, and supported 33 overseas courses and seminars given to about 850 participants. Some of the courses offered through the Washington program include population and development, preparation, evaluation, and management of railway projects, development banking, and rural development projects. The EDI also participates with the United Nations Institute for Training and Research in conducting seminars for the staff of diplomatic missions to the U.N.

EID's overseas activities in South Asia include a cooperative training program with the Bangladesh Institute for Development Studies in Dacca; an experimental seminar in Kathmandu for the supervisors of South Asian participants in previous EDI transportation courses that had been held in Washington, D.C., Bangladesh, and Pakistan; courses given in Pakistan and India on special topics concerned with development policy analysis, decision making, and implementation; and several other courses offered jointly with other institutions on industrial projects in Bangladesh and transportation projects in Pakistan.

INTERNATIONAL RELATIONS DEPARTMENT (IRD)

This department is the bank's lead agency for external cooperation in organizing various aid coordination mechanisms for a number of developing countries that receive assistance from bilateral and multilateral sources. The department also acts as the bank's liaison in its long-standing relations with U.N. agencies and programs concerned with various aspects of development work in the developing countries. In addition, this department manages all technical assistance activities that are integral components of the bank's lending operation.

3. For the Joint Bank Fund Library see entry A22.

4. The World Bank publishes numerous reports and studies, which are listed in the periodically updated *Catalog; World Bank Publications.* For obtaining the bank's free publications, contact the Publication Unit (477-2403). Some of the recent publications of interest include: Inderjit Singh, *Small Farmers and Landless in South Asia* (1979); A. B. Jayarajah, *Bangladesh: Current*

Trends and Development Issues (1979); Rashid R. Faruqee, *Sources of Fertility Decline: Factor Analysis of Inter-country Data* (1979); C. Taylor, *India: Economic Issues in the Power Sector* (1979); Swadesh R. Bose, *Some Aspects of Unskilled Labor Markets for Civil Construction in India: Observations Based on Field Investigation* (1975); Ravi Gulhati, *India's Population Policy: Critical Issues for the Future* (reprint 1978); S. A. Draper, *Pakistan: Forestry Sector Survey* (1978); Lyn Squire et al., *Application of Shadow Pricing to Country Economic Analysis with an Illustration from Pakistan (1979)*; Stephen Guisinger, *Wages, Capital Rental Values and Relative Factor Prices in Pakistan* (1978).

Other useful publications are: *World Bank Annual Report;* the annual *World Development Report;* the quarterly *Finance and Development;* the bimonthly *Report;* the quarterly *World Economic and Social Indicators;* the annual *World Debt Tables: External Public Debt of Developing Countries;* the quarterly *Borrowing in International Capital Markets;* the annual *Commodity Trends and Price Trends;* and the annual *World Bank Atlas.*

While most of the bank publications are publicly available, some special studies are restricted to official use only. All bank documents and records are ultimately deposited in the custody of the Records Management Office (Donald K. Bloomfield, 477-2711) of the Administrative Services Department, which maintains an index of Documentation Available to Staff.

Note: Also see entries A7, F16, and G8.

K9 International Finance Corporation (IFC)

1.   a. *1818 H Street, N.W.*
Washington, D.C. 20433
676-0391

b. Visitors are received by appointment.

c. Judhvir Parmar, Vice President, Asia and the Middle East
676-0385
Torstein Stephansen, Director, Department of Investment, Asia
676-0601
Wilfried E. Kaffenberger, Divisional Manager, South Asia
676-0607

2.   The IFC was established in 1956. An affiliate of the International Bank for Reconstruction and Development (IBRD), the purpose of the corporation is to further economic development by encouraging the growth of productive private enterprise in member countries, particularly in the less-developed areas. Its principal tasks are to provide and bring together financing, technical assistance, and management needed to develop productive investment opportunities in its developing member countries whether from private, mixed, or government enterprises. IFC's capital is provided by its 109 member countries, of which 88 are developing countries. All the countries of South Asia, except the Maldives and Bhutan, are members of the corporation. The IFC occasionally contracts with outside consultants for specific research and policy development tasks.

In fiscal year 1979, IFC loan and equity investment in South Asia supported some 19 projects; types of businesses included shipbuilding, fertilizers, machinery, money and capital market, tourism, chemicals and petrochemicals, development finance, food and food processing, and textiles and fibers. Following is a breakdown of IFC investment in South Asia in fiscal year 1979, expressed in U.S. dollars, in thousands: Bangladesh, $1,565; India, $33,602; Nepal, $3,128; Pakistan, $29,337; and Sri Lanka, $5,420. In responding to the differing needs and circumstances of its member countries, the IFC continues its policy of investing in a wide variety of enterprises.

4. The *IFC Annual Report* summarizes the highlights of its activities for the year. An informative brochure, *IFC General Policies*, is also available from the IFC Information Office (Carl T. Bell, Chief, 676-0391).

K10 International Monetary Fund (IMF)

1. a. *700 19th Street, N.W.*
   Washington, D.C. 20431
   477-3011

   b. The building is not open to the public. Visitors are received by appointment only.

   c. J. de Larosière, Managing Director and Chairman of the Executive Board

2. The International Monetary Fund is an organization of 140 countries that seeks to promote international monetary cooperation and to facilitate the expansion of trade. It makes financing available to members in balance-of-payments difficulties, and provides them with technical assistance to improve their economic management. To enable the IMF to carry out its responsibilities, member countries continually supply it with a broad range of economic and financial information, and the IMF also consults regularly with each member country on its economic situation. All the countries of South Asia, except Bhutan, are members of the IMF and participate in the Special Drawing Rights (SDR). Opportunities for contract research is very limited, but the fund maintains a pool of private, international, fiscal and central banking specialists, who act as advisors to foreign governments.

   Membership in the fund is a prerequisite to membership in the World Bank (see entry K8), and a close working relationship exists between the two organizations as well as between the fund and other international and U.N. agencies.

ASIAN DEPARTMENT
Tun Thim, Director
477-2911

MIDDLE EASTERN DEPARTMENT
A. S. Shaalan, Director
477-4401

The Asian Department, with assigned responsibilities for India, Bangladesh, the Maldives, Nepal, and Sri Lanka, and the Middle Eastern Department, with assigned responsibilities for Afghanistan and Pakistan, serve as the principal operational wings for IMF's South Asian affairs. Country specialists with the departments may confer with researchers: Bangladesh and India (Bruce J. Smith, 477-2923); Nepal (Paul Chabrier, 477-5975); Maldives (Douglas A. Scott, 477-5661); Sri Lanka (John T. Boorman, 477-3342); Afghanistan (Muhammad Yaqub, 477-6531); and Pakistan (F. Drees, 477-6122).

The Asian and Middle Eastern departments advise the IMF's management and executive board on all matters concerning the economics and economic policies of South Asian countries, assist in the formulation of IMF policies in relation to these countries, and, along with other departments of the IMF, provide technical assistance and financial advice on many subjects related to improving the management of the economies of those countries. Following the fund's guideline to help members coordinate their national economic policies internationally, the departments' staff teams make periodic trips to South Asia to collect data, analyze financial trends and policies, and hold policy consultations with national authorities responsible for economic affairs. Both departments compile annual reports on recent economic development in each country under their charge. Country staff reports prepared on the basis of field consultations are not accessible to researchers.

IMF INSTITUTE
Gérard M. Teyssier, Director
477-3727

The IMF Institute was established in 1964 to broaden and coordinate the increasing technical assistance given by the fund. A department of the fund, the institute's purpose is to improve the expertise of officials from member countries in the use of modern tools of economic analysis, in the management of economies, and in IMF procedures and policies. Training courses on financial analysis and policy, balance-of-payments methodology, and public finance are conducted at the institute. Some 2,500 officials, from nearly every member country, have completed such courses since the founding of the institute, which also provides assistance in its areas of competence to regional and national training centers.

RESEARCH DEPARTMENT
William C. Hood, Director
477-2981

IMF's research activities are primarily the responsibility of the Research Department. Although most research is primarily concerned with financial, theoretical, and internal policy questions, occasionally South Asia-related issues are also examined. Researchers may consult the specialists within the department: Commodities Division (Nihad Kaibni, 477-4162); Current Studies Division (Carl P. Blackwell, 477-2893); External Adjustment Division (Jacques Artus, 477-7158); Financial Studies Division (George Von Furstenberg, 477-4316); and Special Studies Division (Anthony Lanyi, 477-2941).

BUREAU OF STATISTICS
Werner Dannemann, Director
477-3395

The bureau's component units are: Balance of Payments Division (Arie C.

Bouter, 477-6054); Data Fund Division (Robert L. Kline, 477-3206); Financial Statistics Division A (Jai B. Gupta, 477-4133); Financial Statistics Division B (Muthusswami Swaminathan, 477-4135); General Statistics Division (Chandrakant A. Patel, 477-3130); and Government Finance Statistics Division (Jonathan V. Levin, 676-0811).

The fund is a principal source of internationally comparable statistics on national economies, including financial and economic data that are relevant to the analysis of countries' monetary and payment problems. Compilations and publications of these vital statistics are the major responsibility of the Bureau of Statistics. In addition to each country's transactions and operations with the fund, the statistics published by the bureau include, among others, data on exchange rates, international reserves, money and banking, prices, production, external trade, wages and employment, balance of payments, government finance, and national accounts. These are all covered in the monthly and annual issues of *International Financial Statistics, Balance of Payments Yearbook, Government Finance Statistics Yearbook, Direction of Trade* (monthly), and similar publications prepared by the bureau. Magnetic tapes relating to these statistical publications are available on subscription.

3. For Joint Bank-Fund Library, see entry A22.

4. The IMF has an active publications program. In addition to various pamphlets and brochures issued from time to time, fund publications include regular and special reports, books, periodicals, and statistical bulletins noted above. The purpose of the fund's publication program is to further its work and to carry out its obligations to act as a center for the collection and to exchange information on monetary and financial problems. A booklet, *The International Monetary Fund Purposes, Structure, and Activities* and a brochure, *Publications, International Monetary Fund* (1979) provide descriptions of all major fund publications. Requests for IMF publications should be addressed to the Publications Section (Amparo Masakayan, Supervisor, 477-2945).

IMF publications include the following. The *Annual Report* reviews the fund's activities and analyzes the developments in the world economy and in the international monetary system. The *Annual Report on Exchange Arrangements and Exchange Restrictions* includes country-by-country descriptions of the exchange systems of most countries of the world. The results of IMF's program of research into economic and financial problems are published in *Staff Papers,* a quarterly economic journal of the fund. Some examples of the staff papers are: Sijbern Cnossen, "Capacity Taxation: the Pakistan Experiment" (Vol. 21, No. 1, 1974); Duncan Ridler and Christopher A. Yandle, "Changes in Patterns and Policies in the International Trade in Rice" (Vol. 19, No. 1, 1972); Omotunde Johnson and Joanne Salop, "Distributional Aspects of Stabilization Programs in Developing Countries" (Vol. 27, No. 1, 1980); and Bijan B. Aghevli and others, "Monetary Policy in Selected Asian Countries" (Vol. 26, No. 4, 1979).

The biweekly *IMF Survey* reports developments in the fund and the international monetary system in the broader context of world economic and financial news, including changes in countries' policies. A quarterly magazine, *Finance and Development,* published jointly by the IMF and the World Bank carries articles on topics related to the interests of the two institutions. *Technical Assistance Service of the International Monetary Fund* (1979) is an informative publication of the Pamphlet Series. Other publications include the 3-volume history of the fund, *The International Monetary Fund, 1945–1965: Twenty Years of International Monetary Cooperation;* and its 2-volume sequel, *The International Monetary Fund, 1966–1971: The System Under Stress.*

All inactive files are held in custody by the Records Management Unit (K. Kyung-Hoy Cho, Chief, 477-6024). It may be noted that most IMF records are confidential.

Note: Also see entry G9.

K11 United Nations Development Program (UNDP)—Washington Office

1.   a. *2101 L Street, N.W.*
        Washington, D.C. 20037
        296-5074

      b. Open to the public, but previous appointment is recommended.

      c. Charles L. Perry, Liaison Officer

2-4.   The Washington Office of the UNDP maintains a small collection of country program reports relating to U.S.-assisted development programs in South Asia. Most of these documents are accessible to researchers. Researchers may request staff assistance in obtaining those records not available at this office from the UNDP headquarters in New York (One, U.N. Plaza, New York, New York 10017).

K12 United Nations Educational, Scientific and Cultural Organization (UNESCO) Liaison Office

1.   a. *918 16th Street, N.W.*
        Washington, D.C. 20006
        457-0770

      b. Open to the public

      c. Herschelle Challenor, Liaison Officer

2-4.   The United Nations Educational, Scientific and Cultural Organization promotes international cooperation in the fields of education, science, mass communication, and culture. This recently established small office acts as liaison with the U.S. Government and other United Nations agencies. A small collection of UNESCO documents is also maintained. Researchers desiring to use the library are advised to call in advance. It may also be noted that some UNESCO publications are available in the Department of State's U.S. National Commission for UNESCO, located at 515 22nd Street, N.W., Washington, D.C. 20520 (Sally Cutting, 632-2767).

L Associations (Academic, Professional, and Cultural)

In this section, an effort has been made to compile a comprehensive list of those academic, cultural, and professional associations that have some pertinence to the field of South Asian studies. Scholars consulting the list of ethnic, social, cultural, and recreational organizations provided in Appendix I of this volume may note that many of these groups are ephemeral, and the contact addresses provided may change as new officials are selected periodically. The wide variety of associations discussed here may prove useful to the scholar interested in South Asian studies. All the associations listed have had some involvement in South Asia-related activities, either directly or indirectly; therefore, most of these associations, in addition to serving as clearinghouses for information, are able to put researchers in touch with other scholars and professionals having research or other relevant expertise in South Asia.

Associations Entry Format (L)

1. *Address; Telephone Numbers*

2. Chief Official and Title

3. Programs and Activities Pertaining to South Asia

4. Library and Reference Collections

5. Publications

L1 Academy for Educational Development (AED)—International Division

1. *1414 22nd Street, N.W.*
   Washington, D.C. 20037
   862-1900

2. Cheryll R. Greenwood, Director

3. This New York-based academy, which was founded in 1961 to help U.S. colleges and universities solve some of their long-range educational, administrative, and financial problems, has expanded steadily over the past years into an international planning and research organization that is currently conducting 53 projects in the developing countries of the world. The primary concern of the International Division is human resources development, particularly in those countries the progress of which has been impeded by illiteracy, poverty, and disease. AED's recent South Asian activities include feasibility and planning studies involving preinvestment analysis for new vocational and technical education programs and facilities in Afghanistan; an operational project in collaboration with three U.S. land-grant universities in assisting Sri Lanka with teaching, research, and outreach programs in agriculture; and occasional studies and assessments in Pakistan, India, and Bangladesh.

4. The division maintains a Clearinghouse on Development Communication, which is designed to serve planners in developing countries and international agencies. The clearinghouse responds to requests for information, provides referral services, and welcomes visitors to use its extensive collection of evaluation and research materials about projects using communication media.

5. The Clearinghouse on Development Communication publishes a quarterly newsletter, *Development Communication Report,* which is circulated internally; a series of succint *Project Files;* and a series of *Information Bulletins,* which treat in some depth the application of communications media to major development problems.

L2 American Anthropological Association (AAA)

1. *1703 New Hampshire Avenue, N.W.*
    Washington, D.C. 20009
    232-8800

2. E. J. Lehman, Executive Director

3. The American Anthropological Association is a professional society of anthropologists, students, educators, and others interested in advancing the discipline of anthropology. The AAA also serves as the administrative headquarters for a number of affiliated professional associations and may be of assistance to scholars in establishing contacts with specialists in American universities across the country. The society also sponsors lectures and conferences and maintains a speaker's bureau.

5. In addition to the *Anthropology Newsletter,* the association publishes two quarterly journals, *American Anthropologist* and the *American Ethnologist,* and various special publications. A publications list as well as information about the various journals of affiliated professional associations are available on request.

L3 American Association for the Advancement of Science (AAAS)

1. *1515 Massachusetts Avenue, N.W.*
    Washington, D.C. 20005
    467-4400

2. William D. Carey, Executive Officer

3. The world's largest federation of scientific and engineering societies, the AAAS—in fulfilling its mission of providing a more systematic direction to scientific research and in securing for scientists increased facilities and wider usefulness—recognizes that the applications of science and technology have global consequences. Largely through its Office of International Science (Denise Weiner, Program Associate, 467-5320), AAAS coordinates many activities of an international scope. In preparation for the 1979 U.N. Conference on Science and Technology for Development (UNCSTD), AAAS cosponsored, with the Indian National Science Academy and the Indian Science Congress Association, a major seminar in New Delhi (October 1978) on the Contribution of Science and Technology to National Development. At the time of this writing, the AAAS was also scheduling a global seminar, in December 1980 in New Delhi, on the Role of Scientific and Engineering Societies in Development.

    The AAAS maintains contact with its sister associations in Pakistan, India, Bangladesh, and Sri Lanka, and extends invitations to them to attend its annual meetings in the U.S.A. The AAAS was also represented in 1979 at scientific meetings in India and Sri Lanka. AAAS is now administering a Science, Engineering, and Diplomacy Fellows Program. Fellows receive one year appointments to work in the State Department's Bureau of Oceans and International Environmental and Scientific Affairs. A major goal of the program is more effective utilization of scientific and technical expertise in shaping foreign policy.

5. AAAS publications include a weekly magazine, *Science,* and the monthly newsletter, *The Consortium Notes.* An informative booklet, *American Association for the Advancement of Science* (1980) may be obtained free. Also available free is a list of AAAS publications.

L4 American Association of Museums (AAM)

1. *1055 Thomas Jefferson Street, N.W.*
    Washington, D.C. 20007
    338-5300

2. Lawrence L. Reger, Director

3-5. The AAM is a service organization for museums and museum professionals since 1906. The International Council of Museums Committee (ICMC), of the AAM (Maria I. Papageorge, Coordinator), receives foreign museum personnel, including those from India, Pakistan, Bangladesh, and Sri Lanka.

The council also publishes a quarterly newsletter that lists current international exhibitions across the U.S. Other AAM publications include the bimonthly *Museum News,* and a monthly newsletter, *Aviso.* A list of *Books and Reprints* (1979) is available free.

L5 American Association of University Women (AAUW)

1. *2401 Virginia Avenue, N.W.*
   Washington, D.C. 20037
   785-7700

2. Q. Brown, Executive Director

3. A national organization for the advancement of women, the AAUW is dedicated to promoting understanding and friendship among university women, encouraging international cooperation, furthering the development of education, and encouraging the full application of members' skills to cultural and community affairs. The AAUW's International Foundation Program offers international fellowships for advanced study in the United States for outstanding women in foreign countries. The first such fellowship was awarded to an Indian woman in 1938–39. Currently the AAUW receives fellows from India, Nepal, and Sri Lanka. AAUW is an affiliate of the International Federation of University Women (IFUW) (Geneva, Switzerland). Through the IFUW, the AAUW maintains contact with its sister organizations in India, Pakistan, Bangladesh, and Sri Lanka. The association sponsors the annual AAUW United Nations Seminar and other conferences on issues involving women's interests.

4. The association has a small library and archival collection on women. Nonmembers may visit the collection through prior arrangements.

5. A bimonthly magazine, *Graduate Women,* is circulated to members only. A *Resource Catalog* lists all AAUW current publications and is available free.

L6 American Catholic Historical Association

1. *The Catholic University of America*
   Washington, D.C. 20064
   635-5079

2. Robert Trisco, Secretary

3. The American Catholic Historical Association was established in 1919 to promote a deeper and more widespread knowledge of the history of the Catholic Church in the U.S.A. and abroad. Members include specialists on the Catholic Church in South Asia.

5. The association publishes a quarterly, *Catholic Historical Review,* which occasionally contains reviews of books on South Asian subjects.

L7 American Council on Education

1. *One Dupont Circle*
   Washington, D.C. 20036
   833-4700

2. J. W. Peltason, Director

3. The American Council on Education, which includes among its membership most U.S. colleges, universities, and professional educational organizations, serves as the chief point of contact between U.S. higher education and the U.S. government. The council's Division of International Educational Relations (Becky Owens, Acting Director, 833-4672) fosters improved relations between educational institutions and the federal government and aims at increasing the funding of federal programs for international education. Through its Council for International Exchange of Scholars (see entry M14), the council administers—for the U.S. International Communication Agency, with supervision from the Board of Foreign Scholarships—the senior scholars program under the provisions of the Fulbright Hays Act.

4. The council's small reference library is available for on-site use by educational researchers. This collection of approximately 4,000 volumes is strong in the history of higher education, educational management, and finance.

L8 American Film Institute (AFI)

1. *John F. Kennedy Center for the Performing Arts*
   2700 F Street, N.W.
   Washington, D.C. 20566
   828-4000

2. Jean Firstenberg, Director

3. The AFI is an independent, nonprofit organization established by the National Endowment for the Arts to preserve the heritage and advance the art of film and television in the U.S. The institute preserves and catalogs films; conducts an advanced conservatory for filmmakers; gives assistance to new American filmmakers through grants and internships with major film educators; distributes film books, periodicals, and reference works; supports basic research in motion picture areas; operates a motion-picture theater in the Kennedy Center; and provides assistance to organizations that present film programs across the country. From time to time AFI has screened several South Asian films, including those of the famous Indian producer-director Satyajit Ray.

4. The institute's reference library (828-4088) maintains a collection of some 2,500 books and 270 periodical titles devoted to film and television. The library maintains vertical files on film and film-making in foreign countries. It also maintains a *Theater File* series that deals with information on films shown by the AFI. The library is open from 9:00 A.M. to 5:00 P.M., Monday through Friday. On-site use of the library is possible through prior arrangement.

5. Publications include: *The Education of the Film-Maker: An International View; American Film Institute Catalog of Feature Films in the U.S. 1893–1970;* the monthly *American Film* and *AFI News;* and the *Fact File* series, volume 10 of which focuses on the *Third World Cinema.* A brochure, *The First Ten Years: The American Film Institute, 1967–1977,* is available on request.

L9 American Foreign Service Association (AFSA)

1. *2101 E Street, N.W.*
   Washington, D.C. 20037
   338-4045

2. Robert Beers, Executive Director

3. The American Foreign Service Association is a professional organization of active, U.S. foreign-service officers. It holds an annual meeting each June in Washington.

5. The AFSA publishes the monthly *Foreign Service Journal,* a newsletter, and a directory of retired members.

L10 American Friends Service Committee (AFSC)—Washington Office

1. *1822 R Street, N.W.*
   Washington, D.C. 20009
   232-3196

2. Tartt Bell, Director

3. Headquartered in Philadelphia, the AFSC is a nonprofit Quaker organization that carries on a variety of service, development, reconciliation, and social-change programs in the U.S. and overseas. AFSC has a long history of association with South Asia. Its current relationship is, however, confined to India and Bangladesh. For further information, contact David Elder, American Friend's Service Committee, 1501 Cherry Street, Philadelphia, Pennsylvania 19102 (215/241-7000).

5. South Asian project reports are available in the committee's Philadelphia office.

L11 American Historical Association (AHA)

1. *400 A Street, S.E.*
   Washington, D.C. 20003
   544-2422

2. Mack Thompson, Executive Director

3. The American Historical Association is a nonprofit membership corporation founded in 1884 for the promotion of historical studies, the collection

and preservation of historical manuscripts, and the dissemination of historical research. As the largest historical society in the U.S., the AHA conducts an active scholarly and professional program for historians interested in every period and geographic area. The AHA also rigorously promotes international liaison with historical societies throughout the world, sponsors joint colloquia with foreign historians, and exchanges publications with foreign historical societies. As a part of its commitment to promoting historical research, the AHA publishes a variety of research materials and offers prizes and fellowships to scholars. AHA has also become involved with the status and rights of historians and their grievances. At the AHA's annual meeting, usually several panels are devoted to South Asian themes.

5. The AHA has traditionally undertaken bibliographic projects to promote historical scholarship. One such bibliography is the *Recently Published Articles*, published 3 times a year on the basis of surveys of some 3,000 journals from around the world. It is the most current bibliography of periodical literature available to historians in all fields. The *American Historical Review*, published 5 times a year, includes scholarly articles and critical reviews of current publications in all fields of history. Through its now discontinued Service Center for Teachers of History, the AHA published a series of highly successful pamphlets intended primarily for use by teachers in schools. This pamphlet series includes: *Asian Religions: An Introduction to the Study of Hinduism, Buddhism, Islam, Confucianism and Taoism* (1967); *The History of India: Its Study and Interpretation* (1965); and *The Near and Middle East* (1959). Another Updated pamphlet is *A History of South Asia* (1973). Other AHA publications of interest include: the *AHA Newsletter; Discussions on Teaching; Employment Information Bulletin; Grants and Fellowships of Interest to Historians;* and *Doctoral Dissertations in History.*

L12 American Political Science Association (APSA)

1. *1527 New Hampshire Avenue, N.W.*
    Washington, D.C. 20036
    483-2512

2. Evron Kirkpatrick, Executive Director

3. The APSA is a national professional association of political scientists that seeks to promote and improve the study and teaching of political science. The association endeavors to realize its objectives largely through publications and conferences. APSA annual conferences often include panels or papers on South Asia-related subjects.

5. The APSA offers the following publications of interest: *The American Political Science Review*, a quarterly journal of scholarly articles and book reviews in political science; *PS*, a quarterly journal of association news and articles of professional concern; *APSA Annual Meeting Proceedings; Guide to Graduate Study in Political Science; Research Support for Political Scientists;* and *Global Dimension in U.S. Education.*

L13 American Psychiatric Association (APA)

1. *1700 18th Street, N.W.*
    Washington, D.C. 20006
    797-4900

2. Donald Langsley, President

3. The APA is a professional organization of practicing psychiatrists. Its Council on International Affairs (Alfred M. Freedman, Chairperson) is responsible for dealing with international questions and problems pertaining to psychiatry and mental health, and for planning all international congresses and conferences that APA sponsors or cosponsors. At the recent APA-sponsored Pacific Congress of Psychiatry, held in Manila, The Philippines (May 1980), several papers of interest were presented; e.g.: "Depression in Old Age in India;" "Strategy for Extending Mental Health Care in Rural Population in India;" "Indian Philosophy and Psychiatry;" "Epidemiology of Depression in General Hospitals in India;" and "Personality Types in Ayurveda." Scholars may be able to obtain copies of these and other papers from the association.

5. The *Catalog of Publications* (1979) lists all major APA publications. A 1978 report, *Culturally Relevant Training for Asian Psychiatric Trainees,* focuses on the particular needs and concerns of Asian physicians participating in psychiatric training programs in the United States. The APA also publishes the quarterly *American Journal of Psychiatry,* the biweekly *Psychiatric News,* and the monthly *Hospital and Community Psychiatry.*

L14 American Psychological Association (APA)

1. *1200 17th Street, N.W.*
    Washington, D.C. 20036
    833-7600

2. Michael Pallak, Executive Director

3. A major professional organization of qualified psychologists, the APA aims to advance psychology as a science, as a profession, and as a means of promoting human welfare. APA's Committee on International Relations in Psychology (Fred Spaner, Chairman, 833-7639) maintains contact with South Asian sister associations and provides information on all international conferences and meetings dealing with psychology.

4. APA maintains a small research collection of books and journals on psychology. The library is open to scholars for on-site use by appointment. APA's Psychological Information Services maintains a computerized data base of abstracts that are scanned from periodicals, technical reports, and monographs, world-wide. For further information, call Lois Granick (833-7624).

5. APA publishes some 22 psychological journals, a monthly newsletter, *APA*

Monitor, and the monthly *Psychological Abstracts,* which compiles non-critical summaries of the world's scientific literature in psychology and related disciplines. Abstracts accumulated since 1967 are also available on magnetic tape for search and retrieval purposes.

L15 American Public Health Association (APHA)

1. *1015 15th Street, N.W.*
    Washington, D.C. 20005
    789-5600

2. William H. McBeath, Executive Director

3. A professional organization of health-care specialists and others interested in the field of community health, the APHA has more recently expanded its expertise to assist developing nations of the world in the evolvement of sound programs for delivering health services. Currently, APHA interest extends to 60 developing countries including India, Bangladesh, Nepal, and Sri Lanka. APHA technical assistance and consultative services in South Asia include the areas of nutrition, rural health, family planning, and re-hydration. At the invitation of the national governments, health programs in many developing countries are intensively studied by teams of APHA experts, who evaluate activities and advise on program methods and priorities. APHA assists educational institutions to improve their curricula for teaching health and family planning techniques and program methodology. For further information, contact Technical Advisory Services International Health Programs (Suzanne Olds, Chief, 789-5691). The APHA serves as the executive secretariat for the World Federation of Public Health Associations (WFPHA), of which India, Pakistan, and Bangladesh are members. The third international congress of WFPHA was scheduled, at the time of this writing, to be held in Calcutta in February 1981.

4-5. The APHA Resource Center (Sally Coughlin, Director, 789-5710) maintains a vertical file of miscellaneous materials on health care delivery systems of different countries of the world. The center is open to the public from 8:30 A.M. to 5:00 P.M., weekdays.

    A list of *Publications of the American Public Health Association* is available free upon request. *Salubritas,* a quarterly newsletter dealing with problems of basic health services in the developing world, is distributed free to persons or institutions involved in the delivery or support of public health services in developing countries. Other publications of interest are the monthly *American Journal of Public Health* and the quarterly *Mothers and Children; The State of the Art of Delivering Low Cost Health Services in Developing Countries* (1971); and *Health Care Financing in Developing Countries* (1979). The APHA *Health Project Capsule* series includes Bangladesh: Ganaseva Kendra Program; India: Gandhi Gram Institute, Indo-Dutch Project for Child Welfare, Maharastra Arogya Mandal, and the Mitraniketan Project; and Nepal: Shanta Bhawan Hospital.

L16 American Society for Public Administration (ASPA)

1. *1225 Connecticut Avenue, N.W.*
   Washington, D.C. 20036
   785-3255

2. Keith Mulrooney, Exeuctive Director

3. The ASPA is a nationwide, nonprofit educational and professional organization dedicated to improved management in public service through exchange, development, and dissemination of information about public administration. The ASPA program includes publications, conferences, education, research, and various special services, all aimed at improved understanding and strengthened administration of public service.

   Within the general framework of ASPA goals, the Section on International and Comparative Administration (SICA) (Dona Wolf, Chairperson, 357-1100) seeks to improve the understanding of the "science, processes, and art" of public administration by bringing an international and comparative perspective into the discourse regarding public administration problems and issues. SICA especially seeks to conduct programs, activities, research, and study in the areas of international, comparative public administration, and to make the functions and research results available to interested ASPA members. The targets of concern include the structure, processes, and outcome of public policy-making and implementation in different economic, political, social, and cultural settings. Within SICA, separate Committees on Asia, International Organizations, and International Professional Exchanges may assist researchers interested in South Asian studies.

5. An *ASPA Publications Price List* is available on request. Of particular interest is the *SICA Newsletter* and the series of *Occasional Papers.* ASPA also publishes a bimonthly journal, *Public Administration Review,* and a biweekly newspaper, *Public Administration Times.*

L17 American Society of International Law (ASIL)

1. *2223 Massachusetts Avenue, N.W.*
   Washington, D.C. 20008
   265-4313

2. Seymour J. Rubin, Executive Director

3. A professional association with membership in some 100 countries, the ASIL is devoted to fostering the study of international law and promoting international relations based on law and justice. Among the many subjects recently dealt with in the society's Research and Study programs are international terrorism; a number of issues in the field of international human rights; the U.S. Constitution and the conduct of foreign policy; international trade institutions; ocean law and management; comparative national treaty law and practice; management of international river basins; the law of state responsibility; and various international environmental problems.

The society has undertaken extensive in-house research on international regulation of activities of a high scientific or technological content, covering such diverse fields as food standards, trade in pharmaceuticals or pesticides, and earth resource satellites, and has recently extended this work into an assessment of the effectiveness of certain United Nations programs. The society also holds ad hoc meetings and conferences of experts in the United States and elsewhere, to examine specific problems of current interest. For further information contact the society's Director of Studies (John Lawrence Hargrove, 265-4313).

4.   The society's library (Helen Philos, Librarian) contains over 22,000 items. It is a collection of treatises and other books, documents, briefs, pamphlets, and periodicals both foreign and domestic, on all aspects of public international law. The library includes basic reference works plus specialized materials, not easily obtainable elsewhere. The library is open to the public from 9:00 A.M. to 5:00 P.M., weekdays, on the basis of a prior appointment. Interlibrary loan and photoduplication services are available.

5.   Publications of the society include: *The American Journal of International Law* (quarterly); the *Proceedings* of the society's annual meeting, which contain discussions by leading authorities on important topics of international concern; the bimonthly *International Legal Materials,* which reproduces current treaties and agreements, legislation and regulations of states, judicial and arbitral decisions, official reports, and resolutions of international organizations; *Occasional Papers* series covering subjects of great variety and interest in transnational legal policy; and the *ASIL Newsletter,* which reports, among other topics, on pending international litigation, and other newsworthy developments in the world of international law. A descriptive brochure, *The American Society of International Law,* is available free.

L18 American Sociological Association (ASA)

1.   *1722 N Street, N.W.*
       Washington, D.C. 20036
       833-3410

2.   Russell Dynes, Executive Officer

3.   A national association of sociologists and professional social workers, the ASA was established in 1905 to further research and teaching in sociology. South Asian scholars may contact the ASA Committee on World Sociology for establishing scholarly contacts.

5.   ASA publications include: *American Sociological Review* (bimonthly); *The American Sociologist* (quarterly); *Sociology of Education* (quarterly); the *Journal of Health and Social Behavior* (quarterly); *ASA Footnotes* (nine issues per year); *Sociological Methodology* (annual); and *Guide to Graduate Departments in Sociology.*

L19 Amnesty International U.S.A.—Washington Office

1. *705 G Street, S.W.*
   Washington, D.C. 20003
   544-0200

2. Patricia L. Rengel, Director

3. Amnesty International (AI) is a world-wide human rights movement which works impartially for the release of prisoners of conscience, men and women detained everywhere for their beliefs, color, ethnic origin, sex, religion or language, provided they have neither used nor advocated violence. Independent of all governments, political factions, ideologies, economic interests, and religious creeds, AI opposes torture and the death penalty in all cases without reservation, and advocates fair and prompt trials for all political prisoners. Recipient of the 1977 Nobel Prize for Peace, the organization has a consultative status with the United Nations. AI's International Secretariat, based in London, pursues news of arrests, carefully investigates cases of prisoners, and follows the political and legal activities in over 100 countries of every political persuasion. The AI also sends fact-finding missions to countries where human rights are believed to have been violated. In recent years, the Amnesty International has been active in evaluating the human-rights status of prisoners in Bangladesh, Sri Lanka, Nepal, India, and Pakistan.

5. The AI publishes the annual *Amnesty International Report,* which surveys human-rights violations throughout the world. Background briefing papers on individual countries include Bangladesh (1977) and Pakistan (1976, 1978). The AI also publishes a monthly newsletter, *Amnesty Action,* and a quarterly bulletin, *Matchbox.* A publication list and a descriptive brochure are available upon request.

L20 Arms Control Association

1. *11 Dupont Circle, N.W.*
   Washington, D.C. 20036
   797-6450

2. William H. Kincade, Executive Director

3. The Arms Control Association is a nonpartisan, membership organization formed in 1971 by a group of concerned individuals to promote understanding of arms control and its contribution to national security.

4. The association's Research and Information Service contains books, periodical literature, and newspaper clippings on international arms control and related subjects including South Asia. The service answers requests for documentation information, consultation, referral, and other research assistance.

5. The association publishes *Arms Control Today,* which occasionally includes materials on South Asia and contains current bibliographies on South Asian

regional security issues. In addition, the association participates in or sponsors the publication of a variety of arms-control materials, such as topical bibliographies and the annual *World Military and Social Expenditures.*

L21 Asia Society—Washington Center

1. *1785 Massachusetts Avenue, N.W.*
    Washington, D.C. 20036
    387-6500

2. Robert B. Oxnam, Vice President and Director

3. A regional branch of the New York-based, nonpolitical, educational organization, the Asia Society provides a forum for diverse views of the countries of East, Southeast, and South Asia, their cultural traditions, contemporary affairs, and relations with the U.S. The center's programs and services include: public lectures and films for general audiences; thematic seminars and topical briefings for more specialized audiences; and small meetings where Asians and Americans can share information and views. In June 1980 the center sponsored a conference—in collaboration with the Middle East Institute and the National Committee to Honor the Fourteenth Centennial of Islam—on the world of Islam, which included various topics related to Islam in South Asia.

4. A small reading room of books and periodicals is available to Asia Society members for reference purposes.

5. A free monthly calendar of events, *Asia in Washington,* lists Washington Center programs and many other Asia-related events and activities in the Washington area. The center is currently compiling a guide to Asia resources in the greater Washington area.

L22 Asian-American Free Labor Institute (AAFLI)

1. *AFL-CIO Building, Suite 406*
    1125 15th Street, N.W.
    Washington, D.C. 20005
    737-3000

2. Morris Paladino, Executive Director

3. The AAFLI was established in 1968 by the American Federation of Labor and Congress of Industrial Organizations (AFL-CIO) to encourage and advance the development of strong, independent trade unions throughout Asia. Educational, social, and impact programs, designed to serve the needs of Asian workers, are administered by the institute in 16 countries including India, Pakistan, Bangladesh, and Sri Lanka. As of 1979, AAFLI had provided basic and special training to more than 5,000 trade-union leaders and officials in South Asia. In addition, the AAFLI, through its special projects, provided modest assistance in the form of medical equipment, office equipment, clothing, construction of union offices, printing and distributing of cooperative educational materials, and food and shelter relief. AAFLI works

very closely with the unions and governments of host countries; its program is developed only after aid has been requested. AAFLI also gives grants to Asian trade unionists for study abroad as part of program development in their countries. Recipients who are nominated by their unions receive grants to study and work with labor organizations in the United States. They also attend labor courses at Harvard University or the University Center for Cooperatives at the University of Wisconsin.

5.   In connection with its varied activities in the education field, the institute has produced some 50 pamphlets, manuals, books, and other published material for use in its own programs as well as in those of the unions with which it cooperates. These materials have appeared in several Asian languages including Bengali. Among the institute's publications, the following two publications may be of special interest: *Building Unions in Asia—A Unique Task;* and *Asia: A Study in Emerging Unions.* The institute also publishes the monthly *AAFLI News,* which includes reports on projects and activities supported by the institute. The institute's annual *Progress Report* provides a brief summary of its activities in South Asian countries.

L23 Asian Benevolent Corporation (ABC)

1.   *2142 F Street, N.W.*
Washington, D.C. 20037
331-0129

2.   Rita O'Donnell, Vice President

3.   ABC is a public, nonprofit organization devoted to the promotion of the arts in the Asian community in the metropolitan Washington area. It maintains a regular gallery of Amerasian art, organizes exhibitions, educational workshops, and seminars on different cultural topics, and holds demonstration classes on various techniques of art. South Asia-related subjects have been occasionally featured in the corporation's program.

L24 Association for Childhood Education International (ACEI)

1.   *3615 Wisconsin Avenue, N.W.*
Washington, D.C. 20016
363-6963

2.   Elvie Lou Luetge, Executive Director

3.   ACEI is a nonprofit membership organization of those concerned with promoting the welfare of children from infancy to early adolescence. The association maintains an international Childhood Education Center to which leading educators, foreign visitors, members, and others come for meetings, research, exhibits, and personal interchange. Currently, the association has 350 affiliates including 10 foreign affiliates.

5.   An *ACEI Publications* list is available free. *Children and International Education* (1974) is a kit of 3 booklets developing appreciation for cultural diversity and for sensitizing teachers to ethnicity. Also available is a 1972

portfolio of 10 leaflets on ways of developing international understanding and fellowship in children and those who work with them. ACEI's educational journal, *Childhood Education,* contains occasional features and information about children's books on South Asia.

L25 Association of American Colleges (AAC)

1. *1818 R Street, N.W.*
   Washington, D.C. 20009
   387-3760

2. Mark H. Curtis, President

3. Established in 1915, the AAC is committed to improving quality in higher education by enhancing and promoting humane and liberating learning. The association is sponsoring the AAC National Assembly on Foreign Language and International Studies (1980), the aim of which is to assist colleges and universities in finding ways to overcome current weaknesses in academic programs in foreign language and international studies. The association has also scheduled a follow-up National Conference in 1981.

4. In addition to several newsletters and magazines, the association's publications include *Asian Studies in Liberal Arts Colleges* (1961), and *Asian Studies in Liberal Education* (1959).

L26 Association of American Geographers (AAG)

1. *1710 16th Street, N.W.*
   Washington, D.C. 20009
   234-1450

2. Patricia McWethy, Executive Director

3. AAG is the national professional association of geographers. The association may be helpful to South Asianists in establishing contacts with specialists in academic as well as nonacademic persuasions. AAG provides small grants to members for research and field work. At the annual meeting of the Association, several South Asia-related panels or papers are often presented.

5. AAG publications include 2 quarterly journals, the *Annals* and the *Professional Geographer;* the *AAG Newsletter;* an annual *Guide to Graduate Departments of Geography in the United States and Canada;* and the *Proceedings* of the annual-meeting papers. Other publications of interest are maps of the *Kingdom of Sikkim, The Underdevelopment and Modernization of the Third World, The Geography of the Third World, The Geography of International Tourism,* and *Triumph or Triage? The World Food Problem in Geographical Perspective.*

L27 Association of Former Intelligence Officers (AFIO)

1. *6723 Whittier Avenue*
    McLean, Virginia 22101
    790-0320

2. John F. Blake, President

3. The AFIO is a private, nonpartisan and nonprofit organization, founded in 1975 by the intelligence professionals concerned with the future of the U.S. intelligence community in the wake of revelations and allegations emanating from the media, Congress, and other sources. Serving as a clearinghouse for the media, the AFIO has been invited to testify before committees of the Congress; its representatives have also appeared as individual witnesses. The AFIO monitors media reporting on intelligence matters and seeks to include its own input. The association assists authors and scholars by providing assistance from the AFIO and its members in preparing books and monographs on matters related to intelligence. The AFIO may assist scholars in contacting former U.S. intelligence officers knowledgeable about South Asian affairs.

4. AFIO is endeavoring to develop a library of works on national security matters for use by AFIO members and legitimate researchers. The collection is open to the public.

5. A periodic publication with limited circulation, *Periscope,* provides news of association activities and useful information on intelligence matters. The association also publishes a membership directory which is not released to nonmembers.

L28 Association on Third World Affairs (ATWA)

1. *2011 Kalorama Road, N.W.*
    Washington, D.C. 20009
    265-7929

2. Lorna Hahn, Executive Director

3. A membership organization established in 1961, the ATWA is composed of educators, lawyers, diplomats, and others who share a common interest in promoting cooperation between Americans and the peoples of developing countries. The organization sponsors ad hoc lectures and panel discussions on subjects of current interest, with guest speakers, at various sites throughout Washington, including foreign embassies.

5. The association publishes a bimonthly newsletter, *Third World Forum,* which often contains materials of interest on South Asia; and a series of occasional papers focusing on current issues.

L29 Center of Concern

1.　*3700 13th Street, N.E.*
Washington, D.C. 20017
635-2757

2.　Peter J. Henriot, Director

3.　In response to an invitation of the United States Catholic Bishops to the International Jesuit Order, the Center of Concern was opened in 1971 as an independent, interdisciplinary team with outreach into the policy-making, religious, and civic communities in the United States and overseas. The center collaborates with a network of social-action and reflection centers in the United States and throughout the world. Holding consultative status with the Economic and Social Council of the United Nations, the center has participated in many international conferences on population, food, women, trade and development, housing, employment, and technology. It also cooperates with the International Labor Organization (ILO) and seeks to build links with international trade-union structures.

　　The Center of Concern also serves as the secretariat of the Interreligious Peace Colloquium (IRPC), a nonprofit, educational, charitable, and religious body incorporated in 1976 to bring together members of the major faiths—Muslims, Jews, Christians, Hindus, and Buddhists—who are policy and decision makers on transnational issues in the fields of politics, economics, media, and education. The colloquium sponsored a symposium on Changing World Economic Order: Challenge to the Five World Faiths (Lisbon, 1977), which was participated in by delegates from Pakistan and Sri Lanka, among others. The IRPC's goal is to establish interfaith groups for peace and justice in different locations in South Asia.

5.　In addition to IRPC occasional papers, such as *Food/Energy and Major Faiths* (1978), which is principally a report and interpretation of the IRPC meeting held in Bellagio, Italy, on "Food Energy Crisis: Challenge to the Five World Faiths;" and the *World Faiths and the New World Order* (1977), which is a summary of papers and discussion notes of IRPC's second conference held in Lisbon in 1977; the center publishes a free bimonthly newsletter *Center Focus*. This newsletter analyzes issues and events such as: current UN conferences, church response to justice issues, the directions of the national and international women's movement, human-rights struggle, population and food, labor and unemployment, and the trade and debt problems of poor countries.

L30 Chamber of Commerce of the United States—International Division

1.　*1615 H Street, N.W.*
Washington, D.C. 20062
659-6111

2.　John L. Caldwell, Vice President, International Division

3.   The world's largest volunteer business federation, the Chamber of Commerce of the United States seeks, through its policies and programs, to advance human progress, private initiative, and international interdependence. In this context, the chamber's International Division works to achieve a freer international flow of goods, services, capital technology, and people. While the division's International Economic Policy Section develops the chamber's positions on all aspects of international economic policy, the International Economic Affairs Section develops and conducts the foreign relations of the national chamber.

In view of India's urgent need for increased employment and income, which could be generated by expanded trade with and investment from the U.S., and considering India's potential as a commercial partner of the U.S., an India-U.S. Business Council was established in 1976, at the request of the two governments, to enable Indian and American business decision-makers to conduct a continuing dialog on bilateral economic relations. Since its inception, the council has sought to stimulate a constructive discussion on Indian-American commercial and economic policy issues, and recommendations on a variety of subjects have been developed for consideration by the appropriate government authorities. In addition, the council has sponsored research and information programs designed to better equip the members of each business community to understand the factors that shape the other country's commercial environment and to assist in identifying and developing specific trade and investment opportunities. For further information, contact council Executive Secretary John G. Sarpa (659-3057).

5.   The International Division publishes the *International Report,* a monthly newsletter; *Trade Negotiation Information Service,* a periodic bulletin; *Foreign Commerce Handbook; International Digest; Guide to Foreign Information Sources;* and *Foreign Investment in the Third World: A Comparative Study of Selected Developing Country Investment Promotion Programs.*

L31 Coordination Council for International Issues (CCII)

1.   *1900 L Street, N.W.*
      Washington, D.C. 20036
      659-9388

2.   B. Coleman, President

3-5. A nonprofit institute established in 1977, the CCII is a minority-controlled organization engaged in research, program evaluation, and development-project implementation and design. The council's goal is to foster links between developing and developed countries, and to promote the human quality of development. The CCII provides speakers on a wide range of topics, and its staff has developed position papers on technology exchange and health-care in developing countries.

In January 1980, the CCII organized a colloquium in Colombo, in collaboration with experts from South Asia, to review the general problems and policy implications of economic development and the promotion of human rights. Recently the CCII staff efforts resulted in the creation of a private human-rights organization, the South Asia Committee on Human Rights Development. This new organization has members from Bangladesh,

India, Nepal, Pakistan, and Sri Lanka. CCII staff has completed a study for AID on the implications of the Foreign Assistance Act of 1961 as amended for AID's Office of Evaluation and Studies. *The Interim CCII Report on the South Asian Colloquium on Human Rights and Development* (1980) is available on request.

L32 Council for International Urban Liaison (CIUL)

1. *818 18th Street, N.W.*
   Washington, D.C. 20006
   223-1434

2. John Garvey, President

3. The CIUL serves as a clearinghouse for information on coping with problems common to urban areas throughout the world. The council monitors developments abroad and reports on them to its member organizations in the United States and Canada. It follows innovations in urban conservation, transportation, finance, planning, and waste management. The council's collection of documents and vertical files may be examined by scholars obtaining prior appointments.

5. CIUL publications include *Urban Innovation Abroad; Urban Transit Abroad;* the *Urban Edge;* and various international *Urban Reports. Urban Edge* features many informative articles on South Asia.

L33 Diplomatic and Consular Officers Retired (DACOR)

1. *1718 H Street, N.W.*
   Washington, D.C. 20006
   298-7848

2. Theodore J. Hadraba, Executive Director

3. DACOR is a membership association of retired foreign-service officers, former ambassadors, and other officials involved in the field of foreign affairs. The organization can be of assistance to scholars interested in contacting former U.S. diplomats in South Asia.

5. The association publishes a monthly newsletter, the *DACOR Bulletin.*

L34 Foreign Policy Association (FPA)—Washington Office

1. *1800 K Street, N.W.*
   Washington, D.C. 20006
   833-2030

2. M. Jon Vondracek, Coordinator

3. Founded in 1918, the New York-based FPA is a private, nonprofit, non-partisan organization the purpose of which is to develop an informed,

thoughtful, and articulate public opinion on international affairs. The association provides educational and informational materials and sponsors meetings designed to increase the interest and knowledge of Americans on foreign-policy issues. The FPA annually conducts approximately 30 seminars and major events and provides its podium for outstanding speakers at meetings that are open to all interested individuals. The FPA prepares reprints of key addresses which are available to interested citizens and organizations. Through its Great Decisions public-opinion survey, FPA solicits and disseminates public views on major international questions each year.

5.   In addition to the *Great Decisions* program book, FPA publishes an annual series of five short topical publications called *Headline Series. Understanding India* (1973), by Phillips Talbot, is such a series publication. Every 4 years, FPA also produces *Foreign Policy Briefs* kits—with briefing cards on current world problems—which are extensively used by voter groups and political candidates. Final reports on Great Decision opinion ballots are circulated through a bulletin, the *Outreacher*.

L35 Foreign Policy Discussion Group

1.   *815 Connecticut Avenue, N.W.*
      Washington, D.C. 20006
      298-8290

2.   Charles T. Mayer, President

3.   A small membership organization of government officials, academicians, and attornies, the group holds monthly meetings featuring distinguished speakers from the realm of foreign policy. Meetings are off the record and closed to nonmembers.

L36 Gandhi Memorial Center

1.   *4748 Western Avenue, N.W.*
      Washington, D.C. 20016
      229-3871

2.   Srimati Kamala, Director

3.   An independent, nonprofit, cultural and educational organization, the Gandhi Memorial Center was founded in 1959 by Swami Premananda of India. The purpose of the center is to disseminate the philosophy, ideal, life, service, and teachings of Mahatma Gandhi as well as the cultural heritage of India. The center sponsors lectures, symposiums, and other educational and cultural programs. Classes are also offered in Indian classical dance and music. A biographical documentary film on the life and mission of Gandhi, produced by Vithal Bhai Jhaveri in 14 parts, totaling 6 hours, may be viewed at the center.

4.   The center's Mahatma Gandhi Memorial Library is open to the public for on-site use and to the members as a lending library on Friday and Saturday

from 10:00 A.M. to 4:00 P.M. The library is closed during the month of July. Special hours for educational groups may be arranged through the director. This collection of over 2,000 volumes, magazines, and pamphlets, which focuses on the life and works of Gandhi, seeks to offer a broad representation of authors and materials from many cultures and times. In addition to being a depository of the works of Mahatma Gandhi, the library also aims at collecting all the publications of the Bharatiya Vidhya Bhavan (Bombay).

5.   The center announces its program and activities through its newsletter, *The Gandhi Message.*

L37   Indo-U.S. Subcommission on Education and Culture—American Secretariat—Washington Office

1.   *The Asia Society*
     1785 Massachusetts Avenue, N.W.
     Washington, D.C. 20036
     387-6500

2.   Lora Redford, Consultant

3.   To promote contacts between India and the U.S., the governments of the two countries created in 1974 the Indo-U.S. Joint Commission on Economic, Commercial, Scientific, Technological, Educational and Cultural Cooperation. To deal with specific issues and fields of cooperation, 3 subcommissions were formed: Education and Culture; Science and Technology; and Economics and Commerce. Subsequently, a Subcommission on Agriculture was added in 1980.
     Within the broad context of the original agreement signed by the U.S. Secretary of State and the Indian Minister for External Affairs, the Subcommission on Education and Culture was instructed to review and recommend programs, plans, and priorities for cooperative efforts to facilitate the interchange of people, materials, and ideas in the broad fields of education, scholarship, and such areas of cultural endeavor as performing arts, fine arts, libraries and museums, sports and mass communications. To implement these goals, the subcommission has established the following Indo-American Fellowship Programs: A Museum Committee, a Joint Committee on Films and Broadcasting, and a Joint Seminar Program. In all its activities, the subcommission seeks to implement its goal of strengthening the patterns of human communication between India and the United States to improve the climate for cooperation amidst conditions of growing interdependence.
     The main office of the American Secretariat of the Subcommission is located at the Asia Society, New York (112 East 64th Street, New York, New York 10021, 212/751-3210). The Indian Secretariat is located in New Delhi, at the Indian Council for Cultural Affairs.

L38 Institute of Public Administration (IPA)

1. *1717 Massachusetts Avenue, N.W.*
    Washington, D.C. 20036
    667-6551

2. Lyle C. Fitch, President

3. The Institute of Public Administration is a nonprofit educational, research, and consultative organization founded in 1906 for the promotion of good government. Its head office is located in New York, but its Washington Office is the operational base for the great majority of the institute's overseas activities. Since the opening of an International Division in 1961, the institute has greatly expanded its activities in public-management training, and research and advisory services in urban development. The IPA's international operations have by now embraced India, Pakistan, and Bangladesh. From 1961 to 1965, the IPA provided assistance to the Calcutta Metropolitan Planning Organization in preparing a development plan and strategies for the Calcutta Metropolitan Region. This Calcutta project concentrated on economic, governmental, and social studies, and on training Indian personnel in techniques of urban analysis. Currently, the institute is involved in a preinvestment study for a Public Administration Training and Management Improvement Project in Bangladesh. Between 1961 and 1979, the institute employed over 180 specialists on 15 major overseas projects.

L39 International Association of Chiefs of Police (IACP)

1. *11 Firstfield Road*
    Gaithersburg, Maryland 20760
    (301) 948-0922

2. Norman Darwick, Executive Director

3. IACP is the world's leading association of police executives representing more than 63 nations of the world including India. Since its inception in 1893, IACP maintains as a primary objective the professionalization of the police service in all parts of the world.
    In 1955, IACP created a Training Division for police officers for the International Cooperation Administration (now the Agency for International Development). The culmination of that effort was the creation of the International Police Academy in Washington (now closed), from which police and intelligence officers from Pakistan and Bangladesh received specialized training.

4. IACP maintains an extensive research library of law enforcement materials for use by members, scholars, journalists, and others who need research assistance in police problems.

5. IACP publications include a monthly, *The Police Chief,* a quarterly, *The*

Journal of Police Science and Administration, and the *Police Yearbook,* which contains the proceedings of the annual conference of the association.

L40 International Hajji Baba Society

1. *7404 Valley Crest Boulevard*
    Annandale, Virginia 22003
    (703) 560-3765

2. H. McCoy Jones, President

3. Founded in 1965, the International Hajji Baba Society is a cultural association the members of which share a common interest in oriental rugs, including those from Afghanistan, Pakistan, and India. The society holds monthly meetings, between September and May, which feature guest speakers addressing topics related to the history, art, manufacture, and cultural significance of oriental carpets and tapestries. Guests of members may attend meetings and membership is open to all interested persons. Lectures are often illustrated.

5. The society's monthly newsletter is distributed to the members of the society. Discounts for the purchase of selected books on oriental rugs are available to members.

L41 International Religious Liberty Association (IRLA)

1. *6840 Eastern Avenue, N.W.*
    Washington, D.C. 20012
    723-0800

2. B. B. Beach, Secretary General

3. The objectives of the IRLA are to disseminate the principles of religious liberty throughout the world and to defend and safeguard, by all legitimate means and agencies, the right of all men to worship or not to worship as each shall individually choose. IRLA, together with the Geneva-based par la Defense de la Liberté Religieuse, sponsored in 1977 the First World Congress on Religious Liberty held in Amsterdam. A second congress is planned for 1981.

4. The IRLA maintains a small library of books and other materials pertaining to its mission. Its journal collection includes *Conscience et Liberté,* which includes many articles on Islam.

5. A bimonthly magazine, *Liberty,* is published by the Seventh Day Adventists, and the Religious Liberty Association of America, the latter of which is an affiliate of the IRLA. It occasionally carries articles of interest on South Asia.

L42 International Road Federation (IRF)

1. *Washington Building*
   15th Street and New York Avenue, N.W.
   Washington, D.C. 20005
   783-6722

2. W. Gerald Wilson, President

3. Established in 1948, the IRF has developed into an impressive international federation consisting of some 66 foreign national associates, including the Indian Roads and Transport Development Association (Bombay) and the Sri Lanka Road and Transport Federation (Colombo). The federation's purpose is to be of service to the people responsible for planning, building, maintaining, managing, and otherwise benefiting from using the world's roads and road systems; and to create understanding of the social and economic benefits provided by good roads. IRF also acts to bring together and to serve as a link between those who have need of and those who can provide expertise. The IRF Fellowship Program for graduate engineers from abroad, which began in 1948, is tailored to the special transport problems and requirements of the countries of the participating fellows. IRF fellowships have been awarded to engineers from India, Pakistan, Bangladesh, Sri Lanka, and Nepal. An *IRF Fellowship Directory* was published in 1978.

5. Each year IRF publishes the *World Survey of Current Research and Development on Roads and Roads Transport.* It is an extensive inventory of highway research and development activities in 77 countries, including India, Pakistan, and Sri Lanka. IRF also publishes a monthly newsletter, *IRF World Highways: the Road and Motor Vehicle Statistics,* which includes data on the number of automobiles, trucks and buses, motorcycles, highway milage, and estimated highway expenditures for the countries of Afghanistan, Pakistan, India, and Sri Lanka. *Limits of Motor Vehicle Sizes and Weights* also covers most countries of South Asia. The annual *Staff Reports* contain much useful information concerning South Asia.

L43 Islamic Center

1. *2551 Massachusetts Avenue, N.W.*
   Washington, D.C. 20008
   332-3451

2. Muhammad Abul Rauf, Director

3. Founded in 1949 and governed by a board composed of 35 Chiefs of Missions from countries with predominately Muslim populations, the Islamic Center is a place of worship for the Muslim community as well as a cultural institution for the dissemination of information on Islam, its history, and culture. It also seeks to enlighten American public-opinion on Islamic countries and peoples and to promote friendly relations between the Muslim world and the Americas. In order to foster greater interest in and understanding of

Islam, the center sponsors a number of programs and activities including lectures, symposia, film presentations, and Arabic language classes. The Islamic Center is also one of the principal sponsors of the National Committee to Honor the Fourteenth Centennial of Islam, a presidentially mandated organization devoting its efforts, over the 1980–1982 period, to promoting an American awareness and knowledge of the world of Islam.

4. The center maintains a small library of some 4,600 titles of standard works on Islam and important commentaries on Islamic law, history, philosophy, traditions, and bibliographies. This predominately Arabic collection contains some 250 books in Urdu. Numerous copies of the *Qur'ān*, including a number of old copies, are available in the library. The library also receives vernacular newspapers from the embassies of the Muslim countries in Washington. The library is open daily from 10:00 A.M. to 4:00 P.M. for on-site use only.

5. A *Bulletin of the Islamic Center* appears twice a year. The center also distributes English and Arabic editions of the *Qur'ān* and a number of titles on *al-Hadith,* the life of the Prophet Muhammad, Islamic beliefs and practices, law and society, and other educational materials.

Note: Also see entry N9.

L44 Members of Congress for Peace Through Law (MCPL)

1. *3523 House Annex 2*
   Washington, D.C. 20515
   225-8550

2. Edith B. Wilkie, Executive Director

3. This bipartisan organization, composed of the members of Congress, promotes and supports legislation to encourage the achievement of world peace through law. It also serves as a catalyst among the ideas, institutions, organizations, and individuals that have impact on international peace. MCPL staff monitors legislation, and organizes meetings and discussions on legislative measures pertaining to defense and foreign policy bearing on the international peace issues. A monthly speakers series presents eminent speakers discussing significant current issues. South Asia-related subjects have been mooted from time to time.

5. MCPL issues the occasional *Fact Sheets* on topics of current interest with legislative implications.

L45 Middle East Institute (MEI)

1. *1761 N Street, N.W.*
   Washington, D.C. 20036
   785-1141

2. L. Dean Brown, President

3. A publicly supported educational institution founded in 1946, the MEI seeks

to promote better understanding between the peoples of the Middle East and the United States. In addition to the annual conference, the institute also provides a variety of public services in the form of panels, lectures, conferences, and seminars. Because of its interest in Islam and developments in Afghanistan and Pakistan, the MEI is a potential research resource for South Asian scholars. The institute cosponsored, with the National Committee to Honor the Fourteenth Centennial of Islam, a conference held in 1980 on the world of Islam, which included several panels and papers of interest to South Asianists.

4. For the institute's library, see entry A25. The institute's Film Library is described in entry F9.

5. The institute publishes the *Middle East Journal,* which includes recent bibliographies on Pakistan and Afghanistan and a chronology of events in those countries. Other publications include several monographs, indexes, occasional *Problem Papers,* summaries of the institute's annual conferences, and a monthly newsletter.

Note: Also see entry P15.

L46 Muslim Women's Association

1. *Islamic Center*
   2551 Massachusetts Avenue, N.W.
   Washington, D.C. 20008
   332-3451

2. Nouha Alhegelan, President
   265-2068

3. The Muslim Women's Association, founded in 1960 under the auspices of the Islamic Center, is an independent, nonpolitical organization of Muslim women drawn from the local community and the diplomatic corps. The objective of the association is to promote cultural, educational, and social activities and services for the Muslim community and to cooperate with other women's groups. The association organizes monthly meetings, bazaars, and occasional panel presentations on aspects of Islamic culture and status of women in Islamic countries.

5. A brief mimeographed history of the association prepared by Sevine Carlson is available upon request.

L47 National Academy of Sciences (NAS)

1. *2101 Constitution Avenue, N.W.*
   Washington, D.C. 20418
   393-8100

2. Philip Handler, President

3. The NAS is a private, nonprofit organization of scientists and engineers dedicated to the furtherance of science and its use for the general welfare.

Upon request, the NAS, through its operating arm, the National Research Council (NRC), serves as the official adviser to the federal government on matters of science and technology. The Board on Science and Technology for International Development (BOSTID), a division of the NRC's Commission on International Relations, is responsible for programs in developing countries. NAS activities in South Asia include:

India: a 1970 workshop in collaboration with the Indian National Science Academy (INSA) on management and organization of industrial research; a 1971 workshop on water in man's life; a 1974 workshop in collaboration with the U.S. Pugwash Committee and Indian Pugwash Committee to discuss future possible areas for Indo-U.S. scientific and technical cooperation; and a 1979 workshop on post-harvest food technology.

Pakistan: a 1976 workshop jointly sponsored with the Pakistan Science Foundation on science and technology planning in the sectoral areas of food, agriculture, water resources, energy, health, industries, minerals, urban planning, environment, transport, telecommunications, and scientific support services.

Sri Lanka: a 1975 workshop on natural product developments; and a 1980 workshop on post-harvest food losses.

Currently, conversations with authorities in Bangladesh are in progress. Furthermore, the Committee on Population and Demography within the NSC Assembly of Social and Behavioral Sciences has three separate study panels on fertility and mortality in Pakistan, India and Bangladesh. While the studies on Bangladesh and India are expected to be published soon, the one on Pakistan is still in a preliminary stage. NAS also receives frequent visitors from South Asia on an informal basis.

4. BOSTID maintains a working library of resource materials related to scientific and technological aspects of economic development.

5. The Fellowship Office of the NSC's Commission on Human Resources has prepared 2 useful booklets: *A Selected List of Major Fellowship Opportunities and Aids to Advanced Education for United States' Citizens,* and *A Selected List of Major Fellowship Opportunities and Aids to Advanced Education for Foreign Nationals.* A list of NAS publications is available on request.

L48 National Association for Foreign Students Affairs (NAFSA)

1. *1860 19th Street, N.W.*
    Washington, D.C. 20009
    462-4811

2. Hugh M. Jenkins, Executive Vice President

3. NAFSA was founded in 1948 with the cooperation of academic institutions and government and private agencies to develop the knowledge and competence of persons concerned with international education. Its goal is the most effective operation of international educational interchange in an effort to assure maximum benefits for individuals, institutions, and society. To achieve these ends, NAFSA provides professional training and information through national and regional conferences, workshops, publications,

and consultations. It also maintains communication with governmental agencies and with public and private organizations, both domestic and foreign; and supports research and development projects.

4.   The association's small collection of books on international student affairs are available to researchers by prior arrangement.

5.   NAFSA issues numerous publications and reports in the field of educational exchange including the *NAFSA Newsletter, NAFSA Directory* of institutions enrolling foreign students, and *Adviser's Manual of Federal Regulations Affecting Foreign Students Publications.*

L49 National Association of State Universities and Land-Grant Colleges (NASULGC)

1.   *One Dupont Circle, N.W.*
       Washington, D.C. 20036
       293-7120

2.   James W. Cowan, Director, International Programs and Studies Office.

3.   The oldest higher-education association in the U.S., the NASULGC is the catalyst through which the collective strength of its entire membership is brought to bear on educational and scientific issues of common concern. Its International Programs and Studies Office serves as a center for information on legislation and governmental and nongovernmental programs related to international education, research, and development. It also serves as a liaison between universities and government agencies, private organizations, and educational associations concerned with international programs and studies. The International Programs and Studies Office works closely with international-program officials at NASULGC member institutions and consortia to help establish and strengthen relationships with developing countries, particularly in the areas of development cooperation and international linkages.

5.   The International Programs and Studies Office publishes a newsletter, *International Letter,* which is distributed to designated officers at member institutions who are especially concerned with international affairs. It reports on proposed legislation in the international field as well as on international-program activities and achievements of member institutions.

L50 National Education Association (NEA)

1.   *1201 16th Street, N.W.*
       Washington, D.C. 20036
       833-4000

2.   Terry Herndon, Executive Director

3.   NEA is a nonprofit membership organization of public school teachers in the U.S. to promote public education in the nation. International programs of the association are coordinated by the Committee on International Re-

lations (Braulio Alonso, 833-4105). NEA maintains cooperative relationships with teachers' organizations around the world, including India, Bangladesh, and Sri Lanka. NEA is an active member of the World Confederation of Organizations of the Teaching Profession.

5. NEA publications include *Today's Education* (issued 4 times during the academic year); *NEA News Service* (monthly); NEA Reporter (monthly); and *Higher Education Newspaper* (7 times a year).

L51 National Geographic Society

1. *1146 16th Street, N.W.*
    Washington, D.C. 20036
    857-7000

2. Robert E. Doyle, President

3. A nonprofit scientific and educational organization established in 1890, the National Geographic Society conducts explorations and research to expand man's knowledge of earth, sea, and sky. The society sends researchers and photographers throughout the world and diffuses the knowledge thus gathered through magazines, maps, books, monographs, lectures, filmstrips, records, and media services.

4. The society's library is described in entry A27.

5. The monthly *National Geographic* frequently publishes articles with photographs on several South Asian themes. A publication list of the society's books, maps, and atlases is available on request.

Note: Also see entries E6 and P18.

L52 National Strategy Information Center (NSIC)—Washington Office

1. *1730 Rhode Island Avenue, N.W.*
    Washington, D.C. 20036
    296-6406

2. Roy Godson, Program Director

3. This New York-based center is a nonprofit and nonpartisan institution organized in 1962 to conduct educational programs in international security affairs. NSIC seeks to encourage civil-military partnership on the grounds that, in a democracy, informed public opinion is necessary for a viable U.S. defense system capable of protecting the nation's vital interests and assisting allies and other free nations determined to maintain their core values of freedom and independence. The center occasionally schedules policy workshops in Washington on resource strategy, geopolitics, military reform, comparative defense budgets, alternatives to détente, and commissions *Agenda Papers* on these topics. It is noted that, in the past, NSIC has established cooperative relations with defense-oriented groups in Pakistan.

5. Publications of interest include: Richard L. Park and Stephen P. Cohen, *India: Emergent Power* (1978); W. A. C. Adie, *Oil Politics and Seapower: The Indian Ocean Vortex* (1975); and George G. Thomson, *Problems of Strategy in the Pacific and Indian Oceans* (1970). A complete *List of Publications* catalog is available upon request.

L53 Overseas Writers

1. *National Press Building*
   14th and F Streets, N.W.
   Washington, D.C. 20045
   737-2934

2. James Anderson, President

3. Overseas Writers is a luncheon club that meets once a month and is composed of newspaper correspondents with overseas experience. A membership list is available. The club can put researchers in touch with members currently working in Washington.

L54 Population Association of America (PAA)

1. *806 15th Street, N.W.*
   Washington, D.C. 20005
   393-3253

2. Edgar M. Bisgyer, Business Manager

3. PAA is a nonprofit, scientific, professional organization established to promote research with respect to problems connected with human population, in both its qualitative and quantitative aspects, and the dissemination and publication of the results of such research. PAA members are interested in all aspects of population and related subjects such as: general demography, family planning, fertility, spatial distribution; trends in population size; marriage, divorce and the family; internal and international migration; population, economic, and social development, and population planning; methods of research and analysis; vital statistics, censuses, and surveys. PAA draws its membership from all parts of the world. At its annual conference, papers are contributed on the different regions of the world.

5. Besides its official newsletter, *PAA Affairs,* the association publishes the quarterly *Demography,* which contains articles related to current population research, including selected papers presented at the most recent PAA annual meeting; and *Population Index,* which contains items of current demographic interest and extensive bibliography of books and scientific articles on population in various parts of the world, and summary tables of population statistics.

L55 Population Crisis Committee (PCC)

1. *1120 19th Street, N.W.*
   Washington, D.C. 20036
   659-1833

2. Fred O. Pinkham, National Chairman

3. A nonprofit educational organization, the PCC develops worldwide support for international population and family programs through public education, policy analysis, and liaison with international leaders and organizations, as well as through direct funding of private family-planning projects overseas. PCC works closely with all appropriate United Nations agencies and maintains a close working relationship with the International Planned Parenthood Federation (IPPF) and its national affiliates.

4. PCC maintains a small collection of population-related literature, newspaper clippings, and reports.

5. PCC publications include *Draper World Population Fund Reports, Briefing Sheets,* and a newsletter, *Population.*

L56 Practical Concepts Incorporated (PCI)

1. *1730 Rhode Island Avenue, N.W.*
   Washington, D.C. 20036
   833-1040

2. Lawrence Posner, Vice President

3. Practical Concepts Incorporated is a management consulting firm committed to helping health managers serve the people. It does this by stressing the practical, not the academic. PCI has provided management services for over 200 projects in some 55 countries including Afghanistan, Bangladesh, India, Nepal, and Pakistan. For example, in Nepal, PCI helped the Royal Government evaluate its methods for using paraprofessionals in rural health clinics. With the aid of the information thus obtained, PCI subsequently helped design a major national rural health plan that combined the contributions of the Health Ministry with those of the several international agencies working in health. In Nepal the PCI also established a 2-way communications link between Katmandu and 8 regional health centers in rural areas. PCI also assists AID in evaluation and design services and health, nutrition, and education services.

5. Some project reports are available for a charge.

L57 Public Administration Service (PAS)

1. *1776 Massachusetts Avenue, N.W.*
   Washington, D.C. 20036
   833-2505

2.   Theodore Sitkoff, President

3.   A nonprofit, private management consulting firm, PAS promotes improvement of public administration through research, publishing, and consultation services. Over the past 2 decades PAS has been involved in a number of fiscal, agricultural, and rural development projects in Afghanistan, Pakistan, India, Nepal, and Bangladesh.

L58 Secretariat for Women in Development (New Transcentury Foundation)

1.   *1789 Columbia Road, N.W.*
Washington, D.C. 20009
328-4422

2.   May Rihani, Director

3.   The Secretariat for Women in Development was created in 1977 to provide services and materials that help integrate women into development programs and processes. The secretariat provides technical assistance to organizations involved in development efforts in the Third World including South Asia. In addition, the secretariat organizes a variety of workshops on the role of women in development, and maintains a roster of qualified women in the Third World, available for consulting work.

4.   The secretariat maintains a Documentation Center (Patricia Harlan McClure, Director, 328-4438), which is open Monday through Friday from 9:00 A.M. to 5:30 P.M. for all interested researchers and field personnel. The center's collection of over 1,300 documents specifically relating to women in development focuses on the Third World. The center also collects published and unpublished documents written by women in the Third World. The collection is divided by region and major subject areas, and is accessible by country. Documents do not circulate, but photoduplication facilities are available.

5.   A listing of some 700 documents in the collection is available as *Women in Development: A Resource List.* An additional 287 documents are listed in *Development As If Women Mattered: An Annotated Bibliography With a Third World Focus.* The secretariat also compiles and publishes information about 100 field projects from nearly 70 countries of the Third World.

L59 Shaybani Society of International Law

1.   *1740 Massachusetts Avenue, N.W.*
Washington, D.C. 20036
785-6257

2.   Majid Khadduri

3.   The society promotes interchange of ideas between scholars and legal experts with expertise or interest in Islamic law, the Islamic law of nations, and international law. The society sponsors a series of luncheon meetings

throughout the year. The series is highlighted by lectures given by guest speakers often on the Islamic dimension of an international legal issue of current interest.

L60 Society for International Development (SID)—Washington Office

1. *1834 Jefferson Place, N.W.*
    Washington, D.C. 20036
    293-2903

2. Alfred Van Huyck, Director

3. SID is a Rome-based, nonprofit, nonpolitical membership organization founded in 1957 to provide a forum for the exchange of ideas, views, and experiences among persons involved with or seriously interested in the vital problems of global social and economic development. The society has consultative status with the United Nations Economic and Social Council and its institutional supporters include the World Bank and the International Monetary Fund. Members of the association represent 130 countries and territories and are affiliated with more than 800 different organizations. SID chapters have been opened in most countries in South Asia. During August 1979, SID's Sixteenth International Conference on Development for the 1980's and Beyond was held in Colombo. The Washington Office sponsors "work groups" on various development themes and other special events, including briefings by senior officials from Washington-based development institutions.

5. The society publishes the quarterly, *International Development Review*, which includes the supplement entitled *Focus—Technical Cooperation*; the bimonthly, *Survey of International Development*; and the *International Roster on Development Skills*.

South Asian Ethnic, Social, Cultural and Recreational Organizations See Appendix 1

L61 United States National Committee (USNC)—World Energy Conference

1. *1620 Eye Street, N.W.*
    Washington, D.C. 20006
    331-0415

2. Robert J. Raudebaugh, Executive Director

3. The USNC was organized over half a century ago in connection with the first World Power Conference held in 1924 in London. A fundamental objective of the USNC is to provide for broad consideration of energy resources, policy, management, technology, and use and conservation as they relate to the total energy picture of the United States and the world. Membership of the World Energy Conference includes India, Pakistan, Nepal, Sri Lanka, and Bangladesh.

L62 World Population Society (WPS)

1. *1337 Connecticut Avenue, N.W.*
   Washington, D.C. 20036
   833-2440

2. Philander P. Claxton, President

3. A nonprofit membership organization of professional populationists dedicated to finding solutions to world population problems, the World Population Society has members in over 60 countries including India, Pakistan, and Bangladesh. WPS organizes international conferences, symposia, and workshops related to action programs to advance the World Population Plan of Action adopted by 136 countries at the 1974 World Population Conference in Bucharest. Several South Asian scholars serve on the Advisory Panel of the society and may be of assistance to South Asian scholars.

5. WPS publications include the *WPS Newsletter,* the monthly *World Population News, World Population Growth and Response, Twenty-two Dimensions to the Population Problem* and the proceedings of its international conferences. WPS plans the creation of a world-wide directory of populationists, with descriptions of their institutions and programs.

L63 World Wildlife Fund—U.S. (WWF-US)

1. *1601 Connecticut Avenue, N.W.*
   Washington, D.C. 20009
   387-0800

2. Russell Train, President

3. A private international organization, the World Wildlife Fund is dedicated to preserving endangered wildlife and wilderness areas throughout the world and to protecting the biological resources upon which human well-being depends. Its priorities and programs are designed to be relevant to the socio-economic needs of peoples everywhere. The fund is represented in 27 countries, including India and Nepal. While in Nepal, the fund supports investigation of the ecology and behavior of tigers and their prey in the Royal Chitawan Park; in India, the WWF-US supports a conservation education program designed to increase public awareness and understanding of conservation issues.

5. Publications include a newsletter, *Focus,* and annual reports.

M Cultural-Exchange and Technical-Assistance Organizations

Many of the nation's cultural-exchange and technical-assistance organizations maintain their offices in the Washington area. Because of their recent or current involvement in various multilateral development or training projects in South Asia, the organizations listed here have acquired a certain level of expertise on that area. Both nonprofit and private consulting firms have been included in the list, although the list of private consulting firms presented here is intended to be representative rather than exhaustive. Because of extensive contract work available with the federal government, particularly with the State Department, the Agency for International Development, and the International Communication Agency, private consulting firms exist in large numbers in the area, although some of them quickly disappear also. Currently, U.S. technical assistance and development projects cover most of South Asia.

Cultural-Exchange and Technical-Assistance Organizations
Entry Format (M)

1. *Address; Telephone Numbers*

2. Chief Official and Title

3. Programs and Activities Pertaining to South Asia

4. Library and Reference Facilities

5. Publications

M1 Agricultural Cooperative Development International (ACDI)

1. *1012 14th Street, N.W.*
   Washington, D.C. 20005
   638-4661

2.   Donald H. Thomas, President

3.   A nonprofit organization, ACDI works under contract with the Agency for International Development in providing technical assistance to agricultural cooperatives in developing countries. ACDI assistance includes advisory and training services in the fields of agricultural credit, cooperative banking, agricultural marketing, supply, education, and policy planning. Currently, ACDI has no contracts in South Asia, but proposals have been submitted for contract grants in Bangladesh and Sri Lanka.

5.   ACDI publications include an *Annual Report,* and a bimonthly *News of Cooperative Development.*

M2 American Association of Collegiate Registrars and Admissions Officers (AACRAO)

1.   *One Dupont Circle*
      Washington, D.C. 20036
      293-9161

2.   J. Douglas Conner, Executive Director

3.   A nonprofit, national, professional association, the AACRAO's International Education Activities Group assists the academic placement offices in U.S. institutions with the credentials of foreign students. It also sponsors workshops on the evaluation of foreign-student credentials, provides credential analysts, consultant sources, and conducts studies designed to improve the selection and admission of AID participants for study in U.S. academic institutions.

5.   AACRAO publishes the *World Education Series* booklets, describing the educational systems of foreign countries, and provides guides to the academic placement of foreign students. The publications are produced with the help of a special grant from the International Communication Agency. There are booklets now available on India, Pakistan, and Afghanistan. A publications brochure is available.

M3 American Council of Young Political Leaders (ACYPL)

1.   *426 C Street, N.E.*
      Washington, D.C. 20002
      546-6010

2.   H. Joseph Farmer, Executive Director

3.   A private, nonprofit organization, the council seeks to provide opportunities for young American and foreign political leaders to gain insight into the vital areas of international affairs and American political processes, respectively, and to foster personal relationships among young political leaders, both American and foreign. With assistance from the International Communication Agency, the ACYPL sends U.S. delegations overseas and receives foreign delegations to the U.S. Since 1966, India has received U.S.

delegates and has sent delegates to the U.S. Other ACYPL programs include foreign policy conferences at the State Department, seminars, and workshops participated in by both American and foreign delegates.

5.   Program information is available upon request.

M4 American Council on International Sports (ACIS)

1.   *817 23rd Street, N.W.*
     Washington, D.C. 20052
     676-7246

2.   Carl A. Troester, Executive Director

3.   A nonprofit, technical-assistance organization capable of providing expertise in sports development and administration, the ACIS is dedicated to enhancing international cooperation and understanding through physical education and sport. In promoting its international activities in physical education and sports, the ACIS receives assistance from relevant U.S. and U.N. agencies.

5.   A council newsletter is available upon request.

M5 American Federation of Labor and Congress of Industrial Organizations (AFL-CIO)—Department of International Affairs

1.   *815 16th Street, N.W.*
     Washington, D.C. 20006
     637-5063

2.   Ernest Lee, Director

3.   The dominant labor organization in the United States, the AFL-CIO, with its 106 affiliated unions, represents approximately 78 percent of the total union membership on various issues of concern to the labor movement. Its Department of International Affairs serves as a liaison office for the various international contacts and activities of the union. The AFL-CIO maintains bilateral ties with India, Sri Lanka, Bangladesh, and Pakistan, and is actively concerned with the labor movements elsewhere in South Asia. South Asian trade-union leaders occasionally visit AFL-CIO member unions; similarly, U.S. trade unionists visit their counterparts in South Asia. The department's Asian Specialist, James Ellenberger, may confer with researchers on the status and developments of labor movements in South Asia.

4.   The AFL-CIO maintains a small library (Dora Kelenson, Librarian, 637-5297), which contains several reference books on international labor movements. The library is open weekdays from 9:00 A.M. to 4:30 P.M. and is accessible to the public.

5.   The semiannual *Executive Council Report to the Convention* outlines the international activities of the AFL-CIO.

M6 American Home Economics Association—International Family Planning Project

1. *2010 Massachusetts Avenue, N.W.*
   Washington, D.C. 20036
   862-8300

2. Elizabeth W. Brabble, Director

3. The International Family Planning Project of the American Home Economics Association is funded by the U.S. Agency for International Development and has as its goal the reduction of fertility through a program of information, education, and communication. The mission of the project is to assist the developing countries' home-economics education systems to integrate family planning and population information into their work. Project activities include: consultation visits; country surveys; in-country workshops and seminars; in-depth training fellowships; publications, research, and pilot projects; an international committee of key home economists in developing countries as contacts, advisors, and leaders for on-going activities of the project; and cooperation with international agencies, such as the International Federation for Home Economics, FAO, UNESCO, and the International Planned Parenthood Federation. Afghanistan, Bangladesh, Nepal, Pakistan, and Sri Lanka have been participating in project activities since 1972.

5. A quarterly newsletter of the International Family Planning Project, *The Link,* serves as an information exchange on its activities, new resources, and research. Project resource materials include: *Resource Catalog: Family Planning and Population Education in Home Economics; Sourcebook for Teachers;* and *Working with Villagers,* a training kit for field workers. Also available is the *Report of a Consultation: Afghanistan* (1976).A list of project publications is available free.

M7 America Red Cross—Office of International Services

1. *17th and D Streets, N.W.*
   Washington, D.C. 20006
   737-8300

2. Joseph Carniglia, Director

3. Operating under Congressional Charter and fulfilling U.S. obligations under certain international treaties, the American Red Cross is a humanitarian disaster-relief and health-education organization. The American Red Cross and the South Asian national Red Cross societies, are affiliated with the world-wide federation of the Geneva-based League of Red Cross Societies. The Office of International Service supervises the donation of supplies, funds, and technical assistance for relief in major natural calamities and man-made disasters abroad. In the past, the American Red Cross has participated in technical assistance and international disaster-relief operations in South Asia and can provide information on these activities.

4. The American Red Cross National Headquarters Library (Edna L.T. Moon, Library Director, 857-3491) is open to the public weekdays from 8:30 A.M. to 4:45 P.M. Photoduplication facilities and interlibrary loan services are available. The collection contains approximately 17,000 books and bound periodicals. In addition, the library maintains numerous records, reports, documents, pamphlets, and periodicals covering the history and current activities of the American Red Cross, the International Red Cross, and the League of Red Cross Societies. A card index to Red Cross periodicals and reports, and an extensive vertical file collection of reports and publications of major national and international voluntary organizations are also available.

5. Publications include the *American Red Cross Annual Report,* which describes the international activities of the Red Cross; a bimonthly periodical *Panorama,* and occasional press releases.

Note: Also see entries B1 and F2.

M8 Asia Foundation—Washington Office

1. *2301 E Street, N.W.*
    Washington, D.C. 20037
    223-5268

2. Allen C. Choate, Representative

3. Headquartered in San Francisco (550 Kearny Street, San Francisco, California 94108, 415/982-4640), the Asia Foundation is a publicly supported, nonprofit, philanthropic organization. The foundation utilizes a small grant approach to respond to Asian-initiated efforts to further economic, social, and cultural growth in their own societies. It also encourages understanding among the peoples of Asia and between Asians and Americans. The foundation assists in the following areas: education, public administration, law, economics, management, community development, communications, family planning, food, nutrition, and health-care delivery. Through its Books for Asia project, the foundation distributes each year hundreds of thousands of donated books and specialized journals to individuals and institutions, ranging from graduate research to rural mobile libraries. The foundation maintains resident representatives in Afghanistan, Pakistan, Nepal, Sri Lanka, and Bangladesh.

5. Publications include a bimonthly, *The Asia Foundation News*; *Asian Student Orientation Handbook*; the *Presidents Review and Annual Report*; and occasional papers on developmental and social changes in Asian countries.

M9 Association for Academic Travel Abroad

1. *1346 Connecticut Avenue, N.W.*
    Washington, D.C. 20036
    785-3412

2. David Parry, Executive Director

3. The association assists academic institutions, museums, and professional organizations in planning and conducting educational travel programs. Tours to South Asia are occasionally arranged by the association.

5. Various information brochures regarding travel programs are available on request.

M10 Baptist World Relief (Baptist World Alliance)

1. *1628 16th Street, N.W.*
    Washington, D.C. 20009
    265-5027

2. Erna Redlich, Assistant Secretary for Relief and Development

3. Baptist World Relief administers the Baptist World Alliance's Relief Fund program. It provides funds to Baptist groups in the Third World for the purchase of equipment needed in local development projects related to schools, clinics, and irrigation projects. In recent years, it has provided relief assistance to Bangladesh, India, and Sri Lanka.

5. The Baptist World Alliance publishes a monthly magazine, the *Baptist World.*

M11 Checchi and Company

1. *1730 Rhode Island Avenue, N.W.*
    Washington, D.C. 20036
    452-9700

2. Vicki Macdonald, Coordinator of International Programs

3. Checchi is a private international consulting and research corporation that specializes in development and management services and works under contract for U.S. government agencies, the World Bank, and other organizations. The company has undertaken technical-assistance project studies in Afghanistan, Bangladesh, Nepal, India, Pakistan, and Sri Lanka.

4. The reports and studies generated by the company are the property of the clients and are available only with the clients' permission. However, reports produced under contract from U.S. government agencies are available from the National Technical Information Service (see entry J6).

M12 Chemonics—International Consulting Division

1. *1120 19th Street, N.W.*
    Washington, D.C. 20036
    466-5340

2. Thurston F. Teele, Director

3. A Phoenix (Arizona)-based conglomerate, the International Consulting

Division provides a wide range of management and consulting services overseas under contracts from the Agency for International Development (AID). The division's recent involvement in technical-assistance programs in South Asia include an AID-financed contract grant in Afghanistan to provide assistance to an Afghanistan fertilizer company and another AID-supported contract grant in Sri Lanka to work with the Mahawali Development Board.

5. A descriptive pamphlet describing the division's programs is available on request.

M13 Cooperative for American Relief Everywhere (CARE)— Washington Field Office

1. *1016 16th Street, N.W.*
    Washington, D.C. 20036
    296-5696

2. Ronwyn Ingraham, Director

3. With its World Headquarters in New York (600 First Avenue, New York, New York 10016, 212/686-3110), CARE is a voluntary, nonprofit and nongovernmental technical-assistance and disaster-relief agency. Its involvement in South Asia includes—Afghanistan: training of medical personnel in surgery, nursing, orthopedics, and community health; Pakistan: housing construction and construction of a food and medical supply warehouse; Nepal: a new operation, programs in exploratory stages; Bangladesh: feeding workers under Food-for-Work programs, agricultural education, development and production, irrigation systems, strengthening of agricultural cooperatives, women's development, including implementation of income-generating projects, and supporting orthopedic and plastic-surgery training programs; India: feeding school children and mothers, feeding workers under Food-for-Peace programs, construction of day-care centers, warehouses, and community centers in urban slums, installation of irrigation pumps, integrated health care and nutrition education, including family planning and education; Sri Lanka: feeding children and mothers, nutrition-education programs, production of fortified blended cereal, nutrition and health services, and soybean food development. Historically, CARE has placed the needs of children in the forefront of its programming and most of its projects either directly or indirectly benefit children.

5. CARE's *Annual Report* and its quarterly newsletter, *CARE World Report*, are available at the Washington Field Office.

M14 Council for International Exchange of Scholars (CIES)

1. *11 Dupont Circle*
    Washington, D.C. 20036
    833-4950

2. Adolph Y. Wilburn, Director

3. CIES was established in 1947 as a private, nonprofit organization to facilitate international exchange in higher education. Under arrangements with the U.S. International Communication Agency, the council cooperates in the administration of the Fulbright-Hays program, which was established in 1961 to increase mutual understanding between the people of the United States and the people of other cultures. Each year, approximately 500 foreign scholars and an equal number of American scholars receive various awards, which the council is responsible for arranging, confirming, and administering, under the Fulbright-Hays program. CIES had aided the exchange of more than 14,000 American scholars from other countries for research, lecturing, and consultation at the university level. The council currently administers exchange programs in Afghanistan, Sri Lanka, Pakistan, and India.

5. The council publishes several information leaflets including the annual *Fulbright Awards Abroad, Fulbright-Hays Opportunities Abroad* and a *Directory of Visiting Fulbright Lecturers and Researchers in the U.S.*

M15 Credit Union National Association (CUNA)—Global Projects Office

1. *1120 19th Street, N.W.*
    Washington, D.C. 20036
    659-4571

2. Thomas R. Carter, Director of Programs

3. An affiliate of the World Council of Credit Unions (WOCCU),CUNA's Global Projects Office provides technical assistance and advisory services to aid in the development of credit unions abroad. Currently, CUNA is exploring the possibilities of developing projects in India.

4. The Global Projects Office receives copies of some of the publications of the World Council of Credit Unions, namely, the *Annual Report, WOCCU Newsletter* (monthly) and *World Reporter* (quarterly).

M16 Experiment in International Living—Washington Office

1. *1346 Connecticut Avenue, N.W.*
    Washington, D.C. 20036
    872-1330

2. Anne Lewis, Director

3. The Experiment in International Living is a nonprofit, international, educational institution dedicated to peaceful relations among people and nations. The experiment seeks to further international understanding through its Homestay Intercultural Exchange Program. Currently India and Sri Lanka participate in these exchanges. At its national headquarters in Brattleboro, Vermont 05301 (802/257-7751), the experiment maintains a School for International Training for teaching people from different nations, cul-

tures, races, and backgrounds to function effectively when moving into a culture alien to their own. In addition, independent study programs are offered in the fall and spring semesters in India and Sri Lanka. Every year approximately 3,000 experimenters from nearly 80 countries visit the U.S. and some 1,100 experimenters from the U.S. visit some 30 different countries on summer programs.

5.   In addition to *Odyssey*, a quarterly newsletter of the experiment, the Washington office circulates a local newsletter periodically.

M17 Foundation for Cooperative Housing (FCH)—International Programs

1.   *2101 L Street, N.W.*
        Washington, D.C. 20037
        857-4100

2.   Charles Dean, President

3.   A people-oriented institution the aim of which is to develop innovative and fresh approaches in response to the shelter needs of the poorer majority, FCH works overseas at the invitation of local governments and cooperative organizations, providing technical advice, training, and collaboration with local technicians in the development of self-help housing, cooperative housing, disaster-relief shelter, rural housing, and special programs for refugees. FCH assists on all phases of project development. Its main concerns are the social and human aspects of shelter programs, concentrating on establishing permanent community-based organizations that allow people to improve their homes and communities over a period of time. Most of the FCH funding is derived from U.S. Agency for International Development's cost-reimbursable contracts. FCH provides consulting services to the United Nations. FCH has assisted Bangladesh in providing immediate shelter and long-term housing reconstruction after natural disasters.

5.   Publications include *FCH International Program, FCH Publication List* and several *Feasibility Studies*.

M18 General Federation of Women's Clubs (GFWC)

1.   *1734 N Street, N.W.*
        Washington, D.C. 20036
        347-3168

2.   Don L. Shide, President

3.   An international organization with membership in 37 countries including India, Pakistan, and Bangladesh, GFWC's International Affairs Program, with cooperation from the Cooperative for American Relief Everywhere (CARE), emphasizes a wide range of educational programs in the developing countries of the world in the fields of nutrition, health-care training, vocational skills, agricultural development, fish production, reforestation, and school construction.

5.   *GF Clubwoman Magazine* is published 9 times a year.

M19 Government Affairs Institute (GAI)

1.   *1776 Massachusetts Avenue, N.W.*
        Washington, D.C. 20036
        833-2505

2.   John Hannah, Executive Director

3.   The Government Affairs Institute is a research, training, and consulting
        organization that operates both in the United States and abroad in the areas
        of agriculture, rural development, public administration, international af-
        fairs, and education. GAI is presently involved in Nepal through its Ag-
        ricultural Sector Implementation Project (ASIP). ASIP is designed to help
        governments of developing countries bridge the gap between agricultural
        planners and farmers by improving the planning, implementation, and
        management capabilities of those in developing countries concerned with
        agriculture and rural development. ASIP is supported by the U.S. Agency
        for International Development.

5.   The ASIP team in Nepal publishes a monthly *ASIP Newsletter,* which is
        available at the GAI Washington office.

M20 Institute of International Education (IIE)—Washington Office

1.   *11 Dupont Circle, N.W.*
        Washington, D.C. 20036
        483-0001

2.   Peter D. Pelham, Director

3.   The Institute of International Education is a private, nongovernment, non-
        profit organization founded in 1919. It maintains its headquarters in New
        York (809 United Nations Plaza, New York, New York 10017). The IIE
        is the largest and most active educational exchange agency in the U.S. It
        administers exchange programs with over 120 countries and provides serv-
        ices to technical-assistance programs overseas, supervises the academic de-
        gree programs of its foreign students, arranging university admission and
        securing financial aid for many of them. Similarly, IIE aids U.S. students
        by running a national competition for grants for graduate study abroad.
        The institute also organizes orientation programs, English-language training
        and other activities that help to make study in the U.S. successful for foreign
        students.
            In addition, the Washington office assists the U.S. Government and other
        institutions, through the International Visitors Program, in arranging ac-
        tivities that range from conference participation to long-term research and
        practical training for visiting foreign leaders. Most IIE activities are funded
        by sponsors—governments, foundations, corporations, international or-
        ganizations, and educational agencies. Afghanistan, Bangladesh, Bhutan,
        India, Pakistan, Nepal, and Sri Lanka are among the nations with which
        IIE has relations through sponsored programs.

5. IIE publications are standard references on international exchange. The institute produces both comprehensive reference works and specialized study guides. A publications list, an *Annual Report*, a summary of *Sponsored Projects*, and a quarterly newsletter, *IIE Reports*, are available on request.

M21 International Center for Dynamics of Development

1. *4201 South 31st Street*
   Arlington, Virginia 22208
   (703) 578-4627

2. Dana D. Reynolds, President

3. The center acts as a catalylist in focusing attention and crystallizing action on policies and programs in the international, national, public, and independent sectors, to broaden participation in political, economic, and social development; and it fosters strategies to promote unity and cooperation among, and within nations. Major South Asia-related activities of the center include: Symposia on Bangladesh Redevelopment (1972); First International Conference on Country Strategies to Involve Peoples in Development (1975), which included several panels and papers on South Asia; and International Symposium on National Strategies to Build Support for Development in the Context of the New International Economic Order (1971). The latter conference also included panels and papers on South Asia and was attended by South Asian officials and scholars. The center's advisory committee has representatives from India, Pakistan, and Sri Lanka.

5. Some conference programs and papers are available.

M22 International Voluntary Services (IVS)

1. *1717 Massachusetts Avenue, N.W.*
   Washington, D.C. 20036
   387-5533

2. John T. Rigby, Executive Director

3. International Voluntary Services is a private nonprofit, independent organization which recruits skilled volunteer technicians from around the world to work on rural development projects in developing countries. Funding for its activities has come from various sources including the U.S. Agency for International Development, Catholic Relief Services, OXFAM, the United Presbyterian Church, and other organizations. Currently the IVS is involved in a community-based program for rural health care and agriculture in Sylhet (Bangladesh).

5. IVS annual reports are available on request.

M23 Jesuit Missions

1. *1717 Massachusetts Avenue, N.W.*
   Washington, D.C. 20036
   387-3720

2.   Simon E. Smith, Executive Secretary

3.   The Jesuits have been actively involved in evangelization, education, and social work in South Asia since the sixteenth century. Current Jesuit activities in South Asia are, however, very modest. Jesuit houses in India, Sri Lanka, Nepal, and Bhutan maintain clinics, hospitals, and schools, and participate in humanitarian and relief operations.

       The Jesuit Mission's special Jesuit Conference Staff (462-0400) maintains liaison with some 6,000 Jesuits in North America. For establishing contact with the Jesuits who have had experience in South Asia, researchers may contact the staff.

5.   Publications include the *JM Newsletter* and Studies in the *International Apostolate of Jesuits*, both of which are produced at irregular times.

M24 League of Women Voters—Overseas Education Fund (OEF)

1.   *2101 L Street, N.W.*
       Washington, D.C. 20037
       466-3430

2.   Louise Montgomery, Director of Field Programs

3.   OEF is a project- and task-oriented organization working in partnership with indigenous organizations to undertake programs in community and human resources development within their own cultural framework. In particular, OEF assistance is directed to the under-utilized potential of women to strengthen the true partnership between women and men in societies where women have been forgotten by the economic system. OEF has been working in nearly 50 countries throughout the world offering technical assistance. OEF activities in South Asia include: training rural and urban low-income women in Sri Lanka in job skills; surveying the child-care constraints for working women in Sri Lanka; and researching the economic and social needs of island women in the Maldives.

5.   A pamphlet series, *Update on Proposed Projects*, is available on request.

M25 Meridian House International (MHI)

1.   *1630 Crescent Place, N.W.*
       Washington, D.C. 20009
       667-6800

2.   Joseph John Jova, President

3.   Meridian House International is a nonprofit corporation, in the field of international affairs, dedicated to supporting international exchange programs. MHI is financed by government contracts and grants, foundation support, and corporate and individual gifts. In addition to providing visitors with reception, orientation, and programming, the MHI conducts a lecture series on world affairs and topical seminars for members of the Washington diplomatic community, and sponsors other educational and cultural pro-

grams. The MHI can provide assistance in some 48 foreign languages including several South Asian languages. Its programs include: the Visitors Program Service (452-0606) and the Washington International Center (332-1025); its affiliates are: the National Council for Community Services to International Visitors (332-1028), the International Visitors Information Service (872-8747), and the Hospitality and Information Service for Diplomats (232-3002).

5.   Publications include the quarterly *MHI Newsletter*.

M26 National 4-H Council

1.   *7100 Connecticut Avenue, N.W.*
Washington, D.C. 20015
656-9000

2.   Melvin J. Thompson, Director, International Programs

3.   National 4-H (Head, Heart, Hands, Health) Council is a private, nonprofit institution dedicated to character- and skill-building youth programs conducted by the Cooperative Extension Service of the U.S. Department of Agriculture. The 4-H's international-exchange programs are designed to promote international understanding and develop better-informed youth leaders, by providing an opportunity to learn about 4-H and youth-development programs, as well as by providing a cross-cultural experience. Over 7,000 individuals representing the U.S. and 80 cooperating countries have participated in 4-H international-exchange programs since they began in 1948. Participating countries in recent years include India, Nepal, Pakistan, and Sri Lanka. International 4-H programs are supported by private funds, and by limited public grants available for use with some countries.

5.   Program literature is available upon request.

M27 National Rural Electric Cooperative Association (NRECA)

1.   *1800 Massachusetts Avenue, N.W.*
Washington, D.C. 20036
857-9500

2.   Samuel Bunker, Coordinator of International Programs

3.   The International Programs Division of NRECA provides technical assistance to foreign-government agencies, utility companies, and cooperatives in the development and operation of rural electric systems and electricity cooperatives. Activities include advisory consulting and training services and preparation of country surveys and feasibility studies. In some projects, the association is involved from the planning stages through implementation. NRECA is presently involved in 6 large AID-assisted projects in Bangladesh. In the past it has also provided technical assistance to Pakistan, Afghanistan, India, Sri Lanka, and Nepal.

5.   Publications include *NRECA Overseas Report; Rural Electrification Mag-*

azine (monthly); and a newsletter, *Rural Electric Coops Overseas*. The numerous studies and reports prepared by the association are for the use of their clients. However, the staff can direct researchers to the appropriate agency to gain access to these materials.

M28 Project HOPE (People-to-People Health Foundation)

1. *Project HOPE Health Sciences Education Center*
   Millwood, Virginia 22646
   (703) 837-2100

2. William B. Walsh, President

3. The People-to-People Health Foundation is an independent, nonprofit corporation, which was formed in 1958 to carry out programs of cooperation in the field of health education between professionals in the U.S. and those in developing countries. Project HOPE brings the skills and techniques developed by the U.S. medical, dental, and allied health professions to the people of other nations, in their own environments, adapted specifically to their needs and ways of life. One of the first programs of Project HOPE was initiated in Sri Lanka. Currently, it has a contract to work in Pakistan.

5. Publications include a quarterly newsletter, *HOPE News*, country program reports, and the *Educational Monographs* series.

M29 Public Welfare Foundation

1. *2600 Virginia Avenue, N.W.*
   Washington, D.C. 20037
   956-1800

2. Davis Haines, President

3. A private, charitable, nonprofit organization, the Public Welfare Foundation strives to improve education, health, living conditions, and human happiness anywhere in the world where circumstances beyond their control have deprived people of development in keeping with their natural abilities. The foundation contributed a small grant in support of cyclone-disaster housing relief in Andhra Pradesh (India) in 1978.

5. Publications include a quarterly newsletter, various country program reports, and an annual report.

M30 Seventh-Day Adventist World Service (SAWS)

1. *6840 Eastern Avenue, N.W.*
   Washington, D.C. 20012
   723-0800

2. Howard D. Burbank, Executive Director

3. The Seventh-Day Adventist World Service is a volunteer relief agency of the General Conference of Seventh-Day Adventists. SAWS has extensive operations in developing countries. It has supplied food, clothing, bedding, and medical supplies in several disaster-relief operations in Bangladesh, Sri Lanka, Nepal, Pakistan, and India.

5. Overseas assistance programs are described in the *SAWS Reporter*.

M31 Sister Cities International (Town Affiliation Association of the U.S.)

1. *1625 Eye Street, N.W.*
   Washington, D.C. 20006
   293-5504

2. Thomas Gittins, Executive Vice President

3. This is a nonprofit, membership organization of city governments and their sister-city communities established to further international cooperation and understanding through sister city links between cities in the U.S. and other nations. The program currently works with nearly 700 U.S. cities and numerous cities in 80 countries in all parts of the world. The program receives grant assistance from the U.S. International Communication Agency. Sister-city links have been established with 6 cities in India, 2 in Pakistan, and 1 in Nepal.

5. The organization publishes the bimonthly, *Sister City News*.

M32 United States Catholic Conference (USCC)

1. *1312 Massachusetts Avenue, N.W.*
   Washington, D.C. 20005
   659-6600

2. J. Bryan Hehir, Associate Secretary, Office of International Justice and Peace

3. USCC's Office of International Justice and Peace within the Department of Social Development and World Peace deals with policy matters regarding human rights, foreign aid for food, and military and political affairs in various regions of the world. For information concerning overseas relief activities contact Catholic Relief Services, 1011 First Avenue, New York, New York 10022 (212/838-4700).

4. The Office of International Justice and Peace maintains a small reference library that is open to scholars during regular hours.

5. Publications include *Developing Communities in the Third World,* by Thomas E. Quigley (1977), a *Publications List*, a monthly newsletter, and a descriptive brochure about the organization.

M33 Volunteer Development Corps

1. *1629 K Street, N.W.*
    Washington, D.C. 20006
    223-2072

2. David W. Angevine, President

3. The Volunteer Development Corps is a private, nonprofit organization that recruits specialists primarily from U.S. agricultural, industrial, and commercial cooperatives in order to provide short-term, voluntary technical assistance to cooperatives and government agencies in developing countries. It is funded mainly by the U.S. Agency for International Development. During the year of 1979 the corps provided assistance to the Government of Sri Lanka in accounting for cooperatives. Currently the corps is exploring the possibilities of extending its involvement to other countries of South Asia.

5. Project summaries and annual reports are available on request.

M34 Volunteers in Technical Assistance (VITA)

1. *3706 Rhode Island Avenue*
    Mt. Rainier, Maryland 20822
    (301) 277-7000

2. Henry Norman, Executive Director

3. A private, nonprofit organization, VITA recruits volunteer consultants to advise on appropriate technology in overseas development projects. Consultants are available in the fields of agriculture, food processing, water resources, renewable energy resources, housing and construction, and small-business management. The organization is partially funded by the U.S. Agency for International Development and has worked under contract with the Peace Corps. VITA's South Asian activities have focused primarily on responding to inquiries from individuals and organizations in need of technical-assistance information.

4. VITA maintains a Documentation Center which is open to the public for on-site use. Researchers may use the collection if they make a prior appointment.

5. In addition to the quarterly, *VITA News*, other publications include various technical manuals, bulletins, and project handbooks. Particularly useful is the *Village Technology Handbook*, which is updated periodically. *A Catalog of Books, Bulletins and Manuals* is available free upon request.

Woodrow Wilson International Center for Scholars (WWICS)
See entry H35

N Religious Organizations

This list of religious organizations and places of worship represents all major religions, religious orders, and sects in South Asia. In addition to Hinduism, Islam, and Sikhism, which are the three dominant religious faiths of the local South Asian community, persons of other religious persuasions have also established their religious organizations for facilitating community worship and cultural efficacy. The list here is only representative and is not exhaustive. Some of the organizations listed in Appendix I (South.Asian Ethnic, Social, Cultural, and Recreational Organizations) also organize religious ceremonies and rituals for their members.

Religious Organizations Entry Format (N)

1. *Address; Telephone Numbers*

2. Chief Official and Title

3. Programs Pertaining to South Asia

4. Publications

N1 American Fazl Mosque

1. *2141 Leroy Place, N.W.*
   Washington, D.C. 20008
   232-3737

2. Mahmud Nasir, Imam

3. Established in 1950, the American Fazl Mosque is a place of worship for the Ahmadiyya community. Open to the public, the mosque holds daily and congregational prayers. The mosque organizes *Qur'ān* classes and religious discussion meetings on Saturdays and Sundays. A small collection of works on the Ahmadiyya movement in Islam, written in Urdu and English, is available for on-site use.

4. An Urdu monthly, *al-Nur*, the quarterly *Muslim Sunrise*, and the monthly *Ahmadiyya Gazette* are disseminated by the mosque.

N2 Buddhist Vihara Society

1. *5017 16th Street, N.W.*
    Washington, D.C. 20011
    723-0773

2. Piyananda, Monk

3. A vihara of the Theravada order of Buddhism with membership predominately drawn from Sri Lanka, the society's objective is to spread the teachings of Gautama Buddha. Meditation meetings and *dharma* discussions are held on Sundays. A religious class for children is also held on Sundays.

4. A *Washington Buddhist* quarterly is distributed by the society.

N3 Dharmadhatu Buddhist Meditation and Study Center

1. *1424 Wisconsin Avenue, N.W.*
    Washington, D.C. 20007
    338-7090

2. David Sable, Director

3. A meditation and study center, Dharmadhatu contains a shrine room and provides classes in Buddhism and sitting practice. The center is mostly patronized by the followers of Gyalwa Karmapa of Tibet, leader of the Kagya Order of Tibetan Buddhism. A large number of the followers of the order have settled in India.

4. A monthly newsletter and a brochure of class schedules are distributed free.

N4 Friends of Buddhism of Washington, D.C.

1. *306 Caroline Street*
    Fredericksburg, Virginia 22401
    (703) 373-2370

2. Kurt F. Leidecker, President
    Virginia Twynham, Secretary, 362-5279

3. Founded in 1952, the Friends of Buddhism is a free association of men and women who are interested in Buddhism and Buddhist communities throughout the world. The association presents opportunities for the study of Buddhist philosophy, art, and way of life. To the Friends of Buddhism, understanding Buddhism is a way of understanding Asia. The society does not commit itself to any particular form of Buddhism; nor does it make the acceptance of Buddhism as a personal way of life or the holdings of any particular philosophy or creed a criterion for admission to membership or participation in meetings. The society organizes monthly lectures, film presentations, and other functions at which scholars, travelers, and lay and clerical Buddhist leaders present their contributions to Buddhism in all its phases.

4.   An irregular newsletter, *Friends of Buddhism*, is circulated to members.

N5 Golden Lotus Temple (Self-Revelation Church of Absolute Monism)

1.   *4748 Western Avenue, N.W.*
      Washington, D.C. 20016
      229-3871

2.   Srimati Kamala, Associate Minister

3.   Open to both men and women, married and unmarried, this church was established by Swami Premananda of India in order to assure the continuity of the philosophy of *Advaita Vedanta*. Every activity of the church, including beautification and maintenance, is the service of dedicated workers in expression of the philosophy of oneness of life, work as worship, and the joy of mutual effort on the path to self-perfection. A small, membership lending-library, containing books on Indian philosophy and religion, is located in the temple. The church holds a Sunday school, Church of Our Children, for the spiritual unfolding of the children.

N6 Guru Nanak Foundation of America

1.   *12917 Old Columbia Pike*
      Silver Spring, Maryland 20904
      (301) 384-2133

2.   Indrajit Singh, Priest

3.   Founded in 1975, the Guru Nanak Foundation is a nonprofit, religious and cultural organization that holds Sunday prayer meetings and other Sikh religious ceremonies. The foundation maintains a small collection of books on religion and conducts a Sunday school for the children.

4.   It disseminates the monthly *Sikh Samachar*.

N7 India House of Worship

1.   *1428 Chilton Drive*
      Silver Spring, Maryland 20904
      384-4090

2.   B. P. Shah, Secretary

3.   The India House of Worship is a nonprofit Hindu religious organization that observes religious ceremonies and festivals. The worshippers gather for monthly meetings at which are featured *bhajan, kirtan,* and recital of the *Gita*. The group hopes to acquire a temple of its own in the future.

N8 International Society for Krishna Consciousness

1. *10310 Oaklyn Road*
   Potomac, Maryland 20854
   (301) 299-2100

2. Sriman Sesadasa, Temple President

3. The International Society for Krishna Consciousness is a religious order to train people according to the precepts of Krishna as provided in the *Bhagavata Gita*. The society holds prayer meetings on Sundays which are open to the public. The society maintains a small collection of Sanskrit texts.

4. The society disseminates a monthly journal *Back to Godhead* and an occasional *Bulletin*.

N9 Islamic Center

1. *2551 Massachusetts Avenue, N.W.*
   Washington, D.C. 20008
   332-3451

2. Muhammad Abdul Rauf, Director

3. A place of worship for the Muslims, the mosque is open for the five daily prayers, the congregational prayer on Friday, and the *Eid al Fitr* and the *Eid al Adha* prayers. The mosque is also open to visitors during the normal working hours of the Islamic Center, 10:00 A.M. to 4:00 P.M., daily.

4. A *Bulletin of the Islamic Center* appears twice a year.

Note: Also see entry L43.

N10 Muslim Community Center

1. *9229 E. Parkhill Drive*
   Bethesda, Maryland 20014
   (301) 530-3678

2. N. S. Dajani, Chairman

3. The Muslim Community Center was established in 1976 for holding religious ceremonies, for imparting religious education to the children, and for promoting cultural activities. The center's master plan includes the construction of a community center for Muslims equipped with a mosque, a school, a social building, and a residence for the staff. A phase of the construction has already commenced. The center runs a Weekend School, organizes *Eid* prayers, and sponsors other social and cultural events.

4. The center issues the bimonthly *MCC Bulletin*.

N11 Muslim Development Corporation

1. *5115 Franconia Road*
    Alexandria, Virginia 22310
    (703) 971-2020

2. Miraj Siddiqi, President

3. The corporation was established in 1976 to build an Islamic community. The project includes the development of a complex consisting of housing units, shopping centers, schools, and a mosque. The corporation is currently trying to acquire 100-plus acres of land for building the complex. The corporation sponsors religious, educational, and recreational activities.

N12 Sikh Temple

1. *3911 Military Road, N.W.*
    Washington, D.C. 20015
    (703) 536-5376

2. Surendra Singh, President

3. Established in 1964, the Sikh Temple is a place of worship for the Sikh community in the Washington metropolitan area. In addition to the prayer meetings, which are held on Sundays, the temple also holds other religious and social ceremonies. The temple organizes a Sunday school for children during the summer.

South Asian Ethnic, Social, Cultural and Recreational Organizations   See Appendix 1

N13 Vedanta Society of Greater Washington

1. *7430 Tower Street*
    Falls Church, Virginia 22046
    (703) 573-4760

2. Shanti Tayal, Executive Secretary

3. The Vedanta Society of Greater Washington is a tax-exempt, nonprofit, philosophical, educational, and spiritual organization that holds open religious and spiritual discussion-sessions once a week. The society follows the spiritual leadership of the Calcutta Ramakrishna Mission and is occasionally visited by an ordained swami. The society also organizes retreats. Sunday school for the children is held as needed. A small reference library of Vedanta literature is available for on-site use.

4. A bimonthly *Bulletin* is circulated to members.

N14 Vedic Cultural Society

1. *2610 East West Highway*
   Chevy Chase, Maryland 20015
   (301) 588-3331

2. L. K. Dhyani, President

3. The Vedic Cultural Society meets the second Sunday of every month at the Gandhi Memorial Center (4748 Western Avenue, N.W., Washington, D.C. 20016) and discusses vedic religion and philosophy. These discussion meetings are usually accompanied by *bhajan* and other classical Indian devotional music.

P Publications and Media

This section lists South Asia-related publications and media not discussed in other sections of the *Guide*. Included here are various newsletters, journals, magazines, and newspapers, some of which are devoted exclusively to South Asian subjects, while others are general publications with some pertinence to South Asia. Also included in this section are the publishing houses in the area producing titles on South Asia or relevant to South Asian studies. All the publications listed here are Washington-based and are in addition to other publications, containing information on South Asia, that have been cited throughout the Organizations division in this volume. In conjunction with this section, which largely describes the U.S. media in Washington, researchers may wish to consult the list of Washington-based South Asian press correspondents, which may be found in Appendix II (South Asian Press Correspondents in Washington, D.C.) of this volume.

Publications and Media Entry Format (P)

1. *Address; Telephone Numbers*

2. Chief Official and Title

3. Programs and Publications Pertaining to South Asia

P1 Air Force Magazine

1. *1750 Pennsylvania Avenue, N.W.*
    Washington, D.C. 20006
    637-3362

2. F. Clifton Berry, Editor

3. A monthly publication of the Air Force Association, the Air Force Magazine began publication in 1948. Particularly useful to South Asian scholars is the December military balance issue of the magazine, which provides comprehensive data on the armed forces of all countries including India, Pakistan, Afghanistan, Sri Lanka, Bangladesh, and Nepal.

P2 American Broadcasting Company (ABC)—Washington Bureau

1. *1124 Connecticut Avenue, N.W.*
   Washington, D.C. 20036
   393-7700

2. Carl Bernstein, Vice President and Bureau Chief

3. Headquartered in New York, ABC is a major, commercial television network. Its evening newscasts, as they are broadcast, are videotaped by the Vanderbilt University Library (Nashville, Tennessee 37203, 615/322-2927), which also produces the *Television News Index and Abstracts,* available commercially.

P3 Armed Forces Journal

1. *1414 22nd Street, N.W.*
   Washington, D.C. 20037
   296-0450

2. Benjamin F. Schemmer, Editor

3. The monthly *Armed Forces Journal,* which began publishing in 1863, occasionally features articles concerning South Asian affairs; e.g., "The Agony of Pakistan" (May 1980) and "India's Business Card" (September 1980).

P4 Asian-American Journal of Commerce

1. *P.O. Box 1933*
   Washington, D.C. 20013
   638-5595

2. Norman Caron, Editor

3. A publication of the Association of Asian-American Chambers of Commerce, established in 1962, the journal is issued quarterly, supplemented by eight newsletters. With its main focus on the trade and commerce of Asia, the *Asian-American Journal of Commerce* reports changes in import and export regulations, joint ventures, living costs, patents, and business climates of various nations. In addition, it also provides information on travel, culture, and other subjects.

P5 Carrollton Press—Declassified Documents Reference System

1. *1911 Fort Myer Drive*
   Arlington, Virginia 22209
   (703) 525-5940

2. Elizabeth Jones, Executive Editor

3.   The Carrollton Press compiles declassified United States government documents and distributes hard and microfiche copies on a subscription basis. Its *Declassified Documents Reference System,* which is published four times a year, has disseminated, to date, some 19,000 documents from the State Department, Central Intelligence Agency, Defense Department, National Security Council, White House, Treasury Department, Federal Bureau of Investigation, and other government agencies. The collection is growing at the rate of 2,000 documents per year. Many of the declassified documents cover important aspects of the United States' relations with South Asia. Finding aids include quarterly cumulative subject-indexes and abstracts of the declassified documents. An irregular newsletter, *Declassified Document News,* may be obtained free upon request. Local subscribers of the *Declassified Documents Reference System* include the Department of State Library, the Georgetown University Library, and the Library of Congress. Other useful Carrollton Press publications include: *Cumulative Index to Her Majesty's Stationary Office Annual Catalogues of Publications, 1922–1972; Combined Retrospective Indexes to Journals in History* (1838–1974), *Political Science* (1886–1974), and *Sociology* (1895–1974); and *Cumulative Subject Index to the Monthly Catalog of United States Government Publications.* Several information brochures and publications lists are available on request.

P6 Columbia Broadcasting System (CBS)—Washington Bureau

1.   *2020 M Street, N.W.*
Washington, D.C. 20036
457-4321

2.   Edwards Fouhy, Vice President and Director, News.

3.   CBS is a national television and radio broadcasting network, and its news coverage of South Asia may be best accessed through the annual *CBS News Index: Key to the Television News Broadcasting,* produced by the Microfilm Corporation of America, located at 21 Harristown Road, Green Rock, New Jersey 07452 (201/447-3000). This index provides comprehensive access to the transcripts of CBS television broadcasts. Every entry consists of a subject heading, a descriptive phrase, and a locator, which guides readers to the verbatim CBS news transcripts. *Television News Index and Abstracts,* produced by the Vanderbilt University Library (Nashville, Tennessee 37203), is another excellent guide to the videotape collection of the network's evening news program. The Vanderbilt videotape collection of the three major commercial television networks—CBS, ABC, and NBC—are available for use to scholars on a loan basis. Scholars may also contact CBS Information Services Manager (Frances Foley Stone) for assistance in retrieving news transcripts and newscast tapes.

P7 Congressional Quarterly

1.   *1414 22nd Street, N.W.*
Washington, D.C. 20037
296-6800

2.   Eugene C. Patterson, Editor and President

3.   An editorial research service and publishing company, the Congressional Quarterly (founded in 1945) serves clients in the fields of news, education, business, and government. It combines specific coverage of Congress, government, and politics. Its basic periodical publication is the *Weekly Report,* which highlights legislation on military, diplomatic, and economic issues, including those relating to South Asia. Editorial Research Reports, an affiliated service of the Quarterly, publishes reference materials on foreign policy, national security, and other topics of news interest.

P8   Foreign Broadcast Information Service (FBIS)—Daily Report

1.   *P. O. Box 2604*
Washington, D.C. 20013
351-3577 (Information)
351-2877 (South Asia)

3.   The U.S. Government's Foreign Broadcast Information Service publishes a series, *Daily Report,* containing current news and commentary monitored by FBIS from foreign broadcasts, news-agency transmissions, newspapers, and periodicals. Items from foreign-language sources are translated by FBIS: those from English-language sources are transcribed, with original phrasing and other characteristics retained. Users of this publication may cite FBIS, provided they do so in a manner clearly identifying it as the secondary source.

   Since April 1980, volume 8 (*South Asia*) of the *Daily Report* includes all the countries of South Asia and Iran. Formerly, South Asia was included in volume 5 (*Middle East and North Africa*). Edited versions of the *Daily Report,* both in hard cover and microfiche, are made available to the public on a subscription basis through the National Technical Information Service. Effective use of this source has in the past been hampered by lack of indexing. Beginning in 1975, however, the Newsbank (P.O. Box 645, 135 East Putnam Avenue, Greenwich, Connecticut 06830, 203/966-1100) has announced the availability of its *Index to the Daily Reports* which is divided into major subject categories, such as agriculture-environment; commerce-industry-finance; government-politics; international relations; and society-culture. Geographic indicators and name indexes make it even more useful. An FBIS reference publication, *Broadcast Stations of the World,* may be obtained from the Government Printing Office.

P9   Foreign Policy

1.   *11 Dupont Circle, N.W.*
Washington, D.C. 20036
797-6420

2.   Charles W. Maynes, Editor

3.   A quarterly journal, *Foreign Policy,* is published by the Carnegie Endowment for International Peace. With its general focus on international affairs,

the journal covers the whole range of political, economic, military, and human issues of concern to policymakers and laymen alike. Articles on South Asian subjects appear from time to time.

P10 Government Printing Office (GPO)

1. *North Capitol and H Streets, N.W.*
   Washington, D.C. 20401
   275-2051

2. John J. Boyle, Public Printer

3. The GPO prints and binds documents for Congress and the departments and agencies of the federal government; distributes and maintains catalogs and a library of government publications; and sells nonconfidential documents to the public. The GPO sells, through mail orders and government bookstores, over 25,000 different publications, and administers the depository library program, through which selected government publications are made available in libraries throughout the country.

   Orders and inquiries concerning publications for sale should be directed to the Assistant Public Printer/Superintendent of Documents (Carl A. LaBarre, 783-3238). An information brochure, *Consumers Guide to Federal Publications,* describes the services provided by the Superintendent of Documents and gives some sources for certain categories of publications not distributed through that office. It is available free, as is a list of depository libraries from the Superintendent of Documents. The *Monthly Catalog of United States Government Publications,* which has semiannual indexes and annual cumulations, lists about 3,000 new titles annually that enter the sales inventory. A total sales catalog, *The GPO Sales Publication Reference File,* is issued bimonthly on microfiche. A useful set of some 270 *Subject Bibliographies* is also available for a wide range of topics including foreign affairs, foreign languages, foreign trade, annual reports, *Country Studies, Background Notes,* maps, national defense and security, and statistics and treaties. The quarterly *Price List 36* is available free upon request.

P11 I&NS Reporter

1. *U.S. Immigration and Naturalization Service*
   425 Eye Street, N.W. (Room 7056)
   Washington, D.C. 20536
   633-2648

2. Janet R. Graham, Editor

3. A quarterly magazine of the U.S. Immigration and Naturalization Service, the *I&NS Reporter,* contains articles on immigration and naturalization topics, recent court and administrative decisions, statistical data, and other relevant materials on immigration. The magazine is of considerable value for ethnic-related studies.

P12 India News

1. *Embassy of India*
    2107 Massachusetts Avenue, N.W.
    Washington, D.C. 20008
    265-5050

2. H. K. Bhasin, First Secretary, Information

3. *India News,* the English language newsletter of the Indian embassy, sum-
    marizes news about recent developments in India and provides job infor-
    mation for Indians living in the United States. *India News* also features
    articles on aspects of Indian culture and biographical studies of prominent
    Indians. Activities of the Indian community in the United States are also
    reported in the newsletter.

P13 Indian Vision

1. *P.O. Box 1716*
    Rockville, Maryland 20850
    (301) 251-9636

2. P. B. Kunjeer, Editor and Publisher

3. *Indian Vision* is a biweekly newsletter that was founded in 1980. The news-
    letter contains information from and about India, and announces social and
    cultural events involving the Indian community in the metropolitan Wash-
    ington area.

P14 Joint Publications Research Service (JPRS)

1. *1000 North Glebe Road*
    Arlington, Virginia 22201
    (703) 841-1050

2. C. P. Braegelmann, Chief

3. The U.S. Joint Publications Research Service provides translations and
    abstracts of foreign-language political and technical publications to various
    federal departments and agencies. While JPRS provides this translation
    support as a service of common concern for the entire government, it is
    directly associated with and funded by the Central Intelligence Agency. In
    providing its services, JPRS contracts with freelance translators with a va-
    riety of language backgrounds, including many from South Asia. JPRS
    publishes, approximately once a week, the *South and East Asia Report,*
    which covers socio-economic, government, political, and technical devel-
    opments in South Asia. JPRS ad hoc publications are announced in the
    Monthly Catalog (GPO) and the *Government Reports Announcements and
    Index* (NTIS). The National Technical Information Service also issues for
    sale an annual *Reference Aid Directory of JPRS Ad Hoc Publications.* A

monthly and an annual cumulation of the index to translations, *Transdex Index,* issued by the JPRS, is available from the Micro Photo Division of Bell and Howell, Old Mansfield Road, Wooster, Ohio 44691. While the monthly index is available in paper form, the annual cumulation may be obtained in either 16 mm microfilm or 105 mm microfiche. Subscriptions are available on a calendar-year basis. The index contains title, bibliographic, key word, and personal-names sections. JPRS publications are available at the Library of Congress and in the JPRS reading room (open 8:00 A.M.–4:30 P.M., Monday–Friday). All JPRS publications in the public domain are sold by NTIS.

P15 Middle East Journal

1.   *Middle East Institute (MEI)*
     1761 N Street, N.W.
     Washington, D.C. 20036
     785-1141

2.   Richard B. Parker, Editor

3.   A quarterly publication of the MEI, the *Middle East Journal,* in addition to articles on Islam and the contemporary Middle East, contains important documents and chronology of daily events in 24 countries including Afghanistan and Pakistan. The journal also features book reviews, a list of recent publications and a bibliography of periodical literature.

P16 National Archives and Records Service—Office of the Federal Register (General Services Administration)

1.   *8th Street and Pennsylvania Avenue, N.W.*
     Washington, D.C. 20408
     523-5240

2.   Ernest J. Galdi, Acting Director

3.   The Office of the Federal Register publishes a number of important publications, primarily concerned with the operations of the United States Government: *United States Government Manual* (annual); *Weekly Compilation of Presidential Documents; Public Papers of the Presidents of the United States; Federal Register* (daily, except weekends and holidays); and *Code of Regulations.* These publications may be ordered from the Government Printing Office (see entry P10).

P17 National Broadcasting Company (NBC)—Washington Bureau

1.   *4001 Nebraska Avenue, N.W.*
     Washington, D.C. 20016
     686-4000

2.   Sid Davis, Vice President, News

3. Scholars may obtain transcripts of newscasts from the NBC headquarters in New York (212/664-4444). Videotapes of the evening newscasts may be accessed through the *Television News Index and Abstracts*, prepared by the Vanderbilt University Library (Nashville, Tennessee 37203).

P18 National Geographic

1. *National Geographic Society*
    17th and M Streets, N.W.
    Washington, D.C. 20036
    857-7000

2. Gilbert M. Grosvenor, Editor

3. *National Geographic* is the monthly journal of the National Geographic Society, a nonprofit, scientific and educational organization. The journal occasionally publishes articles on various South Asia-related subjects. Some examples include: "Bangladesh: Hope Nourishes a New Nation," (September 1972); "India: Subcontinent in Crisis," (May 1963); "Sri Lanka: Time of Testing," (January 1979); and "India's River of Faith: The Ganges," (October 1971).

P19 Pakistan Affairs

1. *Embassy of Pakistan*
    2315 Massachusetts Avenue, N.W.
    Washington, D.C. 20008
    332-8330

2. Farouk el Hussain, Editor

3. Issued by the Information Division of the Embassy of Pakistan, *Pakistan Affairs* is an English-language bi-weekly newsletter, which provides important news about and from Pakistan. It also announces job opportunities in Pakistan and reports the cultural and educational activities of the Pakistanis in the United States. Short biographical studies of prominent Pakistanis, and articles on the culture and people of Pakistan, are also occasionally published in the newsletter.

South Asian Press Correspondents in Washington D.C.
See Appendix II.

P20 Strategic Review

1. *1612 K Street, N.W.*
    Washington, D.C. 20006
    331-1776

2. Walter F. Hahn, Editor-in-Chief

3.   *Strategic Review,* the quarterly publication of the United States Strategic Institute, provides a forum for discussing matters of current significance in the politico-military field. It occasionally carries articles relating to South Asia.

P21 Strategy Week

1.   *2030 M Street, N.W.*
      Washington, D.C. 20036
      223-4934

2.   Gregory R. Copley, Editor and Publisher

3.   This new weekly periodical reviews military and political developments abroad, including South Asia, and supplies related defense-industry information on transfer of arms. The same publisher also produces *Defense and Foreign Affairs,* a monthly magazine examining military and defense-related issues on a world-wide basis. In addition, a newsletter, the *Defense and Foreign Affairs Daily,* and the annual *Defense and Foreign Affairs Handbook* are also published.

P22 Time-Life Books

1.   *777 Duke Street*
      Alexandria, Virginia 22314
      (703) 960-5000

2.   John D. McSweeney, President

3.   A division of Time Incorporated of New York, the Time-Life illustrative documentation publications include a volume on the *China-Burma-India Theater of War* (1978) in the World War II series; and a volume on the city of *Bombay* (1979) in the Great City series. In addition to its research staff, outside scholars are hired on a consulting basis. Brochures describing its publication programs are available on request.

P23 U.S. News & World Report

1.   *2300 N Street, N.W.*
      Washington, D.C. 20037
      333-7400

2.   Marvin L. Stone, Editor

3.   *U.S. News & World Report* is an independent, weekly news magazine that reports and analyzes national and international affairs. Its various stringer bureaus and the bureaus in Peking and Tokyo contribute news and analysis of South Asian affairs. A biennial *U.S. News & World Report Index* includes country and subject headings.

P24 University Press of America

1. *4720 Boston Way*
   Lanham, Maryland 20801
   (301) 459-3366

2. James Lyons, Editor

3. The University Press of America publishes books intended for the academic community that cover a wide range of topics, including anthropology, history, religion, political science, philosophy, and international studies. The press uses a cost-efficient approach, employing a lithographic process to print type-written manuscripts provided by the authors. A list of publications is available on request. A few South Asia-related scholarly titles have been published; e.g., Isaiah Azarish, *Lord Bentinck and Indian Education, Crime and Status of Women* (1978); Sam W. McKinstry, *The Brokerage Role of Rajasthani Lawyers in Three Districts of Rajasthan, India: As Evidenced Through Lawyer-Client Relations: Fact or Fiction?* (1980); and Mizanur Rahman, *Emergence of a New Nation in a Multi-Polar World: Bangladesh* (1978).

P25 University Publications of America (UPA)

1. *44 North Market Street*
   Frederick, Maryland 21701
   (301) 694-0100

2. John Moscato, President

3. University Publications of America publishes both printed and microfilm copies of original works as well as reprints and collections of government documents. UPA publications are designed for the scholarly community and publications cover a wide range of subjects including law, history, economics, foreign affairs, and the sciences. A list of publications is available upon request. Of particular interest to South Asian scholars are the *OSS State Department Intelligence and Research Reports on Asia: China and India* and *China and India: 1950–1961 Supplement.*

P26 Voice of America (VOA)

1. *Health and Human Services Building*
   330 Independence Avenue, S.W.
   Washington, D.C. 20201
   755-4180

2. Mary Bitterman, Director

3. The Voice of America is the global radio network of the U.S. International Communications Agency, which seeks to promote understanding abroad of the United States, its people, culture, and policies. VOA currently broad-

casts some 865 hours per week in 39 languages including Dari, Bengali, Urdu, and Hindi. VOA overseas transmitters are located in Sri Lanka and Thailand, among other locations. Satellite circuits are used to feed VOA overseas relay stations beaming programs to South Asia. The VOA *Broadcasts Schedule* is available upon request.

P27 Washington Monitor

1. *499 National Press Building*
   1529 14th Street, N.W.
   Washington, D.C. 20045
   347-7757

2. Wendy Schaetzel, Executive Editor

3. The Washington Monitor publishes five serials which provide useful reference tools for researchers interested in utilizing the personnel and published resources of the federal government. The *Daily Congressional Monitor* and *Weekly Congressional Monitor* list and report on legislative activities, while the biweekly, *Congress in Print,* lists all committee publications of both houses of Congress and the General Accounting Office, and supplies addresses and phone numbers to be used in ordering items listed. The Washington Monitor also publishes the *Congressional Record Scanner Daily,* which indexes the *Congressional Record,* and the *Weekly Regulatory Monitor,* which indexes the *Federal Register.* The Monitor also issues two telephone books: the *Congressional Yellow Book* (quarterly) and the *Federal Yellow Book* (bimonthly) for Capitol Hill and the top 27,000 federal employees. In addition to its publications, Washington Monitor conducts seminars for Understanding Congress, Understanding the Federal Regulatory Process, and Understanding the News Media. All of these publications and activities can be useful for scholars following congressional and federal activities and publications dealing with South Asia.

P28 Washington Post

1. *1150 15th Street, N.W.*
   Washington, D.C. 20071
   334-6000 (Foreign News)

2. Benjamin Bradlee, Executive Director

3. A daily newspaper, *The Washington Post* provides extensive coverage of international affairs. Its South Asia Bureau, located in New Delhi (Stuart Auerbach, Chief), reports frequently on the political, economic, and diplomatic aspects of South Asian countries as well as on regional developments. The Washington Post Library (Mark Hannan, Librarian) contains over 9,000,000 newspaper clippings, 600,000 photographs, and 20,000 books, as well as cuts, maps, and roll and card microfilm. The newspaper clippings and photographs are arranged alphabetically by name and subject headings. Interlibrary loan and photoduplication services are available. The library is restricted to the use of staff members only. The Bell and Howell Micro

Photo Division (Old Mansfield Road, Wooster, Ohio 44691) publishes a *Newspaper Index to the Washington Post*, 1971–present.

P29 Washington Star

The Washington Star daily newspaper, which ceased publication August 7, 1981, covered national and international news relating to the South Asian countries, often relying on wire services and special correspondents. The Microfilming Corporation of America (21 Harristown Road, Glen Rock, New Jersey 07452) has indexed *The Washington Star* for the period 1852–1973.

P30 World Affairs

1. *American Peace Society*
    4000 Albemarle Street, N.W.
    Washington, D.C. 20016
    362-6445

2. Frank Turley, Managing Editor

3. *World Affairs* is a quarterly journal devoted to international relations and world affairs. Book reviews and articles related to South Asian affairs are occasionally published.

APPENDIXES

Appendix I.   South Asian Ethnic, Social, Cultural, and Recreational Organizations

Association of Indians in America
1120 Fairland Road
Silver Spring, Maryland 20904
A. Joglekar, (301) 384-6980

Bangladesh Association of America
7120 Warbler Lane
McLean, Virginia 22101
Osman Farruk, (703) 893-6033

Bangladesh Council of Metropolitan Washington
7131 Westmoreland Road
Falls Church, Virginia 22042
Enayetur Rahim, (703) 573-7621

Chetna: Indian Women's Organization
58 Devonshire Drive
Bethesda, Maryland 20016
Mrs. Shanta Nanjundiah, (301) 229-2566

Friends of India International
12906 Craiglawn Court
Beltsville, Maryland 20705
R. Gheani, (301) 572-7621

Gujarati Samaj
4607 Barbara Drive
Beltsville, Maryland 20705
Narendra Shah, (301) 937-8569

Guru Nanak Foundation of India
P.O. Box 4013
Chevy Chase, Maryland 20015
Raghubir Singh, (301) 593-4171

India Council
3901 Tunlaw Road, N.W., #403
Washington, D.C. 20007
Thomas Timberg, 333-6480

India School
5502 Durban Road
Bethesda, Maryland 20014
Darshan Krishna, (301) 654-6915

Indian Cultural Coordinating Committee
1710 Tilton Drive
Silver Spring, Maryland 20902
Asit Chatterjee, (301) 593-4725

Indian Medical Association
3700 East West Highway
Hyattsville, Maryland 20782
K. J. Mathew, (301) 762-0983

Kaveri (Kannada Literary and Cultural Association of Metropolitan
Washington)
11810 Rosalinda Drive
Potomac, Maryland 20854
S. Krishanamurthy, (301) 983-0799

Kerala Association
3351 East West Highway
Chevy Chase, Maryland 20015
T. K. Nainan, (301) 986-0642

Marathi Kala Mandal
2318 Malreaux Drive
Vienna, Virginia 22180
Rajani Joglekar, (703) 573-6570

Pakistan Committee
2020 F Street, N.W.
Washington, D.C. 20006
Ashfaq Ishaq, 293-2026

Pakistan Film Club
33 South French Street
Alexandria, Virginia 22304
Mohammad Aslam (703) 751-9210

Pakistan League of America and Canada
P.O. Box 8841
Washington, D.C. 20003
Sam Iftikhar (301) 422-7788

Prabashi
8606 Bradmoore Drive
Bethesda, Maryland 20034
S. N. Banik (301) 530-7539

Sanskriti
1871 Considine Drive
Brookville, Maryland 20729
Reena Chakravarty, (301) 774-2928

Sikh Cultural Society
4452 Spring Dale Street, N.W.
Washington, D.C. 20016
Shamsher Singh, 362-1667

Society of Professional Indian Women
3604 Prospect Street, N.W.
Washington, D.C. 20007
Sudha Haley, 333-5149

Sri Lanka Association of Washington
6100 Robinwood Road
Bethesda, Maryland 20034
C. S. Amersinghe, (301) 229-2766

Subhas Society
2705 Easton Street
Hillcrest Heights, Maryland 20031
Ranjan Borra, (301) 894-4511

Tamil Cultural Association
4210 Mispillon Road
Baltimore, Maryland 21236
P. G. Periasamy, (301) 229-6999

Tamil Sangam of Metropolitan Washington and Baltimore
8302 12th Avenue
Silver Spring, Maryland 20903
I. R. Thomas, (301) 434-4484

Telugu Association
7430 Piney Branch Road
Takoma Park, Maryland 20012
James P. Rao, (301) 565-0100

Young India Forum
P.O. Box 683
Arlington, Virginia 22216
Prakash Kunjeer, (301) 652-3242

Zoroastrian Association of Metropolitan Washington
3710 Leverton Street
Silver Spring, Maryland 20906
Adi Davar, (301) 942-9440

Appendix II. South Asian Press Correspondents in Washington, D.C. (as of October, 1980)

Bombay Samachar
Jehangir B. Dalal
1123 Anesbury Lane
Alexandria, Virginia 22308
(703) 532-7545

Daily Imroze (Lahore, Karachi, and Multan)
Akmal Aleemi
14816 Cloverdale Road
Woodbridge, Virginia 22193
(703) 755-4418

The Hindu (Madras)
N. Ram
4701 Willard Avenue
Chevy Chase, Maryland 20011
(301) 654-9038

Hindustan Samachar (a regional news agency located in New Dehli)
Ram Gehani
12906 Craig Lawn Court
Beltsville, Maryland 20705
(301) 572-7620

Hindustan Times (New Delhi)
N. C. Menon
30 North Beauregard Street
Alexandria, Virginia 22312
(703) 941-5074

Indian Express (Bombay, New Delhi, Chandigarh, Madras, Ahmedabad, Madurai)
T. V. Parasurnam
3723 Emily Street
Kensington, Maryland 20795
(301) 933-2883

Mashriq (Karachi, Lahore, Quetta)
M. A. Khan
6662 South King Highway
Alexandria, Virginia 22306
(703) 755-4418

Statesman of India (Calcutta)
Warren A. Unna
121 6th Street, N.E.
Washington, D.C. 20002
546-3833

The Times of India (Bombay, New Delhi)
Simon Winchester
218 11th Street, N.E.
Washington, D.C. 20002
737-2541

Note: Foreign Press Center (National Press Building, Room 202, Washington, D.C. 20045, 724-1640) may assist scholars in establishing contacts with South Asian press personnel stationed in Washington, D.C.

Appendix III. Library Collections: A Listing by Size of South Asian Holdings

The size of South Asian holdings in the Washington, D.C., area library collections was difficult to determine. The following table provides estimates only and in most cases the estimate is on the conservative side.

More than 300,000 volumes:

Library of Congress

15,000–25,000 volumes:

National Agricultural Library

10,000–15,000 volumes:

State Department Library

5,000–10,000 volumes:

American University Library
Georgetown University Library
Joint Bank-Fund Library
National Library of Medicine
University of Maryland Library

3,500–5,000 volumes:

George Washington University Library
Howard University Library
Middle East Institute Library

2,000–3,500 volumes:

Action Library
Catholic University Library
Development Information Center (Agency for International Development)
Indian Embassy Library
Islamic Center Library
Pakistan Embassy Library
School of Advanced International Studies Library (Johns Hopkins University)

Appendix IV. Bookstores

Very few bookstores in the Washington, D.C., area carry a good selection on South Asia. The following is a selected list of bookstores that may have a few South Asia-related materials, and may assist scholars in obtaining materials through special orders. The bookstores of local universities that offer courses on South Asian themes may carry reference works on South Asia in addition to textbooks. Researchers may contact individual bookstores for information on service hours, discount rates, and related matters. Scholars may also be interested to note that several book sales are held in the Washington area each year including those of the Association of American Foreign Service Wives, Brandeis University, and Vassar College. Information concerning these sales are generally announced in the local newspapers.

American University Book Store
Anderson Hall
Massachusetts and Nebraska Avenues, N.W.
Washington, D.C. 20016
686-2660

Catholic University Bookstore
McMahon Hall
4th Street and Michigan Avenue, N.E.
Washington, D.C. 20064
635-5232

Discount Records and Books
1340 Connecticut Avenue, N.W.
Washington, D.C. 20036
785-1133 (Books)
785-2662 (Records)

This store has a good collection of international records, including a few from South Asia.

George Mason University Bookstore
Student Union
4400 University Drive
Fairfax, Virginia 22030
(703) 323-2696

George Washington University Bookstore
21st and H Streets, N.W.
Washington, D.C. 20052
676-6870

Georgetown University Bookstore
37th and Prospect Streets, N.W.
Washington, D.C. 20057
625-4068

Globe Book Shop
1700 Pennsylvania Avenue, N.W.
Washington, D.C. 20006
393-1490

Howard University Bookstore
2801 Georgia Avenue, N.W.
Washington, D.C. 20059
636-6656

Institute of Modern Languages Bookstore
2125 S Street, N.W.
Washington, D.C. 20009
565-2580

International Learning Center Bookstore
1715 Connecticut Avenue, N.W.
Washington, D.C. 20009
232-4111

Kramer Books
1347 Connecticut Avenue, N.W.
Washington, D.C. 20036
293-2072

Other locations of this store are: 1722 H Street, N.W., 298-8010; 1919 Pennsylvania Avenue, N.W., 466-3111; 1517 Connecticut Avenue, N.W., 387-1400; and 336 Pennsylvania Avenue, S.E., 547-5990.

The Map Store
1636 Eye Street, N.W.
Washington, D.C. 20006
628-2608

Maryland Book Exchange
4500 College Avenue
College Park, Maryland 20740
(301) 927-2510

Modern Language Book and Record Store
3160 O Street, N.W.
Washington, D.C. 20007
338-8963

National Technical Information Service Bookstore
425 13th Street, N.W.
Washington, D.C. 20004
724-3382

Newman Bookstore of Washington
3329 8th Street, N.E.
Washington, D.C. 20017
526-1036

Second Story Books
3236 P Street, N.W.
Washington, D.C. 20007
338-6860

Sidney Kramer Books
1722 H Street, N.W.
Washington, D.C. 20006
298-8010

Smithsonian Institution—Museum Shops
Director of Museum Shops
Natural History Building
12th Street and Constitution Avenue, N.W.
Washington, D.C. 20560
357-1805

Trover Shop Books
277 Pennsylvania Avenue, S.E.
Washington, D.C. 20003
543-8006

Other locations of this store are: 800 15th Street, N.W., 347-2177; 1031
Connecticut Avenue, N.W., 659-8138; 1751 Pennsylvania Avenue, N.W.,
833-2855.

U.S. Government Printing Office (GPO)
Main Bookstore
710 North Capitol Street, N.W.
Washington, D.C. 20402
783-3238

Other locations are:

GPO Bookstore, Commerce Department
14th and E Streets, N.W.
Washington, D.C. 20230
377-3527

GPO Bookstore, Health and Human Services Department
330 Independence Avenue, N.W.
Washington, D.C. 20201
472-7899

GPO Bookstore, International Communication Agency
1776 Pennsylvania Avenue, N.W.
Washington, D.C. 20547
724-9928

GPO State Department Bookstore
21st and C Streets, N.W.
Washington, D.C. 20520
632-1437

University of the District of Columbia Bookstore—Mount Vernon Campus
  Bookstore
529 E Street, N.W.
Washington, D.C. 20004
727-2517

University of Maryland Bookstore
Student Union Building
Campus Drive
College Park, Maryland 20742
(301) 454-3222

Appendix V.   Finding One's Way Around

Visitors to Washington, D.C., might wish to obtain the periodically updated *Newcomers Guide to Metropolitan Washington* (1978), published by *The Washingtonian* magazine and available at local bookstores or at the magazine's office located at 1828 L Street, N.W., Washington, D.C. 20036, 296-3600. A convenient aid in finding one's way around is the *Washington, D.C. and Vicinity Street Maps* (June 1980), which contains some 24 pages of detailed maps plus a street index, published by the Alexandria Drafting Company, 6440 General Greenway, Alexandria, Virginia 22312, (703) 750-0510. Free copies of a metropolitan area map are available from the District of Columbia's Department of Transportation, Room 519, 415 12th Street, N.W., Washington, D.C. 20004, 727-6562. Mail requests must include a stamped, self-addressed 7" × 10" envelope. The office is open from 8:15 A.M. to 4:45 P.M., weekdays.

Appendix VI.   Federal Government Holidays

Federal government offices are closed on the following holidays:

New Year's Day	January 1
Washington's Birthday	3rd Monday in February
Memorial Day	last Monday in May
Independence Day	July 4*
Labor Day	1st Monday in September
Columbus Day	2nd Monday in October
Veteran's Day	November 11*
Thanksgiving	4th Thursday in November
Christmas	December 25*

*If this date is on a Saturday, the holiday is on Friday. If this date is on a Sunday, the holiday is on Monday.

The public areas of the Smithsonian Institution and the General Reading Rooms of the Library of Congress are open on most holidays.

Appendix VII. Standard Entry Formats

A. Libraries Entry Format

1. General Information
    a. *address; telephone numbers*
    b. hours of service
    c. conditions of access (including availability of interlibrary loan and reproduction facilities)
    d. name/title of director and heads of relevant divisions

2. Size of Collection
    a. general
    b. South Asia

3. Description and Evaluation of Collection
    a. narrative assessment of South Asian holdings—subject and area strengths/weaknesses
    b. tabular evaluation of subject strengths:

Subject Categories	*Number of Titles (t)*	*Rating (A-D)**
Philosophy and Religion		
History and Auxiliary Sciences of History		
Geography and Anthropology		
Economics		
Sociology		
Politics and Government		
International Relations		
Law		
Education		
Art and Music		
Language and Literature		
Military Affairs		
Bibliography and Reference		

Afghanistan		
Bangladesh		
Bhutan		
India		
Maldive Islands		
Nepal		

Pakistan
Sri Lanka (Ceylon)

4. Special Collections
   a. periodicals
   b. newspapers
   c. government documents
   d. miscellaneous vertical files
   e. archives and manuscripts
   f. maps
   g. films
   h. tapes

5. Noteworthy Holdings

6. Bibliographic Aids (catalogs, guides, etc.) Facilitating Use of Collection

---

*A—comprehensive collection of primary and secondary sources (Library of Congress collection to serve as standard of evaluation).

B—substantial collection of primary and secondary sources sufficient for some original research (holdings of roughly one-tenth those of the Library of Congress).

C—substantial collection of secondary sources with some primary materials, sufficient to support graduate instruction (holdings of roughly one-half those of the B collection).

D—collection of secondary sources, mostly in English, sufficient to support undergraduate instruction (holdings of roughly one-half those of C collection); collections rated below D are indicated by "D—".

B. Archives and Manuscript Repositories Entry Format

1. General Information
   a. *address; telephone numbers*
   b. hours of service
   c. conditions of access
   d. reproduction services
   e. name/title of director and heads of relevant divisions

2. Size of Holdings Pertaining to South Asia

3. Description of Holdings Pertaining to South Asia

4. Bibliographic Aids (inventories, calendars, etc.) Facilitating Use of Collection

C. Museums, Galleries, and Art Collections Entry Format

1. General Information
   a. *address; telephone numbers*
   b. hours of service
   c. conditions of access
   d. reproduction services

e. name/title of director and heads of relevant divisions

2. Size of Holdings Pertaining to South Asia

3. Description of Holdings Pertaining to South Asia

4. Bibliographic Aids (Inventories, calendars, etc.) Facilitating Use of Collection

---

D. Collections of Music and Other Sound Recordings Entry Format

1. General Information
   a. *address; telephone numbers*
   b. hours of service
   c. conditions of access
   d. name/title of director and key staff members

2. Size of Holdings Pertaining to South Asia

3. Description of Holdings Pertaining to South Asia

4. Facilities for Study and Use
   a. availability of audio equipment
   b. reservation requirements
   c. fees charged
   d. reproduction services

5. Bibliographic Aids Facilitating the Use of Collection

E. Map Collections Entry Format

1. General Information
   a. *address; telephone numbers*
   b. hours of service
   c. conditions of access
   d. reproduction services
   e. name/title of director and heads of relevant divisions

2. Size of Holdings Pertaining to South Asia

3. Description of Holdings Pertaining of South Asia

4. Bibliographic Aids (inventories, calendars, etc.) Facilitating Use of Collection

---

F. Film Collections Entry Format

1. General Information
   a. *address; telephone numbers*
   b. hours of service
   c. conditions of access
   d. name/title of director and key staff members

2. Size of Holdings Pertaining to South Asia

3.   Description of Holdings Pertaining to South Asia

4.   Facilities for Study and Use
  a. availability of audiovisual equipment
  b. reservation requirements
  c. fees charged
  d. reproduction services

5.   Bibliographic Aids Facilitating Use of Collection

G. Data Banks Entry Format

1.   General Information
  a. *address; telephone numbers*
  b. hours of service
  c. conditions of access (including fees charged for information retrieval)
  d. name/title of director and key staff members

2.   Description of Data Files (hard data and bibliographic references) Pertaining to South Asia

3.   Bibliographic Aids Facilitating Use of Storage Media

H. Research Centers Entry Format

1.   *Address; Telephone Numbers*

2.   Name and Title of Chief Official

3.   Programs and Research Activities Pertaining to South Asia

4.   Library and Research Facilities

5.   Publications

I. Academic Programs and Departments Entry Format

1.   *Address; Telephone Numbers*

2.   Chief Official and Title

3.   Degrees and Subjects Offered; Program Activities

4.   Libraries and Research Facilities

J. United States Government Agencies Entry Format*

1.   General Information
  a. *address; telephone numbers*
  b. conditions of access
  c. name/title of director and heads of relevant divisions

2. Functions, Programs, and Research Activities (including in-house research, contract programs, research grants, employment of outside consultants, and international exchange programs)

3. Libraries and Reference Facilities

4. Publications and Records (including unpublished materials, indexes, and vertical files, among other data)

   *In the case of large, structurally complex agencies, each relevant division or bureau is described separately in accordance with the above entry format.

K. South Asian Embassies and International Organizations Entry Format*

1. General Information
   a. *address; telephone numbers*
   b. hours/ conditions of access
   c. names and titles of chief officials

2. Organization Functions, Programs, Research Activities (including in-house research, contract research, research grants, and employment of outside consultants)

3. Library and Reference Facilities

4. Publications and Internal Records (including unpublished research projects)

   *In the case of large, structurally complex international organizations, each relevant division or sub-unit is described separately in accordance with the above entry format.

L. Associations Entry Format

1. *Address; Telephone Numbers*

2. Chief Official and Title

3. Programs and Activities Pertaining to South Asia

4. Library and Reference Collections

5. Publications

M. Cultural-Exchange and Technical-Assistance Organizations Entry Format

1. *Address; Telephone Numbers*

2. Chief Official and Title

3. Programs and Activities Pertaining to South Asia

4.   Library and Reference Facilities

5.   Publications

N. Religious Organizations Entry Format

1.   *Address; Telephone Numbers*

2.   Chief Official and Title

3.   Programs Pertaining to South Asia

4.   Publications

P. Publications and Media Entry Format

1.   *Address; Telephone Numbers*

2.   Chief Official and Title

3.   Programs and Publications Pertaining to South Asia

Bibliography

Reference sources consulted for identification of collections and organizations included in this *Scholars' Guide*.

Akey, Denise, ed. *Encyclopedia of Associations*, 2 vols, 15th ed. Detroit: Gale, 1980.

American Association of Museums. *Official Museum Directory*. Washington, D.C.: American Association of Museums, 1975.

American Council of Voluntary Agencies for Foreign Service, Inc. *U.S. Non-Profit Organizations in Development Assistance Abroad Including Voluntary Agencies, Missions, and Foundations*. New York: Technical Assistance Information Clearing House of the American Council of Voluntary Agencies for Foreign Service, Inc., 1971.

American Library Directory, 32nd ed. 1979. New York: Jacques Cattell Press, 1979.

Andriot, John L., ed. *Guide to U.S. Government Publications*, 2 vols. McLean, Va.: Documents Index, 1980.

Ayer Press. *'80 Ayer Directory of Publications*. Philadelphia: Ayer Press, 1980.

Bhatt, Purnima M. *Scholars' Guide to Washington, D.C. for African Studies*. Washington, D.C.: Smithsonian Institution Press, 1980.

Brown, Allison, ed. *Organizations Serving International Visitors in the National Capital Area*, 4th ed. Washington, D.C.: International Visitors Information Service, 1973.

Brownson, Charles B., comp. *1980 Congressional Staff Directory*. Mount Vernon, Va.: Congressional Staff Directory, 1980.

Case, Margaret H. *South Asian History 1750–1950. A Guide to Periodicals, Dissertations and Newspapers.* Princeton, N.J.: Princeton University Press, 1968.

Chamberlain, Jim, and Ann Hammond. *Directory of the Population Related Community of the Washington, D.C. Area.* Washington, D.C.: World Population Society, D.C. Chapter, April 1978.

Congressional Quarterly, Inc. *Washington Information Directory, 1980–81.* Washington, D.C.: Congressional Quarterly, Inc., 1980.

Dillon, Kenneth J. *Scholars' Guide to Washington, D.C. for Central and East European Studies.* Washington, D.C.: Smithsonian Institution Press, 1980.

Diplomatic List. Washington, D.C.: U.S. Department of State, August 1980.

Downey, James A. *U.S. Federal Official Publications: The International Dimension.* Oxford: Pergamon Press, 1978.

Grant, Steven A. *Scholars' Guide to Washington, D.C. for Russian/Soviet Studies.* Washington, D.C.: Smithsonian Institution Press, 1977.

Green, Shirley L. *Pictorial Resources in the Washington D.C. Area.* Washington, D.C.: Library of Congress, 1976.

Grow, Michael. *Scholars' Guide to Washington, D.C. for Latin American and Caribbean Studies.* Washington, D.C.: Smithsonian Institution Press, 1979.

Hamer, Philip M., ed. *A Guide to Archives and Manuscripts in the United States.* New Haven, Conn.: Yale University Press, 1961.

Jennings, Margaret S., ed. *Library and Reference Facilities in the Area of the District of Columbia,* 10th ed. Washington, D.C.: American Society for Information Science, 1979.

Joyner, Nelson T., Jr. *Joyner's Guide to Official Washington,* 3d ed. Rockville, Md.: Rockville Consulting Group, 1976.

Kim, Hong N. *Scholars' Guide to Washington, D.C. for East Asian Studies.* Washington, D.C.: Smithsonian Institution Press, 1979.

Kruzas, Anthony T., ed. *Encyclopedia of Information Systems and Services,* 1st ed. Ann Arbor: Edward Brothers, 1971.

Martin, Thomas J., comp. *North American Collections of Islamic Manuscripts.* Boston: G. K. Hall, 1978.

Mason, John Brown, ed. *Research Resources: Annotated Guide to the Social Sciences*, 2 vols. Santa Barbara, Calif.: American Bibliographical Center, 1968–71.

Metropolitan Bookstore Guide. Washington, D.C.: Washington Booksellers Association, 1975.

Padolsky, Arthur, and Carolyn R. Smith. *Education Directory: Colleges and Universities, 1978–79*. Washington, D.C.: National Center for Education, Education Division, U.S. Department of Health, Education and Welfare, n.d.

Palmer, Archie M., ed. *Research Centers Directory*, 6th ed. Detroit: Gale Research Co., 1979.

Pearson, J. D., comp. *Oriental Manuscripts in Europe and North America: A Survey*. Bibliotheca Asiatica, No. 7. Switzerland: Interdocumentation Co., 1971.

Rowan, Bonnie G. *Scholars' Guide to Washington, D.C. for Film and Video Collections*. Washington, D.C.: Smithsonian Institution Press, 1980.

Schmeckebier, Laurence Frederick, and Roy B. Eastin. *Government Publications and their Use*, 2d rev. ed. Washington, D.C.: Brookings Institution, 1969.

Schneider, John H., Marvin Gechman, and Stephen E. Furth, eds. *Survey of Commercially Available Computer-Readable Bibliographic Data Bases*. Washington, D.C.: American Society for Information Science, 1973.

Sessions, Vivian S., ed. *Directory of Data Bases in the Social and Behavioral Sciences*. New York: Science Associates/International, 1974.

Smith, David Horton, ed. *Voluntary Transnational Cultural Exchange Organizations of the U.S.: A Selective List*. Washington, D.C.: Center for a Voluntary Society, 1974.

U.S. Congress. *Official Congressional Directory*. Washington, D.C.: Government Printing Office, 1979.

U.S. Department of State. Office of External Research. *Foreign Affairs Research: A Directory of Governmental Resources*. Washington, D.C.: Government Printing Office, 1969.

———. *Government Supported Research on Foreign Affairs: Current Project Information, FY 1976*. Washington, D.C.: Government Printing Office, 1977.

U.S. General Services Administration. National Archives and Records Service. Office of the Federal Register. *United States Government Organizational Manual, 1980–81*. Washington, D.C.: Government Printing Office, 1980.

U.S. National Historical Publications and Records Commission. *Directory of Archives and Manuscript Repositories*. Washington, D.C.: U.S. National Archives and Records Service, 1978.

U.S. Library of Congress, National Referral Center for Science and Technology. *A Directory of Information Resources in the United States Federal Government*. Washington, D.C.: Government Printing Office, 1974.

―――. *A Directory of Information Resources in the United States: Social Sciences*, rev. ed. Washington, D.C.: Government Printing Office, 1973.

Washington V. Washington, D.C.: Potomac Books, 1979.

Wasserman, Paul, ed. *Ethnic Information Sources of the United States*. Detroit: Gale Research Co., 1976.

Weber, Olga S., comp. *North American Film and Video Directory: A Guide to Media Collections and Services*. New York: R. R. Bowker and Co., 1976.

Wynar, Lubomyr Roman. *Encyclopedic Directory of Ethnic Newspapers and Periodicals in the United States*. Littleton, Colo.: Libraries Unlimited, Inc., 1976.

Wynar, Lubomyr Roman, and Lois Buttlar. *Guide to Ethnic Museums, Libraries and Archives in the United States*. Kent, Ohio: The Center for Ethnic Publications, School of Library Science, Kent State University, 1978.

Wynar, Lubomyr Roman, with Lois Buttlar and Anna T. Wynar. *Encyclopedic Directory of Ethnic Organizations in the United States*. Littleton, Colo.: Libraries Unlimited, 1975.

Name Index

(Organizations and Institutions)

Entry symbols correspond to the following sections of the *Guide*:

A—Libraries
B—Archives and Manuscript Repositories
C—Museums, Galleries, and Art Collections
D—Collections of Music and Other Sound Recordings
E—Map Collections
F—Film Collections (Still Photographs and Motion Pictures)
G—Data Banks
H—Research Centers
 I—Academic Programs and Departments
J—United States Government Agencies
K—South Asian Embassies and International Organizations
L—Associations (Academic, Professional, and Cultural)
M—Cultural-Exchange and Technical-Assistance Organizations
N—Religious Organizations
P—Publications and Media

South Asian embassies are indexed alphabetically by their geographic designations although prefixed by their official names as presented in the *Diplomatic List*. Entries that are not in italics refer to the main entries of each collection or organization; entries in italics indicate other references that may also contain relevant material.

Academy for Educational Development
 (AED)—International Division L1
Action Library (Peace Corps Library) A1
Advanced International Studies Institute
 (AISI) (University of Miami) H1
Embassy of the Democratic Republic of
 Afghanistan K1
Agency for International Development
 (AID), A7, *A32*, *B6*, F1, *F12*, G1, G2,
 G3, *G4*, *H11*, *H24*, *H29*, J1, *J6*, *J9*, *J15*,
 J16, *J17*, *J18*, *J32*, *L31*, *M12*, *M17*, *M27*,
 M33
 Bureau for Asia J1
 Office of Bangladesh and India Af-
  fairs J1
 Office of Pakistan, Nepal, and Sri
  Lanka Affairs J1
 Bureau for Development Support J1

Bureau for Near East J1
 Office of Near Eastern/North African
  Affairs—Afghanistan J1
Bureau for Private and Development
 Cooperation J1
 Office of Food for Peace J1
 Office of Labor Affairs J1
 Office of Private and Voluntary Co-
  operation JI
 Office of United States Foreign Dis-
  aster Assistance JI
Bureau for Program and Management
 Services JI
Bureau for Program and Policy Coor-
 dination J1
 Office of Women in Development J1
Bureau of Intergovernmental and In-
 ternational Affairs J1

Economic and Social Data Services
Division (ESDS) G1
Library A7
Office of Development Information and
Utilization (DIU) G2
Office of Public Affairs J1
Photo Collection F1
Program Data Services Division G3
Agricultural Cooperative Development
International (ACDI) M1
Agriculture Department *B6*, *G2*, G4, *J1*,
J2, *J27*
Data Services Center G4
Economics, Policy Analysis and Budget
J2
Economics, Statistics, and Cooperative
Service J2
Agricultural History Branch J2
International Economic Division J2
World Food and Agricultural Out-
look and Situation J2
International Affairs and Commodity
Program J2
Agricultural Stabilization and Con-
servation Service J2
Commodity Credit Corporation J2
Foreign Agricultural Service J2
Agricultural Attachés J2
Commodity Programs J2
Foreign Market Development J2
International Trade Policy J2
Office of the General Sales Man-
ager J2
Office of International Cooperation
and Development J2
Development Project Manage-
ment Center J2
Interagency and Congressional
Affairs J2
International Organization Affairs
J2
International Training Division J2
Reports and Technical Inquiries
Group J2
Scientific and Technical Exchange
Division J2
Technical Assistance Division J2
Library *See* National Agricultural Li-
brary.
Air Force Department *See* Defense De-
partment.
Air Force Magazine P1
American Anthropological Association
(AAA) L2
American Association for the Advance-
ment of Science (AAAS) L3
American Association of Collegiate Re-

gistrars and Admission Officers (AA-
CRAO) M2
American Association of Museums
(AAM) L4
American Association of University
Women (AAUW) L5
American Broadcasting Company
(ABC)—Washington Bureau *A13*, *F5*,
P2
American Catholic Historical Association
L6
American Council of Young Political
Leaders (ACYPL) M3
American Council on Education L7
American Council on International Sports
(ACIS) M4
American Enterprise Institute for Public
Policy Research (AEI) H2
American Fazl Mosque N1
American Federation of Labor and Con-
gress of Industrial Organizations (AFL-
CIO)—Department of International
Affairs *J1*, M5
American Film Institute (AFI) L8
American Foreign Service Association
(AFSA) L9
American Friends Service Committee
(AFSC)—Washington Office L10
American Historical Association (AHA)
L11
American Home Economics Associa-
tion—International Family Planning
Project M6
American Political Science Association
(APSA) L12
American Psychiatric Association (APA)
L13
American Psychological Association
(APA) L14
American Public Health Association
(APHA) L15
American Red Cross B1, F2, *F12*, M7
Archives B1, *F12*
Library M7
Photograph Collection F2
American Society for Public Administra-
tion (ASPA) L16
American Society of International Law
(ASIL) L17
American Sociological Association (ASA)
L18
American University (AU) A2, H3, I1,
I3, *J9*
Academic Programs and Departments
I1
Foreign Area Studies (FAS) H3, *J9*
Library A2

Personal-Papers Index

Library Subject-Strength Index

This index identifies the most useful library collections in the Washington, D.C., area by subject. The evaluations (A through C) presented here are based on the criteria explained at the beginning of Section A and summarized below:

A—comprehensive collection of primary and secondary sources (Library of Congress collection to serve as a standard of evaluation)
B—substantial collection of primary and secondary sources, sufficient for some original research (holdings of roughly one-tenth those of the Library of Congress)
C—substantial collection of secondary sources with some primary materials sufficient to support graduate instruction (holdings of roughly one-half those of the B collection)

The standard Library of Congress subject headings have been used for categorization. Some valuable specialized collections have been included here even though their rating is based on a subcategory of one of the major headings. A listing of library collections according to the size of their South Asian holdings may be found in Appendix III. The subject headings are listed below in the same order as they appear in Section A.

Philosophy and Religion
A collections: A23
B collections: A25
C collections: A15, A34, L43

History and Auxiliary Sciences of History
A collections: A23
B collections: A32
C collections: A1, A2, A34, K3, K5

Geography and Anthropology
A collections: A23
B collections: A12, A27, J30
C collections: A8, A9, A11

Economics
A collections: A23
B collections: A7, A32, J22
C collections: A5, A6, A34, J13, J14, J33

Sociology
A collections: A23
B collections: A34
C collections: A21, A32

Politics and Government
A collections: A23
B collections: A32
C collections: A2, A34

International Relations
A collections: A23, A31, A32
B collections: A2, A34
C collections: A3, A13, A15, A30, K5

Law
A collections: A23
B collections: —
C collections: A32

Education
A collections: A23
B collections: —
C collections: —

Art and Music
A collections: A23
B collections: A34, J30
C collections: A11

Language and Literature
A collections: A23
B collections: —
C collections: —

Military Affairs
A collections: A23
B collections: A32
C collections: —

Bibliography and Reference
A collections: A23
B collections: —
C collections: A32

Afghanistan
A collections: A23
B collections: A7, A15, A22, A26, A32
C collections: A2, A7, A12, A27, A30

Bangladesh
A collections: A23
B collections: A22, A26, A29, A32
C collections: A7, A15, A30, A34

Bhutan
A collections: A23, A26
B collections: A2, A12, A13, A15, A22, A24, A27, A32, A34
C collections: A30

India
A collections: A23
B collections: A22, A26, A29, A32, K3
C collections: A2, A34

Maldive Islands
A collections: A23
B collections: A26, A29, A32
C collections: —

Nepal
A collections: A23
B collections: A7, A22, A26
C collections: A32

Pakistan
A collections: A23
B collections: A7, A22, A26, A32, A34, K5
C collections: A2, A15, A24, A29

Sri Lanka
A collections: A23
B collections: A26, A32
C collections: A2, A7, A24, A27, A29, A34

Subject Index

The subject index that follows employs a topical as well as a geographic approach.

Entry symbols correspond to the following sections of the *Guide*:

A—Libraries
B—Archives and Manuscript Repositories
C—Museums, Galleries, and Art Collections
D—Collections of Music and Other Sound Recordings
E—Map Collections
F—Film Collections (Still Photographs and Motion Pictures)
G—Data Banks
H—Research Centers
I—Academic Programs and Departments
J—United States Government Agencies
K—South Asian Embassies and International Organizations
L—Associations (Academic, Professional, and Cultural)
M—Cultural-Exchange and Technical-Assistance Organizations
N—Religious Organizations
P—Publications and Media

Afghanistan A2, A4, A7, A12, A13, A15, A19, A21, A22, A23, A24, A25, A26, A27, A29, A30, A32, A34, B4, B6, F16, H9, H22, H36, J1, J16, J20, J22, J25, J31, K1, K10, L38, L56, M2, M8, M14, M20, P1, P15
For specific references pertaining to Afghanistan, see:
Academic Programs H8
Anthropology and Sociology F9, H3, J9, J30
Arts C8, L40
Economics J6, K8, L1
Foreign Relations D5, H5, H20, H35, J15
Geography and Maps E3, E4, E5, E6
History J10
Industry J18
Population M6
Religion L45
Statistics J11, J32
Technical Assistance J2, J9
Transportation J9, J32, L42

Ray, Satyajit F5, L8
Recreation
See Parks and Recreation
Religion, Religious Works and Objects A2, A4, A13, A15, A19, A23, A27,
A30, A32, A34, B3, B4, E5, L11, L41, P24,
Buddhism B5, C3, L11, N2, N3, N4
Catholic Church A4, I2, L6, L29, M22, M32
Christianity M10, M22, M30
Hinduism A23, A24, B5, B6, C3, D3, E5, F12, L11, L29, N5, N7, N8,
N13, N14
Islam A4, A8, A11, A15, A23, A24, A25, B5, C3, C11, E5, F9, F14, H2,
H35, J30, K5, L11, L21, L29, L43, L45, L46, L59, N1, N9, N10, N11,
P15
Jainism B5
Jesuits A4, A9, A16, L29, M23
Judaism L29
Parseeism (Zoroastrianism) C8
Sikhism N6, N12
Religion (Academic Course Offerings) I1, I2, I4, I5, I8
Roy, M. N. B6
Rural Development B6, F1, H19, J1, K8, L57, M19

Sanskrit
See Languages
Scholarships, Fellowships, and Grants J10, J20, J24, J30, L5, L7, L22, L42,
L47, M8, M14
Science and Technology A6, A23, B7, F3, G5, G6, H7, J1, J4, J6, J7, J25,
J30, J31, K12, L3, L29, L31, L37, L47 L49, L51
Sculpture A11, C3, C6, F5
Sikhism
See Religion
Sikkim H3, J9, L26
Sindhi
See Languages
Sinhalese
See Languages
Sociology A2, A4, A13, A15, A19, A23, A30, A32, A34, H31, J4, J16, J25,
J31, L18, L60, M21
Space C5, C8, G11, J18, J23, J30, J31, L17
Sports M4
South Asian Languages
See Languages
Sri Lanka A2, A4, A7, A12, A13, A15, A19, A23, A24, A26, A27, A29,
A30, A32, A34, B4, B6, B7, F16, G13, H6, H36, J1, J18, J20, J22, J25,
J31, K6, K10, L3, L4, L5, L29, M8, M14, M16, M20, M21, M24, M26,
P1, P18, P26
For specific references pertaining to Sri Lanka, see:
Agriculture H26, L1, L47, M1
Anthropology and Sociology F10, F12, H24, J9
Development H30, L42
Economics K8, K9
Education L42, L50
Energy L61

The author, Enayetur Rahim, born in 1938, attended Rajshahi University in Bangladesh, receiving his B.A. (Hons) in 1957 and an M.A. in history in 1959. A Fulbright scholar, he attended the University of Pennsylvania where he earned an M.A. in South Asia Regional Studies in 1967. He obtained his Ph.D. from Georgetown University in 1973. Dr. Rahim has taught history at Rajshahi University, St. Cloud State University, and Georgetown University. He is the author of the forthcoming book, *Provincial Autonomy in Bengal, 1937–43* (Institute of Bangladesh Studies, Rajshahi University), and has published a number of articles.

Consultant Purnima M. Bhatt is Assistant Professor of Anthropology and Interdisciplinary Studies at Hood College, Frederick, Maryland.

Consultant Louis A. Jacob is the Head of the Southern Asia Section of the Library of Congress.

Series Editor Zdeněk V. David has been Librarian of the Wilson Center since 1974. Previously, he taught history at Princeton and the University of Michigan, Ann Arbor, and library science at Rutgers University. He served as Slavic Bibliographer of the Princeton University Library from 1966 to 1974.